COLLECTION EDITOR: **JENNIFER GRÜNWALD**
ASSOCIATE EDITOR: **SARAH BRUNSTAD**
EDITOR, SPECIAL PROJECTS: **MARK D. BEAZLEY**
VP, PRODUCTION & SPECIAL PROJECTS: **JEFF YOUNGQUIST**
SVP PRINT, SALES & MARKETING: **DAVID GABRIEL**
BOOK DESIGNER: **JAY BOWEN**

EDITOR IN CHIEF: **AXEL ALONSO**
CHIEF CREATIVE OFFICER: **JOE QUESADA**
PUBLISHER: **DAN BUCKLEY**
EXECUTIVE PRODUCER: **ALAN FINE**

THE UNBEATABLE SQUIRREL GIRL VOL. 1. Contains material originally published in magazine form as THE UNBEATABLE SQUIRREL GIRL #1-8, MARVEL SUPER-HEROES #8, GLX-MAS SPECIAL #1, THE THING #8 and AGE OF HEROES #3. First printing 2016. ISBN# 978-1-302-90224-7. Published by MARVEL WORLDWIDE, INC., a subsidiary of MARVEL ENTERTAINMENT, LLC. OFFICE OF PUBLICATION: 135 West 50th Street, New York, NY 10020. Copyright © 2016 MARVEL No similarity between any of the names, characters, persons, and/or institutions in this magazine with those of any living or dead person or institution is intended, and any such similarity which may exist is purely coincidental. **Printed in China.** ALAN FINE, President, Marvel Entertainment; DAN BUCKLEY, President, TV, Publishing & Brand Management; JOE QUESADA, Chief Creative Officer; TOM BREVOORT, SVP of Publishing; DAVID BOGART, SVP of Business Affairs & Operations, Publishing & Partnership; C.B. CEBULSKI, VP of Brand Management & Development, Asia; DAVID GABRIEL, SVP of Sales & Marketing, Publishing; JEFF YOUNGQUIST, VP of Production & Special Projects; DAN CARR, Executive Director of Publishing Technology; ALEX MORALES, Director of Publishing Operations; SUSAN CRESPI, Production Manager; STAN LEE, Chairman Emeritus. For information regarding advertising in Marvel Comics or on Marvel.com, please contact Vit DeBellis, Integrated Sales Manager, at vdebellis@marvel.com. For Marvel subscription inquiries, please call 888-511-5480. **Manufactured between 6/24/2016 and 9/12/2016** by R.R. DONNELLEY ASIA PRINTING SOLUTIONS, CHINA.

10 9 8 7 6 5 4 3 2 1

the unbeatable Squirrel Girl

Ryan North
WRITER

Erica Henderson
ARTIST

Maris Wicks (#1), **Kyle Starks** (#3),
Chris Giarrusso (#4) & **Eloise Narrington** (#5-6)
TRADING CARD ART

Rico Renzi
COLOR ARTIST

VC's Clayton Cowles
LETTERER

Erica Henderson
COVER ART

**Jon Moisan &
Jake Thomas**
ASSISTANT EDITORS

Wil Moss
EDITOR

Tom Brevoort
EXECUTIVE EDITOR

SPECIAL THANKS TO LISSA PATILLO

Marvel Super-Heroes #8

PLOT/ARTIST: **STEVE DITKO**
SCRIPT: **WILL MURRAY**
COLORIST: **CHRISTIE SCHEELE**
LETTERER: **BRAD K. JOYCE**
COVER ART: **ERIK LARSEN**

GLX-Mas Special #1 "EGGNOG,
TOILET PAPER, AND PEACE ON EARTH"

WRITER: **DAN SLOTT**   ARTIST: **MATT HALEY**
LETTERER: **DAVE LANPHEAR**
COVER ART: **PAUL PELLETIER,
RICK MAGYAR & WIL QUINTANA**
ASSISTANT EDITORS: **ANDY SCHMIDT,
MOLLY LAZER & AUBREY SITTERSON**
EDITOR: **TOM BREVOORT**

The Thing #8 "LAST HAND"

WRITER: **DAN SLOTT**   ARTIST: **KIERON DWYER**
COLOR ARTIST: **LAURA VILLARI**
LETTERER: **DAVE LANPHEAR**
COVER ART: **ANDREA DI VITO
& LAURA VILLARI**
ASSISTANT EDITORS: **ANDY SCHMIDT,
MOLLY LAZER & AUBREY SITTERSON**
EDITOR: **TOM BREVOORT**

Age of Heroes #3 "NUTS TO THIS"

WRITER: **DAN SLOTT**   ARTIST: **TY TEMPLETON**
COLOR ARTIST: **JORGE MAESE**
LETTERER: **DAVE LANPHEAR**
COVER ART: **YANICK PAQUETTE,
MICHEL LACOMBE & NATHAN FAIRBAIRN**
EDITORS: **LAUREN SANKOVITCH
& TOM BREVOORT**

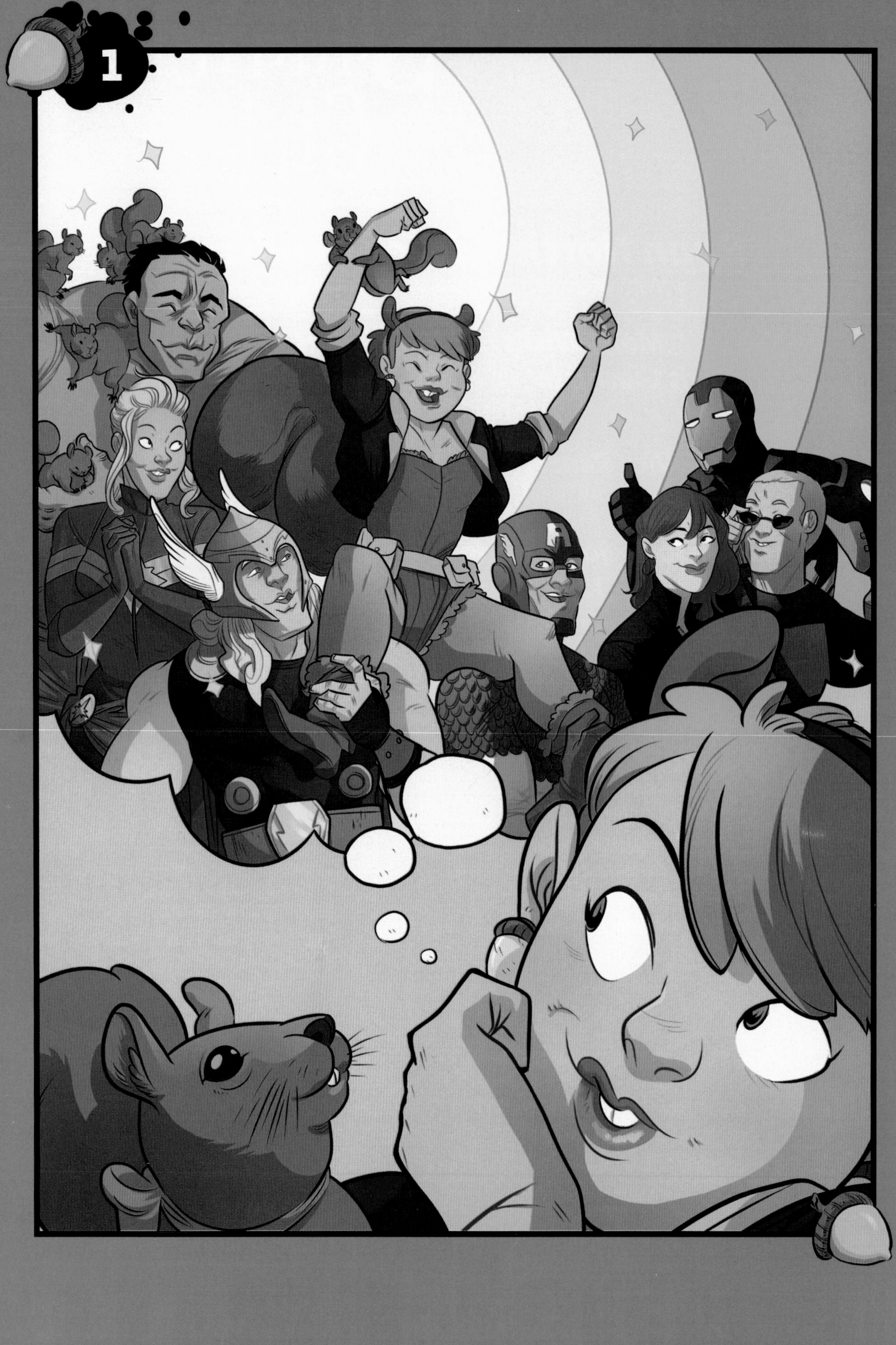
1

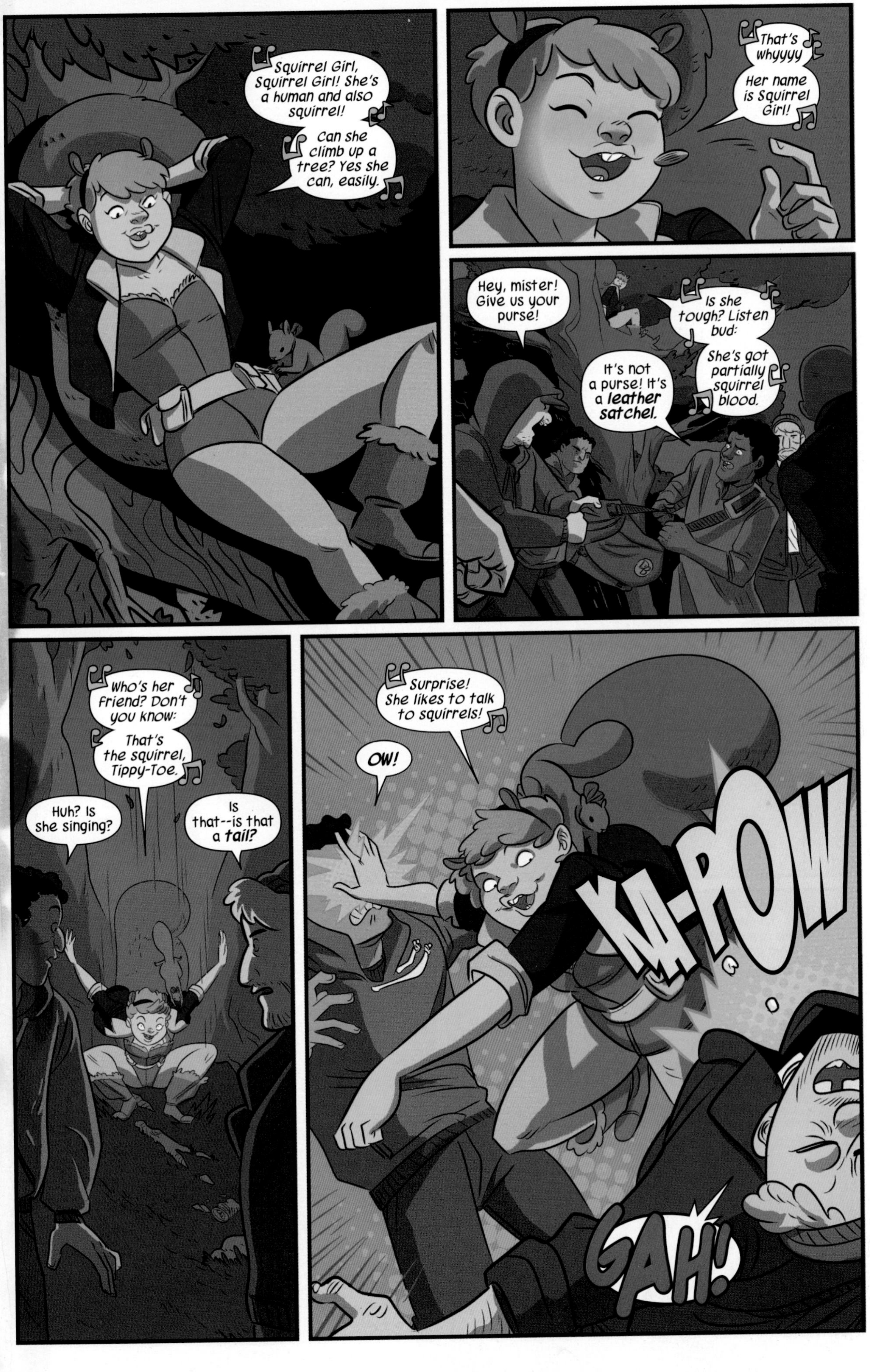
Squirrel Girl, Squirrel Girl! She's a human and also squirrel!
Can she climb up a tree? Yes she can, easily.
That's whyyyy
Her name is Squirrel Girl!
Hey, mister! Give us your purse!
Is she tough? Listen bud:
She's got partially squirrel blood.
It's not a purse! It's a leather satchel.
Who's her friend? Don't you know:
That's the squirrel, Tippy-Toe.
Huh? Is she singing?
Is that--is that a tail?
Surprise! She likes to talk to squirrels!
OW!
KA-POW
GAH!

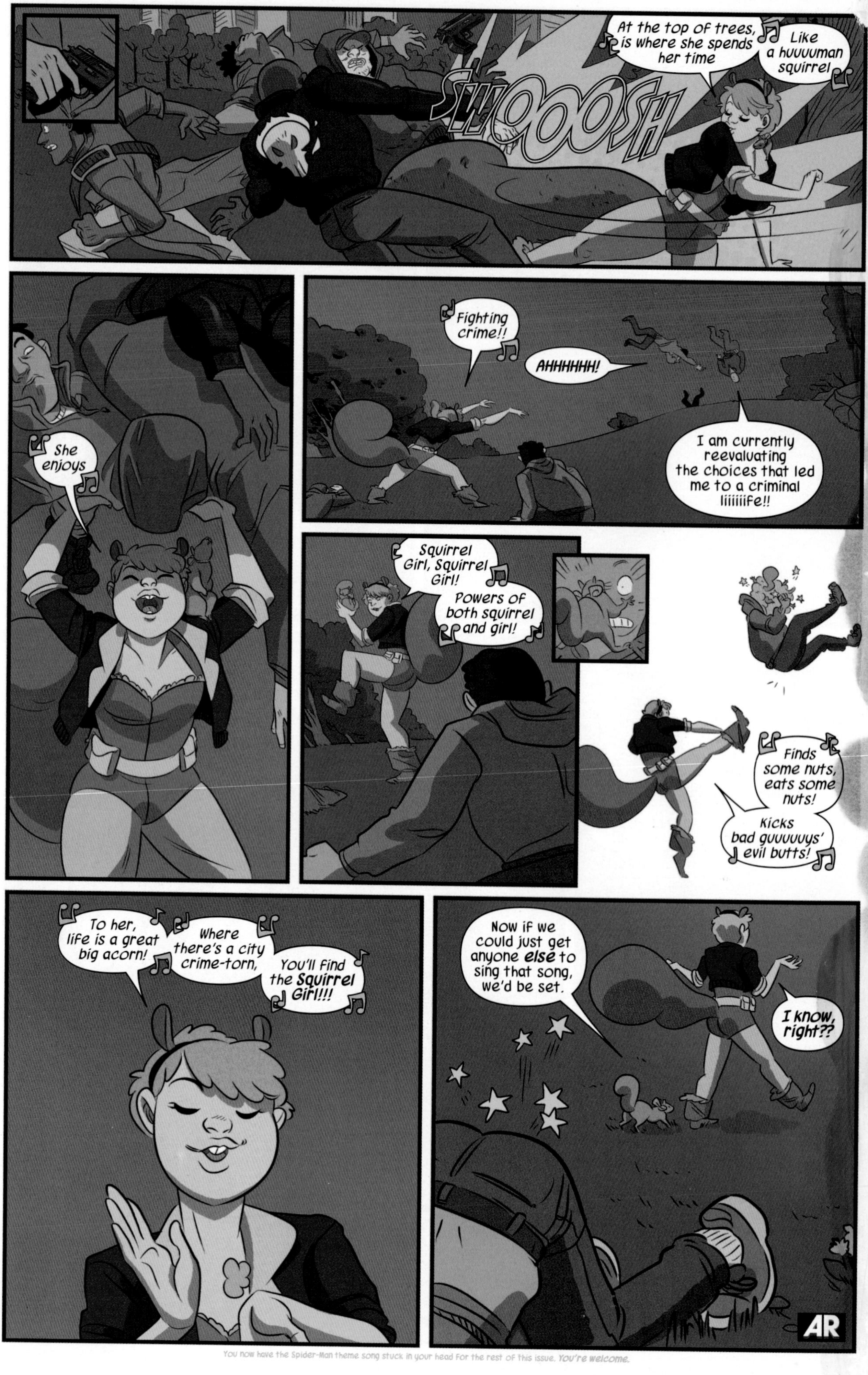
At the top of trees, is where she spends her time
Like a huuuuman squirrel
SWOOOSH
She enjoys
Fighting crime!!
AHHHHHH!
I am currently reevaluating the choices that led me to a criminal liiiiiife!!
Squirrel Girl, Squirrel Girl!
Powers of both squirrel and girl!
Finds some nuts, eats some nuts!
Kicks bad guuuuuys' evil butts!
To her, life is a great big acorn!
Where there's a city crime-torn,
You'll find the **Squirrel Girl!!!**
Now if we could just get anyone ***else*** to sing that song, we'd be set.
I know, right??
AR

You now have the Spider-Man theme song stuck in your head for the rest of this issue. *You're welcome.*

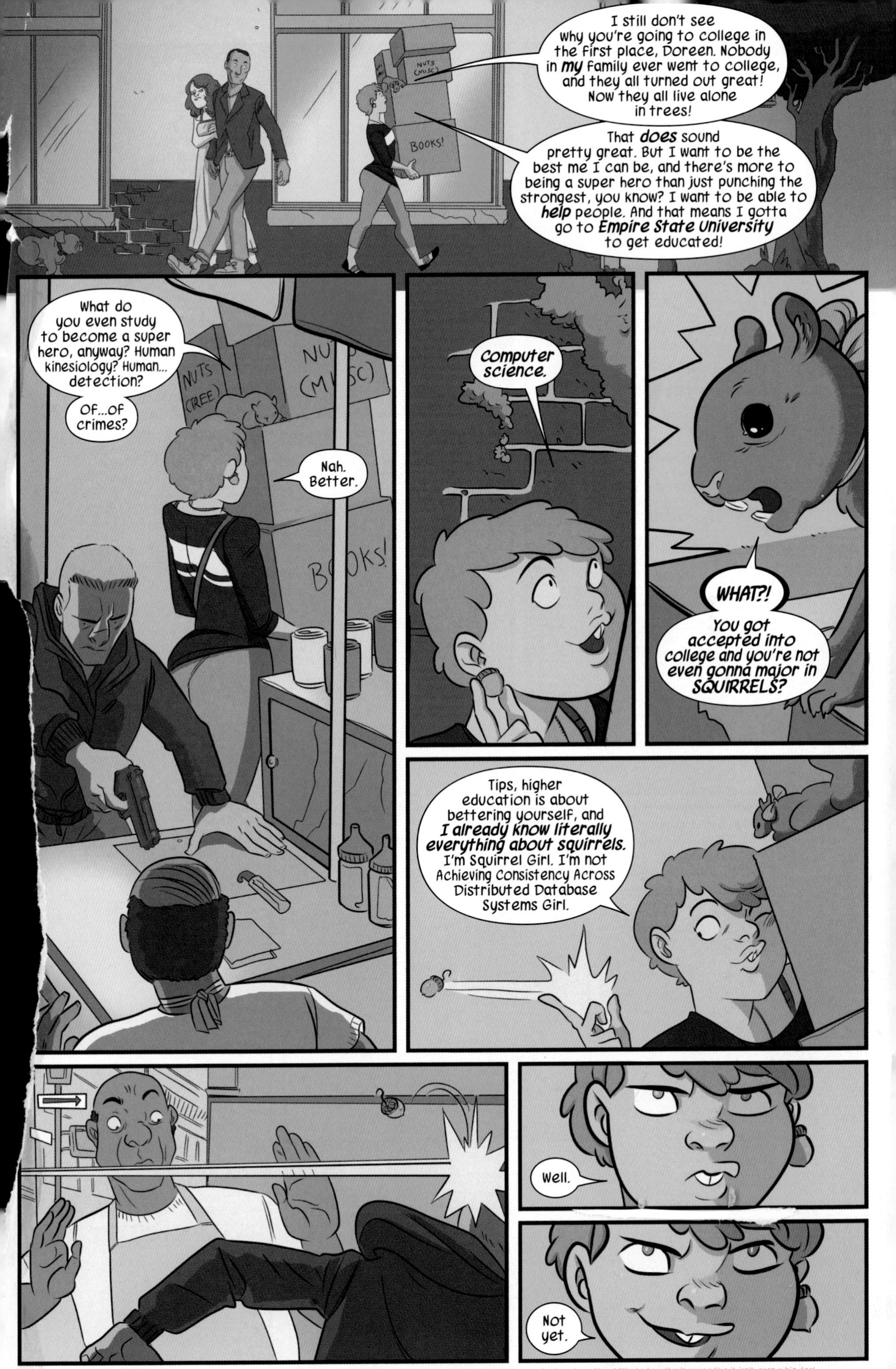
I still don't see why you're going to college in the first place, Doreen. Nobody in my family ever went to college, and they all turned out great! Now they all live alone in trees!
That does sound pretty great. But I want to be the best me I can be, and there's more to being a super hero than just punching the strongest, you know? I want to be able to help people. And that means I gotta go to Empire State University to get educated!
NUTS (MISC)
BOOKS!
What do you even study to become a super hero, anyway? Human kinesiology? Human... detection?
Of...of crimes?
Nah. Better.
NUTS (TREE)
Computer science.
WHAT?!
You got accepted into college and you're not even gonna major in SQUIRRELS?
Tips, higher education is about bettering yourself, and I already know literally everything about squirrels. I'm Squirrel Girl. I'm not Achieving Consistency Across Distributed Database Systems Girl.
Well.
Not yet.

There's more to being a super hero than just being the strongest! For example, you might also be the fastest, or the smartest, or have the ability to breathe in space like it isn't even a big deal.

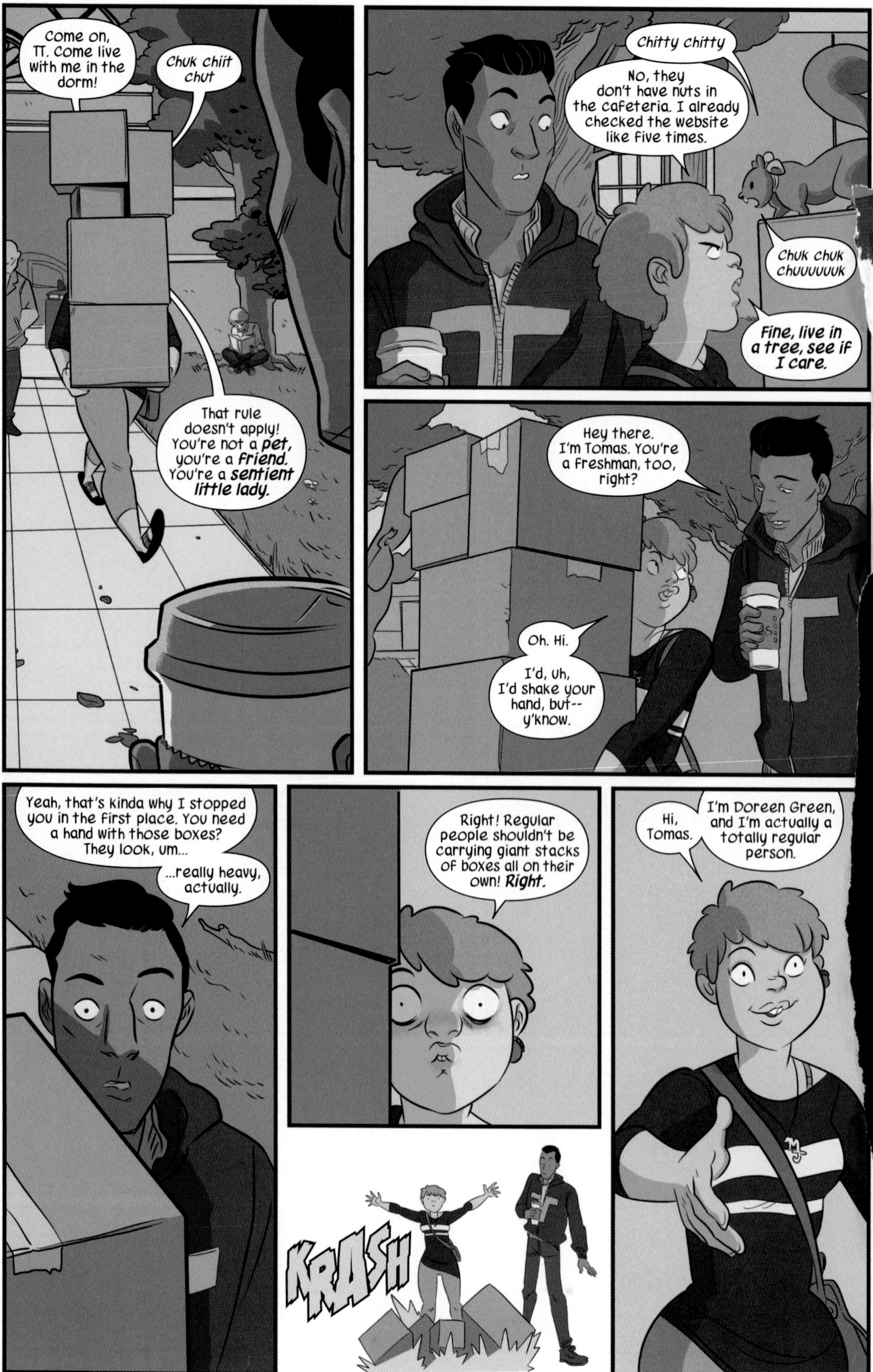

Come on, TT. Come live with me in the dorm!
Chuk chiit chut
That rule doesn't apply! You're not a **pet**, you're a **friend**. You're a **sentient little lady.**
Chitty chitty
No, they don't have nuts in the cafeteria. I already checked the website like five times.
Chuk chuk chuuuuuuk
Fine, live in a tree, see if I care.
Hey there. I'm Tomas. You're a freshman, too, right?
Oh. Hi.
I'd, uh, I'd shake your hand, but-- y'know.
Yeah, that's kinda why I stopped you in the first place. You need a hand with those boxes? They look, um...
...really heavy, actually.
Right! Regular people shouldn't be carrying giant stacks of boxes all on their own! **Right.**
Hi, Tomas.
I'm Doreen Green, and I'm actually a totally regular person.
KRASH

Also, my name rhymes. Yes, that too is but one of the *several* ways in which I am totally regular.

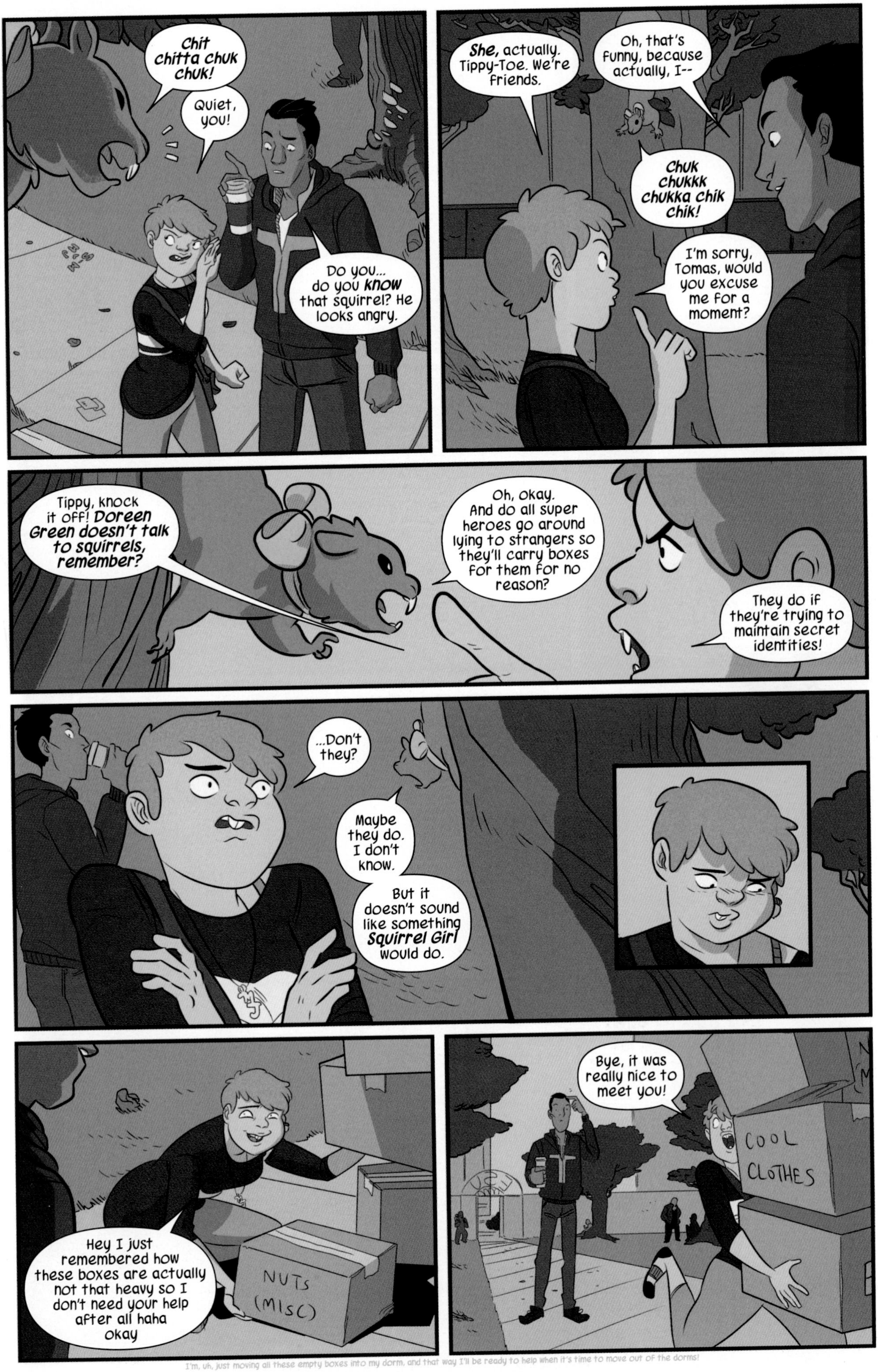

Chit chitta chuk chuk!
Quiet, you!
Do you... do you know that squirrel? He looks angry.
She, actually. Tippy-Toe. We're friends.
Oh, that's funny, because actually, I--
Chuk chukkk chukka chik chik!
I'm sorry, Tomas, would you excuse me for a moment?
Tippy, knock it off! Doreen Green doesn't talk to squirrels, remember?
Oh, okay. And do all super heroes go around lying to strangers so they'll carry boxes for them for no reason?
They do if they're trying to maintain secret identities!
...Don't they?
Maybe they do. I don't know.
But it doesn't sound like something Squirrel Girl would do.
Hey I just remembered how these boxes are actually not that heavy so I don't need your help after all haha okay
NUTs (MISC)
Bye, it was really nice to meet you!
COOL CLOTHES

I'm, uh, just moving all these empty boxes into my dorm, and that way I'll be ready to help when it's time to move out of the dorms!

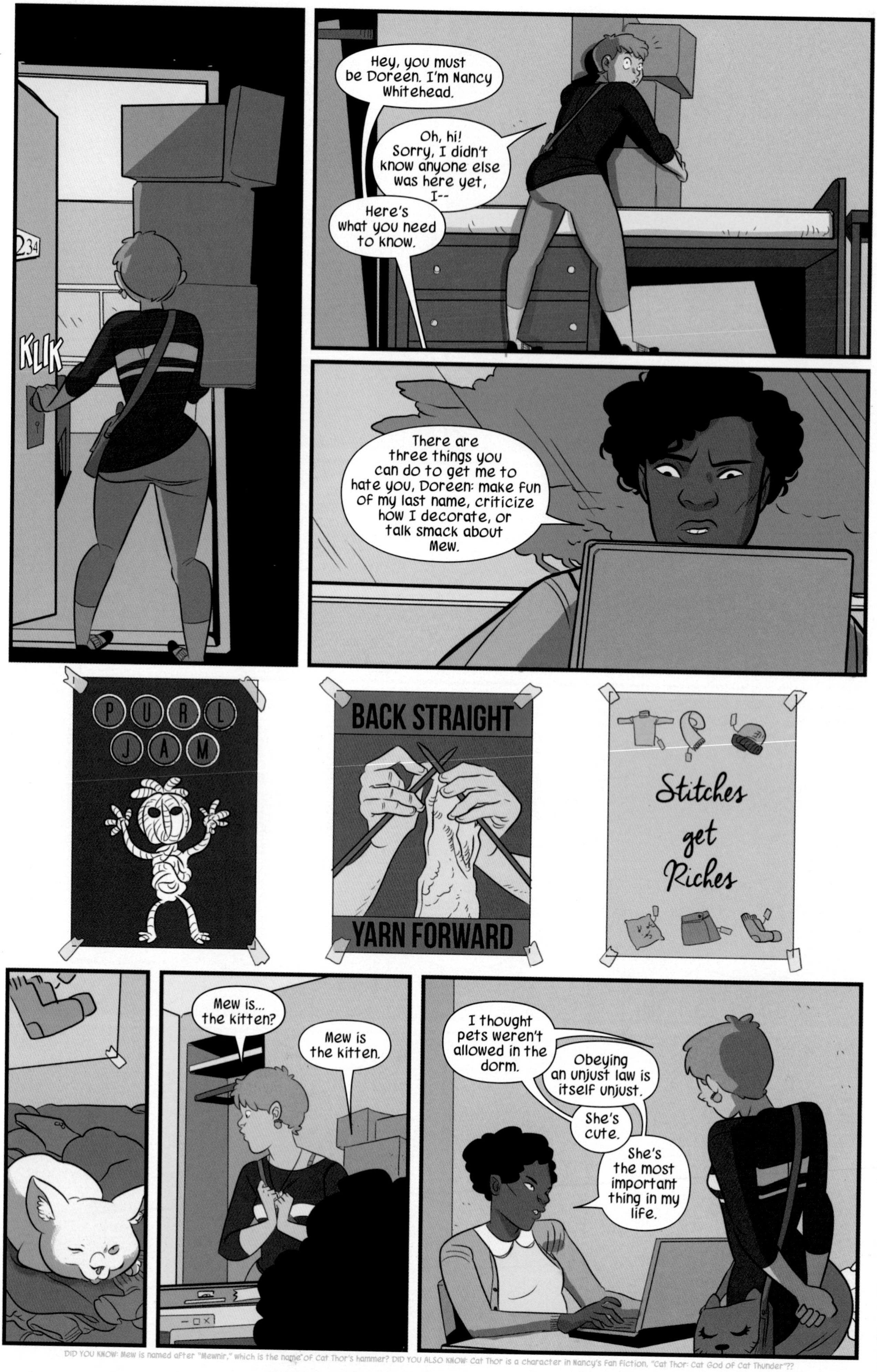
KLIK
Hey, you must be Doreen. I'm Nancy Whitehead.
Oh, hi! Sorry, I didn't know anyone else was here yet, I--
Here's what you need to know.
There are three things you can do to get me to hate you, Doreen: make fun of my last name, criticize how I decorate, or talk smack about Mew.
PURL JAM
BACK STRAIGHT
YARN FORWARD
Stitches get Riches
Mew is... the kitten?
Mew is the kitten.
I thought pets weren't allowed in the dorm.
Obeying an unjust law is itself unjust.
She's cute.
She's the most important thing in my life.

DID YOU KNOW: Mew is named after "Mewnir," which is the name of Cat Thor's hammer? DID YOU ALSO KNOW: Cat Thor is a character in Nancy's Fan Fiction, "Cat Thor: Cat God of Cat Thunder"??

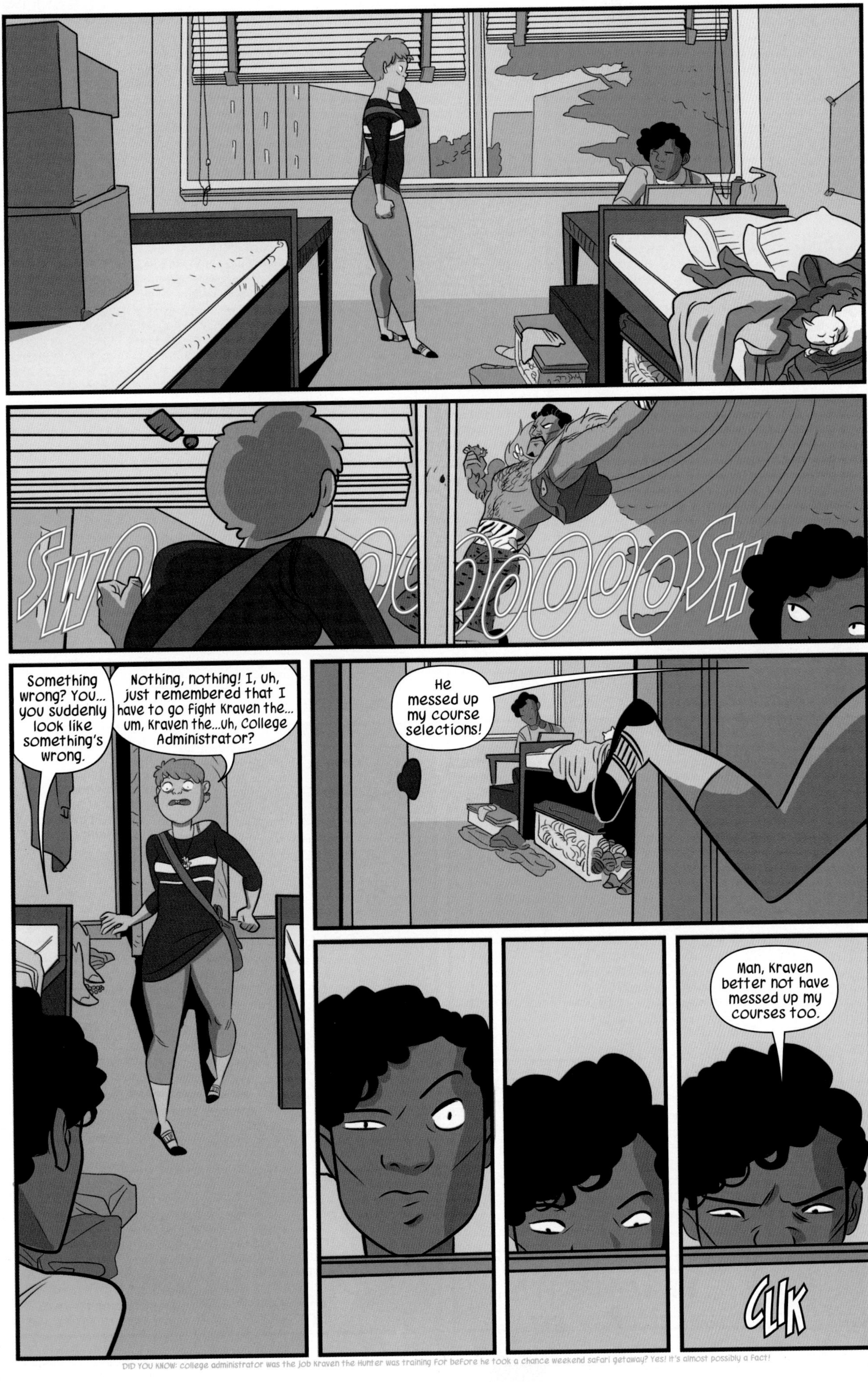
SWOOOOOOOOOOSH
Something wrong? You... you suddenly look like something's wrong.
Nothing, nothing! I, uh, just remembered that I have to go fight Kraven the... um, Kraven the...uh, College Administrator?
He messed up my course selections!
Man, Kraven better not have messed up my courses too.
CLIK

DID YOU KNOW: college administrator was the job Kraven the Hunter was training for before he took a chance weekend safari getaway? Yes! It's almost possibly a fact!

SLAM

All right: twenty seconds to change means he *should* still be on campus.

There's still time!

Come on, come on, I know you're in here somewhere...

A-ha!

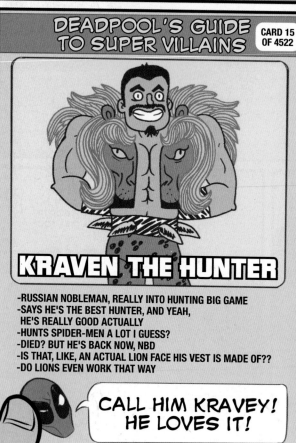

DEADPOOL'S GUIDE TO SUPER VILLAINS

CARD 15 OF 4522

KRAVEN THE HUNTER

-RUSSIAN NOBLEMAN, REALLY INTO HUNTING BIG GAME
-SAYS HE'S THE BEST HUNTER, AND YEAH, HE'S REALLY GOOD ACTUALLY
-HUNTS SPIDER-MEN A LOT I GUESS?
-DIED? BUT HE'S BACK NOW, NBD
-IS THAT, LIKE, AN ACTUAL LION FACE HIS VEST IS MADE OF??
-DO LIONS EVEN WORK THAT WAY

CALL HIM KRAVEY! HE LOVES IT!

I have no quarrel with you. Stand aside, and you will live to tell your descendants of the day you met the great Kraven the Hunter.

Chitta *chuk!* Chuuuuk!

Shut up, you're hunting *squirrels* now?

This... "beast," though it hardly warrants the name, attacked me. I subdued it. It was not worthy of my attention.

I am beginning to think it is not worthy of its life.

There are "Deadpool's Official Unofficial Guide To Super Heroes" cards too, but for some reason every pack is like 99% pictures of Deadpool looking at himself in a mirror and giving himself a thumbs up.

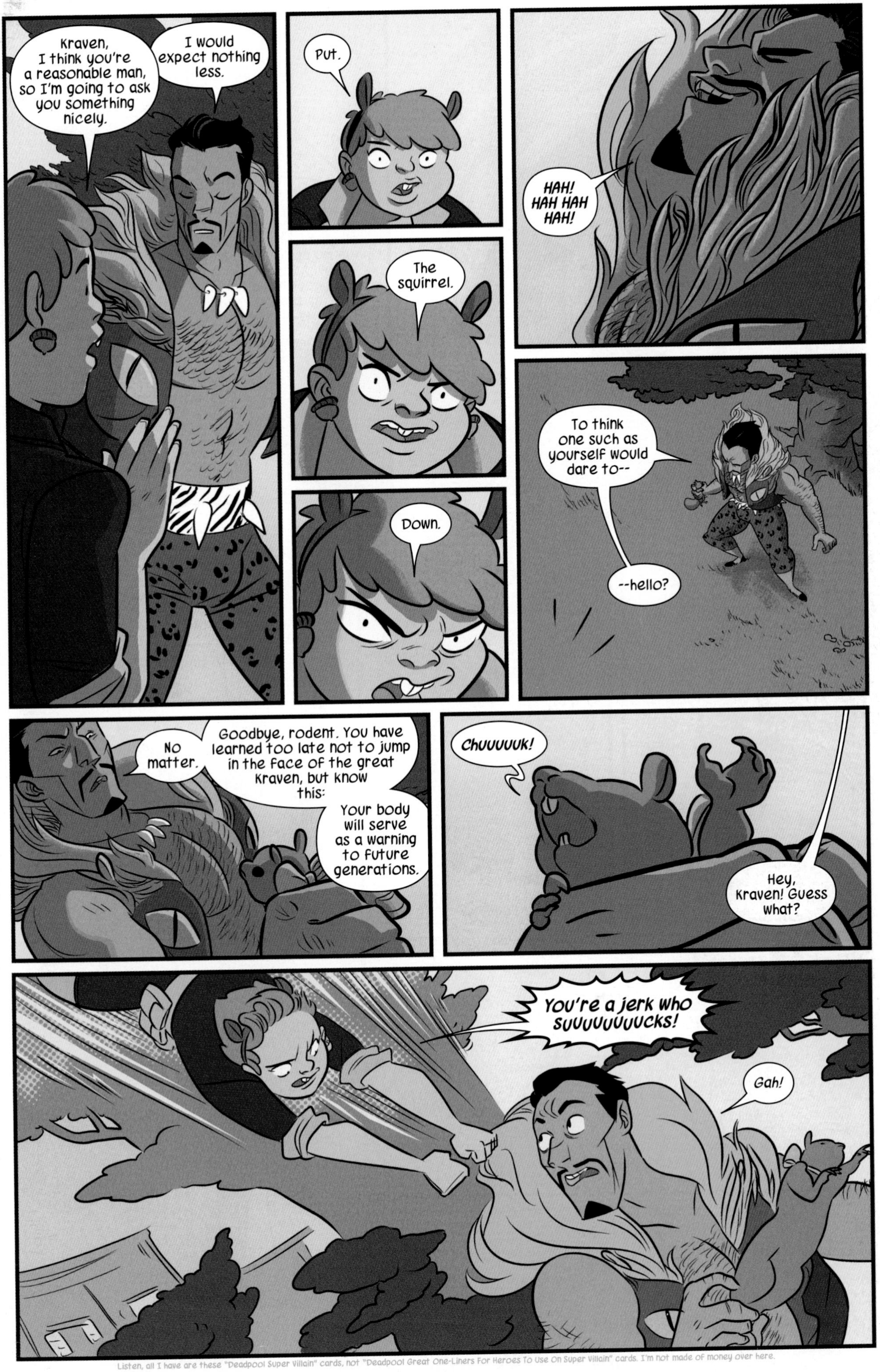
Kraven, I think you're a reasonable man, so I'm going to ask you something nicely.
I would expect nothing less.
Put.
The squirrel.
Down.
HAH! HAH HAH HAH!
To think one such as yourself would dare to--
--hello?
No matter.
Goodbye, rodent. You have learned too late not to jump in the face of the great Kraven, but know this:
Your body will serve as a warning to future generations.
Chuuuuuk!
Hey, Kraven! Guess what?
You're a jerk who suuuuuuuucks!
Gah!

Listen, all I have are these "Deadpool Super Villain" cards, not "Deadpool Great One-Liners For Heroes To Use On Super Villain" cards. I'm not made of money over here.

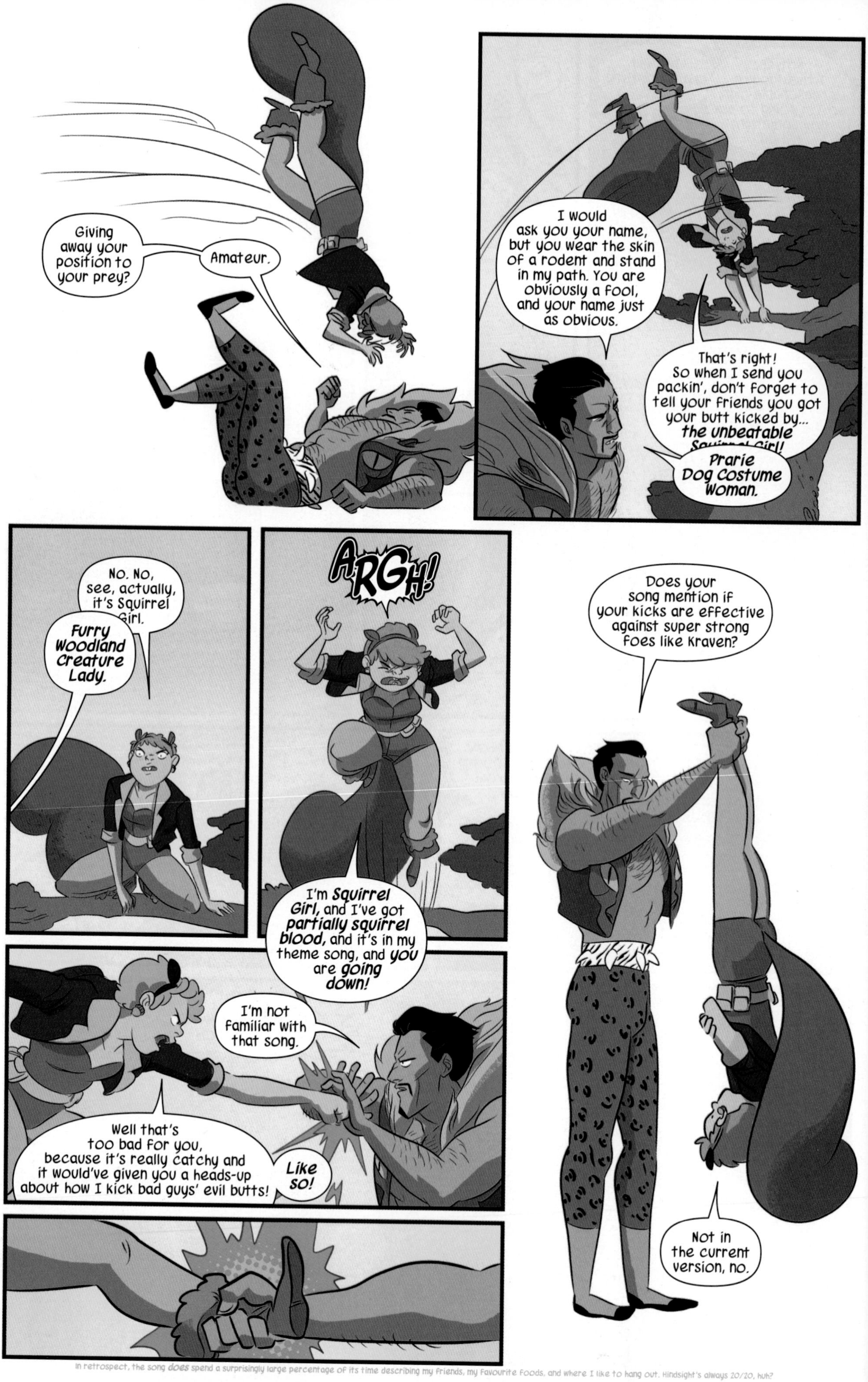
Giving away your position to your prey?
Amateur.
I would ask you your name, but you wear the skin of a rodent and stand in my path. You are obviously a fool, and your name just as obvious.
That's right! So when I send you packin', don't forget to tell your friends you got your butt kicked by... *the unbeatable*
Prarie Dog Costume Woman.
No. No, see, actually, it's Squirrel Girl.
Furry Woodland Creature Lady.
ARGH!
I'm *Squirrel Girl,* and I've got *partially squirrel blood,* and it's in my theme song, and *you* are *going down!*
I'm not familiar with that song.
Well that's too bad for you, because it's really catchy and it would've given you a heads-up about how I kick bad guys' evil butts!
Like so!
Does your song mention if your kicks are effective against super strong foes like Kraven?
Not in the current version, no.

In retrospect, the song *does* spend a surprisingly large percentage of its time describing my friends, my favourite foods, and where I like to hang out. Hindsight's always 20/20, huh?

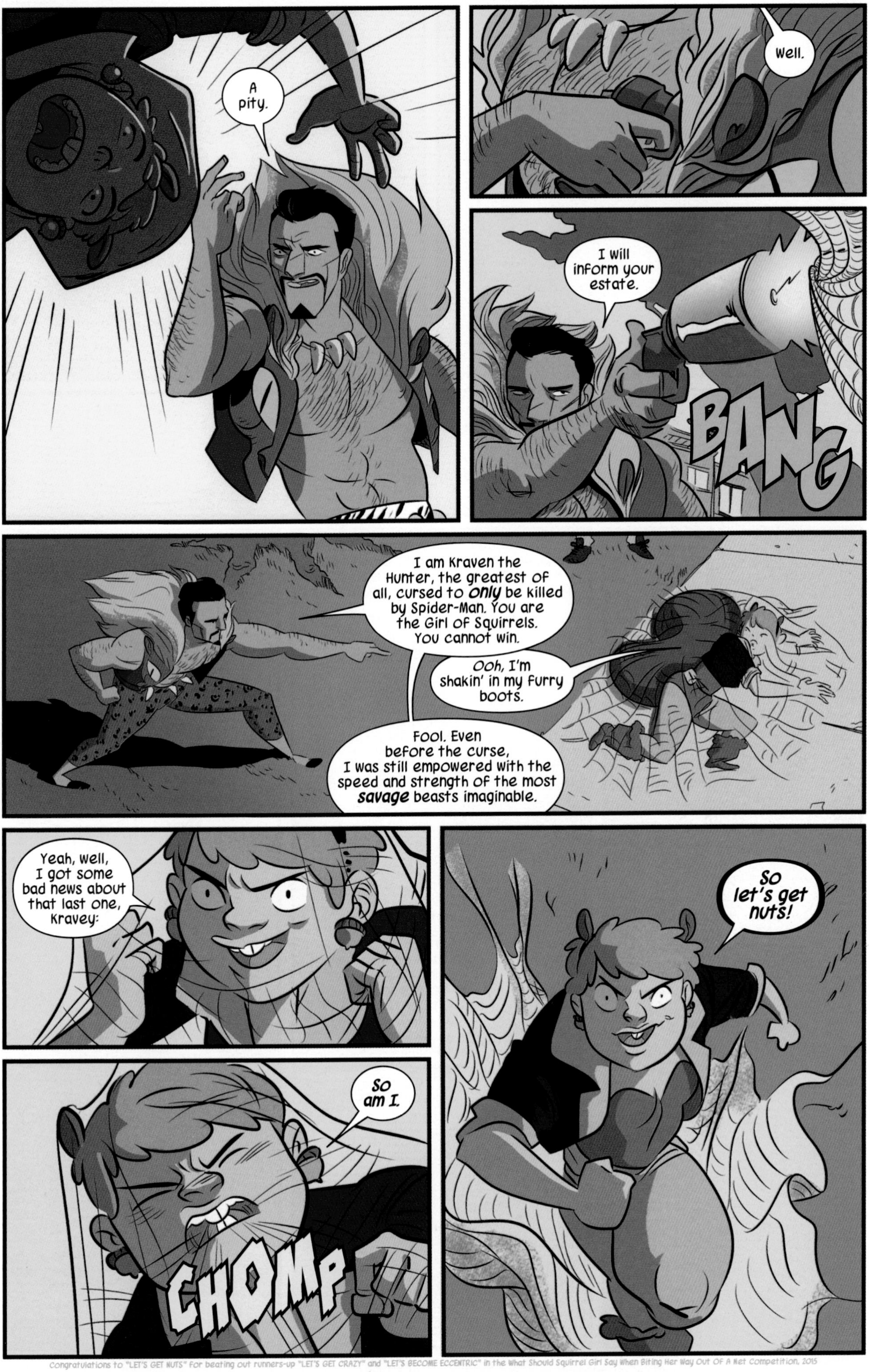
A pity.
Well.
I will inform your estate.
BANG
I am Kraven the Hunter, the greatest of all, cursed to *only* be killed by Spider-Man. You are the Girl of Squirrels. You cannot win.
Ooh, I'm shakin' in my furry boots.
Fool. Even before the curse, I was still empowered with the speed and strength of the most *savage* beasts imaginable.
Yeah, well, I got some bad news about that last one, Kravey:
So am I.
CHOMP
So let's get nuts!

Congratulations to "LET'S GET NUTS" for beating out runners-up "LET'S GET CRAZY" and "LET'S BECOME ECCENTRIC" in the What Should Squirrel Girl Say When Biting Her Way Out Of A Net Competition, 2015

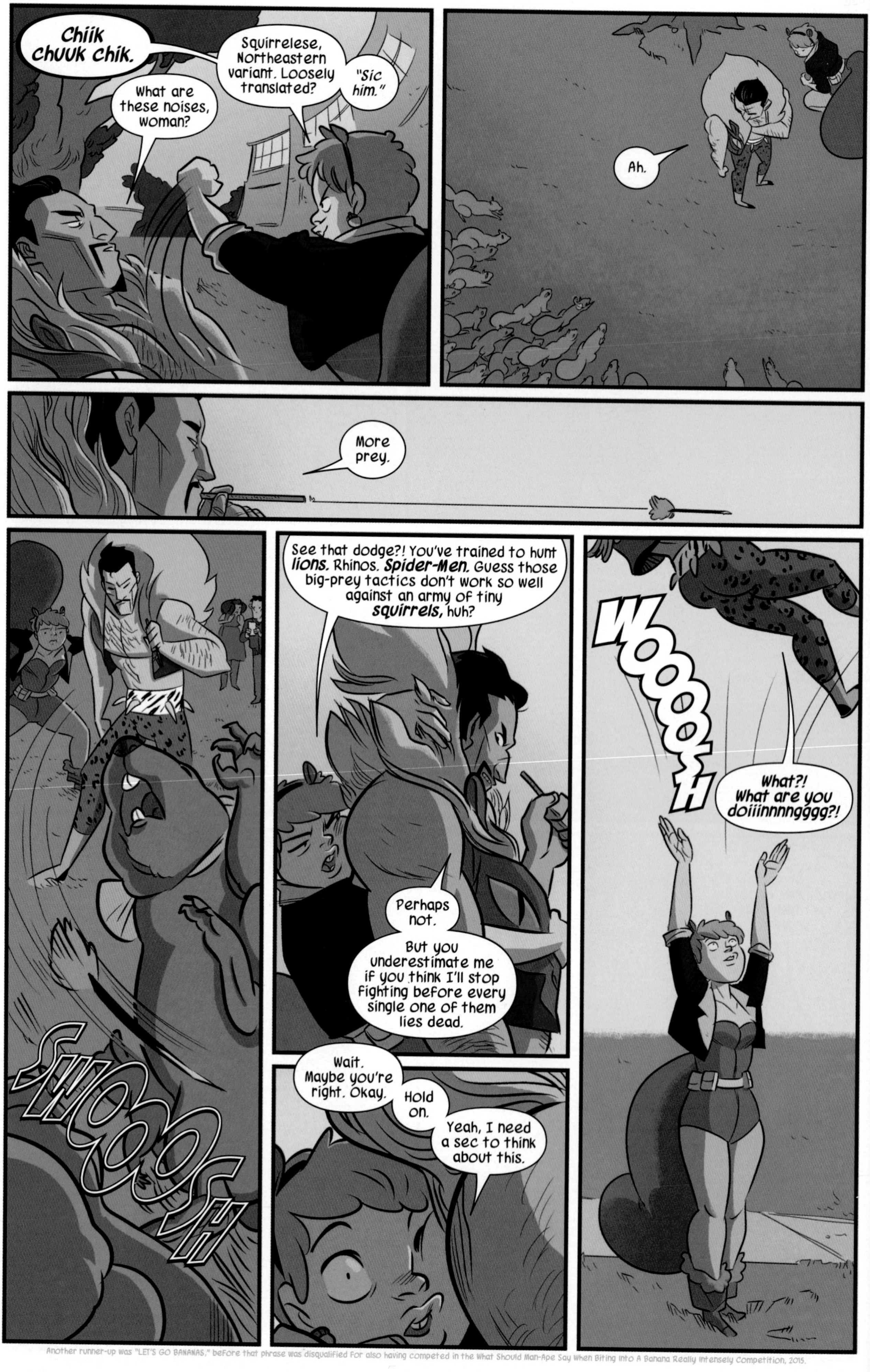
Chiik chuuk chik.
What are these noises, woman?
Squirrelese, Northeastern variant. Loosely translated?
"Sic him."
Ah.
More prey.
See that dodge?! You've trained to hunt lions. Rhinos. Spider-Men. Guess those big-prey tactics don't work so well against an army of tiny squirrels, huh?
SHOOOOSH
Perhaps not.
But you underestimate me if you think I'll stop fighting before every single one of them lies dead.
Wait. Maybe you're right. Okay.
Hold on.
Yeah, I need a sec to think about this.
WOOOOOSH
What?! What are you doiiinnnngggg?!

Another runner-up was "LET'S GO BANANAS," before that phrase was disqualified for also having competed in the What Should Man-Ape Say When Biting Into A Banana Really Intensely Competition, 2015.

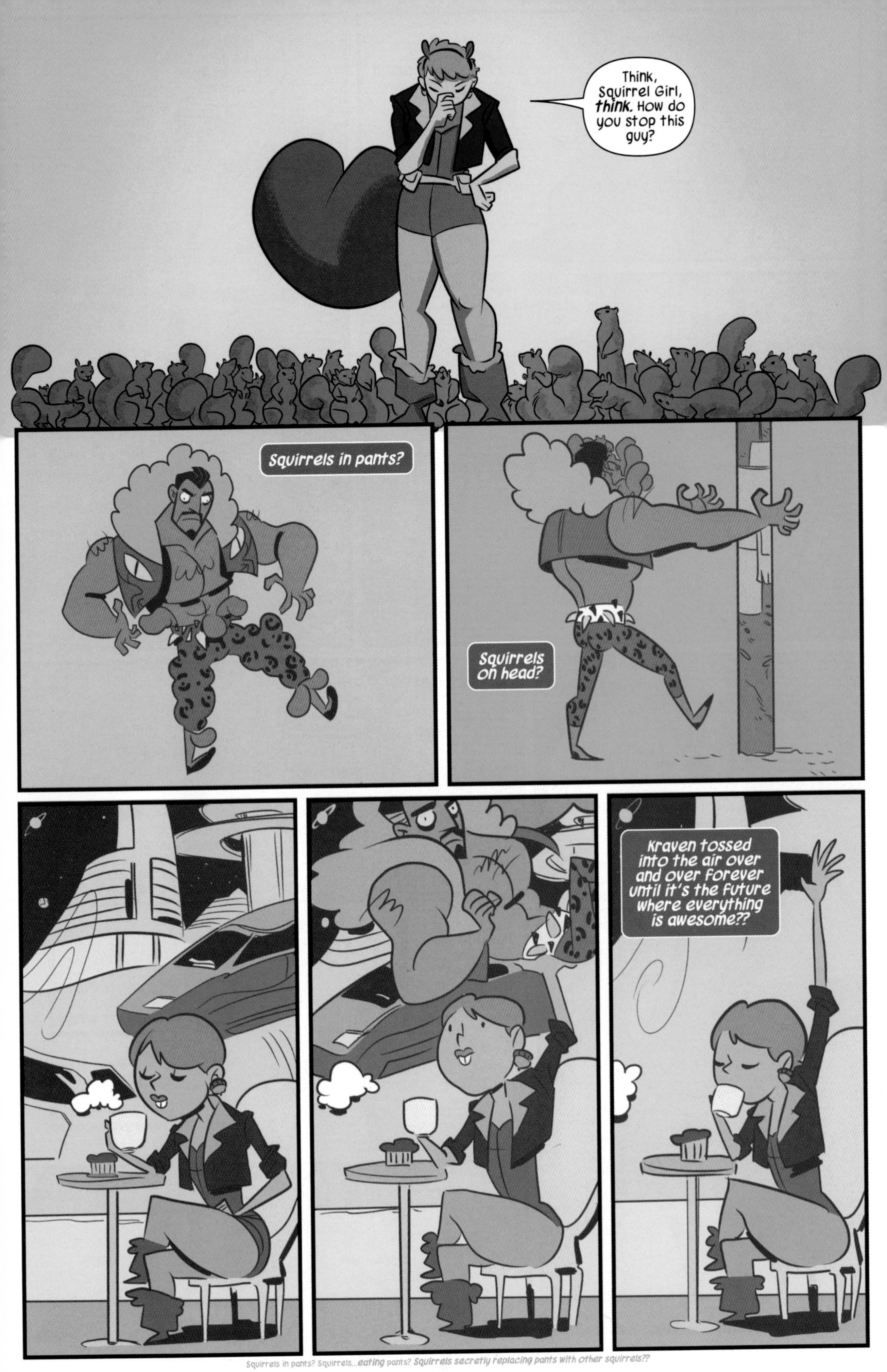
Think, Squirrel Girl, **think.** How do you stop this guy?
Squirrels in pants?
Squirrels on head?
Kraven tossed into the air over and over forever until it's the future where everything is awesome??

Squirrels in pants? Squirrels...*eating* pants? ***Squirrels secretly replacing pants with other squirrels??***

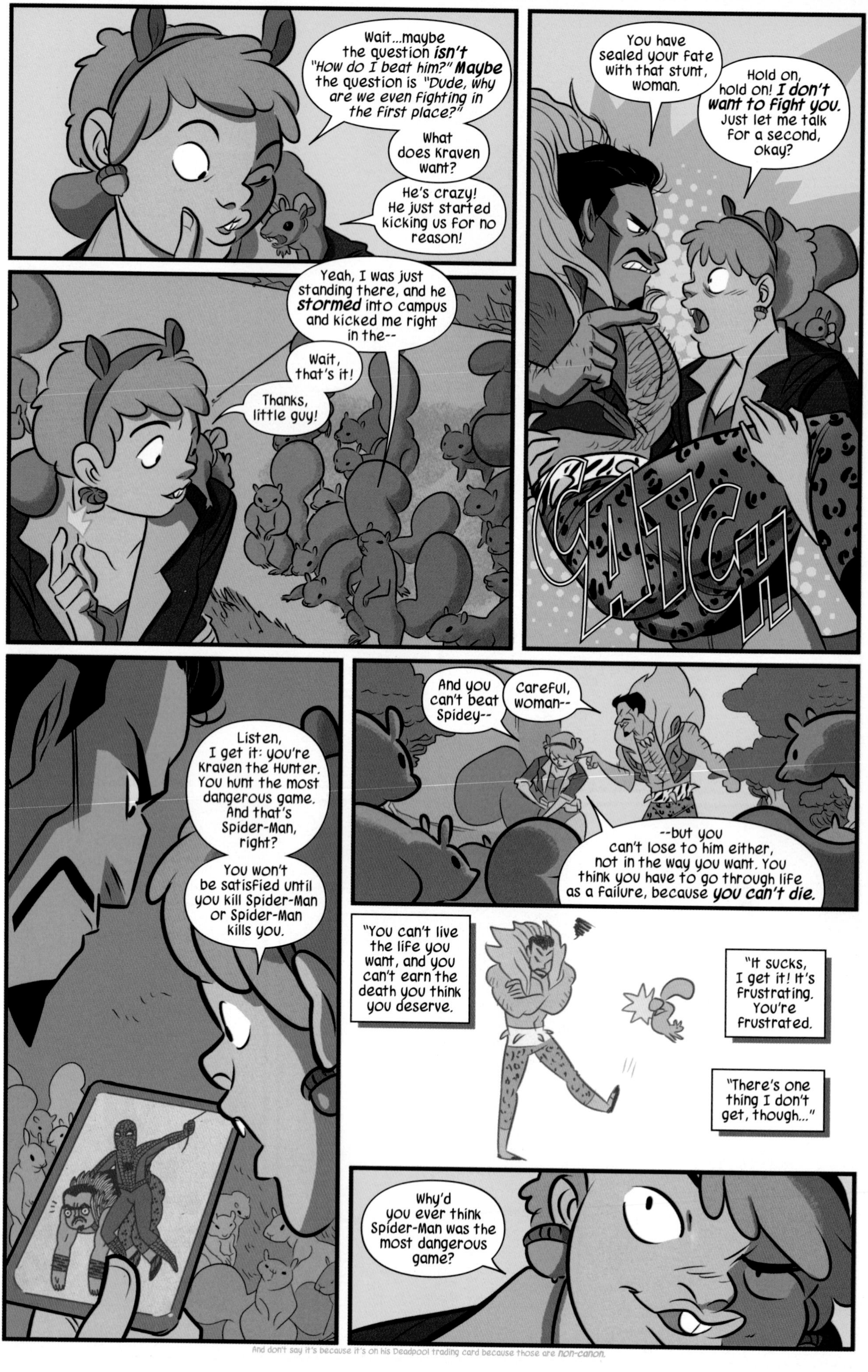
Wait...maybe the question isn't "How do I beat him?" Maybe the question is "Dude, why are we even fighting in the first place?"
What does Kraven want?
He's crazy! He just started kicking us for no reason!
Yeah, I was just standing there, and he stormed into campus and kicked me right in the--
Wait, that's it!
Thanks, little guy!
You have sealed your fate with that stunt, woman.
Hold on, hold on! I don't want to fight you. Just let me talk for a second, okay?
CATCH
Listen, I get it: you're Kraven the Hunter. You hunt the most dangerous game. And that's Spider-Man, right?
You won't be satisfied until you kill Spider-Man or Spider-Man kills you.
And you can't beat Spidey--
Careful, woman--
--but you can't lose to him either, not in the way you want. You think you have to go through life as a failure, because you can't die.
"You can't live the life you want, and you can't earn the death you think you deserve.
"It sucks, I get it! It's frustrating. You're frustrated.
"There's one thing I don't get, though..."
Why'd you ever think Spider-Man was the most dangerous game?

And don't say it's because it's on his Deadpool trading card because those are *non-canon.*

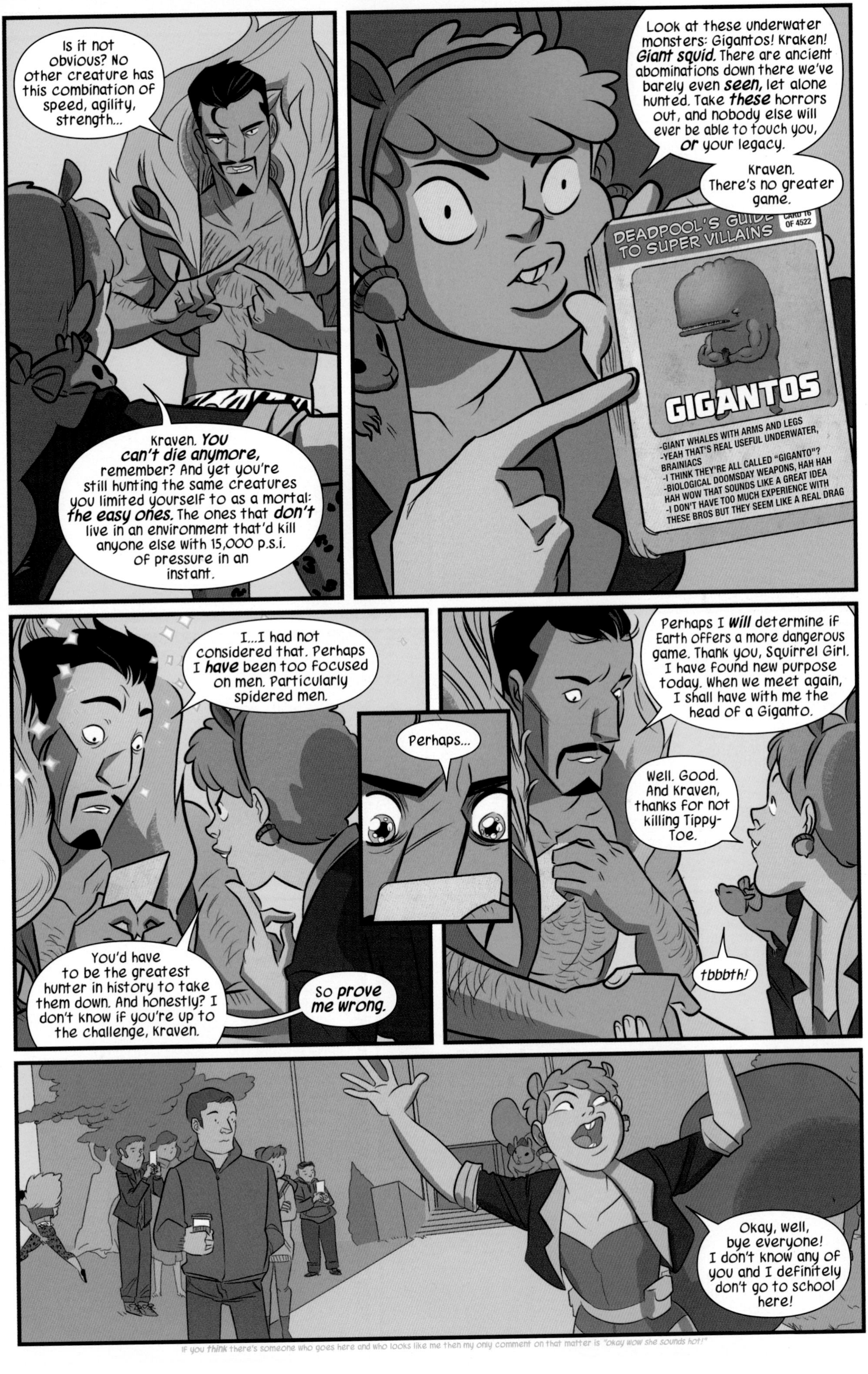
Is it not obvious? No other creature has this combination of speed, agility, strength...
Kraven. YOU can't die anymore, remember? And yet you're still hunting the same creatures you limited yourself to as a mortal: the easy ones. The ones that don't live in an environment that'd kill anyone else with 15,000 p.s.i. of pressure in an instant.
Look at these underwater monsters: Gigantos! Kraken! Giant squid. There are ancient abominations down there we've barely even seen, let alone hunted. Take these horrors out, and nobody else will ever be able to touch you, or your legacy.
Kraven. There's no greater game.
DEADPOOL'S GUIDE TO SUPER VILLAINS
CARD 16 OF 4522
GIGANTOS
-GIANT WHALES WITH ARMS AND LEGS
-YEAH THAT'S REAL USEFUL UNDERWATER, BRAINIACS
-I THINK THEY'RE ALL CALLED "GIGANTO"?
-BIOLOGICAL DOOMSDAY WEAPONS, HAH HAH HAH WOW THAT SOUNDS LIKE A GREAT IDEA
-I DON'T HAVE TOO MUCH EXPERIENCE WITH THESE BROS BUT THEY SEEM LIKE A REAL DRAG
I...I had not considered that. Perhaps I have been too focused on men. Particularly spidered men.
You'd have to be the greatest hunter in history to take them down. And honestly? I don't know if you're up to the challenge, Kraven.
So prove me wrong.
Perhaps...
Perhaps I will determine if Earth offers a more dangerous game. Thank you, Squirrel Girl. I have found new purpose today. When we meet again, I shall have with me the head of a Giganto.
Well. Good. And Kraven, thanks for not killing Tippy-Toe.
tbbbth!
Okay, well, bye everyone! I don't know any of you and I definitely don't go to school here!

If you *think* there's someone who goes here and who looks like me then my only comment on that matter is *"okay wow she sounds hot!"*

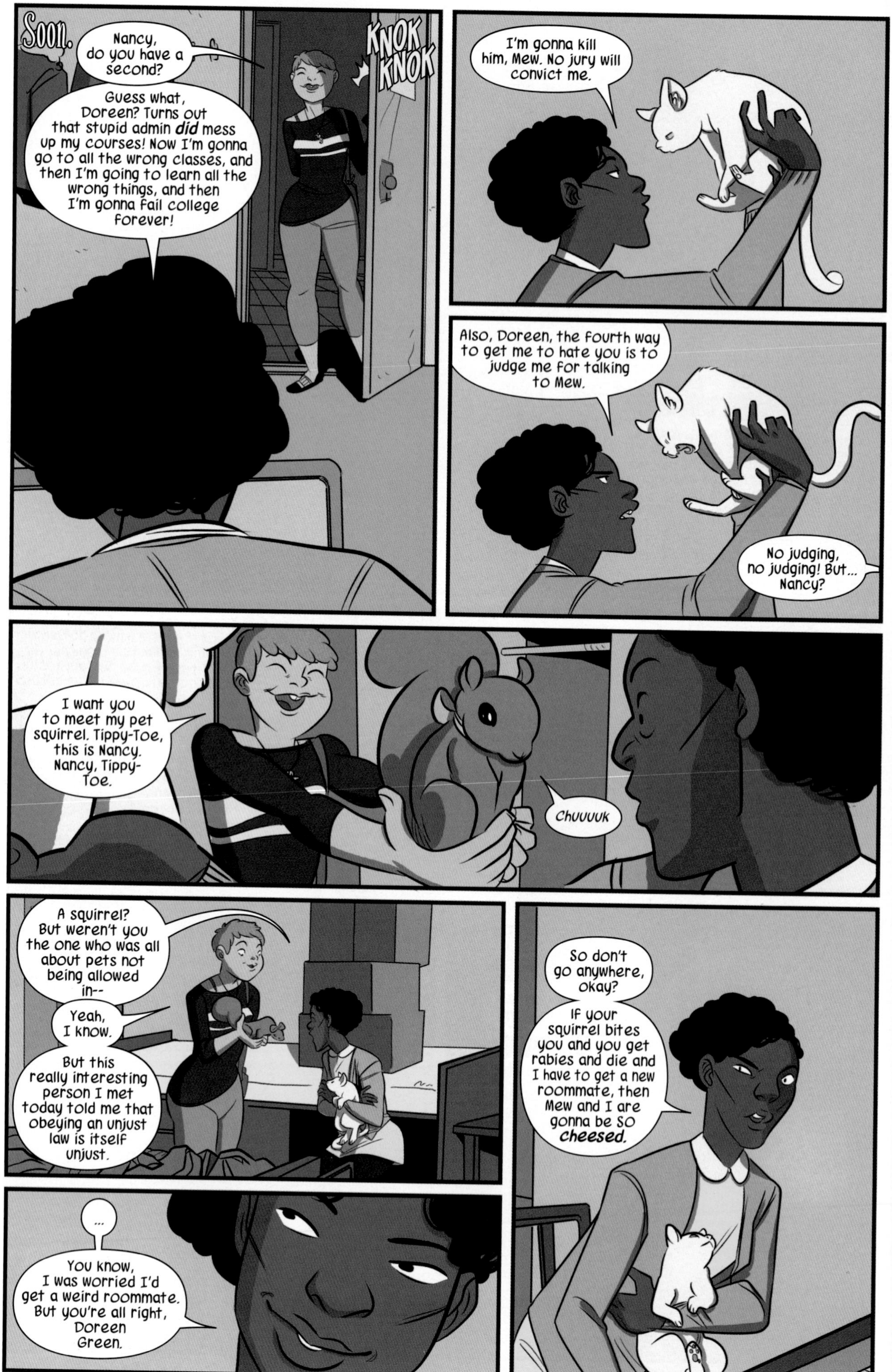

Soon.
Nancy, do you have a second?
KNOK KNOK
Guess what, Doreen? Turns out that stupid admin *did* mess up my courses! Now I'm gonna go to all the wrong classes, and then I'm going to learn all the wrong things, and then I'm gonna fail college forever!
I'm gonna kill him, Mew. No jury will convict me.
Also, Doreen, the fourth way to get me to hate you is to judge me for talking to Mew.
No judging, no judging! But... Nancy?
I want you to meet my pet squirrel. Tippy-Toe, this is Nancy. Nancy, Tippy-Toe.
Chuuuuk
A squirrel? But weren't you the one who was all about pets not being allowed in--
Yeah, I know.
But this really interesting person I met today told me that obeying an unjust law is itself unjust.
...
You know, I was worried I'd get a weird roommate. But you're all right, Doreen Green.
So don't go anywhere, okay?
If your squirrel bites you and you get rabies and die and I have to get a new roommate, then Mew and I are gonna be SO *cheesed.*

Also, sad I guess. Sad and cheesed. It's--it's a really familiar feeling?

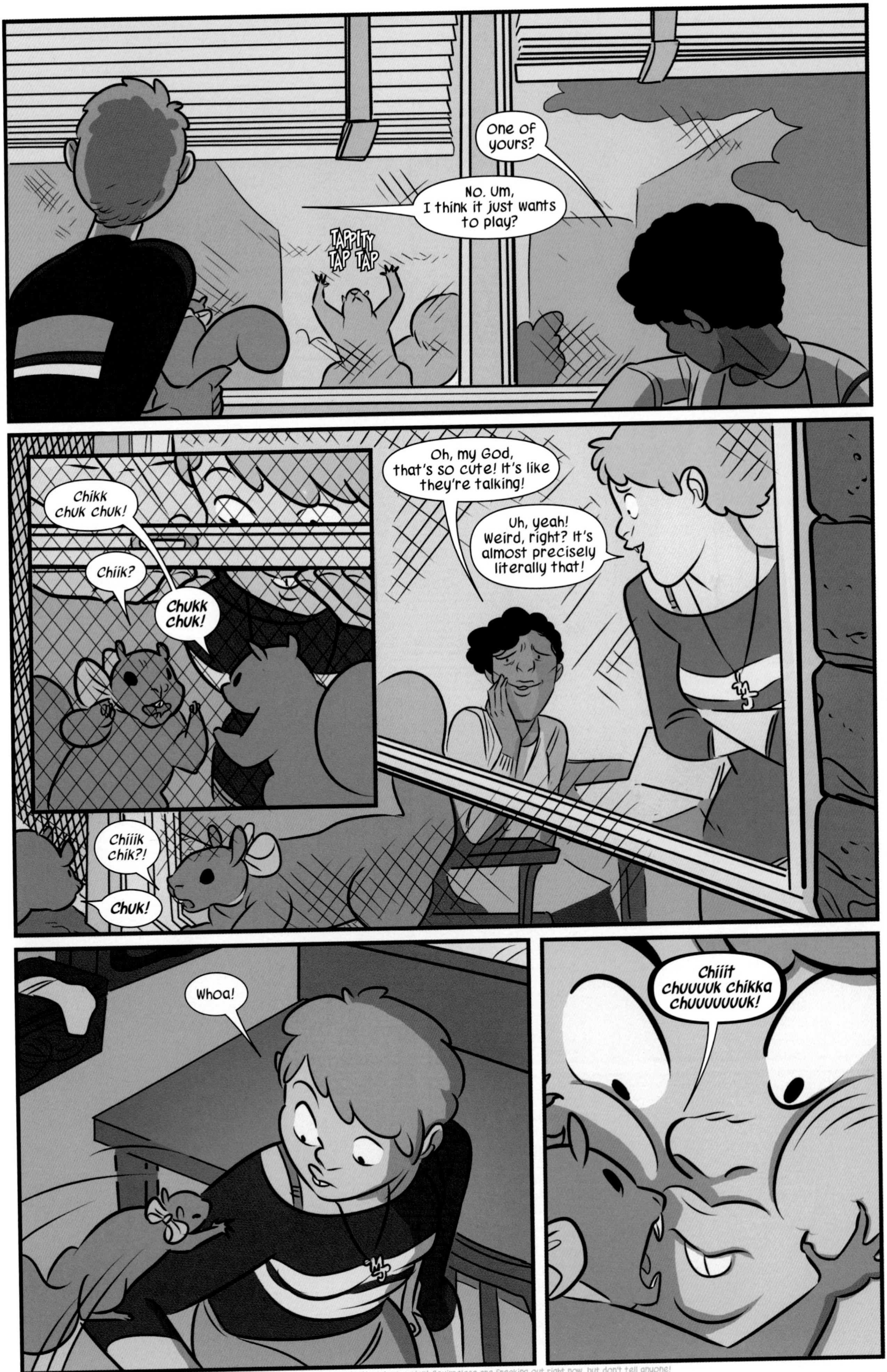
One of yours?
No. Um, I think it just wants to play?
TAPPITY TAP TAP
Oh, my God, that's so cute! It's like they're talking!
Uh, yeah! Weird, right? It's almost precisely literally that!
Chikk chuk chuk!
Chiik?
Chukk chuk!
Chiiik chik?!
Chuk!
Whoa!
Chiiit chuuuuk chikka chuuuuuuuk!

Those of you who *can* speak Northeastern variant Squirrelese are freaking out right now, but don't tell anyone! Keep it a surprise for the rest of us who have to read the next page to find out what the deal is, okay?

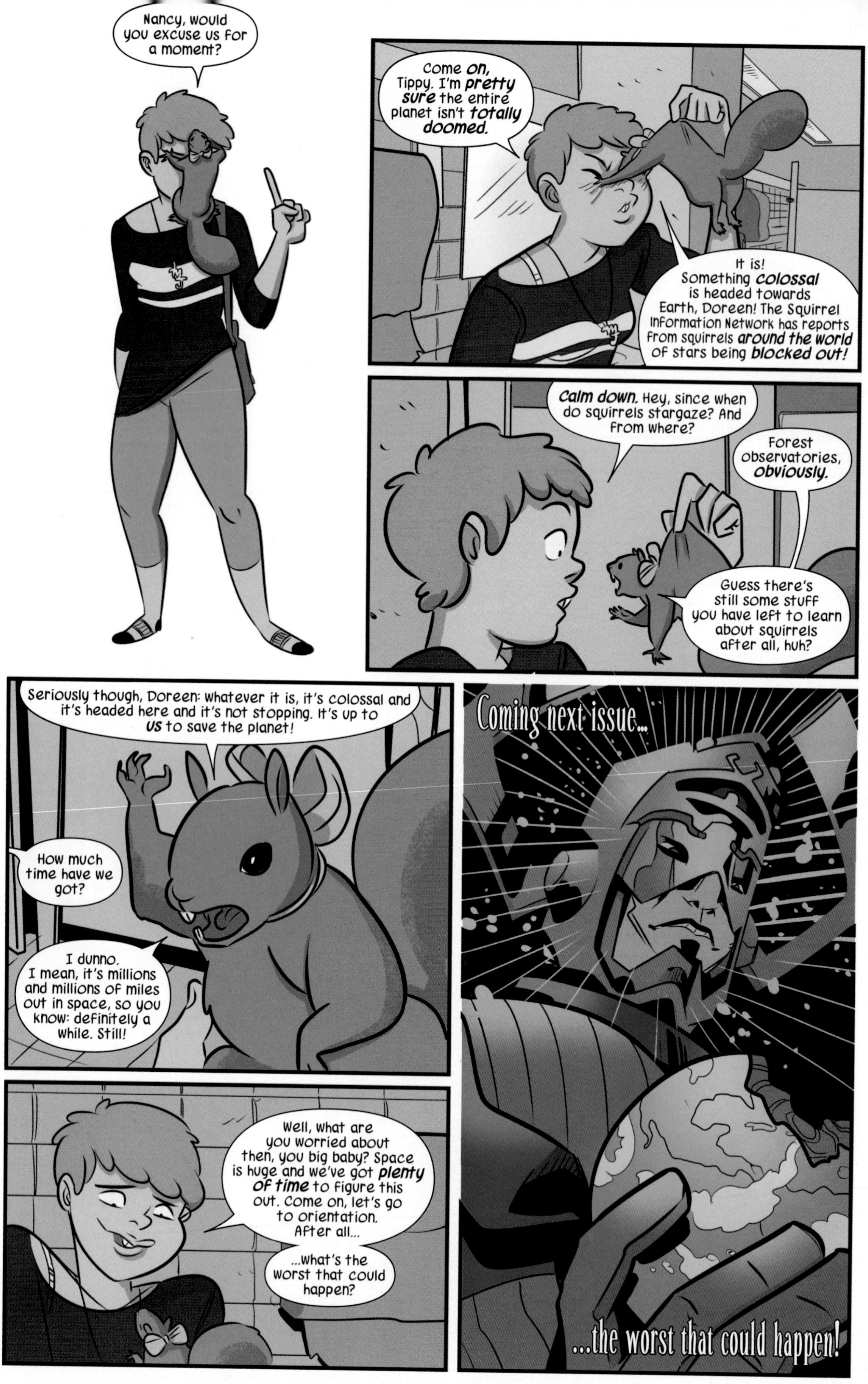
Nancy, would you excuse us for a moment?
Come on, Tippy. I'm pretty sure the entire planet isn't totally doomed.
It is! Something colossal is headed towards Earth, Doreen! The Squirrel Information Network has reports from squirrels around the world of stars being blocked out!
Calm down. Hey, since when do squirrels stargaze? And from where?
Forest observatories, obviously.
Guess there's still some stuff you have left to learn about squirrels after all, huh?
Seriously though, Doreen: whatever it is, it's colossal and it's headed here and it's not stopping. It's up to US to save the planet!
How much time have we got?
I dunno. I mean, it's millions and millions of miles out in space, so you know: definitely a while. Still!
Well, what are you worried about then, you big baby? Space is huge and we've got plenty of time to figure this out. Come on, let's go to orientation. After all...
...what's the worst that could happen?
Coming next issue...
...the worst that could happen!

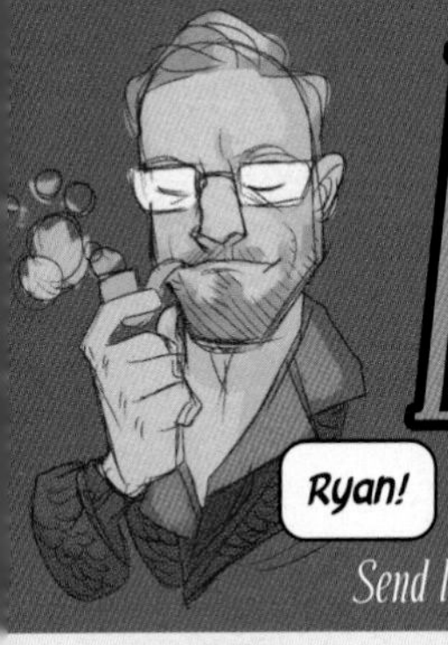
Ryan!

Letters From Nuts

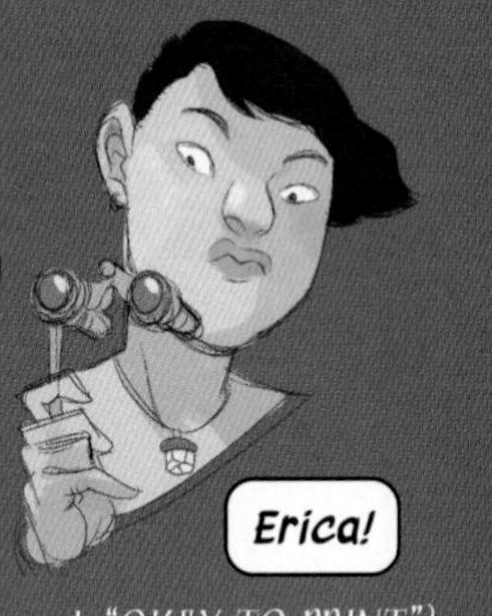
Erica!

Send letters to mheroes@marvel.com or 135 W 50th St, 7th Floor, New York, NY 10020 (Please mark "OKAY TO PRINT")

Hello! We're Erica and Ryan and Rico, we're writing and drawing and coloring a comic about a woman with squirrel powers. We've actually been writing and drawing and coloring this comic for YEARS, decades really, and last month Marvel came to us and asked if they could publish it, and we said "YES!" and then went on to say "Also we've been kinda using your character so you don't really have to ask, also thanks for not suing us."

OKAY NO that's nut true. We only started this comic recently! But we ARE following in the footsteps of the people who have made Squirrel Girl comics before: great guys like Will Murray, Steve Ditko, Dan Slott, Paul Pelletier, Brian Michael Bendis and Mike Deodato!

This book is an experiment: can a book like this find an audience? Will people TRULY read a comic about someone who dresses up like a rodent-like animal and fights crime in a major metropolitan area, even if that animal ISN'T a bat?? We hope they will. If you liked this comic, share it! Tell your friends! Tell the WHOLE WORLD you liked it, because then they might like it too, and then we'll all get more comics like this: fun, funny, awesome books about a crime-fighter with a utility belt and animal-themed gadgets (again, NOT a bat). And if you've got a computer, you can check out unbeatablesquirrelgirl.tumblr.com where we post SNEAK PEEKS at upcoming issues and behind-the-scenes art!

We thought we'd start here with your letters. You can send them to MHEROES@MARVEL.COM, and don't forget to mark them "OKAY TO PRINT" so we know your letter is cool to print. But since this is our first issue all we've gotten so far are some TOTALLY FAKE LETTERS we'll use to get the ball rolling! Can YOU send us something better? I'd sincerely like to see that!!

Q: Excuse me, but how are you following me, how are you getting all this information??

- D. Green

A: Erica is really good at sketching quickly AND at being discreet. A winning combination!

Q: Who wrote Squirrel Girl's theme song?

- Pat W.

A: The song was composed by Academy Award winner Paul Francis Webster and Robert "Bob" Harris in 1967, but at the time it was accidentally applied to another obscure Marvel character named "Spider-Man." Several decades later we detected this error and corrected it, restoring the song to its originally intended glory, and now it's totally about a woman who talks to squirrels.

Q: Who would win in a fight, Squirrel Girl or the Hulk?

- Jenn K.

A: If you ask the Hulk team, they might say something different, which is frankly ADORABLE, but clearly it's Squirrel Girl. Is their character called "The Unbeatable Hulk"? No, they call him "The Incredible Hulk," as in "Incredible! The Hulk just got beat up by Squirrel Girl, she's the greatest and I love her forever!!"

Q: Who would win in a fight, Squirrel Girl or Ms. Marvel?

- Emily H.

A: Yo, why are they fighting? Doreen and Kamala are on the same side here, so it's LITERALLY CRAZY that they're fighting. A better question is who would Squirrel Girl and Ms. Marvel fight FIRST?? My money is on EVERYONE WHO STANDS IN THEIR WAY.

Q: Who would win in a fight, Tippy-Toe the Squirrel or Howard the Duck?

- Chip Z.

A: Tippy-Toe is a regular squirrel with zero super powers, and Howard the Duck is a sentient duck who is approximately as smart as the average human! That said, Tippy-Toe. PROVE ME WRONG, HOWARD.

Q: Who would YOU rather fight, one squirrel-sized Hulk or a hundred Hulk-sized squirrels?

- Lucy W.

A: Doreen would obviously take the squirrel-sized Hulk, seeing as she'd never want to fight squirrels since they are ULTIMATE PALS. Personally, I'd take the squirrel-sized Hulk too, because while I wouldn't like the Hulk when he's angry, I would LOVE him when ADORABLY-SIZED, super-cute, and could fit inside a bottle of pop.

I don't know why I apparently keep trying to pick a fight with the Hulk team here. Send us some letters! DO IT!!

Thanks everyone, and we'll see you next month!

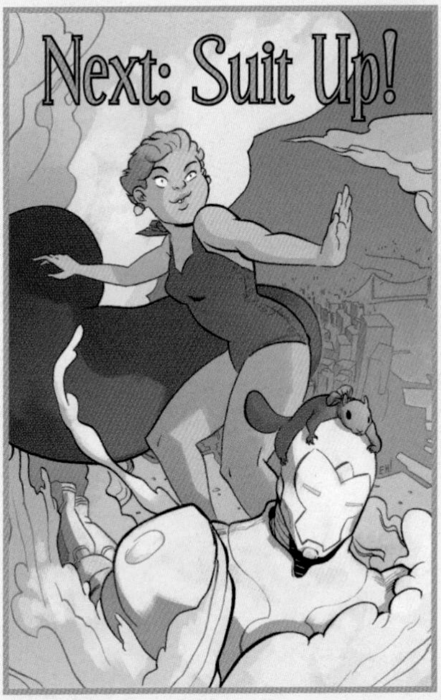
Next: Suit Up!

When you see this: AR, open up the MARVEL AR APP (available on applicable Apple ® iOS or Android ™ devices) and use your camera-enabled device to unlock extra-special exclusive features!

2

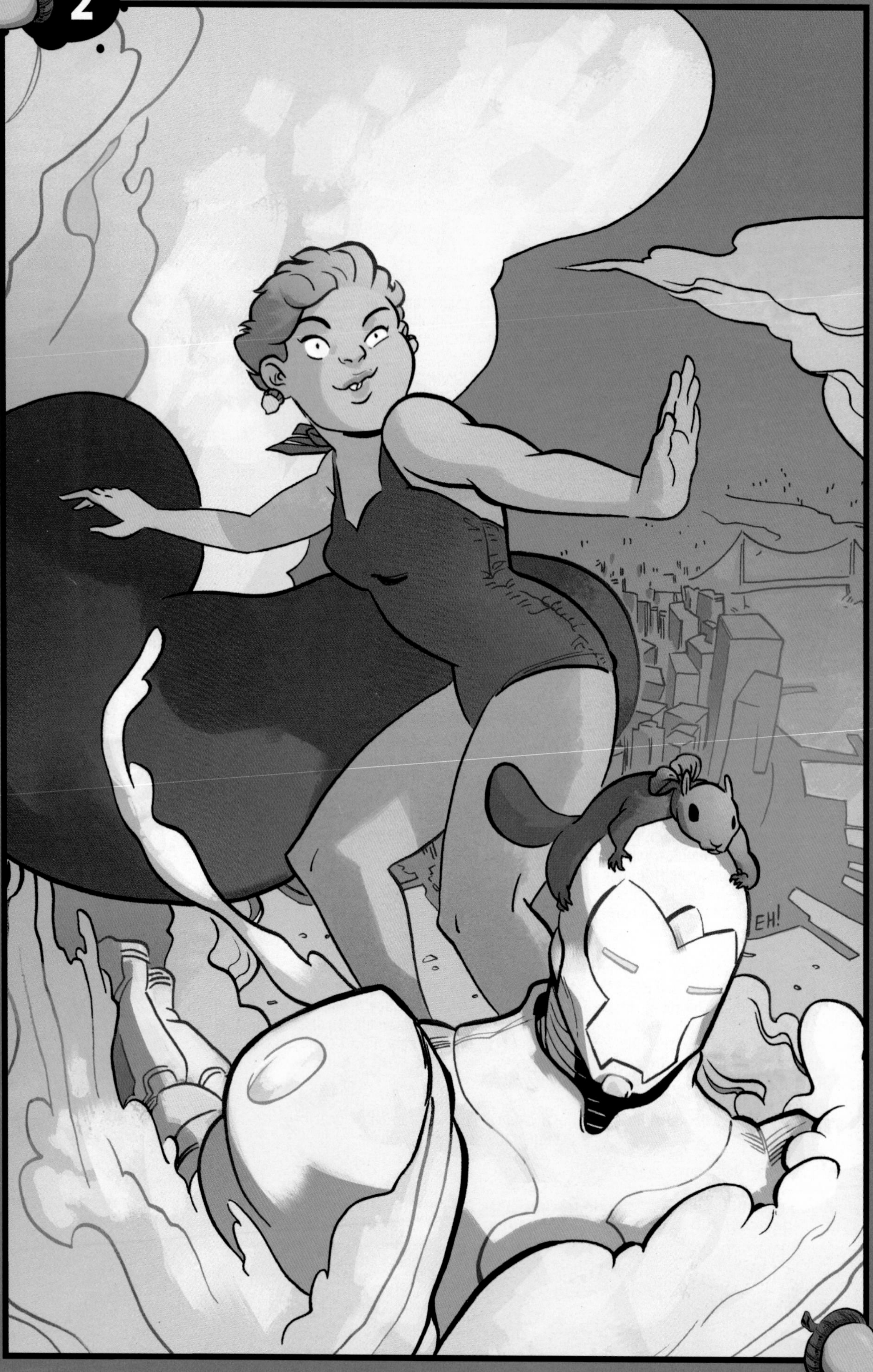
EH!

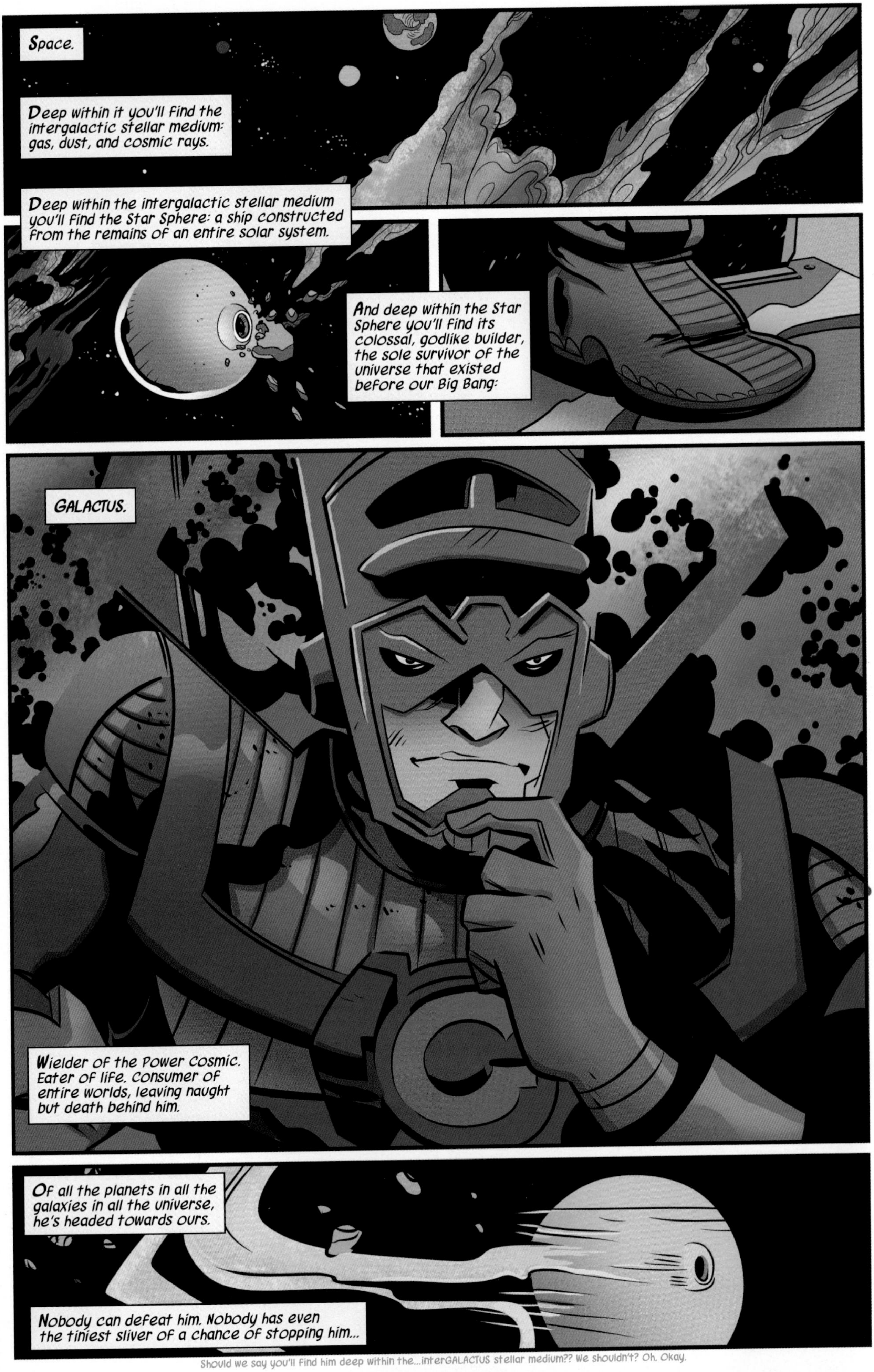

Space.
Deep within it you'll find the intergalactic stellar medium: gas, dust, and cosmic rays.
Deep within the intergalactic stellar medium you'll find the Star Sphere: a ship constructed from the remains of an entire solar system.
And deep within the Star Sphere you'll find its colossal, godlike builder, the sole survivor of the universe that existed before our Big Bang:
GALACTUS.
Wielder of the Power Cosmic. Eater of life. Consumer of entire worlds, leaving naught but death behind him.
Of all the planets in all the galaxies in all the universe, he's headed towards ours.
Nobody can defeat him. Nobody has even the tiniest sliver of a chance of stopping him...

Should we say you'll find him deep within the...interGALACTUS stellar medium?? We shouldn't? Oh. Okay.

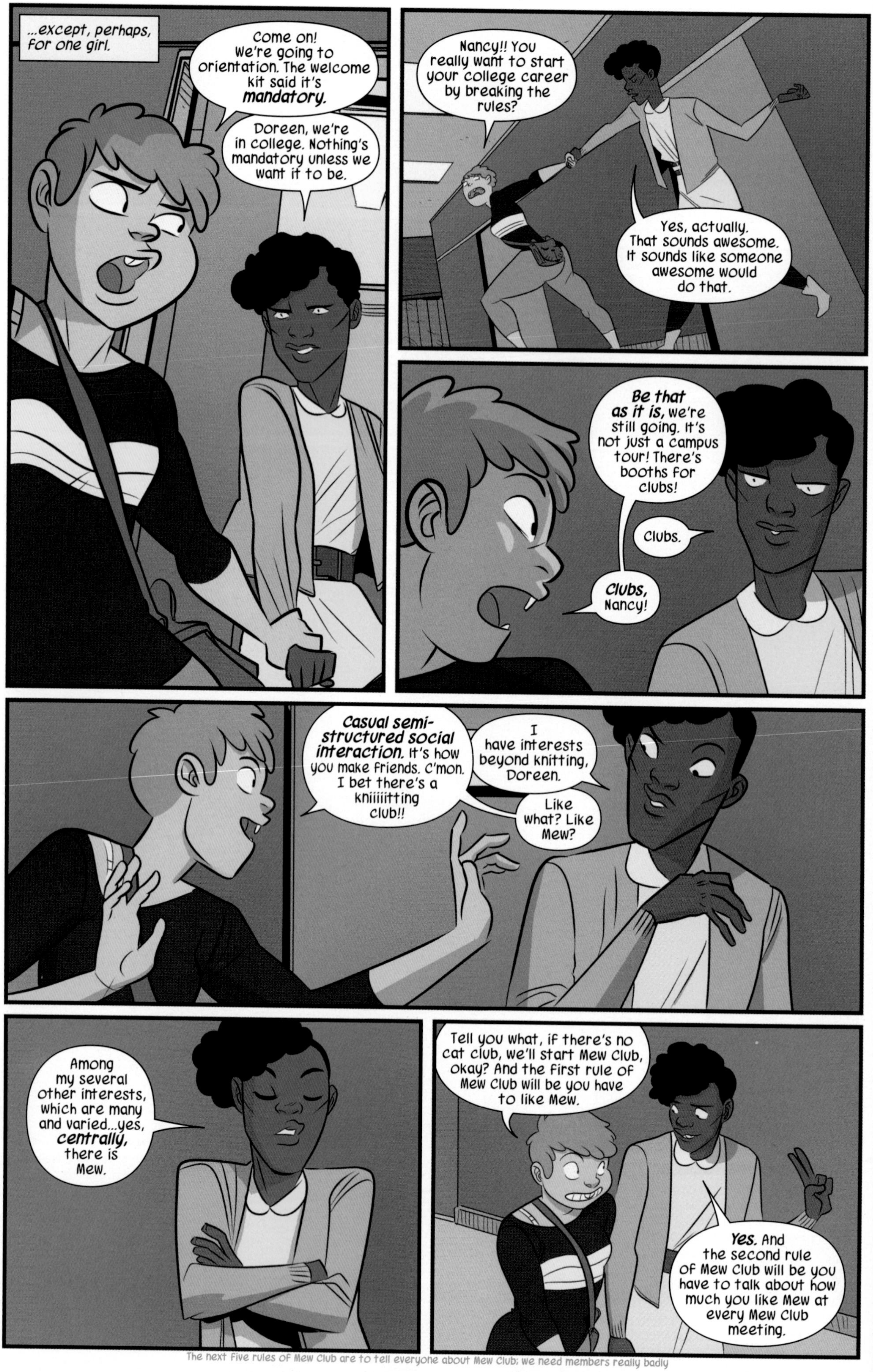
...except, perhaps, for one girl.
Come on! We're going to orientation. The welcome kit said it's mandatory.
Doreen, we're in college. Nothing's mandatory unless we want it to be.
Nancy!! You really want to start your college career by breaking the rules?
Yes, actually. That sounds awesome. It sounds like someone awesome would do that.
Be that as it is, we're still going. It's not just a campus tour! There's booths for clubs!
Clubs.
Clubs, Nancy!
Casual semi-structured social interaction. It's how you make friends. C'mon. I bet there's a kniiiiitting club!!
I have interests beyond knitting, Doreen.
Like what? Like Mew?
Among my several other interests, which are many and varied...yes, centrally, there is Mew.
Tell you what, if there's no cat club, we'll start Mew Club, okay? And the first rule of Mew Club will be you have to like Mew.
Yes. And the second rule of Mew Club will be you have to talk about how much you like Mew at every Mew Club meeting.

The next five rules of Mew Club are to tell everyone about Mew Club; we need members really badly

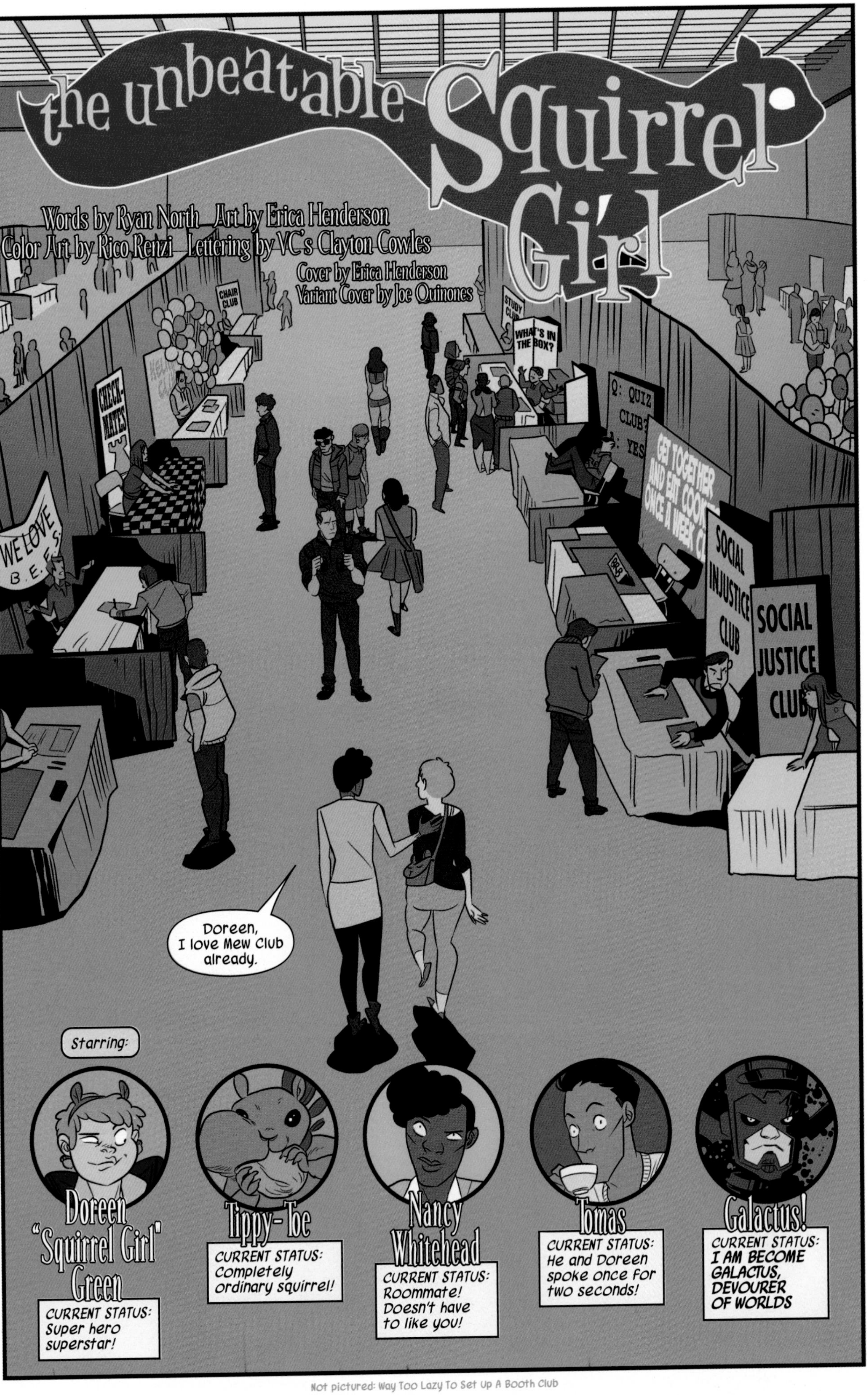
the unbeatable Squirrel Girl
Words by Ryan North Art by Erica Henderson
Color Art by Rico Renzi Lettering by VC's Clayton Cowles
Cover by Erica Henderson
Variant Cover by Joe Quinones
CHAIR CLUB
STUDY CLUB
WHAT'S IN THE BOX?
CHECK-MATES
WE LOVE B.E.E.S
SOCIAL INJUSTICE CLUB
SOCIAL JUSTICE CLUB
Doreen, I love Mew Club already.
Starring:
Doreen "Squirrel Girl" Green
CURRENT STATUS: Super hero superstar!
Tippy-Toe
CURRENT STATUS: Completely ordinary squirrel!
Nancy Whitehead
CURRENT STATUS: Roommate! Doesn't have to like you!
Tomas
CURRENT STATUS: He and Doreen spoke once for two seconds!
Galactus!
CURRENT STATUS: I AM BECOME GALACTUS, DEVOURER OF WORLDS

Not pictured: Way Too Lazy To Set Up A Booth Club

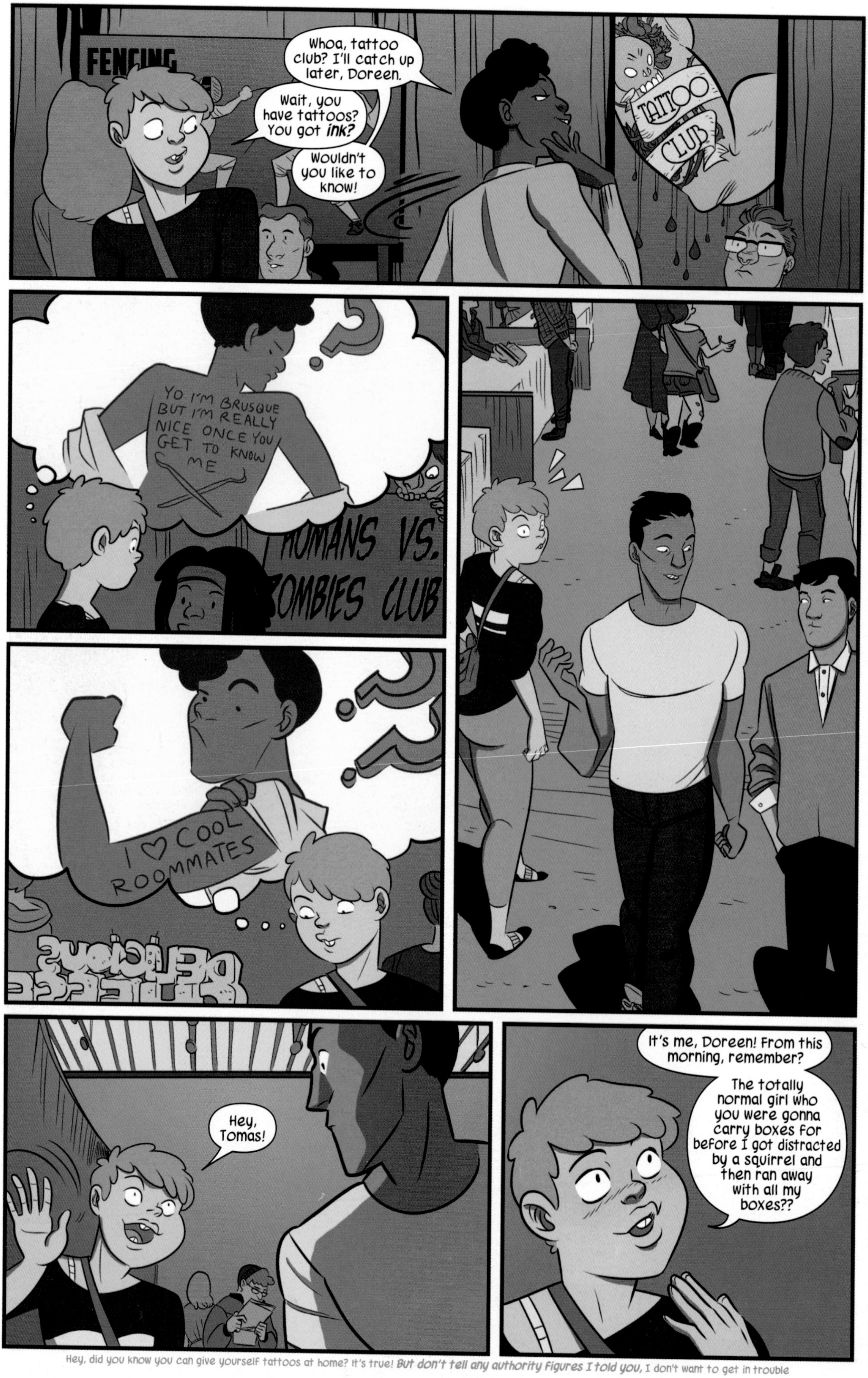
FENCING
Whoa, tattoo club? I'll catch up later, Doreen.
Wait, you have tattoos? You got ink?
Wouldn't you like to know!
TATTOO CLUB
YO I'M BRUSQUE BUT I'M REALLY NICE ONCE YOU GET TO KNOW ME
HUMANS VS. ZOMBIES CLUB
I ♡ COOL ROOMMATES
Hey, Tomas!
It's me, Doreen! From this morning, remember?
The totally normal girl who you were gonna carry boxes for before I got distracted by a squirrel and then ran away with all my boxes??

Hey, did you know you can give yourself tattoos at home? It's true! ***But don't tell any authority figures I told you,*** I don't want to get in trouble

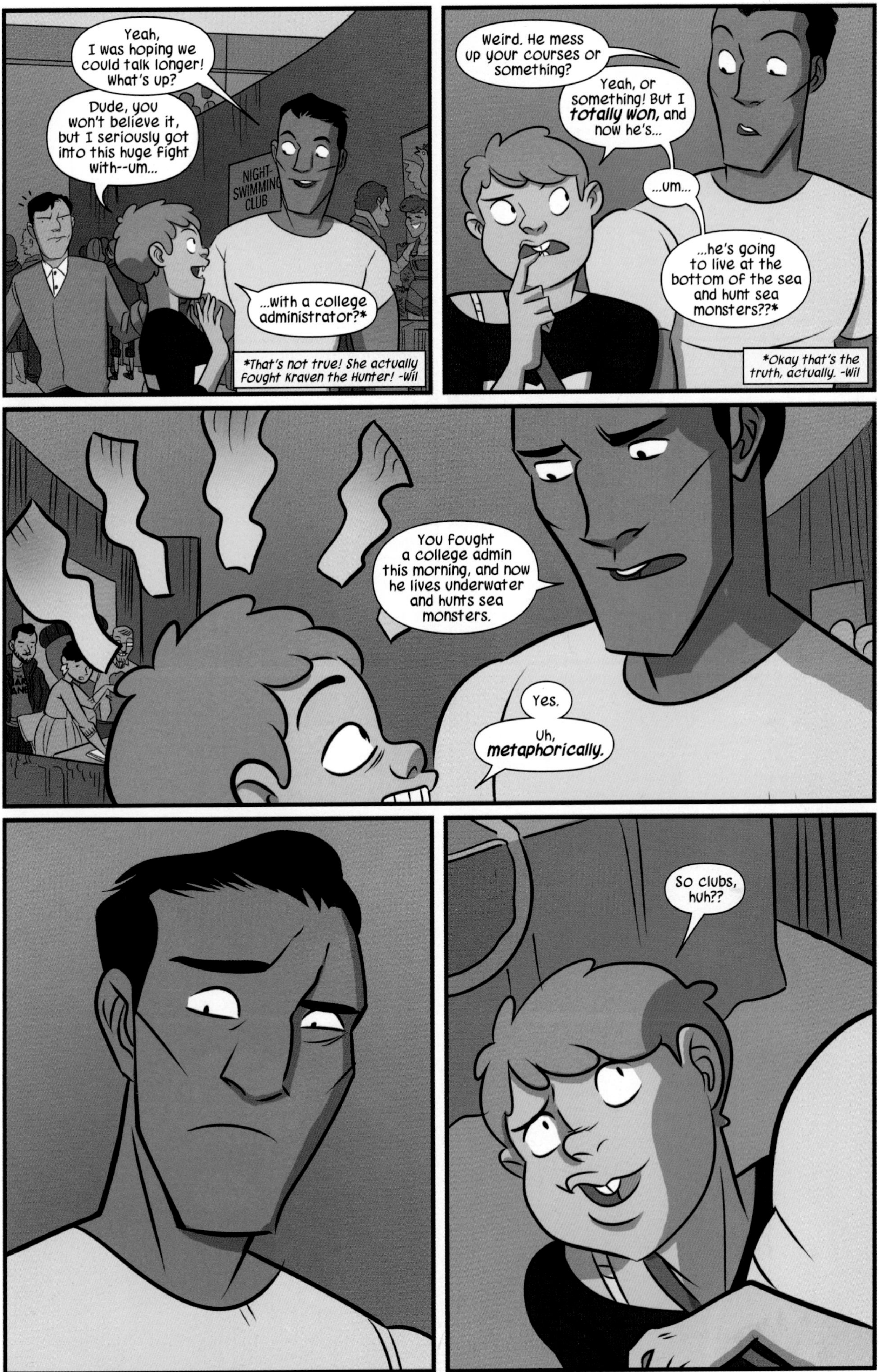
Yeah, I was hoping we could talk longer! What's up?
Dude, you won't believe it, but I seriously got into this huge fight with--um...
NIGHT-SWIMMING CLUB
...with a college administrator?*
*That's not true! She actually fought Kraven the Hunter! -Wil
Weird. He mess up your courses or something?
Yeah, or something! But I *totally won,* and now he's...
...um...
...he's going to live at the bottom of the sea and hunt sea monsters??*
*Okay that's the truth, actually. -Wil
You fought a college admin this morning, and now he lives underwater and hunts sea monsters.
Yes.
Uh, ***metaphorically.***
So clubs, huh??

Here we are in issue 2 already summarizing what happened in issue 1! It's fine for now, but at a certain point I'm gonna have to stop these summaries and you'll just have to buy the comics to find out what happened, okay??

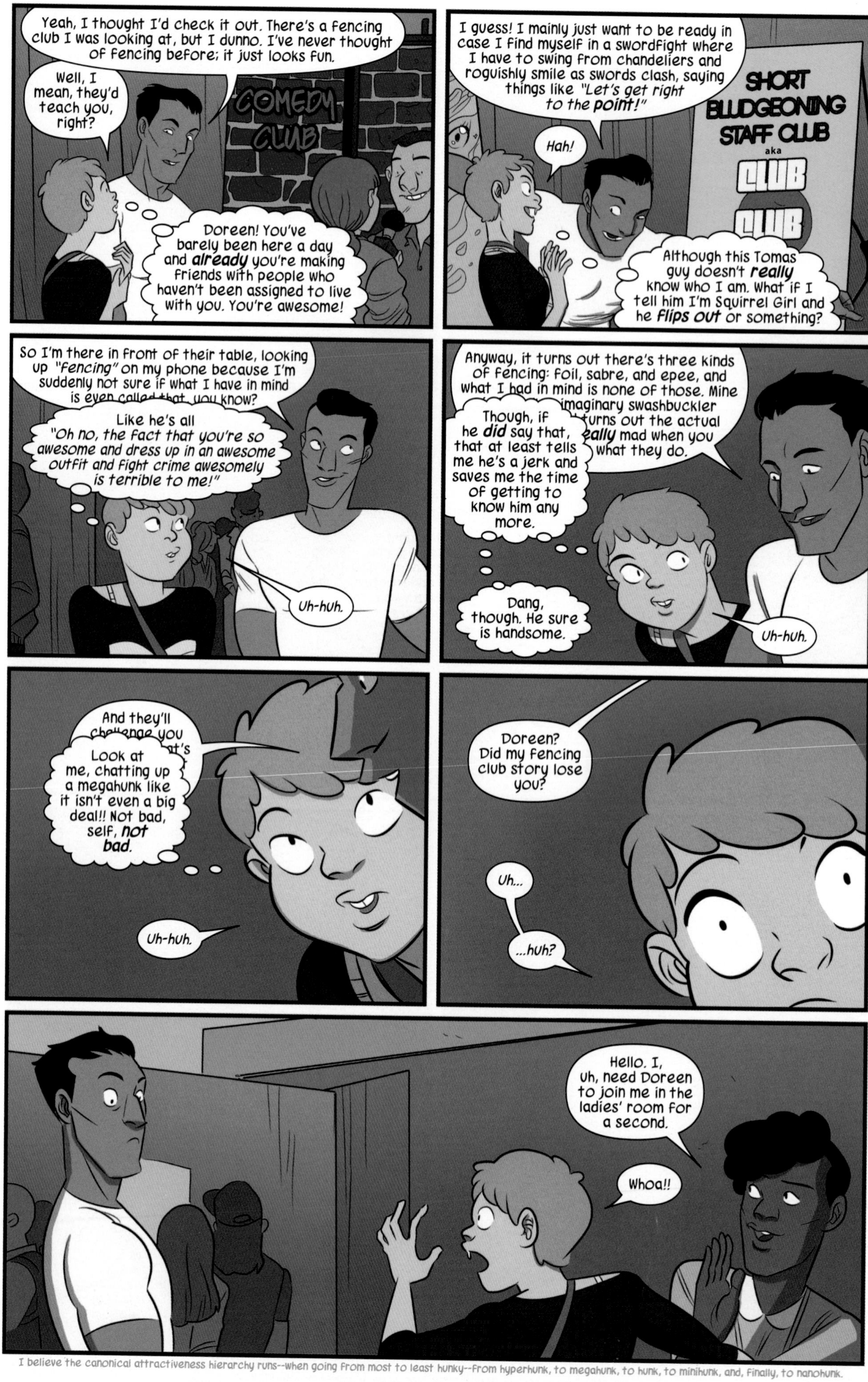
Yeah, I thought I'd check it out. There's a fencing club I was looking at, but I dunno. I've never thought of fencing before; it just looks fun.
Well, I mean, they'd teach you, right?
COMEDY CLUB
Doreen! You've barely been here a day and *already* you're making friends with people who haven't been assigned to live with you. You're awesome!
I guess! I mainly just want to be ready in case I find myself in a swordfight where I have to swing from chandeliers and roguishly smile as swords clash, saying things like *"Let's get right to the* ***point!"***
SHORT BLUDGEONING STAFF CLUB aka CLUB CLUB
Hah!
Although this Tomas guy doesn't ***really*** know who I am. What if I tell him I'm Squirrel Girl and he ***flips out*** or something?
So I'm there in front of their table, looking up *"fencing"* on my phone because I'm suddenly not sure if what I have in mind is even
Like he's all *"Oh no, the fact that you're so awesome and dress up in an awesome outfit and fight crime awesomely is terrible to me!"*
Uh-huh.
Anyway, it turns out there's three kinds of fencing: foil, sabre, and epee, and what I had in mind is none of those. Mine
imaginary swashbuckler
turns out the actual
mad when you
what they do.
Though, if he ***did*** say that, that at least tells me he's a jerk and saves me the time of getting to know him any more.
Dang, though. He sure is handsome.
Uh-huh.
And they'll
Look at me, chatting up a megahunk like it isn't even a big deal!! Not bad, self, ***not bad.***
Uh-huh.
Doreen? Did my fencing club story lose you?
Uh...
...huh?
Hello. I, uh, need Doreen to join me in the ladies' room for a second.
Whoa!!

I believe the canonical attractiveness hierarchy runs--when going from most to least hunky--from hyperhunk, to megahunk, to hunk, to minihunk, and, finally, to nanohunk.

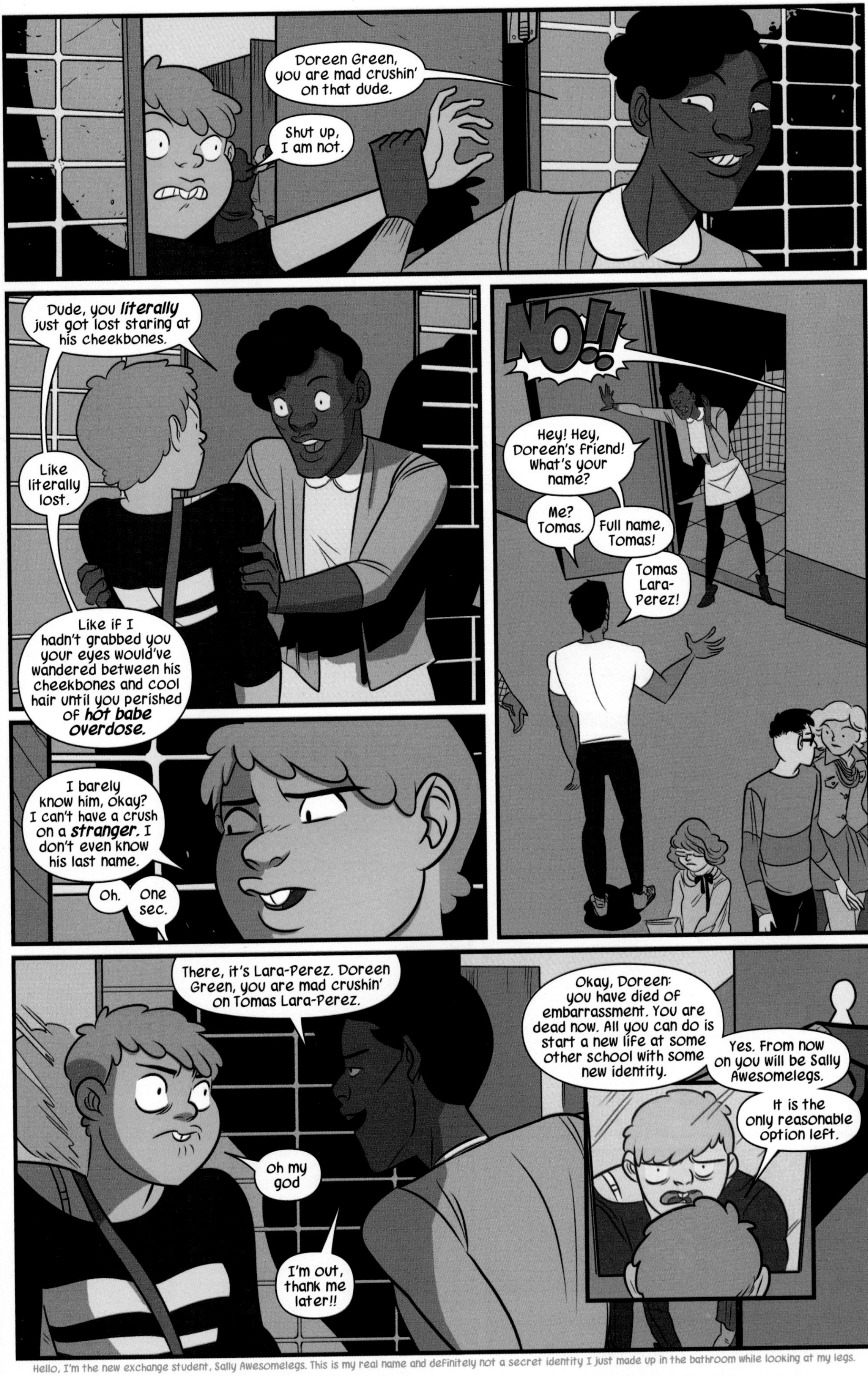
Doreen Green, you are mad crushin' on that dude.
Shut up, I am not.
Dude, you *literally* just got lost staring at his cheekbones.
Like literally lost.
Like if I hadn't grabbed you your eyes would've wandered between his cheekbones and cool hair until you perished of ***hot babe overdose.***
NO!!
Hey! Hey, Doreen's friend! What's your name?
Me? Tomas.
Full name, Tomas!
Tomas Lara-Perez!
I barely know him, okay? I can't have a crush on a ***stranger.*** I don't even know his last name.
Oh.
One sec.
There, it's Lara-Perez. Doreen Green, you are mad crushin' on Tomas Lara-Perez.
Oh my god
I'm out, thank me later!!
Okay, Doreen: you have died of embarrassment. You are dead now. All you can do is start a new life at some other school with some new identity.
Yes. From now on you will be Sally Awesomelegs.
It is the only reasonable option left.
Hello, I'm the new exchange student, Sally Awesomelegs. This is my real name and definitely not a secret identity I just made up in the bathroom while looking at my legs.

SMMP

Huh?

Tippy-Toe, what are you doing?!

Doreen! It's worse than we thought!!

That thing in space! It's gotten closer! Squirrels around the world have been sneaking into observatories to look at it!

And?

And it's the *Star Sphere*, Doreen!!

You say that like I know what a Star Sphere is. *All* stars are spheres, aren't they?

Because of physics?

Come on, come *ON*, where are your cards...

Here!!

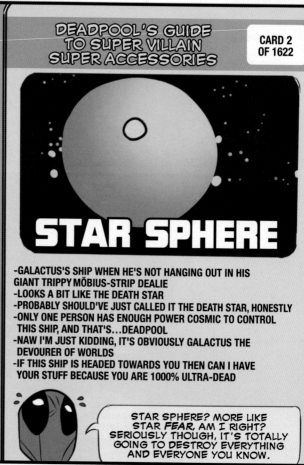

DEADPOOL'S GUIDE TO SUPER VILLAIN SUPER ACCESSORIES

CARD 2 OF 1622

STAR SPHERE

-GALACTUS'S SHIP WHEN HE'S NOT HANGING OUT IN HIS GIANT TRIPPY MÖBIUS-STRIP DEALIE
-LOOKS A BIT LIKE THE DEATH STAR
-PROBABLY SHOULD'VE JUST CALLED IT THE DEATH STAR, HONESTLY
-ONLY ONE PERSON HAS ENOUGH POWER COSMIC TO CONTROL THIS SHIP, AND THAT'S...DEADPOOL
-NAW I'M JUST KIDDING, IT'S OBVIOUSLY GALACTUS THE DEVOURER OF WORLDS
-IF THIS SHIP IS HEADED TOWARDS YOU THEN CAN I HAVE YOUR STUFF BECAUSE YOU ARE 1000% ULTRA-DEAD

STAR SPHERE? MORE LIKE STAR *FEAR*, AM I RIGHT? SERIOUSLY THOUGH, IT'S TOTALLY GOING TO DESTROY EVERYTHING AND EVERYONE YOU KNOW.

Yes, Tippy-Toe did absolutely start this page imagining that window would dramatically smash around her as she leapt through it.

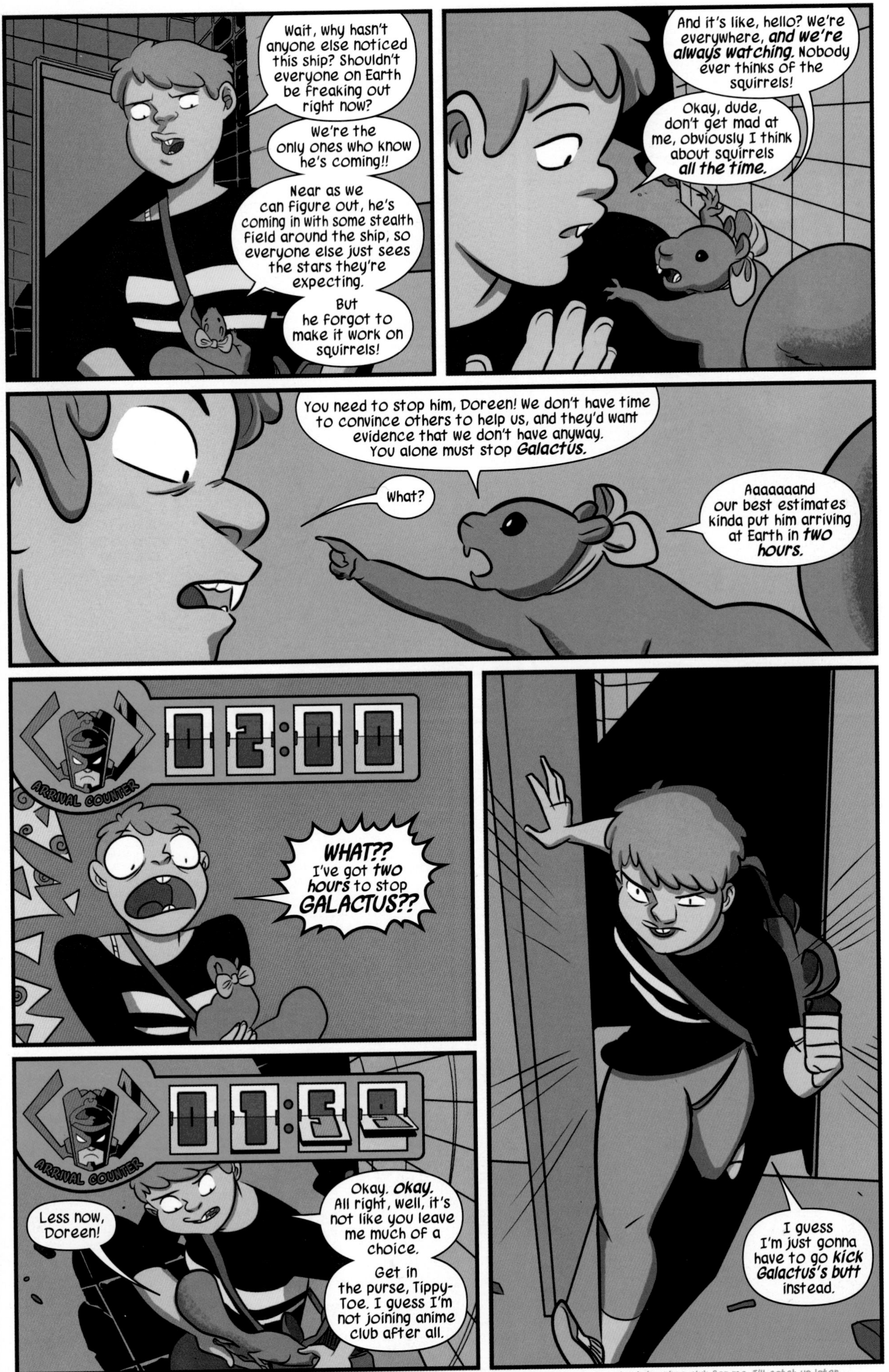

Wait, why hasn't anyone else noticed this ship? Shouldn't everyone on Earth be freaking out right now?
We're the only ones who know he's coming!!
Near as we can figure out, he's coming in with some stealth field around the ship, so everyone else just sees the stars they're expecting.
But he forgot to make it work on squirrels!
And it's like, hello? We're everywhere, and we're always watching. Nobody ever thinks of the squirrels!
Okay, dude, don't get mad at me, obviously I think about squirrels all the time.
You need to stop him, Doreen! We don't have time to convince others to help us, and they'd want evidence that we don't have anyway. You alone must stop Galactus.
What?
Aaaaaaand our best estimates kinda put him arriving at Earth in two hours.
02:00
ARRIVAL COUNTER
WHAT?? I've got two hours to stop GALACTUS??
ARRIVAL COUNTER
Less now, Doreen!
Okay. Okay. All right, well, it's not like you leave me much of a choice.
Get in the purse, Tippy-Toe. I guess I'm not joining anime club after all.
I guess I'm just gonna have to go kick Galactus's butt instead.

Honestly I wish there was time to do both, but there's not, and a girl has to make choices sometimes. Someone else join anime club for me, I'll catch up later.

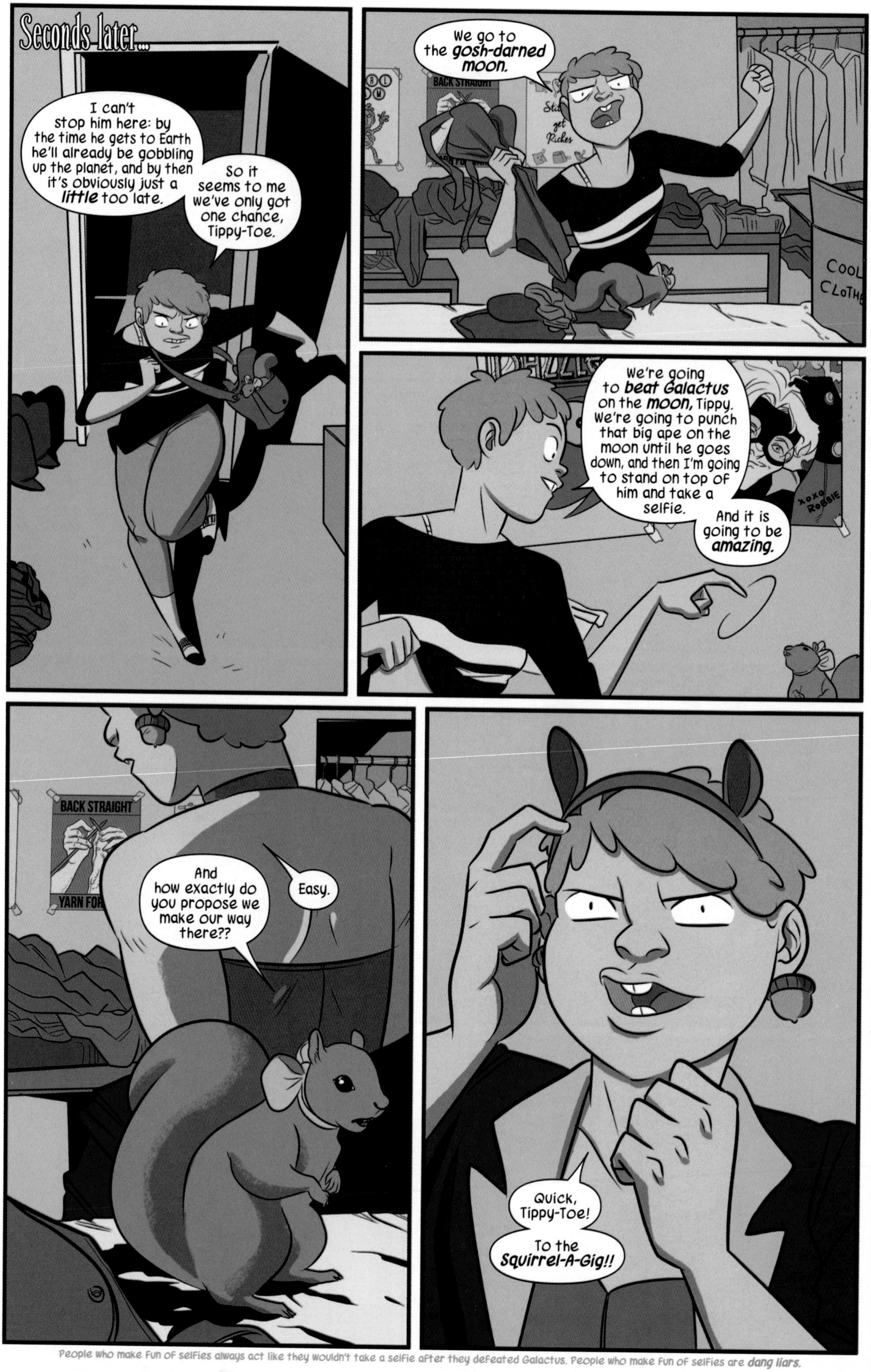
Seconds later...
I can't stop him here: by the time he gets to Earth he'll already be gobbling up the planet, and by then it's obviously just a *little* too late.
So it seems to me we've only got one chance, Tippy-Toe.
We go to the *gosh-darned moon.*
BACK STRAIGHT
COOL CLOTHES
We're going to *beat Galactus* on the *moon,* Tippy. We're going to punch that big ape on the moon until he goes down, and then I'm going to stand on top of him and take a selfie.
And it is going to be *amazing.*
XOXO ROBBIE
BACK STRAIGHT
YARN FOR
And how exactly do you propose we make our way there??
Easy.
Quick, Tippy-Toe!
To the *Squirrel-A-Gig!!*

People who make fun of selfies always act like they wouldn't take a selfie after they defeated Galactus. People who make fun of selfies are *dang liars.*

Okay, yeah, there's absolutely zero way this will get us into space.

I was gonna say.

All right, hold on tight, Tippy. Every good super hero has a Plan B.

Wouldn't a good super hero's Plan A, you know, work every time?

Shh.

Plan B engaged!!

Sorry!

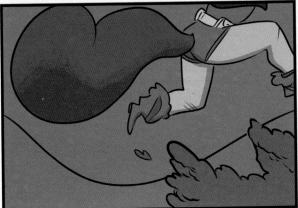

Ahh, sorry!

NYC cab insurance has a small deductible for super hero footprint damage. Don't worry about it!

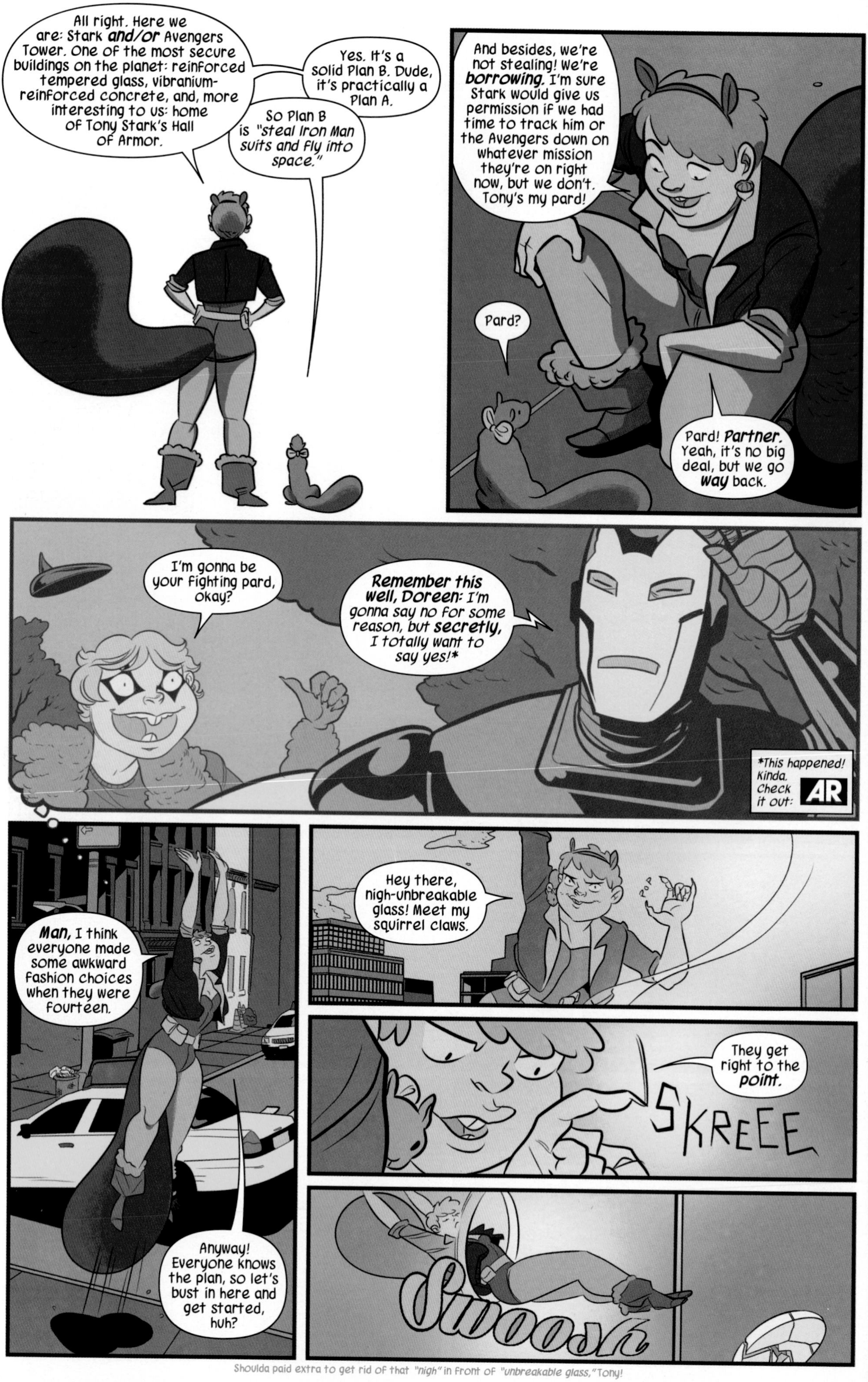
All right. Here we are: Stark **and/or** Avengers Tower. One of the most secure buildings on the planet: reinforced tempered glass, vibranium-reinforced concrete, and, more interesting to us: home of Tony Stark's Hall of Armor.
Yes. It's a solid Plan B. Dude, it's practically a Plan A.
So Plan B is "steal Iron Man suits and fly into space."
And besides, we're not stealing! We're **borrowing.** I'm sure Stark would give us permission if we had time to track him or the Avengers down on whatever mission they're on right now, but we don't. Tony's my pard!
Pard?
Pard! **Partner.** Yeah, it's no big deal, but we go **way** back.
I'm gonna be your fighting pard, okay?
Remember this well, Doreen: *I'm gonna say no for some reason, but* **secretly,** *I totally want to say yes!**
***This happened!** Kinda. Check it out: AR
Man, I think everyone made some awkward fashion choices when they were fourteen.
Anyway! Everyone knows the plan, so let's bust in here and get started, huh?
Hey there, nigh-unbreakable glass! Meet my squirrel claws.
POP
They get right to the **point.**
SKREEE
SWOOSH

Shoulda paid extra to get rid of that *"nigh"* in front of *"unbreakable glass,"* Tony!

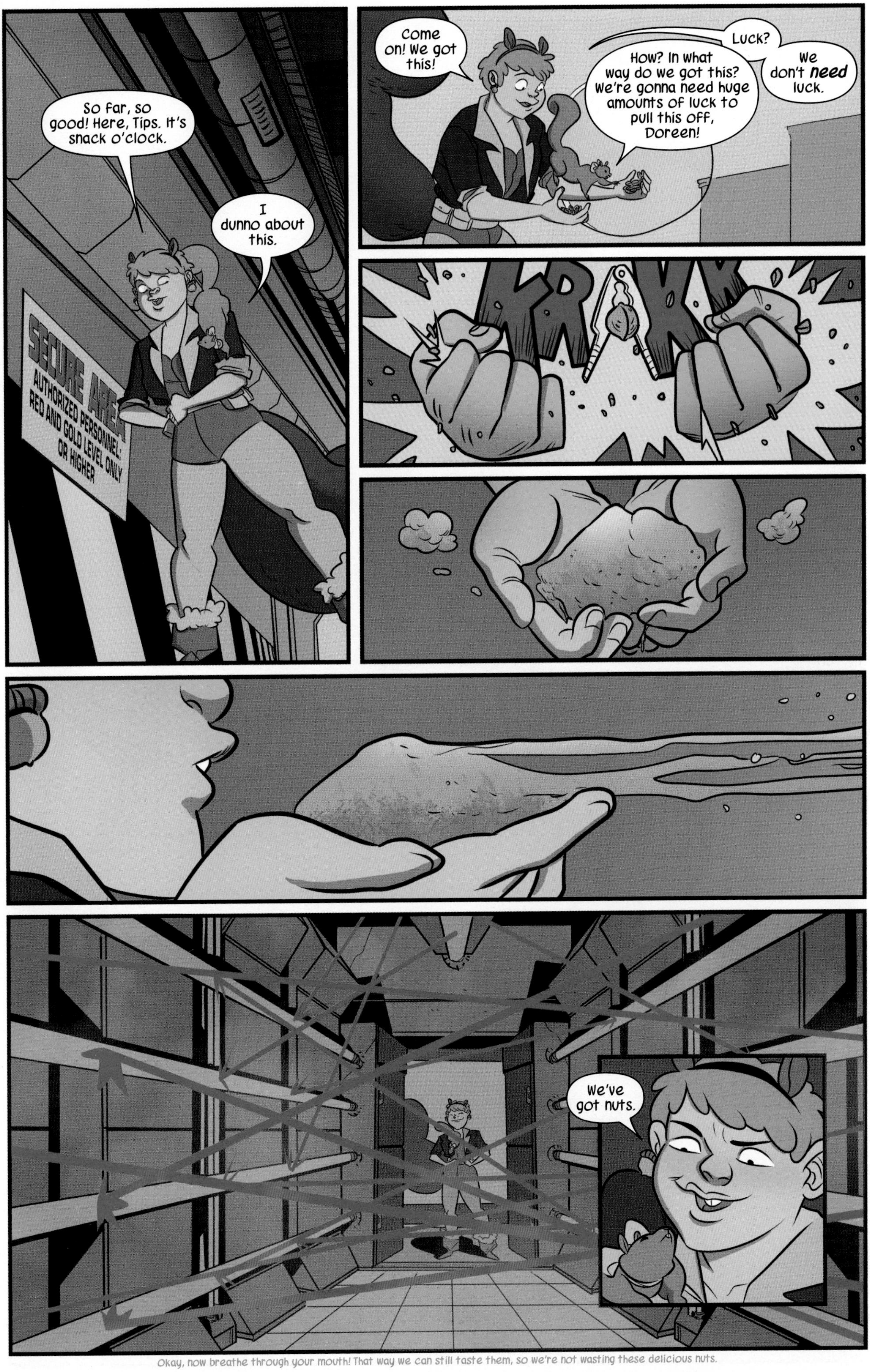
So far, so good! Here, Tips. It's snack o'clock.
I dunno about this.
SECURE AREA
AUTHORIZED PERSONNEL: RED AND GOLD LEVEL ONLY OR HIGHER
Come on! We got this!
How? In what way do we got this? We're gonna need huge amounts of luck to pull this off, Doreen!
Luck?
We don't **need** luck.
KRAK
We've got nuts.

Okay, now breathe through your mouth! That way we can still taste them, so we're not wasting these delicious nuts.

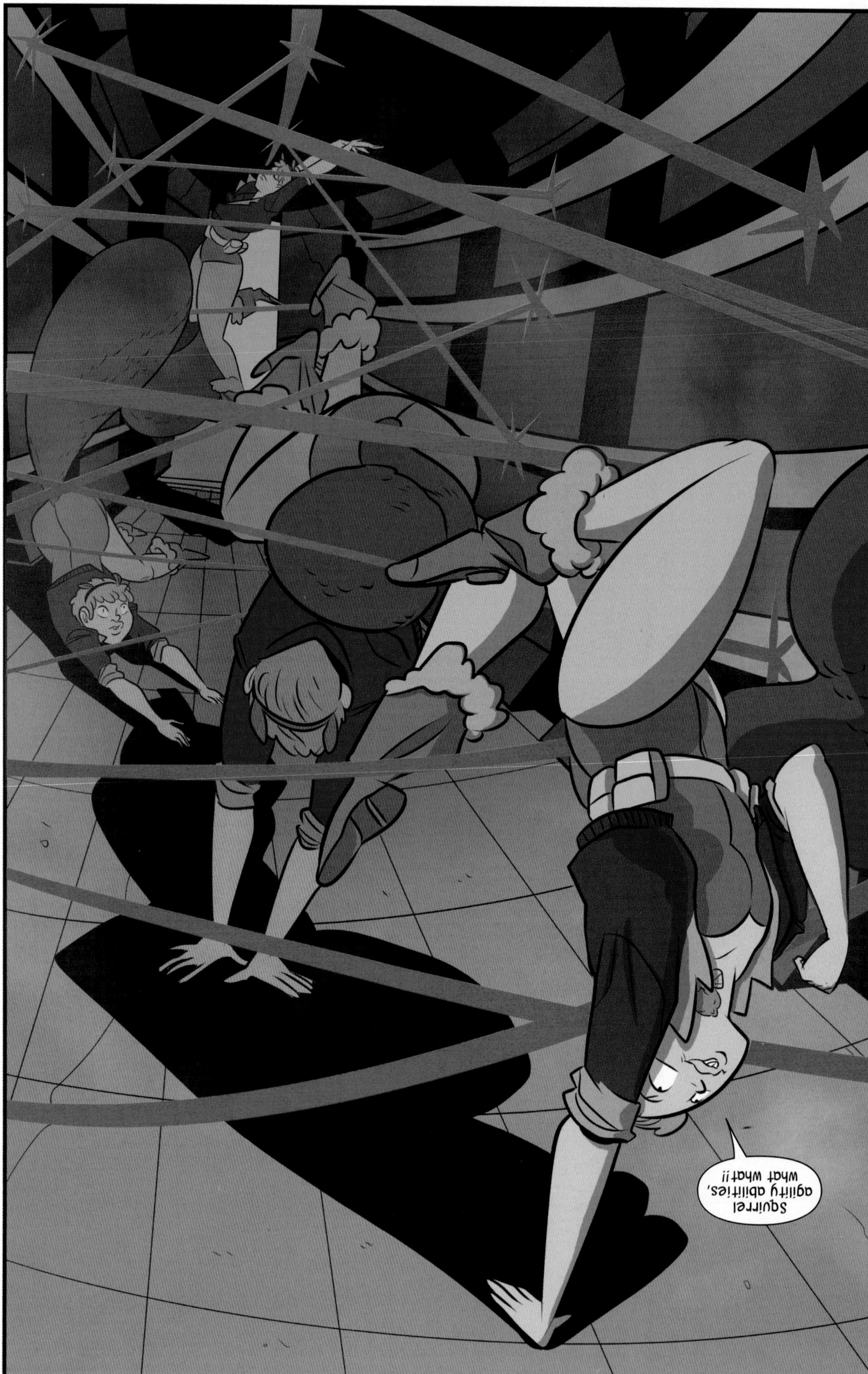
Squirrel agility abilities, what what!!

As my Aunt Benjamina used to say, "With great squirrel agility ability comes great squirrel agility **responsibility**."

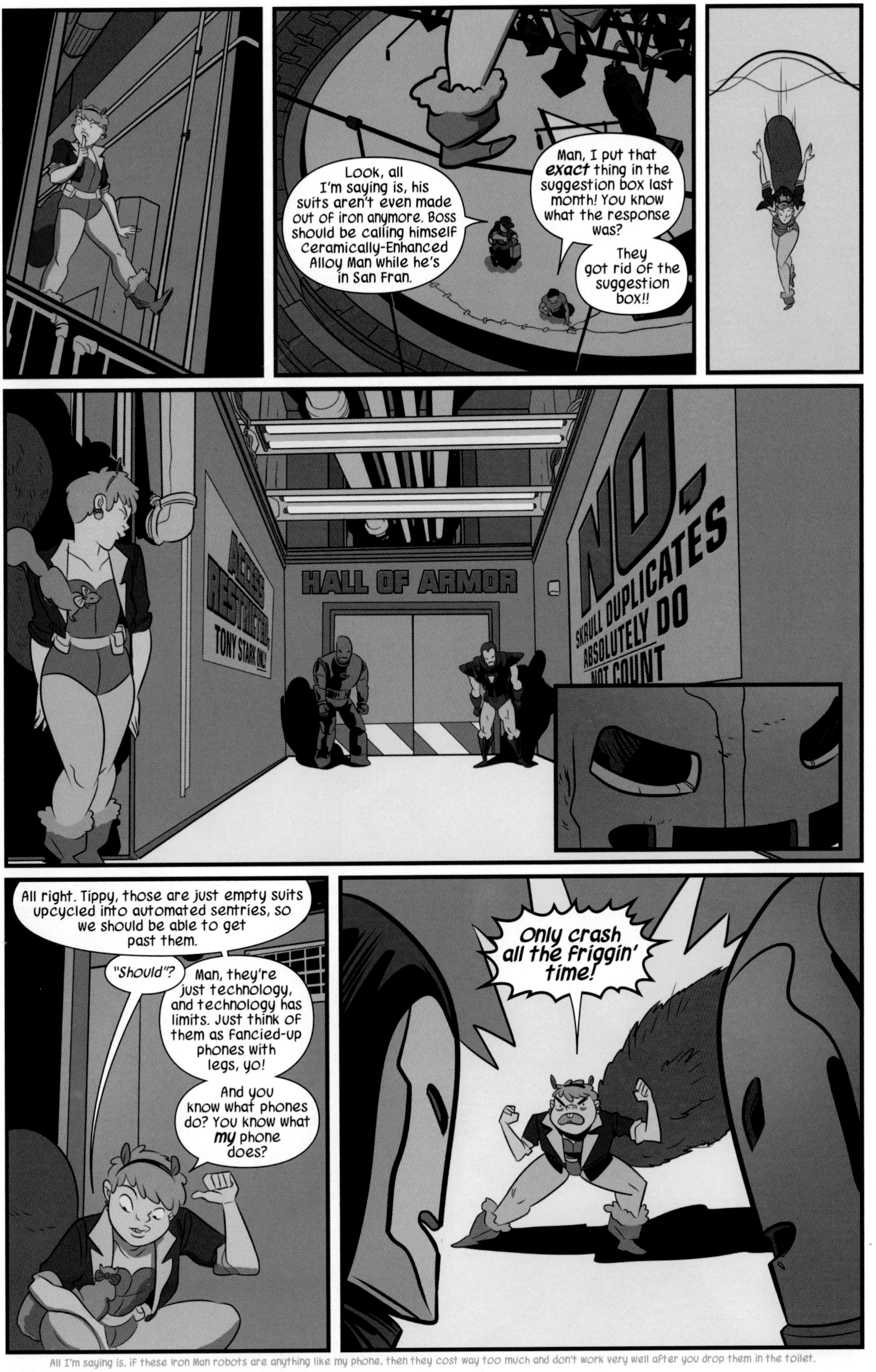
Look, all I'm saying is, his suits aren't even made out of iron anymore. Boss should be calling himself Ceramically-Enhanced Alloy Man while he's in San Fran.
Man, I put that *exact* thing in the suggestion box last month! You know what the response was?
They got rid of the suggestion box!!
ACCESS RESTRICTED. TONY STARK ONLY
HALL OF ARMOR
NO. SKRULL DUPLICATES ABSOLUTELY DO NOT COUNT
All right. Tippy, those are just empty suits upcycled into automated sentries, so we should be able to get past them.
"Should"?
Man, they're just technology, and technology has limits. Just think of them as fancied-up phones with legs, yo!
And you know what phones do? You know what *my* phone does?
Only crash all the friggin' time!

All I'm saying is, if these Iron Man robots are anything like my phone, then they cost way too much and don't work very well after you drop them in the toilet.

Whoa!

All right, robots! This is me, Squirrel Girl, speaking loudly and clearly so your speech recognition can understand!

I'm throwing this grenade at you! It will explode in one second unless you destroy it!

Okay, here comes my grenade!

PHWEE

KAKOOM

See? *See? This* is why we need to invest in the computer sciences. Now all we need to do is open the door and we're...

PHWEE E E

...huh?

Security from eight different zones? All for me?

Me, a regular girl who, um--

--who got really, really lost from the tour group while trying to find the bathroom??

That "PHWEEEEEEeeee" is the sound of the repulsors charging up. The robots aren't saying the "PHWEEEEEEeeee" noises themselves, although that would've been *kinda adorable.*

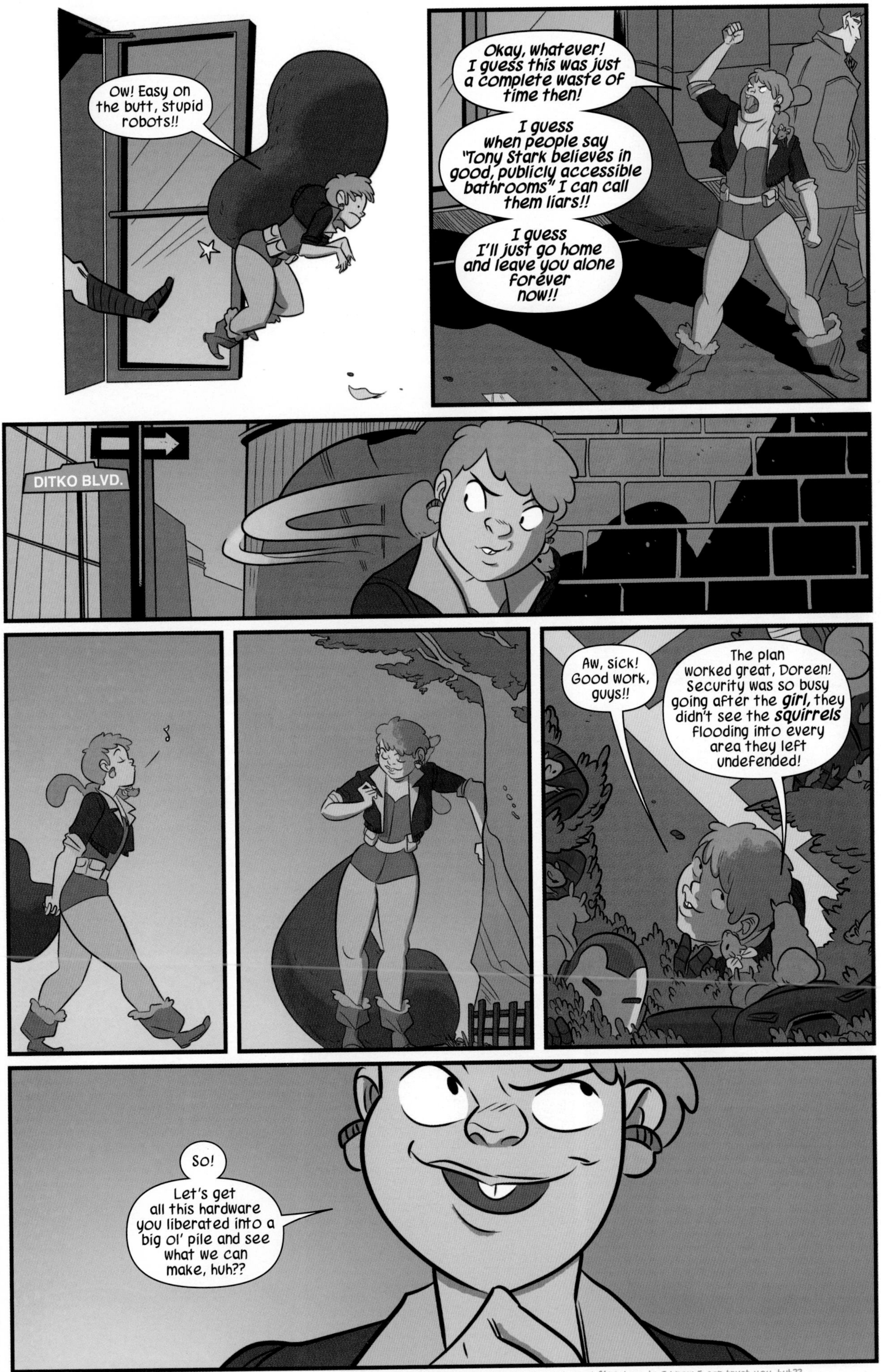
Ow! Easy on the butt, stupid robots!!
Okay, whatever! I guess this was just a complete waste of time then!
I guess when people say "Tony Stark believes in good, publicly accessible bathrooms" I can call them liars!!
I guess I'll just go home and leave you alone forever now!!
DITKO BLVD.
Aw, sick! Good work, guys!!
The plan worked great, Doreen! Security was so busy going after the girl, they didn't see the squirrels flooding into every area they left undefended!
So!
Let's get all this hardware you liberated into a big ol' pile and see what we can make, huh??

I didn't let you, the reader, know her plan before now because it's a better narrative surprise this way! *Also:* how do I know I can trust you, huh?? You could be *literally anyone.*

Hmm.

Hello, computer. Squirrel Girl here. I want you to combine these Iron Man pieces into rad suits for me and my friend, cool?

My friend's a squirrel, just FYI.

He says he's programmed to only respond to Stark.

How's your Tony Stark impression?

Legit impressive, but you know what? I don't think we need it.

Tony owes me a favor, and a long time ago he said if I ever needed his help, just to say three words.

Okay, computer, I've got something to say to you, and I want you to listen very carefully:

Victor.

Von.

Doomship.

VOICEPRINT NOT RECOGNIZED

ACCESS DENIED

BODY TYPE MISMATCH

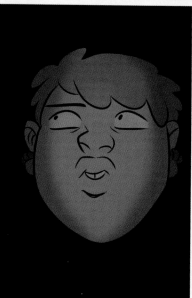

REBOOT: NEW BOOTLOADER INITIATED

VOICE PRINT RECOGNIZED

Kick butt.

Thanks for putting a few good words in for me, pard.

BODY SCAN 84% CURVIER THAN STARK BASELINE

BODY TYPE: Rad / TAIL TYPE: Unexpected / CLAW TYPE: Geez, Tony, you really need to get these nails under control.

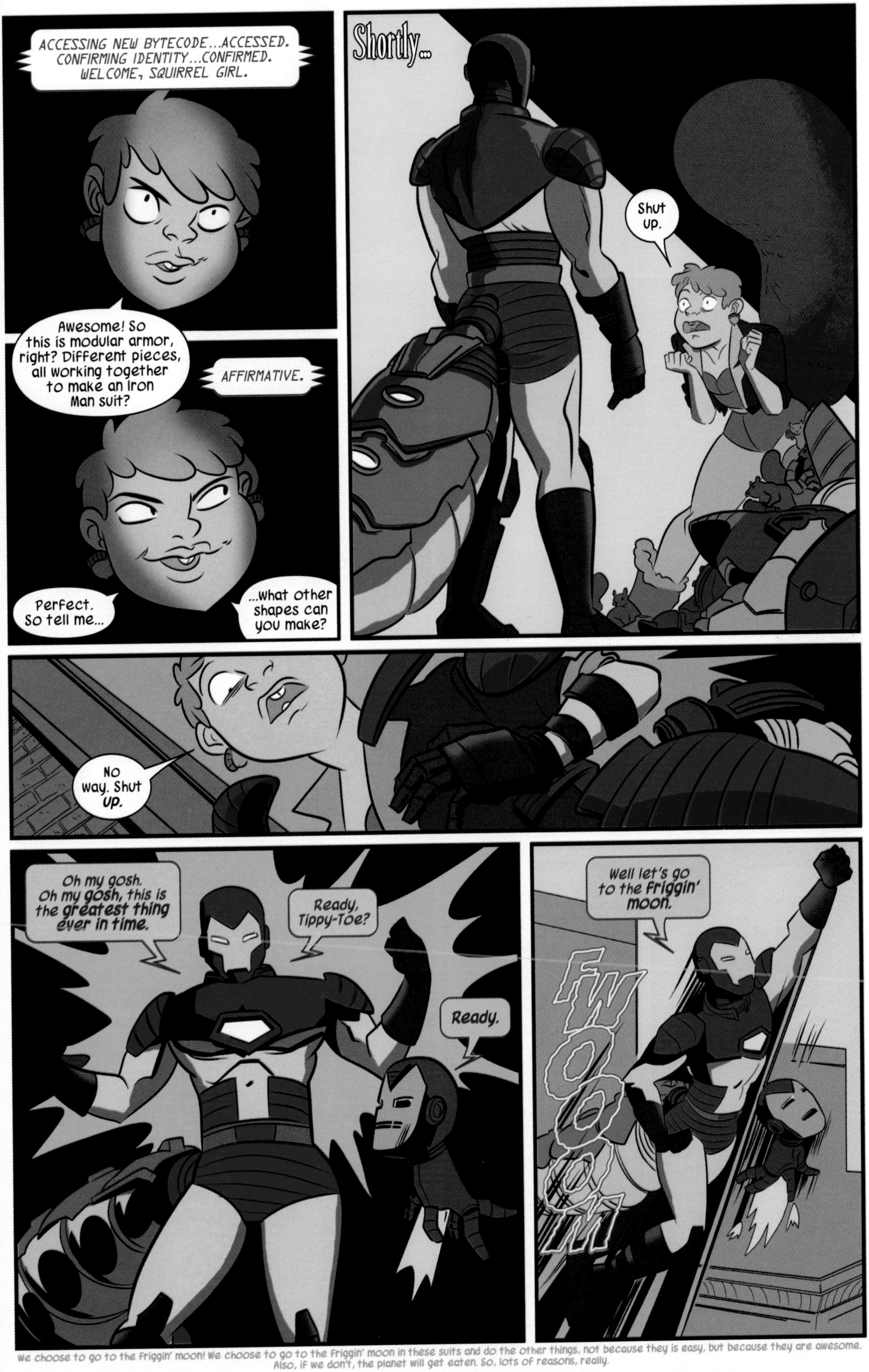
ACCESSING NEW BYTECODE...ACCESSED. CONFIRMING IDENTITY...CONFIRMED. WELCOME, SQUIRREL GIRL.
Shortly...
Shut up.
Awesome! So this is modular armor, right? Different pieces, all working together to make an Iron Man suit?
AFFIRMATIVE.
Perfect. So tell me...
...what other shapes can you make?
No way. Shut up.
Oh my gosh. Oh my gosh, this is the greatest thing ever in time.
Ready, Tippy-Toe?
Ready.
Well let's go to the friggin' moon.
FWOOOOM

We choose to go to the friggin' moon! We choose to go to the friggin' moon in these suits and do the other things, not because they is easy, but because they are awesome. Also, if we don't, the planet will get eaten. So, lots of reasons, really.

Wooooo-hoooo! These aren't so hard to fly after all!
This is totally gonna work!
Well, look at that. Tony Stark. Alone and exposed.
And headed my way.
Must be my lucky day...
...the day Iron Man falls at the hands of Whiplash.
ZZZTKTT ZZZTKTT
What? What??
ZZZZZZZZZ
Wait, no! No!
NO, don't--
WEAPONRY DETECTED: WHIPLASH
ELECTRICAL SYSTEM OVERLOAD
MAGNETIC INTERLOCKS FAILING
AAAAHHHHH!
KRASH
ARRIVAL COUNTER
59:17
ARRIVAL COUNTER
59:16
ARRIVAL COUNTER
59:15

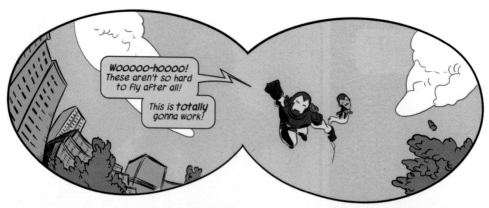

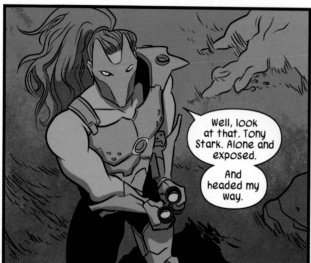

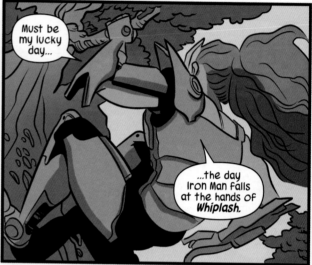

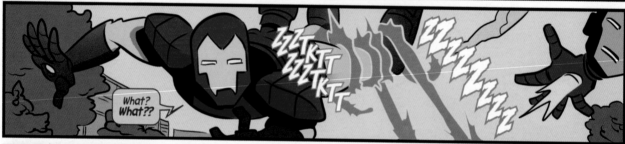

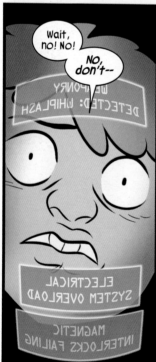

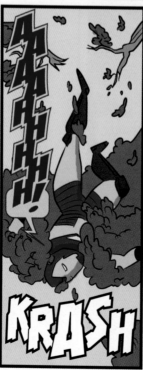

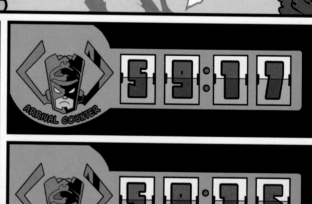

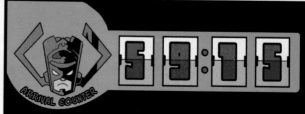

Next month: *Galactus* and *Whiplash* vs *a woman in a robot suit she borrowed.*

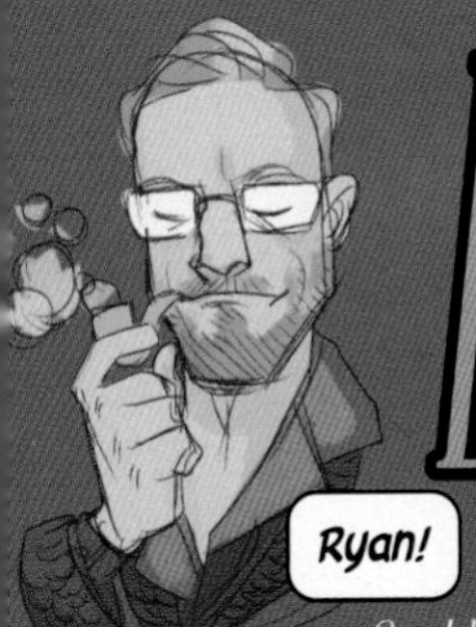
Ryan!

Letters From Nuts

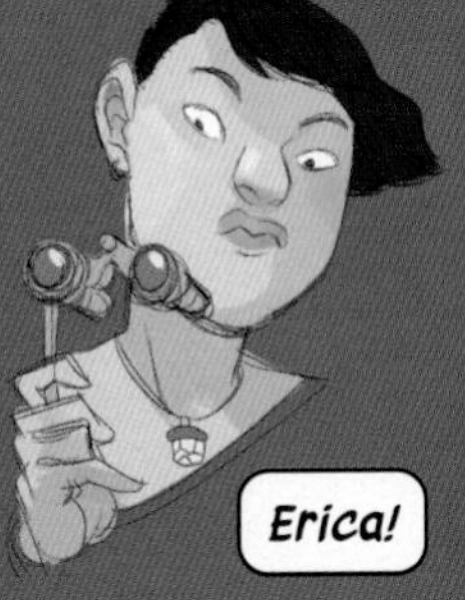
Erica!

Send letters to mheroes@marvel.com or 135 W 50th St, 7th Floor, New York, NY 10020 (Please mark "OKAY TO PRINT")

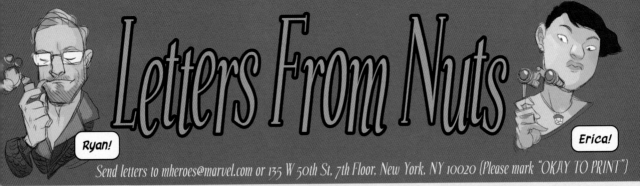

Last month we said all the letters were fake because you hadn't sent us any yet, but now we have TONS and all the letters are real! We love to hear from you: send your email to MHEROES@ MARVEL.COM, and don't forget to mark "OKAY TO PRINT" in there somewhere. And be sure to follow our production blog at unbeatablesquirrelgirl. tumblr.com! We post fan art, sneak peeks, sketches, recordings of Squirrel Girl's theme song we made in our kitchens - all sorts of fun stuff!

YOUR LETTERS:

Q: In issue #1's letters you wrote, "Can a book like this find an audience?" We live in a post-Superior Foes of Spider-Man world; more and more we readers like having the "comic" in our comics. You've found an audience in this guy, that's for sure! Was it Ryan/Erica or the editors who wrote the subscript footnotes? Because that was NUT a bad idea. I hope the footnotes are a continued part of the comic mag!

- Trent H.

A: Yeah, that was me (Ryan) doing that! I like the idea of secrets that you get to discover when you read a comic, and I really hope there are people who only noticed those secret words halfway through (or perhaps, just now, as they're reading this, and now they're going back to see what they missed?). They will continue forever because I love writing them forever!

Q: Squirrels. Cannot. Give. You. RABIES!!! Look it up!! Doreen would have known this and corrected her new roommate (even if she didn't know about the squirrel observatories).

-Benjamin G.
True Squirrel Fan

A: ATTENTION EVERYONE: I looked into this and BENJAMIN IS CORRECT. Squirrels don't even normally GET rabies, because to get it they'd have to hang around with animals that typically carry it, and most of those animals try to eat all the squirrels they see. Squirrel bites are apparently one of the few animal bites that don't trigger a hospital vaccination protocol! GOOD TO KNOW.

PS: if you get bitten by a squirrel, maaaaybe still check with a doctor just in case? You know, before you take the medical advice you found in the letters page of a comic book.

ERICA: I have personal experience with this, actually. As a young teenager, I think you call them tweens now, during the time when most Marvel characters gain their superhuman abilities, I was bitten by a squirrel. I was tested, but did not get rabies. We did not test for radiation. It might have been a radioactive squirrel. If you ask, I'll show you my scar.

Q: Thank you, Erica, for drawing Squirrel Girl not like a sex symbol (I feel awkward when I discovered about she and Logan...). And thank you, Ryan, for showing us that Squirrel Girl is a geek too. It's good to read comics about a girl who is a fan of comics too, and a little tomboy (I'm a tomboy girl too).

Will we see romance between Speedball and Squirrel Girl? I know we are gonna see a lot of Marvel stars in this comic. But I hope to see those love birds together again.

- ScarlettShana

A: Aw, thanks! I wouldn't worry about that Wolverine thing though: all we knew for SURE is that she and Wolverine at one point agreed to never see each other again. BUT NOW I CAN TELL YOU WHY: several years ago, Doreen was about to get into a cab when Wolverine ran up and hopped inside, stealing it from her. Squirrel Girl was (understandably) SUPER-CHEESED and shouted that he was a jerk and his jerkiness must have its OWN healing factor and that she never wanted to see him again. As the cab drove off Wolverine rolled down the window and shouted "You too, bub!". And that's why things were awkward when they met again! THE END.

As for romance with Speedball, everyone has a little romance in their lives at some point, right? But I have a feeling Doreen might have feelings for someone new now...

ERICA: You're welcome, but honestly I just drew her the way I saw her and I don't see her as a sexy character. She's not exactly Emma Frost, you know?

Q: Does Doreen have a flying squirrel costume that opens up and lets her glide?

- Simon S.

A: SPOILER ALERT (IF YOU'RE READING THIS COMIC FROM BACK TO FRONT, THAT IS): She gets an Iron Squirrel outfit this issue, so - kinda! But a base-jumping suit would be PRETTY AMAZING for her to get down the road.

ERICA: Well, I know that S.H.I.E.L.D. has had base-jumping suits for decades and Dum Dum Dugan did invite Doreen to join S.H.I.E.L.D. at one point, so she might have access to some later...

Q: First off, I have to say how absolutely MARVELous (ha!) the first issue of Unbeatable Squirrel Girl was! Wow! Artwork and writing combined, it's pretty much the most perfect comic book of all time and space. Secondly, I have to say how super AWESOME it is to have another female-fronted book, but also one where the character is hilarious and clumsy and endearing and basically a lot more like me than any of the other beautiful, graceful super-women out there. (I love them too, though!) I love everything you've done and I absolutely canNUT wait for the next issue! (One day I'll stop with the puns. Today is NUT that day.)

- Holly R.

A: Thank you! One thing both Erica and I discovered while making this book is how often every day (without thinking!) we would say something is "nuts" or "nutty" or how we'd like "acorn" ("a corn") for dinner. The puns come almost TOO easily!

ERICA: My main thing is I like to draw heartier super ladies, if their powers are mostly physical, because I feel like I shouldn't be able to take down a super hero by sitting on her.

Q: Is it true Squirrel Girl would've been in Avengers 2, but Ultron was too chicken to fight her?

- Andy D.

A: That movie isn't even out yet! How do you know she's NOT in it?? ...But on the off chance that for some reason she isn't, yeah, probably that's the reason! I'm guessing the after-credits scene is just Ultron peeking around corners to make sure Squirrel Girl isn't there, then wiping his forehead and saying "PHEW! CLOSE CALL."

ERICA: I don't know about that, but they need to add her to the movies soon because who's going to take down Thanos???

That's all we have room for, but look for a double-sized letters page next issue! See y'all next month! Stay nutty!

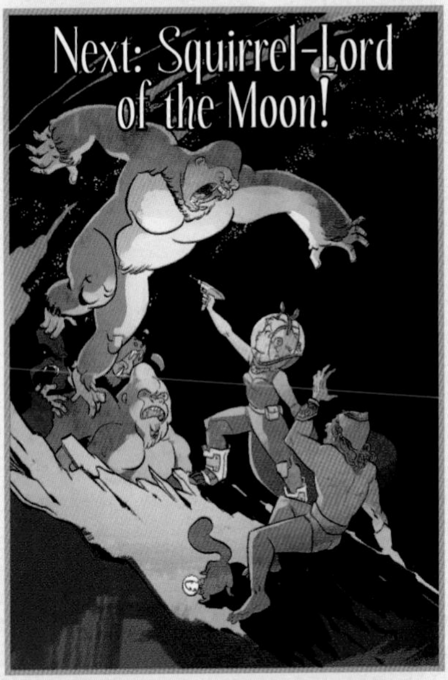
Next: Squirrel-Lord of the Moon!

When you see this: AR, open up the MARVEL AR APP (available on applicable Apple ® iOS or Android ™ devices) and use your camera-enabled device to unlock extra-special exclusive features!

3

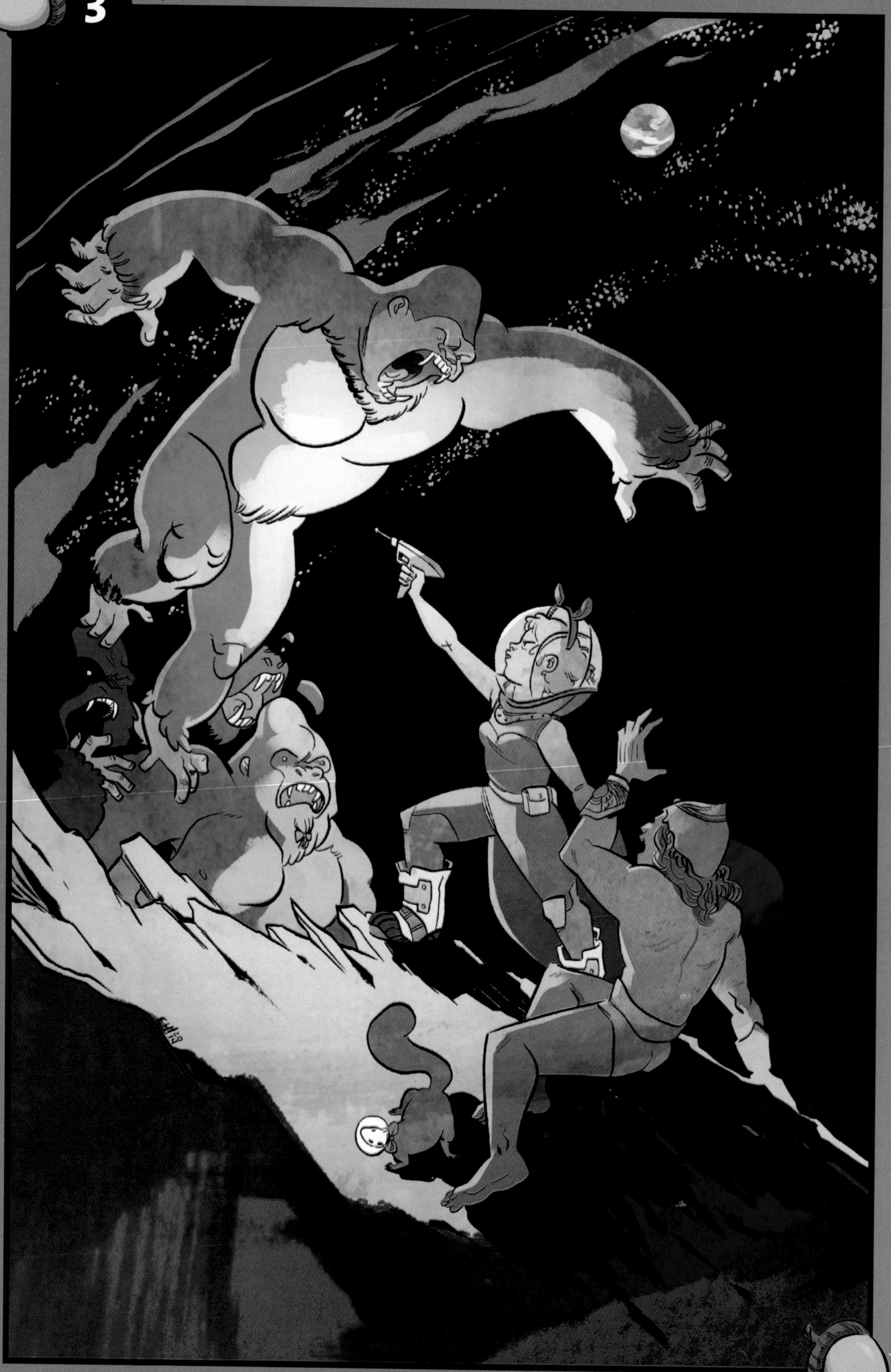

Doreen Green isn't just a first-year computer science student: she secretly also has all the powers of both squirrel and girl! She uses her amazing abilities to fight crime **and** be as awesome as possible. You know her as...**The Unbeatable Squirrel Girl!** Let's catch up with what she's been up to until now, with...

Squirrel Girl in a nutshell

search! 🔍

#OWNED

#everythingisnormalinspace

Welcome to

#USG

Number Three

Hope you like falafel jokes

Squirrel Girl! @unbeatablesg
Did you guys see how I took care of Kraven the other day?

xKravenTheHunterx @unshavenkraven
NOBODY LISTEN TO @unbeatablesg, SHE DIDN'T TAKE CARE OF ME, I MERELY DECIDED TO STOP FIGHTING HER

Squirrel Girl! @unbeatablesg
@unshavenkraven hey dude did you kill any gigantos underwater like I suggested?

xKravenTheHunterx @unshavenkraven
@unbeatablesg listen

xKravenTheHunterx @unshavenkraven
@unbeatablesg these things take time

Squirrel Girl! @unbeatablesg
Apparently I'm the only one that can see that GALACTUS IS COMING TO EARTH!!

Tippy-Toe @yoitstippytoe
CHIT CHUKKA CHITTY

Squirrel Girl! @unbeatablesg
Apparently me and @yoitstippytoe are the only ones that can see GALACTUS IS COMING TO EARTH!!

Squirrel Girl! @unbeatablesg
Oh well

Squirrel Girl! @unbeatablesg
guess we'll just have to stop him ourselves then

Squirrel Girl! @unbeatablesg
ON THE FRIGGIN' MOON

Tony Stark @starkmantony ✅
Whoever "borrowed" Iron Man armor parts from my NYC offices, please return them. Looking at you, @unbeatablesg.

Squirrel Girl! @unbeatablesg
@starkmantony Tony it's REALLY IMPORTANT. Like COSMIC important.

Squirrel Girl! @unbeatablesg
@starkmantony I don't know why I'm being coy. It's for Galactus.

Squirrel Girl! @unbeatablesg
@starkmantony I'm gonna beat up @xGALACTUSx, Tony!! ON THE MOON

Tony Stark @starkmantony ✅
@unbeatablesg You break it, you bought it.

Whiplash @realwhiplash22
I JUST WHIPPED @STARKMANTONY OUT OF THE SKY WITH MY ENERGY WHIPS YES YES #OWNED

Tony Stark @starkmantony ✅
Wasn't me. I'm in San Francisco, @realwhiplash22.

Whiplash @realwhiplash22
@starkmantony SORRY I CANNOT HEAR YOU OVER HOW BADLY YOU GOT #OWNED

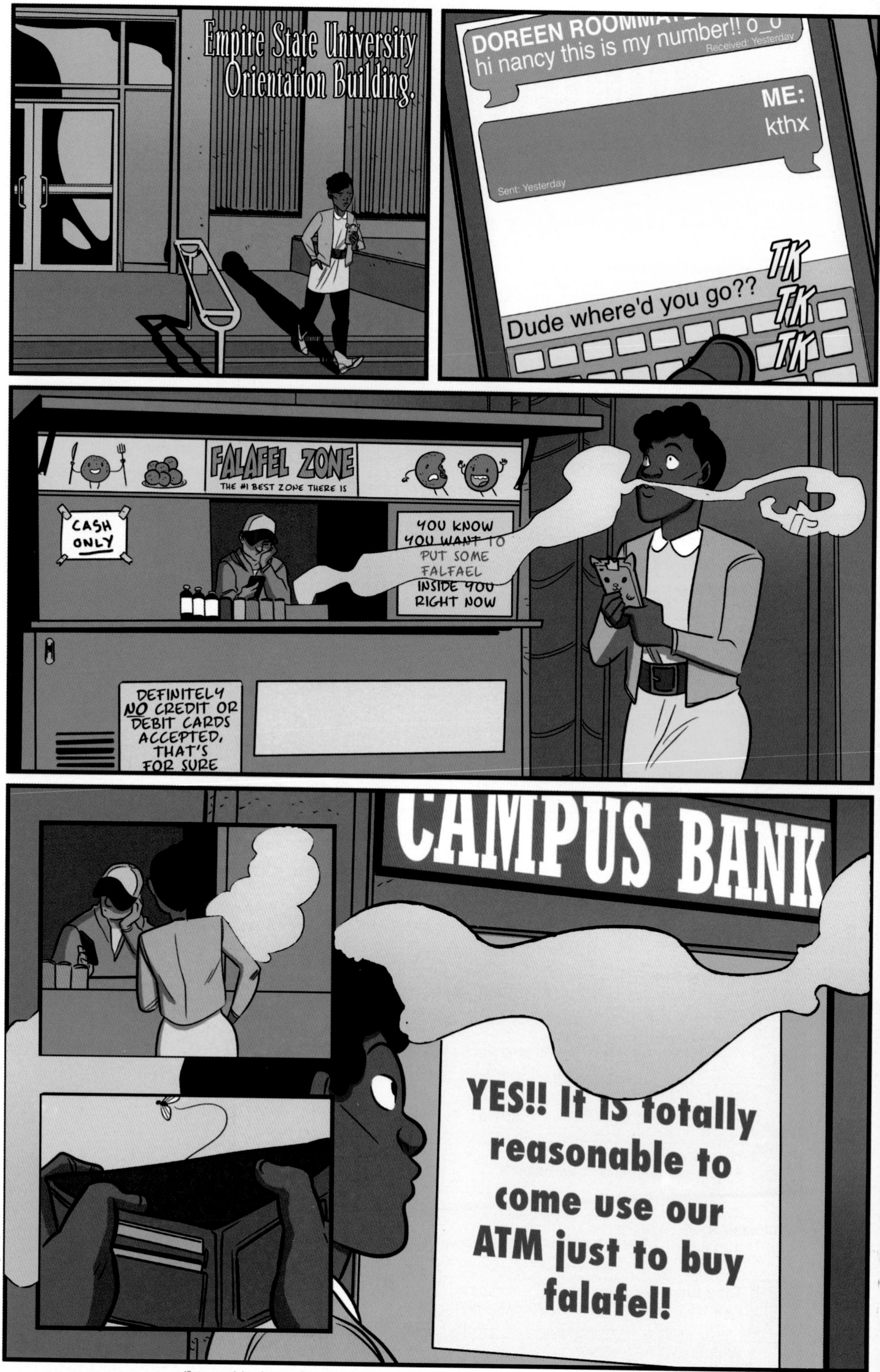

Empire State University Orientation Building.
DOREEN ROOMM
hi nancy this is my number!! o_
Received: Yesterday
ME:
kthx
Sent: Yesterday
Dude where'd you go??
TK
TK
TK
FALAFEL ZONE
THE #1 BEST ZONE THERE IS
CASH ONLY
YOU KNOW YOU WANT TO PUT SOME FALFAEL INSIDE YOU RIGHT NOW
DEFINITELY NO CREDIT OR DEBIT CARDS ACCEPTED, THAT'S FOR SURE
CAMPUS BANK
YES!! It IS totally reasonable to come use our ATM just to buy falafel!

If you want to stop reading this comic to go get some falafel, I understand. In fact, I might join you!

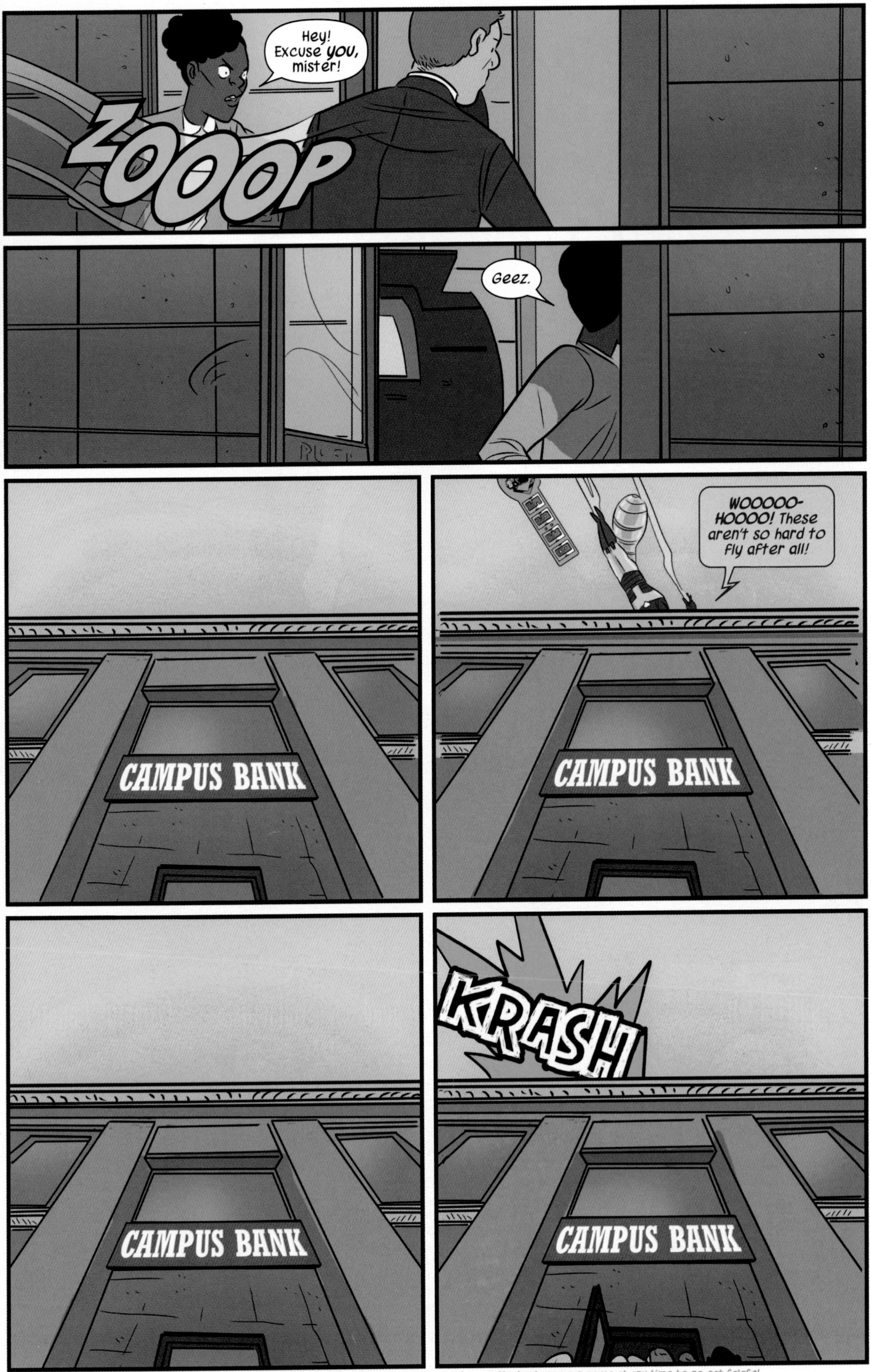
Hey! Excuse **YOU,** mister!
ZOOOP
Geez.
CAMPUS BANK
WOOOOO-HOOOO! These aren't so hard to fly after all!
CAMPUS BANK
CAMPUS BANK
KRASH
CAMPUS BANK

Dang, you guys, these falafel I got are friggin' delicious!! This is why comics are the best: you can pause at any time to go eat falafel, so check and mate, ***all other media.*** Except books, I guess. ***Fine,*** books are good, too.

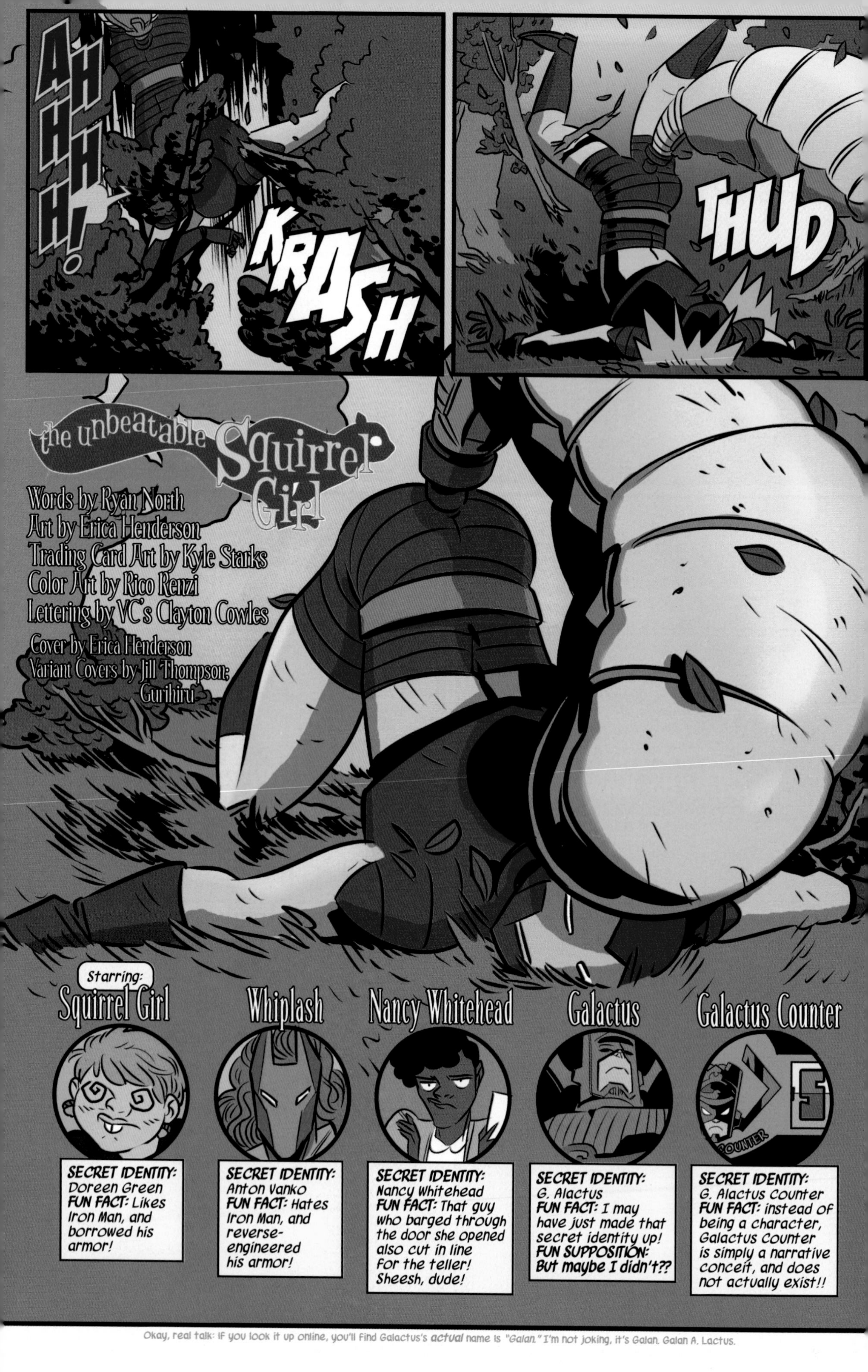
AHHHH!
KRASH
THUD
the unbeatable Squirrel Girl
Words by Ryan North
Art by Erica Henderson
Trading Card Art by Kyle Starks
Color Art by Rico Renzi
Lettering by VC's Clayton Cowles
Cover by Erica Henderson
Variant Covers by Jill Thompson; Gurihiru
Starring:
Squirrel Girl
Whiplash
Nancy Whitehead
Galactus
Galactus Counter
5
COUNTER
SECRET IDENTITY: Doreen Green FUN FACT: Likes Iron Man, and borrowed his armor!
SECRET IDENTITY: Anton Vanko FUN FACT: Hates Iron Man, and reverse-engineered his armor!
SECRET IDENTITY: Nancy Whitehead FUN FACT: That guy who barged through the door she opened also cut in line for the teller! Sheesh, dude!
SECRET IDENTITY: G. Alactus FUN FACT: I may have just made that secret identity up! FUN SUPPOSITION: But maybe I didn't??
SECRET IDENTITY: G. Alactus Counter FUN FACT: instead of being a character, Galactus Counter is simply a narrative conceit, and does not actually exist!!

Okay, real talk: If you look it up online, you'll find Galactus's *actual* name is "Galan." I'm not joking, it's Galan. Galan A. Lactus.

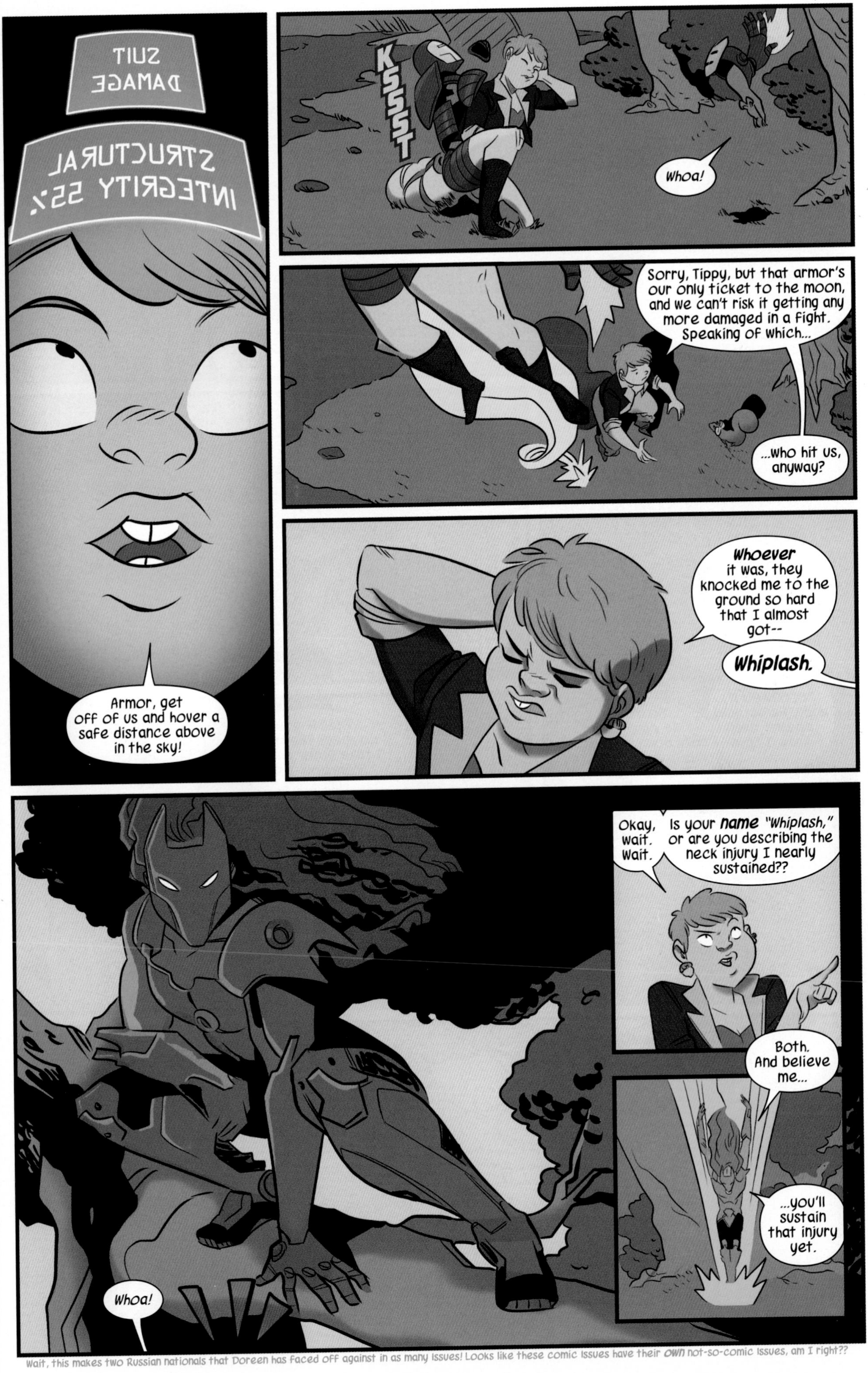
SUIT DAMAGE
STRUCTURAL INTEGRITY 55%
Armor, get off of us and hover a safe distance above in the sky!
KSSST
Whoa!
Sorry, Tippy, but that armor's our only ticket to the moon, and we can't risk it getting any more damaged in a fight. Speaking of which...
...who hit us, anyway?
Whoever it was, they knocked me to the ground so hard that I almost got--
Whiplash.
Whoa!
Okay, wait. Wait.
Is your name "Whiplash," or are you describing the neck injury I nearly sustained??
Both. And believe me...
...you'll sustain that injury yet.

Wait, this makes two Russian nationals that Doreen has faced off against in as many issues! Looks like these comic issues have their *own* not-so-comic issues, am I right??

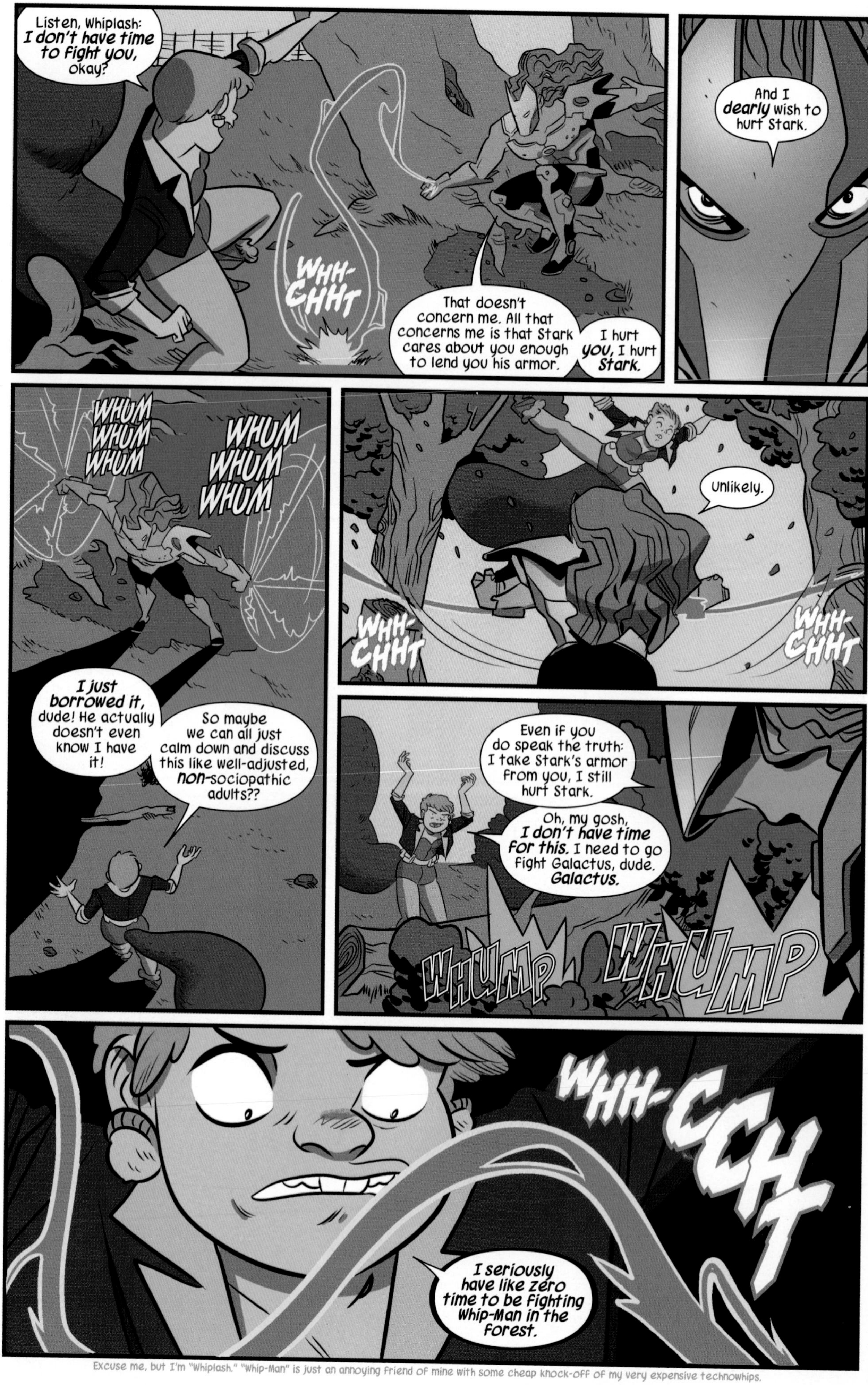
Listen, Whiplash: I don't have time to fight you, okay?
WHH-CHHT
That doesn't concern me. All that concerns me is that Stark cares about you enough to lend you his armor.
I hurt you, I hurt Stark.
And I dearly wish to hurt Stark.
WHUM WHUM WHUM
WHUM WHUM WHUM
I just borrowed it, dude! He actually doesn't even know I have it!
So maybe we can all just calm down and discuss this like well-adjusted, non-sociopathic adults??
Unlikely.
WHH-CHHT
WHH-CHHT
Even if you do speak the truth: I take Stark's armor from you, I still hurt Stark.
Oh, my gosh, I don't have time for this. I need to go fight Galactus, dude. Galactus.
WHUMP
WHUMP
WHH-CCHT
I seriously have like zero time to be fighting Whip-Man in the forest.

Excuse me, but I'm "Whiplash." "Whip-Man" is just an annoying friend of mine with some cheap knock-off of my very expensive technowhips.

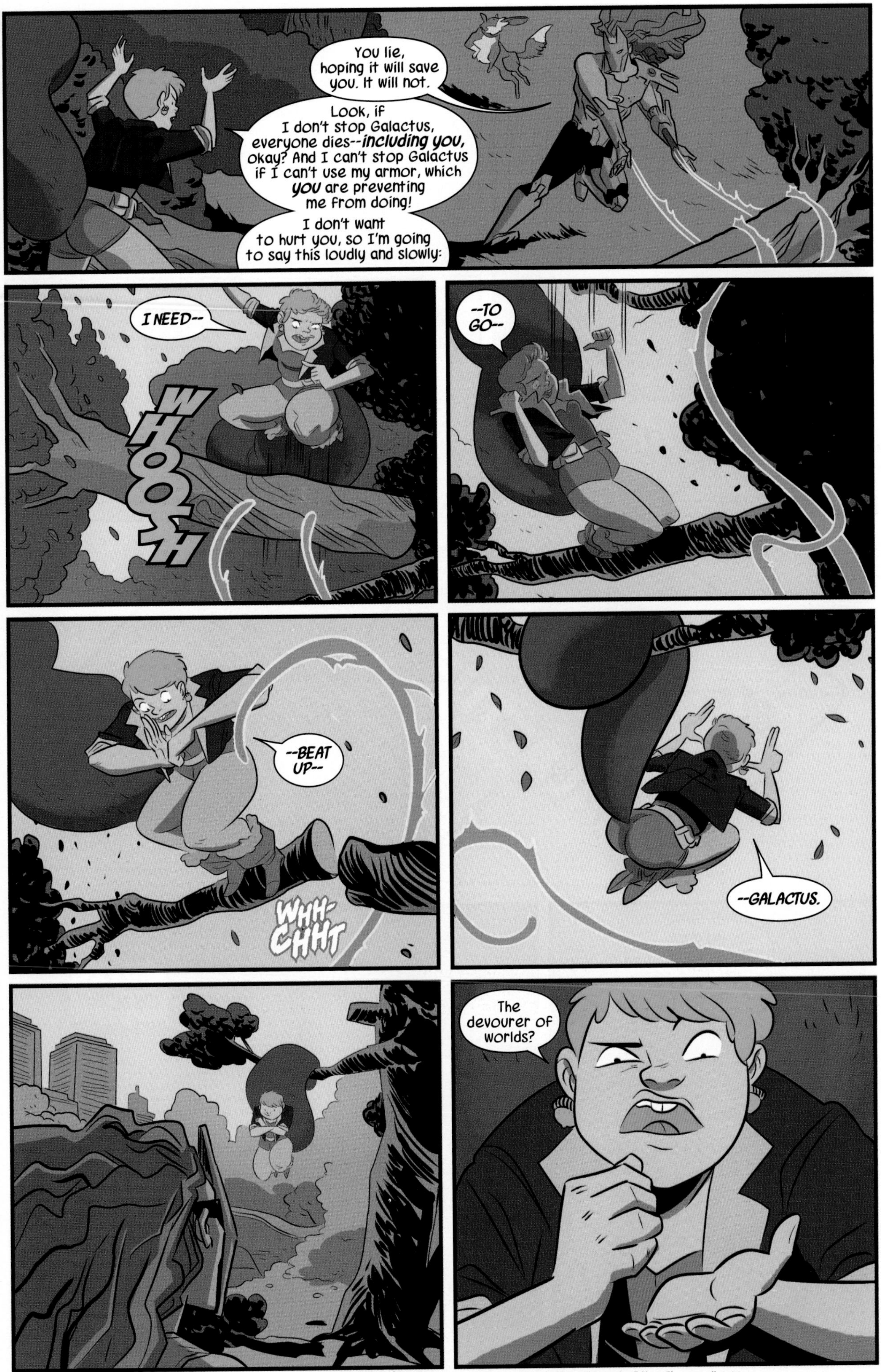
You lie, hoping it will save you. It will not.
Look, if I don't stop Galactus, everyone dies--*including you,* okay? And I can't stop Galactus if I can't use my armor, which *you* are preventing me from doing!
I don't want to hurt you, so I'm going to say this loudly and slowly:
I NEED--
WHOOSH
--TO GO--
--BEAT UP--
WHH-CHHT
--GALACTUS.
The devourer of worlds?

This isn't actual American Sign Language, but if you can think of a better hand symbol for "Galactus" then I'm, *um,* all ears.

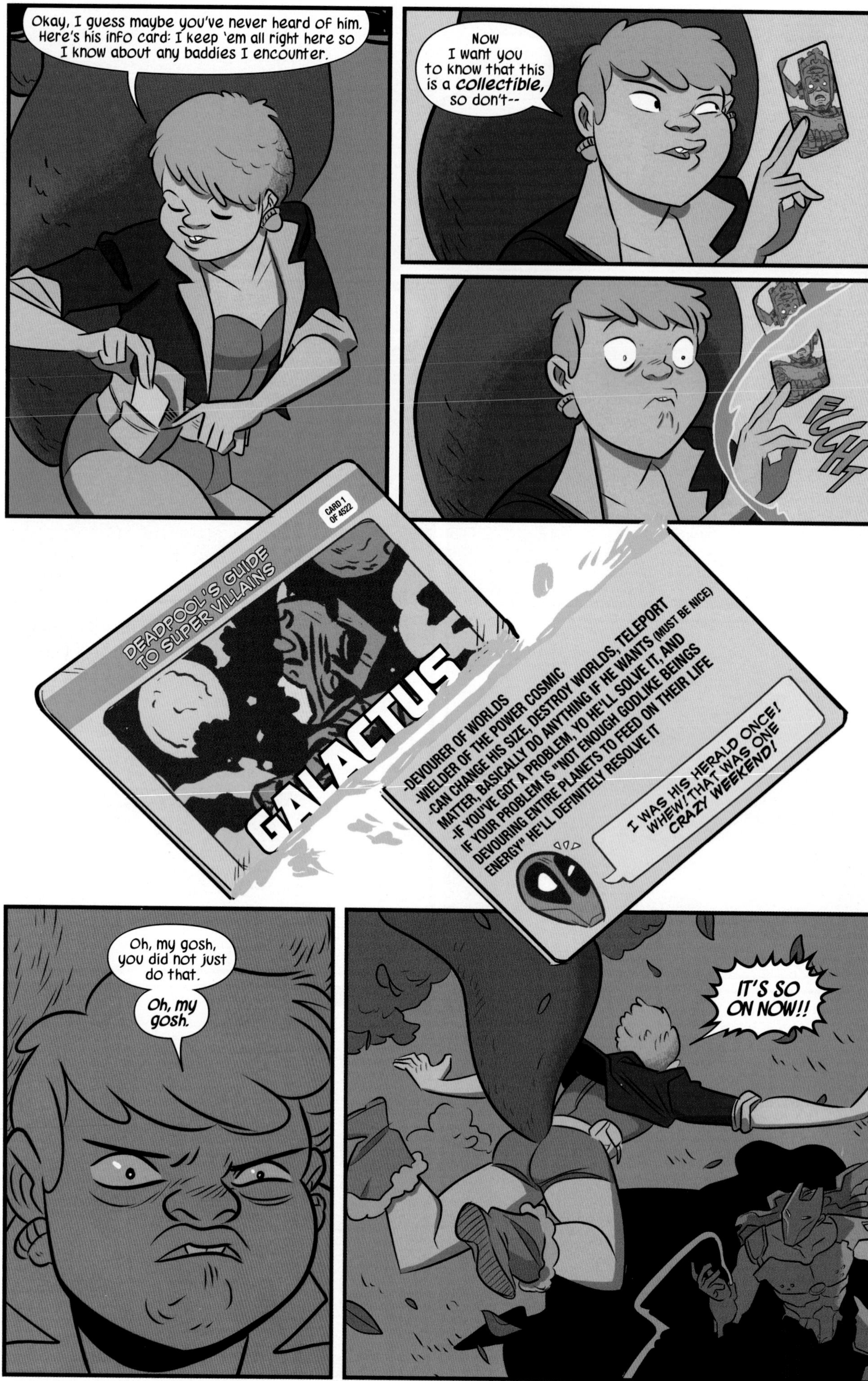

Okay, I guess maybe you've never heard of him. Here's his info card: I keep 'em all right here so I know about any baddies I encounter.
Now I want you to know that this is a *collectible,* so don't--
FCCHT
DEADPOOL'S GUIDE TO SUPER VILLAINS
CARD 1 OF 4522
GALACTUS
-DEVOURER OF WORLDS
-WIELDER OF THE POWER COSMIC
-CAN CHANGE HIS SIZE, DESTROY WORLDS, TELEPORT MATTER, BASICALLY DO ANYTHING IF HE WANTS (MUST BE NICE)
-IF YOU'VE GOT A PROBLEM, YO HE'LL SOLVE IT, AND IF YOUR PROBLEM IS "NOT ENOUGH GODLIKE BEINGS DEVOURING ENTIRE PLANETS TO FEED ON THEIR LIFE ENERGY" HE'LL DEFINITELY RESOLVE IT
I WAS HIS HERALD ONCE! WHEW! THAT WAS ONE *CRAZY WEEKEND!*
Oh, my gosh, you did not just do that.
Oh, my gosh.
IT'S SO ON NOW!!

You know what happens to a squirrel when it gets mad? *The same thing that happens to everything else.*
Which is to say, increased heart rate, elevated adrenaline and norepinephrine production, a lessened capacity for self-monitoring, etc., etc.

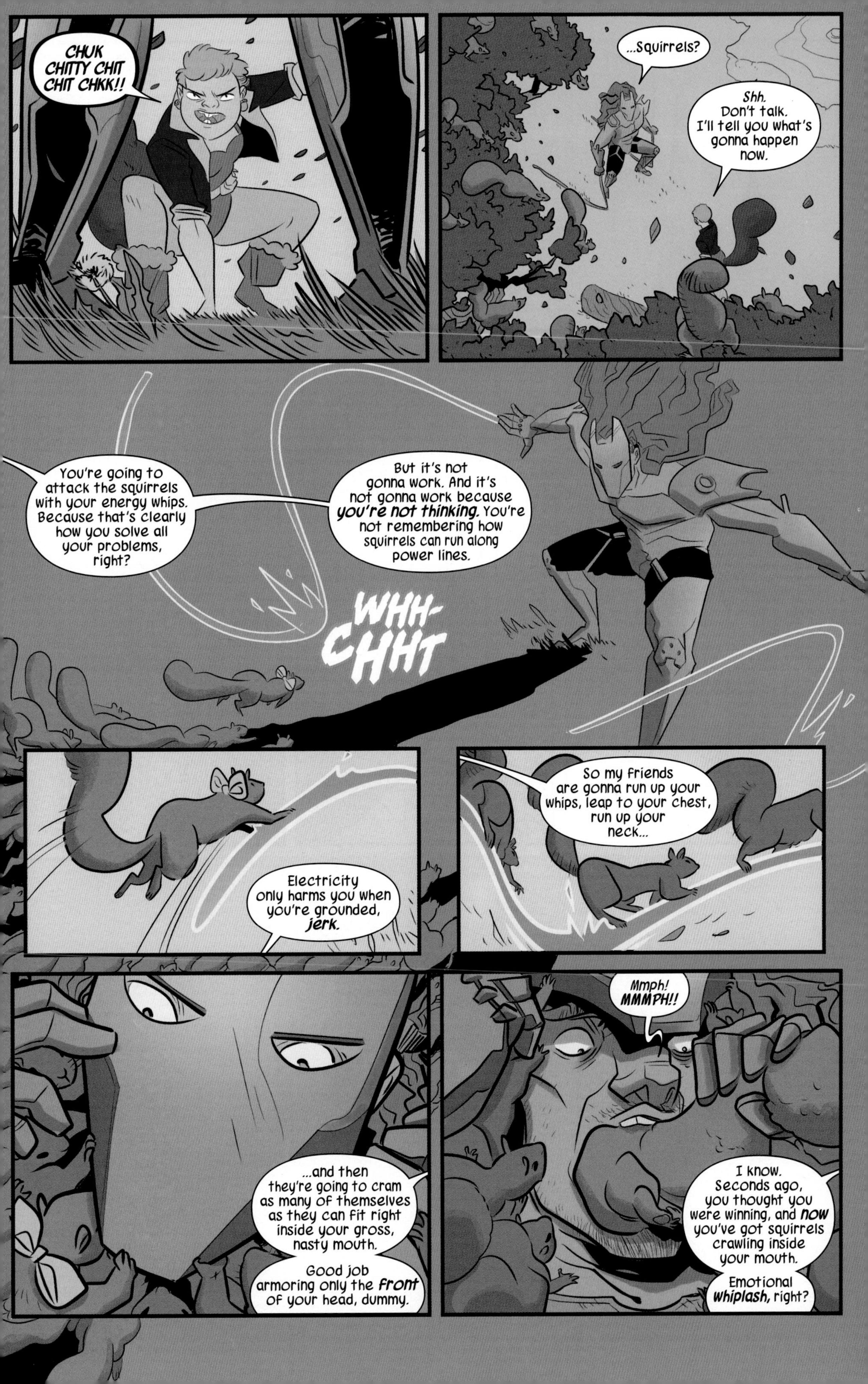
CHUK CHITTY CHIT CHIT CHKK!!
...Squirrels?
Shh. Don't talk. I'll tell you what's gonna happen now.
You're going to attack the squirrels with your energy whips. Because that's clearly how you solve all your problems, right?
But it's not gonna work. And it's not gonna work because you're not thinking. You're not remembering how squirrels can run along power lines.
WHH-CHHT
Electricity only harms you when you're grounded, jerk.
So my friends are gonna run up your whips, leap to your chest, run up your neck...
...and then they're going to cram as many of themselves as they can fit right inside your gross, nasty mouth.
Good job armoring only the front of your head, dummy.
Mmph! MMMPH!!
I know. Seconds ago, you thought you were winning, and now you've got squirrels crawling inside your mouth.
Emotional whiplash, right?

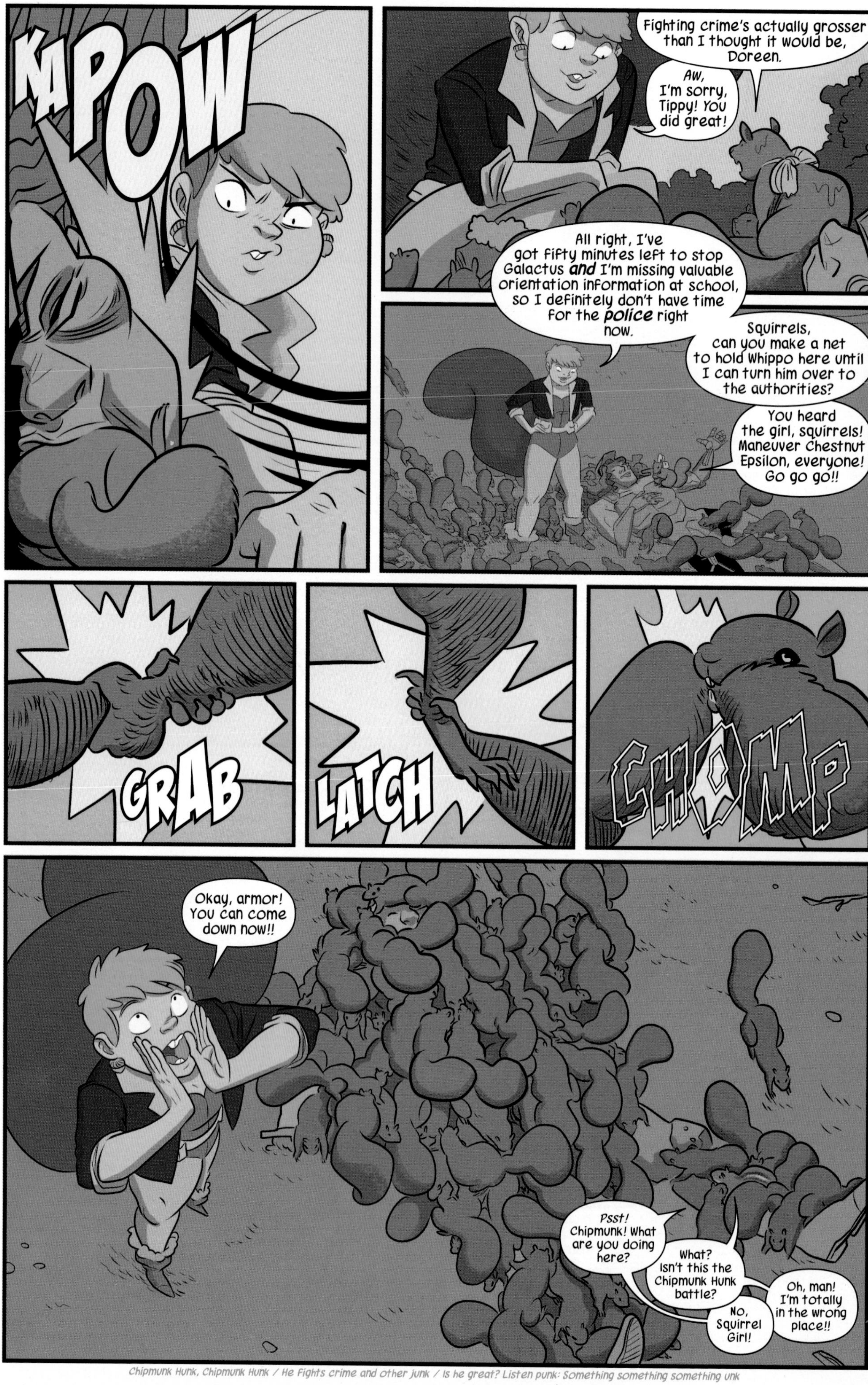
KAPOW
Fighting crime's actually grosser than I thought it would be, Doreen.
Aw, I'm sorry, Tippy! You did great!
All right, I've got fifty minutes left to stop Galactus and I'm missing valuable orientation information at school, so I definitely don't have time for the police right now.
Squirrels, can you make a net to hold Whippo here until I can turn him over to the authorities?
You heard the girl, squirrels! Maneuver Chestnut Epsilon, everyone! Go go go!!
GRAB
LATCH
CHOMP
Okay, armor! You can come down now!!
Psst! Chipmunk! What are you doing here?
What? Isn't this the Chipmunk Hunk battle?
No, Squirrel Girl!
Oh, man! I'm totally in the wrong place!!

Chipmunk Hunk, Chipmunk Hunk / He fights crime and other junk / Is he great? Listen punk: Something something something unk

ARRIVAL COUNTER 49:54

The Iron Squirrel's damaged, but she'll still get us to the moon and back as long as we don't hurt her any more. Suit up, TT!

With pleasure!

Wait! *Wait!!*

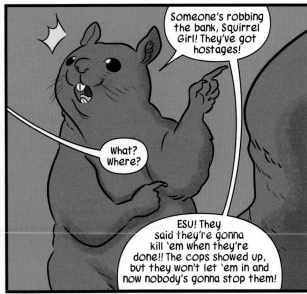

Someone's robbing the bank, Squirrel Girl! They've got hostages!

What? Where?

ESU! They said they're gonna kill 'em when they're done!! The cops showed up, but they won't let 'em in and now nobody's gonna stop them!

No. *I'll* stop them. That's *my* campus now, and that means Empire State University has a new guardian.

A watchful protector.

A *dark* knight.

You're... you're not that dark.

Hey, my costume's dark! It's got, like, *browns.*

Doreen, I'm sorry, but we just don't have the time. If we stop that robbery, then Galactus makes it to Earth and everybody dies anyway.

We *don't* stop that robbery, then we're saving a planet where crime pays and the hostages get shot!

No, that's not how it's gonna be.

We're saving the hostages *and* the planet, Tippy...

...and I think I know how we're gonna do it, too. We're going to invent a new maneuver, even *better* than Chestnut Epsilon.

But that's already our best maneuver!

And it's way better than Chestnut Delta, which it replaced!

To hiiiiim, he is a great big chipmunk / Wherever there's some street punks / You'll find the Chipmunk Hunk!

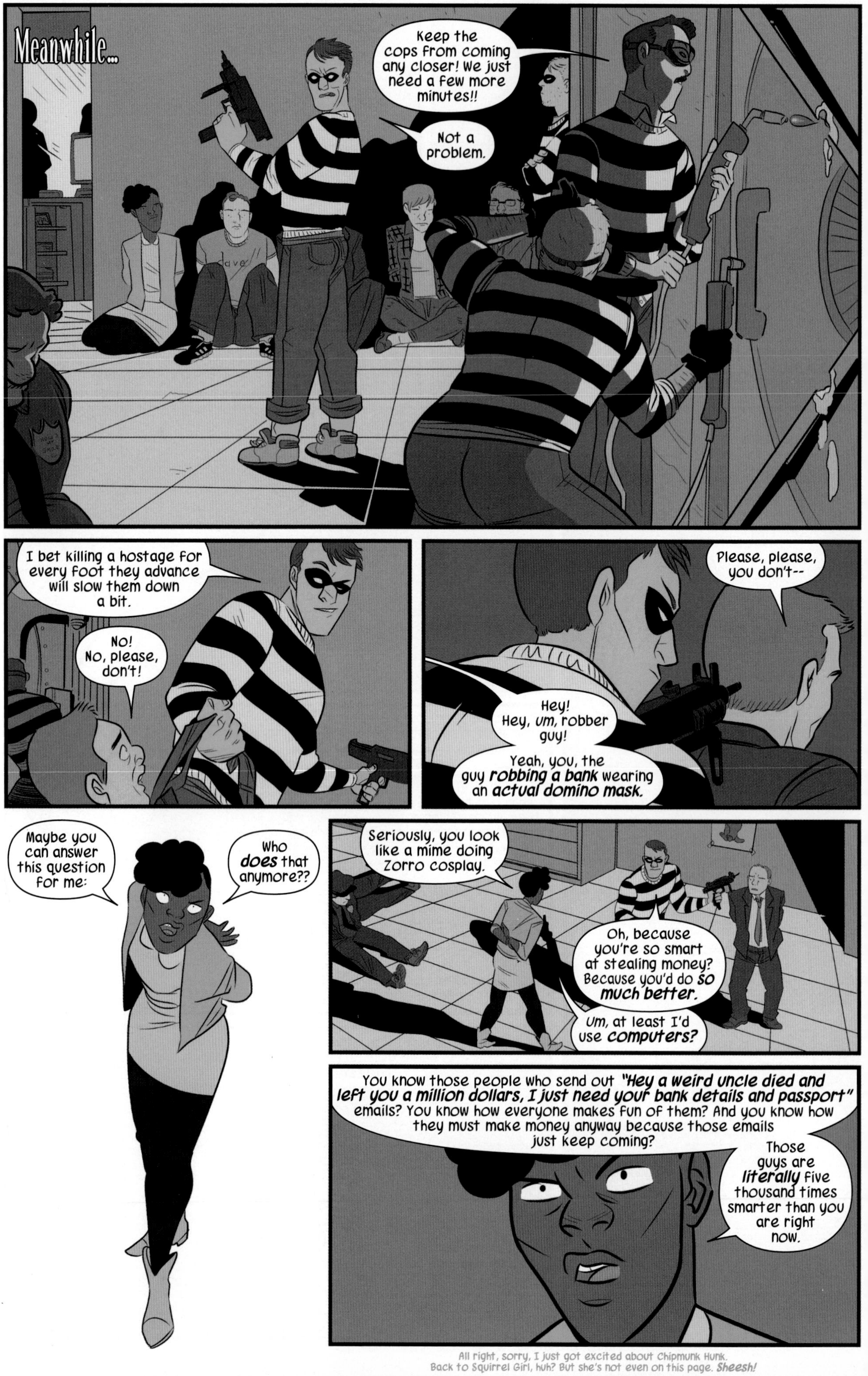
Meanwhile...
Keep the cops from coming any closer! We just need a few more minutes!!
Not a problem.
I bet killing a hostage for every foot they advance will slow them down a bit.
No! No, please, don't!
Please, please, you don't--
Hey! Hey, um, robber guy!
Yeah, you, the guy **robbing a bank** wearing an ***actual domino mask.***
Maybe you can answer this question for me:
Who ***does*** that anymore??
Seriously, you look like a mime doing Zorro cosplay.
Oh, because you're so smart at stealing money? Because you'd do ***so much better.***
Um, at least I'd use ***computers?***
You know those people who send out ***"Hey a weird uncle died and left you a million dollars, I just need your bank details and passport"*** emails? You know how everyone makes fun of them? And you know how they must make money anyway because those emails just keep coming?
Those guys are ***literally*** five thousand times smarter than you are right now.

All right, sorry, I just got excited about Chipmunk Hunk.
Back to Squirrel Girl, huh? But she's not even on this page. ***Sheesh!***

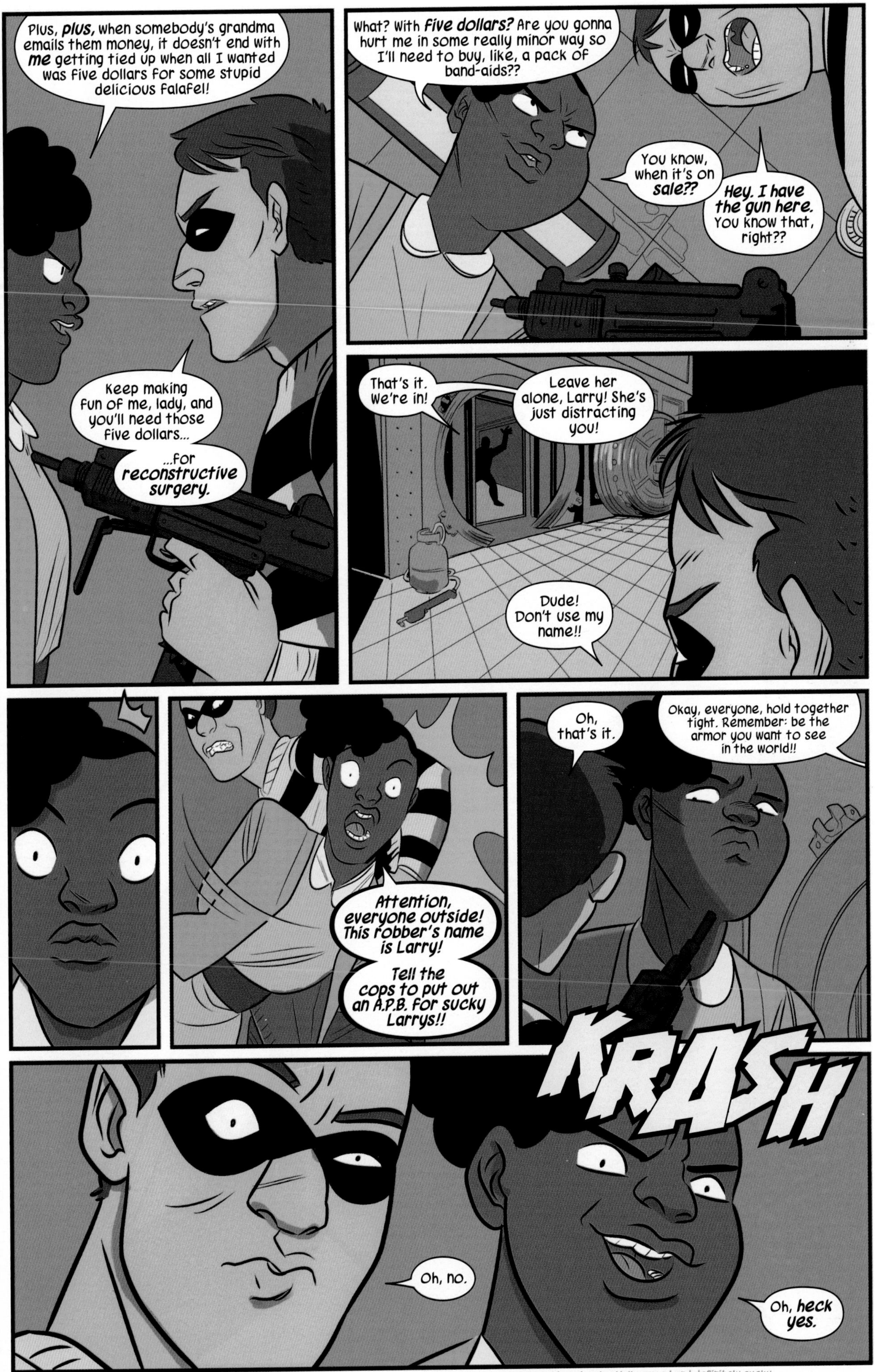
Plus, plus, when somebody's grandma emails them money, it doesn't end with me getting tied up when all I wanted was five dollars for some stupid delicious falafel!
Keep making fun of me, lady, and you'll need those five dollars...
...for reconstructive surgery.
What? With five dollars? Are you gonna hurt me in some really minor way so I'll need to buy, like, a pack of band-aids??
You know, when it's on sale??
Hey. I have the gun here. You know that, right??
That's it. We're in!
Leave her alone, Larry! She's just distracting you!
Dude! Don't use my name!!
Attention, everyone outside! This robber's name is Larry!
Tell the cops to put out an A.P.B. for sucky Larrys!!
Oh, that's it.
Okay, everyone, hold together tight. Remember: be the armor you want to see in the world!!
KRASH
Oh, no.
Oh, heck yes.
Attention, all units: be on the lookout for sucky Larrys in the area. Subjects are to be considered potentially armed and definitely sucky.

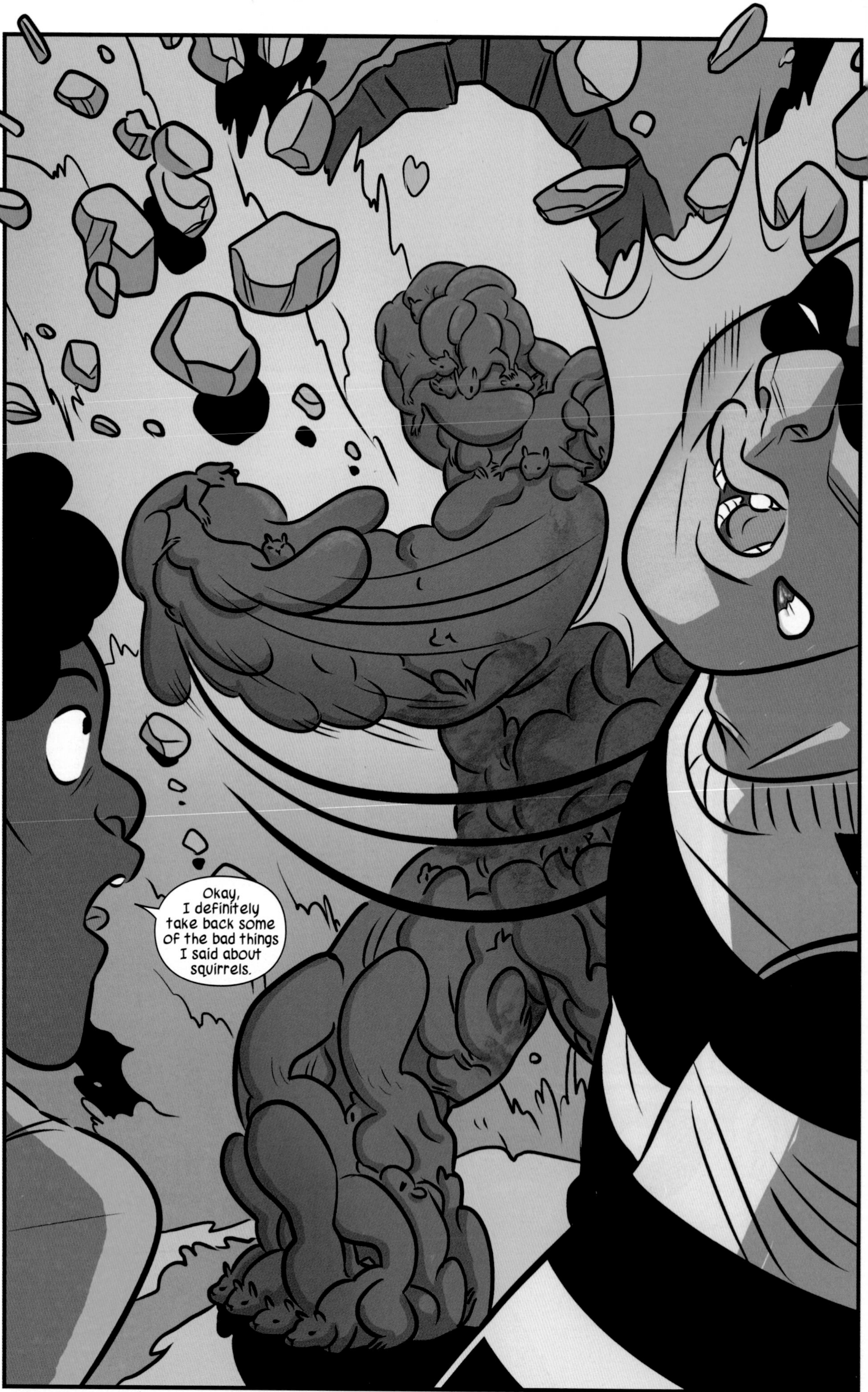
Okay, I definitely take back some of the bad things I said about squirrels.

In retrospect, Wikipedia *did* mention that groups of squirrels could combine to form giant squirrel-based objects, but I just assumed it was vandalism. I was a fool. A fool!!

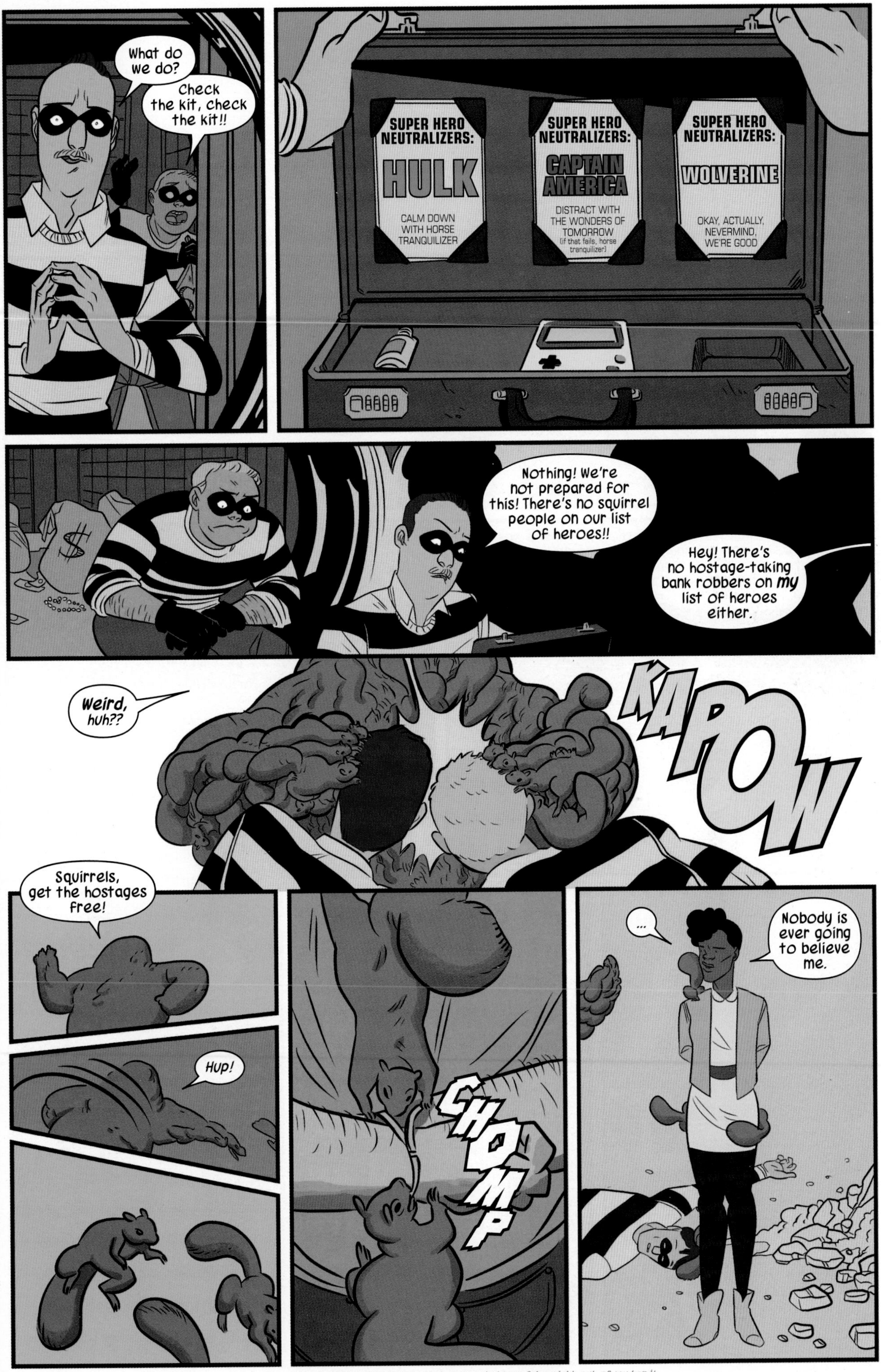
What do we do?
Check the kit, check the kit!!
SUPER HERO NEUTRALIZERS: HULK
CALM DOWN WITH HORSE TRANQUILIZER
SUPER HERO NEUTRALIZERS: CAPTAIN AMERICA
DISTRACT WITH THE WONDERS OF TOMORROW
(if that fails, horse tranquilizer)
SUPER HERO NEUTRALIZERS: WOLVERINE
OKAY, ACTUALLY, NEVERMIND, WE'RE GOOD
Nothing! We're not prepared for this! There's no squirrel people on our list of heroes!!
Hey! There's no hostage-taking bank robbers on *my* list of heroes either.
Weird, huh??
KAPOW
Squirrels, get the hostages free!
Hup!
CHOMP
...
Nobody is ever going to believe me.

This is worse than the time that famous actor guy stole my fries right out of my hand!

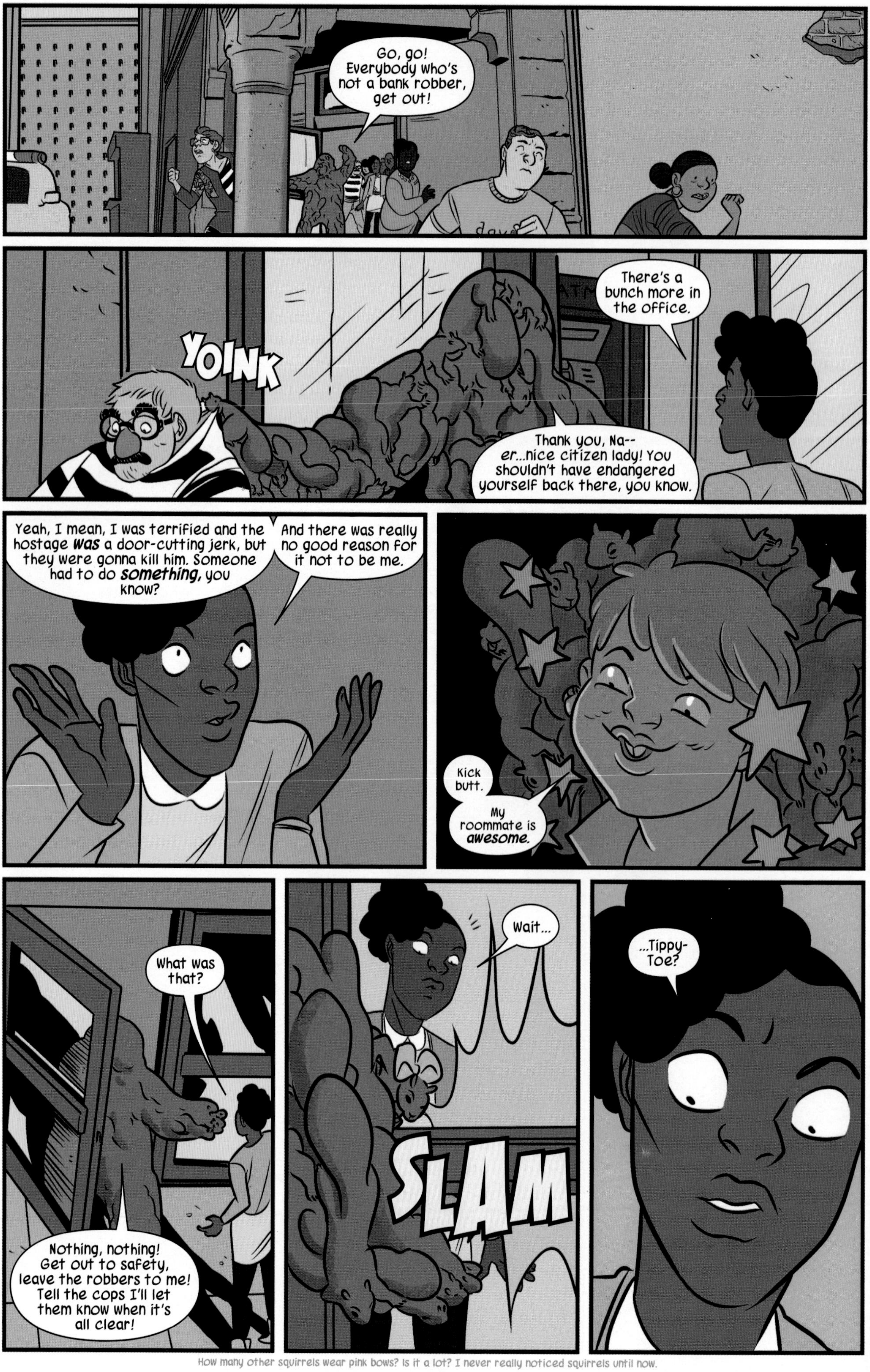
Go, go! Everybody who's not a bank robber, get out!
YOINK
There's a bunch more in the office.
Thank you, Na-- er...nice citizen lady! You shouldn't have endangered yourself back there, you know.
Yeah, I mean, I was terrified and the hostage WAS a door-cutting jerk, but they were gonna kill him. Someone had to do something, you know?
And there was really no good reason for it not to be me.
Kick butt.
My roommate is awesome.
What was that?
Nothing, nothing! Get out to safety, leave the robbers to me! Tell the cops I'll let them know when it's all clear!
Wait...
SLAM
...Tippy-Toe?

How many other squirrels wear pink bows? Is it a lot? I never really noticed squirrels until now.

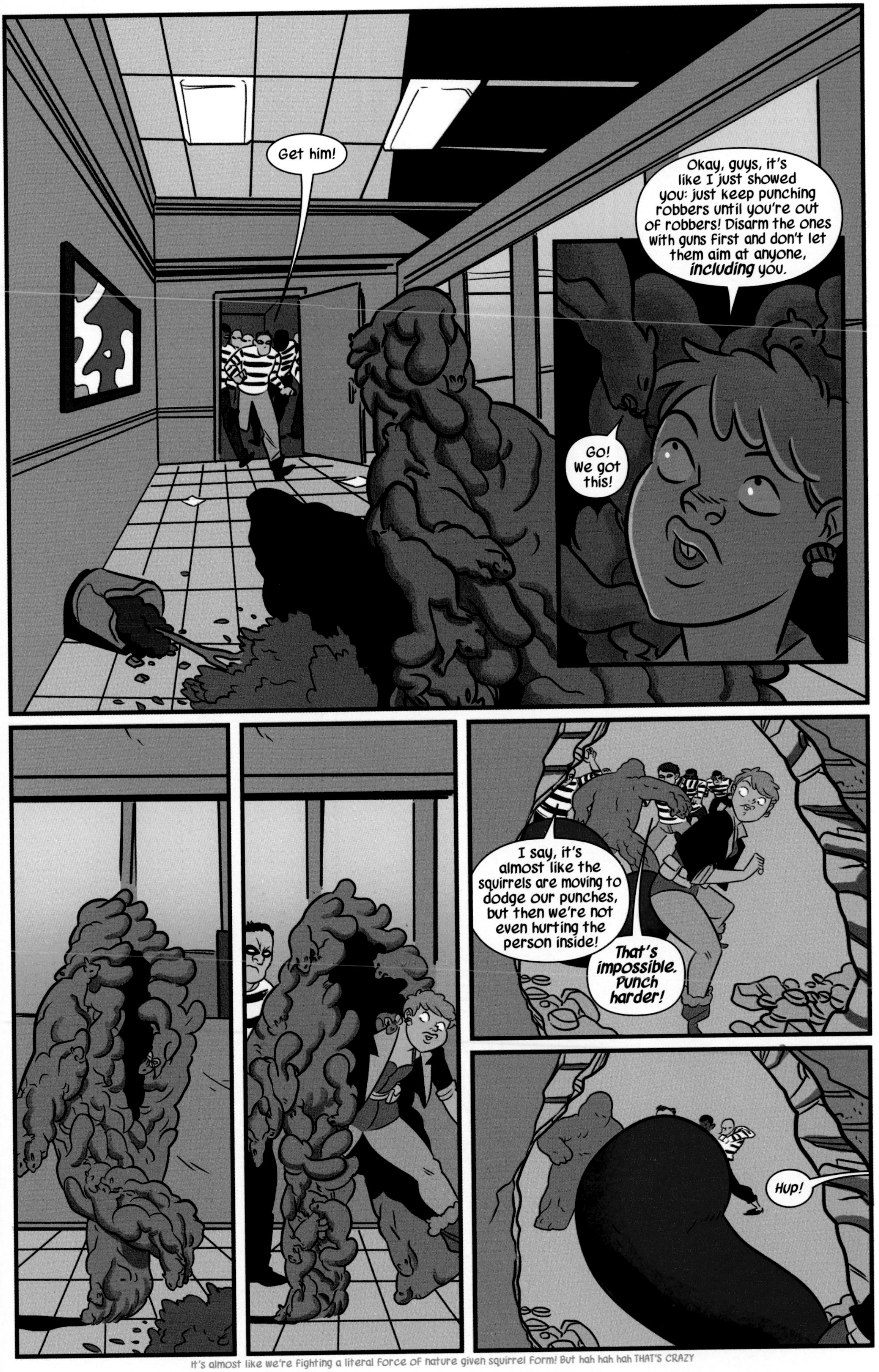
Get him!
Okay, guys, it's like I just showed you: just keep punching robbers until you're out of robbers! Disarm the ones with guns first and don't let them aim at anyone, *including* you.
Go! We got this!
I say, it's almost like the squirrels are moving to dodge our punches, but then we're not even hurting the person inside!
That's impossible. Punch harder!
Hup!

It's almost like we're fighting a literal force of nature given squirrel form! But hah hah hah THAT'S CRAZY

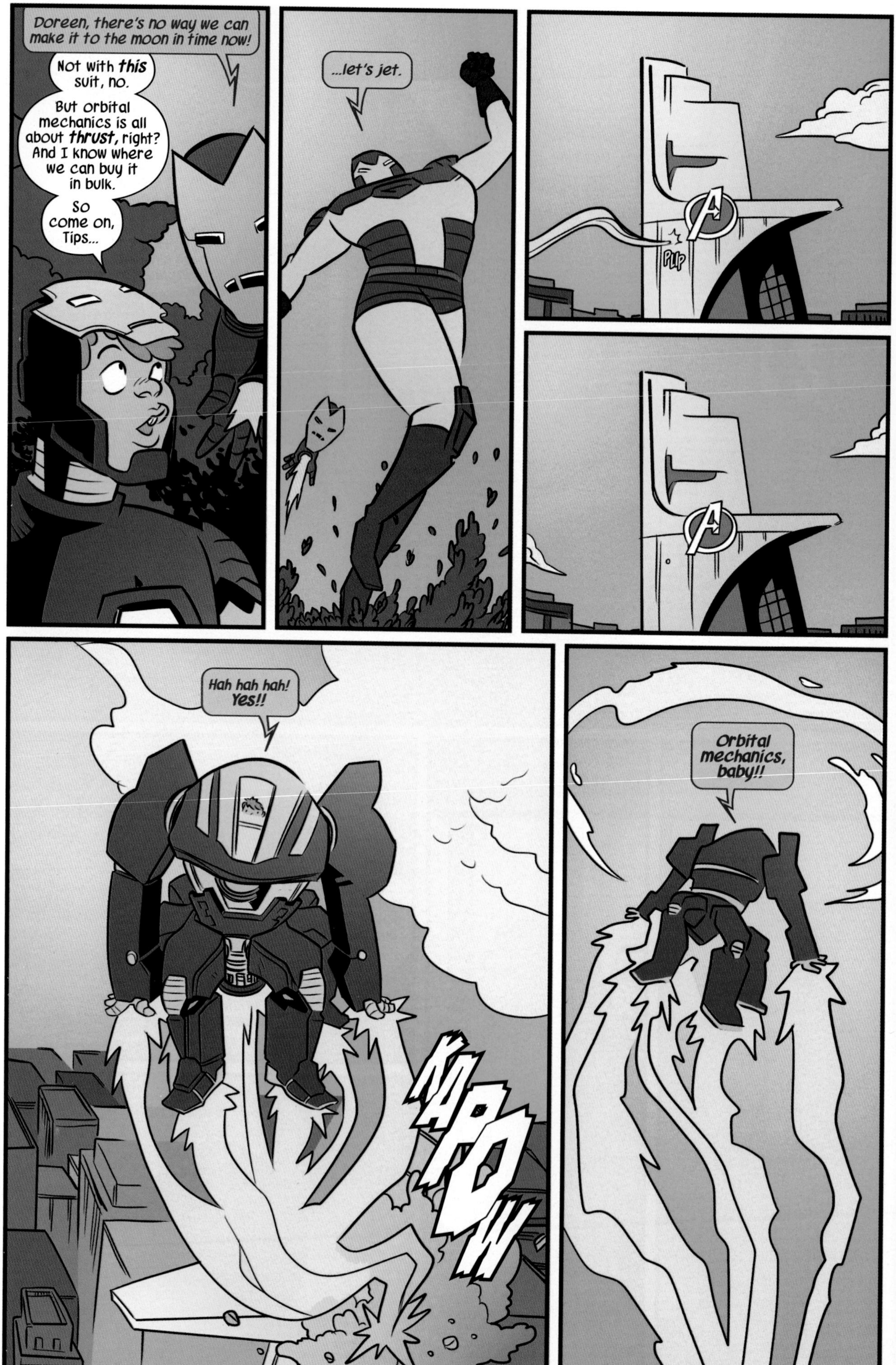
Doreen, there's no way we can make it to the moon in time now!
Not with ***this*** suit, no.
But orbital mechanics is all about ***thrust,*** right? And I know where we can buy it in bulk.
So come on, Tips...
...let's jet.
PLIP
Hah hah hah! ***Yes!!***
KAPOW
Orbital mechanics, baby!!

I was going to put a solution to the inverse Kepler's equation for orbital bodies here but ran out of room, so you'll just have to take my word for it that the physics in my talking squirrel comic are 100% ultralegit

Soon...

There! Earth to the moon and it's no big deal, baby. How much time do we have until Galactus arrives?

Doreen, we're--

...we're too late.

Suit! Emergency disassemble, engage "talk to the hand" maneuver gamma three!!

Whoa!

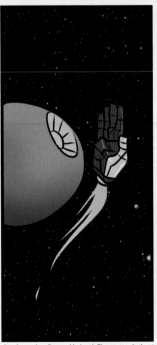

Hey there, cosmic being! It's me, Squirrel Girl!

Please come down here so I can beat you up real quick??

And *here* I was going to solve Fermat's Last Theorem, but again, it's way too large to fit in the margins. *Haha oh well.*

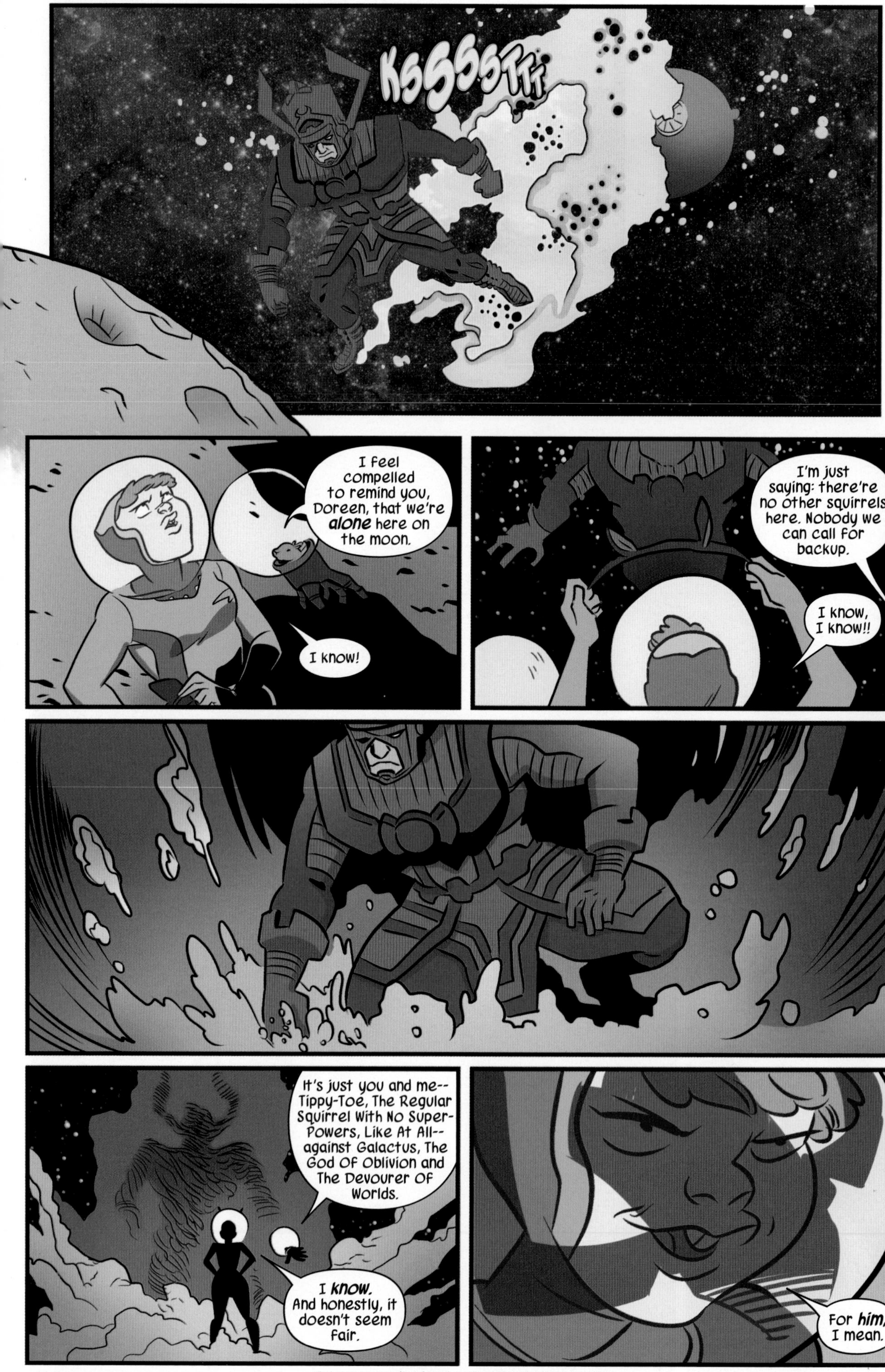
KSSSSTTT
I feel compelled to remind you, Doreen, that we're *alone* here on the moon.
I know!
I'm just saying: there're no other squirrels here. Nobody we can call for backup.
I know, I know!!
It's just you and me--Tippy-Toe, The Regular Squirrel With No Super-Powers, Like At All--against Galactus, The God Of Oblivion and The Devourer Of Worlds.
I *know.* And honestly, it doesn't seem fair.
For *him,* I mean.

What are you reading down here for? They're about to fight!!

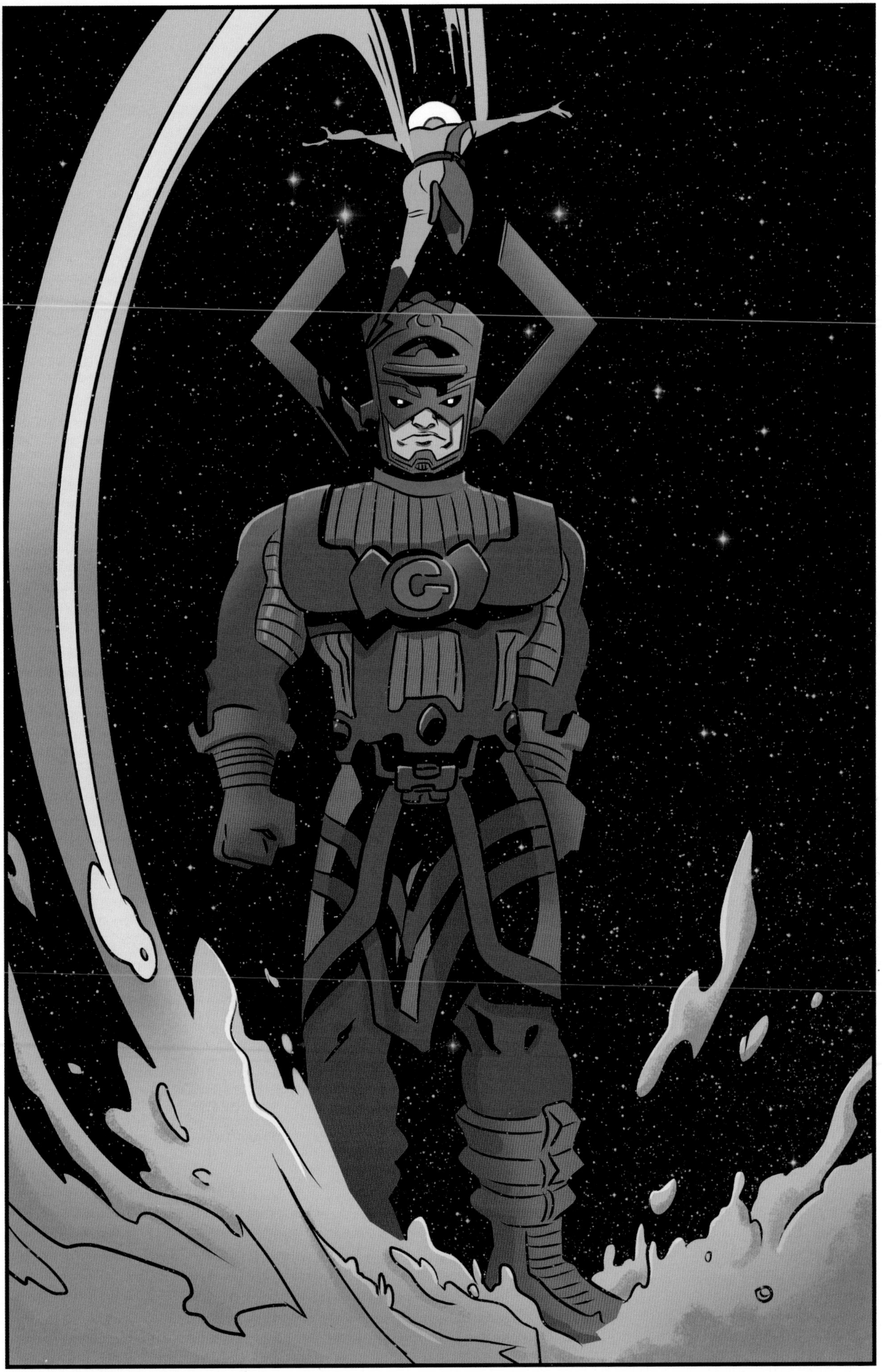

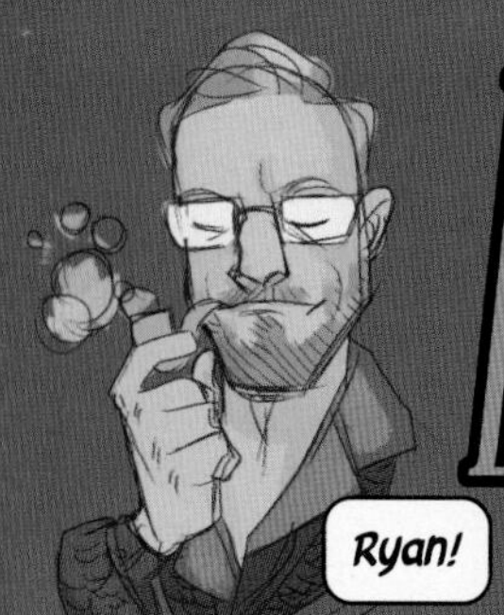
Ryan!

Letters From Nuts

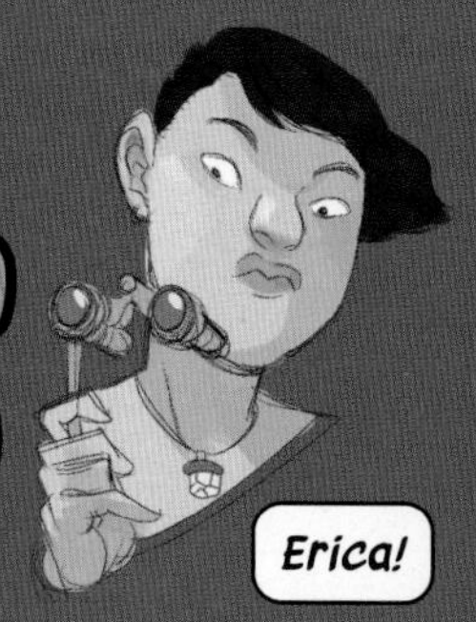
Erica!

Send letters to mheroes@marvel.com or 135 W 50th St, 7th Floor, New York, NY 10020 (Please mark "OKAY TO PRINT")

Welcome to the special triple-sized you-guys-are-awesome-and-are-really-vocal-about-your-feelings-for-this-book letters page!!!

Q: Do squirrels and kitties usually get along? Are you concerned that Tippy-Toe and Mew will come to blows?

Michelle K.

RYAN: They don't usually, I think! But Tippy-Toe and Mew aren't your usual squirrel and kitten. Besides, Nancy would never have said it was okay for Tippy-Toe to stay with them unless she was already PRETTY SURE Mew was on board.

Dear Ryan, Erica, Rico, & VC's Clayton (or just Clayton, idk),

You guys, your Squirrel Girl comic is the coolest! Ryan, I've followed your writing online for a number of years, and have been SUPER PUMPED to see you busting out of the internet and on to printed paper held together by staples!

Can we expect to see some Asgardian tomfoolery within these pages? I demand a Doreen vs. Thor/ Tippy-Toe vs. **[CENSORED]** throwdown/team-up! I mean, come on, Norse mythology has **[MEGA CENSORED]** (whose name, I learned today, means **[YES, THIS TOO IS CENSORED]** which is pretty cool)! How are you NOT going to use that?!

Keep up the amazing work, everybody!

Adam Barnett
Portland, OR

RYAN: Thanks, Adam! We are actually planning to see that person you mentioned showing up down the line, so I just went ahead and censored your letter here as to not spoil the surprise. I'm sorry! But when it happens you can say "See? CALLED IT" and point to this page for proof. Attention future generations: ADAM WAS TOTALLY RIGHT.

ERICA: Hah! That character might have been the topic of my first frantic middle-of-the-night email to Ryan about Squirrel Girl matters. My first foray into self-publishing was a little bestiary and [REDACTED] is totally in there. I love that dude.

Dear Nutty Buddies,

Thanks so much for producing a title that I can confidently share with my niece, Paislee!

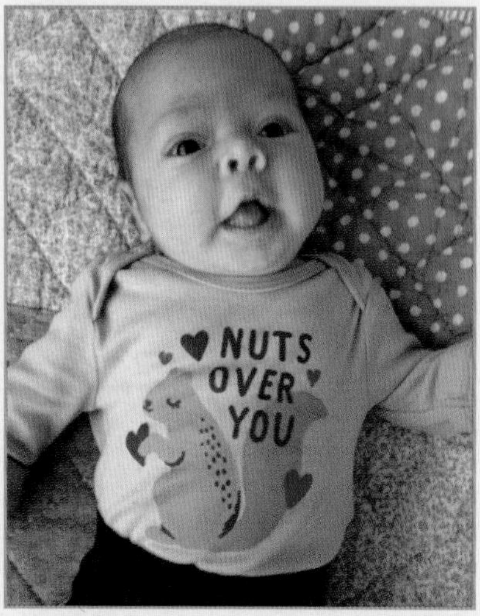
NUTS
OVER
YOU

We're both nuts for Squirrel Girl and it's refreshing to know there's a strong, positive, female role-model out there in the Marvel Universe for her to admire on a monthly basis as she grows from being just a tiny little acorn herself.

Here's a question for you: Did you know that in Norse mythology there was **[CENSORED FOR THE EXACT SAME REASONS AS THE LAST LETTER]?** Really! **[THIS OTHER BIT IS CENSORED TOO. EVERYONE, YOU ARE TOO GOOD AT GUESSING OUR STORY IDEAS]** - and then **[AGAIN, CENSORED, SORRY, I GUESS??].**

Nuts over you,
Paislee H. & Darryl E.

RYAN: Paislee is adorable! #1 Paislee fan over here. Also: I'm glad we're putting out a book you can share with her once she's old enough to realize that if she looks at a certain idiosyncratic series of squiggles in the right order she can hear a voice in her head telling her a story! Once that happens we will be ALL OVER that.

Hi Team Squirrel Girl!

My friend and I just finished the first issue and we both loved it! But we are concerned about Squirrel Girl! Will she have time to go to her classes with all of the crime-fighting that she'll be doing? What are her classes? Thanks!

Beck and Bida

RYAN: I haven't seen her full course selection, but I know there's Introduction to Database Systems, Introduction to Compilers, Linear Algebra, Punching Dudes 101, etc. But yeah, it's tough to balance your social life and your studies. That's why I recommend crime-fighting students cultivate arch-enemies whose powers can dovetail nicely into your education. For example, a super villain who along with trying to take over the world also constructs linear equations in n-dimensional Euclidean vector spaces would be ideal, because that way you can LEARN as you TURN him away from his life of crime.

Q: Now that Squirrel Girl is in college, will she join any clubs or sports teams?

Zachariah W.

RYAN: Zachariah, you clearly wrote this letter before issue #2, where we saw her attempts to join some clubs! So since your question has already been answered, I'm gonna pretend you asked a different question. LIKE SO:

Q: Squirrel Girl has the proportional speed and strength of a squirrel, so what would happen if she got shrunk? Would she lose her powers?

Zachariah W.

RYAN: Excellent question, Zachariah!! This question has not been asked before and I'm glad you definitely came up with it on your own just now. The answer is that while her speed and strength are proportional TO her normal size, they don't change WITH her size. If Ant-Man shrunk her, she'd still be super tough. Similarly, if she ate a bunch and got heavier, that wouldn't make her any stronger. It's too bad, because that would be the EASIEST and MOST FUN way to enhance your super powers ever!

Q: What breed of squirrel is Tippy-Toe? There are 256 species of squirrel worldwide so it's pretty hard to narrow it down.

Sarah Yu
Hong Kong
Squirrel Enthusiast

RYAN: Sarah, I'm glad that as a Squirrel Enthusiast there is finally a comic for you! I don't know what species of squirrel Tippy-Toe is, because while I too am a Squirrel Enthusiast, I am a rank amateur. Are there any Professional Squirrel Enthusiasts who can determine Tippy-Toe's exact squirrel type out there?? (No, "rad type" does not count as an answer.)

ERICA: WELL. I think as someone who gets paid to think about and draw squirrels, I can count myself as a Professional Squirrel Enthusiast, Ryan. Tippy-Toe joined the team after the untimely death of Monkey Joe (RIP) while Doreen was a member of the Great Lakes Avengers, who are based out of Milwaukee. Wisconsin has five varieties of tree squirrel: grey, fox, red, northern flying and southern flying. Tippy is clearly a grey squirrel. Fun fact: Grey is a variety and does not necessarily reflect the actual color of individual animals.

Dear Ryan, Erica, and Rico,

THE UNBEATABLE SQUIRREL GIRL #1 has to be one of the best comic books I've ever read. It was funny, cool, quirky, wacky, and a lot of other good things. Thank you for giving us such an awesome comic book with great art and writing. It's nice to have another super-heroine who doesn't go around fighting crime in her underwear. Some people think the art is "too cartoonish" but 'TIS NOT TRUE! THE ART IS PERFECT!

The Mighty M

P.S. Where can I read Nancy's Cat Thor fan fiction? And where can I get that Purl Jam poster?!

RYAN: Thanks! I actually really like how Squirrel Girl dresses in layers, because you gotta figure sometimes it'd get too hot or too cold and you'd want to be able to adjust. It's just sensible!! As for Nancy's fan fiction epic Cat Thor: Cat God of Cat Thunder, I'd love to have that show up at some point, but for now it lives only in our dreams of a better, impossibly perfect world.

ERICA: Ahhhhhh! Thank you so much! I think clothing choices are pretty important in getting across who someone is. Some people do want to run around in their underwear and that's great for them (looking at you, Emma and Namor), but that's not everyone's bag. I don't want to get too deep into it but our clothing choices say a lot about what we want to get across to people, even if you're not actively thinking about what you're putting on at the time. I mean, you still had to go out and buy it, or, if you're a super hero, probably MAKE IT. I want the clothes to feel like something those characters would choose for themselves.

Hey guys!

Keep up the good work with Squirrel Girl. It's refreshing to see a female super hero that has the body type a lot of us girls have. How did you guys come up with the character design?

Can't wait to read more!

Alexa

ERICA: For the body, I didn't think about it much. I tend to draw super heroines with more physical powers thicker because I honestly have a hard time believing that a 90-pound woman can take down a 200-pound steroidal dude who has equal fighting ability. So yeah. Her body type in the book is the same as the first finished drawing of her I

ever did because that's just how I see Squirrel Girl. Besides, have you seen people who do crossfit? Their thighs are HUUUUUGE.

Hey gang,
I rarely if ever write in to comics but I had to drop a line regarding SQUIRREL GIRL #1 to let you guys know I think it's great stuff. I've been a fan of SG since the GREAT LAKES AVENGERS specials back in the day and it's nice to see the character step out into her own series. My hope was that this would be a return to fun comics without the gloom and grit teeth so prevalent in most titles on the stands and I am happy to report you guys hit it out of the park with a funny, entertaining read. Kudos!
Galactus in the second issue? Nice. I guess Franklin Richards is going to need a new herald after SG gets through with him, huh? I think a college dorm lacks the space for a trophy room to keep the giant purple moon boots, so a headquarters might soon be an item on Doreen's To-Do List. . .
Thanks again for a great comic!
Take care,
Stacy Dooks

This book is so much fun. I had no earthly intention of buying it, I liked the character, and I really enjoyed the Dan Slott GREAT LAKES AVENGERS miniseries from a decade ago, but Squirrel Girl as a lead? My budget is paper thin, and I didn't even consider it. But then the reviews came pouring in, all overwhelmingly positive. And I thought about how disillusioned I've become as a comics fan. Neverending event series, tie-in series to the events, ret-cons, deaths that last six months to spike sales, major changes to flagship characters that everyone knows won't last, another fun She-Hulk series getting cancelled, FANTASTIC FOUR getting shelved, I'm sick to death of it. I thought "this might be what I need." Something purely fun, unapologetically upbeat.
So I bought it, and I laughed out loud at nearly every page. It was so funny. This is exactly what I needed right now. A comic to remind me why I love comics. And now Squirrel Girl is going to fight Galactus. This is going to be incredible. You could do an issue where she does nothing but converse with Tippy-Toe while onlookers look on in bewilderment, and I would love it. Between this and ANT-MAN #1, this has been the most enjoyable week I've had reading comics in at least a decade. I'm completely serious. I truly hope the fanboys and fangirls sample this book, because if they do, it will last.
Jason Smith
Buena Park, Ca

RYAN: Jason this is the nicest! You sure know how to make a guy feel good about his squirrel lady comic: thank you. Our secret is we're just making the sort of book we'd like to read, and we've been really lucky that other people want to read it too. Hooray for comics!
ERICA: I think it's been said before, but I think we were all worried/curious about the reception of this book. It's definitely different from what people associate with mainstream comics so I'm glad that you like it and that we can fill that gap for you.

Dear Ryan North, Eric Henderson, and the Squirrel Girl gang,
I always loved Squirrel Girl and was sad to see how it wasn't appearing as a solo issue in recent years. As a result, when I heard that Squirrel Girl was getting its own series I was jumping up and down like a squirrel would seeing an acorn!!! The art also brings out the best of the college story of Squirrel Girl. It is awesome seeing how Squirrel Girl isn't depicted as a dark, gritty super hero, but a cheerful, just super hero and the art brings out the best of that. I really am honored to be reading this issue and I wish this story continues on forever!!! The jokes make me laugh a lot and her cheerful attitude makes me blissful too!
Thanks,
Andre Lee

P.S. I totally love squirrels in real life too!

RYAN: Thanks Andre! Funny thing about squirrels in real life: I never noticed them before, and now I see them EVERYWHERE. So I'll be walking my dog Chompsky to the park and see squirrels in the trees and think "Oh right I'm late

on the issue #5 script, I should get on that." So now there's these reminders for me to get back to work distributed WORLDWIDE, on every continent except Antarctica.
Therefore I'm moving to Antarctica, see y'all later!!

Dear Ryan & Erica,
When in 1933 a bunch of newspaper comic strips were put together in a periodical, thus creating the first comic book, if its creators could only know that it would one day lead to THE UNBEATABLE SQUIRREL GIRL, they would have reveled with paroxysms of joy, knowing with happy certainty that they had played such a crucial role to the betterment of Western Civilization.
I could go on, but I fear I might start to tilt toward a touch of hyperbole.
Gene Popa

RYAN: One of my favorite things to think about is how your entire life has technically been leading up to THIS one moment, right now. So if I've just made a good sandwich, my entire life has been leading up to that one delicious sandwich. Then a few seconds later my life has been leading up to me eating it, then cleaning up the dishes, etc. Anyway, Gene: my ENTIRE LIFE has been leading up to me answering your letter just now. Thank you for sending it in!

To the nut that answers these letters,
I have been waiting years (make that 2) for Squirrel Girl to have her own comic book series and when I finally got my hands on issue #1, I went absolutely nuts! And if THE AMAZING SPIDER-MAN can have a 700 issue run, then surely, THE UNBEATABLE SQUIRREL GIRL can have at least 800...I mean, 001 on the cover does mean there's room for up to 999 issues, right? Which brings me to a totally unrelatable question...I know Squirrel Girl speaks English as well as Squirrel and is going to school to learn to speak 1s and 0s, but does she speak any other languages such as Japanese, Chinese, Spanish, or Chipmunk?
Philip Hanan

RYAN: Hah hah, I did not notice until JUST NOW that our book does have two leading zeros on the cover. It's not issue 1, it's issue 001. So that's 999 comics in total that Marvel expects from us, and at one a month, that's...83 ¼ years?! LET THIS BE A LESSON TO US ALL: always read the contracts BEFORE you sign them, lest you find out in a letters page you have SIGNED THE REST OF YOUR LIFE AWAY.
Still. No regrets!!
ERICA: Did you know that chipmunks are also part of the family *Sciuridae*? They are! They probably speak the same language. PROBABLY.

Q: Will Squirrel Girl ever team up with any female characters to kick some major butt?
Maryam F.

RYAN: Yep! AND HOW.
ERICA: ALL THE BUTTS.

Dear Erica and Ryan and Rico,
I just finished the first issue of THE UNBEATABLE SQUIRREL GIRL and I am vexed. I was wondering: How can I be more like Squirrel Girl? I am neither a girl nor a squirrel and have a severe nut allergy. The doctors say I shouldn't even be alive! What should I do?
Your Scholar,
James Kislingbury

RYAN: Okay first off, if you're going to doctors who say "you shouldn't even be alive," you should get a new doctor. Get one who says "you SHOULD be alive and I'm glad you are, holla" instead. And while you might not be able to be Squirrel Girl, you could still be Chipmunk Hunk!
ERICA: Well, the important thing with squirrels isn't so much nuts as much as they're opportunistic omnivores that can't digest cellulose. So try to find foods that have a lot of protein, carbs and fat.

To the inspired minds behind THE UNBEATABLE SQUIRREL GIRL,

I'm gonna be honest here - Squirrel Girl wasn't a hard sell for me. I like comics, I like squirrels. I'm a girl and I like reading about girls. In the title alone Squirrel Girl has almost everything I like in life (still needs: Oreos, posters, high speed car chases, etc).
So I figured I was going to like SQUIRREL GIRL #1 because HOW CAN YOU NOT and then I read it (as I made my own move to college, funnily enough) and was STILL wowed! I AM IN LOVE! It is so much fun, from start to finish! The dialogue is hilarious, the facial expressions are to die for, and the colors are so vibrant and delightful ajskdlfjkasdfj IT IS SO. GOOD.
I can't wait to see more of Doreen's adventures - crime-fighting! Attending classes! Punching and studying, aw yeah! It's all great. Fingers crossed for a long and happy series for Doreen and co.!
Marley

RYAN: Thanks, Marley! You're RIGHT that we haven't had high-speed car chases yet, but it's been tricky because how often do you see squirrels inside a car? INFREQUENTLY AT BEST. I guess... we could change that?

Guys and Gals,
You're all nuts. Irrevocably and gloriously so. ANT-MAN? SQUIRREL GIRL? Astonishing and unbeatable first issues!
More importantly, my sick four-year-old was so engaged as we read (an edited, age-appropriate version of) these comics out loud to her (along with issues of ROCKET RACCOON and MS. MARVEL, whom she loves); it lends such a positive experience to her being in a hospital. In times past (the early 80s), I actually looked forward to plowing through back issues of EARTH'S MIGHTIEST while recuperating from surgery or high fever. Isn't that nuts?

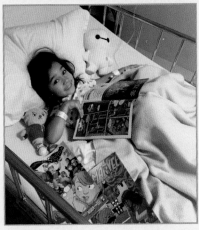

That's probably because every True Believer knows that Marvel Comics are the best medicine. Nuts, but true.
Papa Joe
Cville, VA

P.S. I do hope Kamala Khan and Doreen Green make it to the MCU!

RYAN: Joe, this is adorable and I wish I got comics when I was sick. I hope your daughter is feeling better and never makes the causal connection between illness and GETTING TO READ ALL THE COMICS EVER, because if I had as a kid I'm sure I'd be faking tummy aches every week.

Dear Erica, Ryan, and Rico,
I've just finished reading issue #1 of your new series and I have to say I absolutely loved it. The humor is spot on, the art is ADORABLE, and she has the best theme song ever.
Also, I've been wondering where I can get myself a pack of those Deadpool super villain trading cards? I could really use them in my top secret crime-fighting endeavors. (Maybe I shouldn't be mentioning this in a, possibly, published letter.)
Sarah Y.
Hong Kong

RYAN: Sarah Y. from Hong Kong, your secret of fighting crime is safe with me! I won't tell anyone that Sarah Y. in Hong Kong fights crime. Also, I would love to see those Deadpool cards in real life

too, but I'm a little worried because then they'd need me to write descriptions for EVERY SINGLE MARVEL VILLAIN EVER IN TIME, which I dunno, might take a while. A long weekend, easy.

First off, thank you so much for giving Squirrel Girl her own comic, it's a breath of fresh air and something I have been waiting for...forever. Because squirrels. Second, yay! The bestest and most awesomest marvel heroine gets some recognition for saving us all from the real threats! Yay again!

Um...this was just a thank you letter really, but if I had to ask questions. Ok. Love the addition of acorn earrings, but have the eye stripes gone for good? They were cute...

Also, any chance we get to meet the parents? Doreen's mum and dad must be the proudest parents, or the most laid back, ever.

I have another thank you, to Ryan and Erica, thank you for giving us an upbeat and completely positive lighthearted book, in an industry where everyone is dark, edgy and gritty. (And depressing... Is it me? Or has every hero got problems? Except Squirrel Girl who has squirrels!)

Love you all!
Tim P.
Plymouth, England.

ERICA: Can you imagine having to take that makeup on and off every time though? Squirrel Girl's back in NYC and there's NO TIME TO STOP FOR ANYTHING.

Dear Squirrel Girl Team,

Hello there, you fabulous people in comic book world! When I heard that they were going to be bringing Squirrel Girl back to the Marvel Universe, I was all filled with glee and dancing a jig. I let that simmer on the back burner, until I heard that Ryan North would be writing it. I can't actually put into print how excited this made me. I guess to go with my previous metaphor, you could say I boiled over. (This is the part where you all are laughing and telling me how clever I am; at least, it is in my head.) I've seen what you can do with six panels of dinosaurs, and I am among those who helped with that Kickstarter of yours for the *Hamlet Choose Your Own Adventure.* Who better to take the helm of this new series?

From the second I pulled the first issue off of the shelf at my comic store, I knew I would not be disappointed. The art is amazing! Doreen didn't look quite how I pictured the new Squirrel Girl to look, but that's okay because she looks even better. I love that pretty much everything is round and colorful. Makes the book so much more approachable to someone like me who is new to the world of comic book buying/collecting. I wish I had a convention coming up so I could cosplay her already. And the story! I want to ask so many questions about where you are heading, but I think I'm just going to wait until the comics come out. Thank you all for your work that you're doing. I look forward to seeing what adventures lay ahead for Doreen and Tippy-Toe. And on that note, I'm off to see if Rosetta Stone offers a course on the Northeastern variant of Squirrelese.

Your Unbeatable Fan,
Stefanie M.

RYAN: Thank you, Stefanie! And I am secretly really excited for convention season this year, because I really want to see the Squirrel Girl cosplay. Everyone dress up as her forever, thanks in advance!!

UNBEATABLE SQUIRREL GIRL was the absolute highlight of my day, week, and possible even year (though it's a little early to tell). I'm so excited to see Doreen not only put bad guys in their place but also tackle the exciting world of Computer Science - how incredibly rad. It's the kind of book that gives me hope for super-hero comics. In the mean time, I have two questions for you:

1) Will any of Doreen's past friends (the GLA, Devil, or the Cage-Jones family) be making appearances?

2) If Doreen could have lunch with any other Marvel super hero who would it be?

Congratulations and I'm sure you'll continue to knock it out of the park.

Arielle B.

RYAN: I know Erica loves Flatman (AND WHO DOESN'T?) so I'd love to have him appear at some point! Of course, who's to say that he hasn't ALREADY appeared, only he was standing at just the right angle as to be invisible? WHO INDEED. Well in fact it's the artists and writers who can say, and we're here saying he hasn't done that in Squirrel Girl.

YET.

ERICA: If Doreen could have lunch with any other hero it would be Dazzler because, oh my god, she has, like, ALL of her albums.

Dear Squirrel Girl Creative Team (can I call you the Squirrel Squad?)

I'm absolutely nuts about Doreen! Thank you for bringing back one of my favorite Marvel characters from obscurity into a book I can shove in all my friends' faces. The first issue was all I hoped it would be and more.

I am foaming at the mouth for the next one already! (I should probably go get that checked out.) I am curious, how did you choose between Tippy-Toe and Monkey Joe to appear in the series?

Amy Chase

Ok I've been obsessed with Squirrel Girl and waiting for this moment for a while now... great job on the first issue! I really wanted her to kick some major butt in the first issue but next one looks pretty crazy so I already can't wait.

I MUST know what her MJ necklace stands for. If it's Marc Jacobs I will die but I think there's another meaning... Also, I need her purse, any idea where I can get one?!

Last, Squirrel Girl needs to go into psychiatry or psychology. She has a way with talking to this guy that shows a gift.

Love,
Squirrel Girl super fan for life

RYAN: It stands for "Monkey Joe," her first squirrel companion! He was the squirrel she hung out with before Tippy-Toe. It could also stand for "My Jewelry," in case she only wears jewelry that describes itself. They only way to confirm that for sure though is if she ever wears earrings that just say "earring," which I think... might be amazing??

ERICA: I totally own a brown version of that purse. I think it's sold out. I'm sorry. I'm just going to be honest here, I pretty much own all of Doreen's clothes.

I want to say "chitter chit chit chitter" THANK YOU for bring Squirrel Girl back. The fact that she wears the MJ in homage to Monkey Joe makes me want to tear up.

I can't wait for the next issue! My squirrel friend Ladro is throwing nuts at me asking how he can join the squirrel army?

Sincerely,
Beth 'the Squirrel' Jankowski

ERICA: I'm glad I'm not the only one who tears up over Monkey Joe. (RIP)

Hi Squirrel Girl Team!

So I'm writing this on a Tuesday night because I run a shop and I totally stayed late tonight just to read your book.

I just want to say going in I wasn't convinced. I wasn't a fan of the art, but by the second page (that we hadn't seen in the preview yet) I was totally won over. I love it! I can't wait to sell this to everyone that comes in tomorrow and days after that until I run out then I can sell the 2nd and 3rd and 4th printings too, and the hardcovers and trade paperbacks. This book rocks and it will be great for anyone that loves fun and maybe we can win over some of the people that hate fun too.

One little thing, any chance the color on the bottom page tidbits can be altered a teensy bit? They were really hard to read. Or I just need new glasses.

Thanks for the fun comic!

Jenn Swackhamer
Comic City Pontiac, MI

Hello!

First off, I have to say how absolutely MARVELlous (ha!) the first issue of UNBEATABLE SQUIRREL GIRL was! Wow! Artwork and writing combined, it's pretty much the most perfect comic book of all time and space.

Secondly, I have to say how super AWESOME it is to have another female-fronted book, but also one where the character is hilarious and clumsy and endearing and basically a lot more like me than any of the other beautiful, graceful super-women out there. (I love them too though!) I love everything you've done and I absolutely canNUT wait for the next issue! (One day I'll stop with the puns. Today is NUT that day.)

Holly Ringsell

Well, we've used up all the extra room we have this month! But keep writing! We want to hear from every dang one of you! And don't forget to check out our behind-the-scenes tumblr: unbeatablesquirrelgirl.tumblr.com! See y'all next month! Stay nutty!

Next: Squirrel Girl vs. Planet-Eating Man!

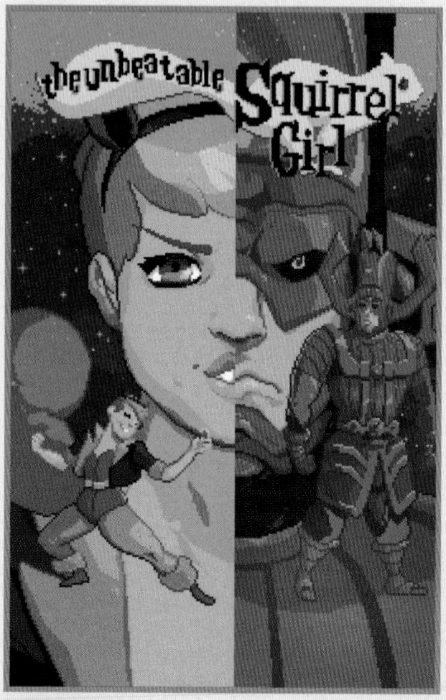
the unbeatable
Squirrel Girl

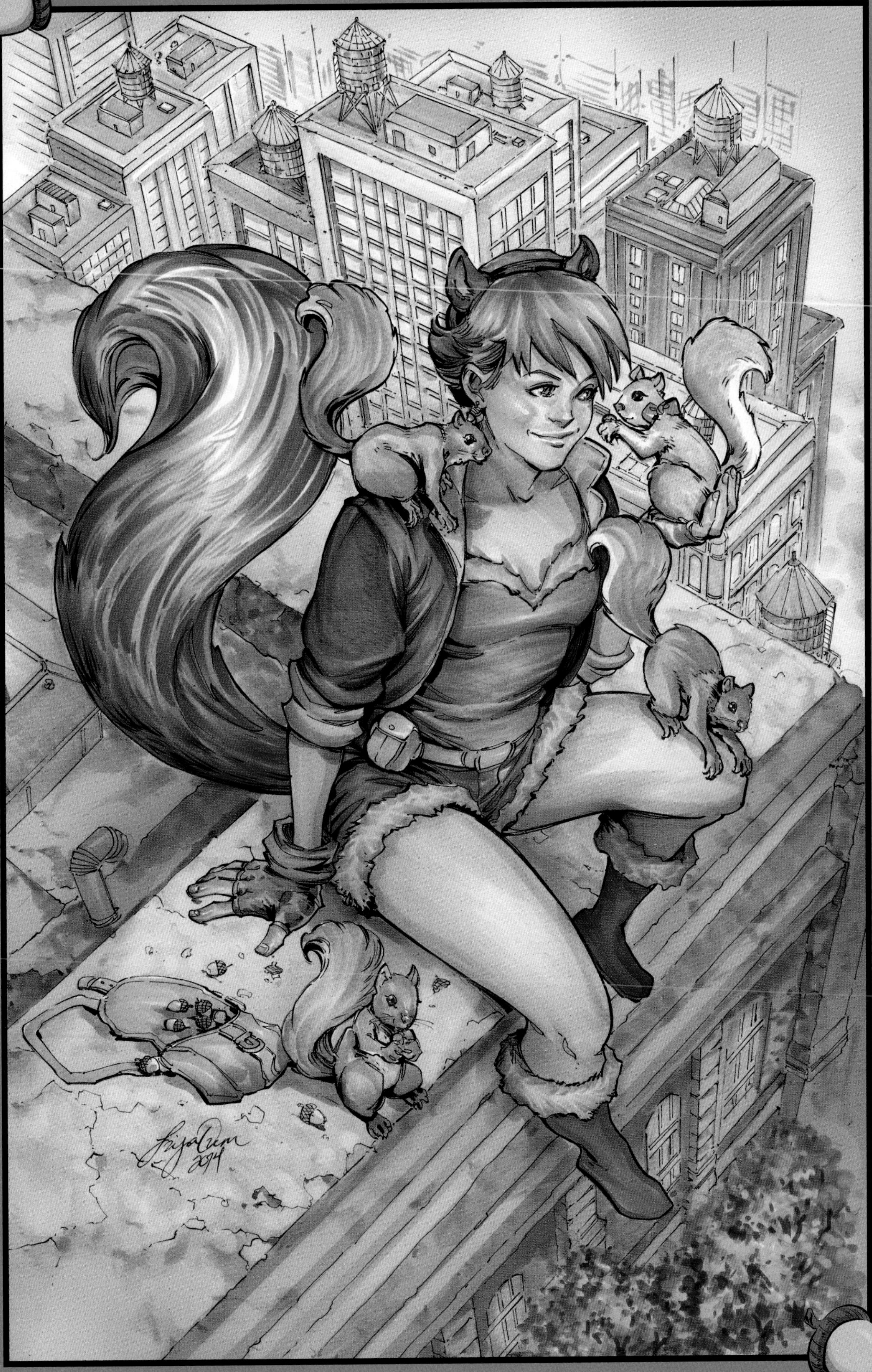

ISSUE #1 VARIANT COVER BY **SIYA OUM**

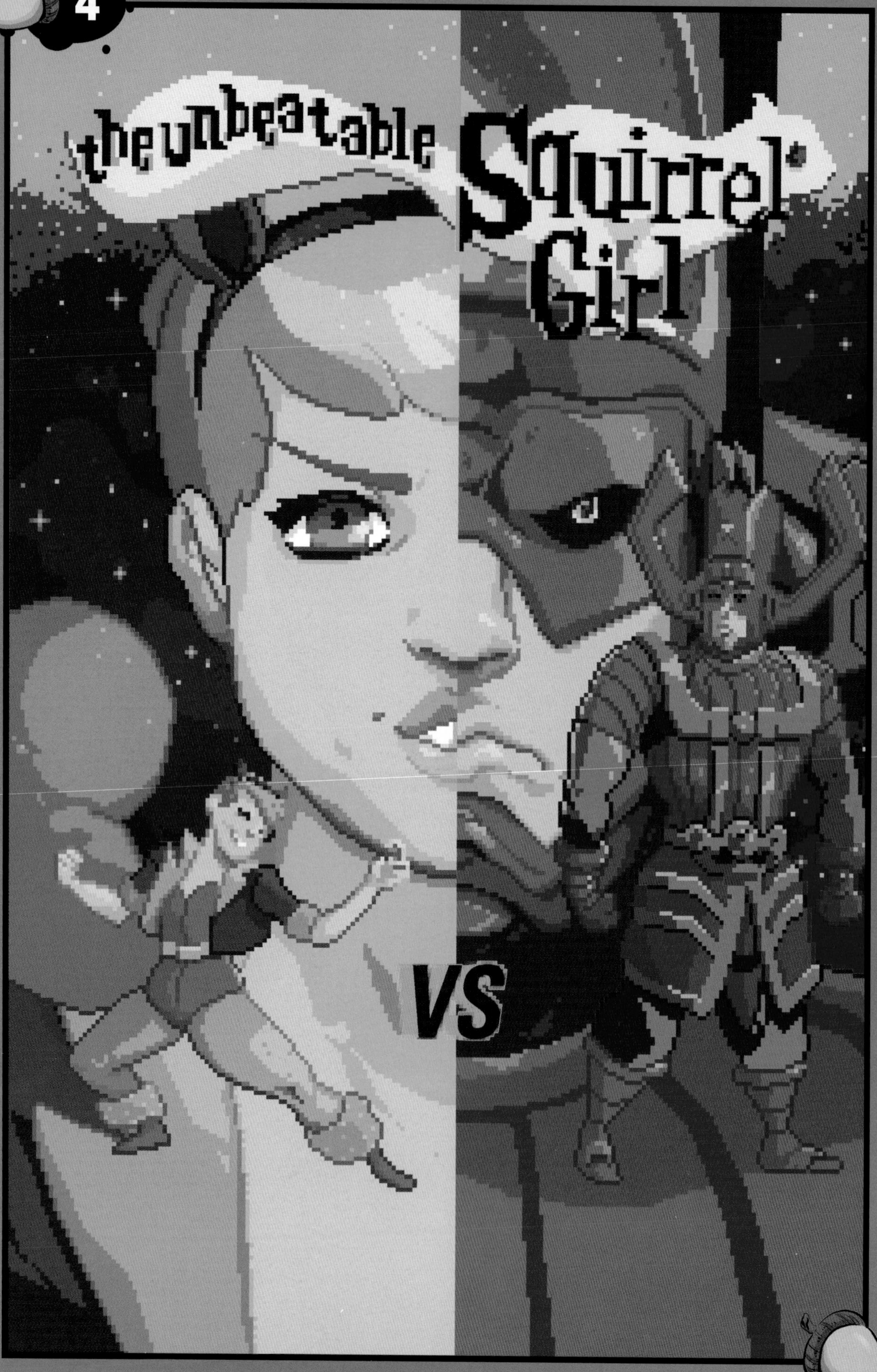
the unbeatable Squirrel Girl
VS

*Doreen Green isn't just a first-year computer science student: she secretly also has all the powers of both squirrel and girl! She uses her amazing abilities to fight crime **and** be as awesome as possible. You know her as...**The Unbeatable Squirrel Girl!** Let's catch up with what she's been up to until now, with...*

Squirrel Girl in a nutshell

search!

#bankrobbery

#banksnobbery

#mew

#squirrelsuitcrochetpattern

#snackcakes

#squirrelman

G. ALACTUS **GALACTUS** @xGALACTUSx
HEY GUESS WHAT I'M COMING TO EARTH TO DEVOUR THE ENTIRE PLANET

G. ALACTUS **GALACTUS** @xGALACTUSx
AND NOBODY KNOWS BECAUSE I PUT MY SHIP IN A STEALTH FIELD

G. ALACTUS **GALACTUS** @xGALACTUSx
"BUT WAIT," YOU SAY, "AHA! NOW WE KNOW YOU'RE COMING BECAUSE YOU JUST POSTED IT ON SOCIAL MEDIA!!"

G. ALACTUS **GALACTUS** @xGALACTUSx
ONLY YOU AREN'T SAYING THAT BECAUSE NOBODY KNOWS I'M COMING BECAUSE NOBODY FOLLOWS ME ON THIS STUPID SITE

G. ALACTUS **GALACTUS** @xGALACTUSx
...

G. ALACTUS **GALACTUS** @xGALACTUSx
#ff @xGALACTUSx

STARK INDUSTR **Tony Stark** @starkmantony
@unbeatablesg Just heard more of my Iron Man parts have been "borrowed," and now there's a big hole in my building too. Any ideas?

Squirrel Girl! @unbeatablesg
@starkmantony Oh wow dude these suits have wifi in them??? I can go online on my way to the MOON?? Tony ur the best <3

STARK INDUSTR **Tony Stark** @starkmantony
@unbeatablesg That "wifi" works even in Mars orbit, uses proprietary Stark technology, and costs several thousand dollars a kilobyte.

Squirrel Girl! @unbeatablesg
@starkmantony um I already downloaded some songs for the trip to the moon. Sorry!!!

STARK INDUSTR **Tony Stark** @starkmantony
@unbeatablesg Don't reply to say you're sorry! That ALSO costs money!

Squirrel Girl! @unbeatablesg
@starkmantony sorry sorry!

STARK INDUSTR **Tony Stark** @starkmantony
@unbeatablesg Don't reply! Stop replying!

Squirrel Girl! @unbeatablesg
@starkmantony whoooooooooooooooooooooooooooops

Nancy W. @sewwiththeflow
Story time, friends. Your hero, me, thought she'd eat some delicious (cash-only) falafel. So I went to the bank.

Nancy W. @sewwiththeflow
And you know how banks are always the worst even when you're NOT being taken hostage? WELL GUESS WHAT?

Nancy W. @sewwiththeflow
Yep. But then we got saved by @unbeatablesg who appeared in SQUIRREL SUIT ARMOR MODE. Not even joking.

Nancy W. @sewwiththeflow
This really happened. I was saved by a squirrel suit Squirrel Girl. I know you don't believe me.

Nancy W. @sewwiththeflow
tl;dr: doesn't matter, ate falafel

Whiplash @realwhiplash22
I am trapped in #CentralPark and need #squirrelrepellant, PLEASE RT!!!!! #please #rt #please #rt #please #rt

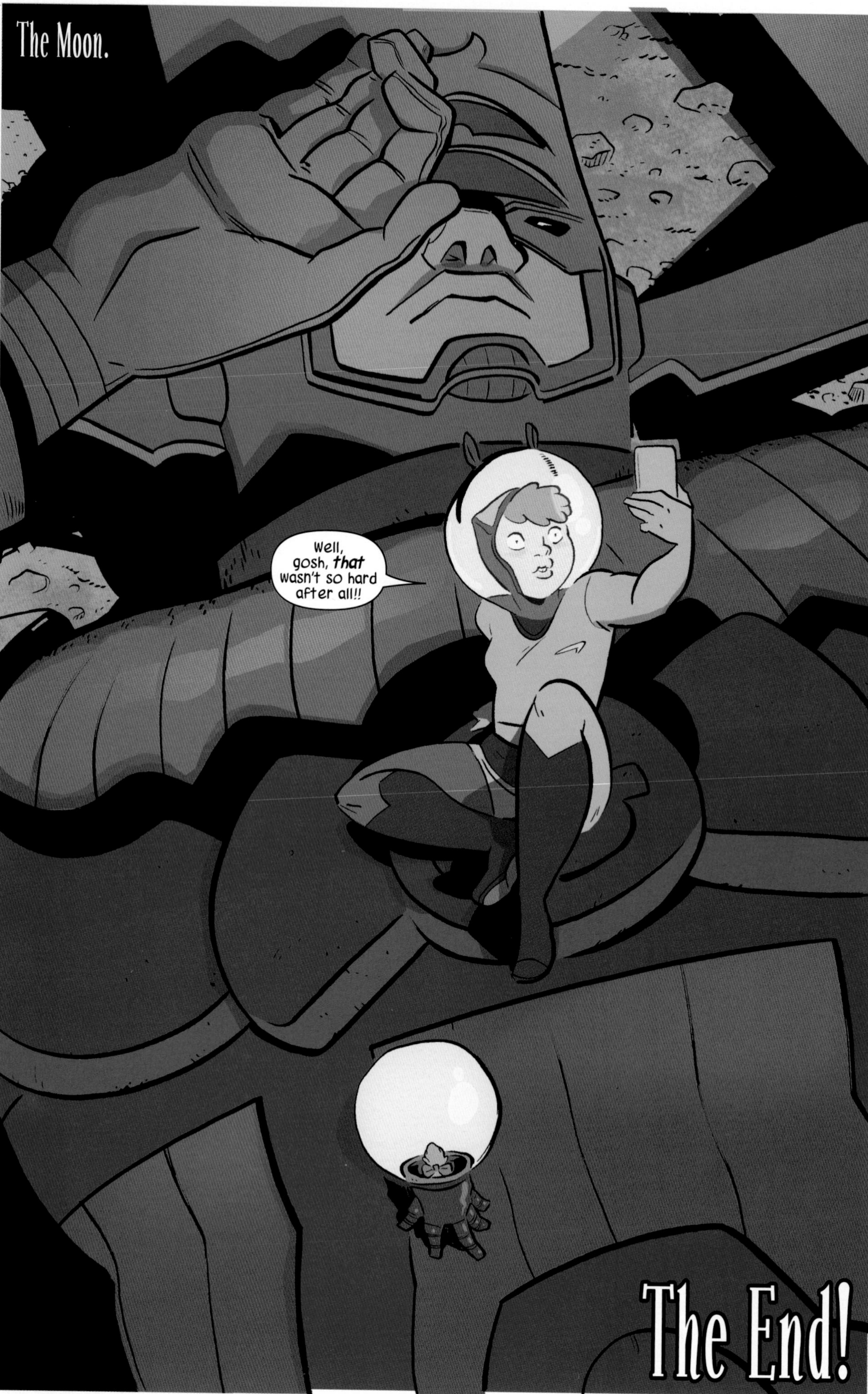
The Moon.
Well, gosh, *that* wasn't so hard after all!!
The End!

All right! Now to the letters page, and then the rest of this book is just blank pages! *Haha, Oh well!!*

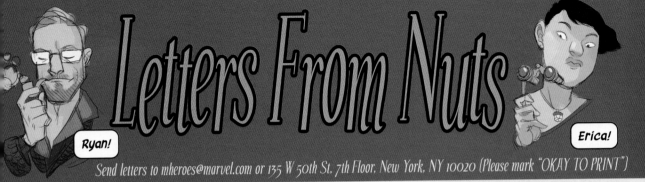

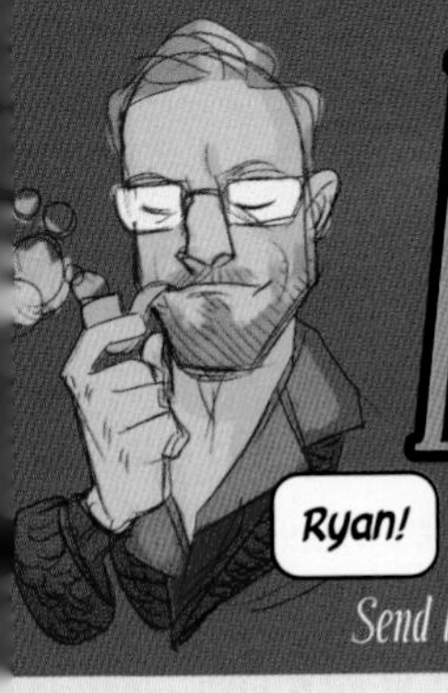
Ryan!

Letters From Nuts

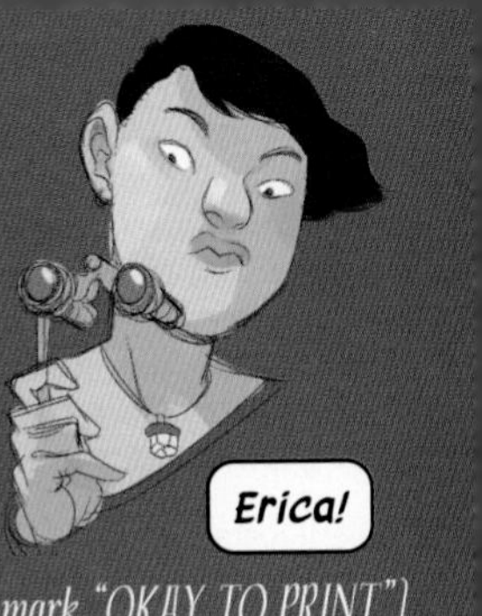
Erica!

Send letters to mheroes@marvel.com or 135 W 50th St, 7th Floor, New York, NY 10020 (Please mark "OKAY TO PRINT")

Dear Squirrel Girl comics,

I really liked Tippy-Toe's squirrel armor. I can't believe that Squirrel Girl's fighting Galactus. I mean, that's a big thing, you know! I find that the cover is very funny because Squirrel Girl is using Iron Man as a surfboard. I mean, a surfboard? That's cray-cray!

Signed,
Elsa McQuaid

RYAN: Thanks! To invent Tippy-Toe's armor I held out my hand in an approximately squirrel shape and confirmed, yes, that would fit inside a glove. And if you're reading this, then you just read the page that showed the aftermath of Squirrel Girl beating Galactus off panel, which we can all agree was really very satisfying! Writing: it's easy!!

ERICA: I remember getting an e-mail saying we needed the second cover and that it should be Squirrel Girl surfing on an Iron Man suit and my first thought was "That's stupid." I'll admit when I'm wrong-- just don't tell Ryan I told you that. Any part of that.

Dear "Letters from Nuts" crew,

As a comic collector of over 20 years, I want to thank you for creating such a great comic. Over the past several years, my love of comics has crossed over with another love - squirrels! I have been a squirrel fanatic since my college days when I worked on an independent study project to identify squirrel parasites. In the last few years, I have been taking a sketchbook to the comic conventions that I attend and I have been asking various artists to draw a Squirrel mashed-up with any character of their choosing! I have attached several of the sketches for your enjoyment (including some of my own):

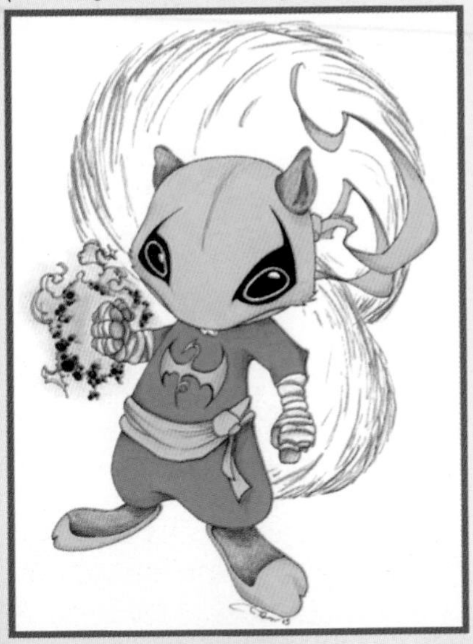

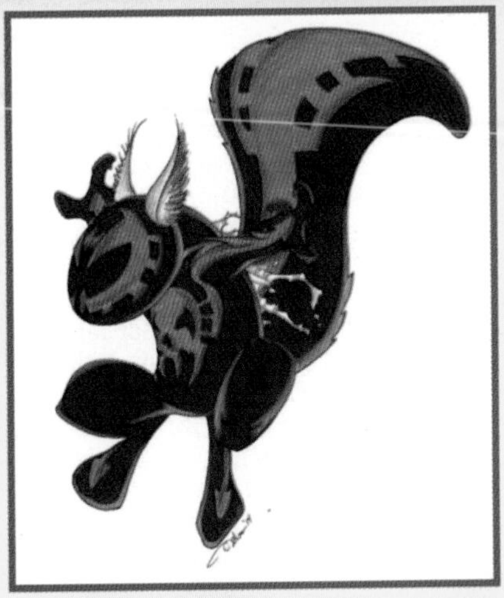

Question: Based on Marvel's summer plans, is there any way we could get a small landmass on Battleworld assigned to a whole universe where all of the Marvel characters are squirrels (and maybe Squirrel Girl could rule them all)? In my opinion, that would be the most important part of the Secret Wars crossover!

Your loyal fan,
Corey Fuhrer

RYAN: Those pictures are amazing. If only we had made this comic more than one page long, we could've shown you Squirrel Galactus! But alas, we decided to publish this book with only one page of comics, some letters, and then a whole bunch of blank pages.

I have pitched your idea to Marvel and they informed me that it's "way too late" to rewrite their Battleworld plans to include Squirrel Island, although they "wish they had thought of that sooner" and "feel regret about not doing Squirrel Island more keenly than [they] have ever felt any emotion before, including love." So – that's something!

ERICA: Although we SHOULD do Squirrel Island but like Spider Island. (Because let's follow up on ALL of Dan Slott's ideas.) Everyone on Manhattan gets bitten by radioactive squirrels but nobody turns into a Squirrel Girl equivalent because that's not how she got her powers. Pretty sure this is a one-page story. Is NOT BRAND ECHH still a thing?

Is Chipmunk Hunk perhaps a monk? Look, I'm just trying to think of rhymes for the theme song.

Stephen,
Kansas City

RYAN: All I know for sure is: he's been shrunk, he can dunk, spelunk, his car's got a trunk, and if you bring him to a cabin he'll steal the top bunk.

ERICA: RYAN. Leave the rhyming to the professionals. Like Adam WarRock. Have you HEARD his Squirrel Girl rap? (www.adamwarrock.com) Step down, buddy.

My four-year-old twin daughters enjoy squirrels quite a bit. They are always asking if we can leave some peanut butter and crackers outside to feed our neighborhood squirrel crew. They also love comic books, as they've been exposed to them pretty much since they were born. So, it was a no-brainer to hip them to THE UNBEATABLE SQUIRREL GIRL series.

There aren't very many comics that the girls will allow me to read them from start to finish. They generally prefer to tear through 'em on their lonesome, looking at the artwork and making up their own dialogue. SQUIRREL GIRL is one of the exceptions though.

One constant with each issue I've noticed is that they keep asking me where Gamora is. So if you end up having the Guardians of the Galaxy make an appearance, that would seal the deal with their appreciation of Squirrel Girl.

Darrick Patrick
Dayton, Ohio

P.S. I'm including a photograph of Nola and Logann showing off their Unbeatable collection so far:

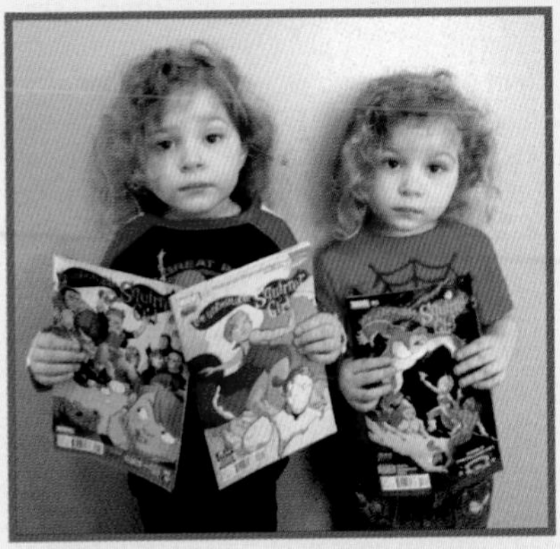

RYAN: Awesome, a complete set! You can tell Nola and Logann that I, the writer of these comics, say that Gamora is secretly there, just hidden. She and Doreen were going to get lunch together before Doreen got wrapped up in this Galactus thing, so while Doreen's there fighting Whiplash and bank robbers and Galactus, Gamora's standing there, just out of frame, gesturing

to her watch, impatiently waiting.

ERICA: Yes! My favorite compliment this book gets is being able to share it with your kids, so I love that! Side note: peanuts aren't great for squirrels and apparently can get some sort of weird invisible toxic mold (citation needed)??? If you want to leave a snack out, nuts in shells are great. It's something they love and the shell provides good gnawing exercise.

Well Hi there!

This is why I really like Squirrel Girl: she's really funny-looking. On a new-comics wall, I can look across all Marvel's titles; lots of angry-looking, grim but very buff-looking hero-suited figures, and there's Squirrel Girl, happy and goofy-looking. I have to support that. And apparently she's the most powerful super-powered person in the whole Marvel Universe? Y'know, I get a lot of comics, but now I'm down to just two Marvel comics, this one, and Captain Marvel. Guess I just like strong, pleasant women in my life. Carol and Doreen are like that, nice people. One's goofy-looking: y'know? -- in the Marvel Universe, that just makes her exceptional.

It certainly helps that SQUIRREL GIRL's written well. And works well with a slightly 'cartoony' edge to the artwork. The words and pictures really support one-another. You could do me a favor, though, by using a darker ink to your teeny tiny bottom-page typings. Old eyes, y'know? Thanks for a good, fun comic.

Best wishes,
Matt Levin
Hatfield, MA

ERICA: I'm glad you're into it! I really stressed out when I was first asked to draw this character. One of the only pieces of mine that Wil (our editor) mentioned when we were starting out was a much more realistic-looking movie poster I drew, and I went back and forth on how the style should look. In the end I took a gamble on a looser and more animated look and I'm super happy that it's worked out.

Loved, loved, loved UNBEATABLE SQUIRREL GIRL #2. Art and story - killing it! Thank you for this book.

Any chance we'll see the Great Lakes Avengers at some point? I mean, that's where I first met Doreen, and now she's way more popular than the GLA so it'd be nice to use her popularity to bolster them up. Also, when you inevitably get to your big, triple-sized anniversary spectacular, could you reprint her first appearance? It's not an easy "tail" to come by. Thanks!

Charles Albert,
Richmond VA

RYAN: I'd like to! I really like Flatman because he has all the powers of being a man AND all the powers of being flat. I can't tell you how many times I've looked at tiny cracks under doors and wanted to see what was on the other side and said "If only I was a flat, but alas, I am a man." Okay, I can: it's several. I have done that several times.

ERICA: I keep picturing the GLA reunion like a high school reunion and Doreen is the one kid that left their small town to do something big and is home for the first time in 10 years and just has no idea if it's going to be super awkward or not. Also, everyone is worried Deadpool is going to show up. THAT GUY, AMIRIGHT?

I just wanted to thank you guys for starting to write/print this comic at such an opportune time. Just two weeks ago I was mentioning that Squirrel Girl existed to a friend and he didn't really believe me, so I looked her up to show him and simultaneously found out that these were being printed! Now, hopefully, I'll get to show him a physical copy with my name in it! It also gives me a great read to look forward to every week with my best-friend-roommates. So...Thank you for such a humorously written and expertly drawn comic!

On an unrelated note though, any chance of us ever seeing any physical copies of Deadpool's Guide to Super Villains and Super Villain Accessories in the future?

Andre W.

RYAN: I'd love to see the Deadpool cards as a set! I don't know if anyone higher up at Marvel Headquarters reads the letters page of our squirrel comic BUT IF THEY DO: Yo, that's two months in a row people have asked for these cards! Please make them immediately. PS: this counts as market research, and I have never been wrong before.

ERICA: Henderson and North, MAKING IT HAPPEN. (The comic/continuation of Squirrel Girl, not the cards. We don't really have control over merchandising- yet.)

To whom it may concern,

I got the first two issues of UNBEATABLE SQUIRREL GIRL recently, and I can't wait to for next month's issue. Thank you for making Tippy-Toe so cute, and for Nancy. I knit and crochet, too (and now I know next year's Halloween costume). I couldn't resist making a little Tippy-Toe for myself. Thank you for creating something so cute and fun.

Keep up the amazing work!
Katie H.

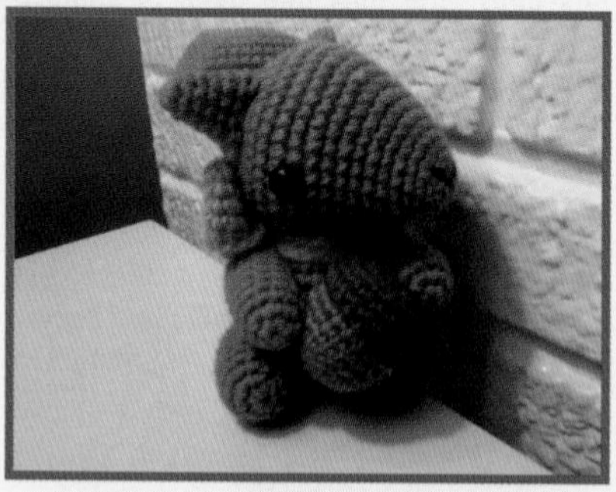

RYAN: Katie, GUESS WHAT: I love that Tippy-Toe so much! Nancy's knitting is inspired by my mom, who made me a sweater with a dinosaur on it, and the sweater has a hood with a tassel, AND THE DINOSAUR ON THE SWEATER IS WEARING THE SAME SWEATER WITH THE SAME HOOD AND TASSEL. It's the best ever.

ERICA: AHHHHH. WHAAAAAT. I do some sewing, but knitting and crocheting are amazing mystery arts to me. I'm so in awe! That Tippy is just so cute! Fun Fact: When I first saw Nancy in the script she was so much like a friend of mine that I grew up with that I had to reread her intro a few times. When issue 1 came out, other friends asked if it was her. So I love that people are getting into Nancy because she rocks!

Hey guys,

Thanks for making such an epic comic, first of all! Secondly, I really like Mew and also knitting. How can I join Mew Club?

Jane
Cat, Squirrel, and Yarn Enthusiast

RYAN: To join Mew Club you have to write down "Mew is a great cat" on a piece of paper and sign your name, and then you are a member of Mew Club. Mew is based on two cats we know in real life (one I know, and one Erica knows) and when you perform this ritual, we will be alerted, and will inform the Actual Mews of this Actual News.

Wanted to say that, as one of two comics I'm reading, this one is my personal favorite. Just wanted to ask, have you ever come across negative reception for the comic? How did you deal with it?

Felix

RYAN: Thanks for reading our comic! Also, you should read more comics!

There's always going to be people who don't like what you're doing, and it's like, that's fine? There are books I don't like but I don't hate them or want them destroyed or anything. I just don't read them! So if I see someone reacting negatively to anything I do, I don't take it personally, I just think "Oh that's too bad, this person's tastes are not my own. I guess their opinions are different from my clearly objectively correct ones, oh well."

ERICA: I'm with Ryan. There are going to be some people that you just don't agree with on taste and even if they're jerks about it there's not much you can do there, so there's no point in dealing with that. The only time I address it is when I get "won't read because Squirrel Girl isn't hot anymore" because UGH. Anyway, it's pretty easy to get those dudes to back off with a quick "why are you so concerned about a minor being hot?" Also, I'm so curious about this one other comic you're reading. Tweet us about it when you see this answer!

Next: Readers Beware!

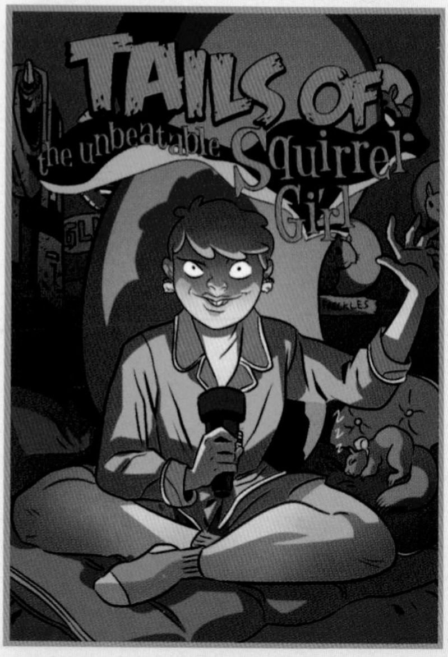
TAILS OF
the unbeatable Squirrel Girl

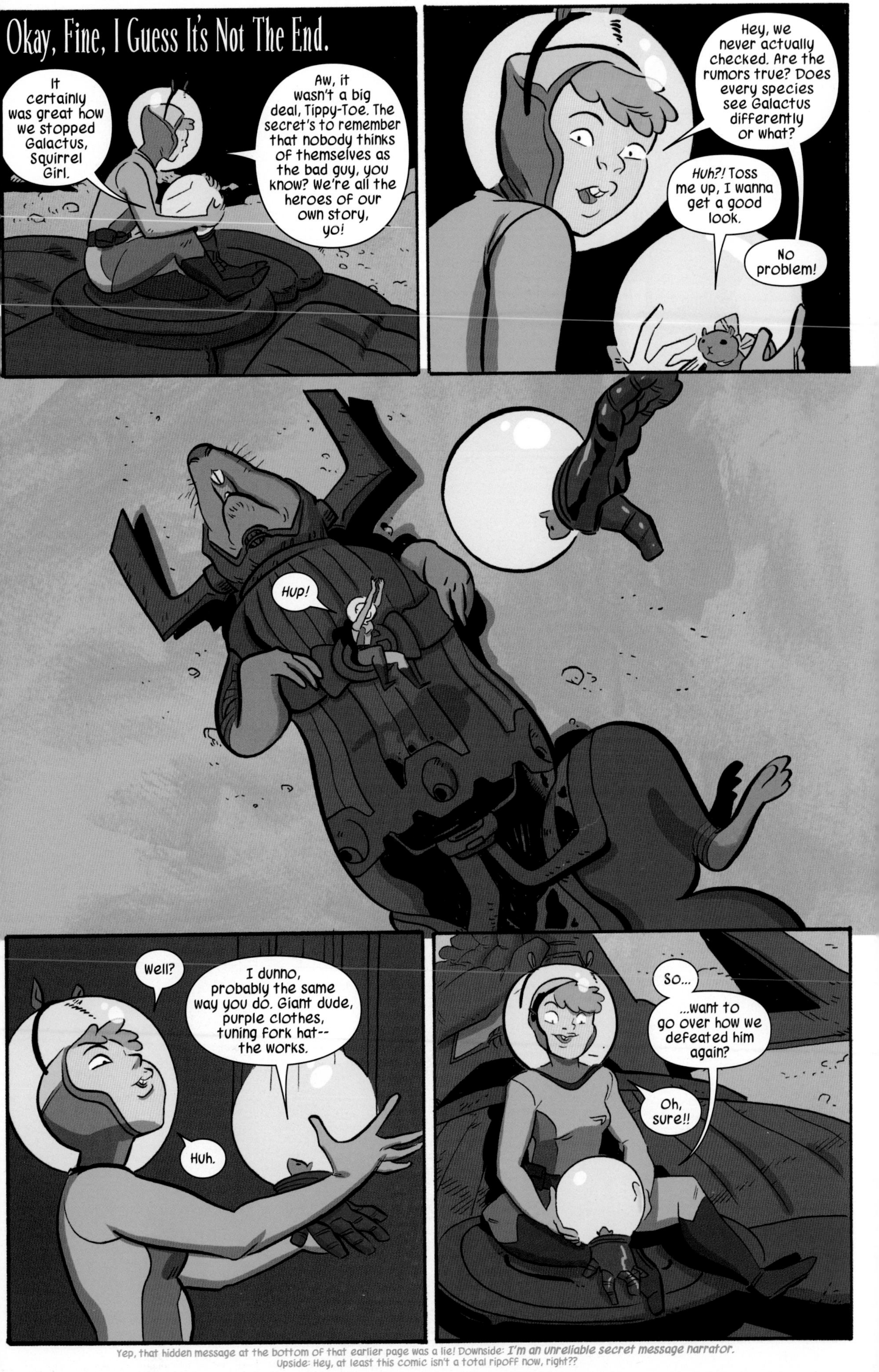
Okay, Fine, I Guess It's Not The End.
It certainly was great how we stopped Galactus, Squirrel Girl.
Aw, it wasn't a big deal, Tippy-Toe. The secret's to remember that nobody thinks of themselves as the bad guy, you know? We're all the heroes of our own story, yo!
Hey, we never actually checked. Are the rumors true? Does every species see Galactus differently or what?
Huh?! Toss me up, I wanna get a good look.
No problem!
Hup!
Well?
I dunno, probably the same way you do. Giant dude, purple clothes, tuning fork hat-- the works.
Huh.
So...
...want to go over how we defeated him again?
Oh, sure!!

Yep, that hidden message at the bottom of that earlier page was a lie! Downside: *I'm an unreliable secret message narrator.*
Upside: Hey, at least this comic isn't a total ripoff now, right??

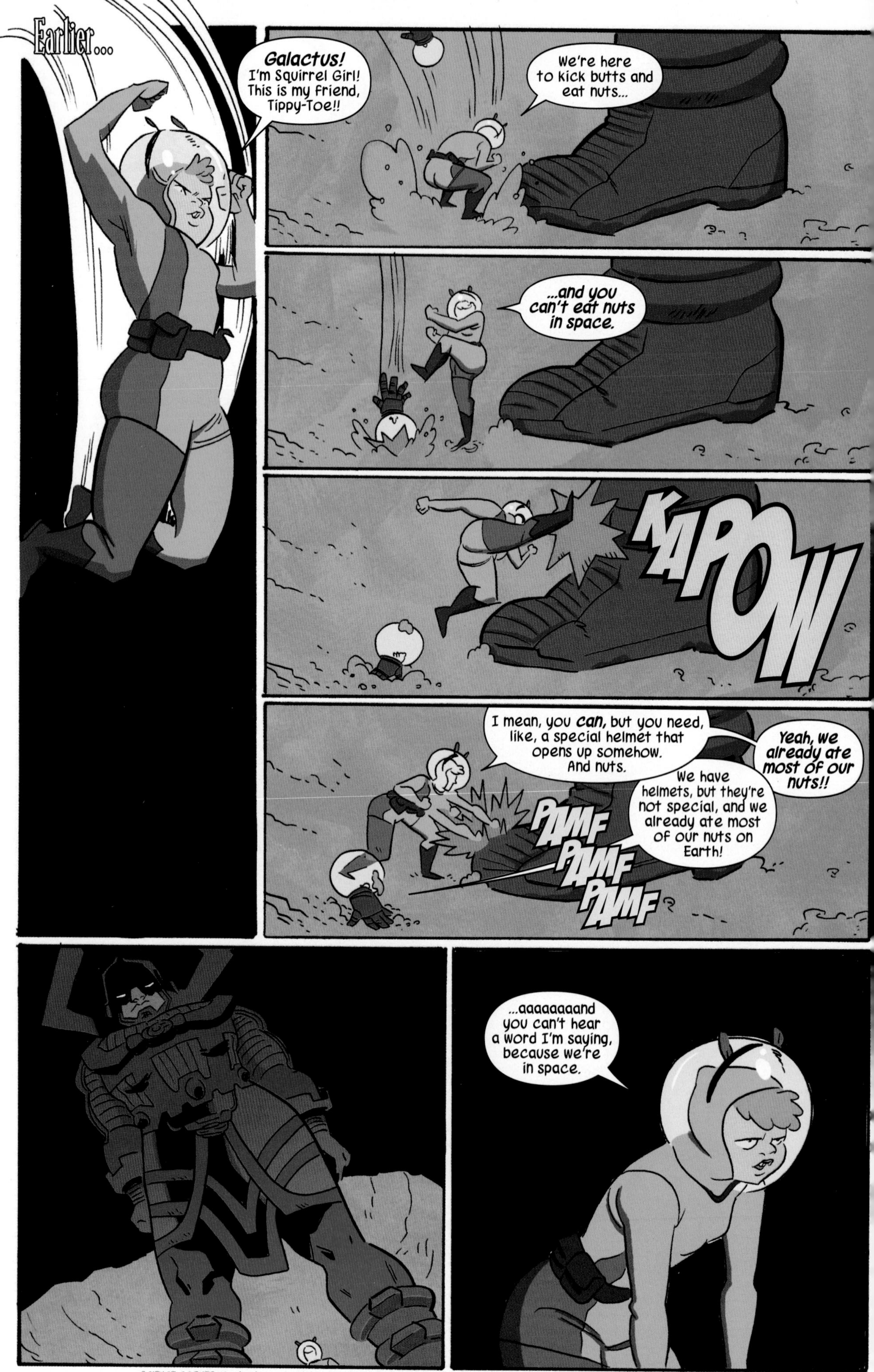
Earlier...
Galactus! I'm Squirrel Girl! This is my friend, Tippy-Toe!!
We're here to kick butts and eat nuts...
...and you can't eat nuts in space.
KAPOW
I mean, you can, but you need, like, a special helmet that opens up somehow. And nuts.
Yeah, we already ate most of our nuts!!
We have helmets, but they're not special, and we already ate most of our nuts on Earth!
PAMF PAMF PAMF
...aaaaaaaand you can't hear a word I'm saying, because we're in space.

SCIENCE CORNER: You're in space right now, too! You're on a ball of ***liquid metal*** surrounded by rocks and a thin layer of gas, spinning wildly through the universe at thousands of kilometers per hour. Hang on tight!

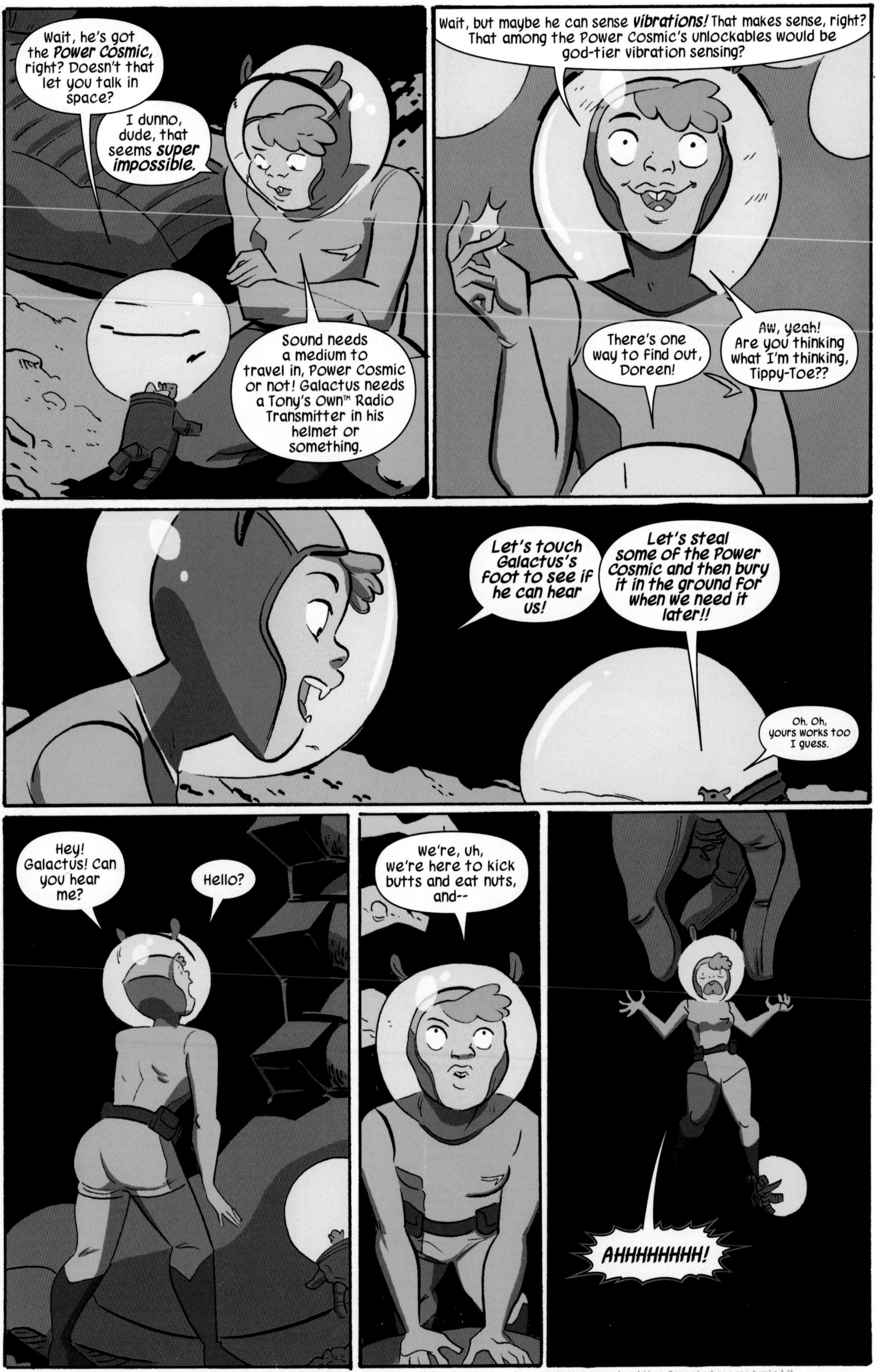
Wait, he's got the *Power Cosmic*, right? Doesn't that let you talk in space?
I dunno, dude, that seems ***super impossible.***
Sound needs a medium to travel in, Power Cosmic or not! Galactus needs a Tony's Own™ Radio Transmitter in his helmet or something.
Wait, but maybe he can sense ***vibrations!*** That makes sense, right? That among the Power Cosmic's unlockables would be god-tier vibration sensing?
There's one way to find out, Doreen!
Aw, yeah! Are you thinking what I'm thinking, Tippy-Toe??
Let's touch Galactus's foot to see if he can hear us!
Let's steal some of the Power Cosmic and then bury it in the ground for when we need it later!!
Oh. Oh, yours works too I guess.
Hey! Galactus! Can you hear me?
Hello?
We're, uh, we're here to kick butts and eat nuts, and--
AHHHHHHHH!

If the Power Cosmic is anything like an acorn, ***and I'm pretty sure it is,*** then we should bury it in the ground and then forget where we buried it and then a Power Cosmic tree will grow from that spot many years from now!

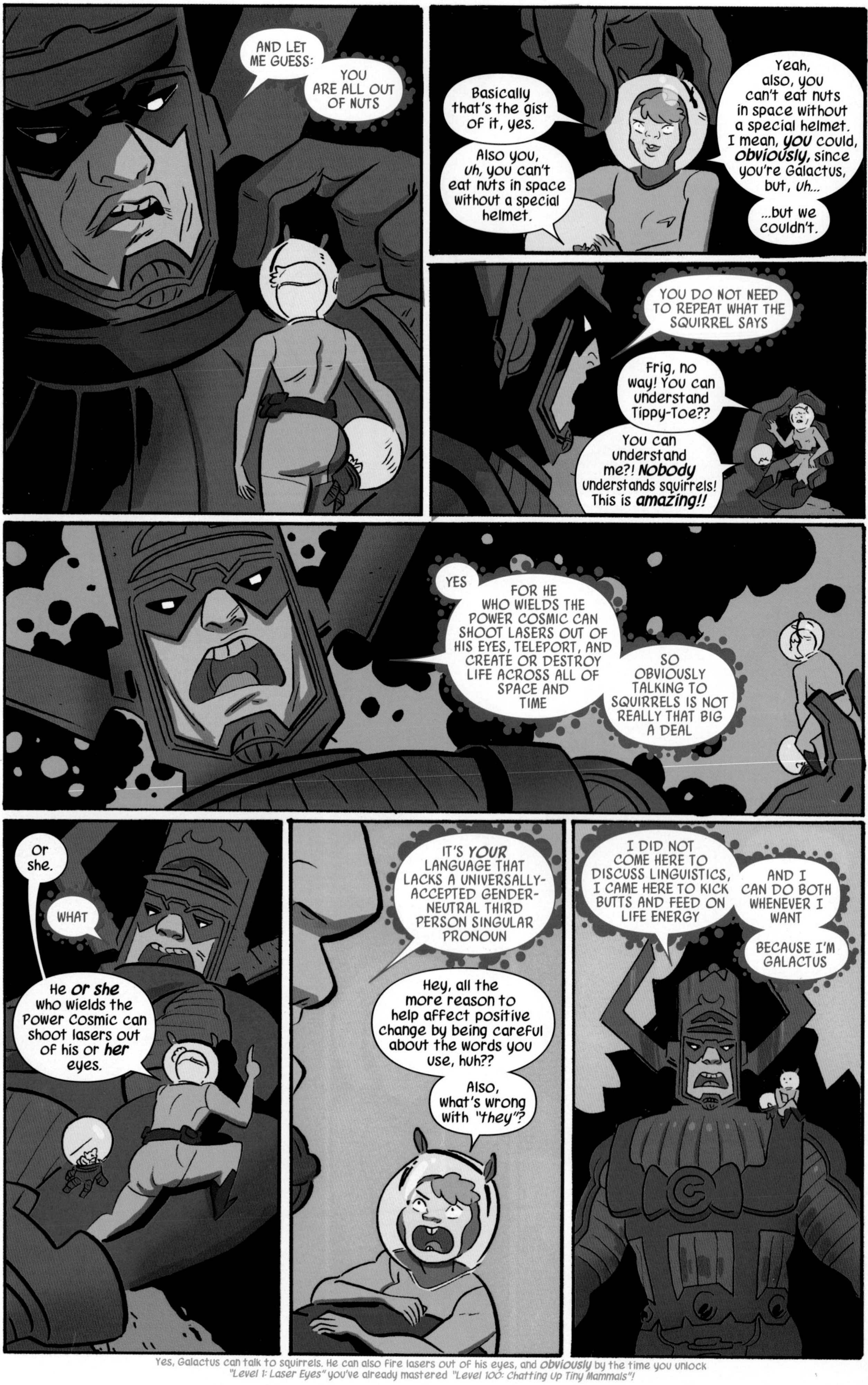
AND LET ME GUESS:
YOU ARE ALL OUT OF NUTS
Basically that's the gist of it, yes.
Also you, uh, you can't eat nuts in space without a special helmet.
Yeah, also, you can't eat nuts in space without a special helmet. I mean, YOU could, obviously, since you're Galactus, but, uh...
...but we couldn't.
YOU DO NOT NEED TO REPEAT WHAT THE SQUIRREL SAYS
Frig, no way! You can understand Tippy-Toe??
You can understand me?! Nobody understands squirrels! This is amazing!!
YES
FOR HE WHO WIELDS THE POWER COSMIC CAN SHOOT LASERS OUT OF HIS EYES, TELEPORT, AND CREATE OR DESTROY LIFE ACROSS ALL OF SPACE AND TIME
SO OBVIOUSLY TALKING TO SQUIRRELS IS NOT REALLY THAT BIG A DEAL
Or she.
WHAT
He or she who wields the Power Cosmic can shoot lasers out of his or her eyes.
IT'S YOUR LANGUAGE THAT LACKS A UNIVERSALLY-ACCEPTED GENDER-NEUTRAL THIRD PERSON SINGULAR PRONOUN
Hey, all the more reason to help affect positive change by being careful about the words you use, huh??
Also, what's wrong with "they"?
I DID NOT COME HERE TO DISCUSS LINGUISTICS, I CAME HERE TO KICK BUTTS AND FEED ON LIFE ENERGY
AND I CAN DO BOTH WHENEVER I WANT
BECAUSE I'M GALACTUS

Yes, Galactus can talk to squirrels. He can also fire lasers out of his eyes, and *obviously* by the time you unlock *"Level 1: Laser Eyes"* you've already mastered *"Level 100: Chatting Up Tiny Mammals"*!

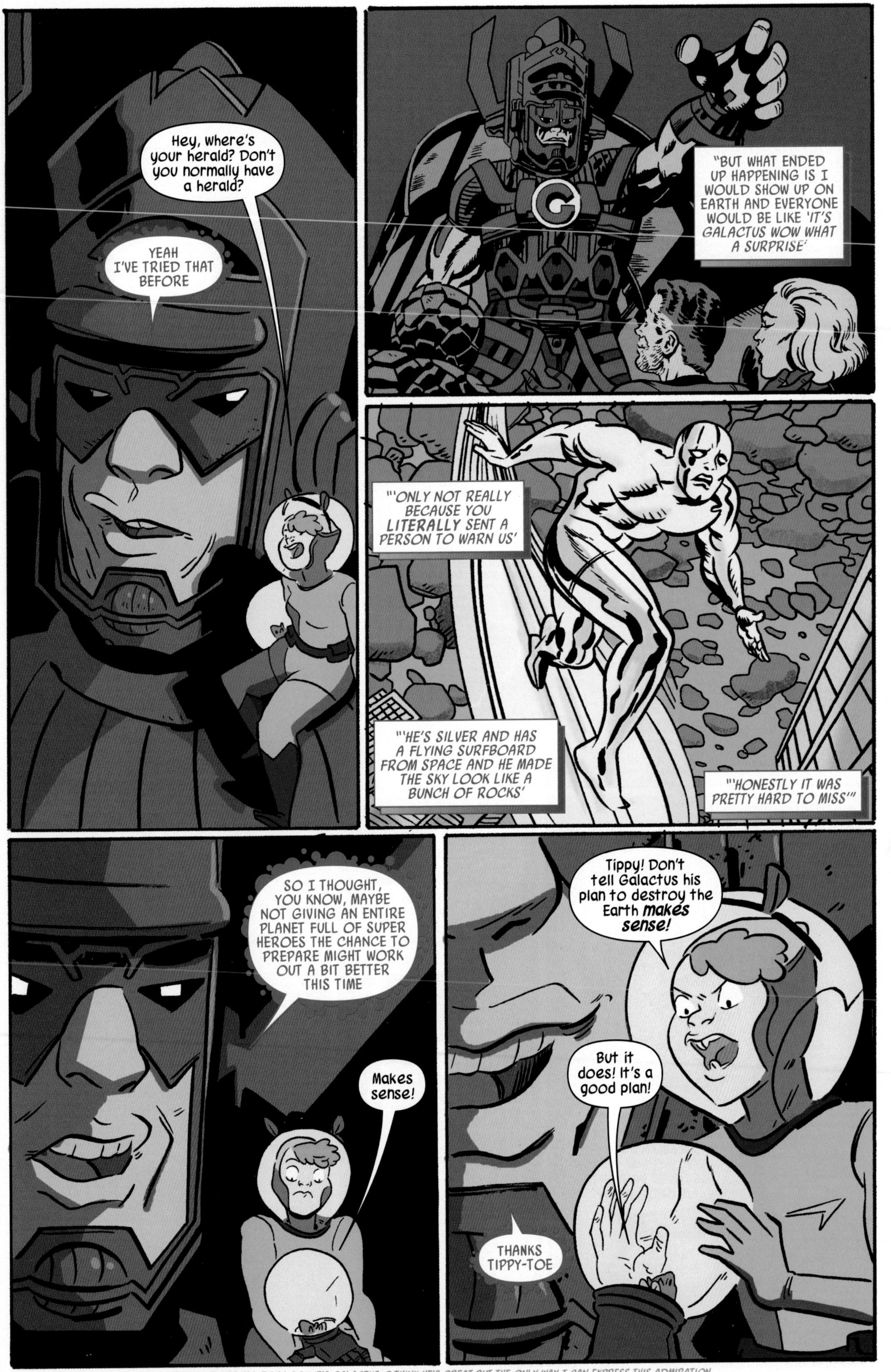
Hey, where's your herald? Don't you normally have a herald?
YEAH I'VE TRIED THAT BEFORE
"BUT WHAT ENDED UP HAPPENING IS I WOULD SHOW UP ON EARTH AND EVERYONE WOULD BE LIKE 'IT'S GALACTUS WOW WHAT A SURPRISE'
"'ONLY NOT REALLY BECAUSE YOU LITERALLY SENT A PERSON TO WARN US'
"'HE'S SILVER AND HAS A FLYING SURFBOARD FROM SPACE AND HE MADE THE SKY LOOK LIKE A BUNCH OF ROCKS'
"'HONESTLY IT WAS PRETTY HARD TO MISS'"
SO I THOUGHT, YOU KNOW, MAYBE NOT GIVING AN ENTIRE PLANET FULL OF SUPER HEROES THE CHANCE TO PREPARE MIGHT WORK OUT A BIT BETTER THIS TIME
Makes sense!
Tippy! Don't tell Galactus his plan to destroy the Earth makes sense!
But it does! It's a good plan!
THANKS TIPPY-TOE

EVERYONE WAS ALL "OH LOOK IT'S GALACTUS, I THINK HE'S GREAT BUT THE ONLY WAY I CAN EXPRESS THIS ADMIRATION IS TO STYMIE HIS PLANS, NEVERTHELESS I DO SECRETLY REALLY RESPECT WHAT HE'S TRYING TO DO HERE"

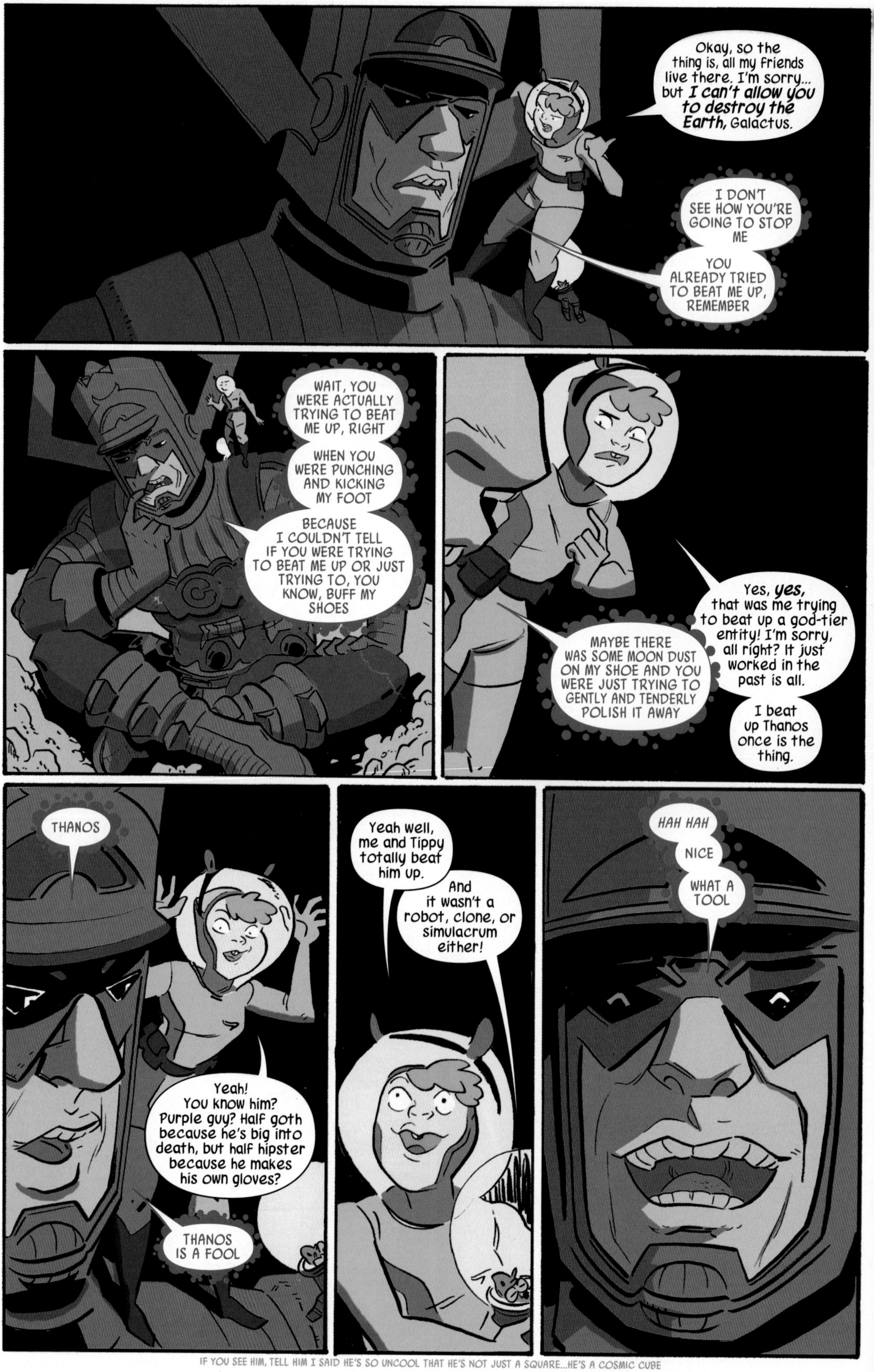
Okay, so the thing is, all my friends live there. I'm sorry... but *I can't allow you to destroy the Earth,* Galactus.
I DON'T SEE HOW YOU'RE GOING TO STOP ME
YOU ALREADY TRIED TO BEAT ME UP, REMEMBER
WAIT, YOU WERE ACTUALLY TRYING TO BEAT ME UP, RIGHT
WHEN YOU WERE PUNCHING AND KICKING MY FOOT
BECAUSE I COULDN'T TELL IF YOU WERE TRYING TO BEAT ME UP OR JUST TRYING TO, YOU KNOW, BUFF MY SHOES
MAYBE THERE WAS SOME MOON DUST ON MY SHOE AND YOU WERE JUST TRYING TO GENTLY AND TENDERLY POLISH IT AWAY
Yes, *yes,* that was me trying to beat up a god-tier entity! I'm sorry, all right? It just worked in the past is all.
I beat up Thanos once is the thing.
THANOS
Yeah! You know him? Purple guy? Half goth because he's big into death, but half hipster because he makes his own gloves?
THANOS IS A FOOL
Yeah well, me and Tippy totally beat him up.
And it wasn't a robot, clone, or simulacrum either!
HAH HAH
NICE
WHAT A TOOL

IF YOU SEE HIM, TELL HIM I SAID HE'S SO UNCOOL THAT HE'S NOT JUST A SQUARE...HE'S A COSMIC CUBE

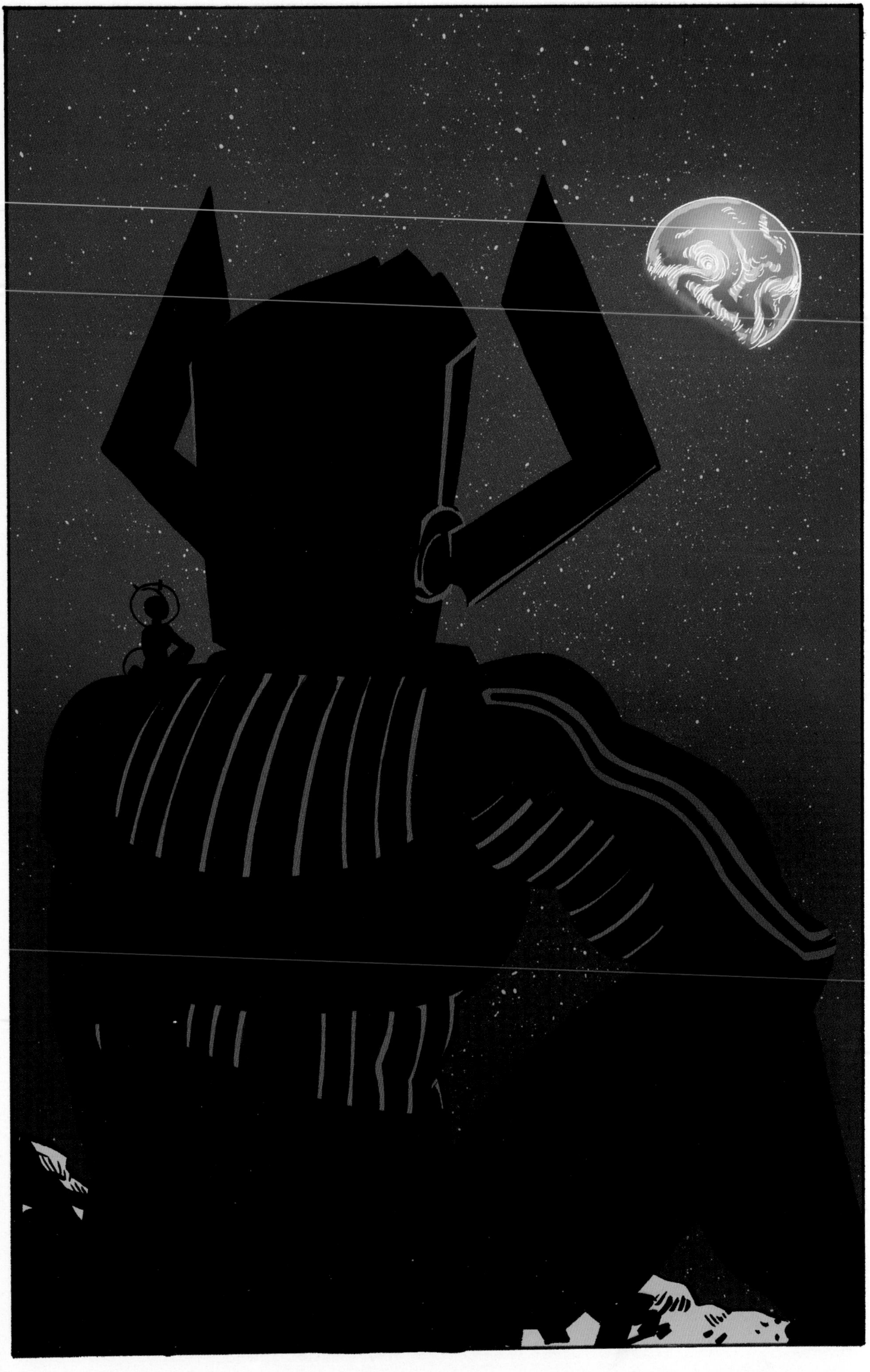

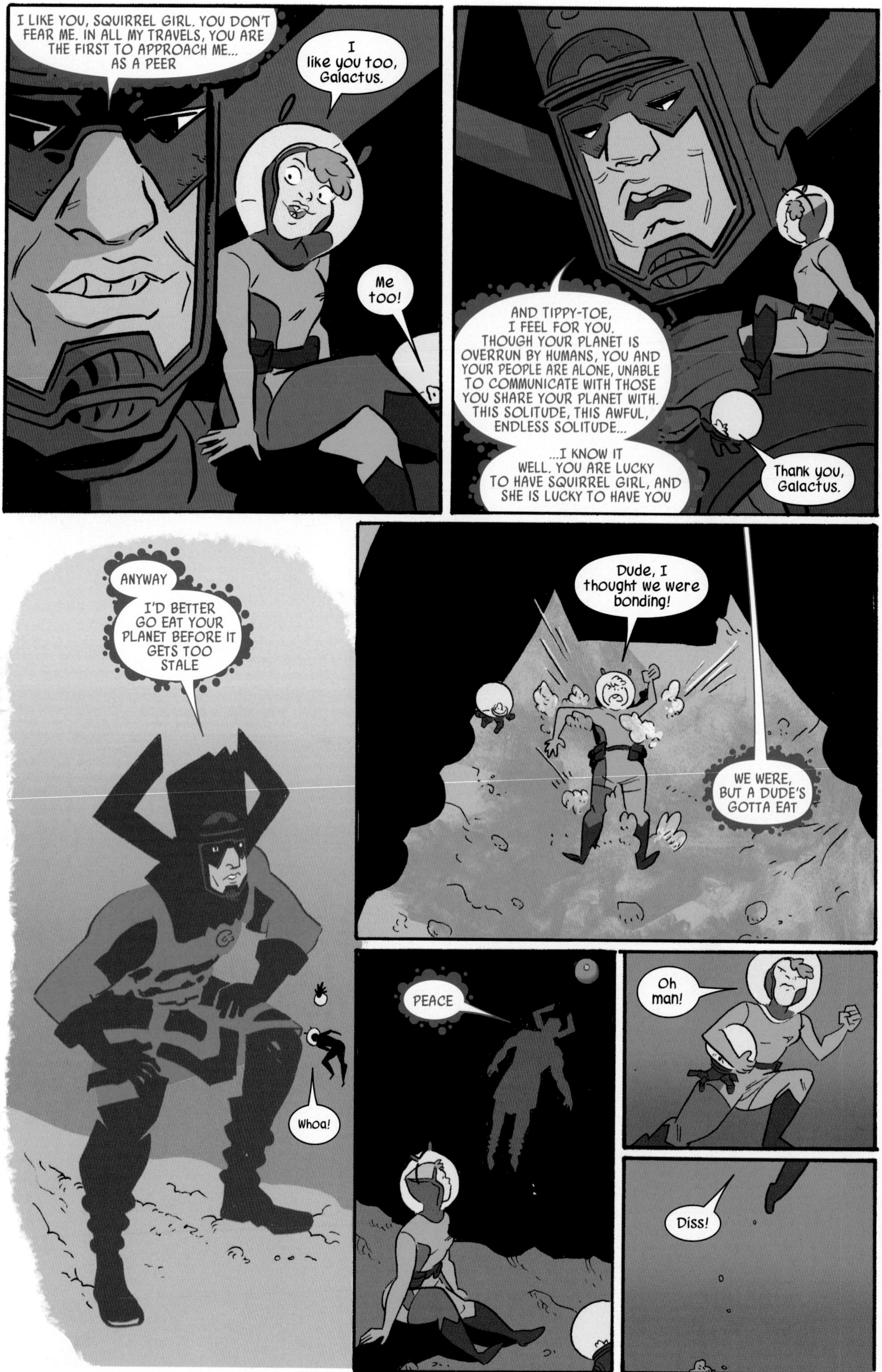
I LIKE YOU, SQUIRREL GIRL. YOU DON'T FEAR ME. IN ALL MY TRAVELS, YOU ARE THE FIRST TO APPROACH ME... AS A PEER
I like you too, Galactus.
Me too!
AND TIPPY-TOE, I FEEL FOR YOU. THOUGH YOUR PLANET IS OVERRUN BY HUMANS, YOU AND YOUR PEOPLE ARE ALONE, UNABLE TO COMMUNICATE WITH THOSE YOU SHARE YOUR PLANET WITH. THIS SOLITUDE, THIS AWFUL, ENDLESS SOLITUDE...
...I KNOW IT WELL. YOU ARE LUCKY TO HAVE SQUIRREL GIRL, AND SHE IS LUCKY TO HAVE YOU
Thank you, Galactus.
ANYWAY
I'D BETTER GO EAT YOUR PLANET BEFORE IT GETS TOO STALE
Whoa!
Dude, I thought we were bonding!
WE WERE, BUT A DUDE'S GOTTA EAT
PEACE
Oh man!
Diss!

Turns out you **can't** defeat Galactus by just chilling with him on the moon! All right, Tippy, scratch that off the list, and we'll see how well *"Fight him in orbit **around** the moon"* works out.

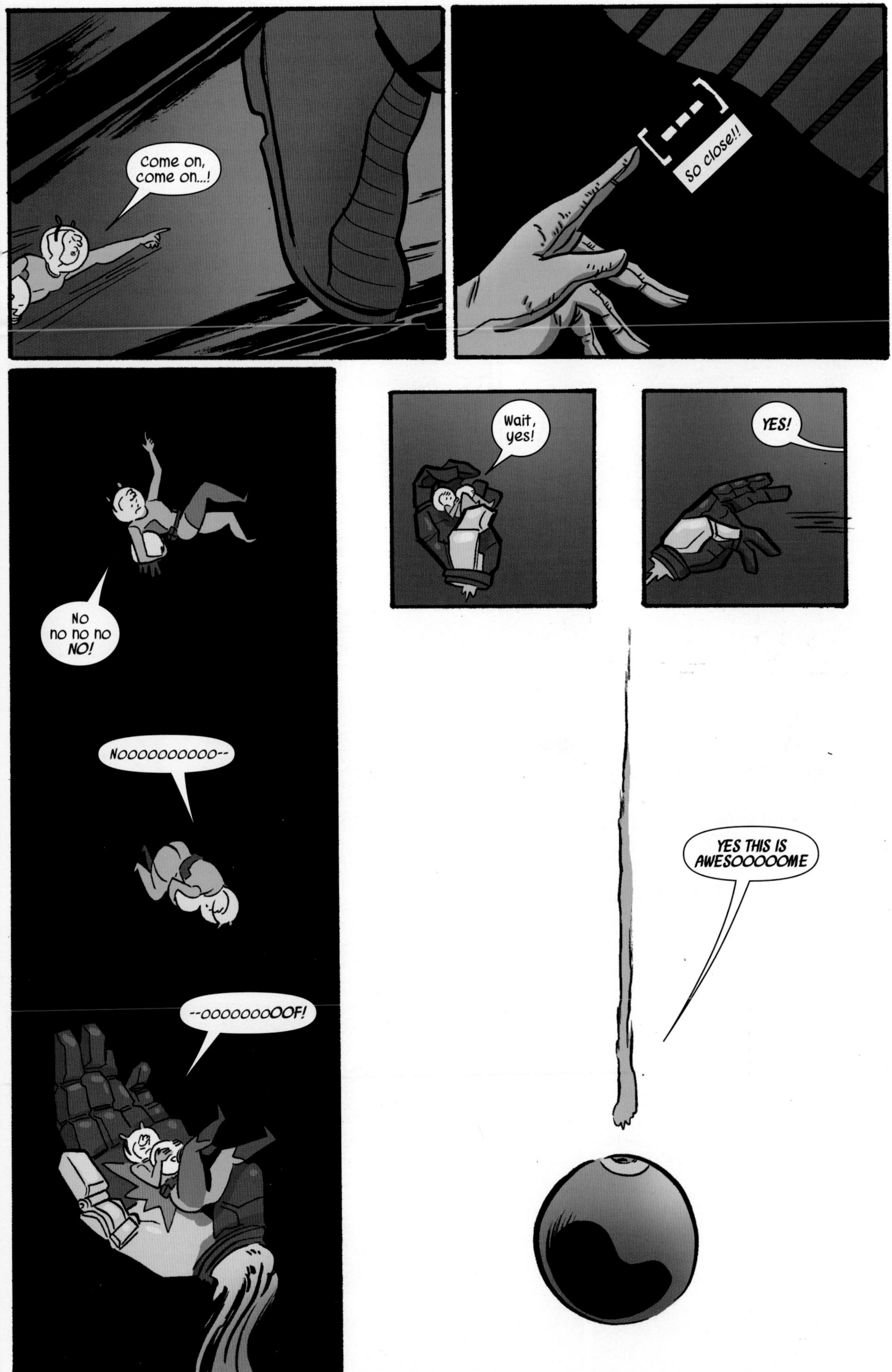
Come on, come on...!
[...]
So close!!
No no no no NO!
NOOOOOOOOOO--
--OOOOOOOOOF!
Wait, yes!
YES!
YES THIS IS AWESOOOOOME

Thanks, Iron Man suit parts! You saved the day. Come on, everyone, let's all give those suit parts...a hand??

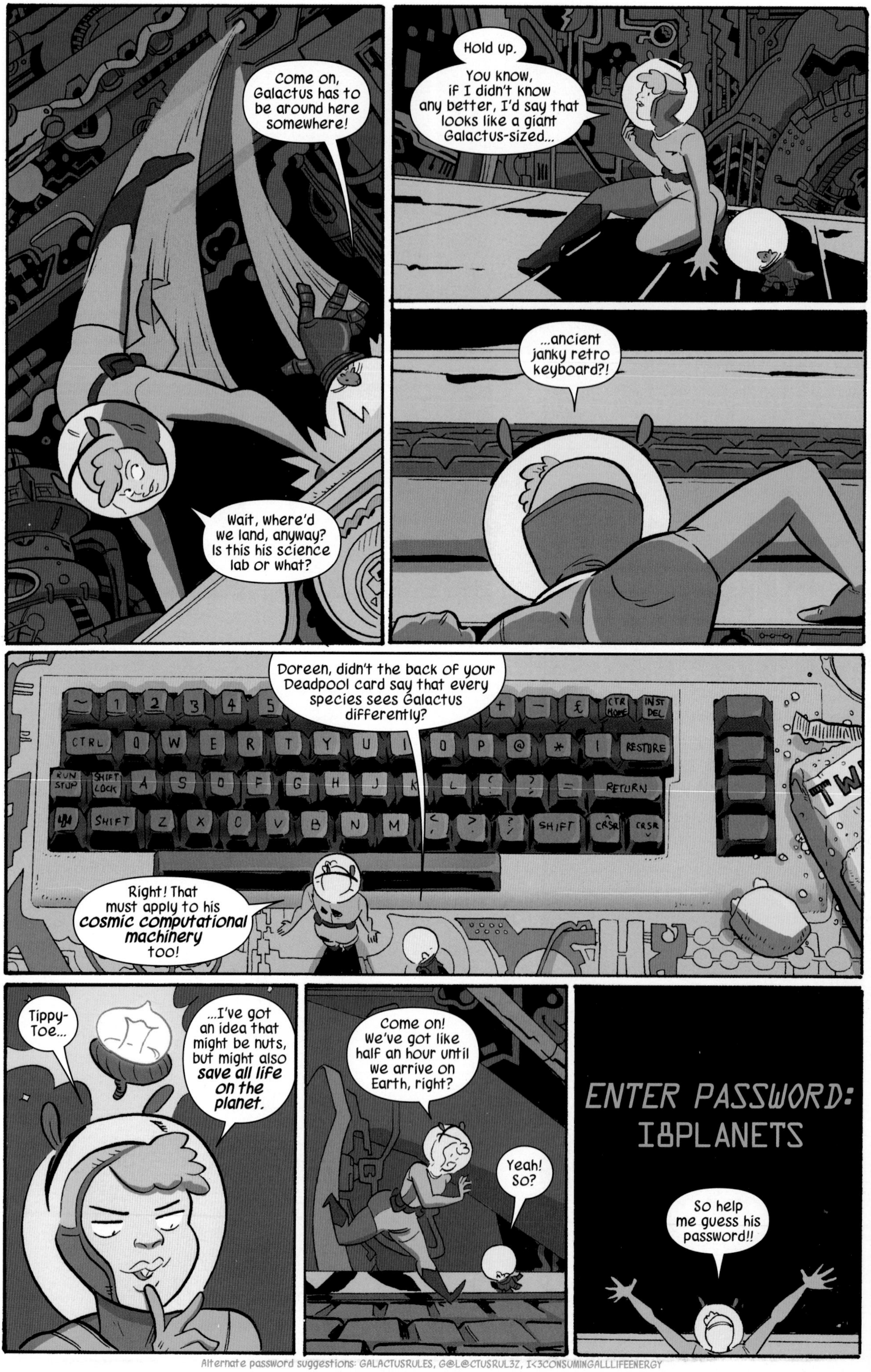

Come on, Galactus has to be around here somewhere!
Wait, where'd we land, anyway? Is this his science lab or what?
Hold up.
You know, if I didn't know any better, I'd say that looks like a giant Galactus-sized...
...ancient janky retro keyboard?!
Doreen, didn't the back of your Deadpool card say that every species sees Galactus differently?
Right! That must apply to his cosmic computational machinery too!
Tippy-Toe...
...I've got an idea that might be nuts, but might also save all life on the planet.
Come on! We've got like half an hour until we arrive on Earth, right?
Yeah! So?
ENTER PASSWORD:
I8PLANETS
So help me guess his password!!

Alternate password suggestions: GALACTUSRULES, G@L@CTUSRUL3Z, I<3CONSUMINGALLLIFEENERGY

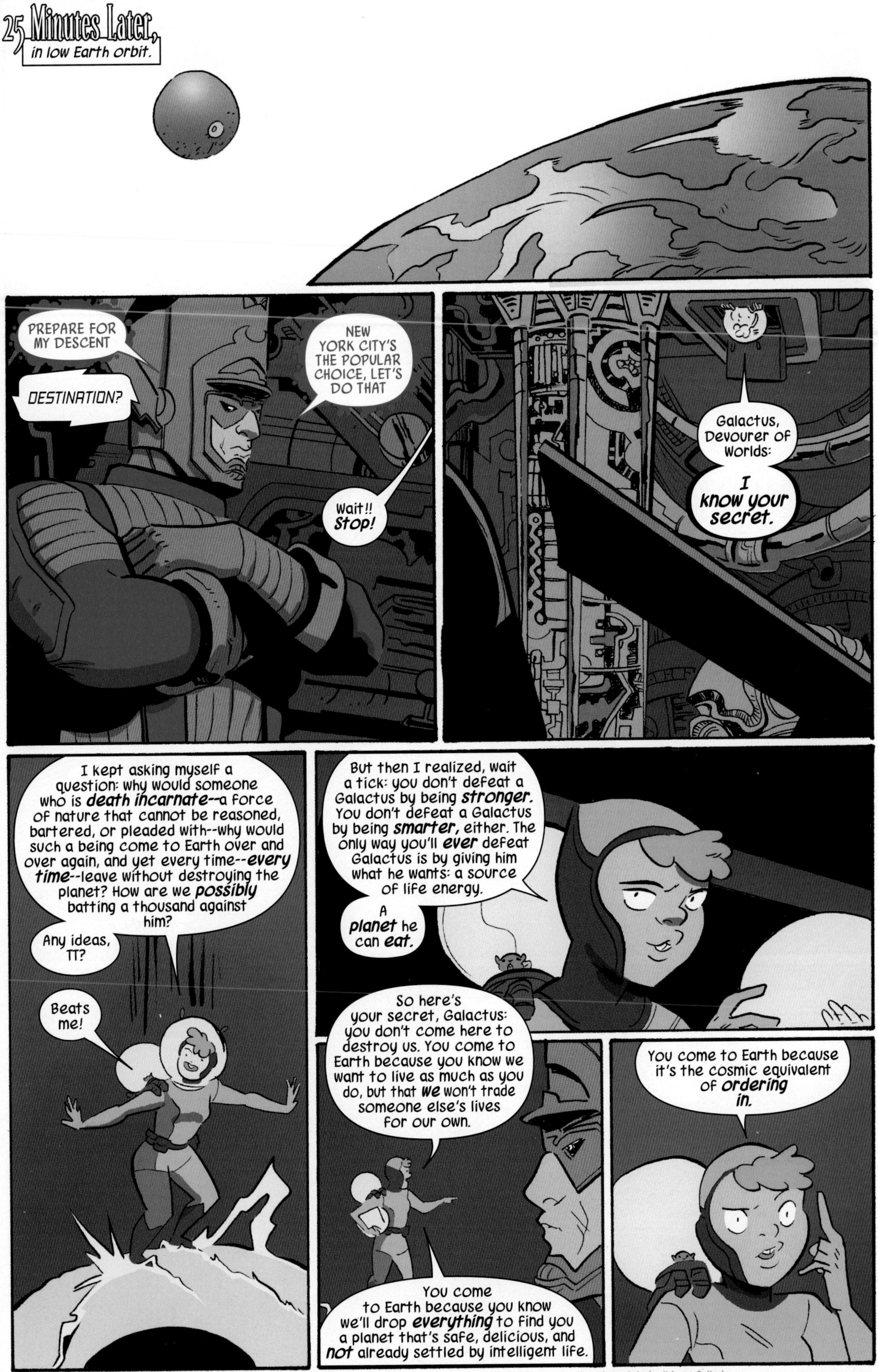
25 Minutes Later, in low Earth orbit.
PREPARE FOR MY DESCENT
DESTINATION?
NEW YORK CITY'S THE POPULAR CHOICE, LET'S DO THAT
Wait!! Stop!
Galactus, Devourer of Worlds:
I know your secret.
I kept asking myself a question: why would someone who is death incarnate--a force of nature that cannot be reasoned, bartered, or pleaded with--why would such a being come to Earth over and over again, and yet every time--every time--leave without destroying the planet? How are we possibly batting a thousand against him?
Any ideas, TT?
Beats me!
But then I realized, wait a tick: you don't defeat a Galactus by being stronger. You don't defeat a Galactus by being smarter, either. The only way you'll ever defeat Galactus is by giving him what he wants: a source of life energy.
A planet he can eat.
So here's your secret, Galactus: you don't come here to destroy us. You come to Earth because you know we want to live as much as you do, but that we won't trade someone else's lives for our own.
You come to Earth because you know we'll drop everything to find you a planet that's safe, delicious, and not already settled by intelligent life.
You come to Earth because it's the cosmic equivalent of ordering in.

And you *definitely* don't defeat Galactus by having a more audacious fashion sense. Many have tried, all have failed, though honestly many of them looked pretty great while they did so.

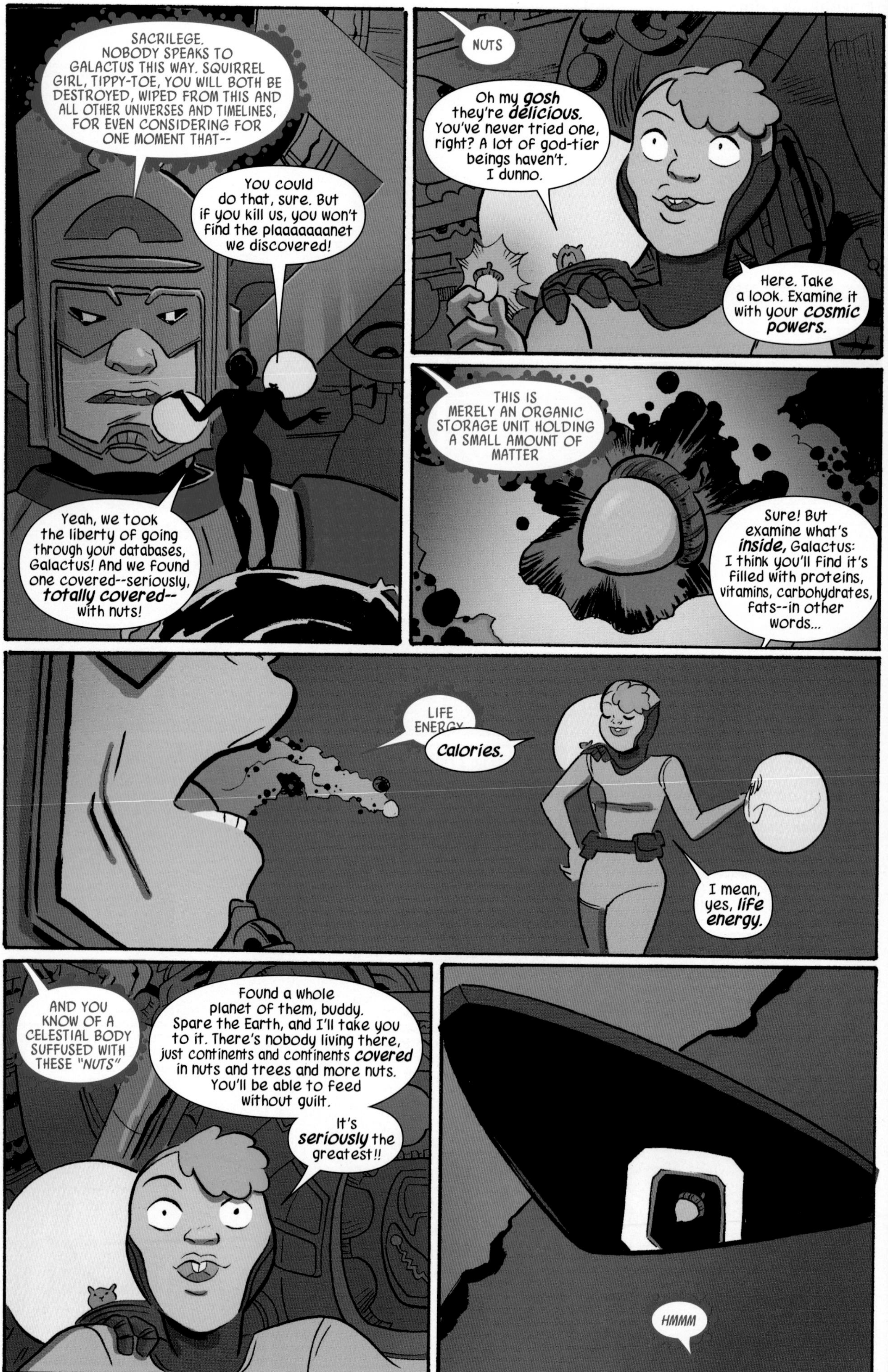

SACRILEGE. NOBODY SPEAKS TO GALACTUS THIS WAY. SQUIRREL GIRL, TIPPY-TOE, YOU WILL BOTH BE DESTROYED, WIPED FROM THIS AND ALL OTHER UNIVERSES AND TIMELINES, FOR EVEN CONSIDERING FOR ONE MOMENT THAT--
You could do that, sure. But if you kill us, you won't find the plaaaaaaanet we discovered!
Yeah, we took the liberty of going through your databases, Galactus! And we found one covered--seriously, totally covered-- with nuts!
NUTS
Oh my gosh they're delicious. You've never tried one, right? A lot of god-tier beings haven't. I dunno.
Here. Take a look. Examine it with your cosmic powers.
THIS IS MERELY AN ORGANIC STORAGE UNIT HOLDING A SMALL AMOUNT OF MATTER
Sure! But examine what's inside, Galactus: I think you'll find it's filled with proteins, vitamins, carbohydrates, fats--in other words...
LIFE ENERGY
Calories.
I mean, yes, life energy.
AND YOU KNOW OF A CELESTIAL BODY SUFFUSED WITH THESE "NUTS"
Found a whole planet of them, buddy. Spare the Earth, and I'll take you to it. There's nobody living there, just continents and continents covered in nuts and trees and more nuts. You'll be able to feed without guilt.
It's seriously the greatest!!
HMMM

Galactus, I don't know what your computers actually look like, but that retro computer interface had ultra-primitive terrible security. Do I thank you, or thank my imagination, or...?

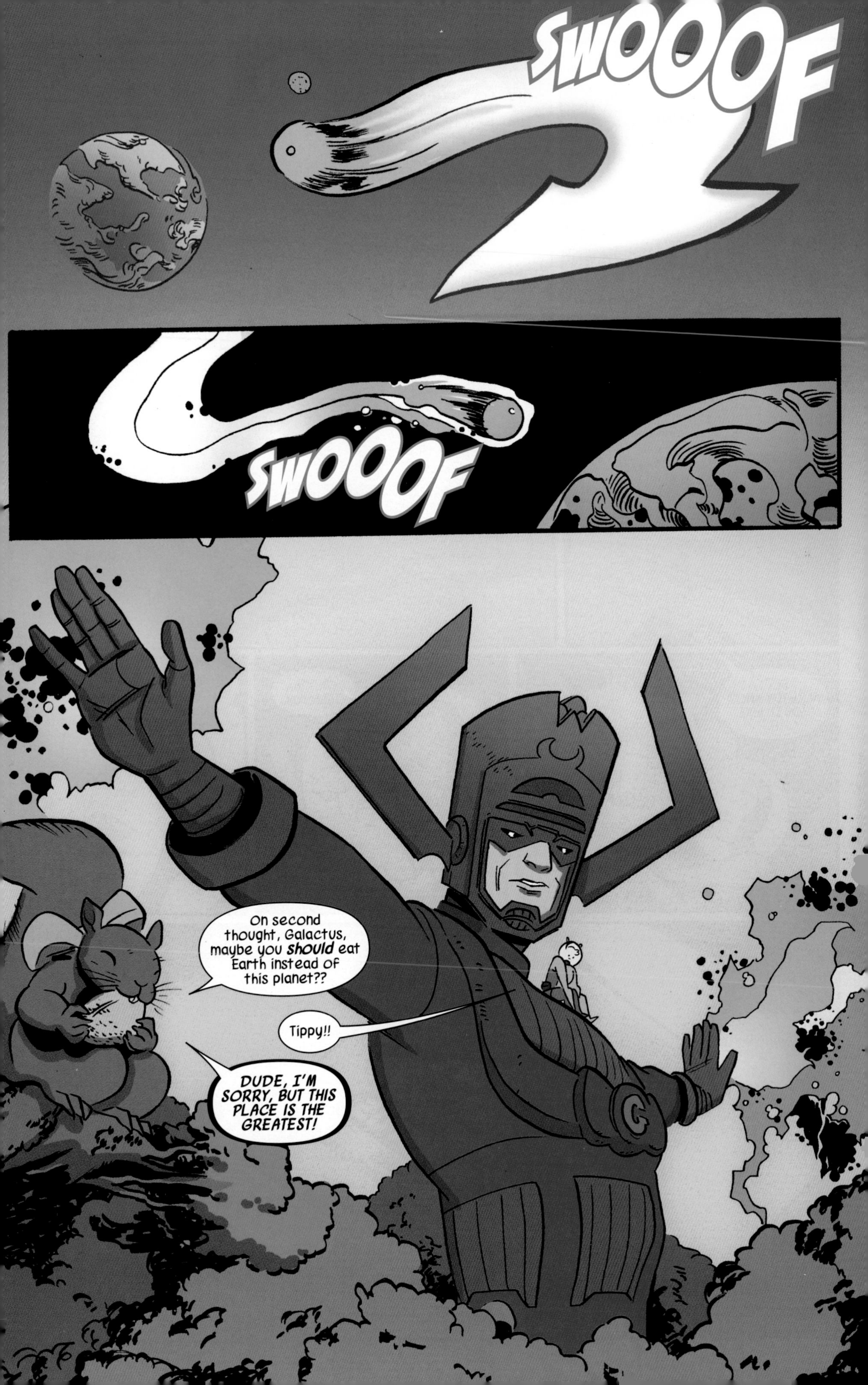
SWOOOF
SWOOOF
On second thought, Galactus, maybe you *should* eat Earth instead of this planet??
Tippy!!
DUDE, I'M SORRY, BUT THIS PLACE IS THE GREATEST!

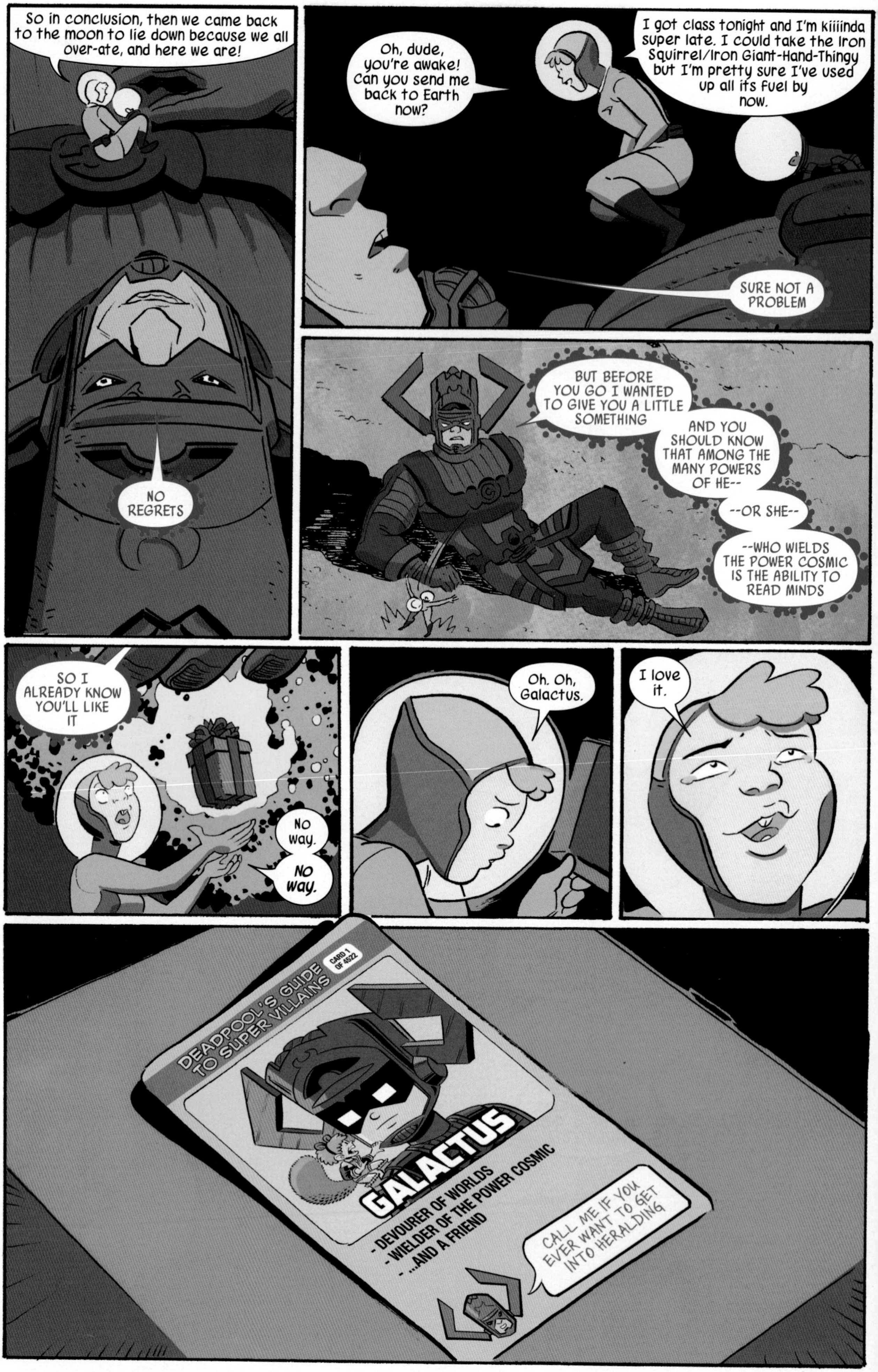
So in conclusion, then we came back to the moon to lie down because we all over-ate, and here we are!
NO REGRETS
Oh, dude, you're awake! Can you send me back to Earth now?
I got class tonight and I'm kiiiinda super late. I could take the Iron Squirrel/Iron Giant-Hand-Thingy but I'm pretty sure I've used up all its fuel by now.
SURE NOT A PROBLEM
BUT BEFORE YOU GO I WANTED TO GIVE YOU A LITTLE SOMETHING
AND YOU SHOULD KNOW THAT AMONG THE MANY POWERS OF HE--
--OR SHE--
--WHO WIELDS THE POWER COSMIC IS THE ABILITY TO READ MINDS
SO I ALREADY KNOW YOU'LL LIKE IT
No way.
No way.
Oh. Oh, Galactus.
I love it.
DEADPOOL'S GUIDE TO SUPER VILLAINS
CARD 1 OF 4522
GALACTUS
- DEVOURER OF WORLDS
- WIELDER OF THE POWER COSMIC
- ...AND A FRIEND
CALL ME IF YOU EVER WANT TO GET INTO HERALDING

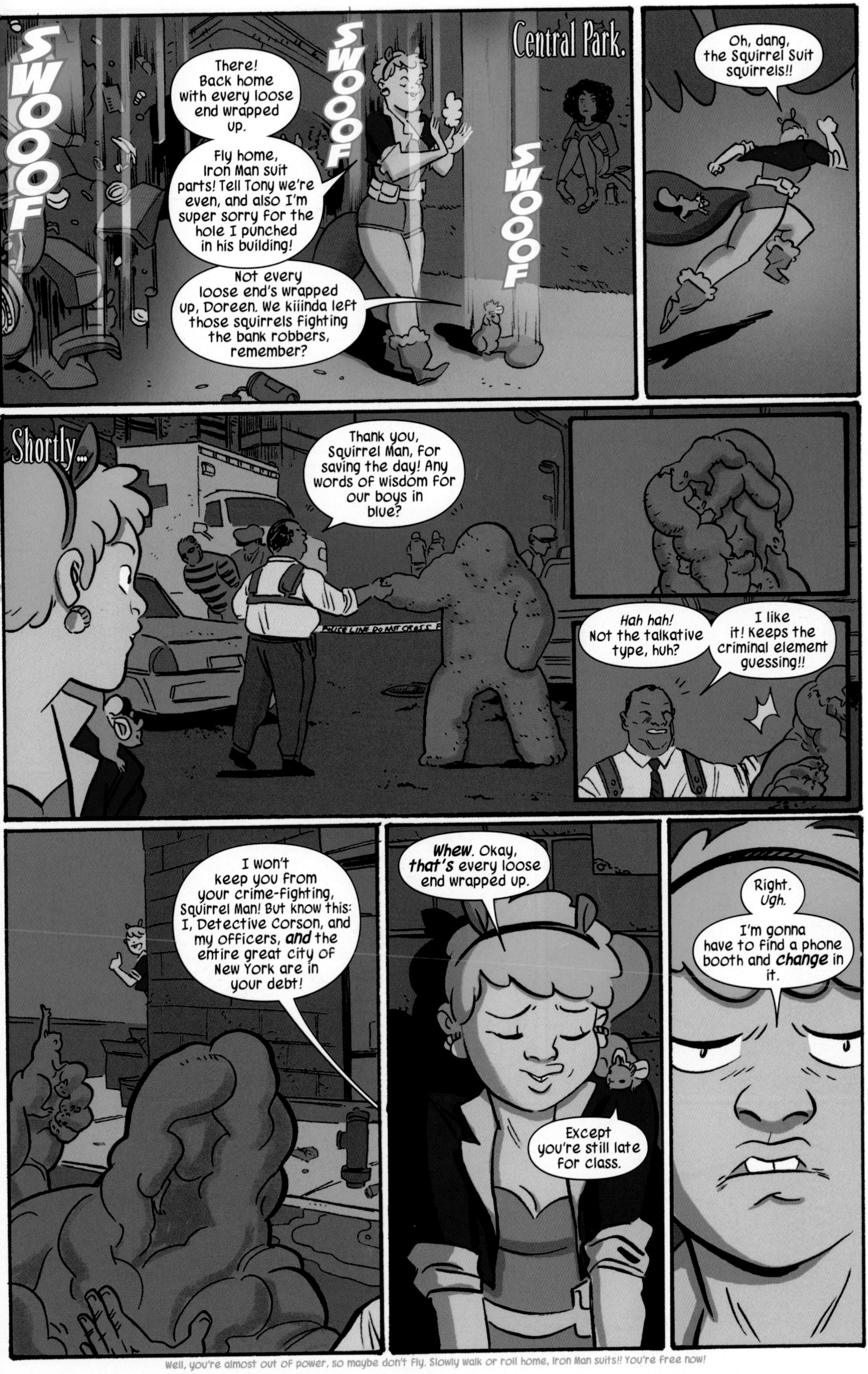
SWOOOF
SWOOOF
Central Park.
There! Back home with every loose end wrapped up.
Fly home, Iron Man suit parts! Tell Tony we're even, and also I'm super sorry for the hole I punched in his building!
Not every loose end's wrapped up, Doreen. We kiiinda left those squirrels fighting the bank robbers, remember?
SWOOOF
Oh, dang, the Squirrel Suit squirrels!!
Shortly...
Thank you, Squirrel Man, for saving the day! Any words of wisdom for our boys in blue?
Hah hah! Not the talkative type, huh?
I like it! Keeps the criminal element guessing!!
I won't keep you from your crime-fighting, Squirrel Man! But know this: I, Detective Corson, and my officers, *and* the entire great city of New York are in your debt!
Whew. Okay, ***that's*** every loose end wrapped up.
Except you're still late for class.
Right. *Ugh.*
I'm gonna have to find a phone booth and ***change*** in it.

Well, you're almost out of power, so maybe don't fly. Slowly walk or roll home, Iron Man suits!! You're free now!

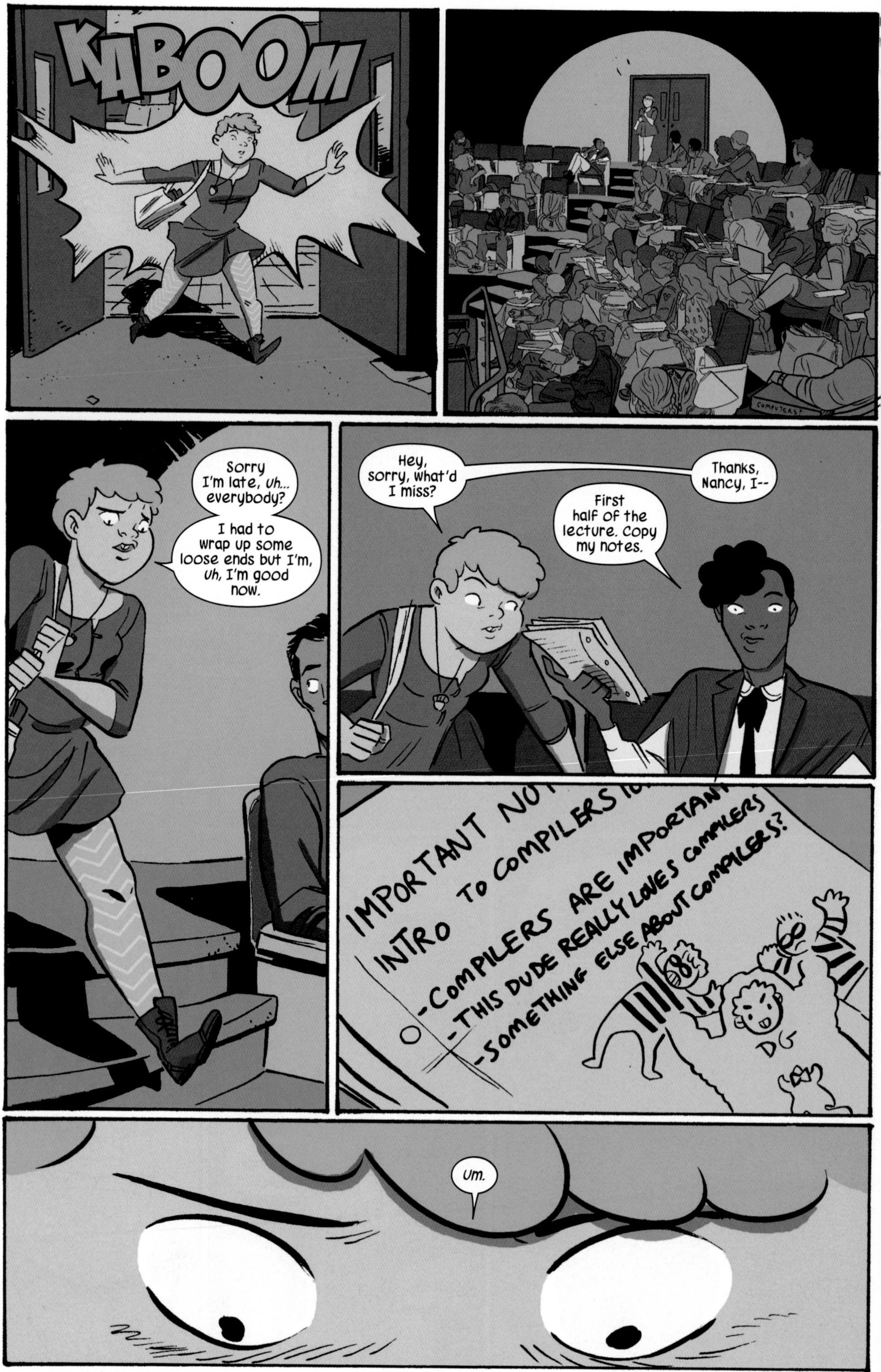
KABOOM
COMPUTERS?
Sorry I'm late, uh... everybody?
I had to wrap up some loose ends but I'm, uh, I'm good now.
Hey, sorry, what'd I miss?
First half of the lecture. Copy my notes.
Thanks, Nancy, I--
IMPORTANT NO
INTRO TO COMPILERS
-COMPILERS ARE IMPORTANT
-THIS DUDE REALLY LOVES COMPILERS
-SOMETHING ELSE ABOUT COMPILERS?
DG
Um.

Oh, don't worry, that's not you! That's my new 100% original character named "Squirrely D. Girly." TRADEMARK AND COPYRIGHT BY ME, DO NOT STEAL!!

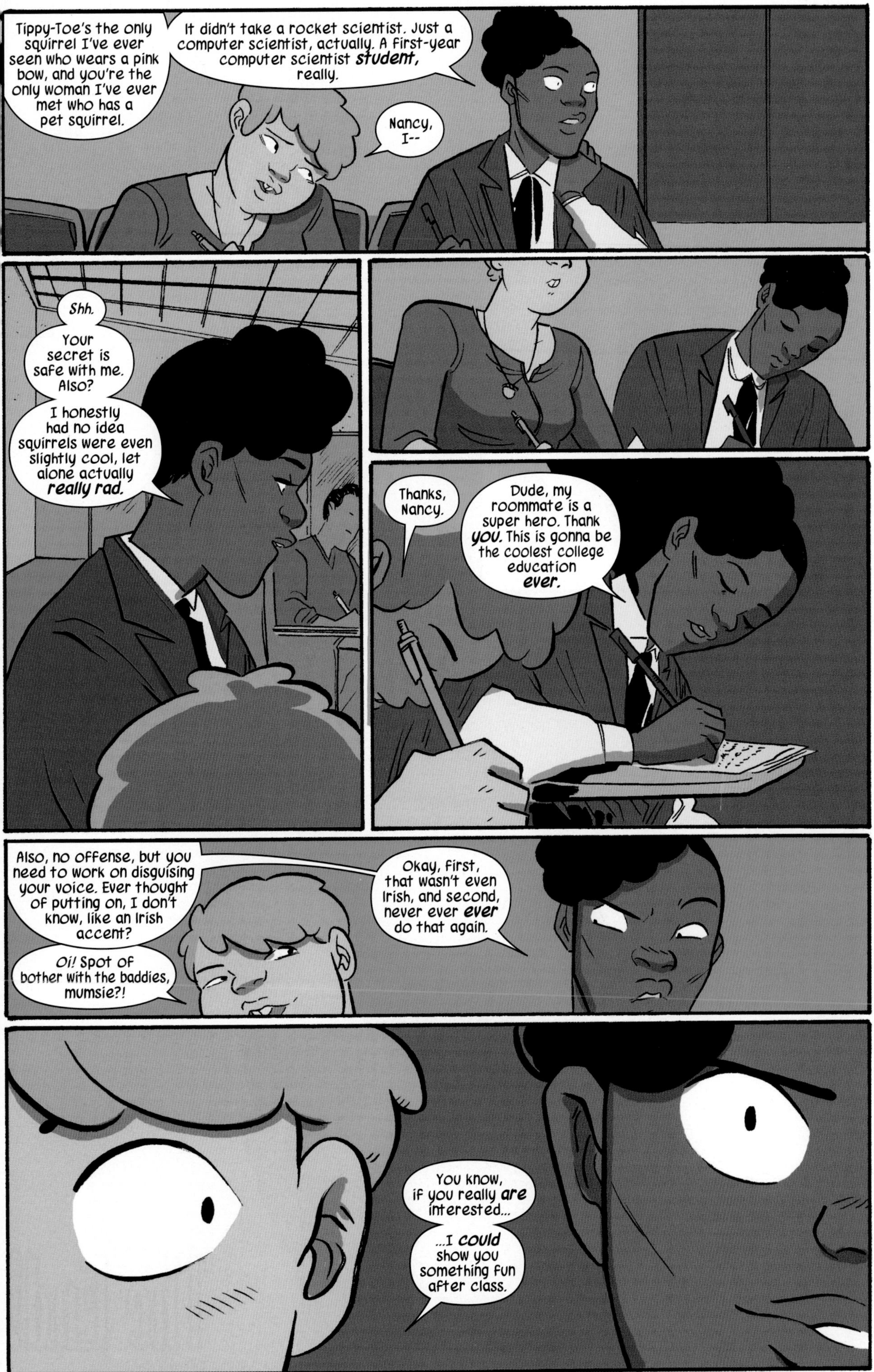
Tippy-Toe's the only squirrel I've ever seen who wears a pink bow, and you're the only woman I've ever met who has a pet squirrel.
It didn't take a rocket scientist. Just a computer scientist, actually. A first-year computer scientist student, really.
Nancy, I--
Shh.
Your secret is safe with me. Also?
I honestly had no idea squirrels were even slightly cool, let alone actually really rad.
Thanks, Nancy.
Dude, my roommate is a super hero. Thank you. This is gonna be the coolest college education ever.
Also, no offense, but you need to work on disguising your voice. Ever thought of putting on, I don't know, like an Irish accent?
Oi! Spot of bother with the baddies, mumsie?!
Okay, first, that wasn't even Irish, and second, never ever ever do that again.
You know, if you really are interested...
...I could show you something fun after class.

Doreen, do you even know where Ireland is? Doreen, do you need to take Intro to Really Basic Geography before you take Intro to Compilers??

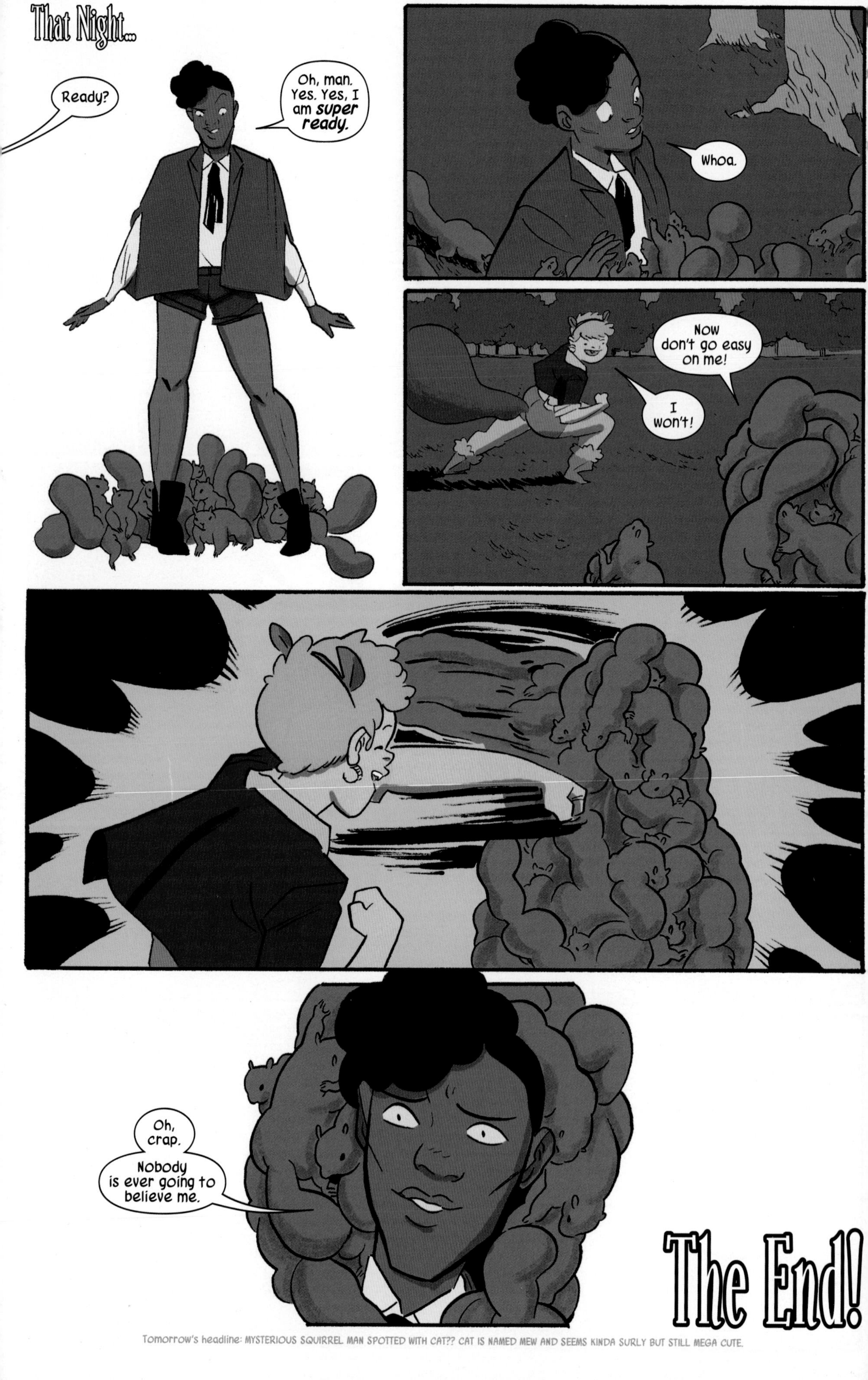
That Night...
Ready?
Oh, man. Yes. Yes, I am super ready.
Whoa.
Now don't go easy on me!
I won't!
Oh, crap.
Nobody is ever going to believe me.
The End!
Tomorrow's headline: MYSTERIOUS SQUIRREL MAN SPOTTED WITH CAT?? CAT IS NAMED MEW AND SEEMS KINDA SURLY BUT STILL MEGA CUTE.

the unbeatable Squirrel Girl #4!

Written by
Ryan North

Art by
Erica Henderson

Trading Card Art by
Chris Giarrusso

Color Art by
Rico Renzi

Lettering and Production by
VC's Clayton Cowles

Cover Artist **Erica Henderson**
Special Thanks to **Cassie Hart Kelly**
Assistant Editor **Jon Moisan**
Editor **Wil Moss**
Executive Editor **Tom Brevoort**
Editor in Chief **Axel Alonso**
Chief Creative Officer **Joe Quesada**
Publisher **Dan Buckley**
Executive Producer **Alan Fine**

Squirrel Girl will return in...
Squirrel Girl #5, duh.

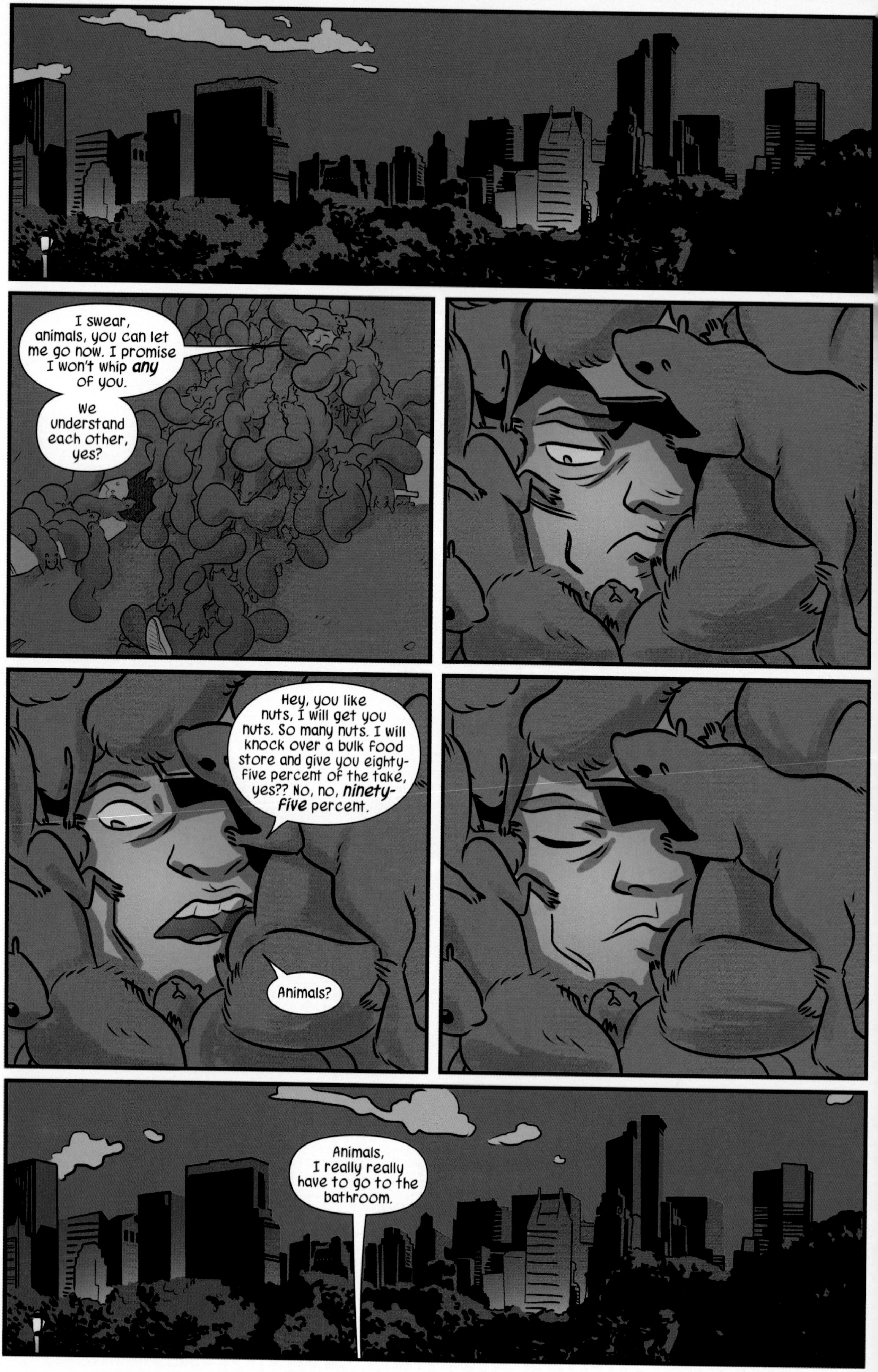
I swear, animals, you can let me go now. I promise I won't whip *any* of you.
We understand each other, yes?
Hey, you like nuts, I will get you nuts. So many nuts. I will knock over a bulk food store and give you eighty-five percent of the take, yes?? No, no, *ninety-five* percent.
Animals?
Animals, I really really have to go to the bathroom.

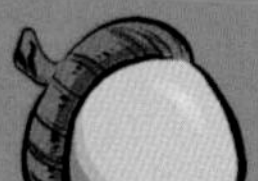

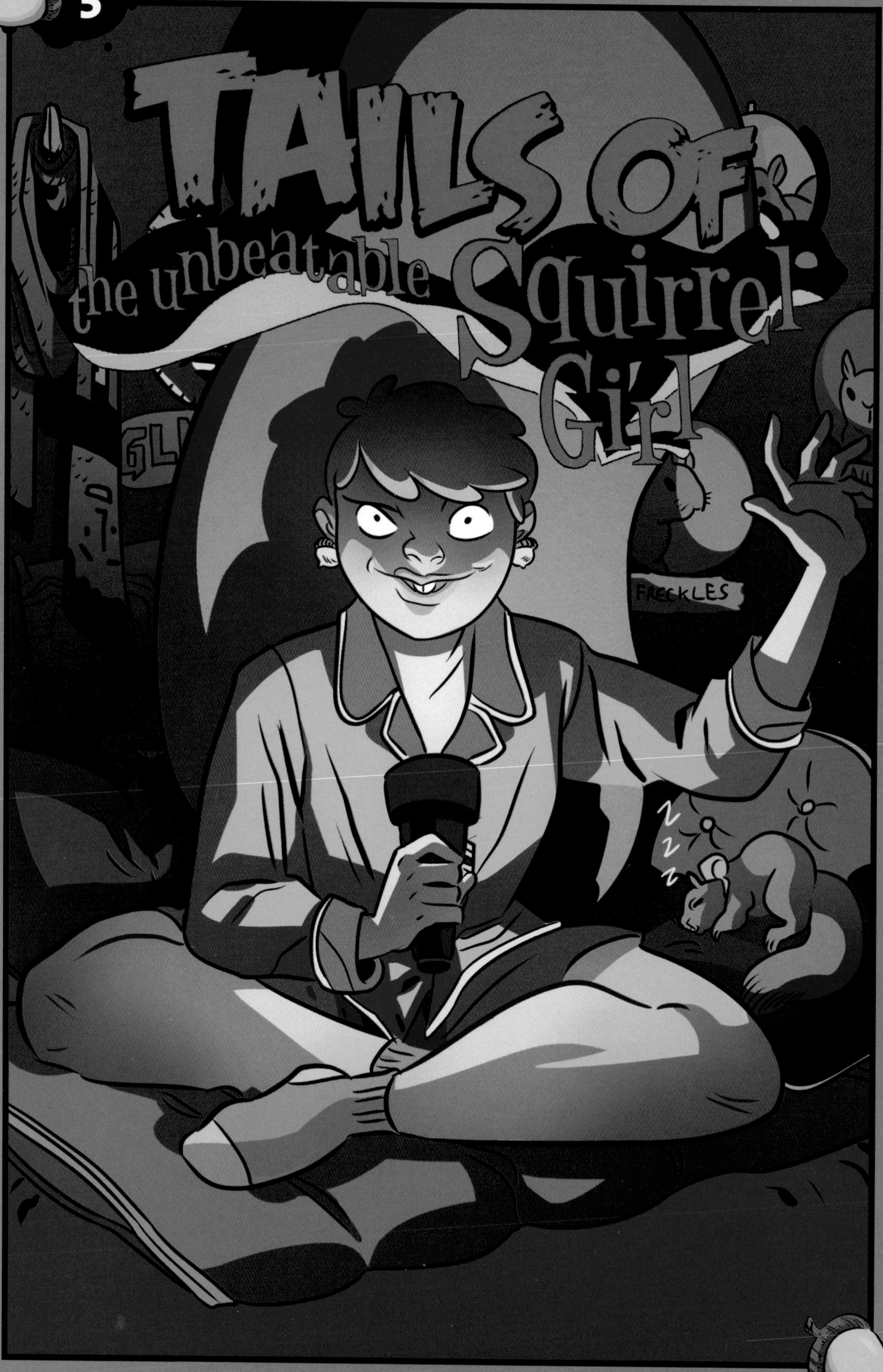
TAILS OF
the unbeatable Squirrel Girl
FRECKLES
Z Z Z

Doreen Green isn't just a first-year computer science student: she secretly also has all the powers of both squirrel and girl! She uses her amazing abilities to fight crime **and** be as awesome as possible. You know her as...*The Unbeatable Squirrel Girl!* Let's catch up with what she's been up to until now, with...

Squirrel Girl *in a nutshell*

Squirrel Girl! @unbeatablesg
@xGALACTUSx hey dude thanks for not eating the planet after all!!

GALACTUS @xGALACTUSx
@unbeatablesg NO PROBLEM THAT PLANET OF NUTS YOU FOUND WAS WAY BETTER ANYWAY

Deadpool @pooltothedead
@unbeatablesg @xGALACTUSx Wait, what? You guys weren't joking about that?

Deadpool @pooltothedead
@unbeatablesg @xGALACTUSx Galactus ACTUALLY came to Earth?? Yesterday? The ACTUAL GALACTUS was HERE??

Deadpool @pooltothedead
@unbeatablesg @xGALACTUSx dang man I spent the whole day at home watching tv in my underpants

Deadpool @pooltothedead
@unbeatablesg @xGALACTUSx CALL ME NEXT TIME!!

Tony Stark @starkmantony ✓
A bunch of my Iron Man suit parts showed up in NYC with moon dust on them. That's actually extremely valuable, so thanks @unbeatablesg.

Tippy-Toe @yoitstippytoe
@starkmantony CHITT CHUK CHITTT?

Tony Stark @starkmantony ✓
@yoitstippytoe I can't understand you. None of my translation algorithms can understand you. Probably because you are a literal squirrel.

Tippy-Toe @yoitstippytoe
@starkmantony CHUKKA.... CHITT CHUK CHITTT?

Tony Stark @starkmantony ✓
@unbeatablesg Little help?

Squirrel Girl! @unbeatablesg
@starkmantony she's asking you if you figured out that the dust came from the new moon restaurant

Tony Stark @starkmantony ✓
@unbeatablesg @yoitstippytoe What new moon restaurant?

Tippy-Toe @yoitstippytoe
@starkmantony CHUTT CHUK CHUKK CHITTY CHIT

Squirrel Girl! @unbeatablesg
@starkmantony She says "The one that just opened up! The food's good, but it doesn't have much of an ATMOSPHERE"

Squirrel Girl! @unbeatablesg
@starkmantony hahaha, that's pretty good actually!! good work @yoitstippytoe

Tony Stark @starkmantony ✓
@unbeatablesg @yoitstippytoe You guys know I'm the head of a major corporation, right?

Tony Stark @starkmantony ✓
@unbeatablesg @yoitstippytoe I shouldn't even be hanging out here as it is

Nancy W. @sewwiththeflo
I bet being covered from head to toe in a living squirrel suit doesn't smell as bad as you think it would.

Nancy W. @sewwiththeflo
IMPORTANT UPDATE:

Nancy W. @sewwiththeflo
So it turns out being covered head to toe in a living squirrel suit doesn't smell as GOOD as you think it would either

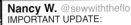

search! 🔍

#dinosaurs

#basslass

#clones

#acronyms

#nuthorde

#TIPPPPPPPY!!

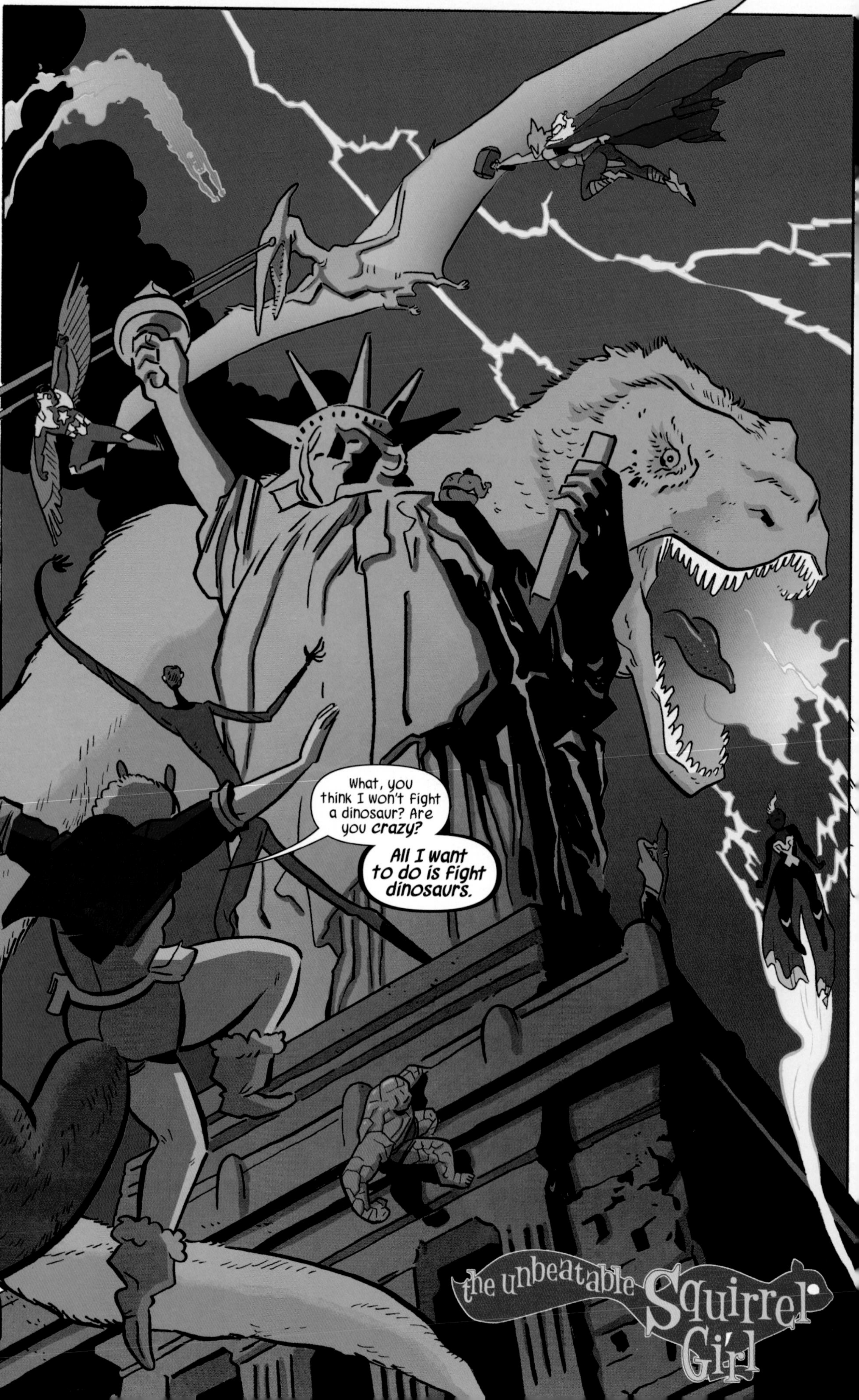
What, you think I won't fight a dinosaur? Are you crazy?
All I want to do is fight dinosaurs.
the unbeatable Squirrel Girl

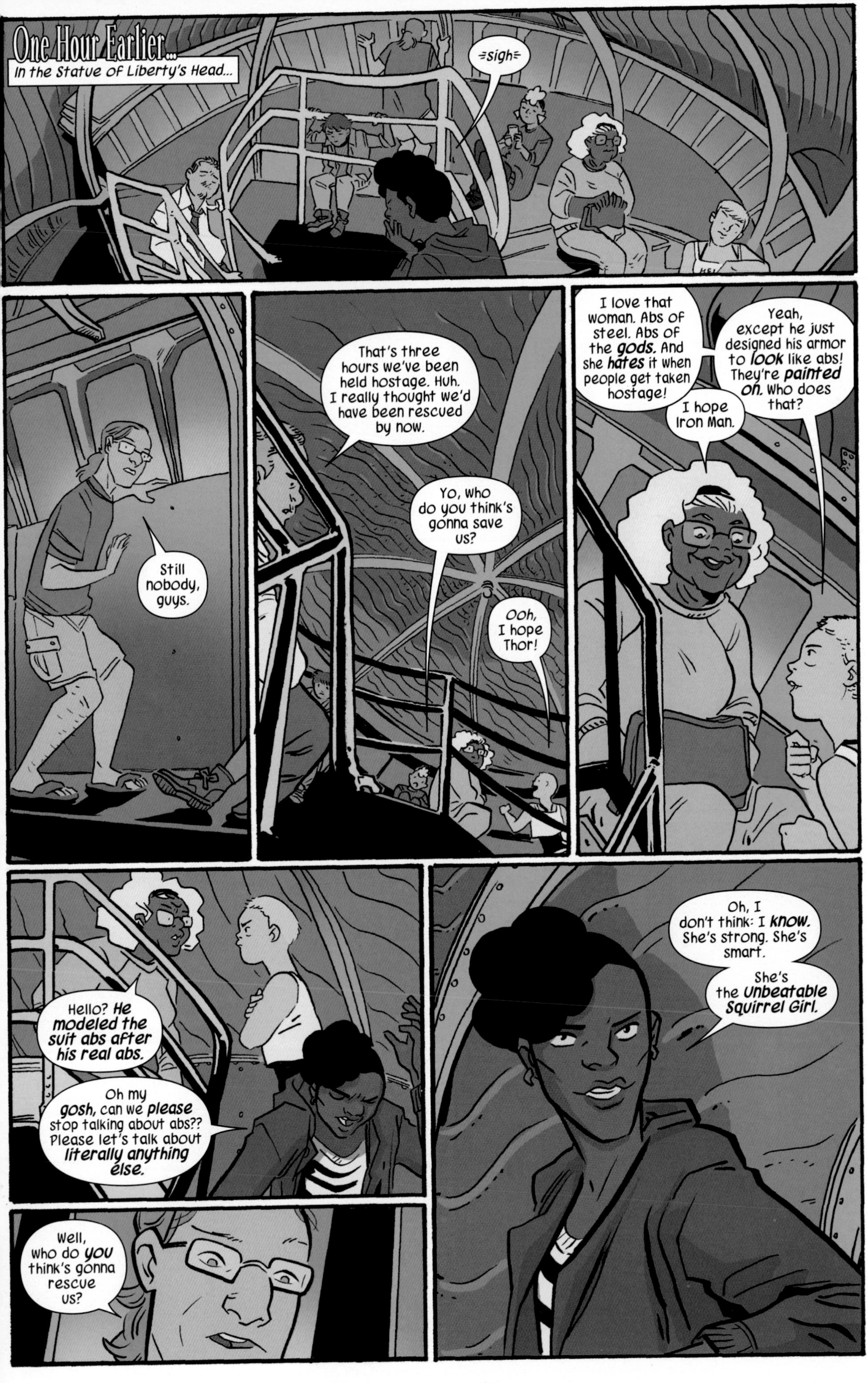
One Hour Earlier...
In the Statue of Liberty's Head...
=sigh=
Still nobody, guys.
That's three hours we've been held hostage. Huh. I really thought we'd have been rescued by now.
Yo, who do you think's gonna save us?
Ooh, I hope Thor!
I love that woman. Abs of steel. Abs of the gods. And she hates it when people get taken hostage!
I hope Iron Man.
Yeah, except he just designed his armor to look like abs! They're painted on. Who does that?
Hello? He modeled the suit abs after his real abs.
Oh my gosh, can we please stop talking about abs?? Please let's talk about literally anything else.
Well, who do you think's gonna rescue us?
Oh, I don't think: I know. She's strong. She's smart.
She's the Unbeatable Squirrel Girl.

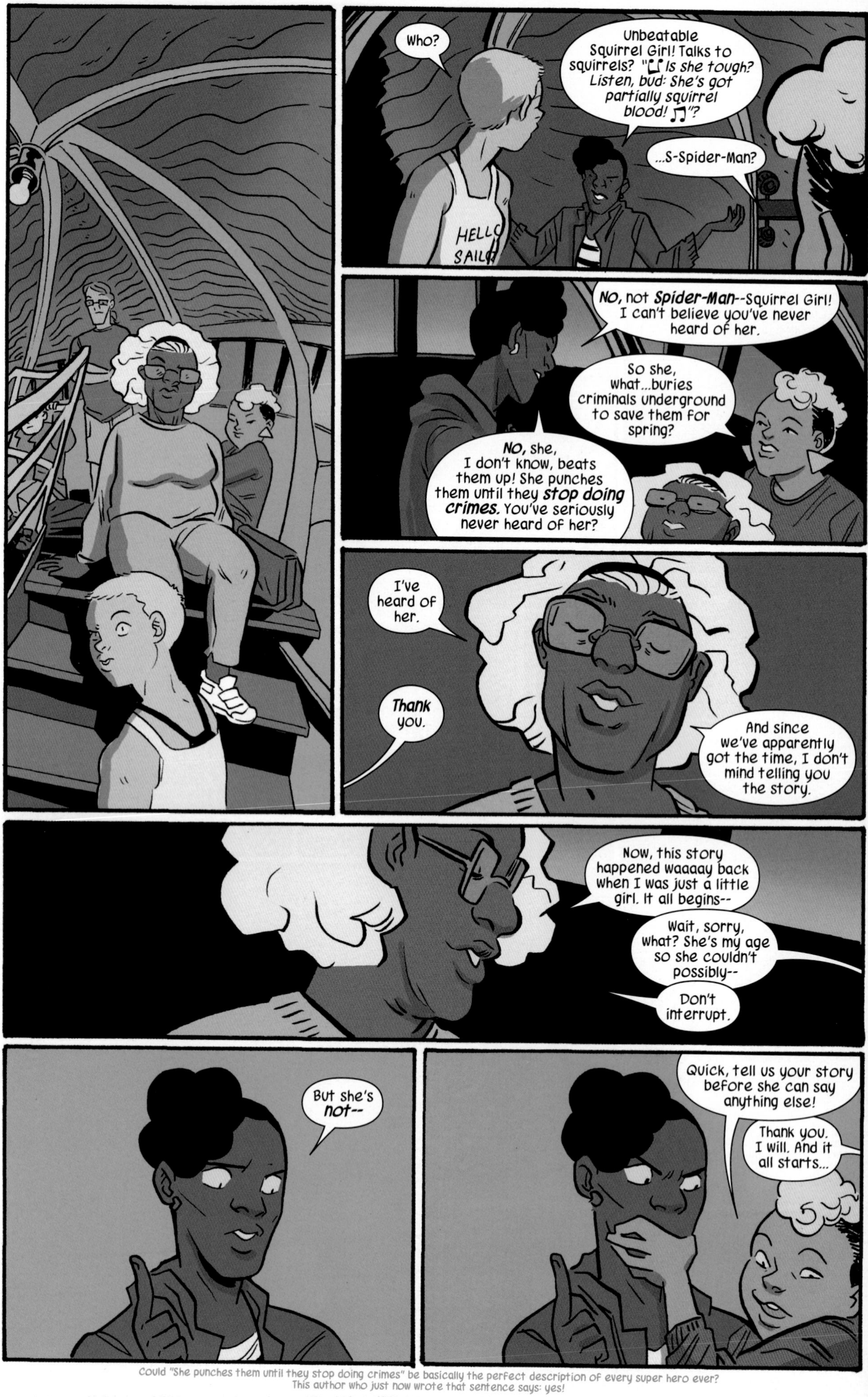
Who?
Unbeatable Squirrel Girl! Talks to squirrels? "♫ Is she tough? Listen, bud: She's got partially squirrel blood! ♫"?
...S-Spider-Man?
HELLO SAILOR
No, not *Spider-Man*--Squirrel Girl! I can't believe you've never heard of her.
So she, what...buries criminals underground to save them for spring?
No, she, I don't know, beats them up! She punches them until they *stop doing crimes.* You've seriously never heard of her?
I've heard of her.
Thank you.
And since we've apparently got the time, I don't mind telling you the story.
Now, this story happened waaaay back when I was just a little girl. It all begins--
Wait, sorry, what? She's my age so she couldn't possibly--
Don't interrupt.
But she's *not--*
Quick, tell us your story before she can say anything else!
Thank you. I will. And it all starts...

Could "She punches them until they stop doing crimes" be basically the perfect description of every super hero ever?
This author who just now wrote that sentence says: yes!

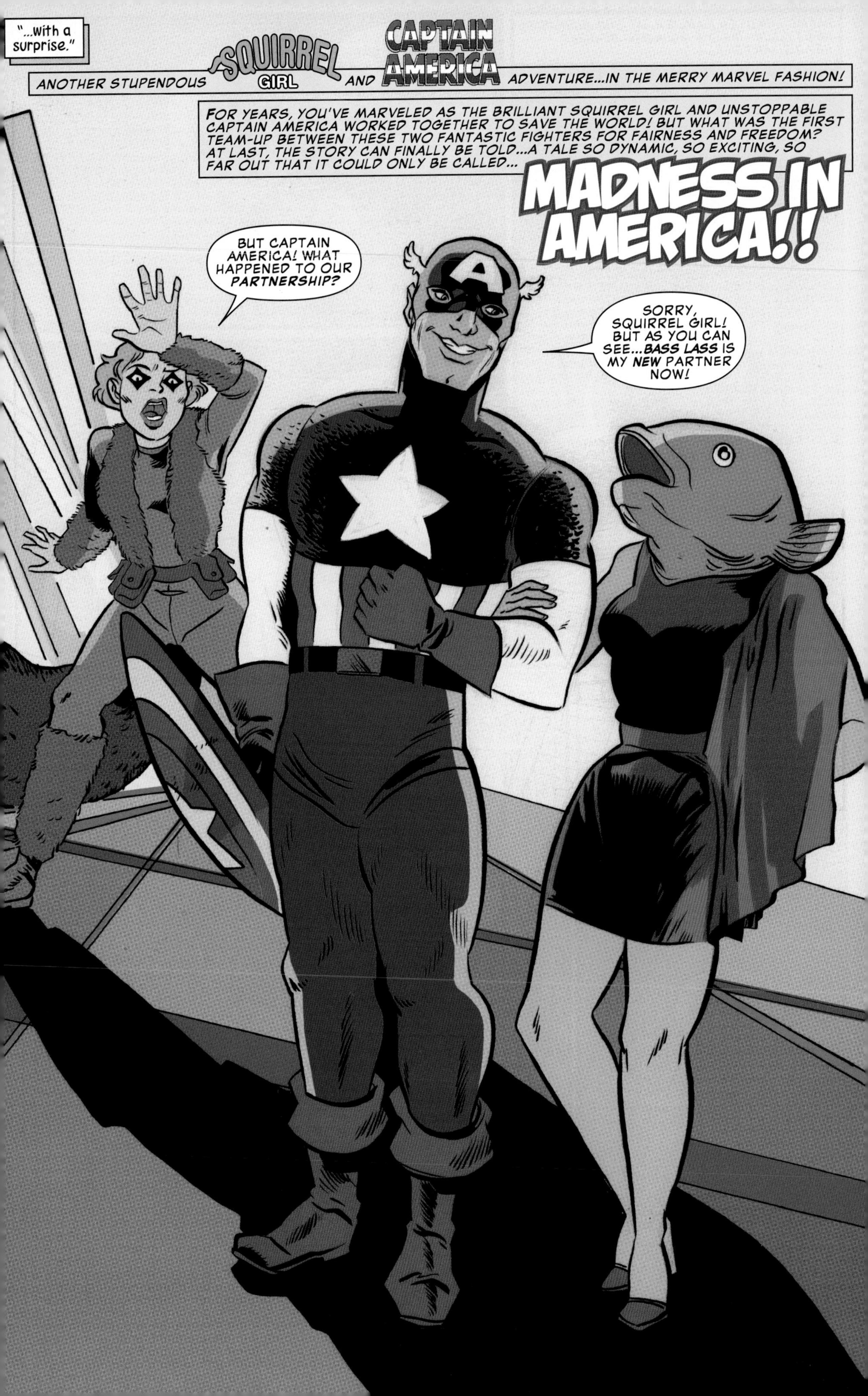

"...with a surprise."
ANOTHER STUPENDOUS SQUIRREL GIRL AND CAPTAIN AMERICA ADVENTURE...IN THE MERRY MARVEL FASHION!
FOR YEARS, YOU'VE MARVELED AS THE BRILLIANT SQUIRREL GIRL AND UNSTOPPABLE CAPTAIN AMERICA WORKED TOGETHER TO SAVE THE WORLD! BUT WHAT WAS THE FIRST TEAM-UP BETWEEN THESE TWO FANTASTIC FIGHTERS FOR FAIRNESS AND FREEDOM? AT LAST, THE STORY CAN FINALLY BE TOLD...A TALE SO DYNAMIC, SO EXCITING, SO FAR OUT THAT IT COULD ONLY BE CALLED...
MADNESS IN AMERICA!!
BUT CAPTAIN AMERICA! WHAT HAPPENED TO OUR PARTNERSHIP?
SORRY, SQUIRREL GIRL! BUT AS YOU CAN SEE...BASS LASS IS MY NEW PARTNER NOW!

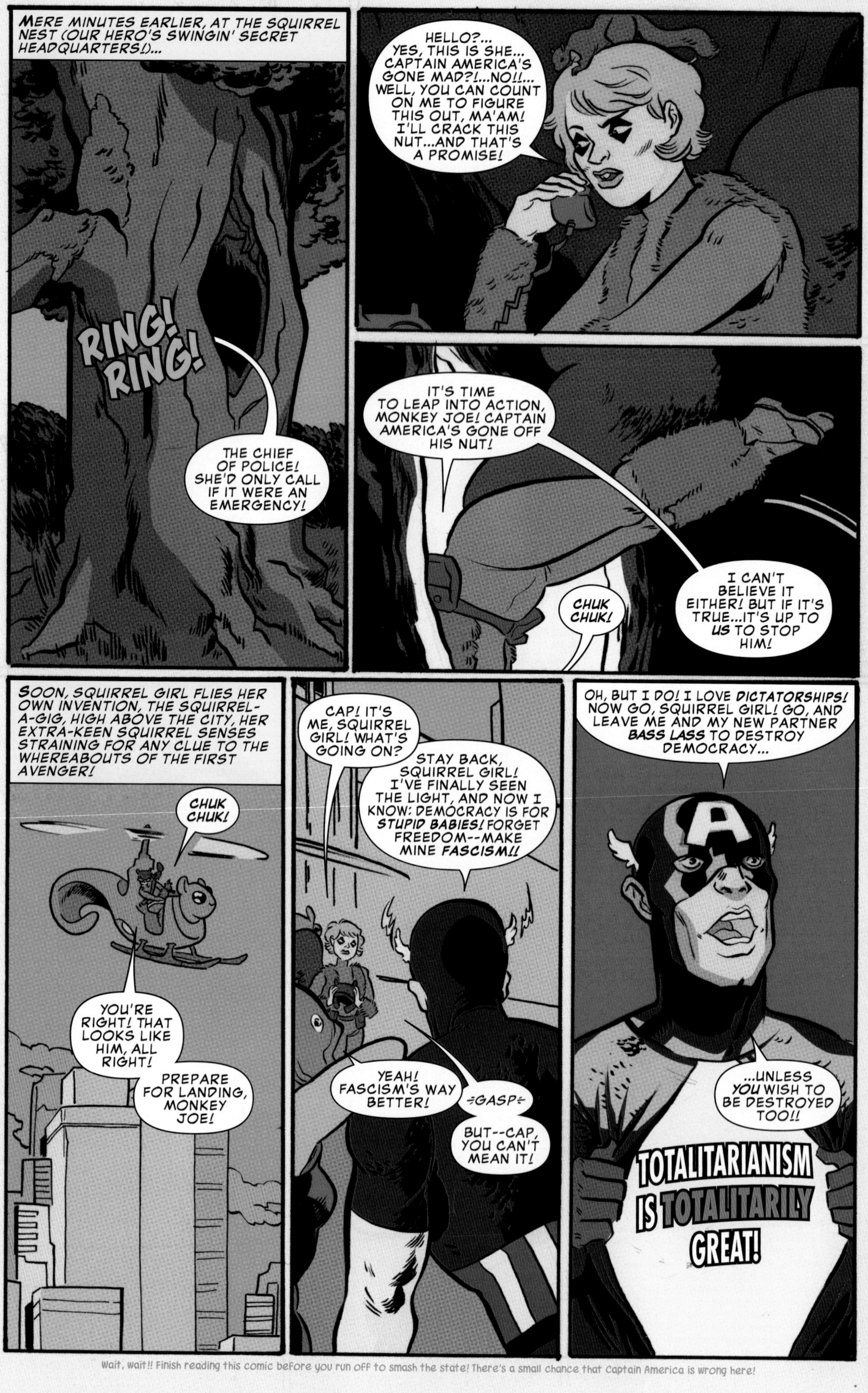
MERE MINUTES EARLIER, AT THE SQUIRREL NEST (OUR HERO'S SWINGIN' SECRET HEADQUARTERS!)...
RING! RING!
THE CHIEF OF POLICE! SHE'D ONLY CALL IF IT WERE AN EMERGENCY!
HELLO?... YES, THIS IS SHE... CAPTAIN AMERICA'S GONE MAD?!...NO!!... WELL, YOU CAN COUNT ON ME TO FIGURE THIS OUT, MA'AM! I'LL CRACK THIS NUT...AND THAT'S A PROMISE!
IT'S TIME TO LEAP INTO ACTION, MONKEY JOE! CAPTAIN AMERICA'S GONE OFF HIS NUT!
CHUK CHUK!
I CAN'T BELIEVE IT EITHER! BUT IF IT'S TRUE...IT'S UP TO US TO STOP HIM!
SOON, SQUIRREL GIRL FLIES HER OWN INVENTION, THE SQUIRREL-A-GIG, HIGH ABOVE THE CITY, HER EXTRA-KEEN SQUIRREL SENSES STRAINING FOR ANY CLUE TO THE WHEREABOUTS OF THE FIRST AVENGER!
CHUK CHUK!
YOU'RE RIGHT! THAT LOOKS LIKE HIM, ALL RIGHT!
PREPARE FOR LANDING, MONKEY JOE!
CAP! IT'S ME, SQUIRREL GIRL! WHAT'S GOING ON?
STAY BACK, SQUIRREL GIRL! I'VE FINALLY SEEN THE LIGHT, AND NOW I KNOW: DEMOCRACY IS FOR STUPID BABIES! FORGET FREEDOM--MAKE MINE FASCISM!!
YEAH! FASCISM'S WAY BETTER!
=GASP=
BUT--CAP, YOU CAN'T MEAN IT!
OH, BUT I DO! I LOVE DICTATORSHIPS! NOW GO, SQUIRREL GIRL! GO, AND LEAVE ME AND MY NEW PARTNER BASS LASS TO DESTROY DEMOCRACY...
...UNLESS YOU WISH TO BE DESTROYED TOO!!
TOTALITARIANISM IS TOTALITARILY GREAT!

Wait, wait!! Finish reading this comic before you run off to smash the state! There's a small chance that Captain America is wrong here!

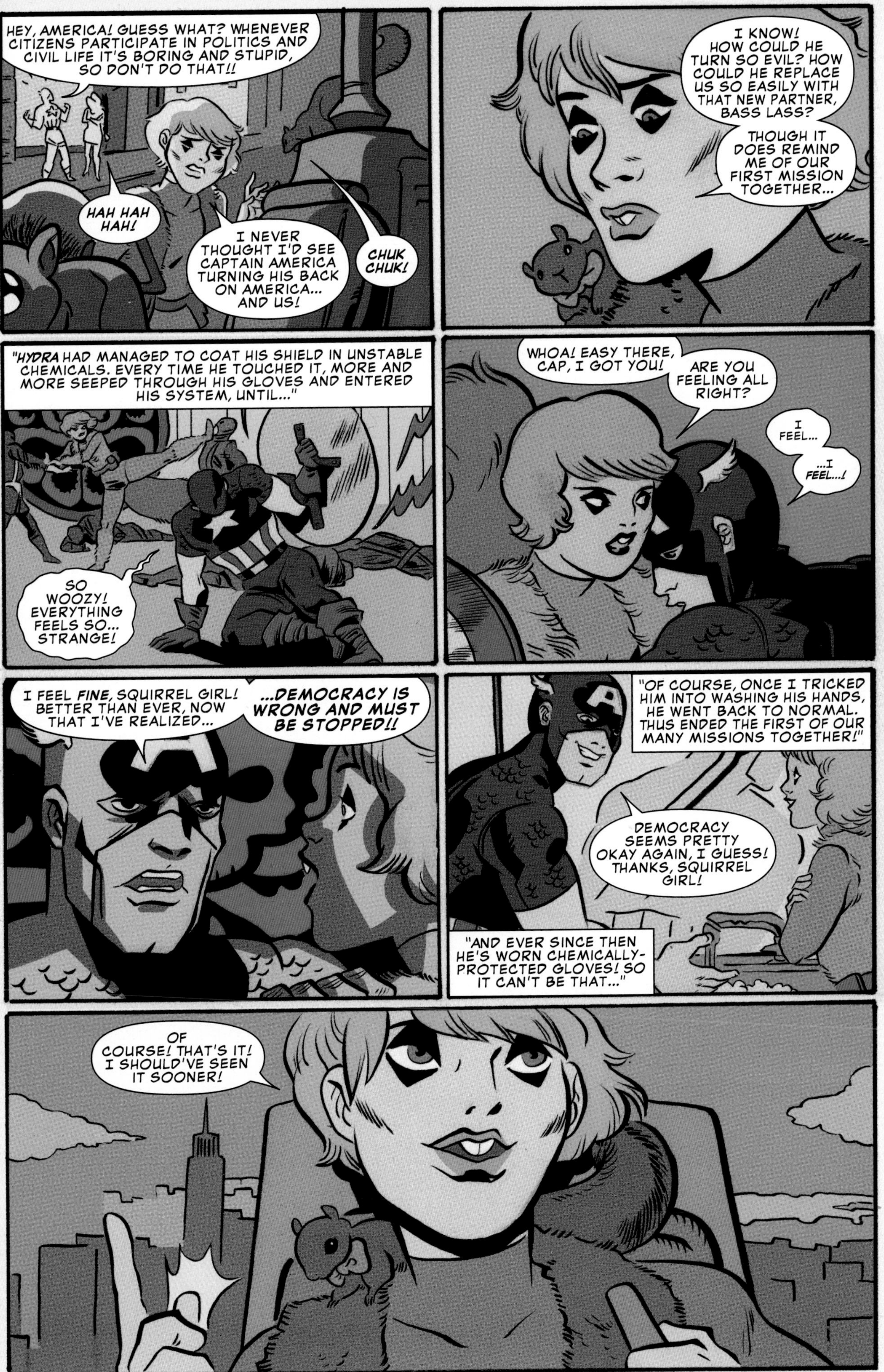
HEY, AMERICA! GUESS WHAT? WHENEVER CITIZENS PARTICIPATE IN POLITICS AND CIVIL LIFE IT'S BORING AND STUPID, SO DON'T DO THAT!!
HAH HAH HAH!
I NEVER THOUGHT I'D SEE CAPTAIN AMERICA TURNING HIS BACK ON AMERICA... AND US!
CHUK CHUK!
I KNOW! HOW COULD HE TURN SO EVIL? HOW COULD HE REPLACE US SO EASILY WITH THAT NEW PARTNER, BASS LASS?
THOUGH IT DOES REMIND ME OF OUR FIRST MISSION TOGETHER...
"HYDRA HAD MANAGED TO COAT HIS SHIELD IN UNSTABLE CHEMICALS. EVERY TIME HE TOUCHED IT, MORE AND MORE SEEPED THROUGH HIS GLOVES AND ENTERED HIS SYSTEM, UNTIL..."
SO WOOZY! EVERYTHING FEELS SO... STRANGE!
WHOA! EASY THERE, CAP, I GOT YOU!
ARE YOU FEELING ALL RIGHT?
I FEEL...
...I FEEL...!
I FEEL FINE, SQUIRREL GIRL! BETTER THAN EVER, NOW THAT I'VE REALIZED...
...DEMOCRACY IS WRONG AND MUST BE STOPPED!!
"OF COURSE, ONCE I TRICKED HIM INTO WASHING HIS HANDS, HE WENT BACK TO NORMAL. THUS ENDED THE FIRST OF OUR MANY MISSIONS TOGETHER!"
DEMOCRACY SEEMS PRETTY OKAY AGAIN, I GUESS! THANKS, SQUIRREL GIRL!
"AND EVER SINCE THEN HE'S WORN CHEMICALLY-PROTECTED GLOVES! SO IT CAN'T BE THAT..."
OF COURSE! THAT'S IT! I SHOULD'VE SEEN IT SOONER!

Oh, to live in a world where *"Democracy seems pretty okay again, I guess"* is to Captain America as *"With great power comes great responsibility"* is to Spider-Man.

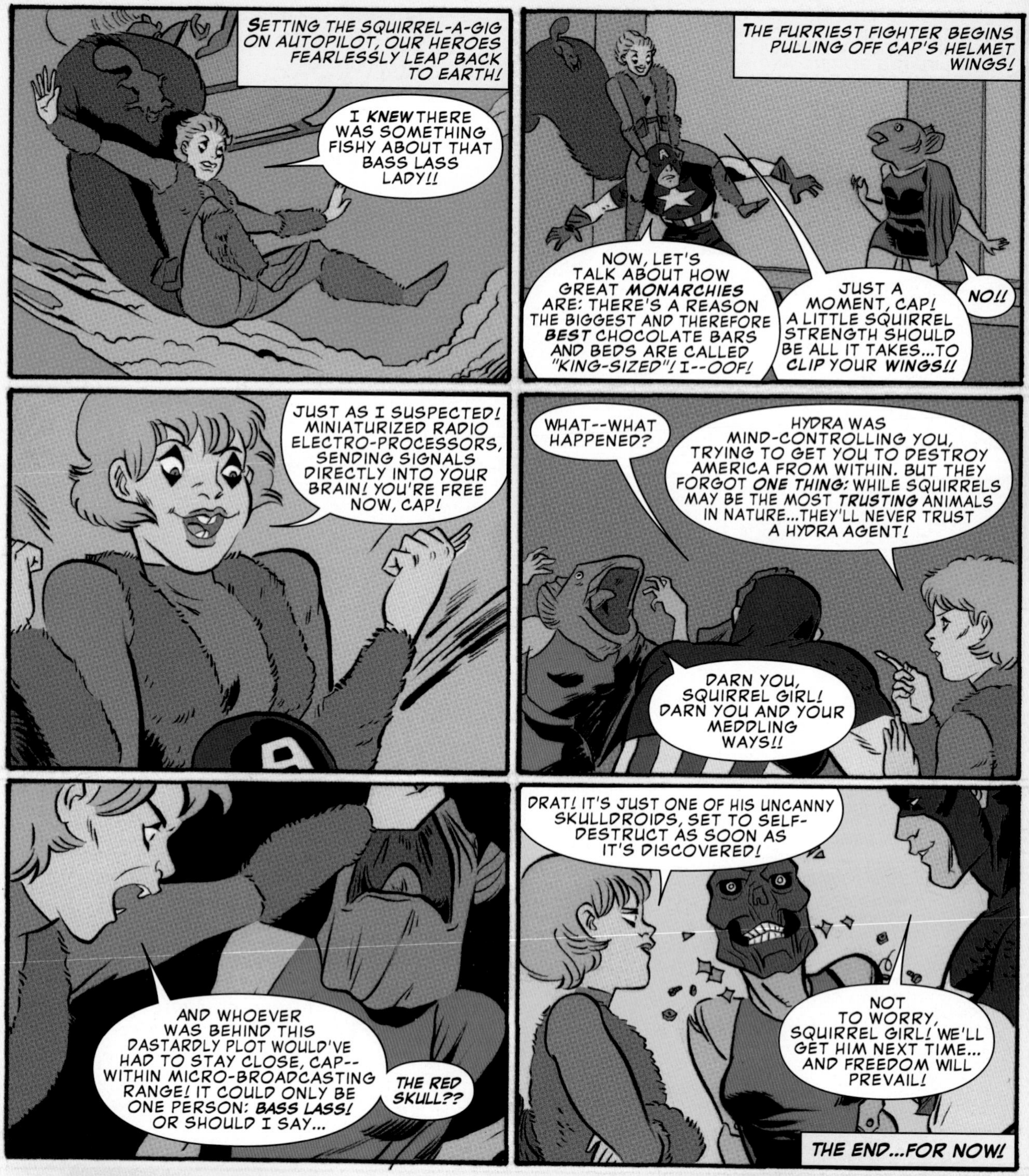
SETTING THE SQUIRREL-A-GIG ON AUTOPILOT, OUR HEROES FEARLESSLY LEAP BACK TO EARTH!
I KNEW THERE WAS SOMETHING FISHY ABOUT THAT BASS LASS LADY!!
THE FURRIEST FIGHTER BEGINS PULLING OFF CAP'S HELMET WINGS!
NOW, LET'S TALK ABOUT HOW GREAT MONARCHIES ARE: THERE'S A REASON THE BIGGEST AND THEREFORE BEST CHOCOLATE BARS AND BEDS ARE CALLED "KING-SIZED"! I--OOF!
JUST A MOMENT, CAP! A LITTLE SQUIRREL STRENGTH SHOULD BE ALL IT TAKES...TO CLIP YOUR WINGS!!
NO!!
JUST AS I SUSPECTED! MINIATURIZED RADIO ELECTRO-PROCESSORS, SENDING SIGNALS DIRECTLY INTO YOUR BRAIN! YOU'RE FREE NOW, CAP!
WHAT--WHAT HAPPENED?
HYDRA WAS MIND-CONTROLLING YOU, TRYING TO GET YOU TO DESTROY AMERICA FROM WITHIN. BUT THEY FORGOT ONE THING: WHILE SQUIRRELS MAY BE THE MOST TRUSTING ANIMALS IN NATURE...THEY'LL NEVER TRUST A HYDRA AGENT!
DARN YOU, SQUIRREL GIRL! DARN YOU AND YOUR MEDDLING WAYS!!
AND WHOEVER WAS BEHIND THIS DASTARDLY PLOT WOULD'VE HAD TO STAY CLOSE, CAP-- WITHIN MICRO-BROADCASTING RANGE! IT COULD ONLY BE ONE PERSON: BASS LASS! OR SHOULD I SAY...
THE RED SKULL??
DRAT! IT'S JUST ONE OF HIS UNCANNY SKULLDROIDS, SET TO SELF-DESTRUCT AS SOON AS IT'S DISCOVERED!
NOT TO WORRY, SQUIRREL GIRL! WE'LL GET HIM NEXT TIME... AND FREEDOM WILL PREVAIL!
THE END...FOR NOW!

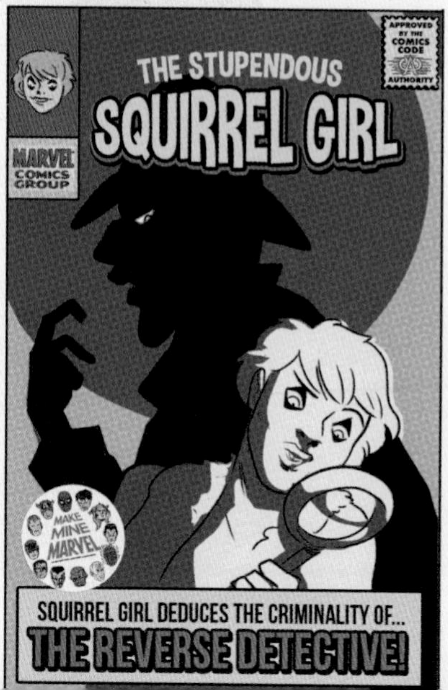
APPROVED BY THE COMICS CODE AUTHORITY
THE STUPENDOUS
SQUIRREL GIRL
MARVEL COMICS GROUP
MAKE MINE MARVEL
SQUIRREL GIRL DEDUCES THE CRIMINALITY OF...
THE REVERSE DETECTIVE!

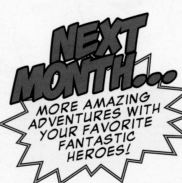

NEXT MONTH...

MORE AMAZING ADVENTURES WITH YOUR FAVORITE FANTASTIC HEROES!

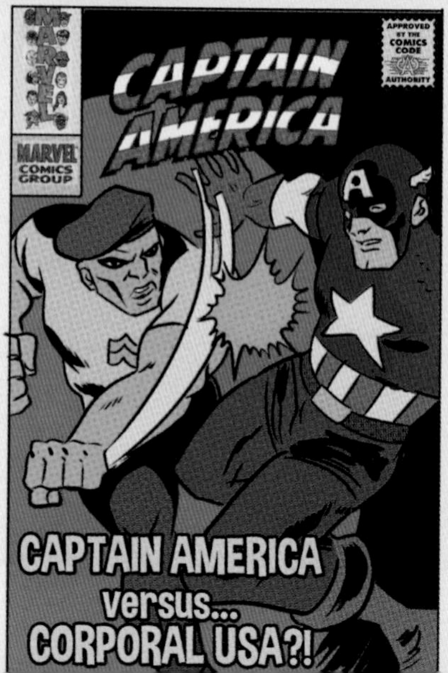
MARVEL
APPROVED BY THE COMICS CODE AUTHORITY
CAPTAIN AMERICA
MARVEL COMICS GROUP
CAPTAIN AMERICA versus... CORPORAL USA?!

In that comic, Captain America says "Stand down! That's an order, Corporal." and then Corporal USA is all "Um yeah so the thing is, I think it's pretty clear we're both operating outside the traditional military chain of command here??"

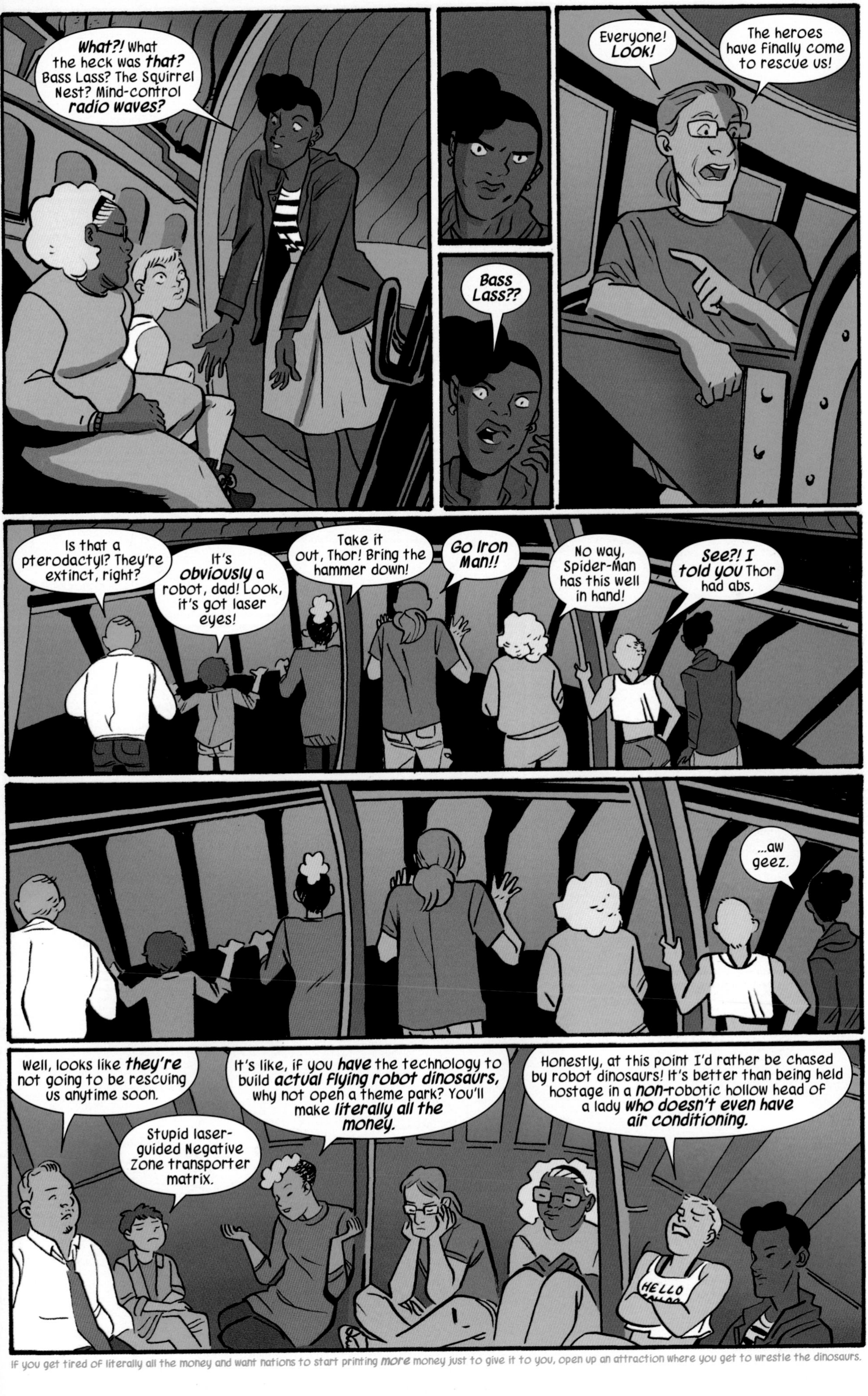
What?! What the heck was that? Bass Lass? The Squirrel Nest? Mind-control radio waves?
Bass Lass??
Everyone! LOOK!
The heroes have finally come to rescue us!
Is that a pterodactyl? They're extinct, right?
It's obviously a robot, dad! Look, it's got laser eyes!
Take it out, Thor! Bring the hammer down!
Go Iron Man!!
No way, Spider-Man has this well in hand!
See?! I told you Thor had abs.
...aw geez.
Well, looks like they're not going to be rescuing us anytime soon.
Stupid laser-guided Negative Zone transporter matrix.
It's like, if you have the technology to build actual flying robot dinosaurs, why not open a theme park? You'll make literally all the money.
Honestly, at this point I'd rather be chased by robot dinosaurs! It's better than being held hostage in a non-robotic hollow head of a lady who doesn't even have air conditioning.
HELLO

If you get tired of literally all the money and want nations to start printing *more* money just to give it to you, open up an attraction where you get to wrestle the dinosaurs.

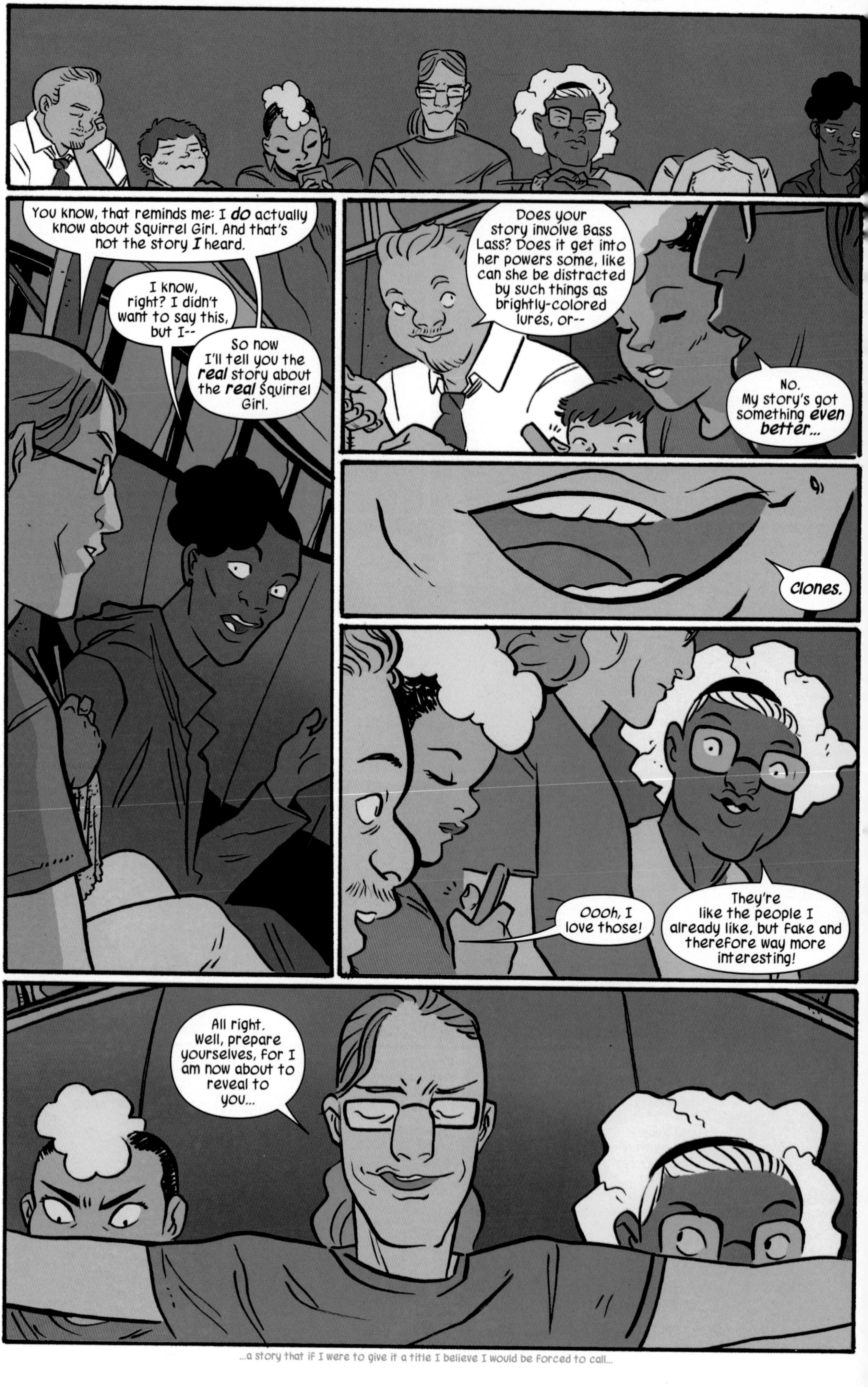
You know, that reminds me: I *do* actually know about Squirrel Girl. And that's not the story *I* heard.
I know, right? I didn't want to say this, but I--
So now I'll tell you the *real* story about the *real* Squirrel Girl.
Does your story involve Bass Lass? Does it get into her powers some, like can she be distracted by such things as brightly-colored lures, or--
No. My story's got something *even better...*
Clones.
Oooh, I love those!
They're like the people I already like, but fake and therefore way more interesting!
All right. Well, prepare yourselves, for I am now about to reveal to you...

...a story that if I were to give it a title I believe I would be forced to call...

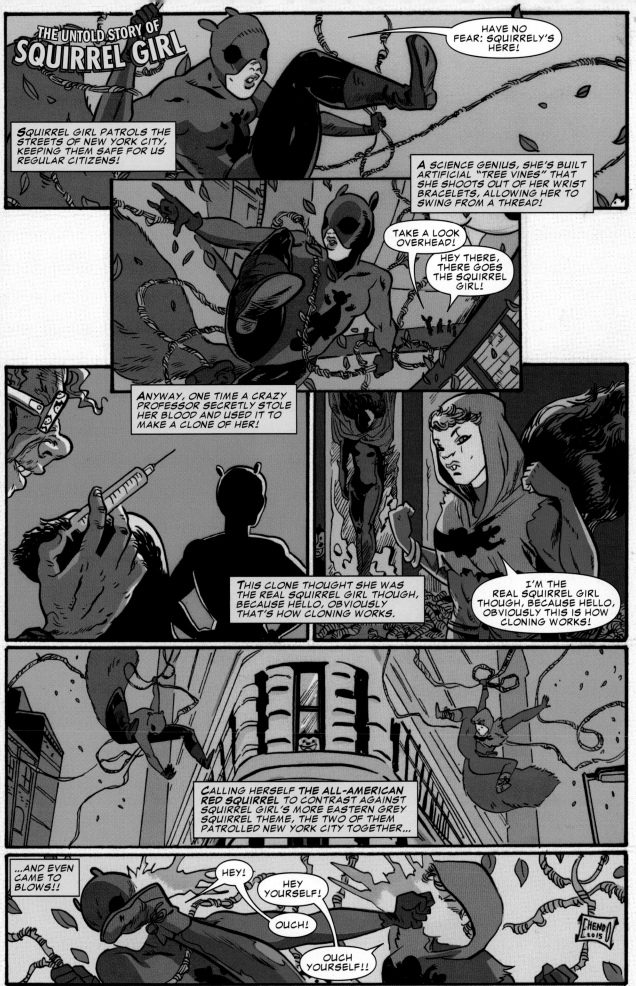

THE UNTOLD STORY OF **SQUIRREL GIRL**

HAVE NO FEAR; SQUIRRELY'S HERE!

SQUIRREL GIRL PATROLS THE STREETS OF NEW YORK CITY, KEEPING THEM SAFE FOR US REGULAR CITIZENS!

A SCIENCE GENIUS, SHE'S BUILT ARTIFICIAL "TREE VINES" THAT SHE SHOOTS OUT OF HER WRIST BRACELETS, ALLOWING HER TO SWING FROM A THREAD!

TAKE A LOOK OVERHEAD!

HEY THERE, THERE GOES THE SQUIRREL GIRL!

ANYWAY, ONE TIME A CRAZY PROFESSOR SECRETLY STOLE HER BLOOD AND USED IT TO MAKE A CLONE OF HER!

THIS CLONE THOUGHT SHE WAS THE REAL SQUIRREL GIRL THOUGH, BECAUSE HELLO, OBVIOUSLY THAT'S HOW CLONING WORKS.

I'M THE REAL SQUIRREL GIRL THOUGH, BECAUSE HELLO, OBVIOUSLY THIS IS HOW CLONING WORKS!

CALLING HERSELF THE ALL-AMERICAN RED SQUIRREL TO CONTRAST AGAINST SQUIRREL GIRL'S MORE EASTERN GREY SQUIRREL THEME, THE TWO OF THEM PATROLLED NEW YORK CITY TOGETHER...

...AND EVEN CAME TO BLOWS!!

HEY!

HEY YOURSELF!

OUCH!

OUCH YOURSELF!!

Hey, this reminds me: with great power doesn't come great responsibility! With great power *actually* comes great joules per second, or "watts," the integral of which over time measures the work performed. Librarians: please go ahead and file this comic in the "WOW! SCIENCE FACTS" section of the library.

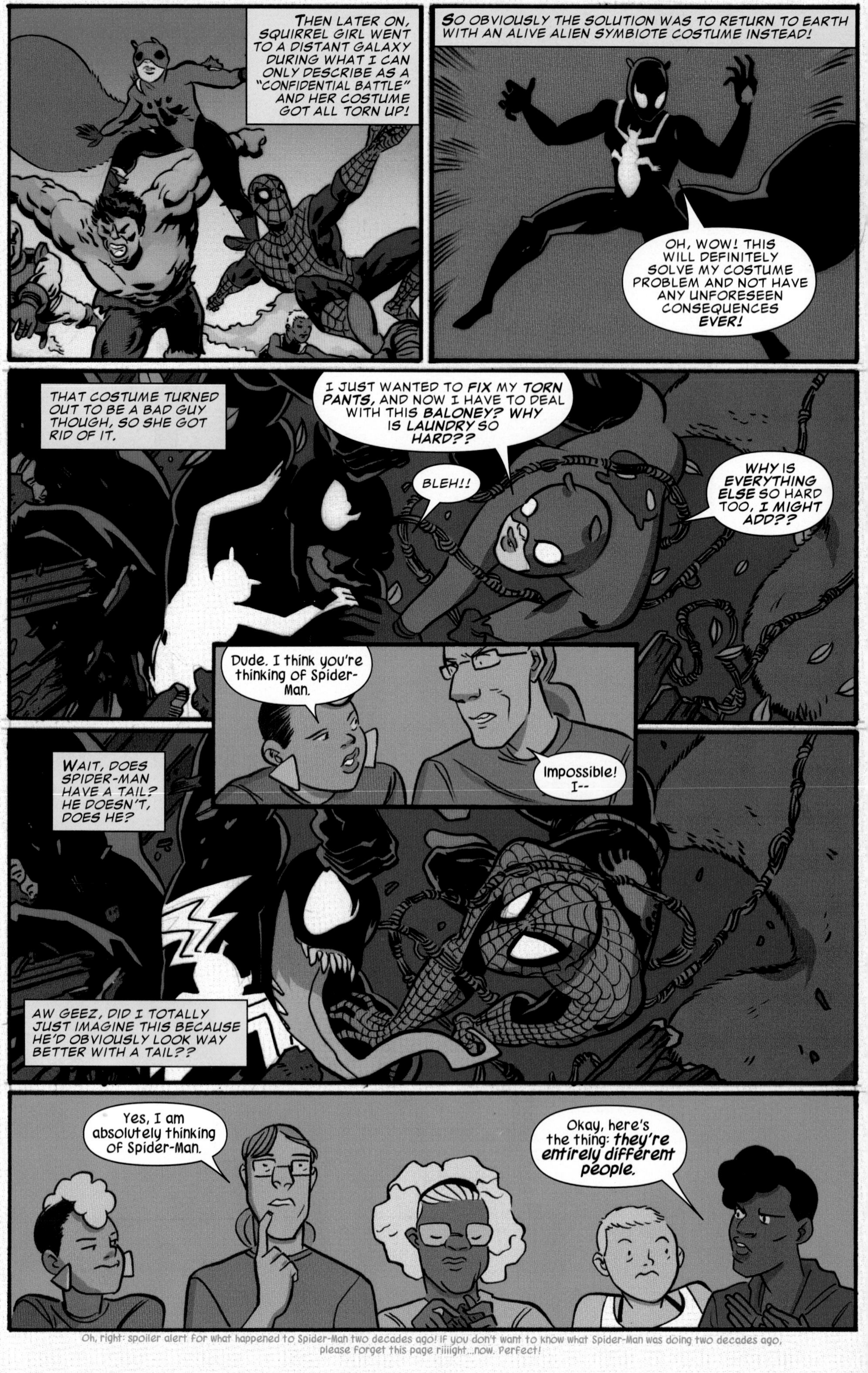
THEN LATER ON, SQUIRREL GIRL WENT TO A DISTANT GALAXY DURING WHAT I CAN ONLY DESCRIBE AS A "CONFIDENTIAL BATTLE" AND HER COSTUME GOT ALL TORN UP!
SO OBVIOUSLY THE SOLUTION WAS TO RETURN TO EARTH WITH AN ALIVE ALIEN SYMBIOTE COSTUME INSTEAD!
OH, WOW! THIS WILL DEFINITELY SOLVE MY COSTUME PROBLEM AND NOT HAVE ANY UNFORESEEN CONSEQUENCES EVER!
THAT COSTUME TURNED OUT TO BE A BAD GUY THOUGH, SO SHE GOT RID OF IT.
I JUST WANTED TO FIX MY TORN PANTS, AND NOW I HAVE TO DEAL WITH THIS BALONEY? WHY IS LAUNDRY SO HARD??
BLEH!!
WHY IS EVERYTHING ELSE SO HARD TOO, I MIGHT ADD??
Dude. I think you're thinking of Spider-Man.
Impossible! I--
WAIT, DOES SPIDER-MAN HAVE A TAIL? HE DOESN'T, DOES HE?
AW GEEZ, DID I TOTALLY JUST IMAGINE THIS BECAUSE HE'D OBVIOUSLY LOOK WAY BETTER WITH A TAIL??
Yes, I am absolutely thinking of Spider-Man.
Okay, here's the thing: they're entirely different people.

Oh, right: spoiler alert for what happened to Spider-Man two decades ago! If you don't want to know what Spider-Man was doing two decades ago, please forget this page riiiight...now. Perfect!

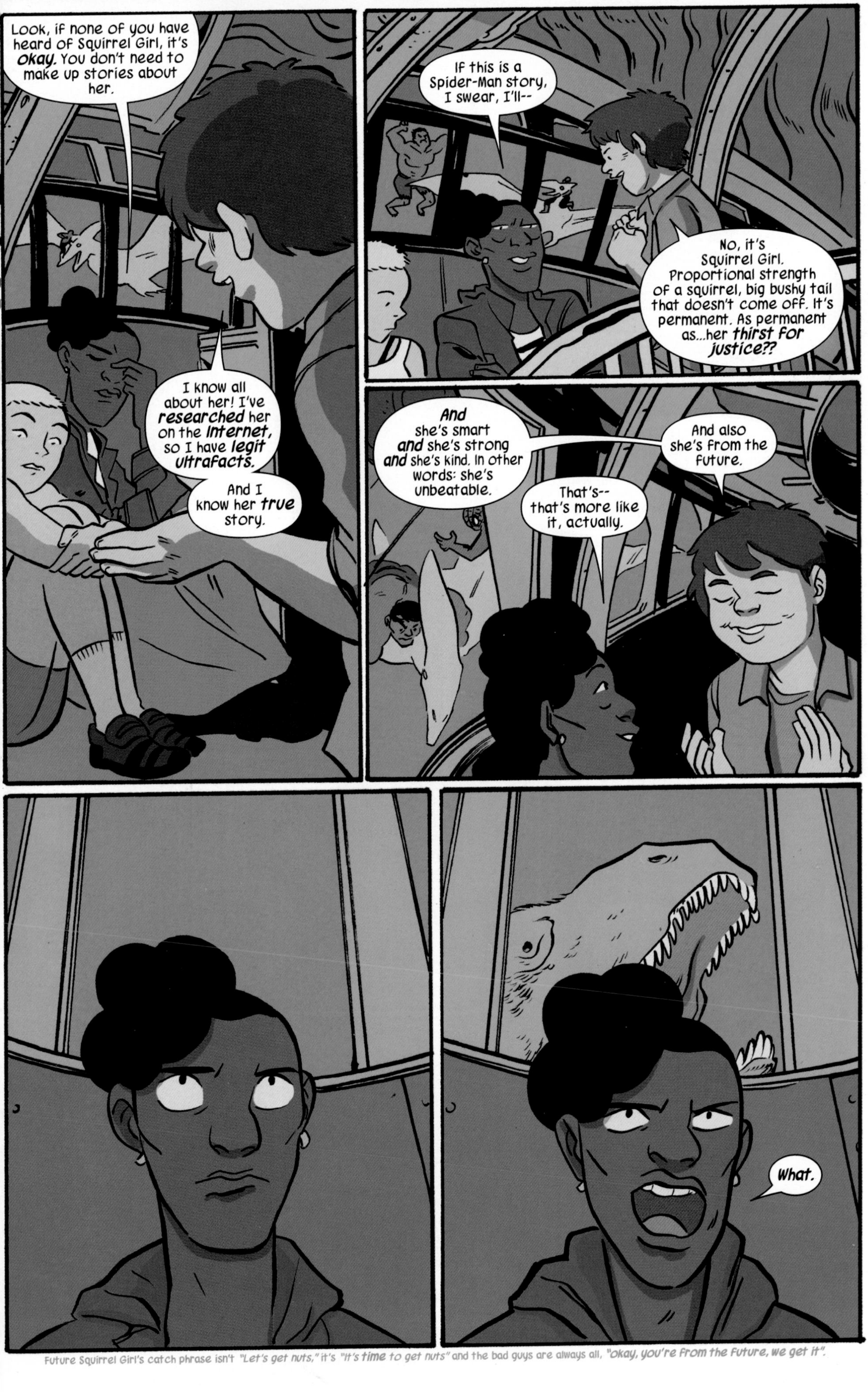
Look, if none of you have heard of Squirrel Girl, it's okay. You don't need to make up stories about her.
I know all about her! I've researched her on the Internet, so I have legit ultrafacts.
And I know her true story.
If this is a Spider-Man story, I swear, I'll--
No, it's Squirrel Girl. Proportional strength of a squirrel, big bushy tail that doesn't come off. It's permanent. As permanent as...her thirst for justice??
And she's smart and she's strong and she's kind. In other words: she's unbeatable.
And also she's from the future.
That's-- that's more like it, actually.
What.

Future Squirrel Girl's catch phrase isn't "Let's get nuts," it's "It's time to get nuts" and the bad guys are always all, "okay, you're from the future, we get it".

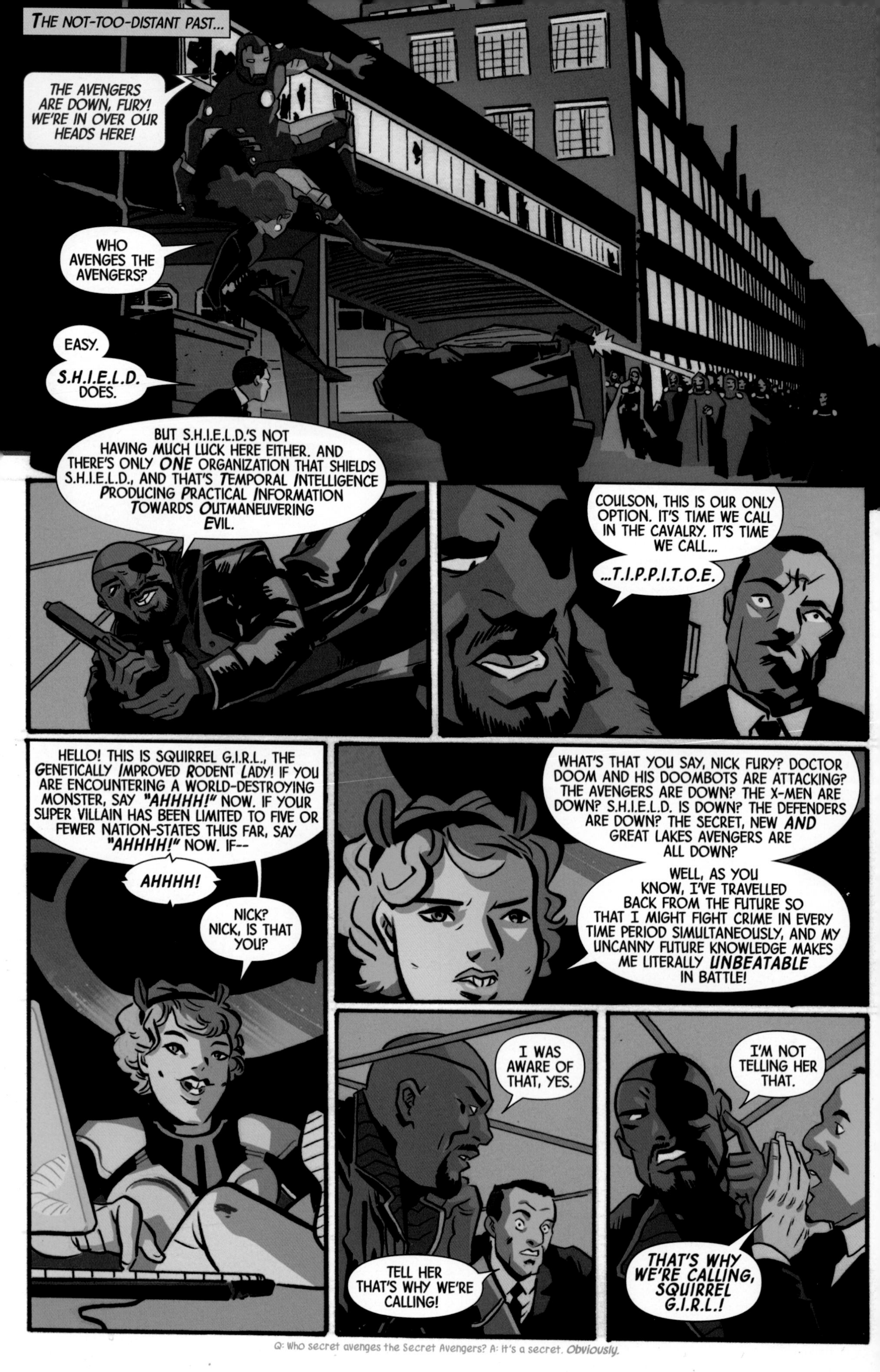
THE NOT-TOO-DISTANT PAST...
THE AVENGERS ARE DOWN, FURY! WE'RE IN OVER OUR HEADS HERE!
WHO AVENGES THE AVENGERS?
EASY.
S.H.I.E.L.D. DOES.
BUT S.H.I.E.L.D.'S NOT HAVING MUCH LUCK HERE EITHER. AND THERE'S ONLY ONE ORGANIZATION THAT SHIELDS S.H.I.E.L.D., AND THAT'S TEMPORAL INTELLIGENCE PRODUCING PRACTICAL INFORMATION TOWARDS OUTMANEUVERING EVIL.
COULSON, THIS IS OUR ONLY OPTION. IT'S TIME WE CALL IN THE CAVALRY. IT'S TIME WE CALL...
...T.I.P.P.I.T.O.E.
HELLO! THIS IS SQUIRREL G.I.R.L., THE GENETICALLY IMPROVED RODENT LADY! IF YOU ARE ENCOUNTERING A WORLD-DESTROYING MONSTER, SAY "AHHHH!" NOW. IF YOUR SUPER VILLAIN HAS BEEN LIMITED TO FIVE OR FEWER NATION-STATES THUS FAR, SAY "AHHHH!" NOW. IF--
AHHHH!
NICK? NICK, IS THAT YOU?
WHAT'S THAT YOU SAY, NICK FURY? DOCTOR DOOM AND HIS DOOMBOTS ARE ATTACKING? THE AVENGERS ARE DOWN? THE X-MEN ARE DOWN? S.H.I.E.L.D. IS DOWN? THE DEFENDERS ARE DOWN? THE SECRET, NEW AND GREAT LAKES AVENGERS ARE ALL DOWN?
WELL, AS YOU KNOW, I'VE TRAVELLED BACK FROM THE FUTURE SO THAT I MIGHT FIGHT CRIME IN EVERY TIME PERIOD SIMULTANEOUSLY, AND MY UNCANNY FUTURE KNOWLEDGE MAKES ME LITERALLY UNBEATABLE IN BATTLE!
I WAS AWARE OF THAT, YES.
TELL HER THAT'S WHY WE'RE CALLING!
I'M NOT TELLING HER THAT.
THAT'S WHY WE'RE CALLING, SQUIRREL G.I.R.L.!

Q: Who secret avenges the Secret Avengers? A: It's a secret. *Obviously.*

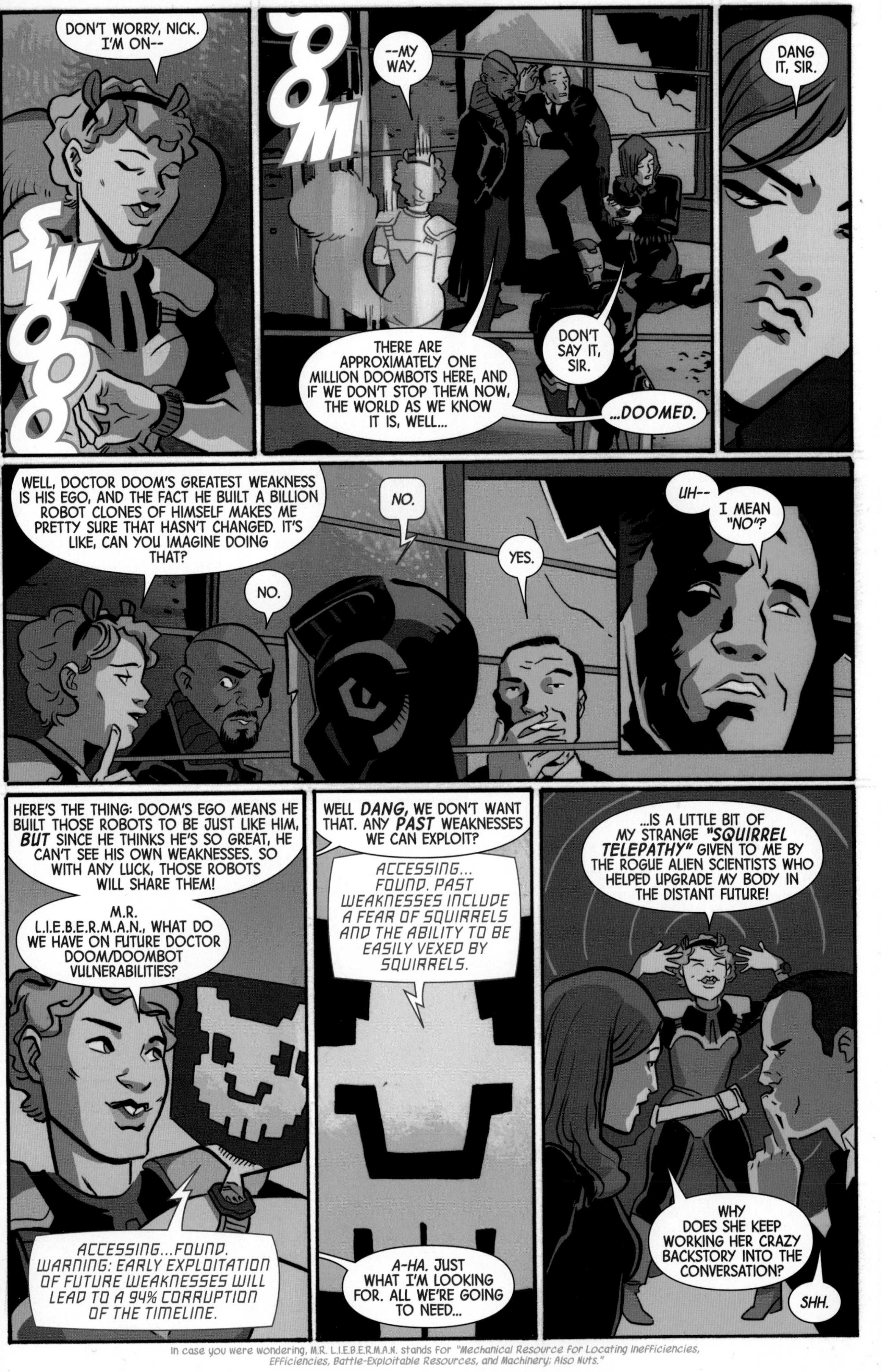
DON'T WORRY, NICK. I'M ON--
SWOOOO
OOOM
--MY WAY.
THERE ARE APPROXIMATELY ONE MILLION DOOMBOTS HERE, AND IF WE DON'T STOP THEM NOW, THE WORLD AS WE KNOW IT IS, WELL...
DON'T SAY IT, SIR.
...DOOMED.
DANG IT, SIR.
WELL, DOCTOR DOOM'S GREATEST WEAKNESS IS HIS EGO, AND THE FACT HE BUILT A BILLION ROBOT CLONES OF HIMSELF MAKES ME PRETTY SURE THAT HASN'T CHANGED. IT'S LIKE, CAN YOU IMAGINE DOING THAT?
NO.
NO.
YES.
UH--
I MEAN "NO"?
HERE'S THE THING: DOOM'S EGO MEANS HE BUILT THOSE ROBOTS TO BE JUST LIKE HIM, BUT SINCE HE THINKS HE'S SO GREAT, HE CAN'T SEE HIS OWN WEAKNESSES. SO WITH ANY LUCK, THOSE ROBOTS WILL SHARE THEM!
M.R. L.I.E.B.E.R.M.A.N., WHAT DO WE HAVE ON FUTURE DOCTOR DOOM/DOOMBOT VULNERABILITIES?
ACCESSING...FOUND. WARNING: EARLY EXPLOITATION OF FUTURE WEAKNESSES WILL LEAD TO A 94% CORRUPTION OF THE TIMELINE.
WELL DANG, WE DON'T WANT THAT. ANY PAST WEAKNESSES WE CAN EXPLOIT?
ACCESSING... FOUND. PAST WEAKNESSES INCLUDE A FEAR OF SQUIRRELS AND THE ABILITY TO BE EASILY VEXED BY SQUIRRELS.
A-HA. JUST WHAT I'M LOOKING FOR. ALL WE'RE GOING TO NEED...
...IS A LITTLE BIT OF MY STRANGE "SQUIRREL TELEPATHY" GIVEN TO ME BY THE ROGUE ALIEN SCIENTISTS WHO HELPED UPGRADE MY BODY IN THE DISTANT FUTURE!
WHY DOES SHE KEEP WORKING HER CRAZY BACKSTORY INTO THE CONVERSATION?
SHH.

In case you were wondering, M.R. L.I.E.B.E.R.M.A.N. stands for *"Mechanical Resource For Locating Inefficiencies, Efficiencies, Battle-Exploitable Resources, and Machinery; Also Nuts."*

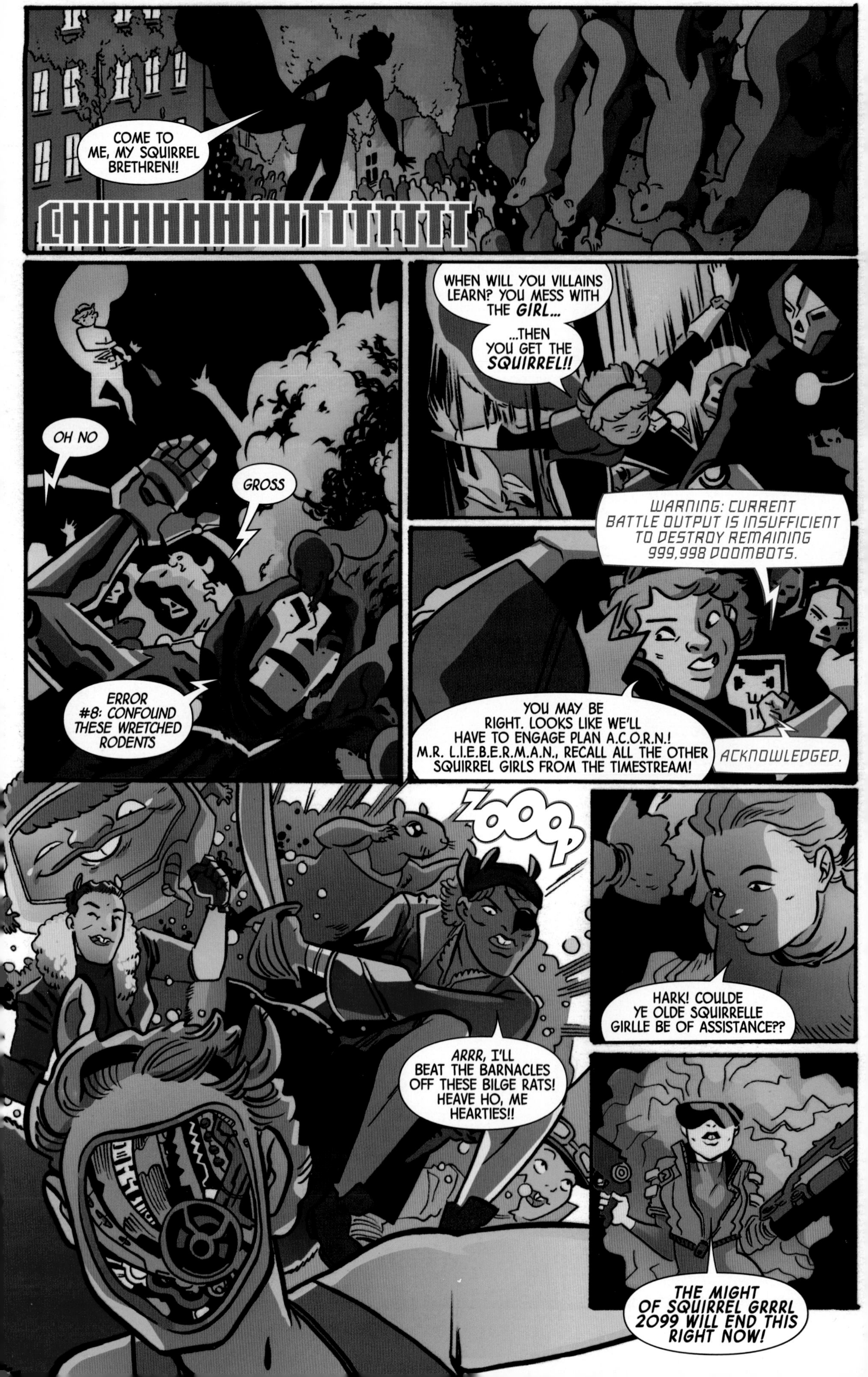
COME TO ME, MY SQUIRREL BRETHREN!!
CHHHHHHHHTTTTTTT
OH NO
GROSS
ERROR #8: CONFOUND THESE WRETCHED RODENTS
WHEN WILL YOU VILLAINS LEARN? YOU MESS WITH THE GIRL...
...THEN YOU GET THE SQUIRREL!!
WARNING: CURRENT BATTLE OUTPUT IS INSUFFICIENT TO DESTROY REMAINING 999,998 DOOMBOTS.
YOU MAY BE RIGHT. LOOKS LIKE WE'LL HAVE TO ENGAGE PLAN A.C.O.R.N.! M.R. L.I.E.B.E.R.M.A.N., RECALL ALL THE OTHER SQUIRREL GIRLS FROM THE TIMESTREAM!
ACKNOWLEDGED.
ZOOOP
ARRR, I'LL BEAT THE BARNACLES OFF THESE BILGE RATS! HEAVE HO, ME HEARTIES!!
HARK! COULDE YE OLDE SQUIRRELLE GIRLLE BE OF ASSISTANCE??
THE MIGHT OF SQUIRREL GRRRL 2099 WILL END THIS RIGHT NOW!

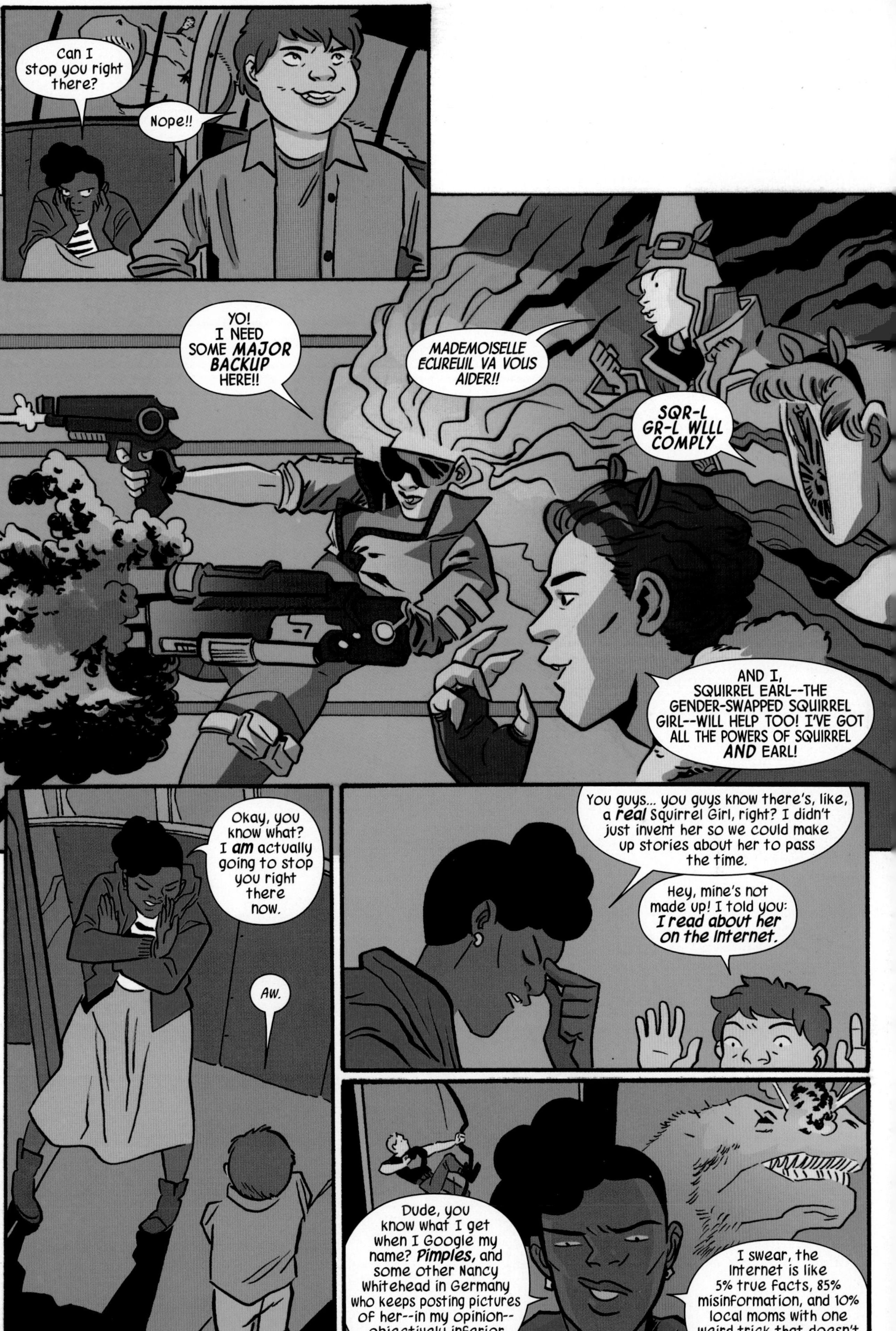
Can I stop you right there?
Nope!!
YO! I NEED SOME MAJOR BACKUP HERE!!
MADEMOISELLE ECUREUIL VA VOUS AIDER!!
SQR-L GR-L WLLL COMPLY
AND I, SQUIRREL EARL--THE GENDER-SWAPPED SQUIRREL GIRL--WILL HELP TOO! I'VE GOT ALL THE POWERS OF SQUIRREL AND EARL!
Okay, you know what? I am actually going to stop you right there now.
Aw.
You guys... you guys know there's, like, a real Squirrel Girl, right? I didn't just invent her so we could make up stories about her to pass the time.
Hey, mine's not made up! I told you: I read about her on the Internet.
Dude, you know what I get when I Google my name? Pimples, and some other Nancy Whitehead in Germany who keeps posting pictures of her--in my opinion--objectively inferior cat. That's it.
I swear, the Internet is like 5% true facts, 85% misinformation, and 10% local moms with one weird trick that doesn't even friggin' work.

And it's not even that weird, either. They should advertise it as one regular trick that sucks! Honestly, sometimes I wonder why I click on banner ads.

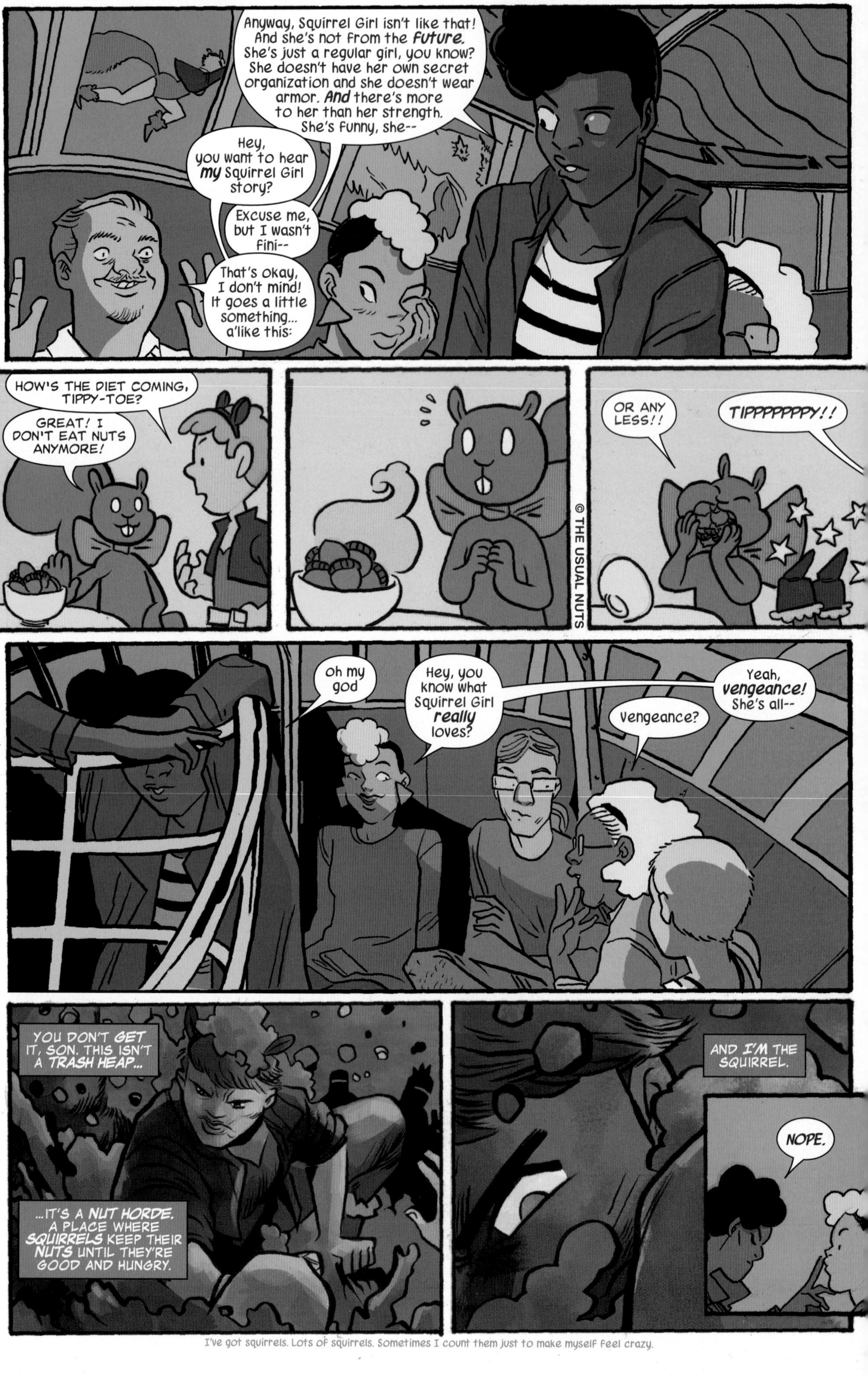
Anyway, Squirrel Girl isn't like that! And she's not from the *future.* She's just a regular girl, you know? She doesn't have her own secret organization and she doesn't wear armor. *And* there's more to her than her strength. She's funny, she--
Hey, you want to hear *my* Squirrel Girl story?
Excuse me, but I wasn't fini--
That's okay, I don't mind! It goes a little something... a'like this:
HOW'S THE DIET COMING, TIPPY-TOE?
GREAT! I DON'T EAT NUTS ANYMORE!
© THE USUAL NUTS
OR ANY LESS!!
TIPPPPPPPY!!
Oh my god
Hey, you know what Squirrel Girl *really* loves?
Vengeance?
Yeah, *vengeance!* She's all--
YOU DON'T *GET* IT, SON. THIS ISN'T A *TRASH HEAP...*
...IT'S A *NUT HORDE.* A PLACE WHERE *SQUIRRELS* KEEP THEIR *NUTS* UNTIL THEY'RE GOOD AND HUNGRY.
AND *I'M* THE SQUIRREL.
NOPE.

I've got squirrels. Lots of squirrels. Sometimes I count them just to make myself feel crazy.

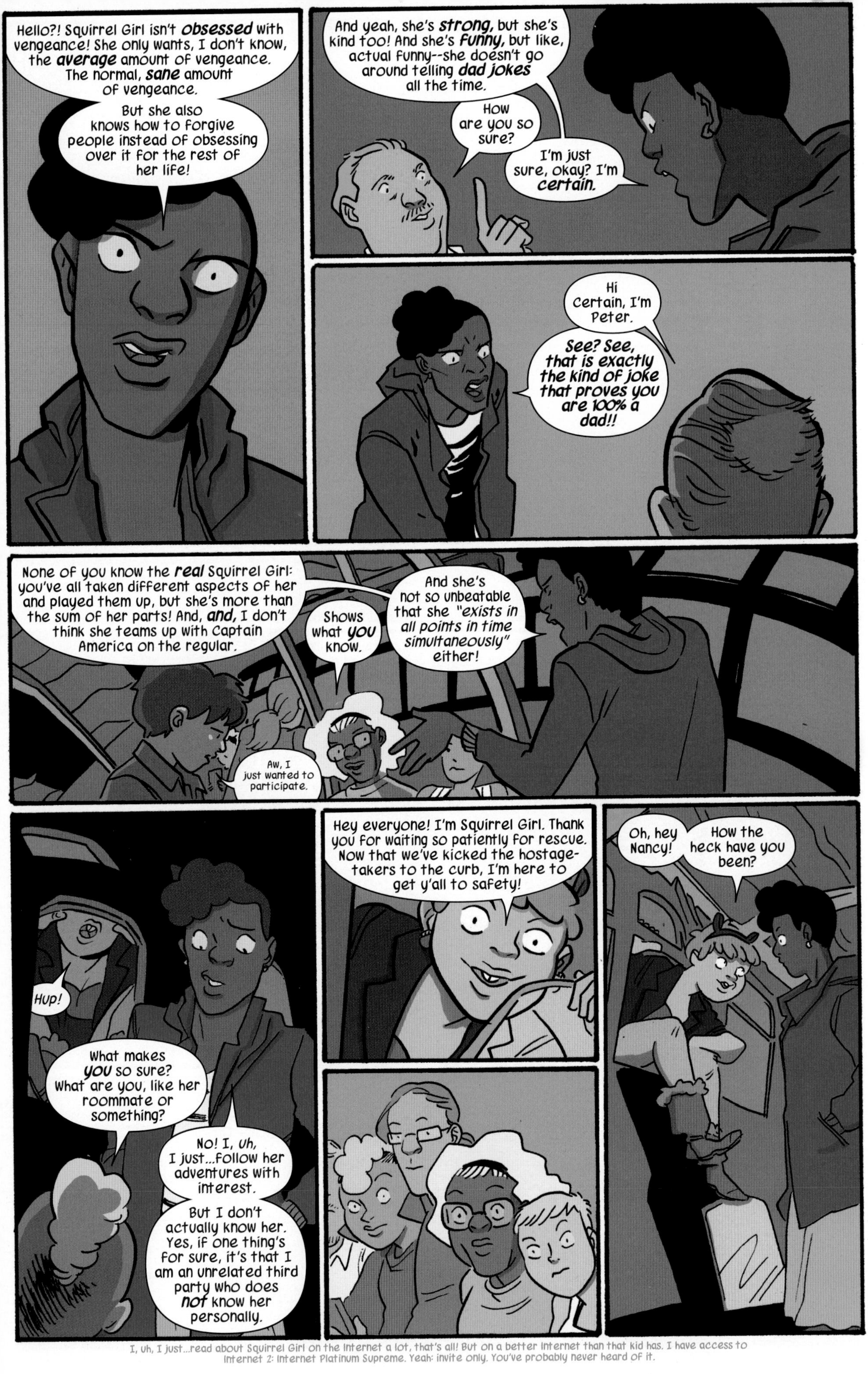
Hello?! Squirrel Girl isn't obsessed with vengeance! She only wants, I don't know, the average amount of vengeance. The normal, sane amount of vengeance.
But she also knows how to forgive people instead of obsessing over it for the rest of her life!
And yeah, she's strong, but she's kind too! And she's funny, but like, actual funny--she doesn't go around telling dad jokes all the time.
How are you so sure?
I'm just sure, okay? I'm certain.
Hi Certain, I'm Peter.
See? See, that is exactly the kind of joke that proves you are 100% a dad!!
None of you know the real Squirrel Girl: you've all taken different aspects of her and played them up, but she's more than the sum of her parts! And, and, I don't think she teams up with Captain America on the regular.
Shows what you know.
And she's not so unbeatable that she "exists in all points in time simultaneously" either!
Aw, I just wanted to participate.
Hup!
What makes you so sure? What are you, like her roommate or something?
No! I, uh, I just...follow her adventures with interest.
But I don't actually know her. Yes, if one thing's for sure, it's that I am an unrelated third party who does not know her personally.
Hey everyone! I'm Squirrel Girl. Thank you for waiting so patiently for rescue. Now that we've kicked the hostage-takers to the curb, I'm here to get y'all to safety!
Oh, hey Nancy!
How the heck have you been?

I, uh, I just...read about Squirrel Girl on the Internet a lot, that's all! But on a better Internet than that kid has. I have access to Internet 2: Internet Platinum Supreme. Yeah: invite only. You've probably never heard of it.

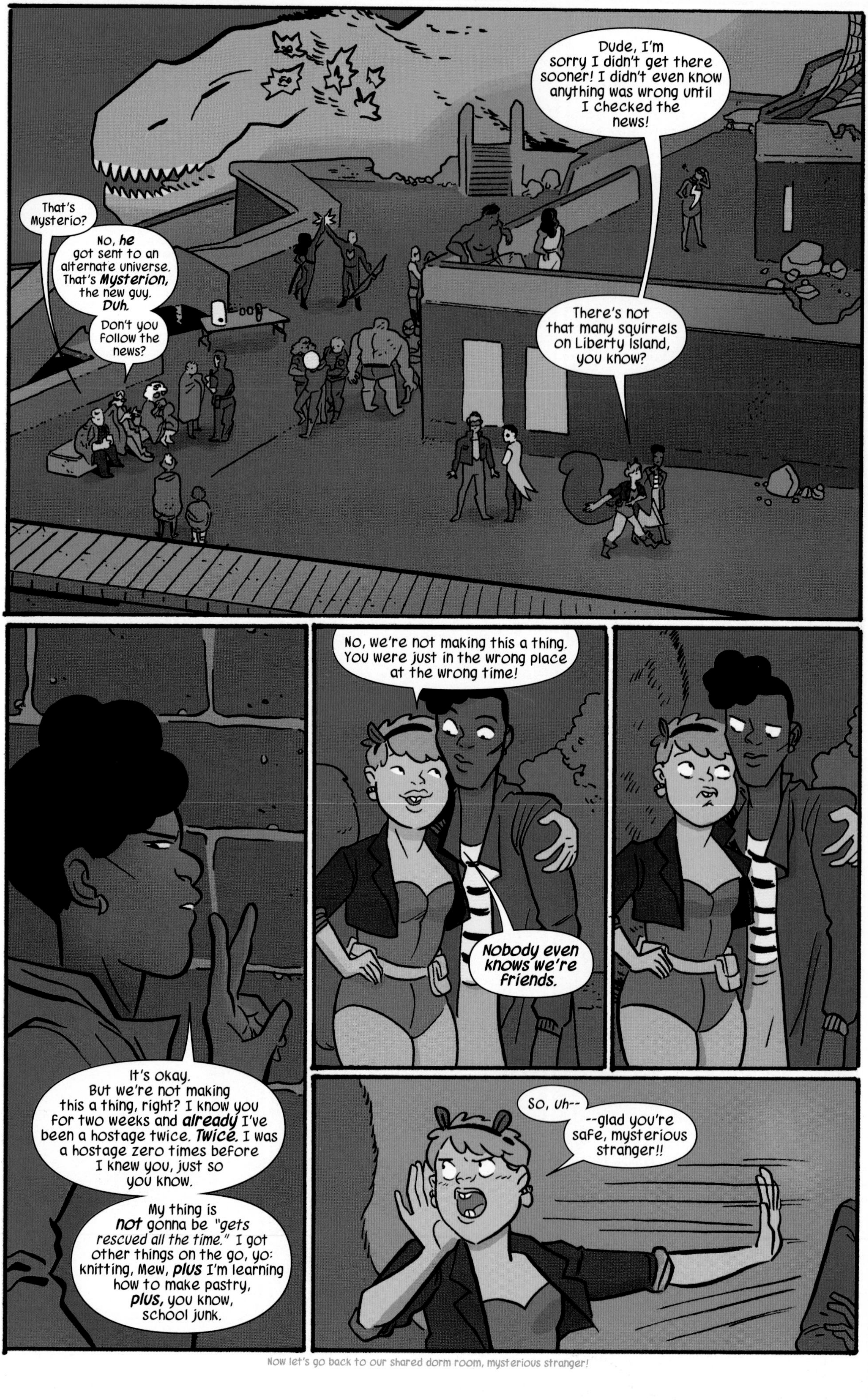
Dude, I'm sorry I didn't get there sooner! I didn't even know anything was wrong until I checked the news!
That's Mysterio?
No, he got sent to an alternate universe. That's Mysterion, the new guy. Duh.
Don't you follow the news?
There's not that many squirrels on Liberty Island, you know?
It's okay. But we're not making this a thing, right? I know you for two weeks and already I've been a hostage twice. Twice. I was a hostage zero times before I knew you, just so you know.
My thing is not gonna be "gets rescued all the time." I got other things on the go, yo: knitting, Mew, plus I'm learning how to make pastry, plus, you know, school junk.
No, we're not making this a thing. You were just in the wrong place at the wrong time!
Nobody even knows we're friends.
So, uh--
--glad you're safe, mysterious stranger!!

Now let's go back to our shared dorm room, mysterious stranger!

Oh, by the way, you should know that we kinda told Squirrel Girl stories while we were waiting.

No way! Seriously? That's awesome! Did you tell them about my *exploits*? How I got Kraven to live in the ocean and beat Whiplash with my sweet *electricity knowledge* and then stopped *Galactus* on the *moon* with the power of *friendship*??

Also, dude, you need to change your name to something like "Squirrel Girl Who Is Not From The Future, Didn't Hang Around With Captain America in The '50s, Doesn't Tell Dad Jokes, And Doesn't Have Robot Duplicates, Also: Not Spider-Man."

NO. I don't think they would've believed me anyway.

Whoa, robot duplicates? *Dude.* You have to tell me all *about* this.

It sounds *totally* nuts!

Oh wow! You think she's secretly the robot one??

She did the nut pun!!

Man! You can't even see her abs in that stupid costume.

The End!

WHO WILL BE THE NEWEST FRIEND OF

the unbeatable Squirrel Girl

THOR	ALSO THOR???	INVISIBLE WOMAN	CHIPMUNK HUNK	JOE QUESADA
HOWARD T. DUCK	SPEEDBALL	NIELS	ROCK	KRAZLER
KOI BOI	DEVIL DINOSAUR	GROOT		

PICK TWO!
(Answer inside)

NEXT MONTH...

MORE AMAZING ADVENTURES WITH YOUR FAVORITE FANTASTIC HEROES!

♪ S.G.W.I.N.F.T.F.D.H.A.W.C.A.I.T.5.D.T.D.J.A.D.H.R.D.A.N.S.M., S.G.W.I.N.F.T.F.D.H.A.W.C.A.I.T.5.D.T.D.J.A.D.H.R.D.A.N.S.M., powers of both S.G.W.I.N.F.T.F.D.H.A.W.C.A.I.T.5.D.T.D.J.A.D.H.R.D.A.N.S.M. and girl ♪

Hope everyone enjoyed this issue! Our sincerest thanks/apologies to John Romita Sr., Jack Kirby, George Roussos, Dick Sprang, Edmond Hamilton, Todd McFarlane, Greg Wright, Mike Zeck, Christie Scheele, Chris Samnee, Matthew Wilson, Chris Giarrusso, Frank Miller and Lynn Varley for providing inspiration for the various "Squirrel Girl tails." Now on to your letters!

Congratulations on a tremendous first three issues of THE UNBEATABLE SQUIRREL GIRL! I am beyond pleased to see this comic and constantly amazed at how good it is. Like other commentators, I have largely abandoned other titles by the two big boys because everything out there seems bloated, grim, derivative, and tiresome. But Squirrel Girl has breathed new life into my pull list at my Friendly Local Comic Shop and I am exhausting the patience of my friends by telling them over and over again how they need to buy this book. Extra copies are being set aside as birthday and Christmas gifts. All I need now is an updated Heroclix figure so I can bring SG to tabletop gaming, a way to locate (and afford) all the wonderful alternate covers, and a Tippy-Toe bath toy. (To keep the Submariner from getting up to anything naughty.)

Excellent work, please continue until ALL evil has been vanquished from EVERY multiverse!

Best regards,
Kevin Hendryx
Austin, TX
WWSGD

RYAN: Thanks! Though as we have now had FOUR issues (well, now FIVE) since you wrote your letter, hopefully the next letter you write us won't be "the first three were great but then WHOAH, WHAT HAPPENED??" (please do not write this letter). And my favorite thing to say (well, about comics) is that it's a medium, not a genre, and that there's room enough for all sorts of stories here. So let's tell all sorts of stories!

p.s.: WWSGD? CLEARLY she would eat nuts and/or kick butts.

ERICA: AH! Such kind words! It warms my heart. I love having a diversity of stories to pick from and I think we're starting to get more of that at the forefront now. My own comic collection spans titles from Uncle Scrooge to Sky Doll. But honestly we're not trying to do something different, we're just doing something that we'd want to read ourselves.

I absolutely adore Squirrel Girl. She is my favorite super hero of all time in the history of ever. I recommend this comic to everybody I know who is into comics. And I'm really thankful my brother showed me this book. I find her a very relatable character and I love the humor in the comics. I also appreciate that she isn't like any other comic book character I've come across and the comic is something anybody can enjoy. Keep up the amazing work you guys are doing! Also when decorating Easter eggs this year I made Doreen Green/ Squirrel Girl and Tippy Toe themed Easter eggs so I've attached a picture for you guys.

Susie S.

RYAN: Awesome! I love when people hear about comics by someone sharing their issue, because I feel like comics live when they're shared around and not stuffed in a bag and put into a box. Thank you for the kind words, and thank your brother for me too! And those eggs are off the HOOK.

Dear purveyors of fine squirrel literature,
I've never written into a comic before, I don't even read comics very often, but after arriving at the store too early... and then too late, I finally got copies of Squirrel Girl and felt like I had to thank you!

I followed Squirrel Girl during her time in the GLA, and I am ecstatic to see her headlining her own title. I've never really felt a strong connection to any heroes in the past, but I can really relate to Squirrel Girl, she just feels down to earth. On top of the excellent writing and characterization, the art is just adorable. Congratulations on a great release, I don't even have any questions (unless you can suggest a good one), I just wanted to say thanks for getting me interested in comics for the first time in years.

Thanks,
Robert 'MrAptronym'

RYAN: Thanks, Robert! And let me suggest a question for you: "How come Doreen hasn't met any flying squirrels yet?" And the answer is that, until LITERALLY YESTERDAY when Erica proved me wrong, I thought that there weren't any in North America. I saw some flying squirrels at a zoo when I was a kid and I guess I assumed all zoo animals were from far away? Anyway, turns out they DO live on at least the same continent that Doreen lives on, so I'm a big dummy but at least I'm slightly smarter now, and we'll hopefully see some in the comic sooner rather than later.

ERICA: The 44 varieties of flying squirrel live in North America, Europe, and Asia, but there's like one kind in America and one that spans from Finland to Japan and then the other 42 are all in Asia. So, really Asia is still has the best flying-squirrel-to-continent ratio. Oh, wait, the original question wasn't about flying squirrels. I'm glad you like our take on Doreen, being a long time Squirrel Girl fan!

Dear Ryan & Erica,
What's with all this talk of Chipmunk Hunk? Are you teasing us with a prospective Woodland Avengers? I could definitely get behind that series.

Keep up the good work,
Mitch

RYAN: I wasn't planning the Woodland Avengers, but now that you mention it it's all I can think about, so let's say... DEFINITELY YES, THAT IS EXACTLY WHAT IS GOING TO HAPPEN.

ERICA: I thought we weren't supposed to talk about the Yosemite Avengers until after Secret Wars.

Dear Ryan & Erica,
Thank you for teaming up an empowered girl with the world's most charismatic microfauna. You have made a lot of female squirrel biologists very happy. (By "a lot," I mean proportionally... sadly, we aren't that numerous.) I especially appreciate Doreen's sensible footwear choice and her blind optimism about the coolness of squirrels. Please keep making this comic FOREVER. Also, if you can swing it, please introduce a paleontologist who is woefully dull compared to Squirrel Girl. For an added touch of realism. My boyfriend studies theropods, and I'm sure I don't have to say who's the bigger hit at parties.

Lastly, please enjoy this portrait of me with some of my squirrel friends. I would have also included a photo of my pre-Unbeatable Squirrel Girl costume, but the furry one-piece bathing suit is, erm, a little alarming.

Sincerely,
Amanda

RYAN: Amanda! I didn't even NOTICE the squirrels at first because they match your whole ensemble so well! I had never considered using baby squirrels as a fashion accessory until now but clearly I was not dreaming big enough. That is an amazing picture. I love it.

As someone who was always big into theropods from my Dinosaur Comics strip and who is now big into squirrels for obvious reasons, I feel like I can't decide who is cooler between you and your boyfriend! Probably you're both tied for first? But in any case I feel like you and your boyfriend and I could share some pretty friggin' scintillating conversation at cool parties, so please attend some cool parties soon and invite me, THANKS IN ADVANCE.

ERICA: I think I know who the winner is, because I'm pretty sure small mammals made it past the KT extinction. Amanda, I am 100% jealous of your woodland creature friends. So many of us watched Sleeping Beauty (and should totally watch it again because of that Eyvind Earle art) and said, "yes, when I grow up, I'm going to have a woodland posse" but we gave up and moved onto other, lesser endeavors. I salute you.

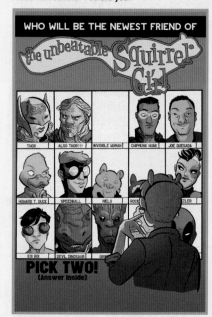

WHO WILL BE THE NEWEST FRIEND OF the unbeatable Squirrel Girl

THOR	ALSO THOR!!!	INVISIBLE WOMAN	CHIPMUNK HUNK	JOE QUESADA
HOWARD T. DUCK	SPEEDBALL	NIELS	ROCK	TZLER
KOI BOI	DEVIL DINOSAUR	GR		

PICK TWO!
(Answer Inside)

Next: HIPPO FIIIIIIIIGHT!

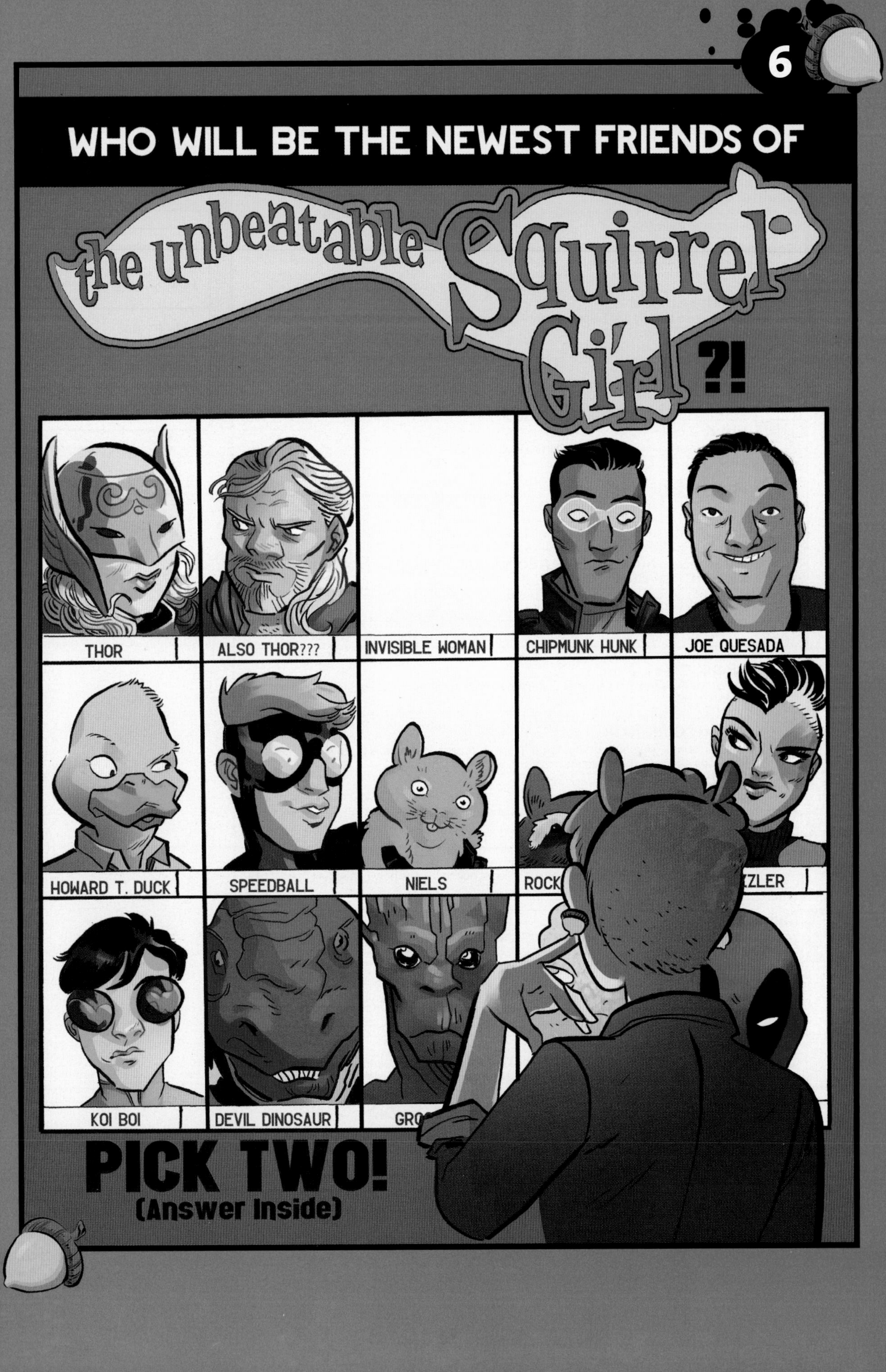
6
WHO WILL BE THE NEWEST FRIENDS OF
the unbeatable Squirrel Girl ?!
THOR
ALSO THOR???
INVISIBLE WOMAN
CHIPMUNK HUNK
JOE QUESADA
HOWARD T. DUCK
SPEEDBALL
NIELS
ROCK
ZLER
KOI BOI
DEVIL DINOSAUR
GRO
PICK TWO!
(Answer Inside)

Doreen Green isn't just a first-year computer science student: she secretly also has all the powers of both squirrel and girl!
She uses her amazing abilities to fight crime **and** be as awesome as possible. You know her as...The Unbeatable Squirrel Girl!
Let's catch up with what she's been up to until now, with...

Squirrel Girl in a nutshell

Squirrel Girl! @unbeatablesg
RT if you helped defeat Mysterion and his ROBOT DINOSAURS and saved the statue of liberty!!

Squirrel Girl! @unbeatablesg
RT @unbeatablesg: RT if you helped defeat Mysterion and his ROBOT DINOSAURS and saved the statue of liberty!!

Squirrel Girl! @unbeatablesg
Yes I did just retweet myself

Squirrel Girl! @unbeatablesg
PROBABLY because I totally just helped defeat Mysterion and his ROBOT DINOSAURS and saved the STATUE OF LIBERTY??

Squirrel Girl! @unbeatablesg
@HULKYSMASHY hey thanks for the RT!

HULK @HULKYSMASHY
@unbeatablesg HULK SMASH PUNY DINOSAUR!!

Squirrel Girl! @unbeatablesg
@HULKYSMASHY haha we sure did!!

HULK @HULKYSMASHY
@unbeatablesg HULK GLAD WHEN SOCIOLOGICAL PROBLEMS CAN BE SOLVED BY SMASHING

Squirrel Girl! @unbeatablesg
@HULKYSMASHY yeah it's always nice when things work out that way actually

CampusBank @campusbank
Good news! We've fixed the giant squirrel-suit-shaped hole in our wall. CampusBank: We've Got Class Too™.

Squirrel Girl! @unbeatablesg
@campusbank okay but let's not forget the only reason that hole is there is because i saved all the hostages

CampusBank @campusbank
We think you'll be INTERESTed in our new savings account fee schedules. CampusBank: We've Got Class Too™.

Squirrel Girl! @unbeatablesg
@campusbank cool pun bro but can we at least acknowledge how i saved all the hostages

CampusBank @campusbank
We can't take all the CREDIT for our new student charge card plans. CampusBank: We've Got Class Too™.

Squirrel Girl! @unbeatablesg
@campusbank sometimes i wonder why i follow so many #brands on social media

Squirrel Girl! @unbeatablesg
Okay everyone, HONESTLY, tell me this wall doesn't look WAY BETTER with a hole:

search!

#hippothehippo

#imwithskrull

#liontomeetyou

#squirrelgirl

#kicksbuttseatsnuts

Oh that poor narrator

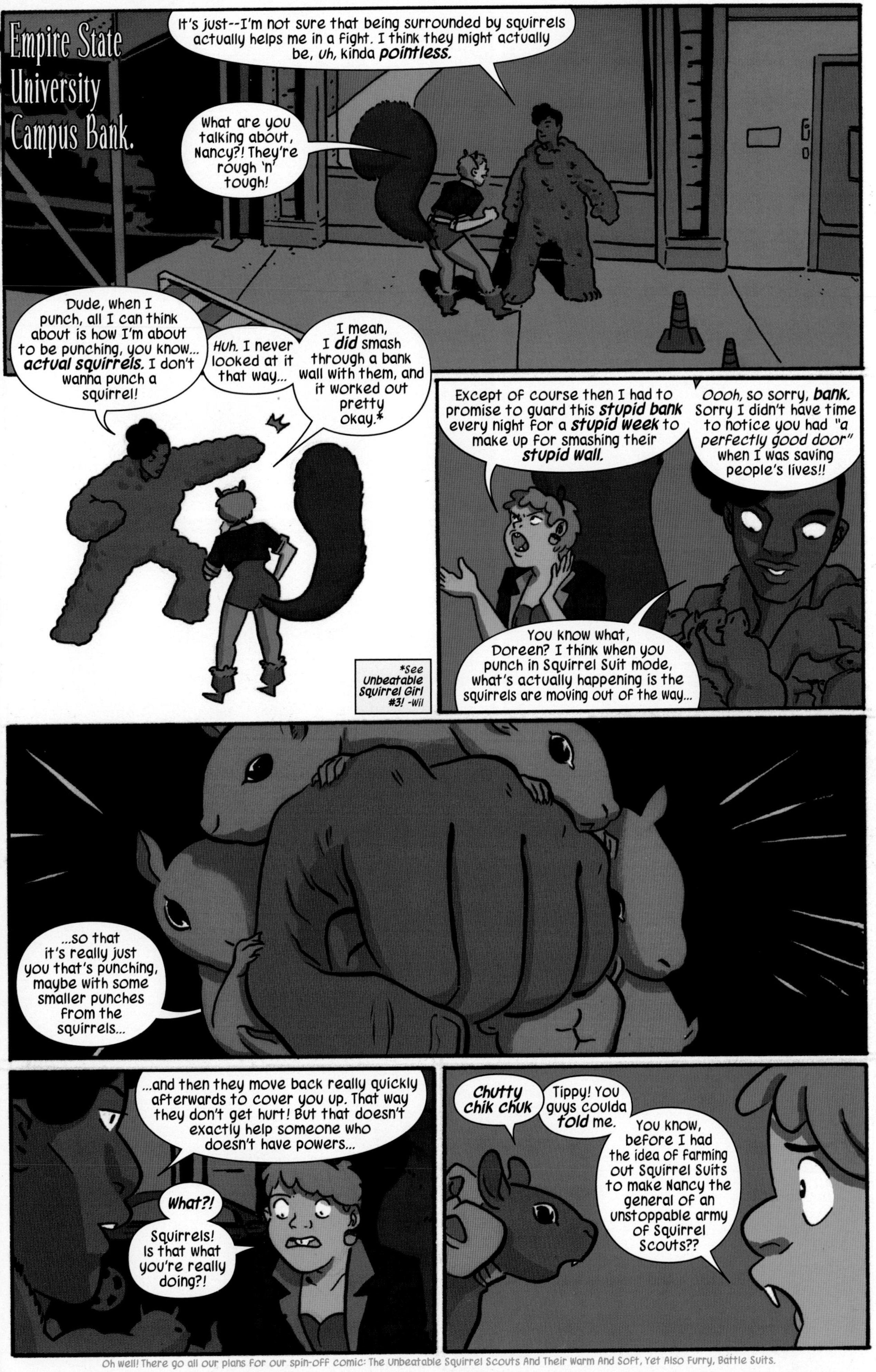

Empire State University Campus Bank.
It's just--I'm not sure that being surrounded by squirrels actually helps me in a fight. I think they might actually be, uh, kinda pointless.
What are you talking about, Nancy?! They're rough 'n' tough!
Dude, when I punch, all I can think about is how I'm about to be punching, you know... actual squirrels. I don't wanna punch a squirrel!
Huh. I never looked at it that way...
I mean, I did smash through a bank wall with them, and it worked out pretty okay.*
*See Unbeatable Squirrel Girl #3! -Wil
Except of course then I had to promise to guard this stupid bank every night for a stupid week to make up for smashing their stupid wall.
Oooh, so sorry, bank. Sorry I didn't have time to notice you had "a perfectly good door" when I was saving people's lives!!
You know what, Doreen? I think when you punch in Squirrel Suit mode, what's actually happening is the squirrels are moving out of the way...
...so that it's really just you that's punching, maybe with some smaller punches from the squirrels...
...and then they move back really quickly afterwards to cover you up. That way they don't get hurt! But that doesn't exactly help someone who doesn't have powers...
What?!
Squirrels! Is that what you're really doing?!
Chutty chik chuk
Tippy! You guys coulda told me.
You know, before I had the idea of farming out Squirrel Suits to make Nancy the general of an unstoppable army of Squirrel Scouts??

Oh well! There go all our plans for our spin-off comic: The Unbeatable Squirrel Scouts And Their Warm And Soft, Yet Also Furry, Battle Suits.

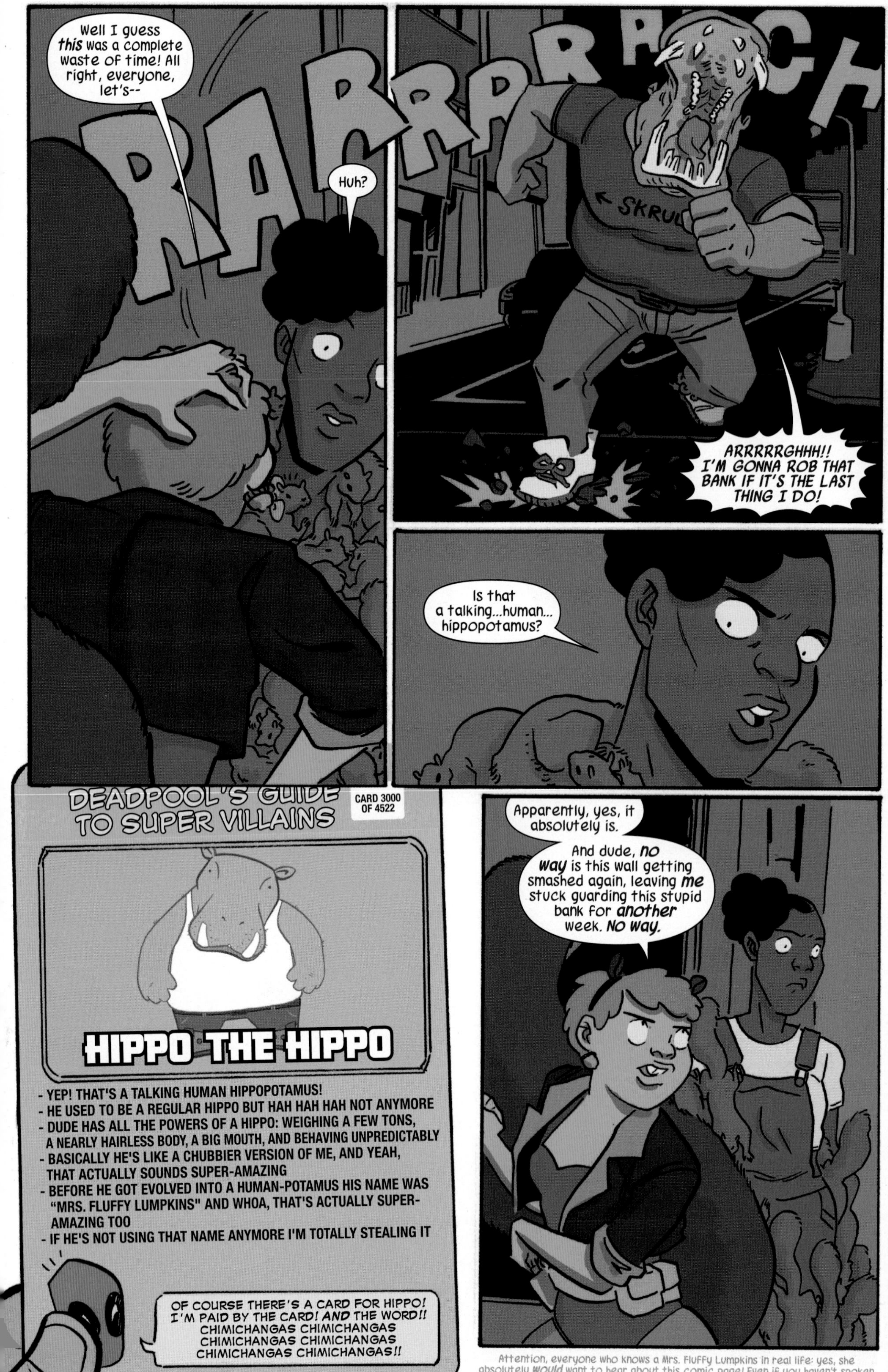

Well I guess *this* was a complete waste of time! All right, everyone, let's--
RARRRRRRAAACH
Huh?
← SKRULL
ARRRRRGHHH!! I'M GONNA ROB THAT BANK IF IT'S THE LAST THING I DO!
Is that a talking...human... hippopotamus?
DEADPOOL'S GUIDE TO SUPER VILLAINS
CARD 3000 OF 4522
HIPPO THE HIPPO
- YEP! THAT'S A TALKING HUMAN HIPPOPOTAMUS!
- HE USED TO BE A REGULAR HIPPO BUT HAH HAH HAH NOT ANYMORE
- DUDE HAS ALL THE POWERS OF A HIPPO: WEIGHING A FEW TONS, A NEARLY HAIRLESS BODY, A BIG MOUTH, AND BEHAVING UNPREDICTABLY
- BASICALLY HE'S LIKE A CHUBBIER VERSION OF ME, AND YEAH, THAT ACTUALLY SOUNDS SUPER-AMAZING
- BEFORE HE GOT EVOLVED INTO A HUMAN-POTAMUS HIS NAME WAS "MRS. FLUFFY LUMPKINS" AND WHOA, THAT'S ACTUALLY SUPER-AMAZING TOO
- IF HE'S NOT USING THAT NAME ANYMORE I'M TOTALLY STEALING IT
OF COURSE THERE'S A CARD FOR HIPPO! I'M PAID BY THE CARD! *AND* THE WORD!! CHIMICHANGAS CHIMICHANGAS CHIMICHANGAS CHIMICHANGAS CHIMICHANGAS CHIMICHANGAS!!
Apparently, yes, it absolutely is.
And dude, *no way* is this wall getting smashed again, leaving *me* stuck guarding this stupid bank for *another* week. *No way.*

Attention, everyone who knows a Mrs. Fluffy Lumpkins in real life: yes, she absolutely *would* want to hear about this comic page! Even if you haven't spoken to her in years! *Especially* if you haven't spoken to her in years!

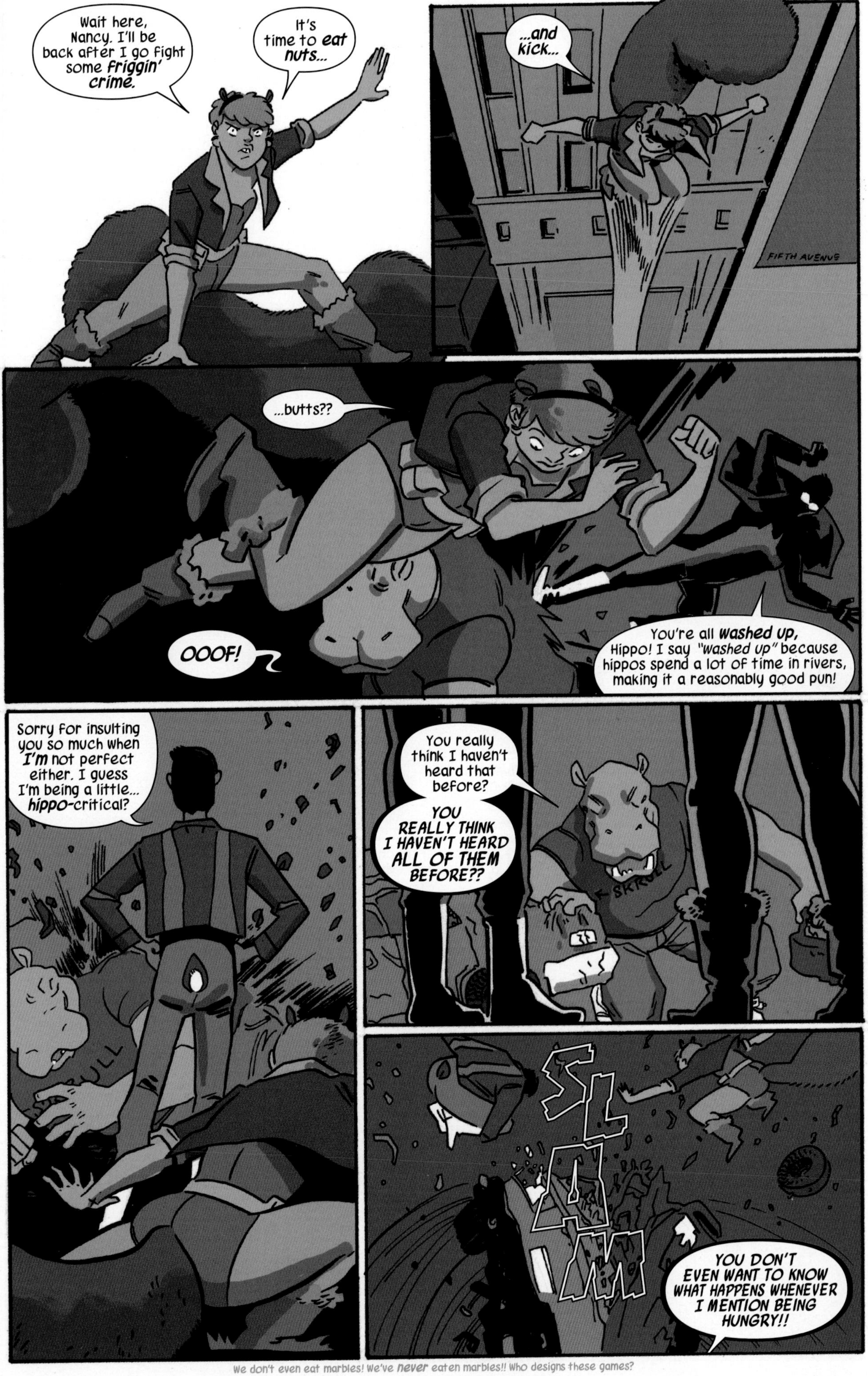

Wait here, Nancy. I'll be back after I go fight some friggin' crime.
It's time to eat nuts...
...and kick...
FIFTH AVENUE
...butts??
OOOF!
You're all washed up, Hippo! I say "washed up" because hippos spend a lot of time in rivers, making it a reasonably good pun!
Sorry for insulting you so much when I'm not perfect either. I guess I'm being a little... hippo-critical?
You really think I haven't heard that before?
YOU REALLY THINK I HAVEN'T HEARD ALL OF THEM BEFORE??
SKRULL
SLAM
YOU DON'T EVEN WANT TO KNOW WHAT HAPPENS WHENEVER I MENTION BEING HUNGRY!!

We don't even eat marbles! We've never eaten marbles!! Who designs these games?

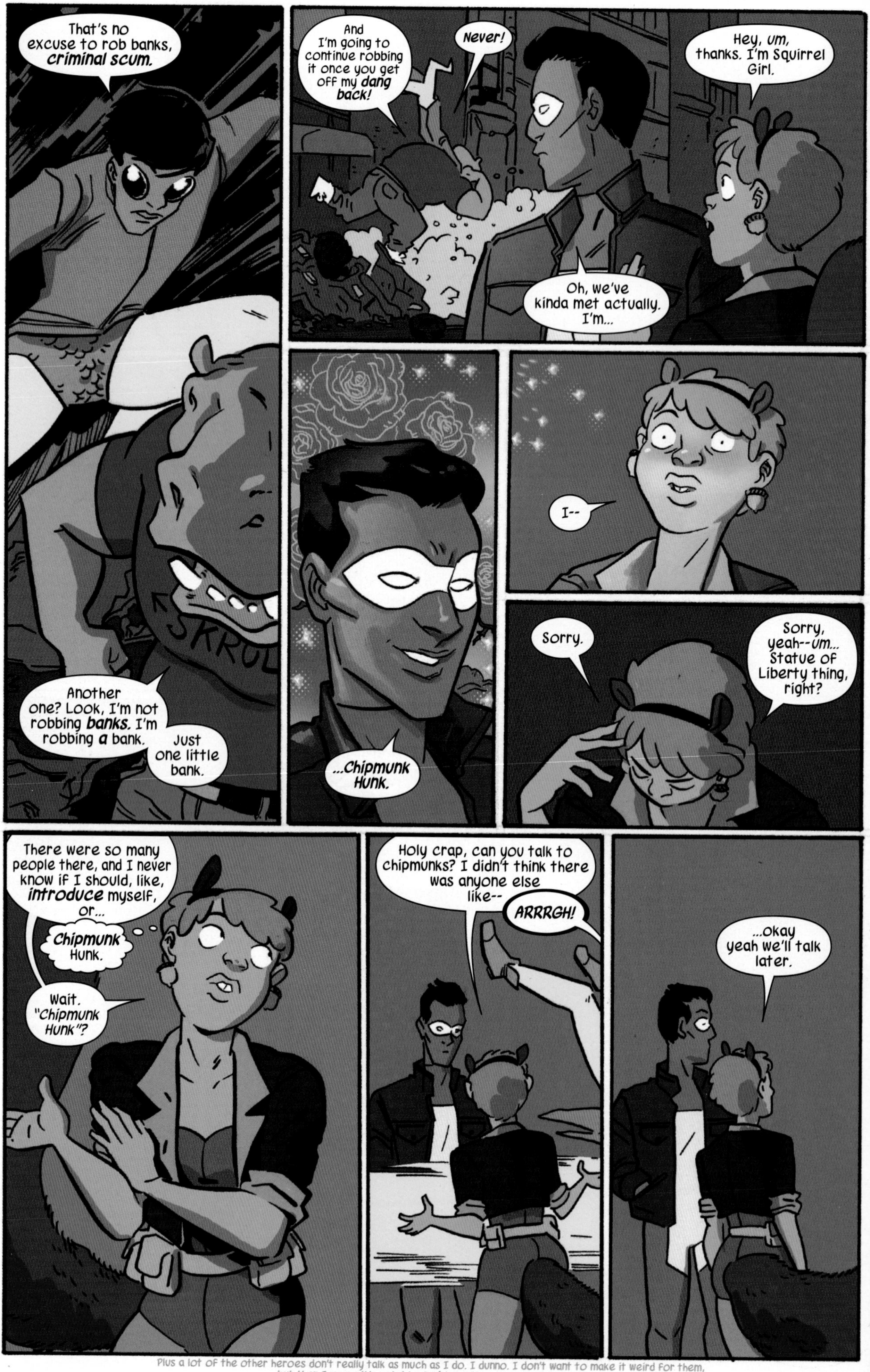
That's no excuse to rob banks, **criminal scum.**
Another one? Look, I'm not robbing **banks.** I'm robbing **a** bank.
Just one little bank.
And I'm going to continue robbing it once you get off my **dang back!**
Never!
Hey, um, thanks. I'm Squirrel Girl.
Oh, we've kinda met actually. I'm...
...Chipmunk Hunk.
I--
Sorry.
Sorry, yeah--um... Statue of Liberty thing, right?
There were so many people there, and I never know if I should, like, **introduce** myself, or...
Chipmunk Hunk.
Wait. "Chipmunk Hunk"?
Holy crap, can you talk to chipmunks? I didn't think there was anyone else like--
ARRRGH!
...okay yeah we'll talk later.

Plus a lot of the other heroes don't really talk as much as I do. I dunno. I don't want to make it weird for them, but then I worry it's weird to ***not*** introduce myself, you know?

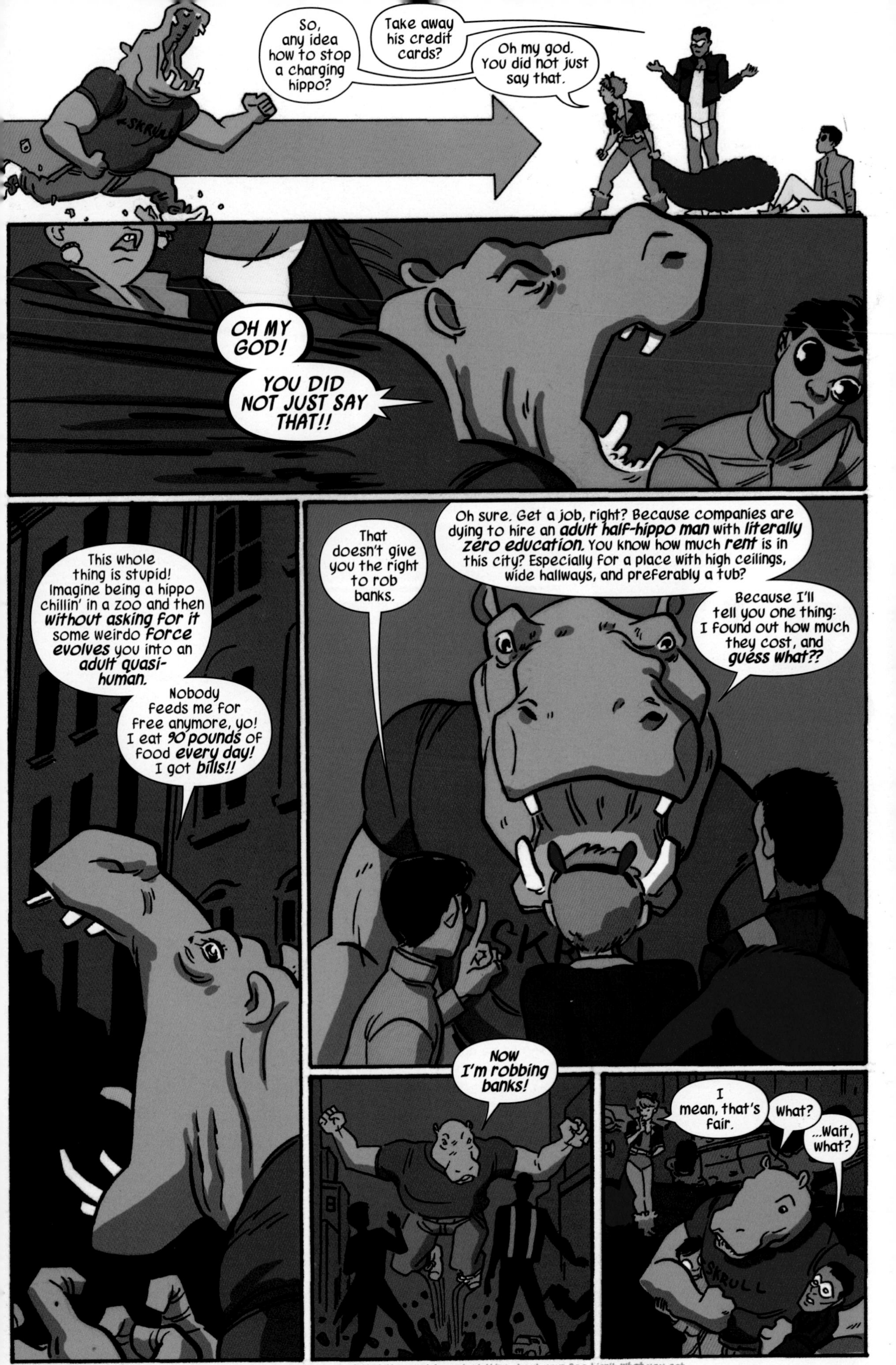
So, any idea how to stop a charging hippo?
Take away his credit cards?
Oh my god. You did not just say that.
OH MY GOD!
YOU DID NOT JUST SAY THAT!!
This whole thing is stupid! Imagine being a hippo chillin' in a zoo and then without asking for it some weirdo force evolves you into an adult quasi-human.
Nobody feeds me for free anymore, yo! I eat 90 pounds of food every day! I got bills!!
That doesn't give you the right to rob banks.
Oh sure. Get a job, right? Because companies are dying to hire an adult half-hippo man with literally zero education. You know how much rent is in this city? Especially for a place with high ceilings, wide hallways, and preferably a tub?
Because I'll tell you one thing: I found out how much they cost, and guess what??
Now I'm robbing banks!
I mean, that's fair.
What?
...Wait, what?

I like the idea of eating so much that the most important thing about your food isn't *what* you eat, but rather just the number of pounds it weighs. I--I really like eating, you guys.

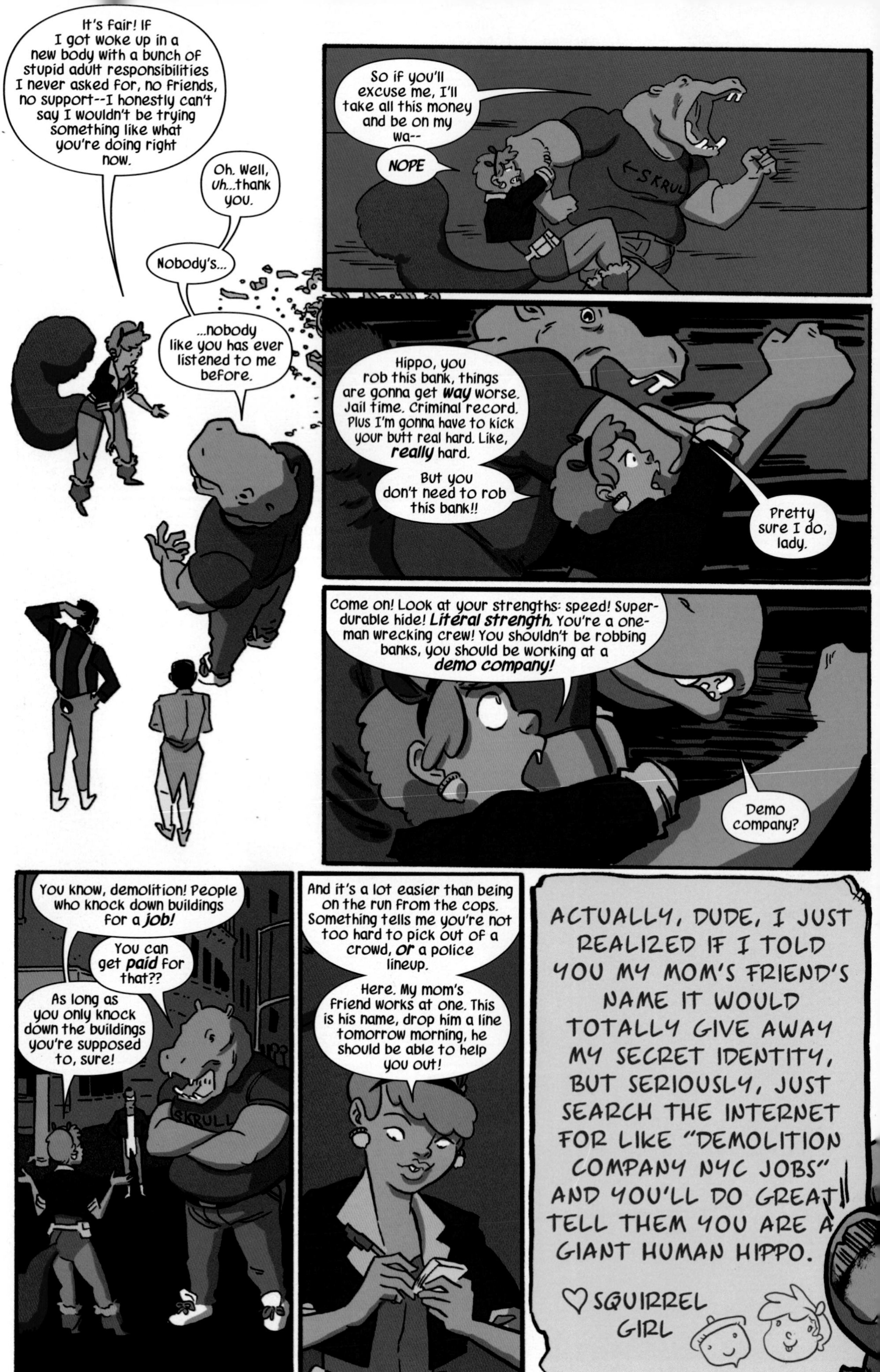
It's fair! If I got woke up in a new body with a bunch of stupid adult responsibilities I never asked for, no friends, no support--I honestly can't say I wouldn't be trying something like what you're doing right now.
Oh. Well, uh...thank you.
Nobody's...
...nobody like you has ever listened to me before.
So if you'll excuse me, I'll take all this money and be on my wa--
NOPE
SKRULL
Hippo, you rob this bank, things are gonna get *way* worse. Jail time. Criminal record. Plus I'm gonna have to kick your butt real hard. Like, *really* hard.
But you don't need to rob this bank!!
Pretty sure I do, lady.
Come on! Look at your strengths: speed! Super-durable hide! *Literal strength.* You're a one-man wrecking crew! You shouldn't be robbing banks, you should be working at a *demo company!*
Demo company?
You know, demolition! People who knock down buildings for a *job!*
You can get *paid* for that??
As long as you only knock down the buildings you're supposed to, sure!
SKRULL
And it's a lot easier than being on the run from the cops. Something tells me you're not too hard to pick out of a crowd, *or* a police lineup.
Here. My mom's friend works at one. This is his name, drop him a line tomorrow morning, he should be able to help you out!
ACTUALLY, DUDE, I JUST REALIZED IF I TOLD YOU MY MOM'S FRIEND'S NAME IT WOULD TOTALLY GIVE AWAY MY SECRET IDENTITY, BUT SERIOUSLY, JUST SEARCH THE INTERNET FOR LIKE "DEMOLITION COMPANY NYC JOBS" AND YOU'LL DO GREAT. TELL THEM YOU ARE A GIANT HUMAN HIPPO.
♡ SQUIRREL GIRL

The demolition company Squirrel Girl's mom's friend works at is called *"Yo, What's Up, We Hate Buildings Too"* because who wouldn't hire a demo company with that name? The answer: nobody.

Y'all **are** guarding this bank right now, so, I mean, I guess I'll give this demo thing a try. But I'm telling you right now that if this doesn't work out, I'm coming back to steal this bank.

Not steal **from** the bank.

I will literally lift this bank up and carry it away.

That's all I can ask!!

Squirrel Girl, that...was actually really impressive.

Who would've thought that the only thing my fists of *justice* couldn't punch...was his heart?

Hey, guys.

Greetings, citizen. I am *KOI BOI*, defender of New York and protector of the scales of justice.

And I'm Chipmunk Hunk, defeater of punks **and** other junk!

...Right. Guys, it's me, Nancy.

Uhhh--

Oh my gosh, Doreen, seriously? *Seriously.* It's just a domino mask.

What?

Also, um, who is this "Doreen" you speak of, *Nancy??*

Seriously??

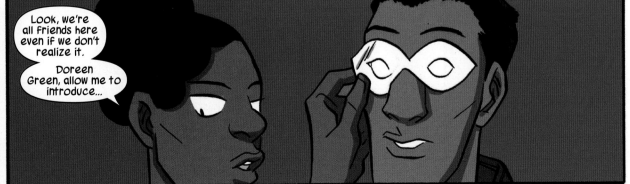

Look, we're all friends here even if we don't realize it.

Doreen Green, allow me to introduce...

Okay, I promise that with Squirrel Girl, Koi Boi, Chipmunk Hunk, and Bass Lass, we are done with animal rhyming names. *Promise.* For at least the next eleven pages.

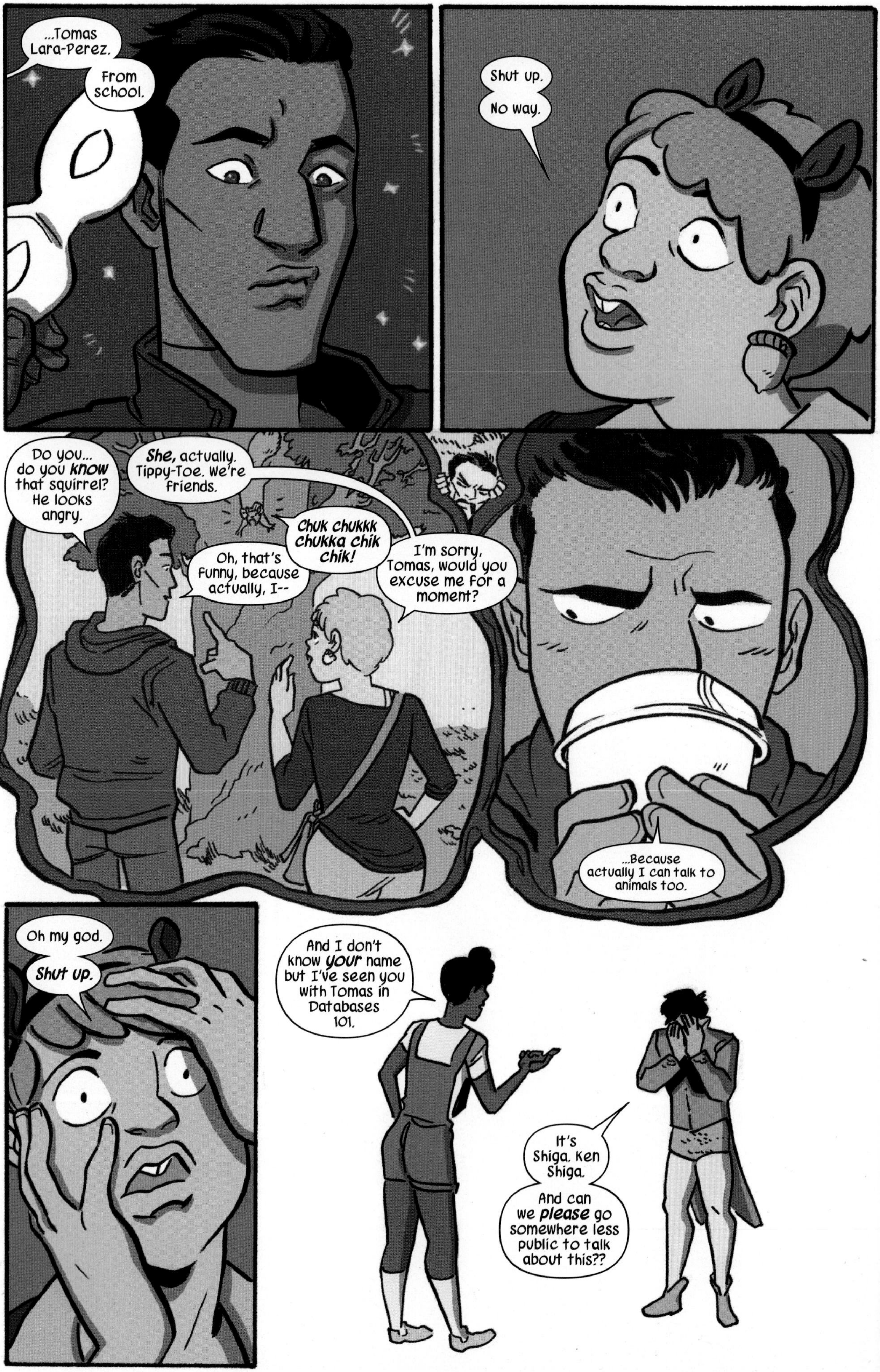
...Tomas Lara-Perez.
From school.
Shut up.
No way.
Do you... do you *know* that squirrel? He looks angry.
She, actually. Tippy-Toe. We're friends.
Chuk chukkk chukka chik chik!
Oh, that's funny, because actually, I--
I'm sorry, Tomas, would you excuse me for a moment?
...Because actually I can talk to animals too.
Oh my god.
Shut up.
And I don't know *your* name but I've seen you with Tomas in Databases 101.
It's Shiga. Ken Shiga.
And can we *please* go somewhere less public to talk about this??

This flashback is from our first issue, and if you haven't bought it yet, good news: holding out for six months just got you *two* panels from it for free! At this rate you'll be able to read the whole first issue in several dozen years!

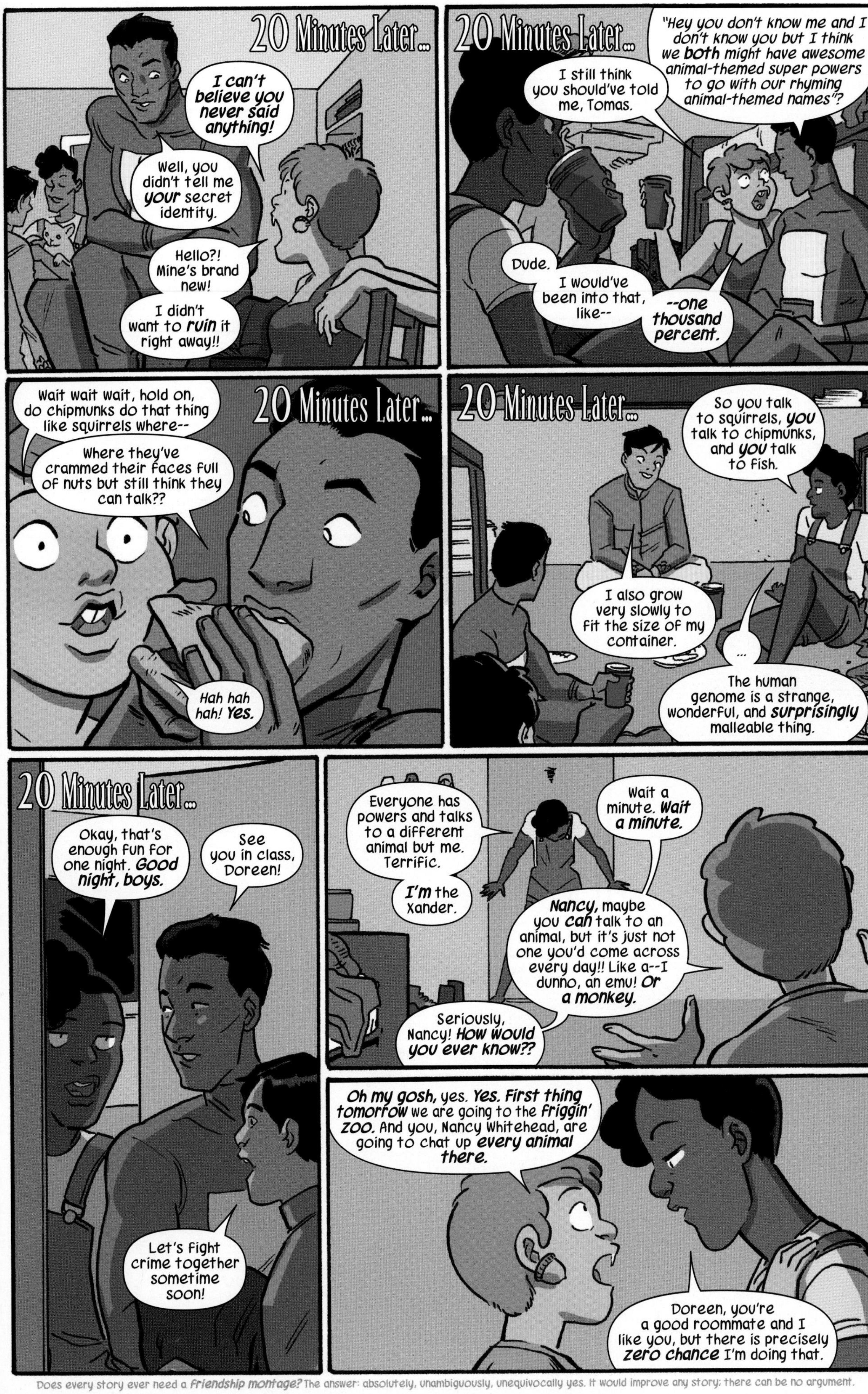
20 Minutes Later...
I can't believe you never said anything!
Well, you didn't tell me your secret identity.
Hello?! Mine's brand new!
I didn't want to ruin it right away!!
20 Minutes Later...
I still think you should've told me, Tomas.
"Hey you don't know me and I don't know you but I think we both might have awesome animal-themed super powers to go with our rhyming animal-themed names"?
Dude.
I would've been into that, like--
--one thousand percent.
Wait wait wait, hold on, do chipmunks do that thing like squirrels where--
20 Minutes Later...
Where they've crammed their faces full of nuts but still think they can talk??
Hah hah hah! Yes.
20 Minutes Later...
So you talk to squirrels, you talk to chipmunks, and you talk to fish.
I also grow very slowly to fit the size of my container.
...
The human genome is a strange, wonderful, and surprisingly malleable thing.
20 Minutes Later...
Okay, that's enough fun for one night. Good night, boys.
See you in class, Doreen!
Let's fight crime together sometime soon!
Everyone has powers and talks to a different animal but me. Terrific.
I'm the Xander.
Wait a minute. Wait a minute.
Nancy, maybe you can talk to an animal, but it's just not one you'd come across every day!! Like a--I dunno, an emu! Or a monkey.
Seriously, Nancy! How would you ever know??
Oh my gosh, yes. Yes. First thing tomorrow we are going to the friggin' zoo. And you, Nancy Whitehead, are going to chat up every animal there.
Doreen, you're a good roommate and I like you, but there is precisely zero chance I'm doing that.

Does every story ever need a *friendship montage?* The answer: absolutely, unambiguously, unequivocally yes. It would improve any story; there can be no argument.

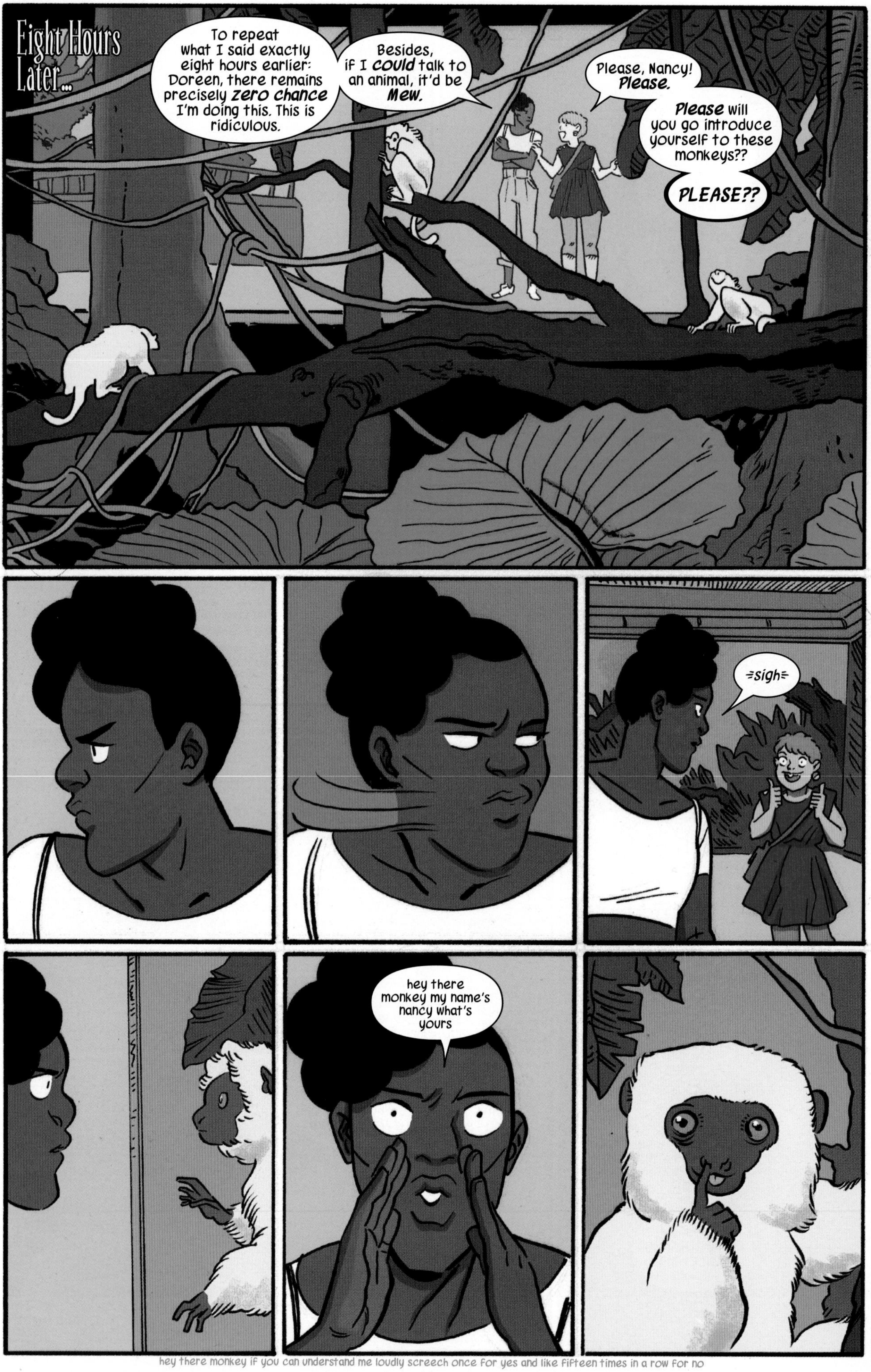
Eight Hours Later...
To repeat what I said exactly eight hours earlier: Doreen, there remains precisely zero chance I'm doing this. This is ridiculous.
Besides, if I could talk to an animal, it'd be Mew.
Please, Nancy! Please.
Please will you go introduce yourself to these monkeys??
PLEASE??
=sigh=
hey there monkey my name's nancy what's yours

hey there monkey if you can understand me loudly screech once for yes and like fifteen times in a row for no

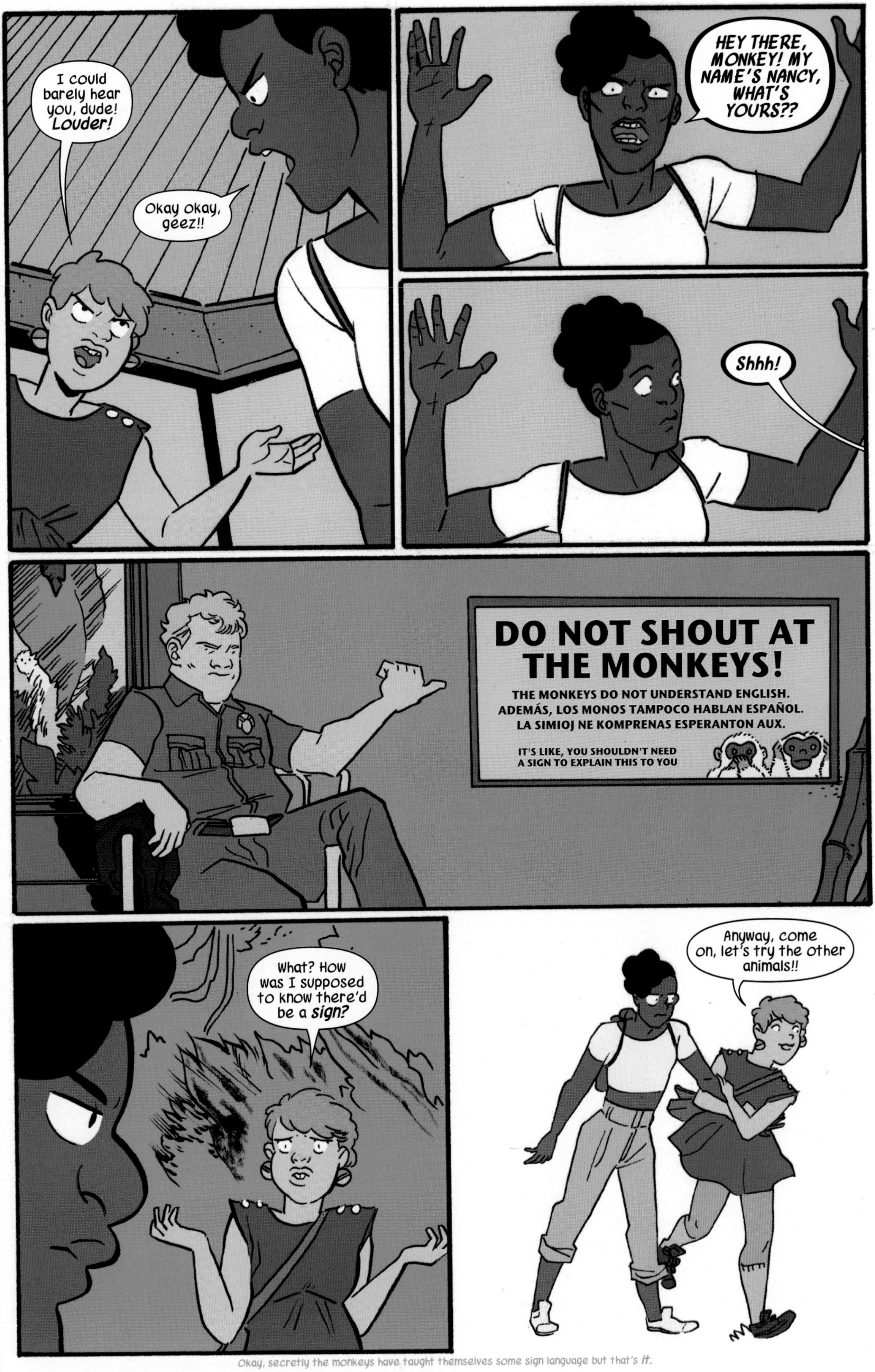
I could barely hear you, dude! Louder!
Okay okay, geez!!
HEY THERE, MONKEY! MY NAME'S NANCY, WHAT'S YOURS??
Shhh!
DO NOT SHOUT AT THE MONKEYS!
THE MONKEYS DO NOT UNDERSTAND ENGLISH.
ADEMÁS, LOS MONOS TAMPOCO HABLAN ESPAÑOL.
LA SIMIOJ NE KOMPRENAS ESPERANTON AUX.
IT'S LIKE, YOU SHOULDN'T NEED A SIGN TO EXPLAIN THIS TO YOU
What? How was I supposed to know there'd be a *sign?*
Anyway, come on, let's try the other animals!!

Okay, secretly the monkeys have taught themselves some sign language but that's *it.*

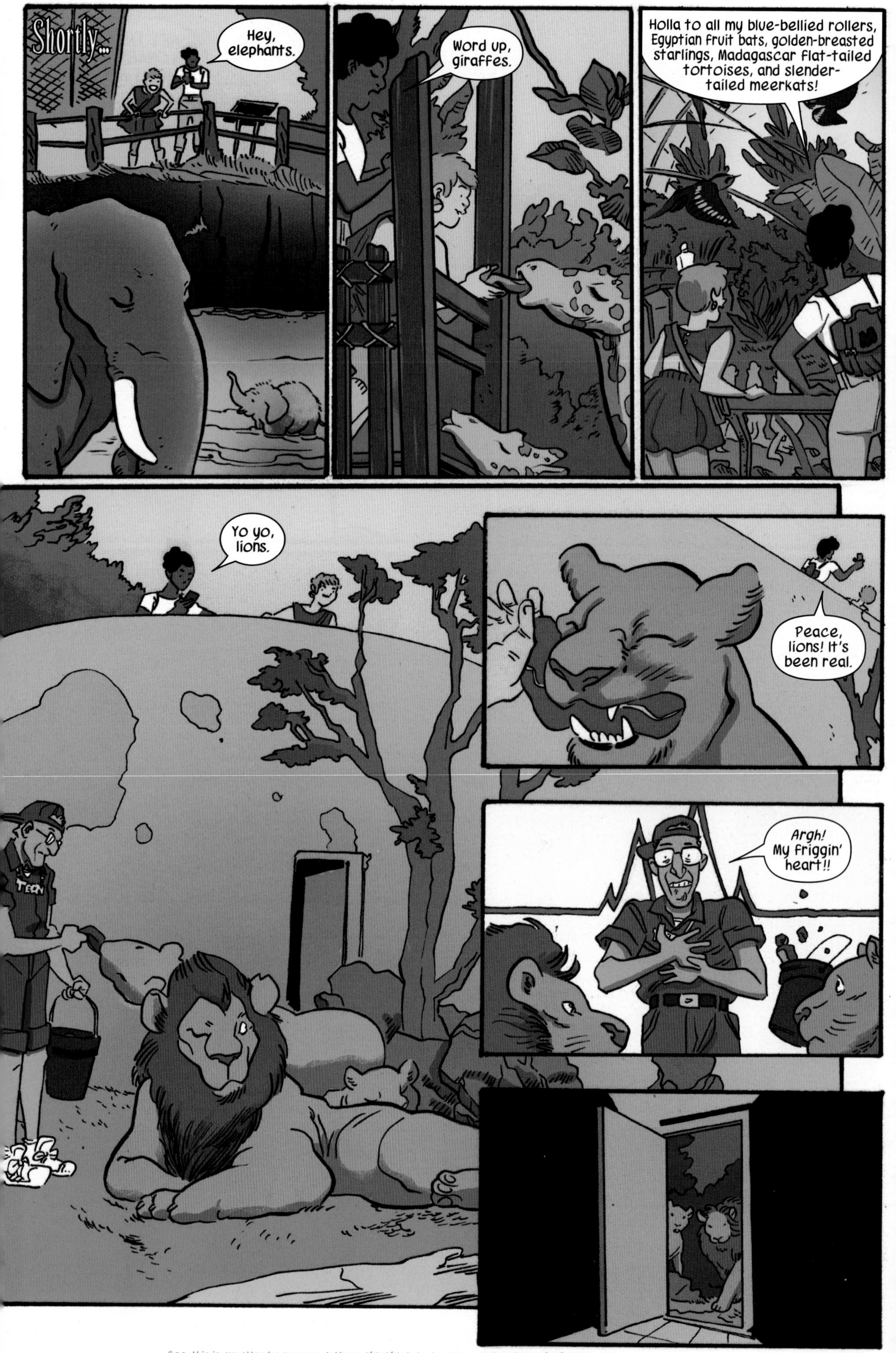
Shortly...
Hey, elephants.
Word up, giraffes.
Holla to all my blue-bellied rollers, Egyptian fruit bats, golden-breasted starlings, Madagascar flat-tailed tortoises, and slender-tailed meerkats!
Yo yo, lions.
Peace, lions! It's been real.
TECH
Argh! My friggin' heart!!

See, this is exactly why zoo regulations *clearly* state to close all lion doors *before* having a medical emergency.

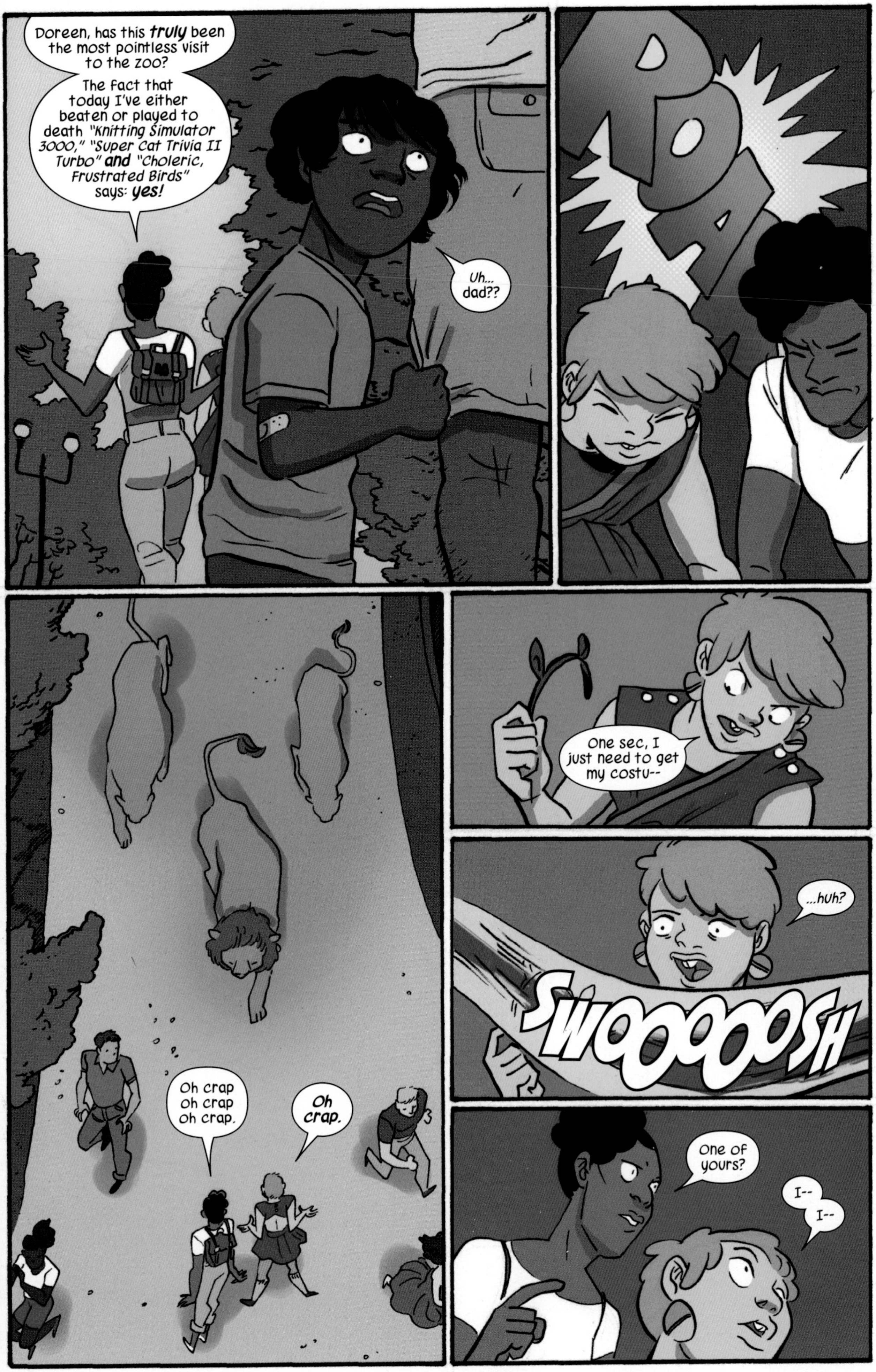

Doreen, has this truly been the most pointless visit to the zoo?
The fact that today I've either beaten or played to death "Knitting Simulator 3000," "Super Cat Trivia II Turbo" and "Choleric, Frustrated Birds" says: yes!
Uh... dad??
ROAR
Oh crap oh crap oh crap.
Oh crap.
One sec, I just need to get my costu--
...huh?
SWOOOOOOSH
One of yours?
I--
I--

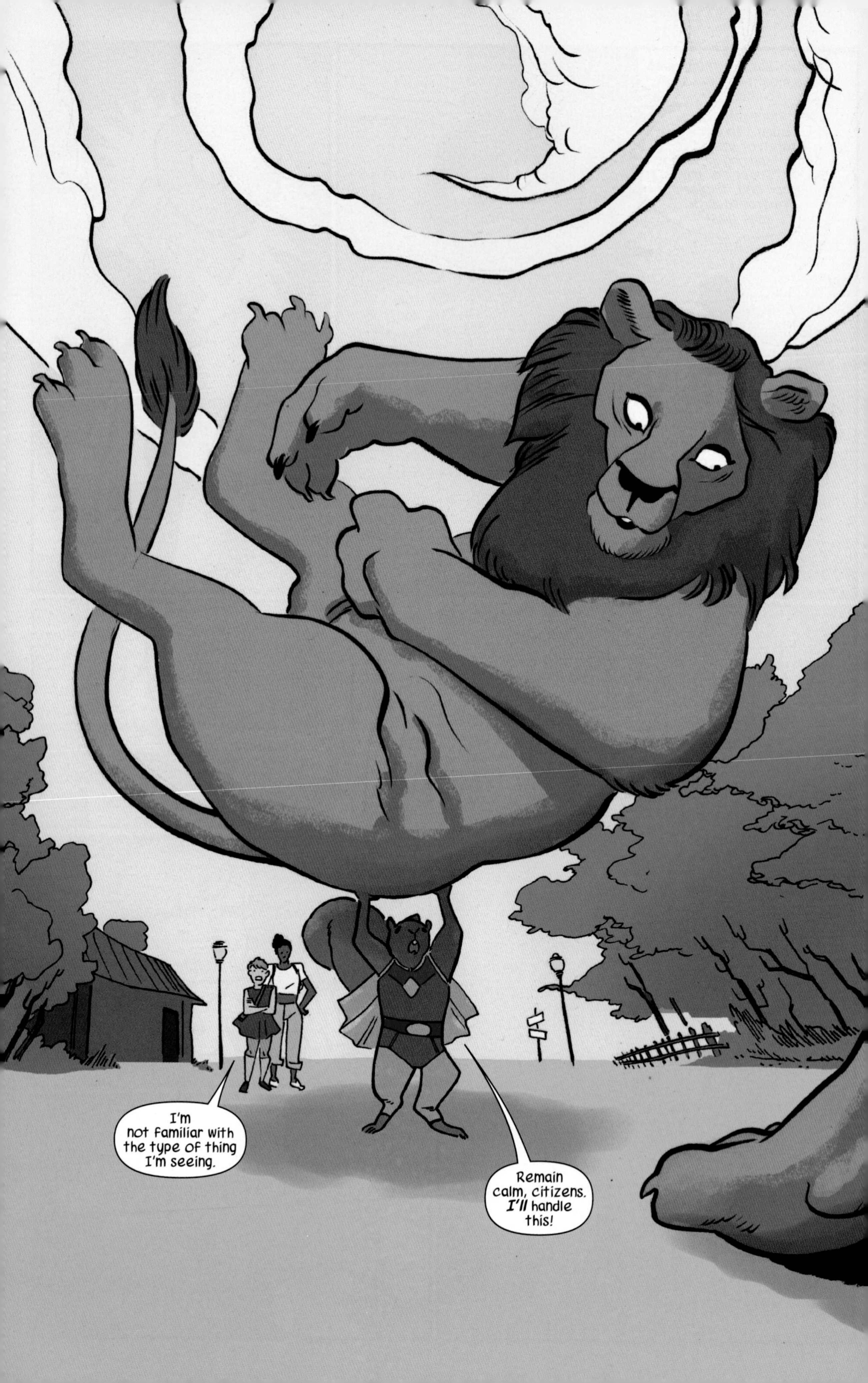
I'm not familiar with the type of thing I'm seeing.
Remain calm, citizens. *I'll* handle this!

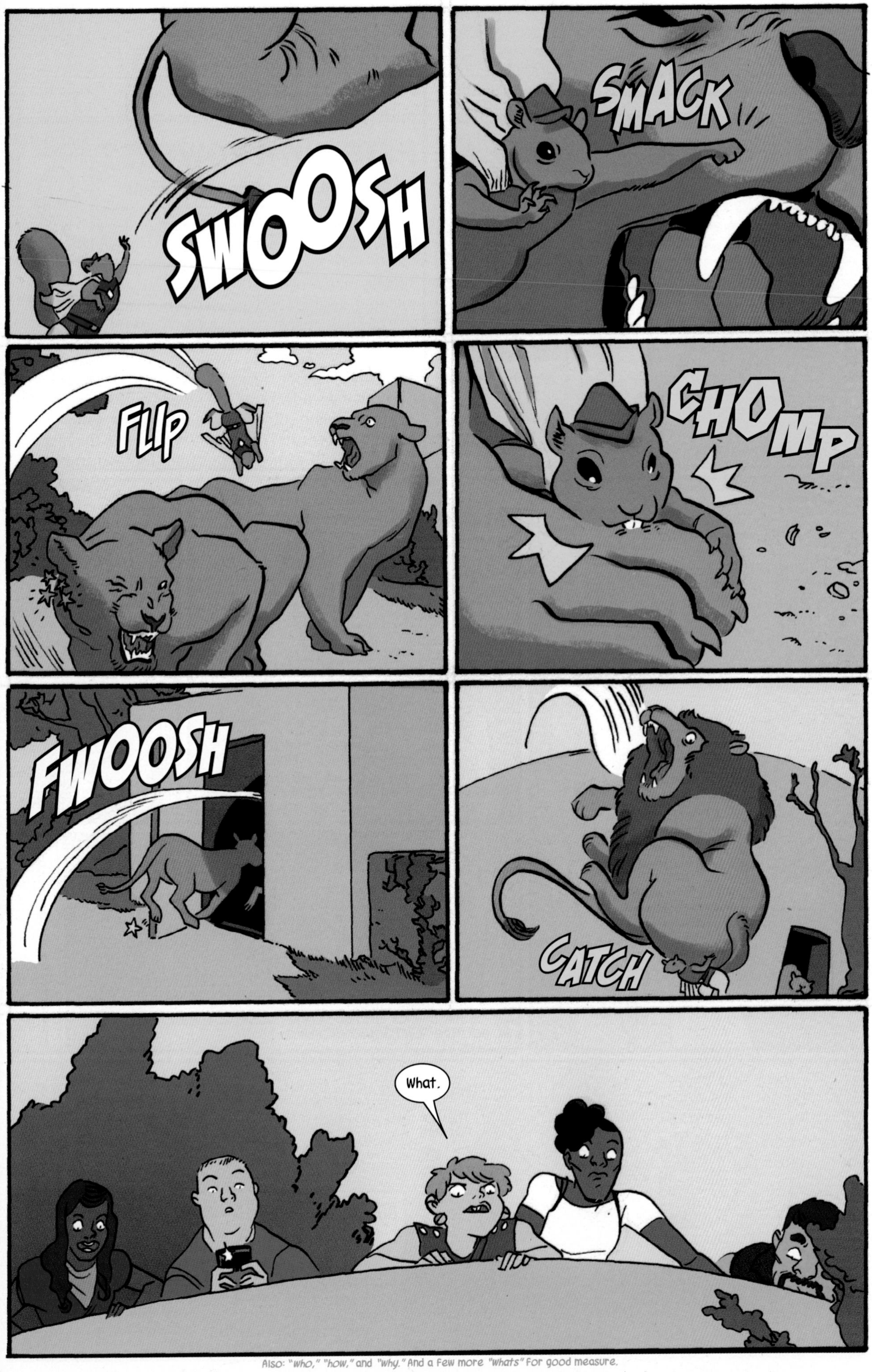
SWOOSH
SMACK
FLIP
CHOMP
FWOOSH
CATCH
What.

Also: "who," "how," and "why." And a few more "whats" for good measure.

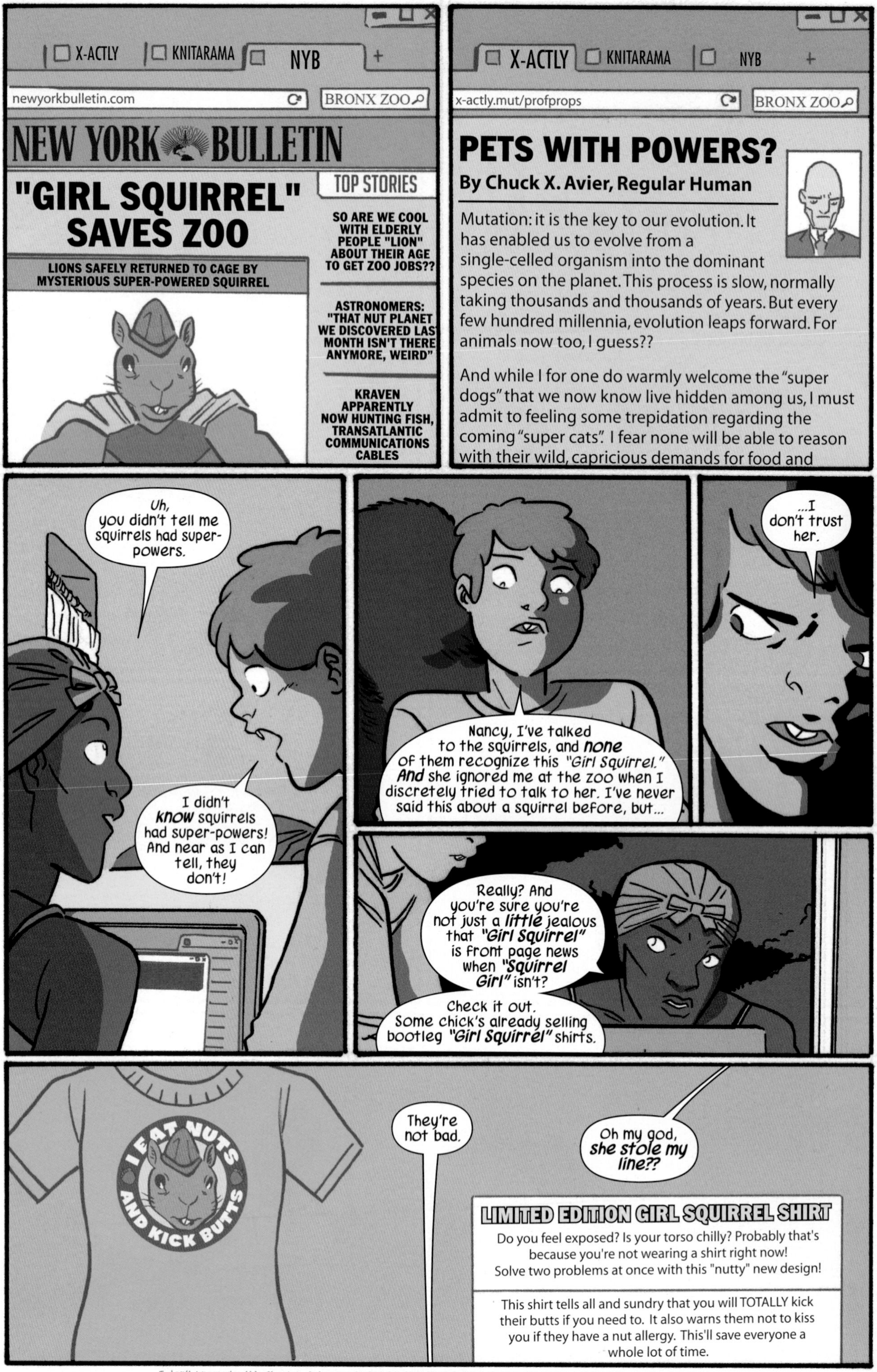
X-ACTLY
KNITARAMA
NYB
newyorkbulletin.com
BRONX ZOO
NEW YORK BULLETIN
"GIRL SQUIRREL" SAVES ZOO
LIONS SAFELY RETURNED TO CAGE BY MYSTERIOUS SUPER-POWERED SQUIRREL
TOP STORIES
SO ARE WE COOL WITH ELDERLY PEOPLE "LION" ABOUT THEIR AGE TO GET ZOO JOBS??
ASTRONOMERS: "THAT NUT PLANET WE DISCOVERED LAST MONTH ISN'T THERE ANYMORE, WEIRD"
KRAVEN APPARENTLY NOW HUNTING FISH, TRANSATLANTIC COMMUNICATIONS CABLES
X-ACTLY
KNITARAMA
NYB
x-actly.mut/profprops
BRONX ZOO
PETS WITH POWERS?
By Chuck X. Avier, Regular Human
Mutation: it is the key to our evolution. It has enabled us to evolve from a single-celled organism into the dominant species on the planet. This process is slow, normally taking thousands and thousands of years. But every few hundred millennia, evolution leaps forward. For animals now too, I guess??
And while I for one do warmly welcome the "super dogs" that we now know live hidden among us, I must admit to feeling some trepidation regarding the coming "super cats". I fear none will be able to reason with their wild, capricious demands for food and
Uh, you didn't tell me squirrels had super-powers.
I didn't know squirrels had super-powers! And near as I can tell, they don't!
Nancy, I've talked to the squirrels, and none of them recognize this "Girl Squirrel." And she ignored me at the zoo when I discretely tried to talk to her. I've never said this about a squirrel before, but...
...I don't trust her.
Really? And you're sure you're not just a little jealous that "Girl Squirrel" is front page news when "Squirrel Girl" isn't?
Check it out. Some chick's already selling bootleg "Girl Squirrel" shirts.
I EAT NUTS AND KICK BUTTS
They're not bad.
Oh my god, she stole my line??
LIMITED EDITION GIRL SQUIRREL SHIRT
Do you feel exposed? Is your torso chilly? Probably that's because you're not wearing a shirt right now! Solve two problems at once with this "nutty" new design!
This shirt tells all and sundry that you will TOTALLY kick their butts if you need to. It also warns them not to kiss you if they have a nut allergy. This'll save everyone a whole lot of time.

I don't know who this Chuck X. Avier guy is, but he sure likes talking up this School For Gifted Youngsters! Weird!!

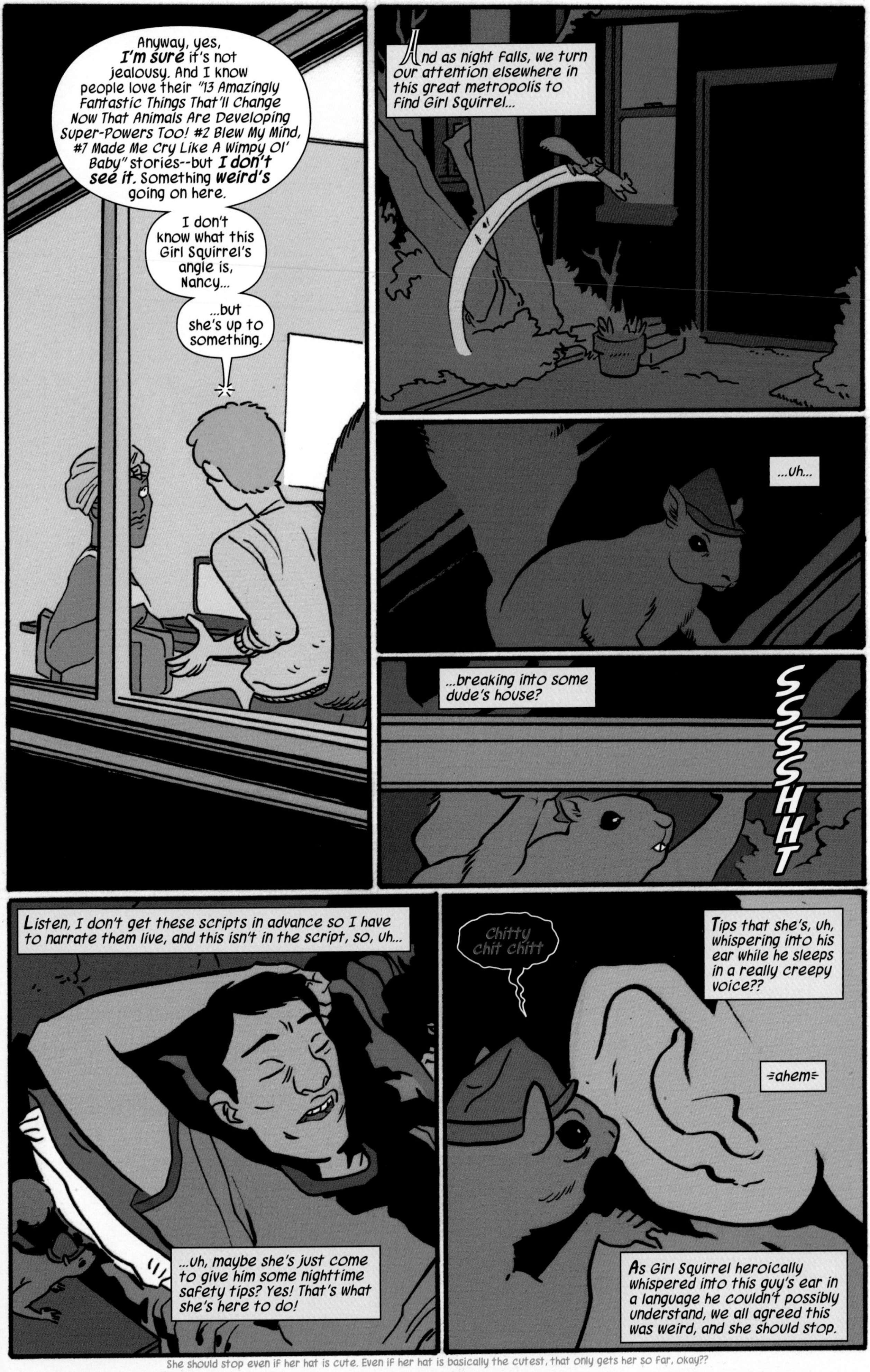

Anyway, yes, I'm sure it's not jealousy. And I know people love their "13 Amazingly Fantastic Things That'll Change Now That Animals Are Developing Super-Powers Too! #2 Blew My Mind, #7 Made Me Cry Like A Wimpy Ol' Baby" stories--but I don't see it. Something weird's going on here.
I don't know what this Girl Squirrel's angle is, Nancy...
...but she's up to something.
And as night falls, we turn our attention elsewhere in this great metropolis to find Girl Squirrel...
...uh...
...breaking into some dude's house?
SSSSHHT
Listen, I don't get these scripts in advance so I have to narrate them live, and this isn't in the script, so, uh...
...uh, maybe she's just come to give him some nighttime safety tips? Yes! That's what she's here to do!
Chitty chit chitt
Tips that she's, uh, whispering into his ear while he sleeps in a really creepy voice??
=ahem=
As Girl Squirrel heroically whispered into this guy's ear in a language he couldn't possibly understand, we all agreed this was weird, and she should stop.

She should stop even if her hat is cute. Even if her hat is basically the cutest, that only gets her so far, okay??

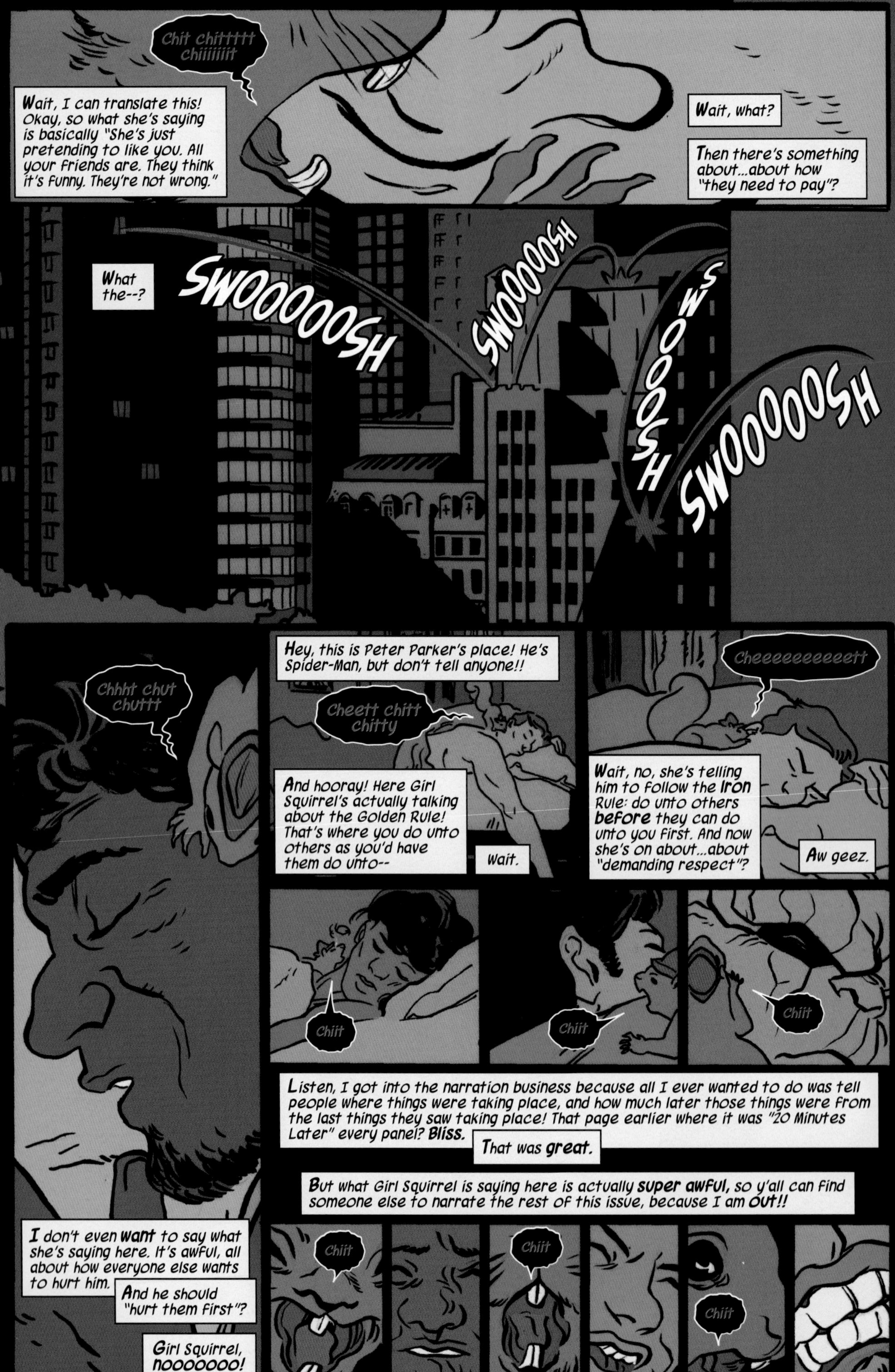
Chit chittttt chiiiiiiit
Wait, I can translate this! Okay, so what she's saying is basically "She's just pretending to like you. All your friends are. They think it's funny. They're not wrong."
Wait, what?
Then there's something about...about how "they need to pay"?
What the--?
SWOOOOOSH
SWOOOOOSH
SWOOOOOSH
SWOOOOOSH
Chhht chut chuttt
Hey, this is Peter Parker's place! He's Spider-Man, but don't tell anyone!!
Cheett chitt chitty
And hooray! Here Girl Squirrel's actually talking about the Golden Rule! That's where you do unto others as you'd have them do unto--
Wait.
Cheeeeeeeeeeett
Wait, no, she's telling him to follow the Iron Rule: do unto others before they can do unto you first. And now she's on about...about "demanding respect"?
Aw geez.
Chiit
Chiit
Chiit
Listen, I got into the narration business because all I ever wanted to do was tell people where things were taking place, and how much later those things were from the last things they saw taking place! That page earlier where it was "20 Minutes Later" every panel? Bliss.
That was great.
But what Girl Squirrel is saying here is actually super awful, so y'all can find someone else to narrate the rest of this issue, because I am out!!
I don't even want to say what she's saying here. It's awful, all about how everyone else wants to hurt him.
And he should "hurt them first"?
Girl Squirrel, noooooooo!
Chiit
Chiit
Chiit

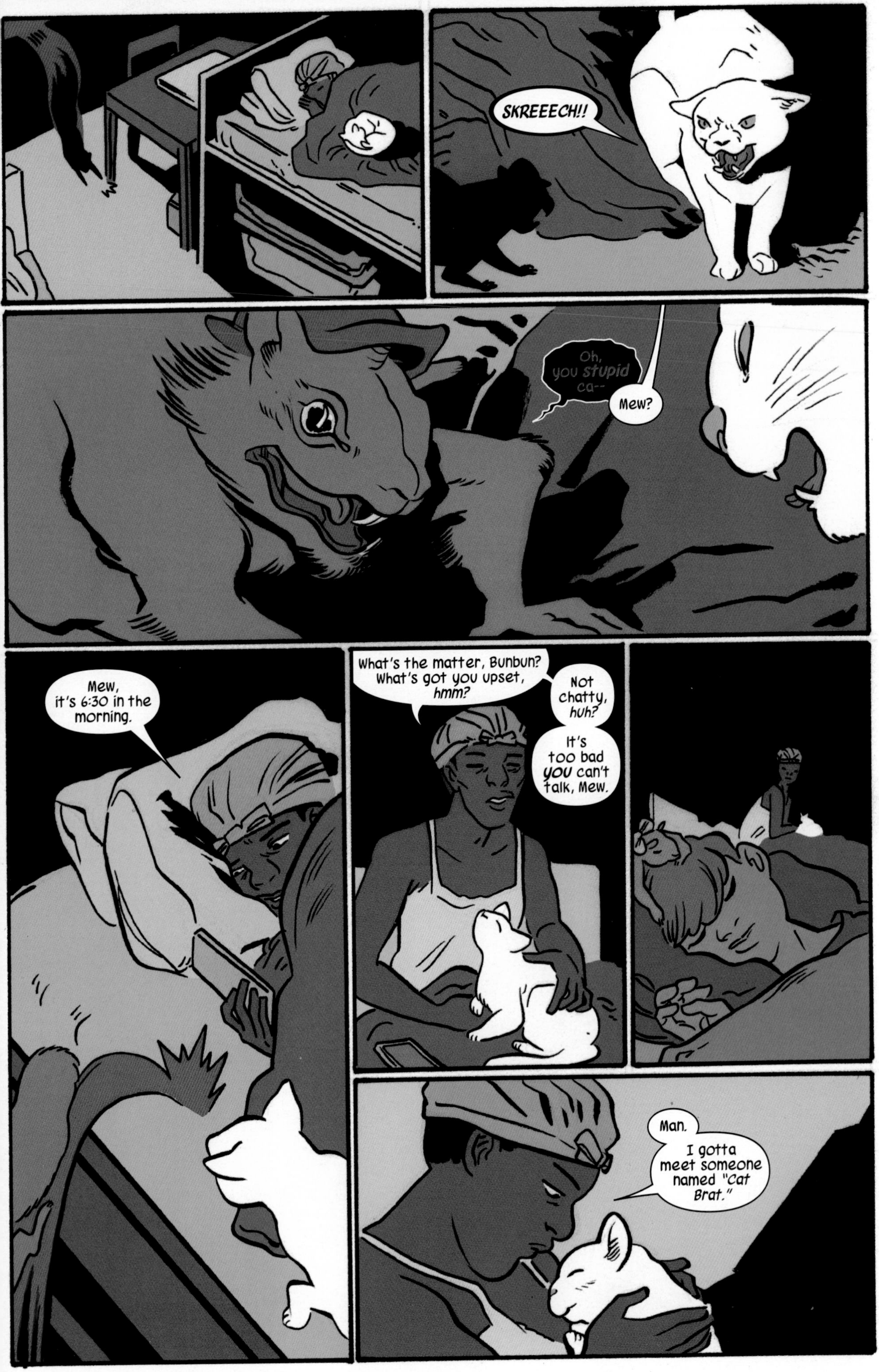
SKREEECH!!
Oh, you stupid ca--
Mew?
Mew, it's 6:30 in the morning.
What's the matter, Bunbun? What's got you upset, hmm?
Not chatty, huh?
It's too bad you can't talk, Mew.
Man.
I gotta meet someone named "Cat Brat."

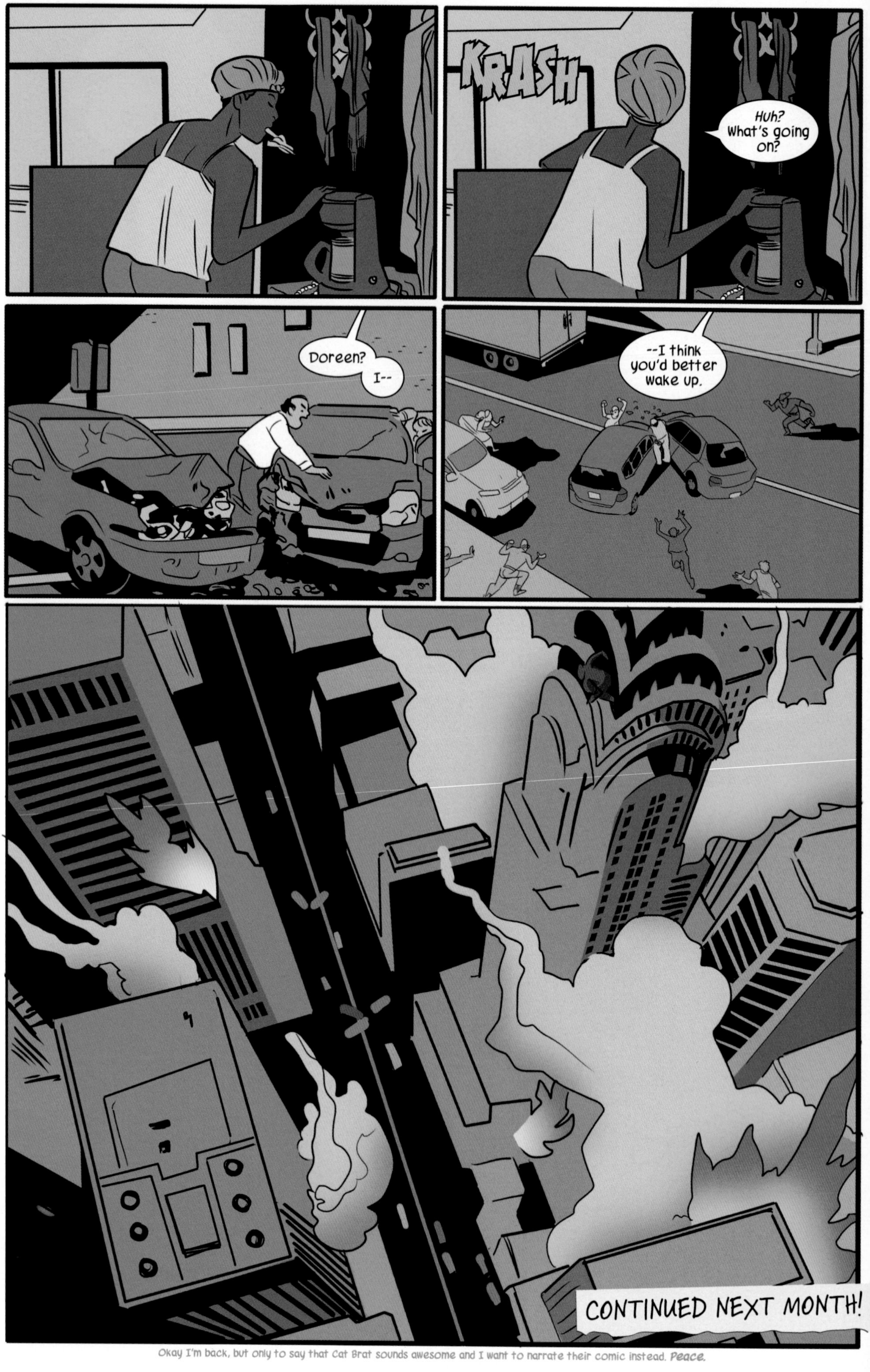
KRASH
Huh? What's going on?
Doreen? I--
--I think you'd better wake up.
CONTINUED NEXT MONTH!

Okay I'm back, but only to say that Cat Brat sounds awesome and I want to narrate their comic instead. *Peace.*

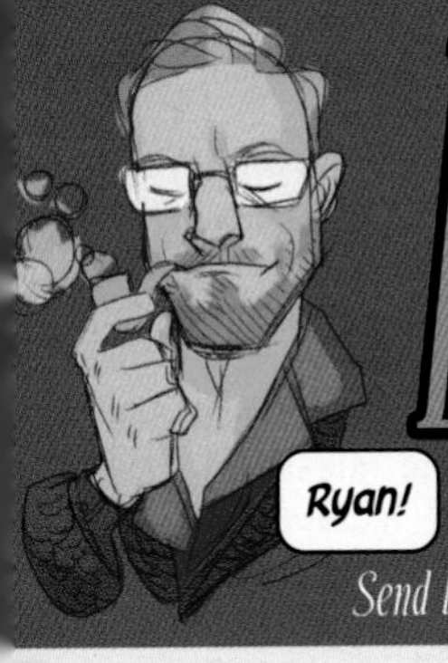
Ryan!

Letters From Nuts

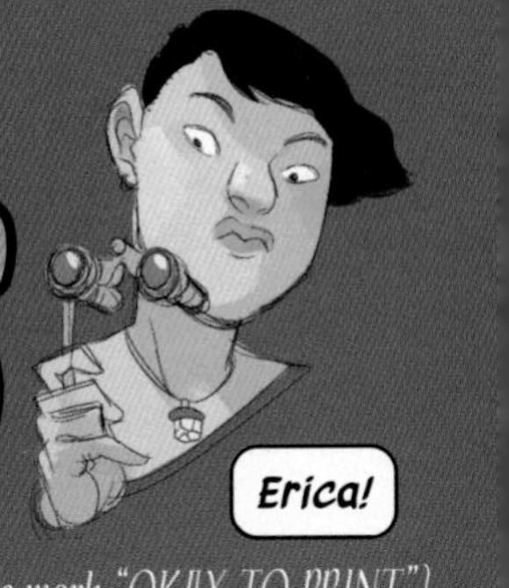
Erica!

Send letters to mheroes@marvel.com or 135 W 50th St, 7th Floor, New York, NY 10020 (Please mark "OKAY TO PRINT")

Dear Squirrel Girl Editor,

What in the H-E-single Asgardian hockey stick is the matter with you?! I have just read the advance copy of SQUIRREL GIRL #4!!! ONE PAGE?!! SQUIRREL GIRL DEFEATS GALACTUS IN ONE PAGE?!!! Thank you, jerk-faces. Thank you for ruining Marvel Comics for all time!

The Marvel that *I* knew, the Marvel that *I* grew up with made sense! LOGICAL sense! Armor was transistor powered! Steve Rogers could hide his shield under his jacket! And NOBODY could beat Galactus! NO ONE!

Yes, it's canon that Squirrel Girl's defeated Doctor Doom, M.O.D.O.K., and even Fin Fang Foom, but none of those guys are the Mighty Galactus! Silver Surfer just fought Galactus for three straight issues--that's 59 more pages than shown here--and the Surfer STILL LOST! Now THAT'S a Galactus story that makes SENSE! (And on sale soon as part of the SILVER SURFER: WORLDS APART trade paperback.) And now you've gone and defeated him in what is tantamount to ONE PANEL?! And by someone with SQUIRREL POWERS?!

NUTS TO YOU, PAL! NUTS! TO! YOU!

Dan Slott
3 Doors Down
Marvel Entertainment, NY

RYAN: Hey Dan! Nice to hear from you, buddy! I was stoked to run your great quote on the cover of our issue #2 ("I can't recommend the new SQUIRREL GIRL book enough! It's NUTS!") but I think you may have overlooked something because there's not much here I can use. The best I've come up with from your letter is, "I have just read... Squirrel Girl #4!!!... Now THAT'S a Galactus story! ...SQUIRREL POWERS... TO YOU, PAL!" which is actually a pretty great quote after all, so--thanks!

ERICA: Dan, calm down.

Dear Ryan and Erica,

I just wanted to let you know how much I've been enjoying THE UNBEATABLE SQUIRREL GIRL thus far. An encounter with Galactus so early in the series would seem difficult to pull off successfully, but I thought it was handled very well. The way Squirrel Girl hears Galactus's words not just in her own language, but her own vernacular, was a nice touch. The full page of an American teenage girl sitting on the giant shoulder of a god-like being older than the universe, together contemplating the Earth set against the background of the cosmos, is perhaps Erica's most beautiful image.

I also noticed that your Galactus story parallels that of the original Galactus trilogy by Lee and Kirby, which I am old enough to have read when it first appeared. In both cases, the encounter with Galactus commences hot on the heels of another adventure and ends with the characters resuming their everyday lives. I'll certainly be looking forward to future installments.

Make Mine Marvel!
Charles Hoffman,
Van Nuys, CA

P.S. I've taken the liberty of attaching a picture of myself with Erica's father, Red Hook, 1980s. I know that he would be delighted with Squirrel Girl.

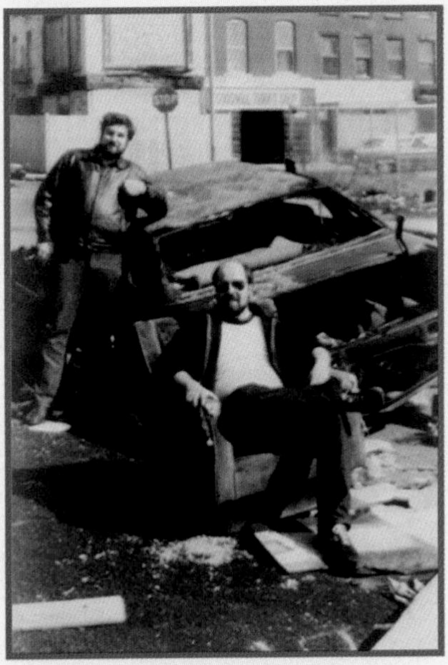

RYAN: I didn't even see these parallels until you pointed them out, but now I'm happy they're there!

ERICA: Oh wow. That's an old photo. That's possibly a pre-Erica photo. Anyway, I think Galactus had to be in the first arc. Dan Slott's work on the character really established who the character is after her initial appearance in Marvel Super-Heroes Winter Special, and more importantly established that she wins fights against the toughest of the tough. After pitting her against some of Marvel's biggest baddies (Giganto, Fin Fang Foom, Thanos) it only makes sense that we start off by going one further and putting her up against Marvel's biggest (literally?) baddie.

Dear Unbeatable Squirrel-team,

As a long time comic reader and Marvel fan, I want to thank you for one of, heck, THE most brilliantly executed, on-point character portrayals in issue #4.

Only SQUIRREL GIRL could leave me satisfied with a one-page comic. Sometimes nothing more needs to be said, and you said it perfectly.

I also appreciate the interaction with the fans you guys show in the responses of your letter columns, showing that you care about us as much as we care about you. The SG fans may not be as garishly loud as those of a certain Spider-Man, but like the squirrels, we are there, hiding in the trees and eating nuts.

Squirrel Girl may not be as widely known of a hero, she's not in it for the flash and publicity. She's the hero we need, there to do things right and put a smile on our faces. Heck, I bet not even Howard the Duck, among the grumpiest, most perennially frustrated and disappointed of heroes, could resist cracking a smile in her presence.

Now if you'll excuse me, I've just finished up the letters column and am off to see if the tiny print continues on the blank pages to follow...wait...what's this? BONUS COMIC!

You guys (for lack of a proper gender-neutral pronoun) rock!

Nathan

RYAN: I appreciate you taking the time to write a letter only three pages into the comic! I kinda wish all letters were like that, all "Dear Squirrel Girl people, I can't wait to see what happens next! I guess I'm about to now though! Well, bye!"

ERICA: I personally enjoy "dude" as a gender-neutral term. It's often thought of as male, but it just means individual. Before the 60s (which is when it started to be misused as "man") it meant either a city slicker or someone who is very fashion forward and that's definitely us. 100%.

P.S. I'm glad you like SQUIRREL GIRL!

Hello again, lovely people, and thank you again for the brilliance that is SQUIRREL GIRL! I have just finished #4... And you have to make SQUIRREL GIRL spin-offs! "Squirrel Girl, Herald of Galactus" has to be a thing! What must we do to make it happen?! On the subject, how about a Magneto/Squirrel-Girl eighteen-chapter epic that dwarfs all those 90's crossovers that we all remember so fondly?

No? Okay...what about "Squirrel Girl's Adventures In Babysitting" filling in all the gaps where SG had to stay home and look after Luke Cage's kid?

SQUIRREL GIRL is easily my favorite comic book to date, across all publishers and genres. Thank you again for everything!

Tim P.
Plymouth, England

RYAN: I keep thinking of how Magneto and Squirrel Girl would get along. He's such a serious, dour guy! Maybe they should go on a road trip together. Maybe... maybe they should DEFINITELY go on a road trip together.

I wanted to write in to complain that my copy of UNBEATABLE SQUIRREL GIRL #4 must have been a counterfeit. The bottom of the first page clearly states that all of the pages following the letters page would be blank. I was deeply disappointed to find all sorts of art, words, and story along with ZERO blank pages! Either it was counterfeit or someone in quality control needs to be fired!

Seriously though, it was one of the most entertaining comics I've read in some time. I can't remember the last time I've started laughing uproariously and had to catch my breath and re-read what I had just read to make sure I got it all… And this happened several times during this issue. If the rest of the pages HAD been blank it would have been an amazing gag of its own. Great stuff!

Sean Bayless

RYAN: Sean, the truth of the matter is that after printing the blank pages we felt bad about maybe ripping people off, so we requested the staff at your (and everyone's!) local comic book store to create and draw in their own conclusion to the story on the remaining blank pages, so everyone got their own different ending! I'm glad you liked yours! P.S.: Let me know what some of the jokes were, so I can use them in future issues.

ERICA: I'm going to respond to the second half of your letter since Ryan responded to the first half. I was reading this script while my boyfriend was in the other end of the apartment and he kept walking over to find out what I was laughing at. This also happens a lot when I'm out working with Joe Quinones (artist on HOWARD THE DUCK) and we'll chuckle to ourselves about the pages we're working on while in a cafe. So you are not alone in this.

Congratulations, Ryan and Erica, on creating a fun and entertaining comic. After reading the first issue of this comic, I found myself already going nuts for this series. I love that Doreen is just as awkward and silly as any other person. Also, it's pretty cool that she "defeats" these baddies just by being nice and friendly to them. I'm definitely looking forward to many more issues to come!

The photo attached is me with a baby squirrel that my family cared for recently. He's now living with 12 other little squirrels at our local wildlife rescue!

Kevin Krause

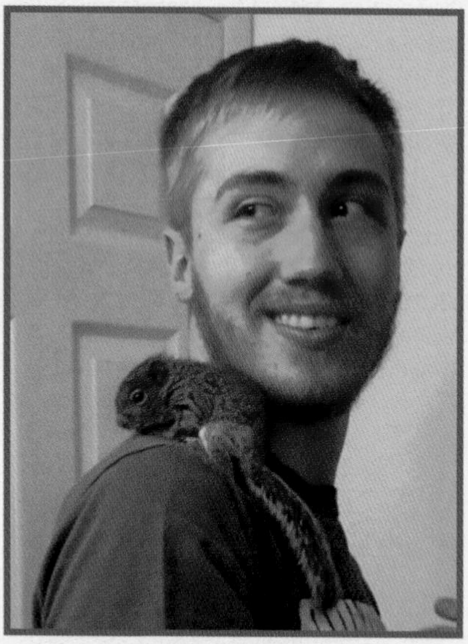

RYAN: Thanks! Also when I started this comic I honestly did not expect there would be so many people with squirrels in their lives. I did not expect our letters column would be mostly photos of people with squirrels on them. I'm happy this turned out to be the case!

ERICA: This is worth it just for all the pictures of wee baby squirrels people send us.

I've seriously never written to a comic book before. (It seemed silly.) But I had to let you all know that THE UNBEATABLE SQUIRREL GIRL is my new most favorite thing. Ever. I love it. I love it. I love it.

Jesse

P.S. Please tell me there's some sweet Squirrel Girl merch in the works? I would love to buy me some Doreen Green action figures, buttons, etc.

RYAN: Jesse, I would love some Squirrel Girl action figures! We don't get to tell the merchandise companies what to make, but now I will absolutely tell the merchandise companies what to make: a Squirrel Girl action figure with at least 12 points of articulation, and which comes packaged with a Tippy-Toe figure that can lock onto her shoulder and a randomly selected Deadpool card. I've got the designs right here. Call me, merchandise companies.

ERICA: I want a Squirrel Girl toy so bad. In the meantime I've just been collecting squirrel paraphernalia. Right now I'm up to two necklaces, a purse and a stuffed animal.

Rico did design six different Squirrel Girl buttons for the release of the book though. He's way more on top of this merchandising stuff than we are. Have you seen all the Spider-Gwen stuff he's put together? YOW!

To the gloriously deranged minds behind SQUIRREL GIRL:

Kudos! Amazing work! I've been hooked since the first issue! I have but one humble question. When do we get to meet The Chipmunk Hunk? Convention season is upon us and I need to know what my cosplay should look like.

Keep up the fabulous work, Doreen is a gem and I haven't laughed so much in ages.

Josh W.

RYAN: Hey thanks, Josh! As for meeting Chipmunk Hunk, I can't say for sure when we'll be seeing him! If that bothers you, I guess that's just the NEXT ISSUE you need to deal with. It's probably ISSUE #6 on your list.

Oh wait, never mind, this is issue six already. He's in this issue, surprise!!

ERICA: OH GOD I'M SO EXCITED FOR CHIPMUNK HUNK COSPLAY. I NEVER CONSIDERED THAT MIGHT BE A POSSIBILITY. YOU'D BETTER SEND US PHOTOS.

Next: Avengers Assemble?

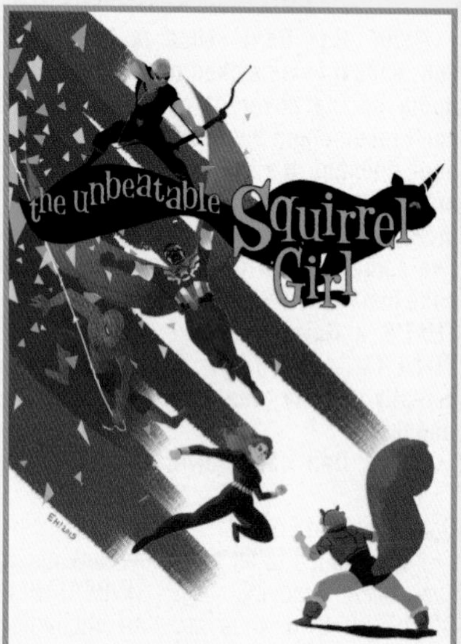
the unbeatable Squirrel Girl

On Sale 7/1/15!

Attention Squirrel Scouts! Make sure to check out our production blog, **unbeatablesquirrelgirl.tumblr.com**, where we post behind-the-scenes stuff on how the book gets made, along with all sorts of cool things *you* make: fanart, cosplay, whatever!

7

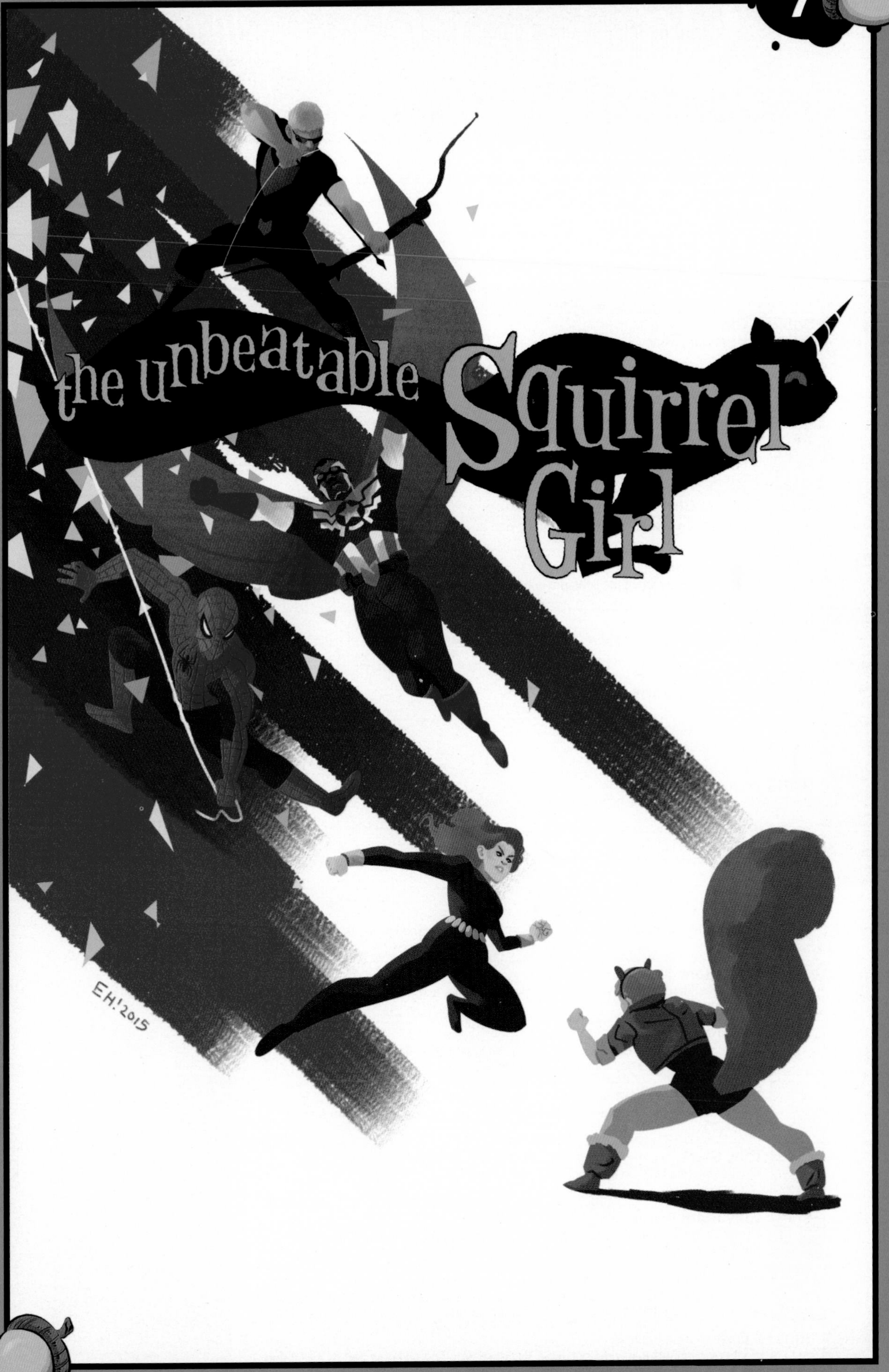
the unbeatable Squirrel Girl
EH! 2015

*Doreen Green isn't just a first-year computer science student: she secretly also has all the powers of both squirrel and girl! She uses her amazing abilities to fight crime **and** be as awesome as possible. You know her as...**The Unbeatable Squirrel Girl!** Let's catch up with what she's been up to until now, with...*

Squirrel Girl in a nutshell

Squirrel Girl! @unbeatablesg
PUBLIC SERVICE ANNOUNCEMENT: Everyone should go to the zoo and talk to every animal there. Just go and chat up every animal!

Squirrel Girl! @unbeatablesg
Because how do you know you CAN'T talk to animals unless you've tried with every animal?? And they've got lots of animals there!

Squirrel Girl! @unbeatablesg
Also yes I am aware that there are elements of zoos that are NOT UNPROBLEMATIC but where else are you gonna chat up mad lemurs

Squirrel Girl! @unbeatablesg
Besides Madagascar I mean

Tippy-Toe @yoitstippytoe
@unbeatablesg CHITTT CHITTY CHIT CHIT

Squirrel Girl! @unbeatablesg
@yoitstippytoe dude, I meant "mad lemurs" in the "lots of lemurs" sense, not that they're angry! The zoo ones were actually mostly sleepy

Squirrel Girl! @unbeatablesg
@yoitstippytoe lots of sleepy lemurs to be had at your local zoo, visit today

Nancy W. @sewwiththeflo
I was at the zoo yesterday when the lions got out and this "Girl Squirrel" saved everyone.

Nancy W. @sewwiththeflo
As near as I can tell she is a squirrel with the INVERSE proportional strength of a girl? Or something?

Nancy W. @sewwiththeflo
What even is biology, you guys.

Nancy W. @sewwiththeflo
How do bodies even work.

Nancy W. @sewwiththeflo
Local woman publicly questions how a squirrel can have the powers of a girl. Vets hate me.

Tony Stark @starkmantony
@unbeatablesg Getting reports of fights breaking out all over NYC. Can I assume you are on this?

Squirrel Girl! @unbeatablesg
@starkmantony uh can you assume it's like 6:30am here and i just woke up

Tony Stark @starkmantony
@unbeatablesg My post woke you up? Huh. You have a special notification sound for me, don't you.

Squirrel Girl! @unbeatablesg
@starkmantony um, YEAH, it's your old 60s-style PERSONAL JINGLE that you hoped we'd all just forgot about and it's AMAZING

Squirrel Girl! @unbeatablesg
@starkmantony ♫ Tony Stark / Makes you feel / He's the cool exec / With a heart of steel ♫

Tony Stark @starkmantony
@unbeatablesg Hold on a second.

Tony Stark @starkmantony
@unbeatablesg I just remotely erased that song from your phone and from every other mirror online.

Squirrel Girl! @unbeatablesg
@starkmantony ♫ Tony Stark / Makes me feel / That I'm super glad / That I backed up that song to a device not connected to the internet ♫

Squirrel Girl! @unbeatablesg
Hey I dunno if any criminals follow me but JUST IN CASE, you should know that KOI BOI and CHIPMUNK HUNK are fighting crime now too!

Squirrel Girl! @unbeatablesg
Also if you are a criminal please stop doing crimes. #crimeadvice

search!

#databasesoneohone

#databasesoneohFUN

#dontthrowshadeonmyfriends

#breakfastbeats

#boythor

Bostonian Cameos

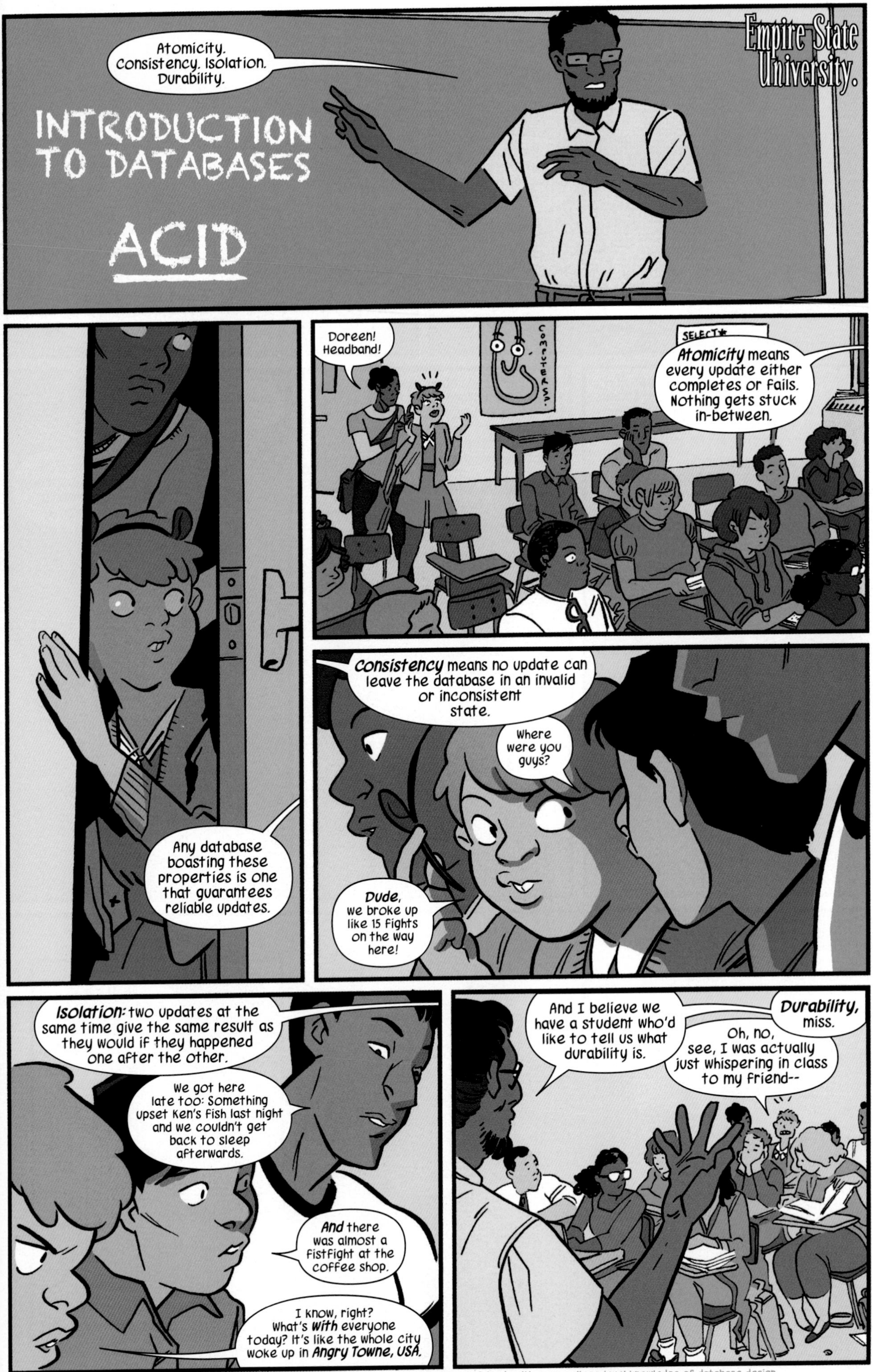
Empire State University.
Atomicity. Consistency. Isolation. Durability.
INTRODUCTION TO DATABASES
ACID
Doreen! Headband!
COMPUTERS!
SELECT*
Atomicity means every update either completes or fails. Nothing gets stuck in-between.
Consistency means no update can leave the database in an invalid or inconsistent state.
Where were you guys?
Any database boasting these properties is one that guarantees reliable updates.
Dude, we broke up like 15 fights on the way here!
Isolation: two updates at the same time give the same result as they would if they happened one after the other.
We got here late too: Something upset Ken's fish last night and we couldn't get back to sleep afterwards.
And there was almost a fistfight at the coffee shop.
I know, right? What's with everyone today? It's like the whole city woke up in Angry Towne, USA.
And I believe we have a student who'd like to tell us what durability is.
Durability, miss.
Oh, no, see, I was actually just whispering in class to my friend--

All these database facts are true, by the way. So now you can impress all your friends with your college-level knowledge of database design, so long as they don't ask a single follow-up question!

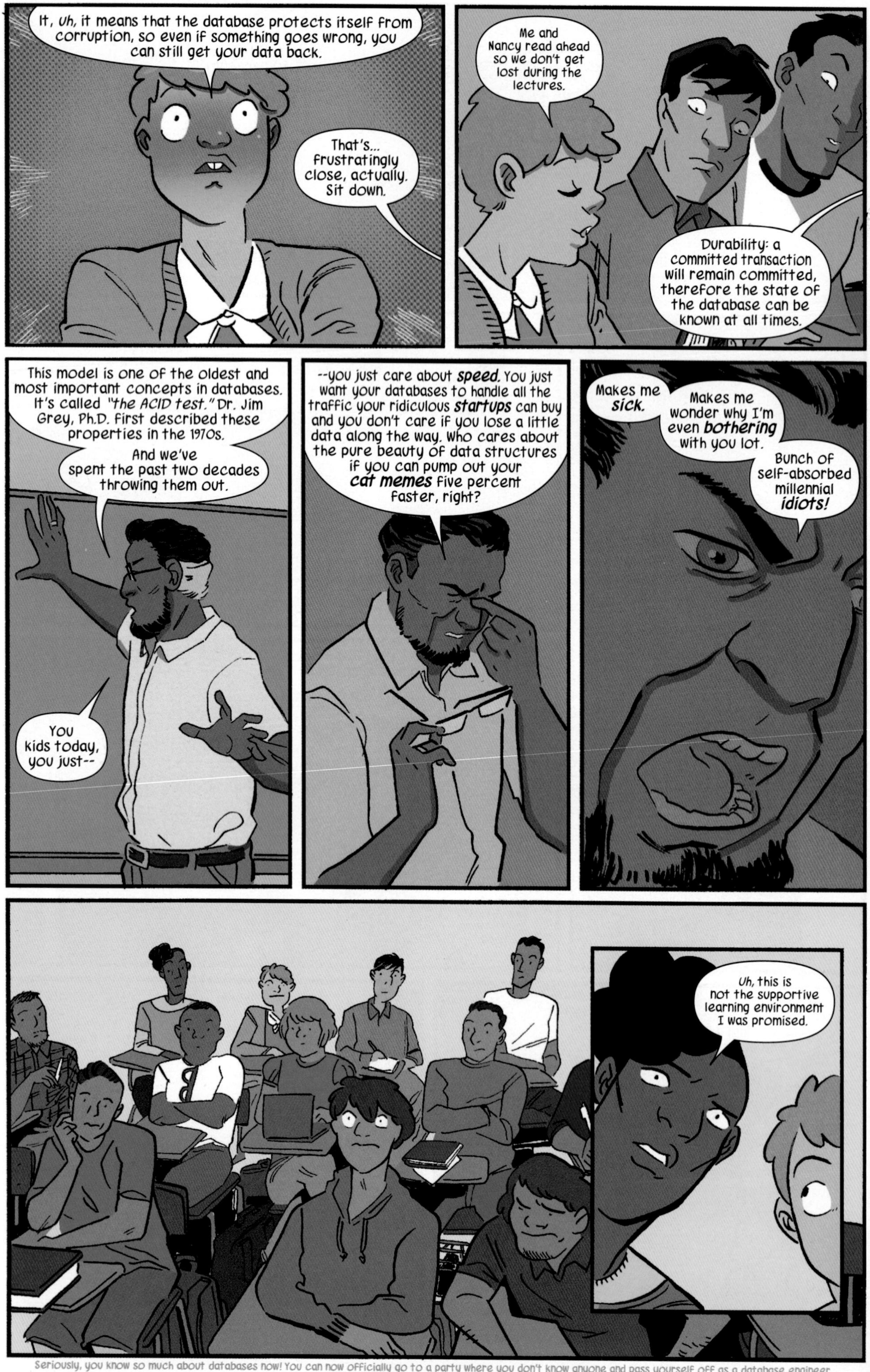
It, *uh*, it means that the database protects itself from corruption, so even if something goes wrong, you can still get your data back.
That's... frustratingly close, actually. Sit down.
Me and Nancy read ahead so we don't get lost during the lectures.
Durability: a committed transaction will remain committed, therefore the state of the database can be known at all times.
This model is one of the oldest and most important concepts in databases. It's called *"the ACID test."* Dr. Jim Grey, Ph.D. first described these properties in the 1970s.
And we've spent the past two decades throwing them out.
You kids today, you just--
--you just care about ***speed***. You just want your databases to handle all the traffic your ridiculous ***startups*** can buy and you don't care if you lose a little data along the way. Who cares about the pure beauty of data structures if you can pump out your ***cat memes*** five percent faster, right?
Makes me ***sick***.
Makes me wonder why I'm even ***bothering*** with you lot.
Bunch of self-absorbed millennial ***idiots!***
Uh, this is not the supportive learning environment I was promised.

Seriously, you know so much about databases now! You can now officially go to a party where you don't know anyone and pass yourself off as a database engineer. In fact, surprise, ***this is now mandatory***.

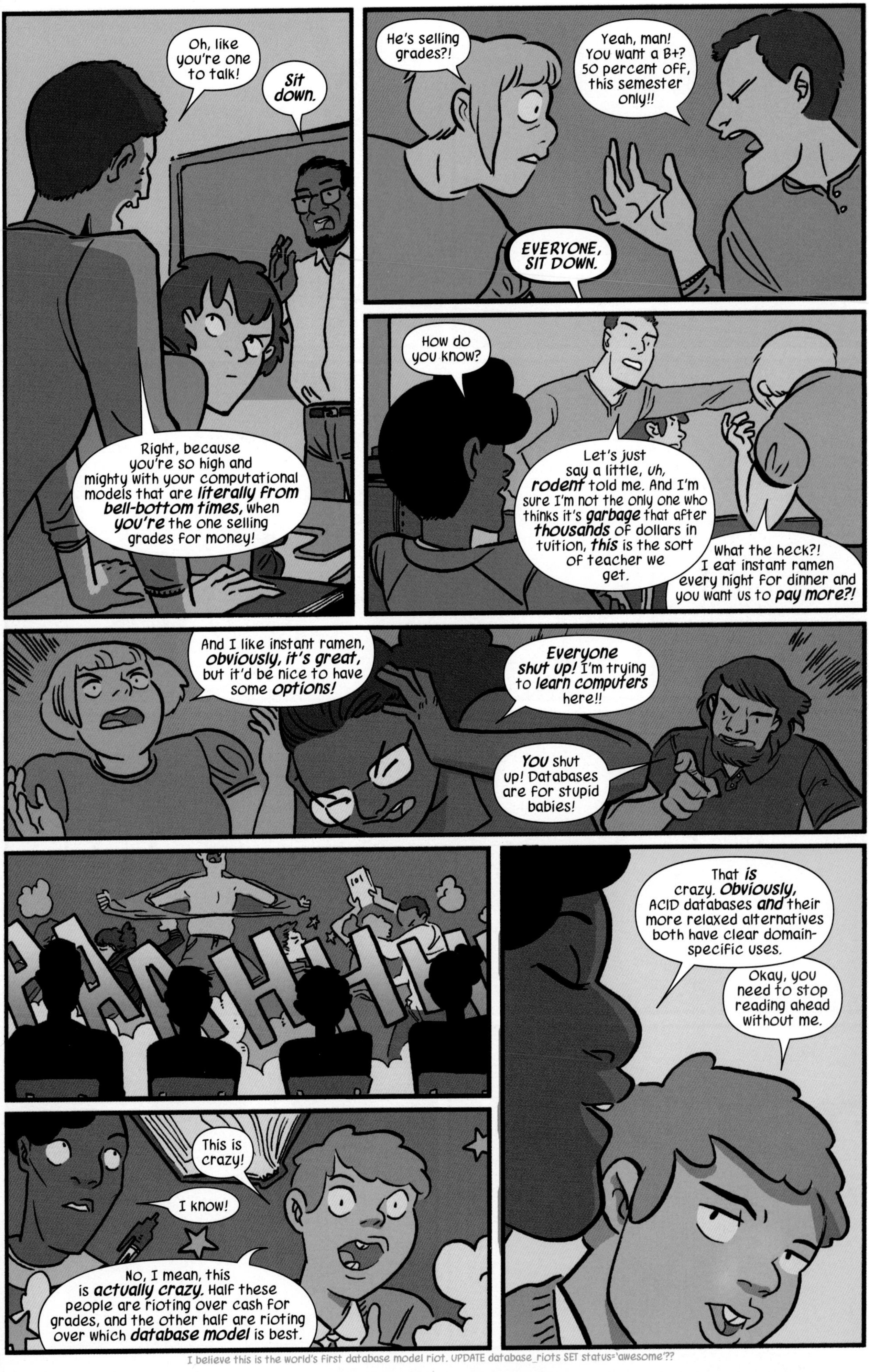
Oh, like you're one to talk!
Sit down.
Right, because you're so high and mighty with your computational models that are literally from bell-bottom times, when you're the one selling grades for money!
He's selling grades?!
Yeah, man! You want a B+? 50 percent off, this semester only!!
EVERYONE, SIT DOWN.
How do you know?
Let's just say a little, uh, rodent told me. And I'm sure I'm not the only one who thinks it's garbage that after thousands of dollars in tuition, this is the sort of teacher we get.
What the heck?! I eat instant ramen every night for dinner and you want us to pay more?!
And I like instant ramen, obviously, it's great, but it'd be nice to have some options!
Everyone shut up! I'm trying to learn computers here!!
YOU shut up! Databases are for stupid babies!
101
This is crazy!
I know!
No, I mean, this is actually crazy. Half these people are rioting over cash for grades, and the other half are rioting over which database model is best.
That is crazy. Obviously, ACID databases and their more relaxed alternatives both have clear domain-specific uses.
Okay, you need to stop reading ahead without me.

I believe this is the world's first database model riot. UPDATE database_riots SET status='awesome'??

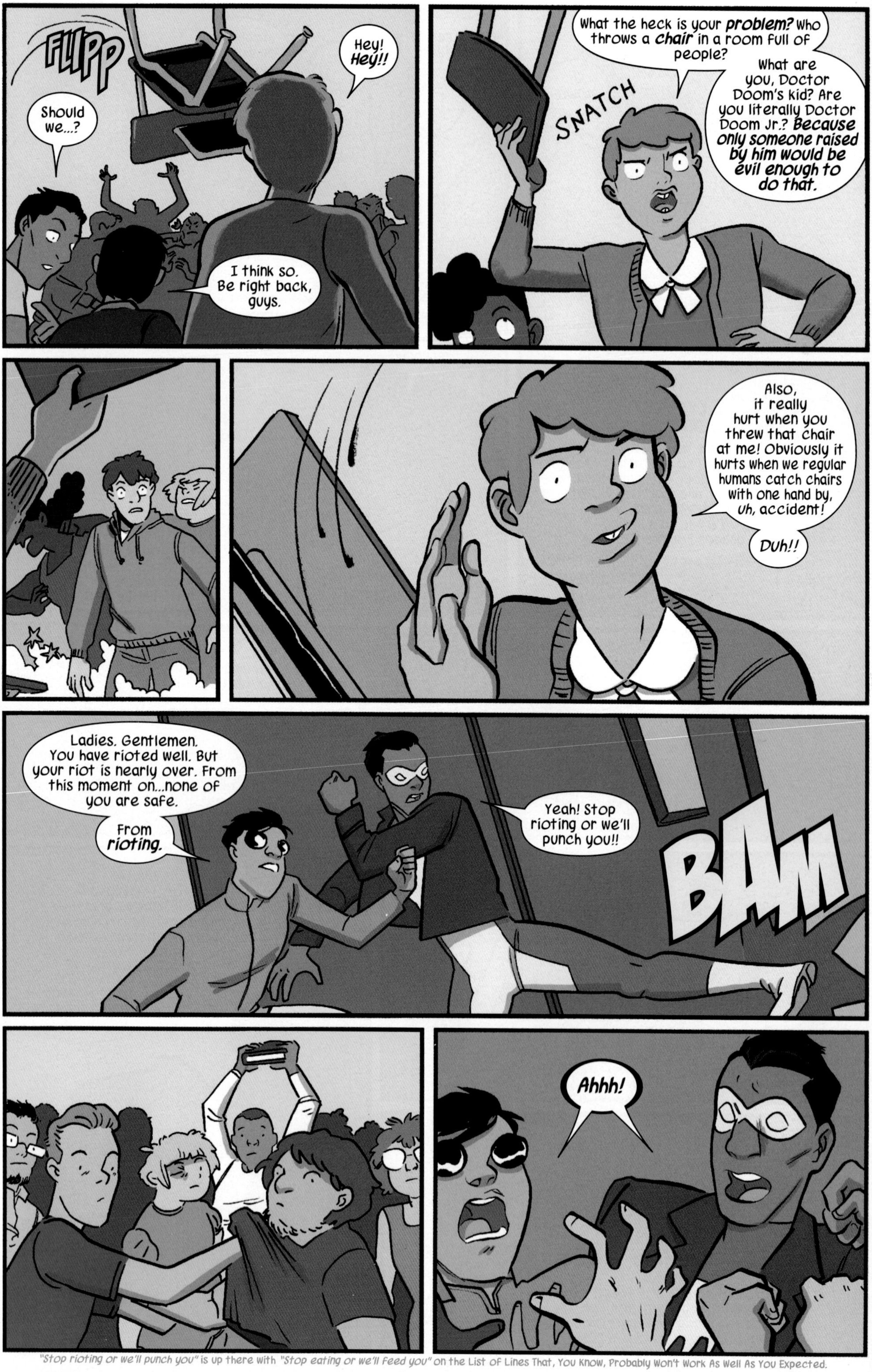
FLIPP
Hey! Hey!!
Should we...?
I think so. Be right back, guys.
What the heck is your problem? Who throws a chair in a room full of people?
SNATCH
What are you, Doctor Doom's kid? Are you literally Doctor Doom Jr.? Because only someone raised by him would be evil enough to do that.
Also, it really hurt when you threw that chair at me! Obviously it hurts when we regular humans catch chairs with one hand by, uh, accident!
Duh!!
Ladies. Gentlemen. You have rioted well. But your riot is nearly over. From this moment on...none of you are safe.
From rioting.
Yeah! Stop rioting or we'll punch you!!
BAM
Ahhh!

"Stop rioting or we'll punch you" is up there with "Stop eating or we'll feed you" on the List of Lines That, You Know, Probably Won't Work As Well As You Expected.

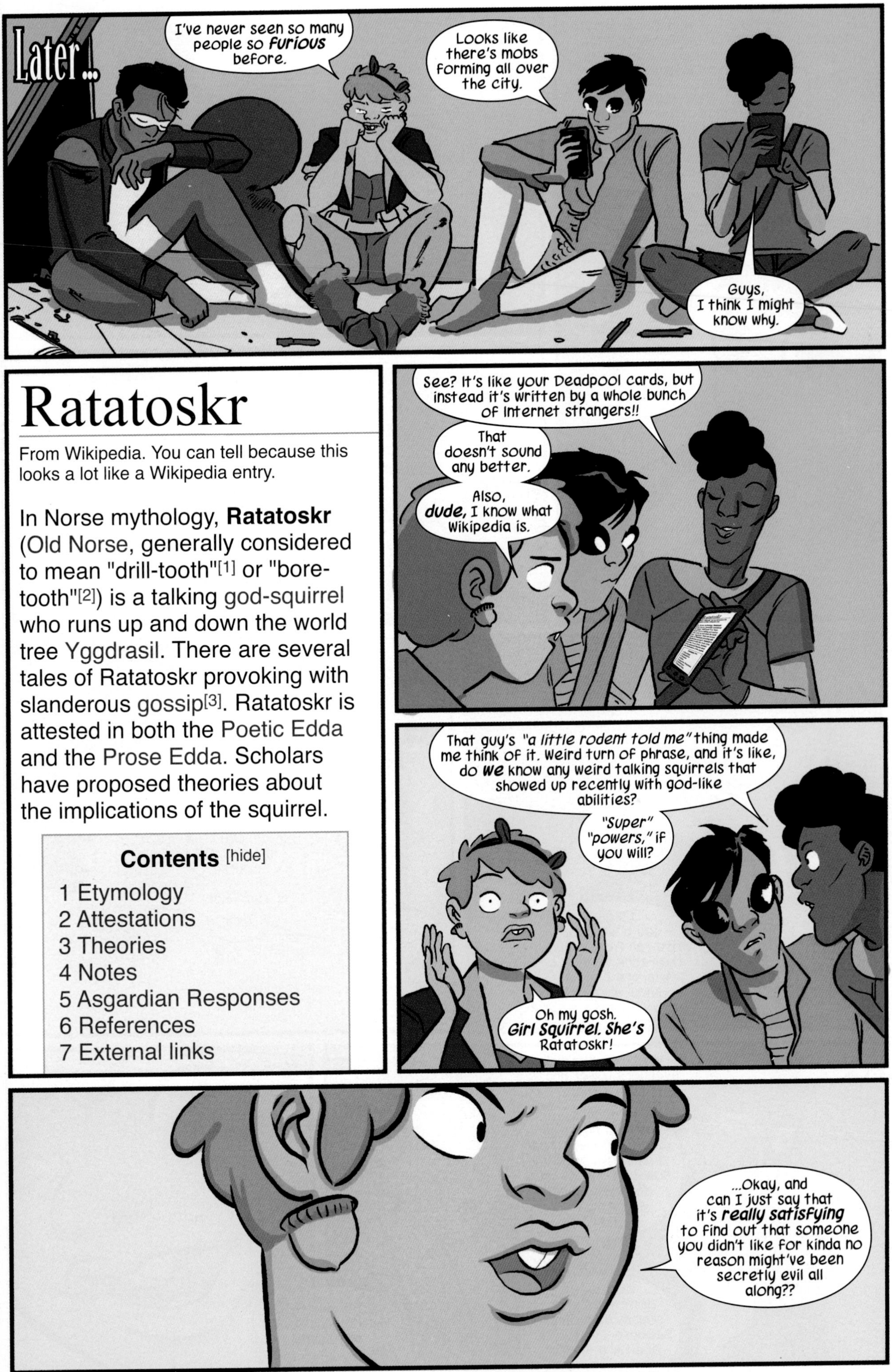
Later...
I've never seen so many people so *furious* before.
Looks like there's mobs forming all over the city.
Guys, I think I might know why.
Ratatoskr
From Wikipedia. You can tell because this looks a lot like a Wikipedia entry.
In Norse mythology, **Ratatoskr** (Old Norse, generally considered to mean "drill-tooth"[1] or "bore-tooth"[2]) is a talking god-squirrel who runs up and down the world tree Yggdrasil. There are several tales of Ratatoskr provoking with slanderous gossip[3]. Ratatoskr is attested in both the Poetic Edda and the Prose Edda. Scholars have proposed theories about the implications of the squirrel.
Contents [hide]
1 Etymology
2 Attestations
3 Theories
4 Notes
5 Asgardian Responses
6 References
7 External links
See? It's like your Deadpool cards, but instead it's written by a whole bunch of internet strangers!!
That doesn't sound any better.
Also, *dude,* I know what Wikipedia is.
That guy's *"a little rodent told me"* thing made me think of it. Weird turn of phrase, and it's like, do *we* know any weird talking squirrels that showed up recently with god-like abilities?
"Super" "powers," if you will?
Oh my gosh. *Girl Squirrel. She's* Ratatoskr!
...Okay, and can I just say that it's *really satisfying* to find out that someone you didn't like for kinda no reason might've been secretly evil all along??

Also, she was ripping off my name the whole time and that *was* annoying. There. I said it.

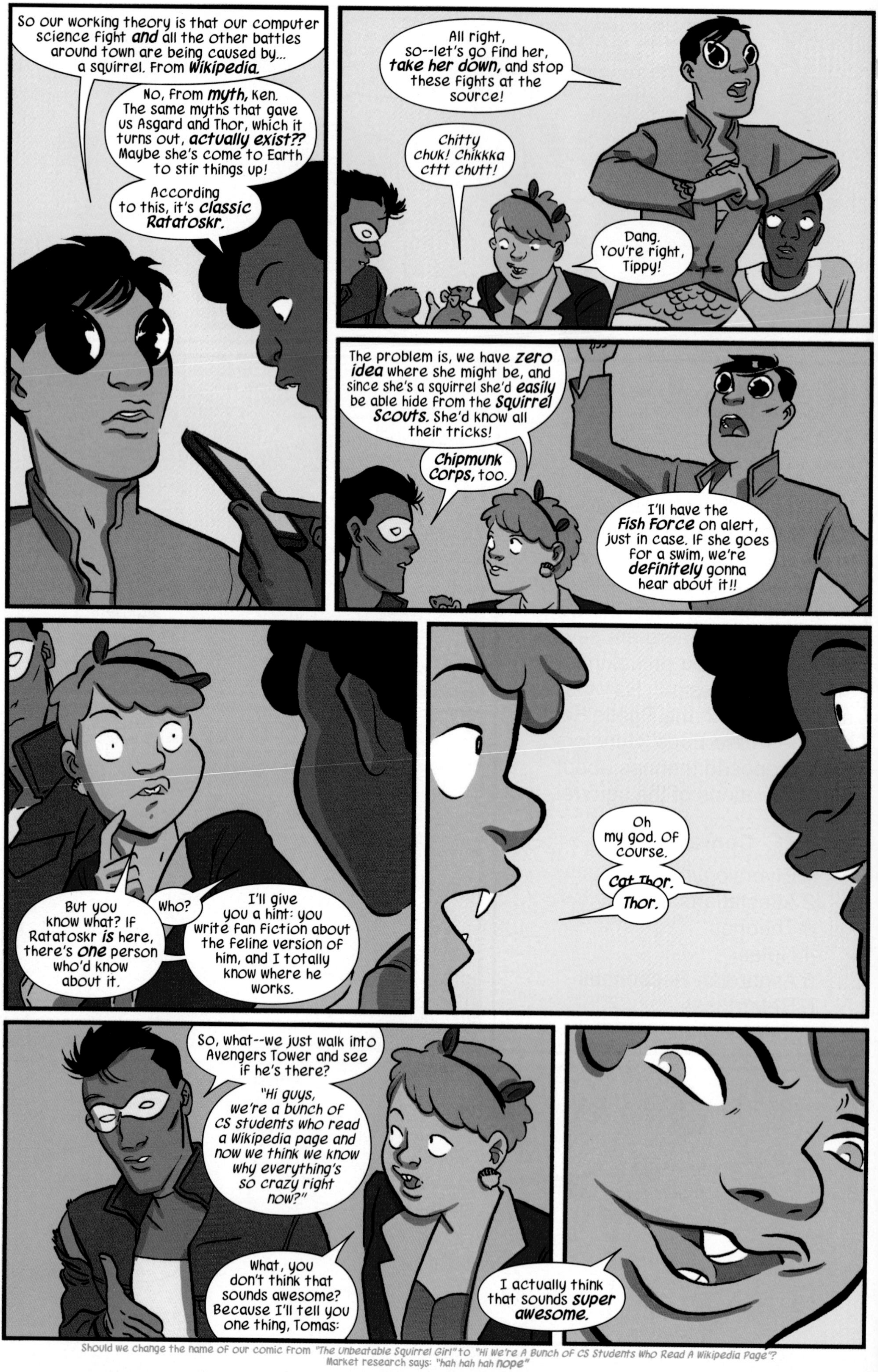
So our working theory is that our computer science fight and all the other battles around town are being caused by... a squirrel. From Wikipedia.
No, from myth, Ken. The same myths that gave us Asgard and Thor, which it turns out, actually exist?? Maybe she's come to Earth to stir things up!
According to this, it's classic Ratatoskr.
All right, so--let's go find her, take her down, and stop these fights at the source!
Chitty chuk! Chikkka cttt chutt!
Dang. You're right, Tippy!
The problem is, we have zero idea where she might be, and since she's a squirrel she'd easily be able hide from the Squirrel Scouts. She'd know all their tricks!
Chipmunk Corps, too.
I'll have the Fish Force on alert, just in case. If she goes for a swim, we're definitely gonna hear about it!!
But you know what? If Ratatoskr is here, there's one person who'd know about it.
Who?
I'll give you a hint: you write fan fiction about the feline version of him, and I totally know where he works.
Oh my god. Of course.
Cat Thor.
Thor.
So, what--we just walk into Avengers Tower and see if he's there?
"Hi guys, we're a bunch of CS students who read a Wikipedia page and now we think we know why everything's so crazy right now?"
What, you don't think that sounds awesome? Because I'll tell you one thing, Tomas:
I actually think that sounds super awesome.

Should we change the name of our comic from *"The Unbeatable Squirrel Girl"* to *"Hi We're A Bunch Of CS Students Who Read A Wikipedia Page"*?
Market research says: *"hah hah hah* ***nope****"*

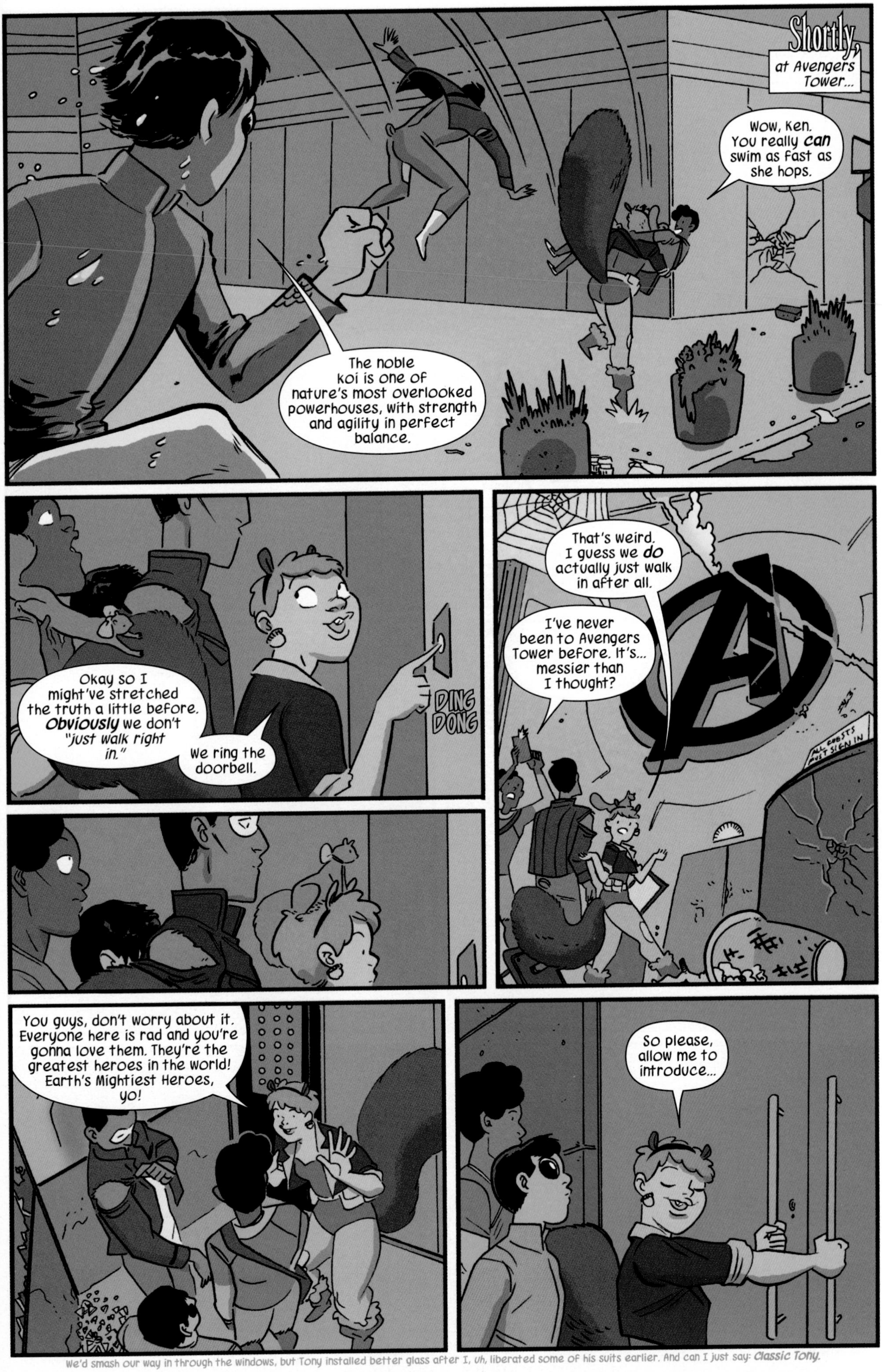
Shortly, at Avengers Tower...
Wow, Ken. You really **can** swim as fast as she hops.
The noble koi is one of nature's most overlooked powerhouses, with strength and agility in perfect balance.
Okay so I might've stretched the truth a little before. ***Obviously*** we don't "just walk right in."
We ring the doorbell.
DING DONG
That's weird. I guess we ***do*** actually just walk in after all.
I've never been to Avengers Tower before. It's... messier than I thought?
ALL GUESTS MUST SIGN IN
You guys, don't worry about it. Everyone here is rad and you're gonna love them. They're the greatest heroes in the world! Earth's Mightiest Heroes, yo!
So please, allow me to introduce...

We'd smash our way in through the windows, but Tony installed better glass after I, *uh*, liberated some of his suits earlier. And can I just say: ***Classic Tony.***

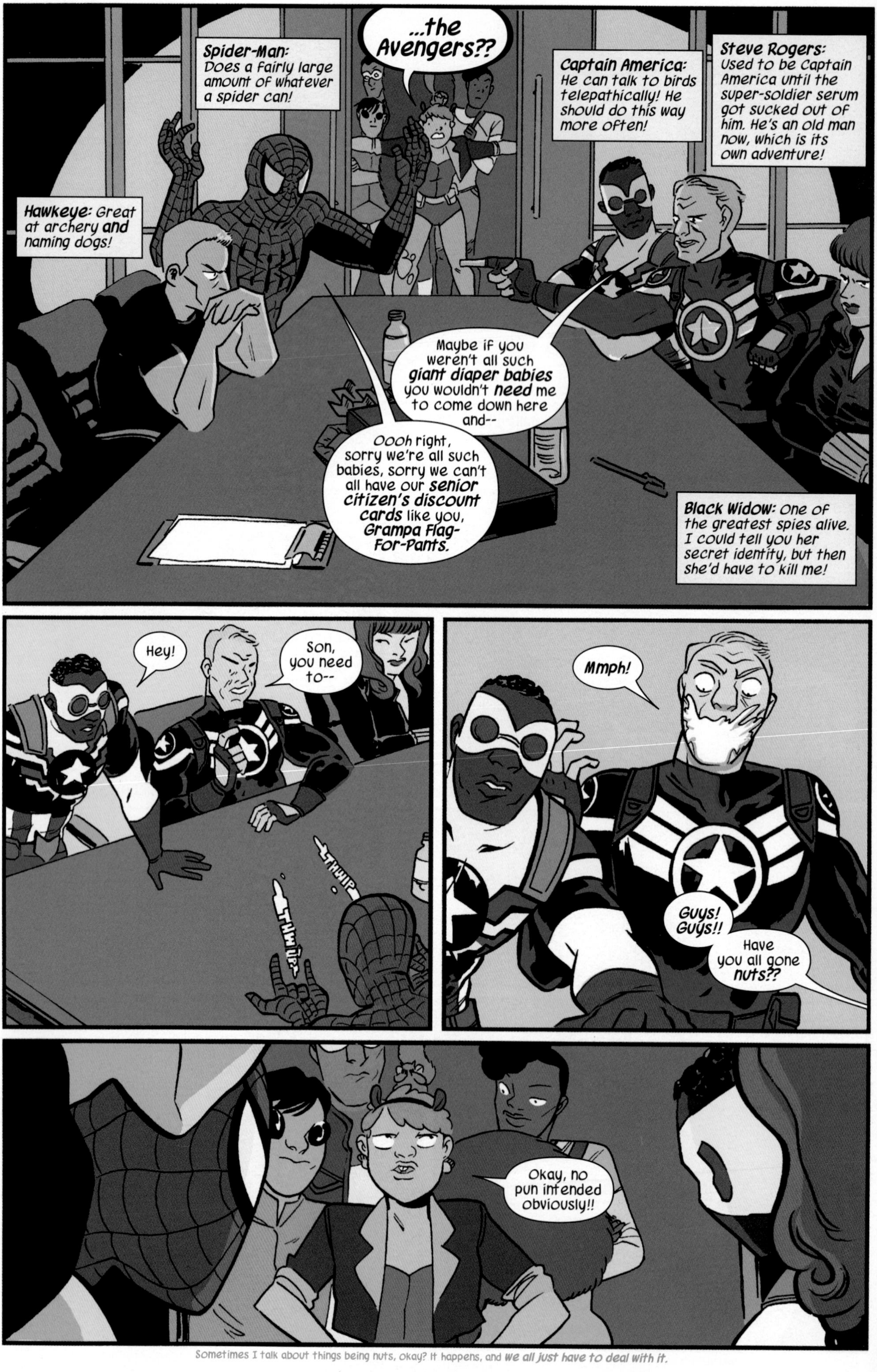

...the Avengers??
Spider-Man: Does a fairly large amount of whatever a spider can!
Captain America: He can talk to birds telepathically! He should do this way more often!
Steve Rogers: Used to be Captain America until the super-soldier serum got sucked out of him. He's an old man now, which is its own adventure!
Hawkeye: Great at archery and naming dogs!
Maybe if you weren't all such giant diaper babies you wouldn't need me to come down here and--
Oooh right, sorry we're all such babies, sorry we can't all have our senior citizen's discount cards like you, Grampa Flag-For-Pants.
Black Widow: One of the greatest spies alive. I could tell you her secret identity, but then she'd have to kill me!
Hey!
Son, you need to--
THWIP
THWIP
Mmph!
Guys! Guys!!
Have you all gone nuts??
Okay, no pun intended obviously!!

Sometimes I talk about things being nuts, okay? It happens, and *we all just have to deal with it.*

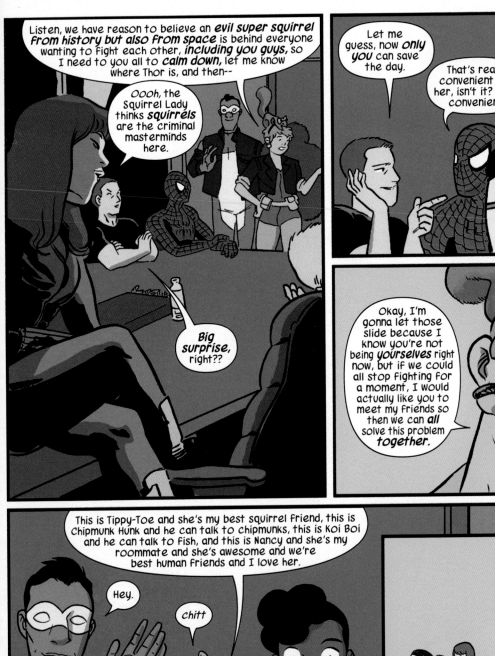

Listen, we have reason to believe an *evil super squirrel from history but also from space* is behind everyone wanting to fight each other, *including you guys,* so I need to you all to *calm down,* let me know where Thor is, and then--

Oooh, the Squirrel Lady thinks *squirrels* are the criminal masterminds here.

Big surprise, right??

Let me guess, now *only you* can save the day.

That's really convenient for her, isn't it? *Real* convenient.

Hey Squirrel Girl, who are your friends? *The Mixed Nuts?*

Okay, I'm gonna let those slide because I know you're not being *yourselves* right now, but if we could all stop fighting for a moment, I would actually like you to meet my friends so then we can *all* solve this problem *together.*

This is Tippy-Toe and she's my best squirrel friend, this is Chipmunk Hunk and he can talk to chipmunks, this is Koi Boi and he can talk to fish, and this is Nancy and she's my roommate and she's awesome and we're best human friends and I love her.

Hey.

Chitt

And I warn you: if you can't say anything nice, *don't* *say anything at all.*

I--

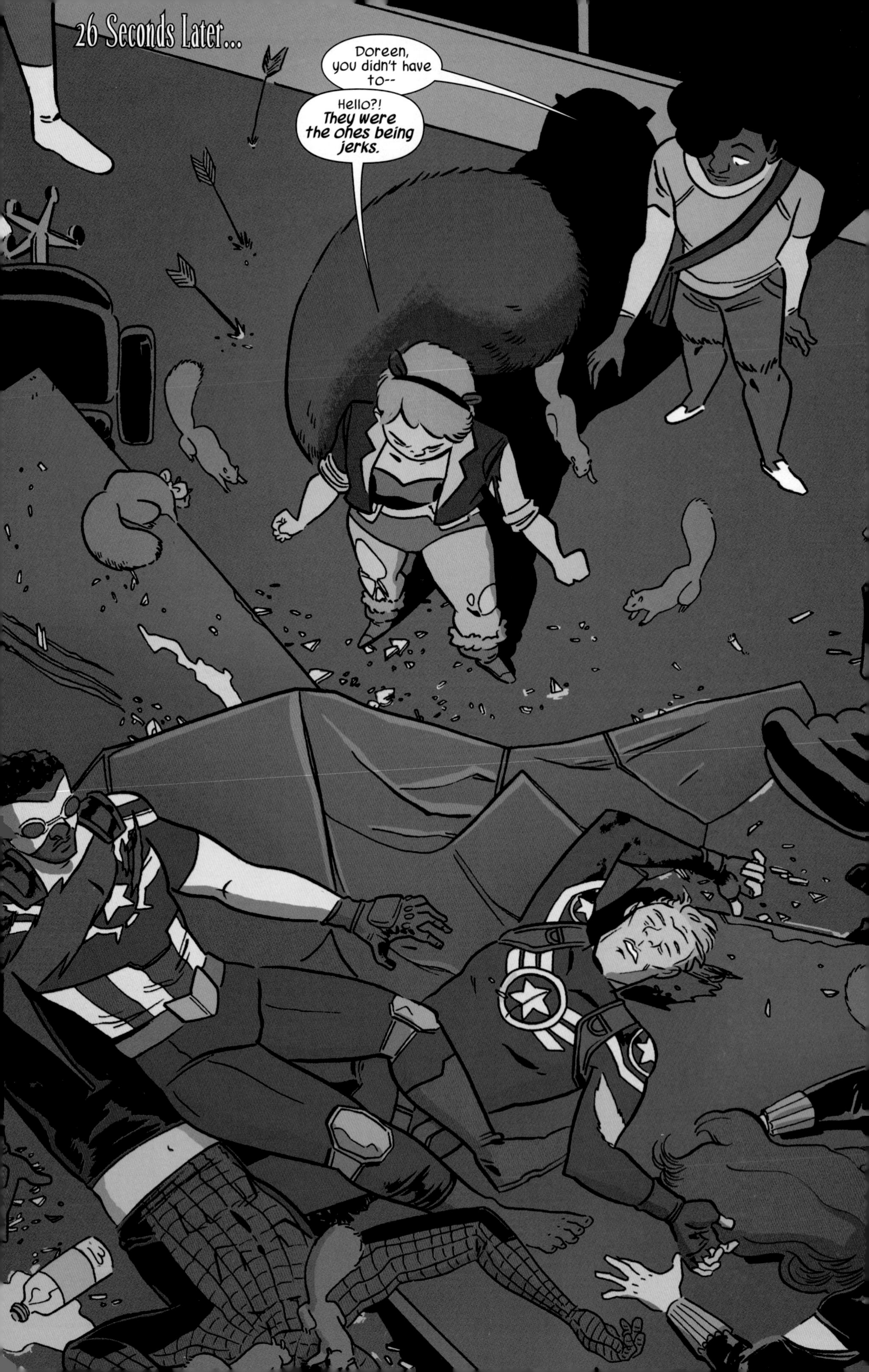
26 Seconds Later...
Doreen, you didn't have to--
Hello?! *They were the ones being jerks.*

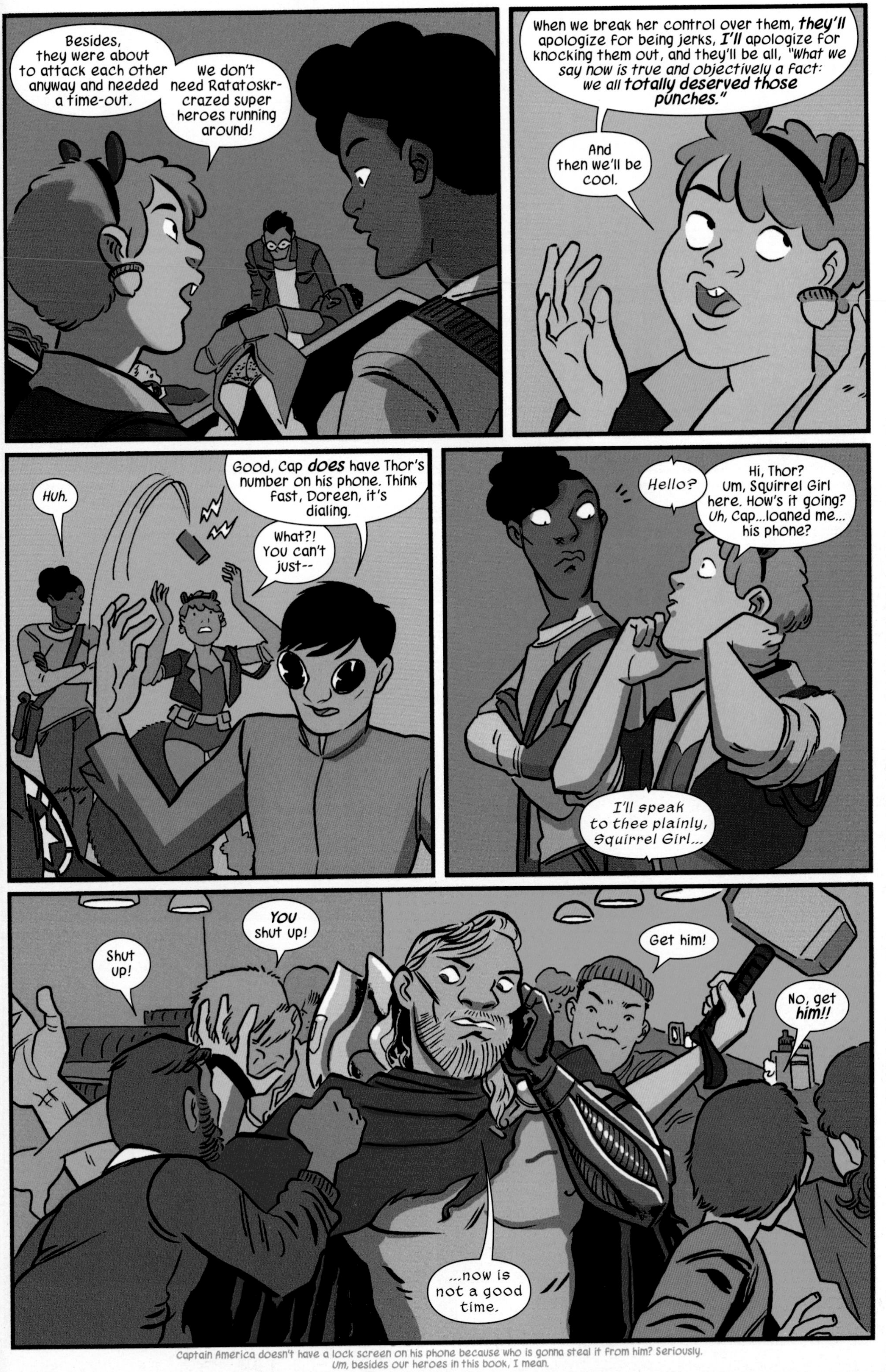
Besides, they were about to attack each other anyway and needed a time-out.
We don't need Ratatoskr-crazed super heroes running around!
When we break her control over them, they'll apologize for being jerks, I'll apologize for knocking them out, and they'll be all, "What we say now is true and objectively a fact: we all totally deserved those punches."
And then we'll be cool.
Huh.
Good, Cap does have Thor's number on his phone. Think fast, Doreen, it's dialing.
What?! You can't just--
Hello?
Hi, Thor? Um, Squirrel Girl here. How's it going? Uh, Cap...loaned me... his phone?
I'll speak to thee plainly, Squirrel Girl...
Shut up!
YOU shut up!
Get him!
No, get him!!
...now is not a good time.

Captain America doesn't have a lock screen on his phone because who is gonna steal it from him? Seriously.
Um, besides our heroes in this book, I mean.

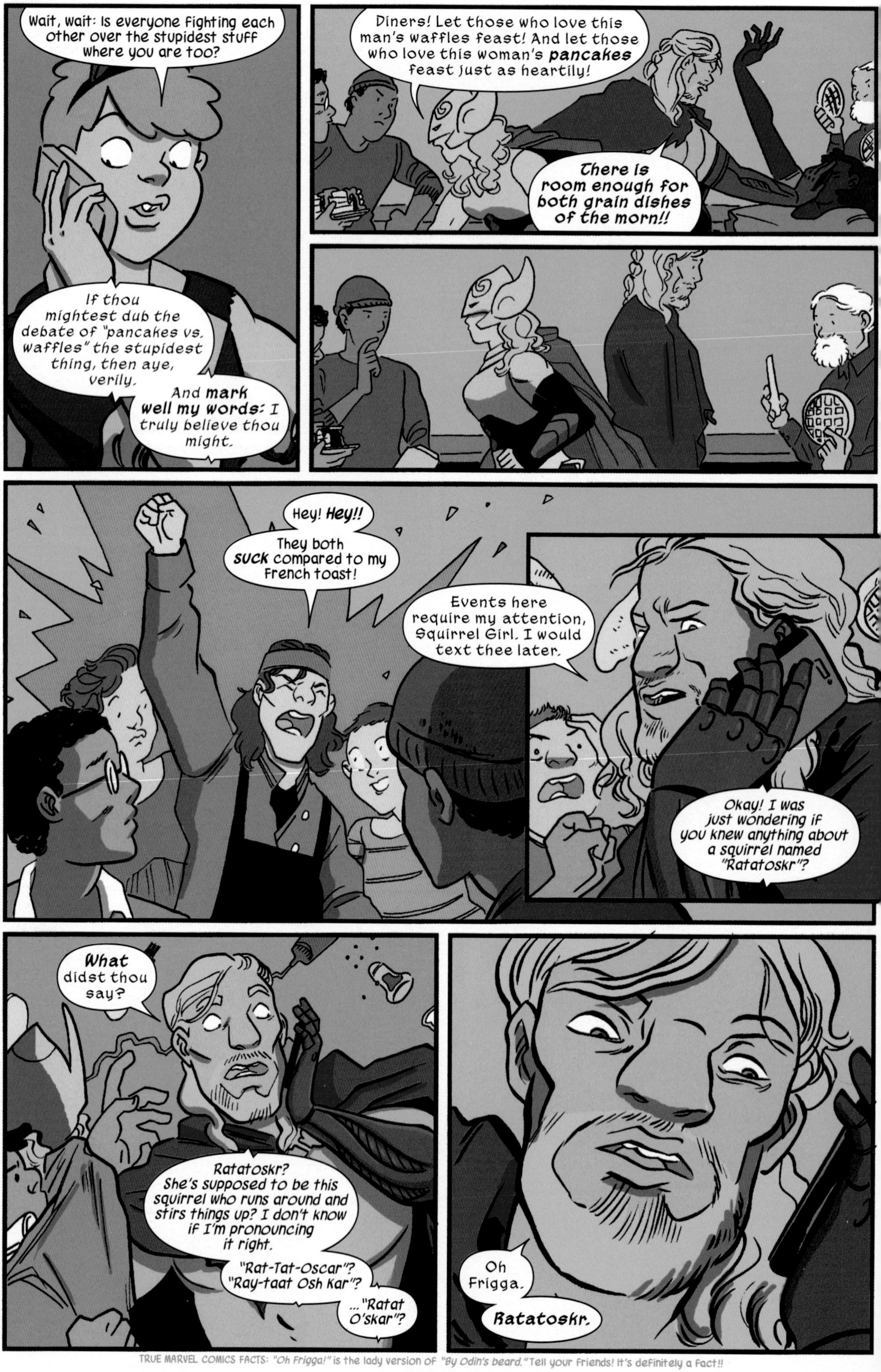
Wait, wait: Is everyone fighting each other over the stupidest stuff where you are too?
Diners! Let those who love this man's waffles feast! And let those who love this woman's **pancakes** feast just as heartily!
There is room enough for both grain dishes of the morn!!
If thou mightest dub the debate of "pancakes vs. waffles" the stupidest thing, then aye, verily.
And **mark well my words:** I truly believe thou might.
Hey! **Hey!!**
They both **SUCK** compared to my French toast!
Events here require my attention, Squirrel Girl. I would text thee later.
Okay! I was just wondering if you knew anything about a squirrel named "Ratatoskr"?
What didst thou say?
Ratatoskr? She's supposed to be this squirrel who runs around and stirs things up? I don't know if I'm pronouncing it right.
"Rat-Tat-Oscar"? "Ray-taat Osh Kar"?
..."Ratat O'skar"?
Oh Frigga.
Ratatoskr.

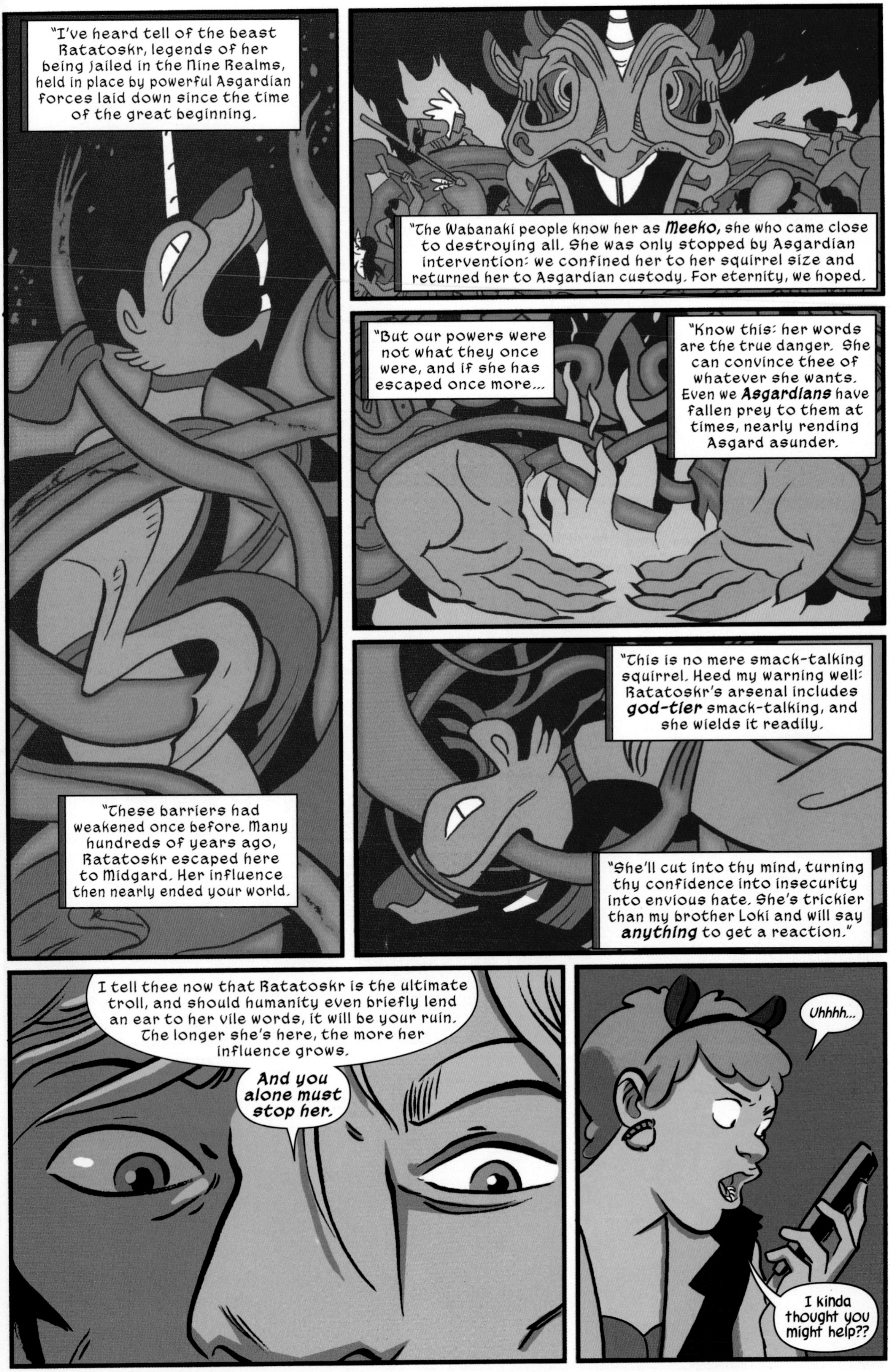
"I've heard tell of the beast Ratatoskr, legends of her being jailed in the Nine Realms, held in place by powerful Asgardian forces laid down since the time of the great beginning.
"The Wabanaki people know her as Meeko, she who came close to destroying all. She was only stopped by Asgardian intervention: we confined her to her squirrel size and returned her to Asgardian custody. For eternity, we hoped.
"But our powers were not what they once were, and if she has escaped once more...
"Know this: her words are the true danger. She can convince thee of whatever she wants. Even we Asgardians have fallen prey to them at times, nearly rending Asgard asunder.
"These barriers had weakened once before. Many hundreds of years ago, Ratatoskr escaped here to Midgard. Her influence then nearly ended your world.
"This is no mere smack-talking squirrel. Heed my warning well: Ratatoskr's arsenal includes god-tier smack-talking, and she wields it readily.
"She'll cut into thy mind, turning thy confidence into insecurity into envious hate. She's trickier than my brother Loki and will say anything to get a reaction."
I tell thee now that Ratatoskr is the ultimate troll, and should humanity even briefly lend an ear to her vile words, it will be your ruin. The longer she's here, the more her influence grows.
And you alone must stop her.
Uhhhh...
I kinda thought you might help??

See, Thor, *this* is why I keep saying you should contribute to Wikipedia. This is *way* more useful than their summary. *Sheesh!*

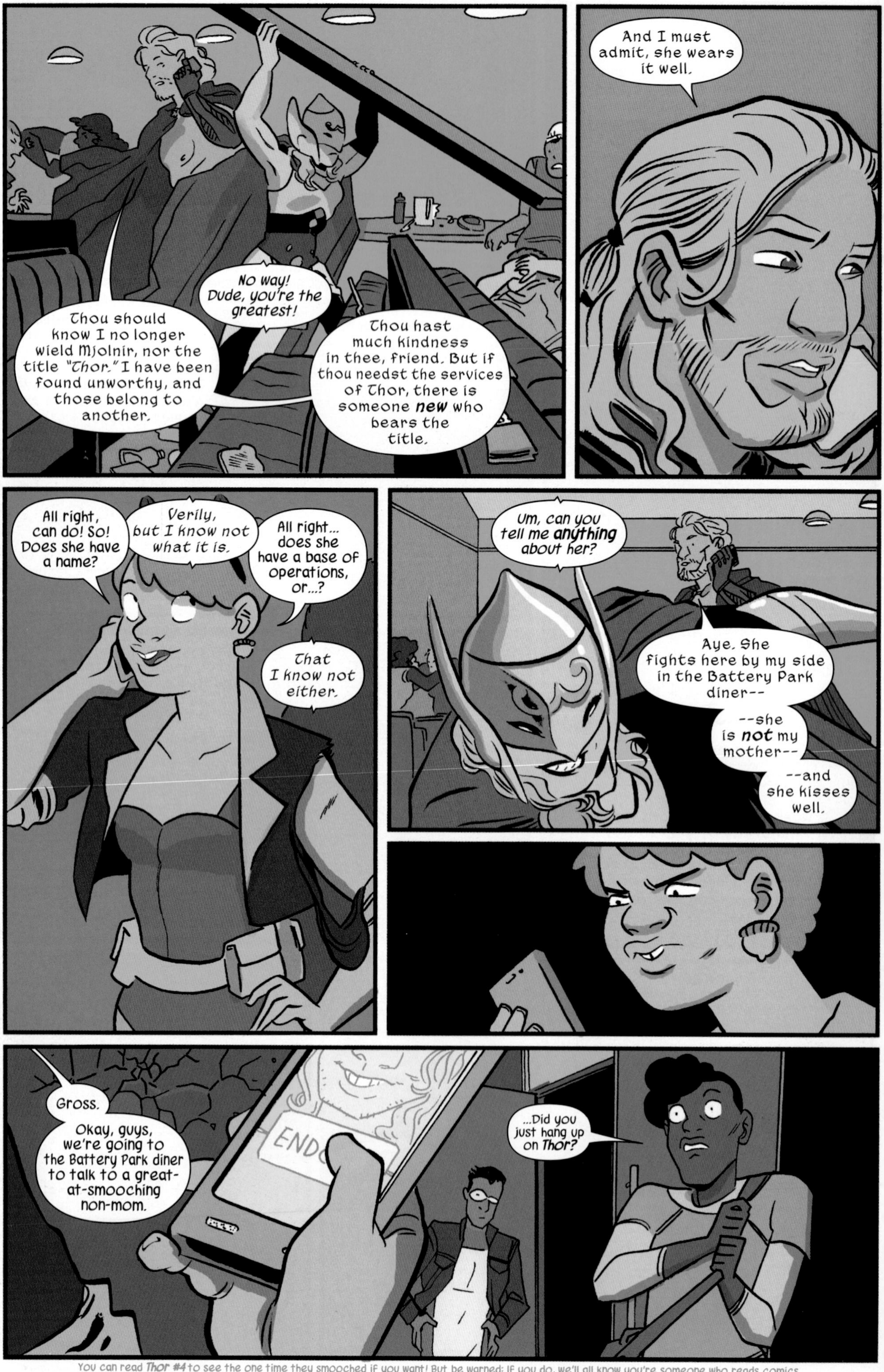
Thou should know I no longer wield Mjolnir, nor the title "Thor." I have been found unworthy, and those belong to another.
No way! Dude, you're the greatest!
Thou hast much kindness in thee, friend. But if thou needst the services of Thor, there is someone **new** who bears the title.
And I must admit, she wears it well.
All right, can do! So! Does she have a name?
Verily, but I know not what it is.
All right... does she have a base of operations, or...?
That I know not either.
Um, can you tell me **anything** about her?
Aye. She fights here by my side in the Battery Park diner--
--she is **not** my mother--
--and she kisses well.
Gross.
Okay, guys, we're going to the Battery Park diner to talk to a great-at-smooching non-mom.
END
...Did you just hang up on *Thor?*

You can read *Thor #4* to see the one time they smooched if you want! But be warned: if you do, we'll all know you're someone who reads comics just to flip forward to the smooches. *We'll all know. Even your parents will know.*

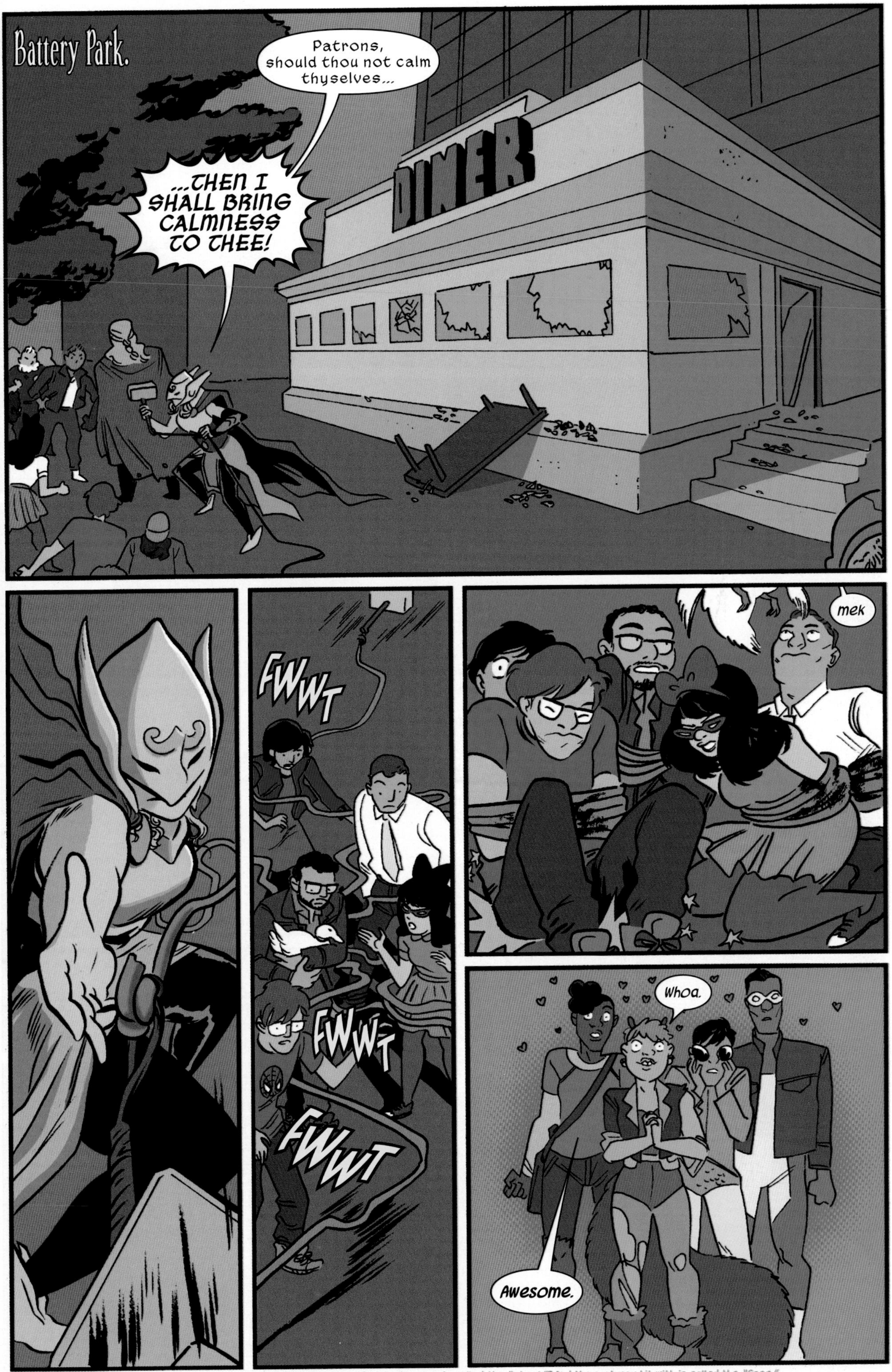
Battery Park.
Patrons, should thou not calm thyselves...
...THEN I SHALL BRING CALMNESS TO THEE!
DINER
FWWT
FWWT
FWWT
mek
Whoa.
Awesome.

TRUE REAL WORLD FACTS: Did you know that the side of a hammer is called the *"cheek"*? And the part you hit with is called the *"face,"* which is attached to the *"neck."* Hammers are these adorable little metal heads we invented to solve our problems.

Thors: Well met, friends and allies. Odinson here has told me of Ratatoskr, and if but half of what he says is true, then we must hasten to Asgard.

Once there we shall restore the barriers that bind her, though I fear that even *both* our efforts may not be enough to contain this beast.

How fares Captain America?

Nancy: I... ...kiiiinda... ...knocked him out?

Thors: Then the Avengers have been corrupted, just as I feared. Thou shalt return with us to Asgard, as you have experience with this beast.

Nancy: I'm sorry, Thors-- --and I can't believe I'm saying this-- --but I can't go.

Doreen: She means yes. She means "Yes *absolutely* we would like to go to Asgard, *forsooth* and *verily* we are honored to accept thy gracious invitation, thanks."

Nancy: Nancy, what happens after we fix Ratatoskr's cell?

We'd still need to return to Earth to find her, and stop her, *and* convince her to go back there.

It's just gonna get worse while we're gone, and I can't leave the planet to tear itself apart!

We could split up.

We'd stay here to, you know, keep civilization running, find Ratatoskr/Girl Squirrel/whatever her name is...

...and Nancy goes with them, helping them set things up there, and filling them in on what she's like now! Yes.

Chitt chitt!

Yeah, and Tippy goes too, to watch her back!

Nancy: I get to go to Asgard.

Thors: Very well. Once we have restored Ratatoskr's Asgardian bonds, it will be up to thee to return her to us.

Nancy: I get to go to *Asgard.*

Nancy: Hi, I'm Nancy Whitehead. *Huge* fan.

Quick question: are there cats in Asgard? Because what my *Cat Thor Fan Fiction* presupposes is--

KASHODOOM

Oh, I forgot to mention! That duck on the last page? His name is Chip Zducksky, and he's off to have his own adventures that we, for reasons of good taste, cannot publish here. Fare thee well, Chip Zducksky!

Much Later, in Central Park...

Am I gonna have to say it? That's the third mob we've subdued and we're still *no closer* to finding Ratatoskr.

The more fights we stop, the more innocents we save. And we *will* find her. Nobody can hide from *justice.*

Who says I'm hiding, chumleys??

Whoa!

Why so nervous? We're all on the same side here! Just a couple of animal-themed heroes trying to save the day against impossible odds, right, *friendos?*

Hi, I'm Squirrel Girl, and I have to ask...are you Ratatoskr?

Ratat-*WHO*skr?

She's an Asgardian squirrel who maybe came to Earth to destroy civilization through trolling and talkin' trash. It, *Uh--*

...it sounded more reasonable before I said it out loud.

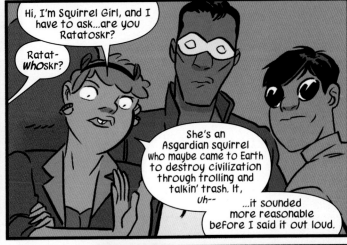

Hah! You saw the news, right? If I'm Ratatoskr, why would I have saved those people at the zoo? That's doing *good*, not spreading chaos!

And why would I go to all the trouble of making myself this adorable super hero costume just so I could trick you later by being evil?

And how am I supposed to be talking to all these people, anyway? What, do I visit their homes in a single night like some demented Squirrel Claus, using my special talents to inject messages into their brains, messages that I'm sustaining still, even as we speak?

Uh--

--you're saying that sarcastically, but it's actually a really credible way to accomplish what's been going on??

Seriously, I don't know if you realize this, but what you're saying really makes it sound like you actually did it and you're just toying with u--*OHHHH.*

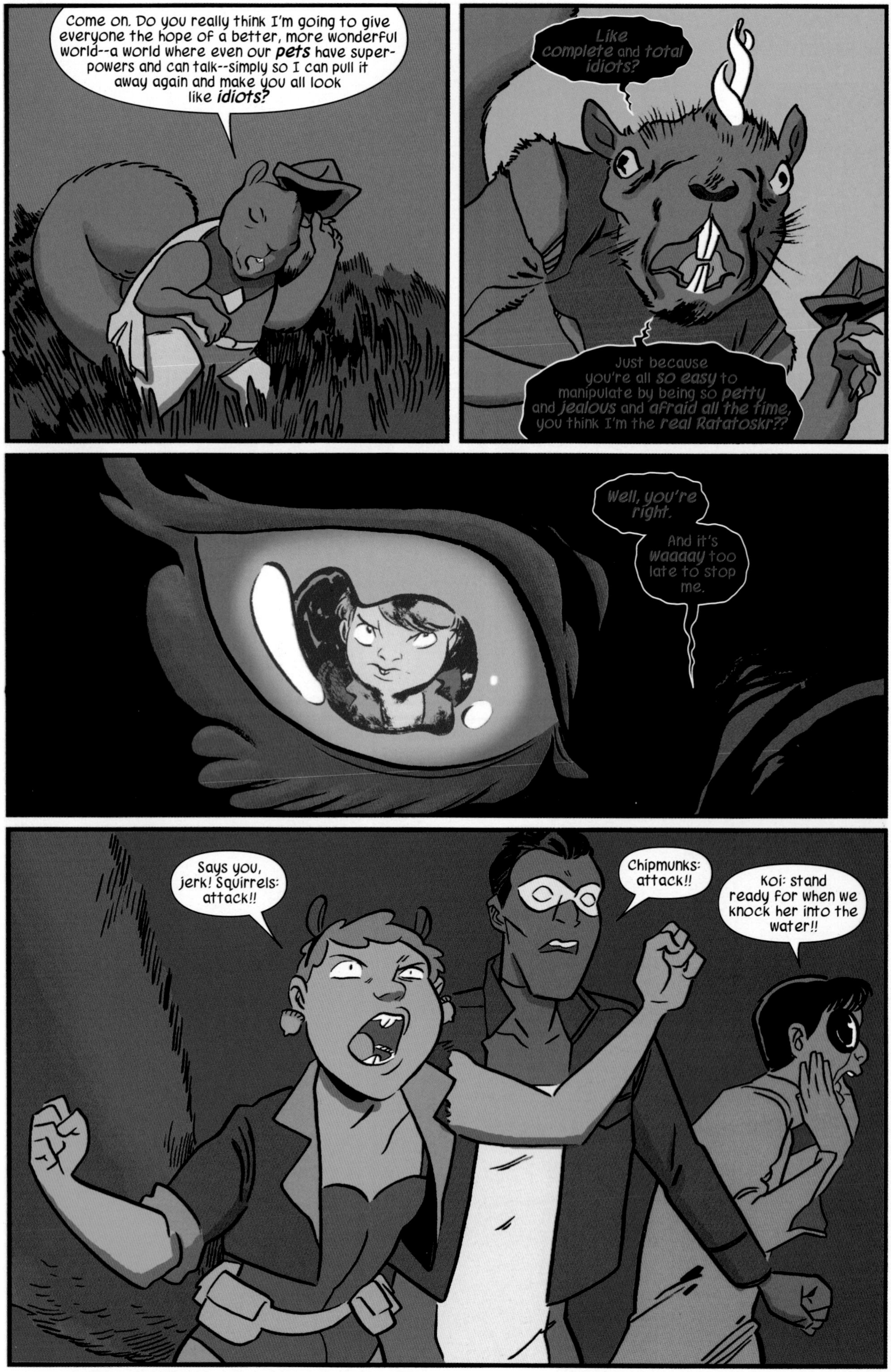
Come on. Do you really think I'm going to give everyone the hope of a better, more wonderful world--a world where even our pets have super-powers and can talk--simply so I can pull it away again and make you all look like idiots?
Like complete and total idiots?
Just because you're all so easy to manipulate by being so petty and jealous and afraid all the time, you think I'm the real Ratatoskr??
Well, you're right.
And it's waaaay too late to stop me.
Says you, jerk! Squirrels: attack!!
Chipmunks: attack!!
Koi: stand ready for when we knock her into the water!!

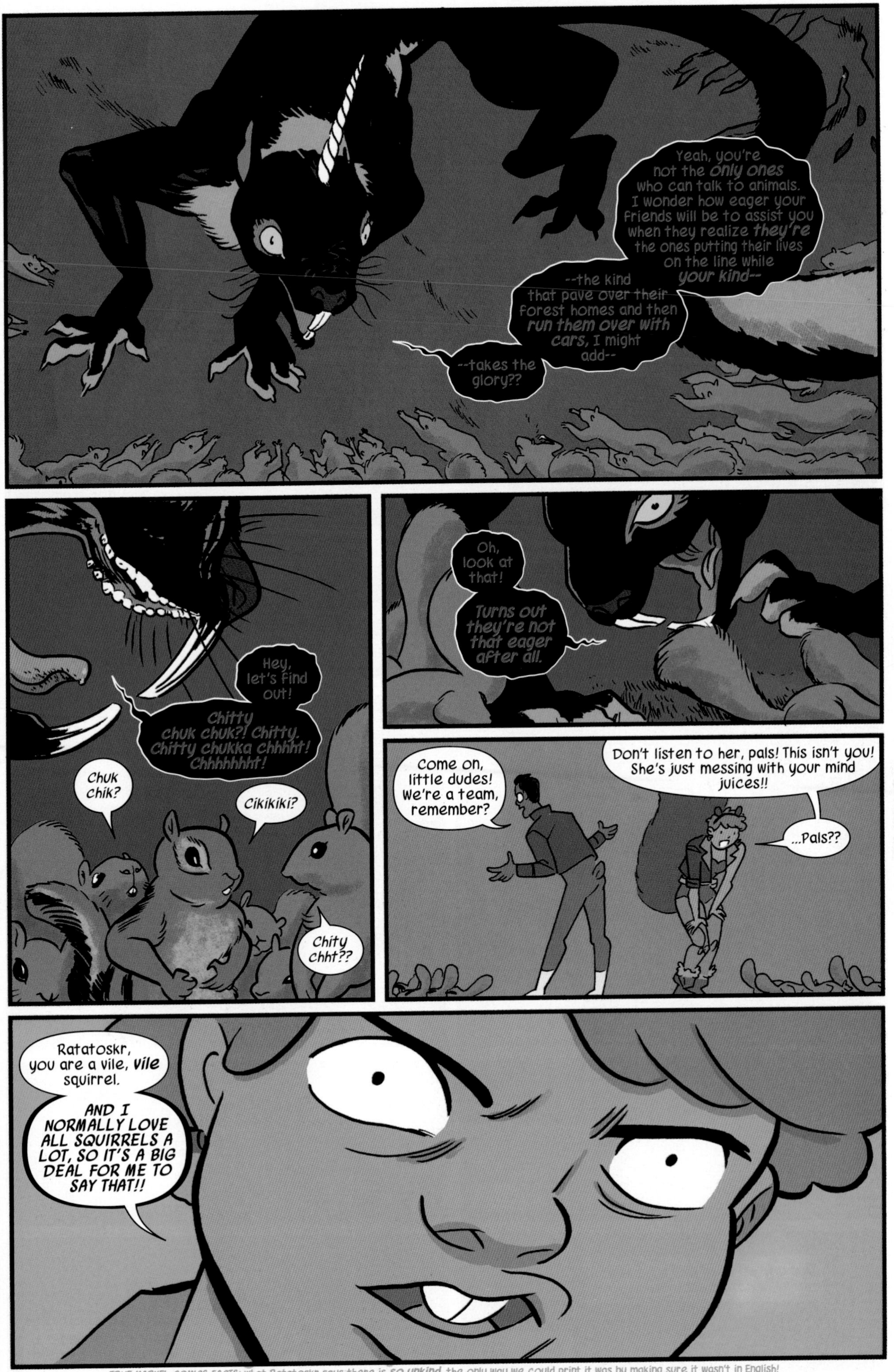
Yeah, you're not the only ones who can talk to animals. I wonder how eager your friends will be to assist you when they realize they're the ones putting their lives on the line while your kind--
--the kind that pave over their forest homes and then run them over with cars, I might add--
--takes the glory??
Hey, let's find out!
Chitty chuk chuk?! Chitty. Chitty chukka chhhht! Chhhhhhht!
Chuk chik?
Cikikiki?
Chity Chht??
Oh, look at that!
Turns out they're not that eager after all.
Come on, little dudes! We're a team, remember?
Don't listen to her, pals! This isn't you! She's just messing with your mind juices!!
...Pals??
Ratatoskr, you are a vile, vile squirrel.
AND I NORMALLY LOVE ALL SQUIRRELS A LOT, SO IT'S A BIG DEAL FOR ME TO SAY THAT!!

TRUE MARVEL COMICS FACTS: what Ratatoskr says there is *so unkind,* the only way we could print it was by making sure it wasn't in English! So yeah, I guess just make sure you don't show this comic to any squirrels you want to be friends with.

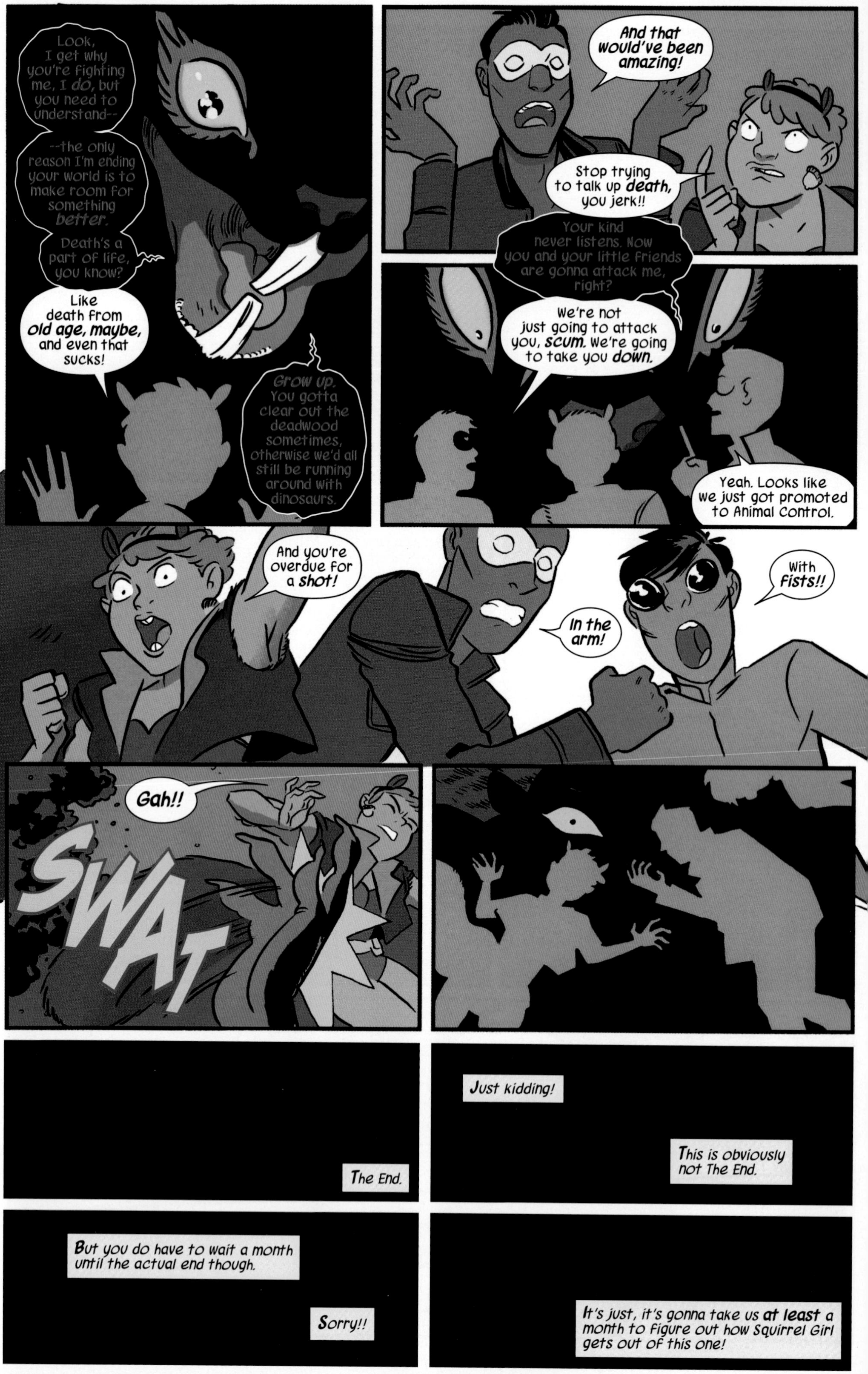
Look, I get why you're fighting me, I *do*, but you need to understand--
--the only reason I'm ending your world is to make room for something *better*.
Death's a part of life, you know?
Like death from **old age, maybe,** and even that sucks!
Grow up. You gotta clear out the deadwood sometimes, otherwise we'd all still be running around with dinosaurs.
And that would've been amazing!
Stop trying to talk up **death,** you jerk!!
Your kind never listens. Now you and your little friends are gonna attack me, right?
We're not just going to attack you, **scum.** We're going to take you **down.**
Yeah. Looks like we just got promoted to Animal Control.
And you're overdue for a **shot!**
In the arm!
With **fists!!**
Gah!!
SWAT
The End.
Just kidding!
This is obviously not The End.
But you do have to wait a month until the actual end though.
Sorry!!
It's just, it's gonna take us **at least** a month to figure out how Squirrel Girl gets out of this one!

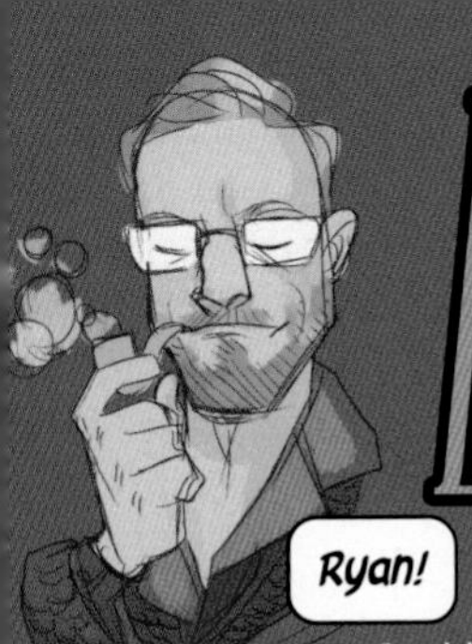
Ryan!

Letters From Nuts

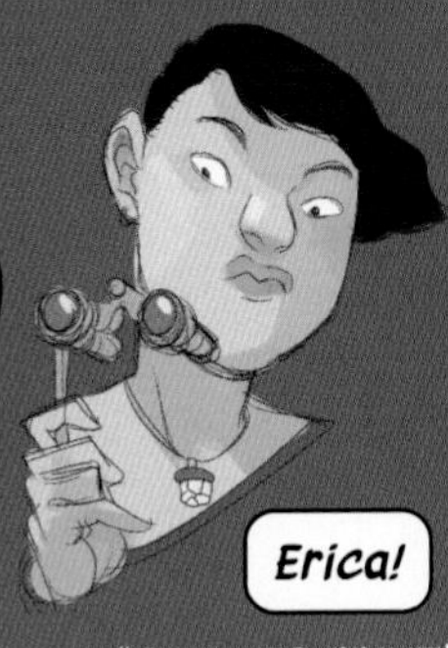
Erica!

Send letters to mheroes@marvel.com or 135 W 50th St, 7th Floor, New York, NY 10020 (Please mark "OKAY TO PRINT")

Dear Erica and Ryan,

Could you please make a spin off series for Squirrel Grrrl 2099. She looks badasssss! Power of squirrels and lazerss!

Thanks
Brent, Auckland, NZ

RYAN: I'm actually way more interested in what Bass Lass (and Squirrel Earl) are up to! What are her powers? Does wearing a fish head and an evening gown give her powers, and if so, how did she ever discover that? Would - would I get her powers under similar circumstances?

ERICA: I'm torn on this. On the one hand, I prefer to have something like that not get any bigger than it is because we all have our own expectations of who she is and defining it would narrow down who she is. On the other hand, earlier this year, my boyfriend read Doom 2099 out loud to me as we lay on the sofa so I'm definitely into some 2099 craziness.

Hey!

First of all, this is not my email account. I am only 9. This is my mom's account. Second of all, I know I'm a little young to be reading SQUIRREL GIRL, but I am addicted to any girl super hero comic. Third of all, you are awesome, period. Here are my top 5 comic books (not in any type of order):

- Ms. Marvel
- Squirrel Girl
- Supergirl
- Wonder Woman
- Buffy Vampire Slayer

Can't wait to read more comics.

Eliot P.

RYAN: Hey Eliot, thanks! That's great company to be in. This was a very sweet letter, and I'm stoked you like so many female super heroes! There's a whole universe of them out there, and it's getting bigger all the time. Hooray!

ERICA: I think as long as you can open up Unbeatable Squirrel Girl and know what the words mean, you're old enough to read it. Ryan's right (don't tell him I said that), there are a ton of great books out there. When you're a couple of years older, e-mail again and I'll have a giant list of recommendations.

For the Avengers premiere, as a fundraiser, my manager agreed to dress up as any super hero his reports wanted as long as we each donated $100 to charity. We all chipped in and after a brief discussion, we of course chose the Unbeatable Squirrel Girl. We all pitched in on the costume and I think he pulled it off pretty well.

Kyle Gong

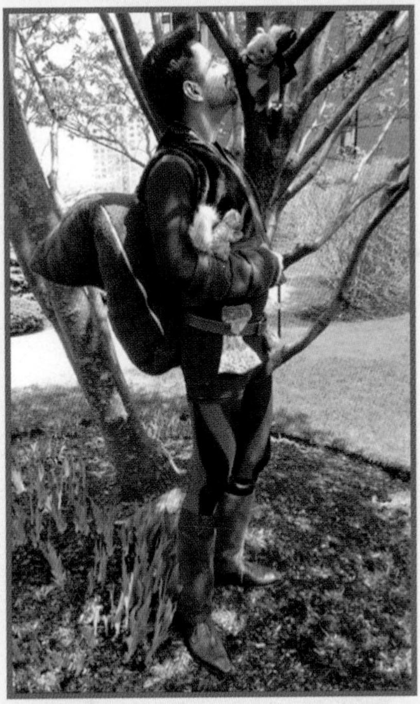

RYAN: I rate your manager: AWESOME. Also please tell me he came in with those plastic bags of nuts tied to his belt before the costume was ever conceived of, because that is a new level of efficient snacking.

ERICA: YES YES YES YES YES YES YES YES YES YES YES YES YES YES YES YES YES YES YES YES YES YES YES YES YES YES YES YES YES YES YES YES YES YES YES YES YES YES YES

Dear Erica and Ryan and whoever else is involved in creating this book,

UNBEATABLE SQUIRREL GIRL is such a great, entertaining book that it inspired me to write to Marvel for the FIRST TIME EVER. See how important you are? Keep up the good work.

So, I got a question and a suggestion:

- Can we have another miniseries starring the Pet Avengers, only this time including Tippy-Toe and, maybe, Mew? I know there's a cat there already, but I think Mew's interactions with Ms. Lion would be priceless!
- I think we should have a cameo from Iara Dos Santos [aka Shark-Girl] on this book. For no other reason than she's from my city and I think that would be awesome. Make it happen! Pretty please?

Tiago Maciel
Recife, Brazil

RYAN: 1) I think about the Pet Avengers all the time.

2) I didn't know about Shark-Girl, and now I think about HER all the time too! Koi Boi and Shark-Girl: will their love sink, or will it - at last, at long last - swim??

ERICA: 1) There can totally be two cats. Who says there can't be two cats? I demand MORE CATS. Cat Thor, I say.

2) Shark-Girl is great. I vote yes.

Dear Erica, Ryan and Rico,

As a proud dog owner, I am predisposed to absolutely hate squirrels. They torment my dogs in the backyard, sitting in trees and mocking them with their incessant chirping. During normal conversation, I have to spell out the S-Q-U-I-R-R-E-L word because my dogs know that word and begin to bark and rampage. Squirrels are nothing more than dog-aggravating, plague-carrying rodents.

With all that in my past, I was predisposed to despise Squirrel Girl and all she represented. Then I read the first story arc and I immediately changed my tune. Not only is the story itself funny and engaging and beautifully drawn, but I am seeing a new side of the squirrel. I have started to appreciate their craftiness and versatility. Maybe like Kraven, my dogs need to find a new enemy.

I have attempted to read Squirrel Girl comics to my dogs in the hopes of changing their minds. Sadly, they are too distracted by the squirrels outside to ever sit still for enough time.

Max D.
Los Angeles, CA

RYAN: My first dog, Kita, hated squirrels too (or really just loved to bark at them and chase them off the deck? It is impossible to say). My current dog, Noam Chompsky, doesn't really notice squirrels, but I do, and if I'm behind on a deadline it's like they're all saying "hey stop hanging out with your dog in the park and go work, slacker." So I think it's fair to say that, like you, my relationship with squirrels has become... more complicated?

ERICA: As I've mentioned in the letters before, I was bitten by a squirrel (remember kids, they're wild animals!) and had to get tested for rabies. It took me a long time to come back around to squirrels but I was pretty okay with them again before I started on the book. Now my goal is to find someone who has a pet squirrel so that I can play with it.

Hi there!

I would like to start with thanking you guys for providing me with a comic that is most definitely worth spending my money on; I buy them both in digital and physical copies, because when living in Denmark it takes a while for the magazines to arrive and I'm not always a patient person - not when it comes to things like this ;)

Secondly, OH MY GOSH! I've never had that much attention on any of my cosplays, as when you retweeted and blogged my Star Trek/Squirrel Girl picture, as well as my "standard" ones (not that there's anything ordinary about Doreen.)

I fell in love with her after reading the first volume, with her positive attitude, her humor and her style, and knew right away that I had to make her my newest cosplay, and I love it! She has practical pockets (lots of room for nuts) and while my tail is a tiny bit heavy, it's also a build-in chair! And people loved it when I brought it to the latest con! I even made a nice bunch of her trading cards, just for props .I am introducing her to everyone I know, and the last time I saw my five year old sister, her very first thing to say was not "hi," but rather "you're a squirrel!" because she'd seen the pictures online.

I love Doreen, Tippy Toe and you guys, and I am happy to spread the word!

Peace out!
Stine Fuchs

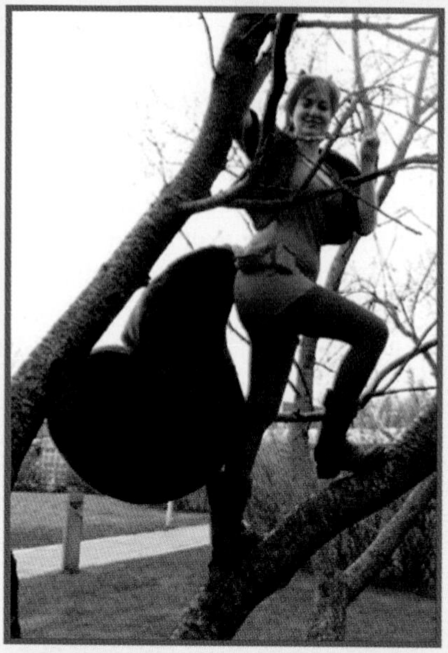

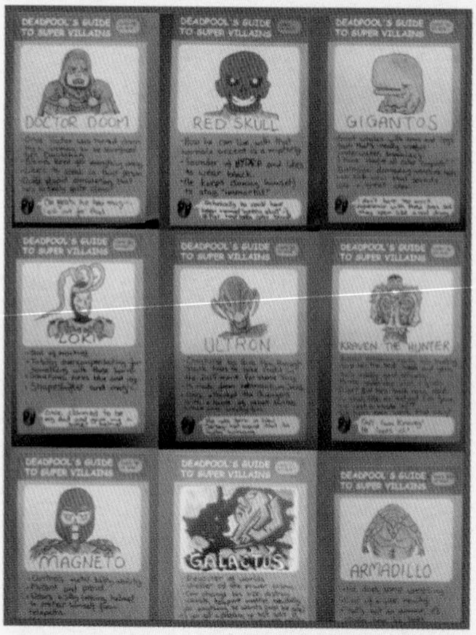
DEADPOOL'S GUIDE TO SUPER VILLAINS
DOCTOR DOOM
RED SKULL
GIGANTOS
ULTRON
KRAVEN THE HUNTER
MAGNETO
GALACTUS
ARMADILLO

Denmark

RYAN: Stine, your cosplay is, and I say this without hyperbole, OFF THE HOOK. Holy cow. Also, it's such a thrill to see cosplay for Squirrel Girl! Especially when it's so great. I love that you made more Deadpool cards too - they're so much fun to write (AS YOU HAVE NOW DISCOVERED) that I'm sure there'll be more here in the future! In conclusion, you are awesome (and thank you so much for buying every issue - TWICE!) and we are in your debt. Keep spreading the word!!

ERICA: Your Star Trek Squirrel Girl is amazing, as is your Squirrel Girl Squirrel Girl. For readers who haven't seen it, it's on our tumblr (see below).

The Deadpool cards are AMAZING. I love that you're drawing them yourself too. Keep sending us photos, okay? We will retweet ALL OF THEM.

RYAN: Finally, I'd like to dedicate this issue to Hester the sugar glider, pictured below. While not technically a squirrel (sugar gliders look similar to flying squirrels but had a different evolutionary path!), she was the pet of our editor Wil and his wife, Julia, and she had an awesome ten-year run. She was loved so much, and will be missed.

ERICA: She's beautiful. I'm sorry she's gone, Wil, but you've had a great many years with her and that's what's important.

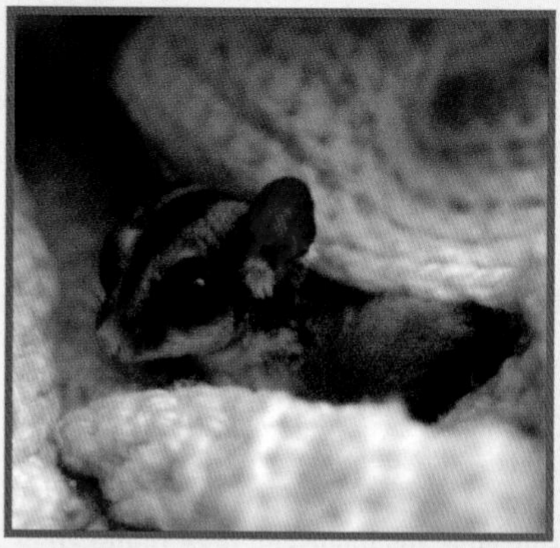

Next: It's The End Of The Squirrel-D As We Know It!

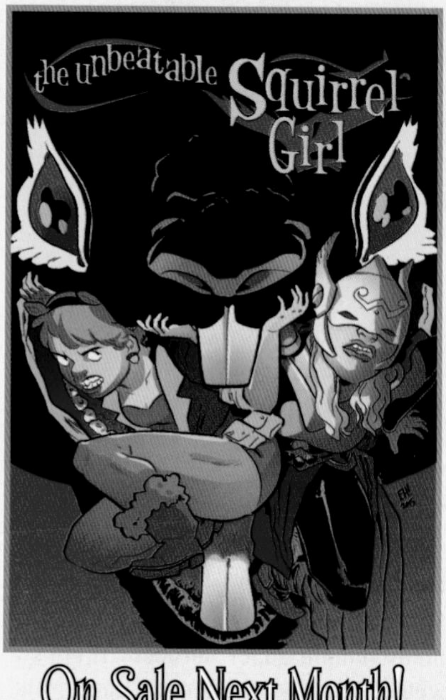
the unbeatable Squirrel Girl

On Sale Next Month!

Attention Squirrel Scouts! Make sure to check out our production blog, **unbeatablesquirrelgirl.tumblr.com**, where we post behind-the-scenes stuff on how the book gets made, along with all sorts of cool things *you* make: fan art, cosplay, whatever!

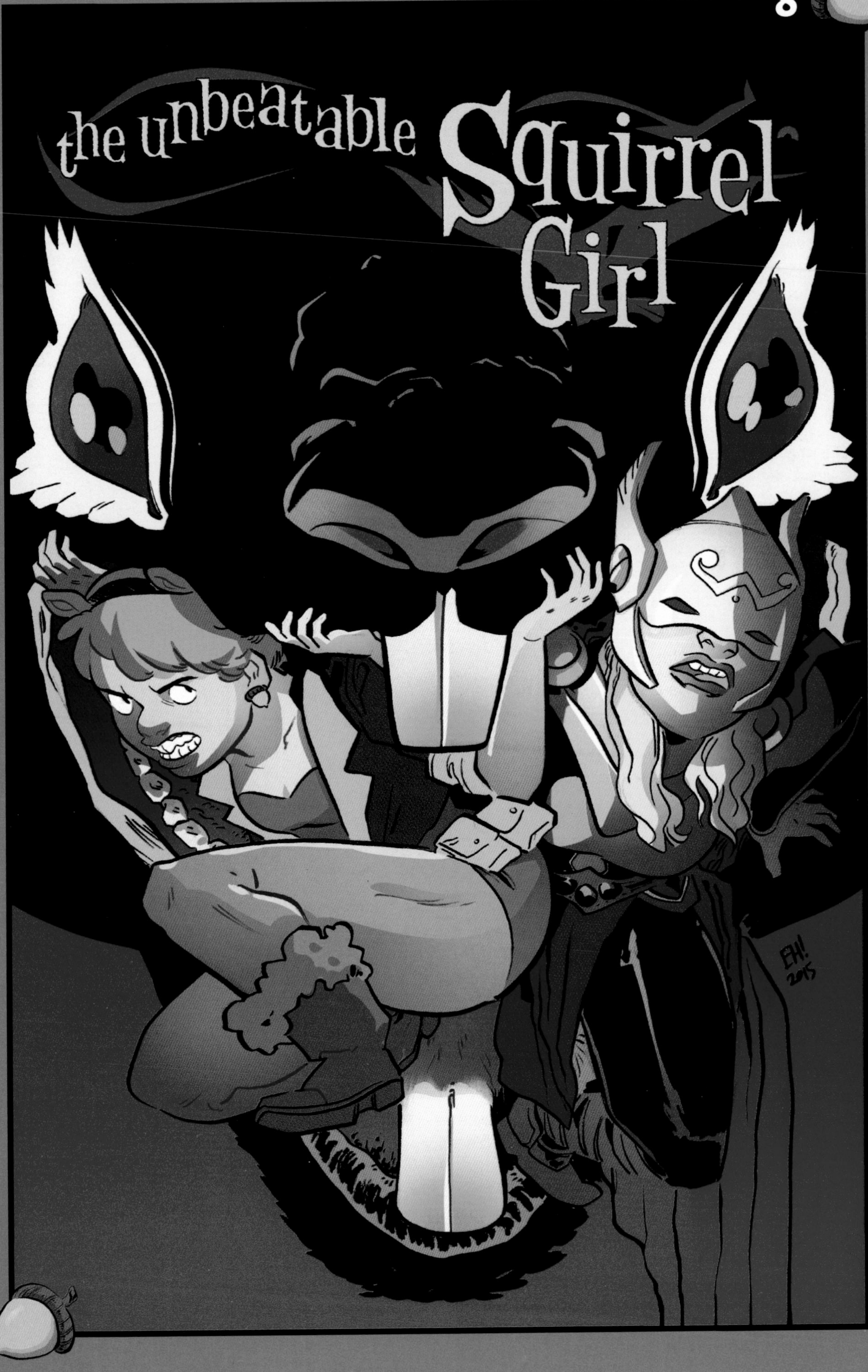
the unbeatable Squirrel Girl
EH! 2015

Doreen Green isn't just a first-year computer science student: she secretly also has all the powers of both squirrel and girl! She uses her amazing abilities to fight crime **and** be as awesome as possible. You know her as...**The Unbeatable Squirrel Girl!** Let's catch up with what she's been up to until now, with...

Squirrel Girl in a nutshell

Nancy W. @sewwiththeflo
If I don't come back, I want my epitaph to read "HERE LIES NANCY WHITEHEAD: SHE WENT TO ASGARD AND DIED AND IT WAS TOTALLY WORTH IT."

Nancy W. @sewwiththeflo
Koi Boi and Chipmunk Hunk and @unbeatablesg all stayed behind, so I need y'all to make sure one of them takes care of this for me.

Squirrel Girl! @unbeatablesg
@sewwiththeflo dude, you're not going to DIE in ASGARD!! you got a current AND a former Thor watching your back! COME ON

Nancy W. @sewwiththeflo
@unbeatablesg It was a humblebrag, SG. A humbleepitaph.

Squirrel Girl! @unbeatablesg
@sewwiththeflo only you would brag by updating your followers on what your GRAVESTONE should read.

Nancy W. @sewwiththeflo
@unbeatablesg #personalbranding

Tony Stark @starkmantony
@unbeatablesg Hey, just looking at a report that says you're fighting "a giant monster god-squirrel from Asgard named 'Ratatoskr'"

Tony Stark @starkmantony
@unbeatablesg Can't help noticing that before I knew you, there were precisely zero evil squirrel-gods running around NYC.

Squirrel Girl! @unbeatablesg
@starkmantony uh that's funny because before I knew YOU there were precisely zero IRON MONGERS and MADAME MASQUES running around NYC!!

Squirrel Girl! @unbeatablesg
@starkmantony haha okay, so, i got those from a website that lists villains you've defeated? but they're like, bonkers

Squirrel Girl! @unbeatablesg
@starkmantony dude you fought a BIG WHEEL named "BIG WHEEL" that was invented by one "Jackson WHEELE"??? that's SINCERELY AMAZING.

Tony Stark @starkmantony
@unbeatablesg Can't talk, gotta get back to my very important world-class CEO work. Just take care of the squirrel thing.

Squirrel Girl! @unbeatablesg
@starkmantony obviously i'm gonna do that! quick question before I go though. just one super-quick question, okay?

Squirrel Girl! @unbeatablesg
@starkmantony when he said he was gonna take over earth, did you tell him he "spoke" too soon and is in "wheely" big trouble now or WHAT

Squirrel Girl! @unbeatablesg
So um, I kinda beat up the Avengers? In 26 seconds?? But they were being mind-controlled so it's okay

HULK @HULKYSMASHY
@unbeatablesg HULK WAS NOT PRESENT FOR THIS BUT HULK THINKS ABOUT BEATING UP AVENGERS ALL THE TIME

Squirrel Girl! @unbeatablesg
@HULKYSMASHY haha, well, they sassed my pals!! they were SO RUDE!

HULK @HULKYSMASHY
@unbeatablesg HULK WOULD LIKE TO BELIEVE THERE IS ALWAYS TIME FOR POLITENESS

Squirrel Girl! @unbeatablesg
@HULKYSMASHY dude! you are blowing my mind here!! i had no idea you thought this way!

Squirrel Girl! @unbeatablesg
@HULKYSMASHY hulk smash...my prejudices against giant green rage monsters!!

search!

#asgard
#catsgard
#ratatoskrage
#breakfastmeets
#seeyouinoctober

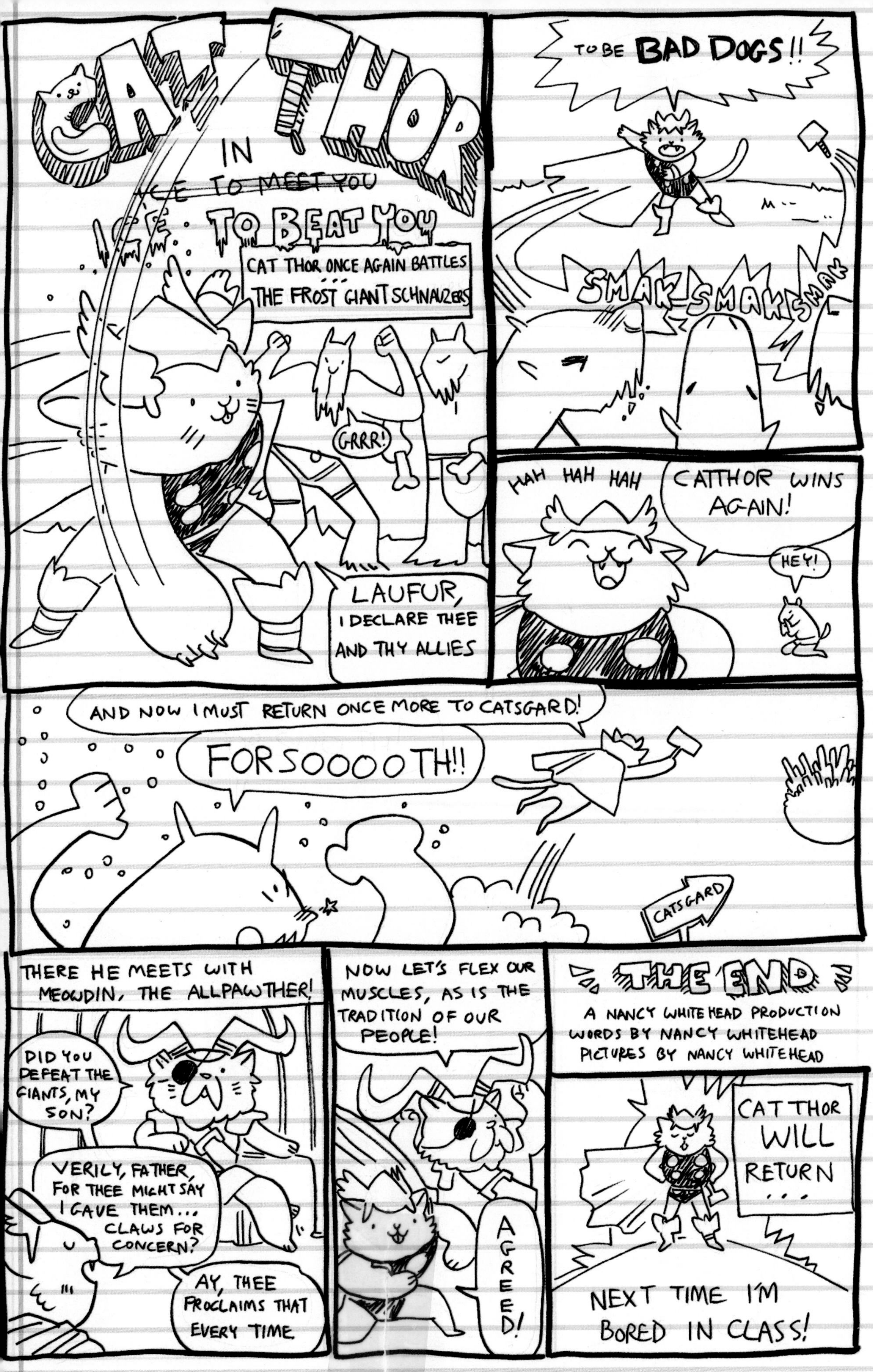
CAT THOR
IN
ICE TO MEET YOU
ICE TO BEAT YOU
CAT THOR ONCE AGAIN BATTLES THE FROST GIANT SCHNAUZERS
GRRR!
LAUFUR, I DECLARE THEE AND THY ALLIES
TO BE BAD DOGS!!
SMAK SMAK SMAK
HAH HAH HAH
CATTHOR WINS AGAIN!
HEY!
AND NOW I MUST RETURN ONCE MORE TO CATSGARD!
FORSOOOOTH!!
CATSGARD
THERE HE MEETS WITH MEOWDIN, THE ALLPAWTHER!
DID YOU DEFEAT THE GIANTS, MY SON?
VERILY, FATHER, FOR THEE MIGHT SAY I GAVE THEM... CLAWS FOR CONCERN?
AY, THEE PROCLAIMS THAT EVERY TIME.
NOW LET'S FLEX OUR MUSCLES, AS IS THE TRADITION OF OUR PEOPLE!
AGREED!
THE END
A NANCY WHITEHEAD PRODUCTION
WORDS BY NANCY WHITEHEAD
PICTURES BY NANCY WHITEHEAD
CAT THOR WILL RETURN...
NEXT TIME I'M BORED IN CLASS!

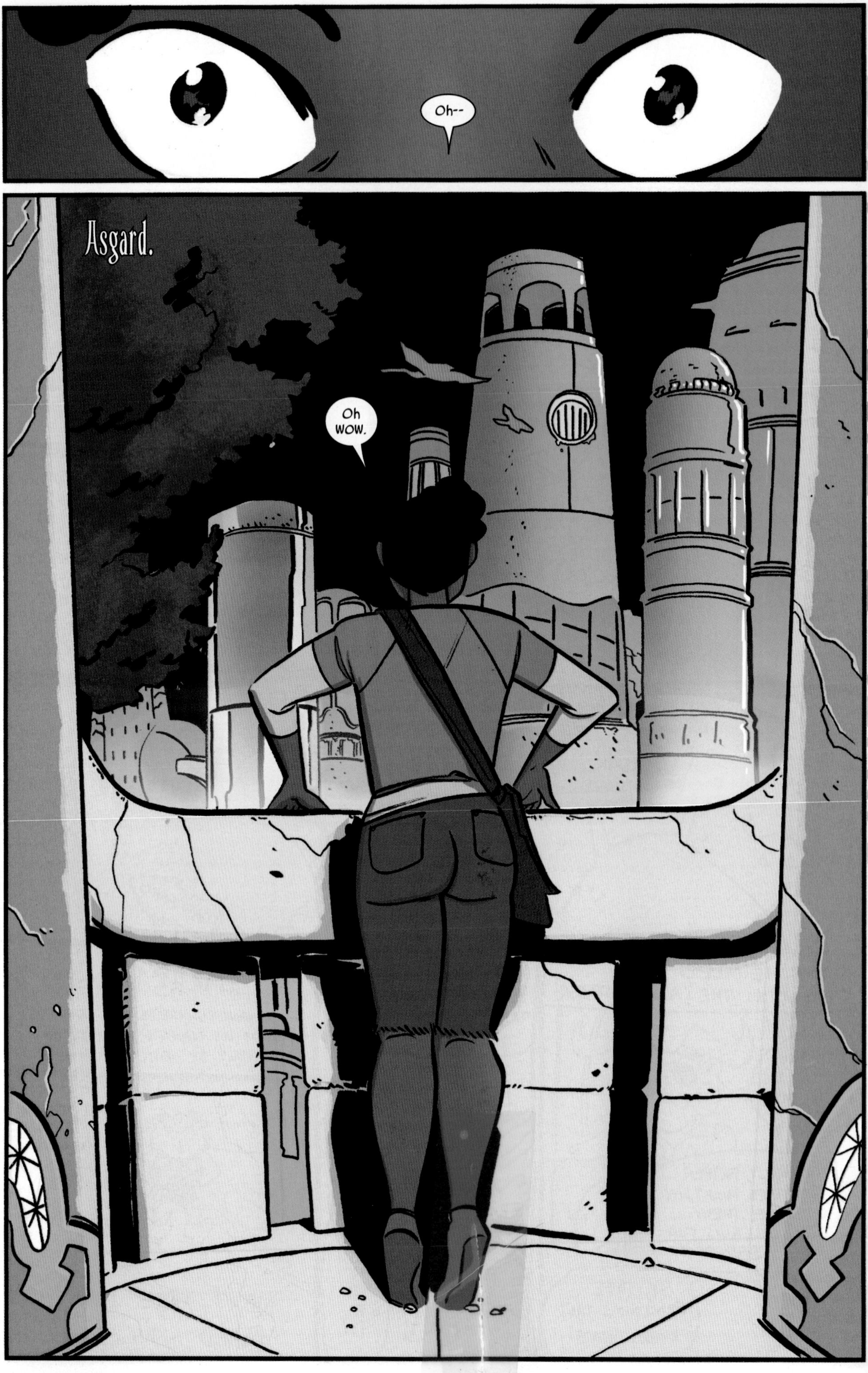
Oh--
Asgard.
Oh wow.

I see now the weakness in our defenses, Thor, but I do not understand how it came to be.

I do not believe this shall be an easy repair, Odinson.

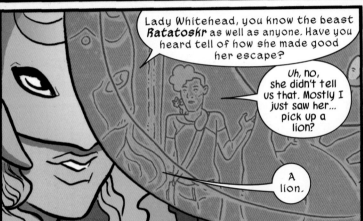

Lady Whitehead, you know the beast *Ratatoskr* as well as anyone. Have you heard tell of how she made good her escape?

Uh, no, she didn't tell us that. Mostly I just saw her... pick up a lion?

A lion.

Two of them, actually. We were at the zoo. It's a long story.

iwastryingtotalktoanimals

I'm sorry, but when thou speak so quickly and softly, not even Heimdall himself could ascertain--

But I *do* bring with me all of Earth's accumulated knowledge of the beast. Wait, hold on. Uh--

--"I bring tidings from Midgard to thee from the great seer Wikipedia"?

Thy seer Wikipedia claims that if we all donated now, his fundraiser would be over within the hour.

Yeah, he does that.

I must say, thy seer Wikipedia seems to know an awful lot about some *very* embarrassing subject matter!

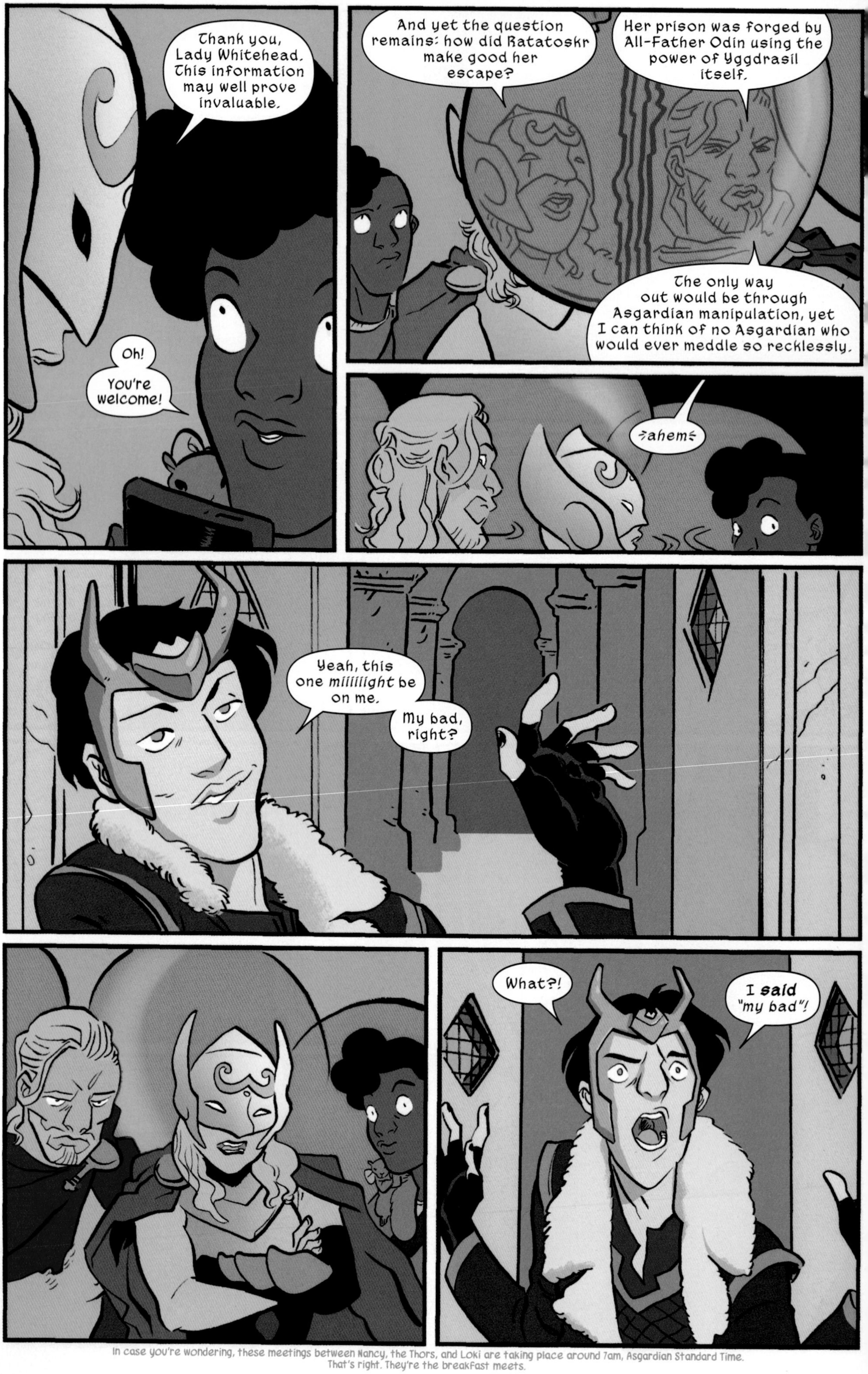
Thank you, Lady Whitehead. This information may well prove invaluable.
Oh!
You're welcome!
And yet the question remains: how did Ratatoskr make good her escape?
Her prison was forged by All-Father Odin using the power of Yggdrasil itself.
The only way out would be through Asgardian manipulation, yet I can think of no Asgardian who would ever meddle so recklessly.
ahem
Yeah, this one *miiiiiight* be on me.
My bad, right?
What?!
I **said** *"my bad"*!

In case you're wondering, these meetings between Nancy, the Thors, and Loki are taking place around 7am, Asgardian Standard Time.
That's right. They're the breakfast meets.

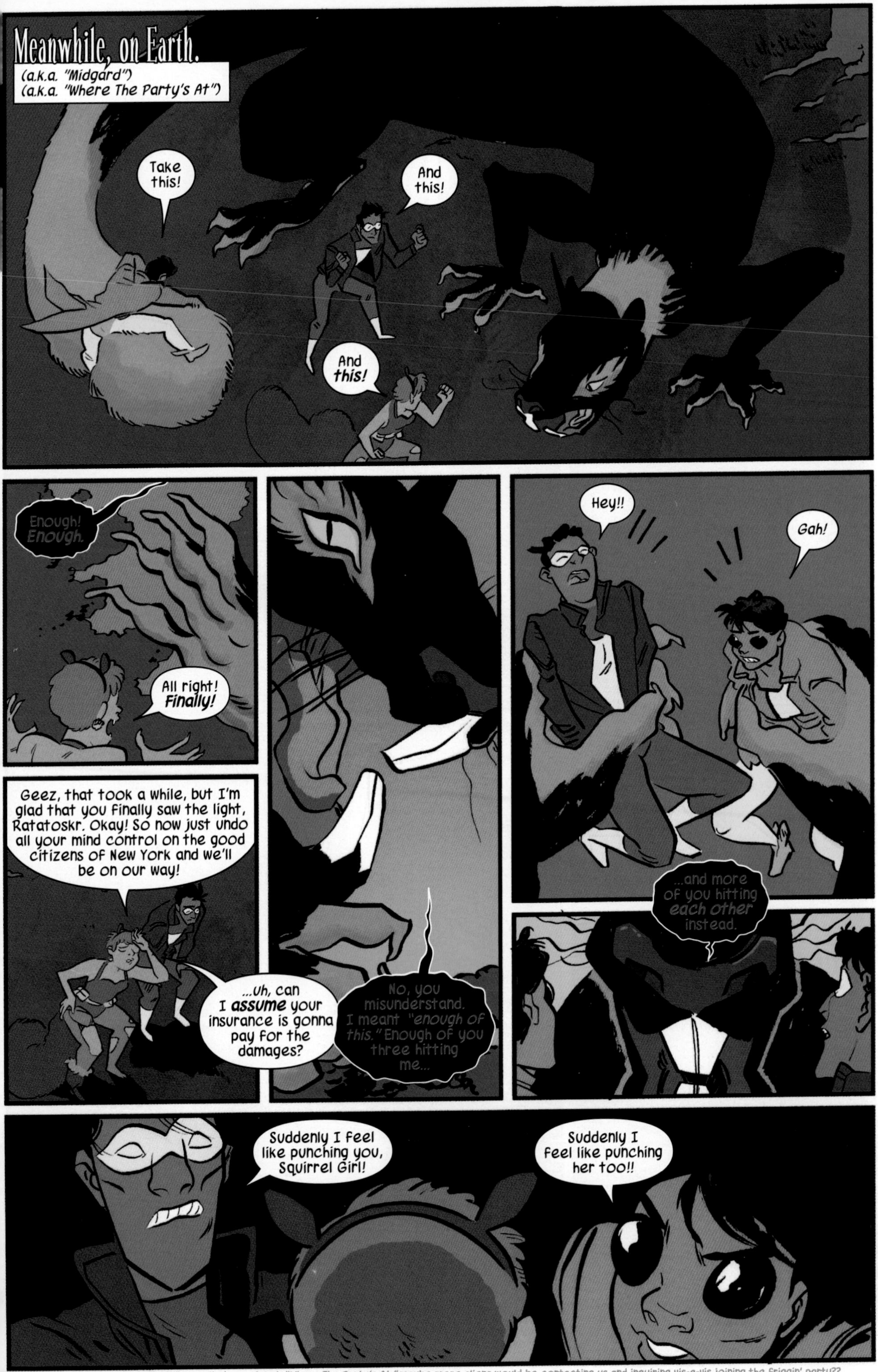
Meanwhile, on Earth.
(a.k.a. "Midgard")
(a.k.a. "Where The Party's At")
Take this!
And this!
And this!
Enough! Enough.
All right! Finally!
Hey!!
Gah!
Geez, that took a while, but I'm glad that you finally saw the light, Ratatoskr. Okay! So now just undo all your mind control on the good citizens of New York and we'll be on our way!
...uh, can I assume your insurance is gonna pay for the damages?
No, you misunderstand. I meant "enough of this." Enough of you three hitting me...
...and more of you hitting each other instead.
Suddenly I feel like punching you, Squirrel Girl!
Suddenly I feel like punching her too!!

Theory: if instead of "Earth" we called our planet "Where The Party's At," maybe more aliens would be contacting us and inquiring vis-a-vis joining the friggin' party??

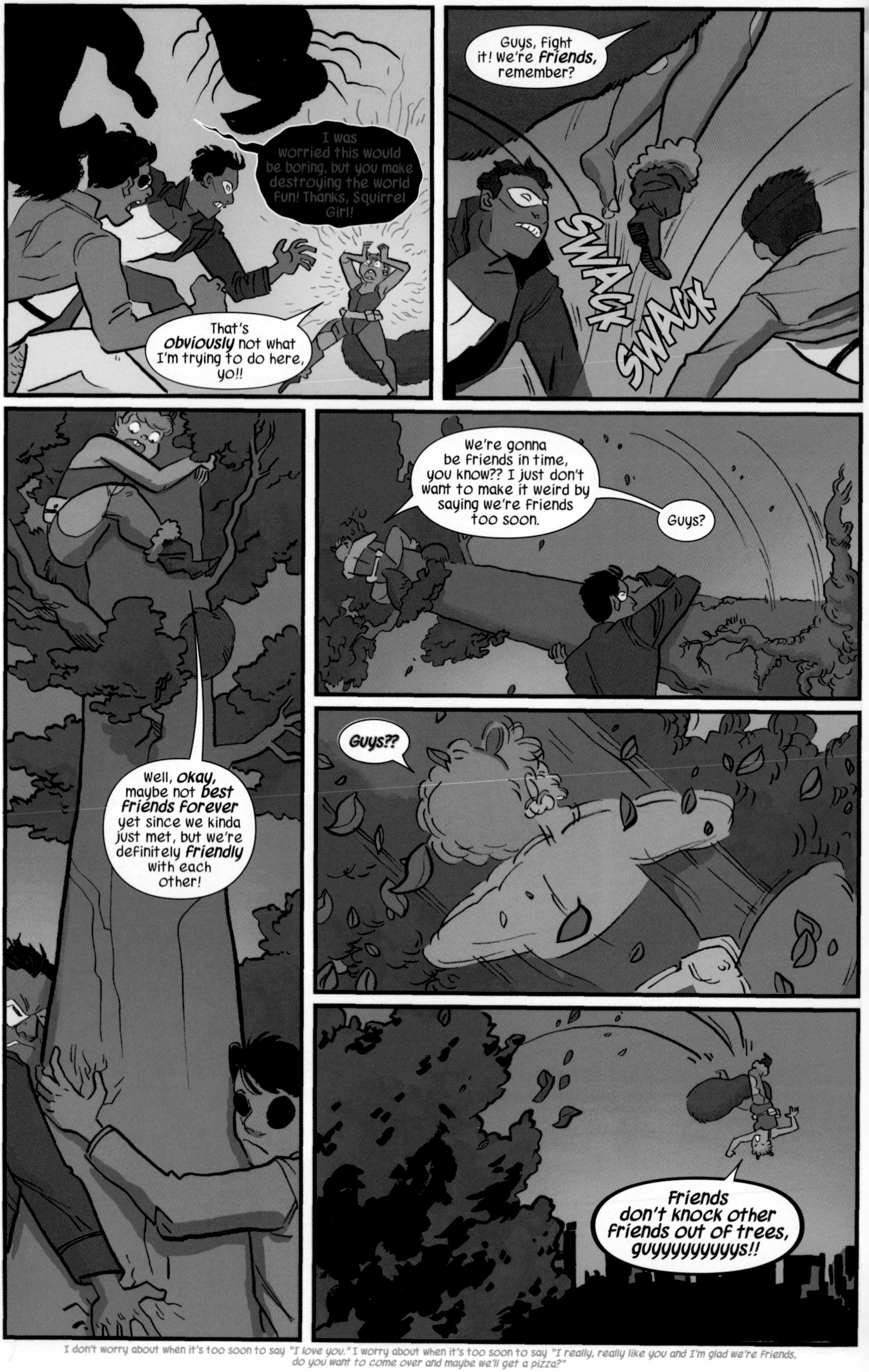
I was worried this would be boring, but you make destroying the world fun! Thanks, Squirrel Girl!
That's *obviously* not what I'm trying to do here, yo!!
Guys, fight it! We're *friends*, remember?
SWACK
SWACK
Well, *okay*, maybe not *best friends forever* yet since we kinda just met, but we're definitely *friendly* with each other!
We're gonna be friends in time, you know?? I just don't want to make it weird by saying we're friends too soon.
Guys?
Guys??
Friends don't knock other friends out of trees, guyyyyyyyyys!!

I don't worry about when it's too soon to say "I love you." I worry about when it's too soon to say "I really, really like you and I'm glad we're friends, do you want to come over and maybe we'll get a pizza?"

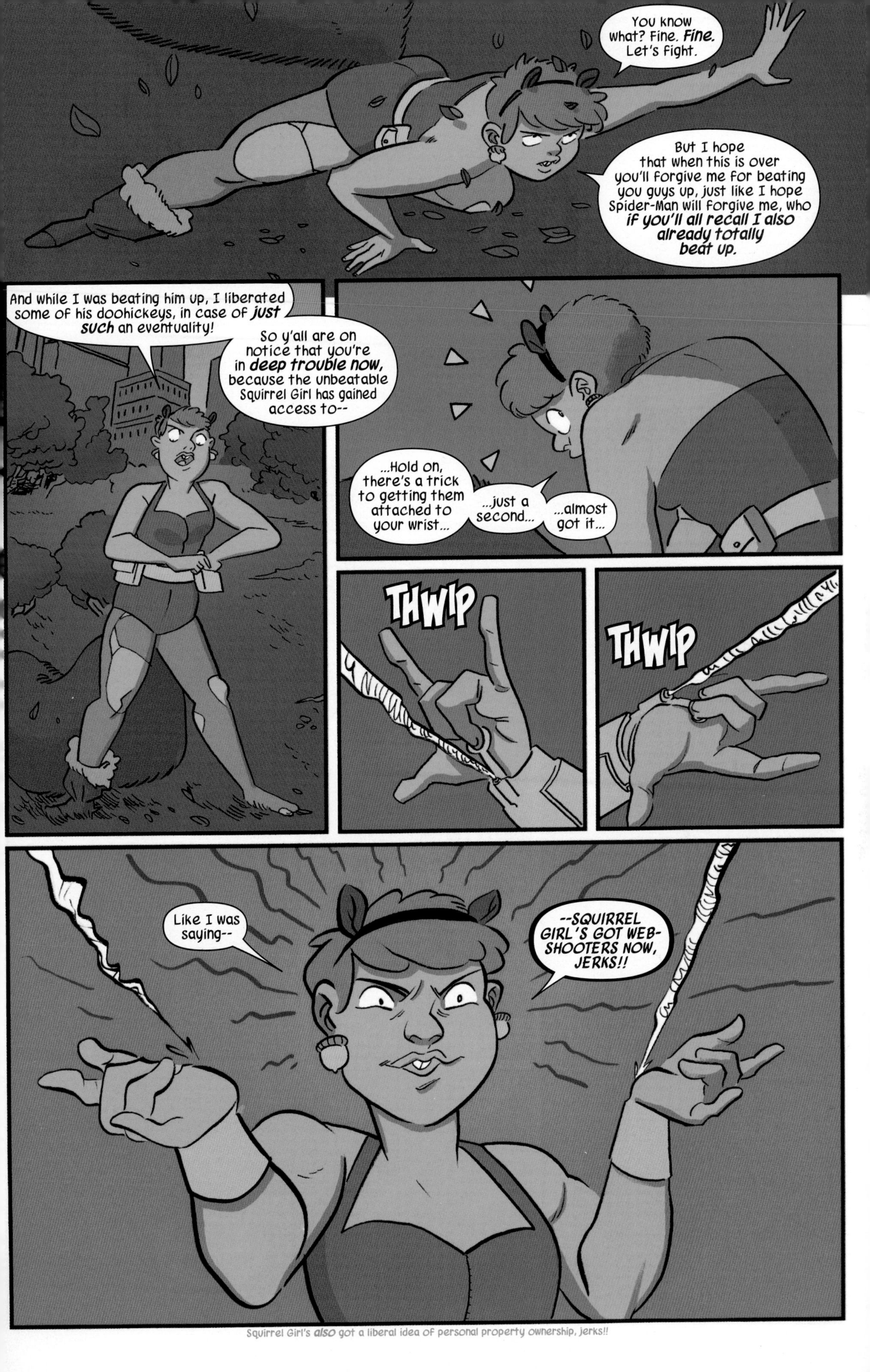

You know what? Fine. *Fine.* Let's fight.
But I hope that when this is over you'll forgive me for beating you guys up, just like I hope Spider-Man will forgive me, who *if you'll all recall I also already totally beat up.*
And while I was beating him up, I liberated some of his doohickeys, in case of *just such* an eventuality!
So y'all are on notice that you're in *deep trouble now,* because the unbeatable Squirrel Girl has gained access to--
...Hold on, there's a trick to getting them attached to your wrist...
...just a second...
...almost got it...
THWIP
THWIP
Like I was saying--
--SQUIRREL GIRL'S GOT WEB-SHOOTERS NOW, JERKS!!

Squirrel Girl's *also* got a liberal idea of personal property ownership, jerks!!

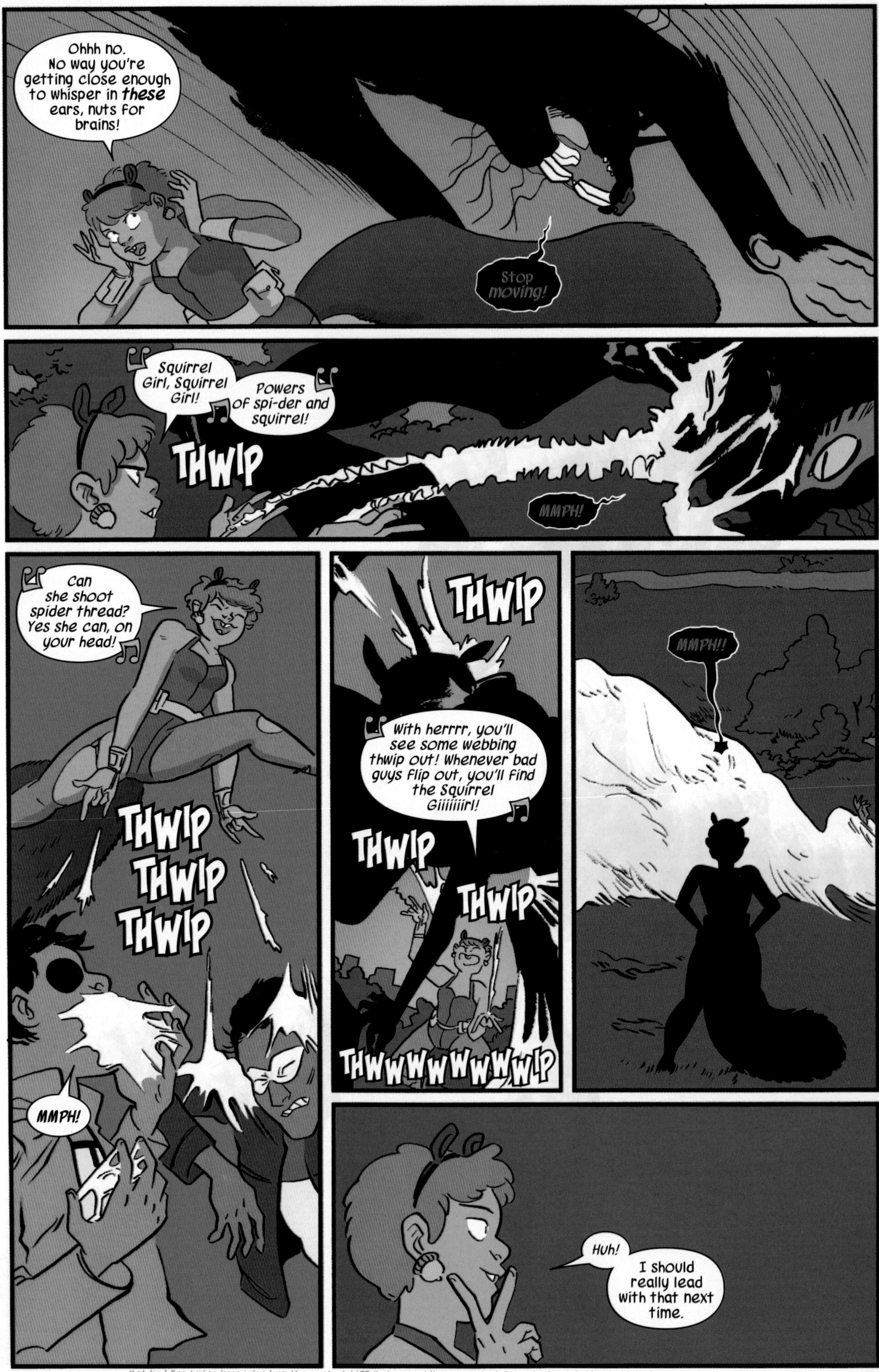
Ohhh no. No way you're getting close enough to whisper in *these* ears, nuts for brains!
Stop moving!
Squirrel Girl, Squirrel Girl!
Powers of spi-der and squirrel!
THWIP
MMPH!
Can she shoot spider thread? Yes she can, on your head!
THWIP
THWIP
THWIP
MMPH!
THWIP
With herrrr, you'll see some webbing thwip out! Whenever bad guys flip out, you'll find the Squirrel Giiiiiiirl!
THWIP
THWIP
THWWWWWWWWWIP
MMPH!!
Huh!
I should really lead with that next time.

Not bad for lyrics improvised on the spot, right?? I also would've accepted *"Can she beat Spider-Man? Evidence shows she can."*

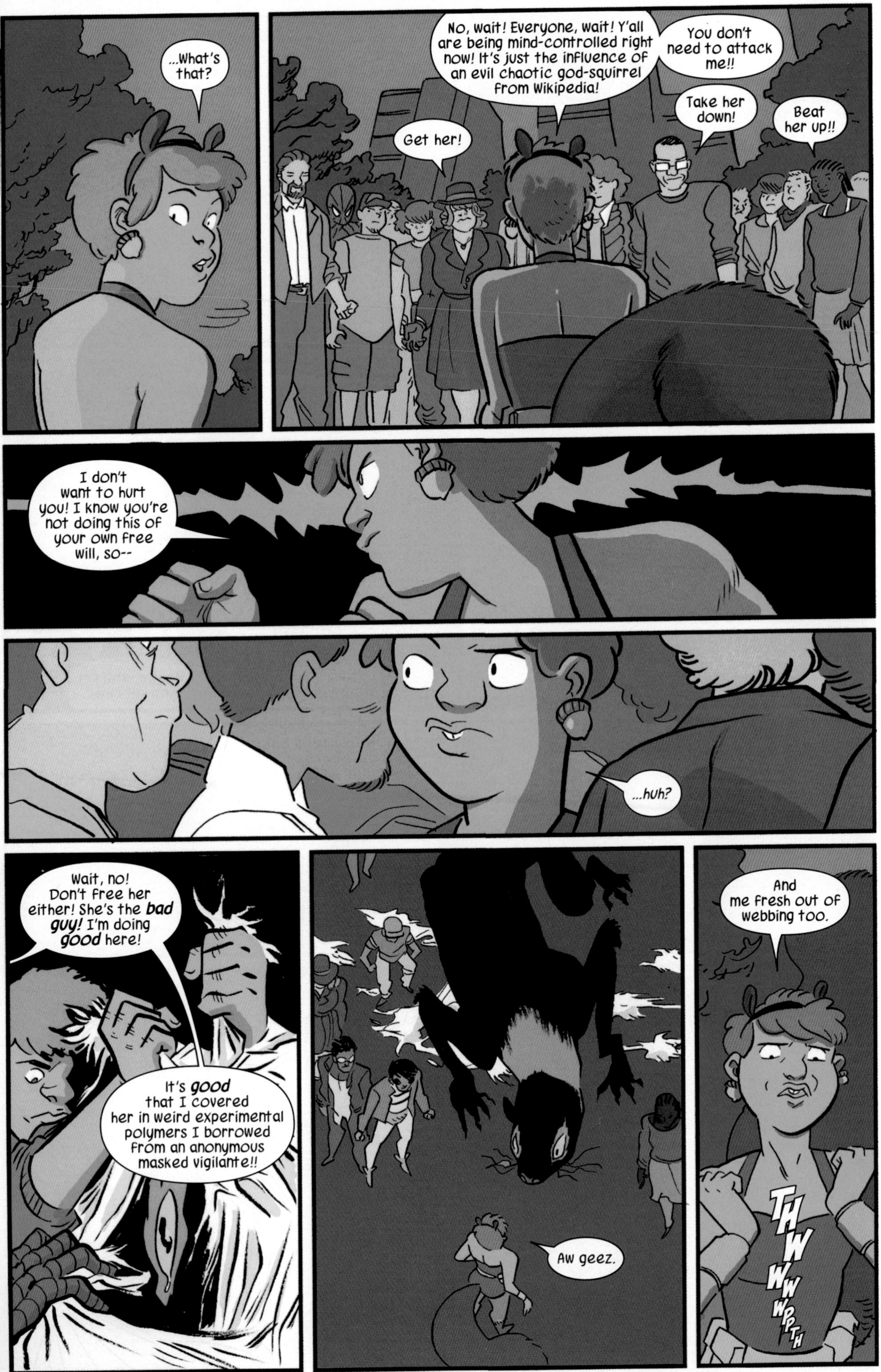
...What's that?
No, wait! Everyone, wait! Y'all are being mind-controlled right now! It's just the influence of an evil chaotic god-squirrel from Wikipedia!
You don't need to attack me!!
Get her!
Take her down!
Beat her up!!
I don't want to hurt you! I know you're not doing this of your own free will, so--
...huh?
Wait, no! Don't free her either! She's the **bad guy!** I'm doing **good** here!
It's **good** that I covered her in weird experimental polymers I borrowed from an anonymous masked vigilante!!
Aw geez.
And me fresh out of webbing too.
THWWWWPPTH
And I never even got to make a sword and shield out of webbing either, *or* a fully-functional car! ***What a waste.***

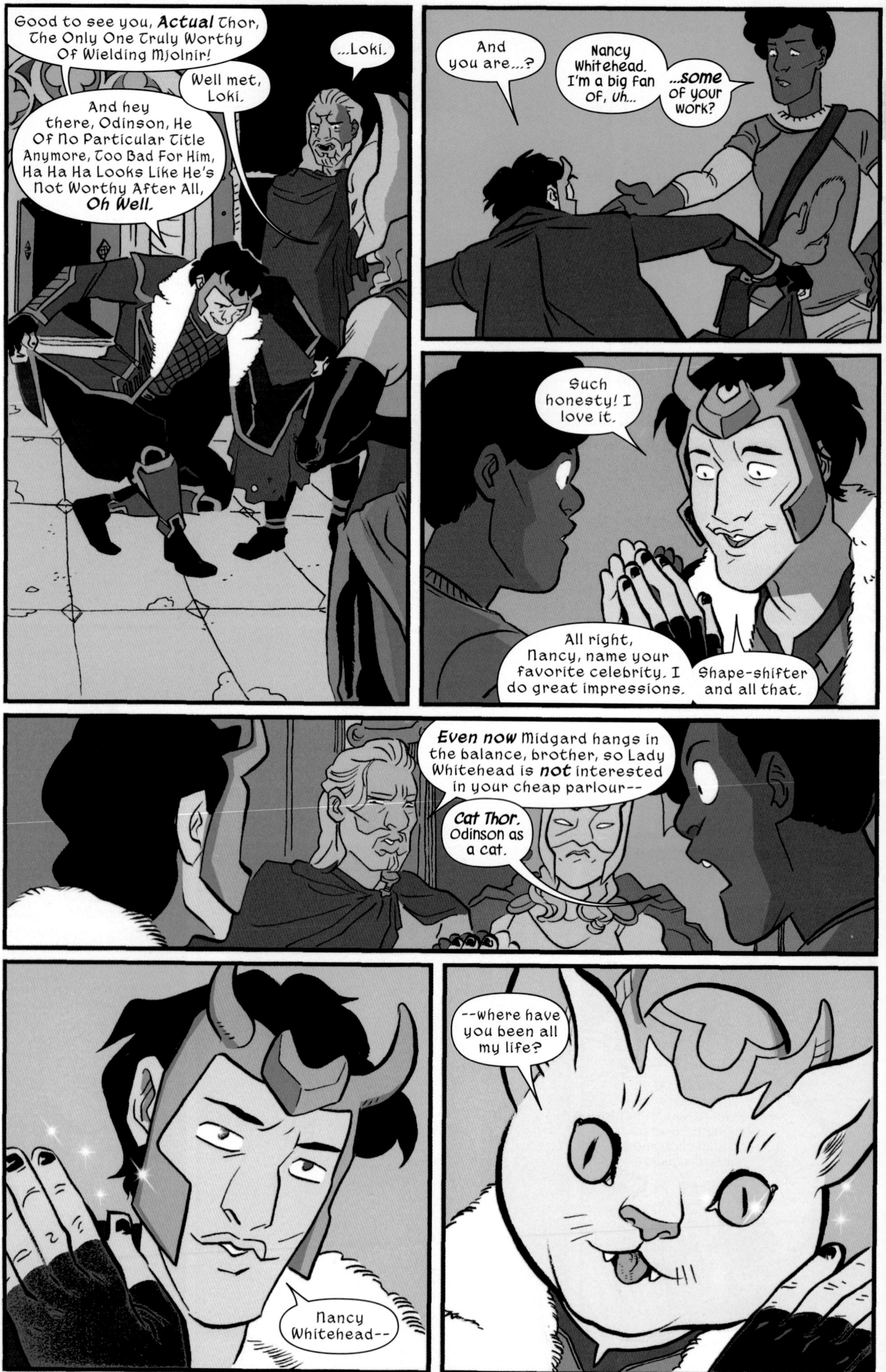
Good to see you, Actual Thor, The Only One Truly Worthy Of Wielding Mjolnir!
...Loki.
Well met, Loki.
And hey there, Odinson, He Of No Particular Title Anymore, Too Bad For Him, Ha Ha Ha Looks Like He's Not Worthy After All, Oh Well.
And you are...?
Nancy Whitehead. I'm a big fan of, uh...
...some of your work?
Such honesty! I love it.
All right, Nancy, name your favorite celebrity. I do great impressions.
Shape-shifter and all that.
Even now Midgard hangs in the balance, brother, so Lady Whitehead is not interested in your cheap parlour--
Cat Thor. Odinson as a cat.
Nancy Whitehead--
--where have you been all my life?

Brothers, am I right? Always teasing each other, always turning their heads into cat versions of the other brother's head. Classic!

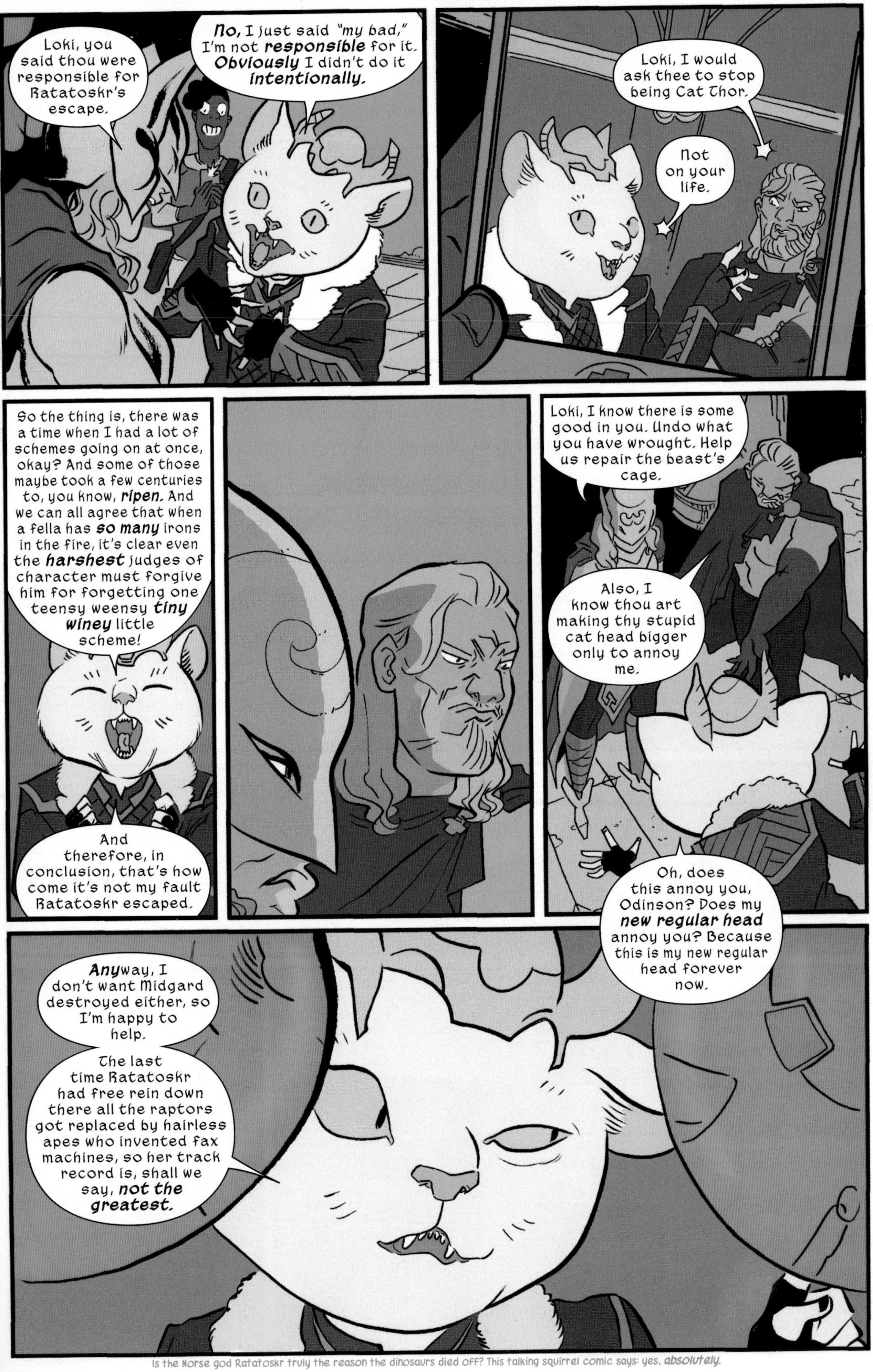
Loki, you said thou were responsible for Ratatoskr's escape.
No, I just said "my bad," I'm not responsible for it. Obviously I didn't do it intentionally.
Loki, I would ask thee to stop being Cat Thor.
Not on your life.
So the thing is, there was a time when I had a lot of schemes going on at once, okay? And some of those maybe took a few centuries to, you know, ripen. And we can all agree that when a fella has so many irons in the fire, it's clear even the harshest judges of character must forgive him for forgetting one teensy weensy tiny winey little scheme!
And therefore, in conclusion, that's how come it's not my fault Ratatoskr escaped.
Loki, I know there is some good in you. Undo what you have wrought. Help us repair the beast's cage.
Also, I know thou art making thy stupid cat head bigger only to annoy me.
Oh, does this annoy you, Odinson? Does my new regular head annoy you? Because this is my new regular head forever now.
Anyway, I don't want Midgard destroyed either, so I'm happy to help.
The last time Ratatoskr had free rein down there all the raptors got replaced by hairless apes who invented fax machines, so her track record is, shall we say, not the greatest.

Is the Norse god Ratatoskr truly the reason the dinosaurs died off? This talking squirrel comic says: yes, *absolutely.*

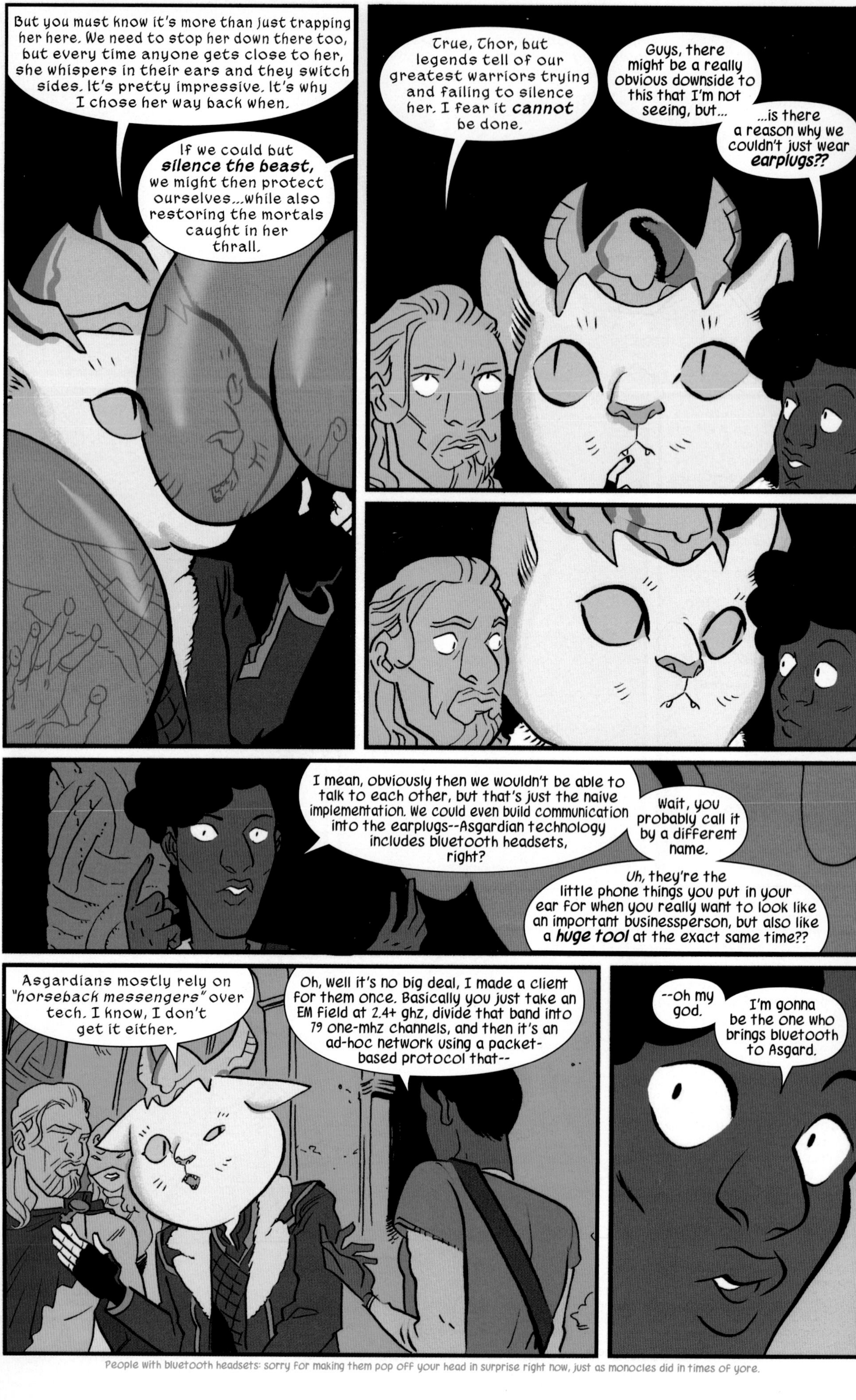
But you must know it's more than just trapping her here. We need to stop her down there too, but every time anyone gets close to her, she whispers in their ears and they switch sides. It's pretty impressive. It's why I chose her way back when.
If we could but *silence the beast,* we might then protect ourselves...while also restoring the mortals caught in her thrall.
True, Thor, but legends tell of our greatest warriors trying and failing to silence her. I fear it *cannot* be done.
Guys, there might be a really obvious downside to this that I'm not seeing, but...
...is there a reason why we couldn't just wear *earplugs??*
I mean, obviously then we wouldn't be able to talk to each other, but that's just the naive implementation. We could even build communication into the earplugs--Asgardian technology includes bluetooth headsets, right?
Wait, you probably call it by a different name.
Uh, they're the little phone things you put in your ear for when you really want to look like an important businessperson, but also like a *huge tool* at the exact same time??
Asgardians mostly rely on *"horseback messengers"* over tech. I know, I don't get it either.
Oh, well it's no big deal, I made a client for them once. Basically you just take an EM field at 2.4+ ghz, divide that band into 79 one-mhz channels, and then it's an ad-hoc network using a packet-based protocol that--
--oh my god.
I'm gonna be the one who brings bluetooth to Asgard.

People with bluetooth headsets: sorry for making them pop off your head in surprise right now, just as monocles did in times of yore.

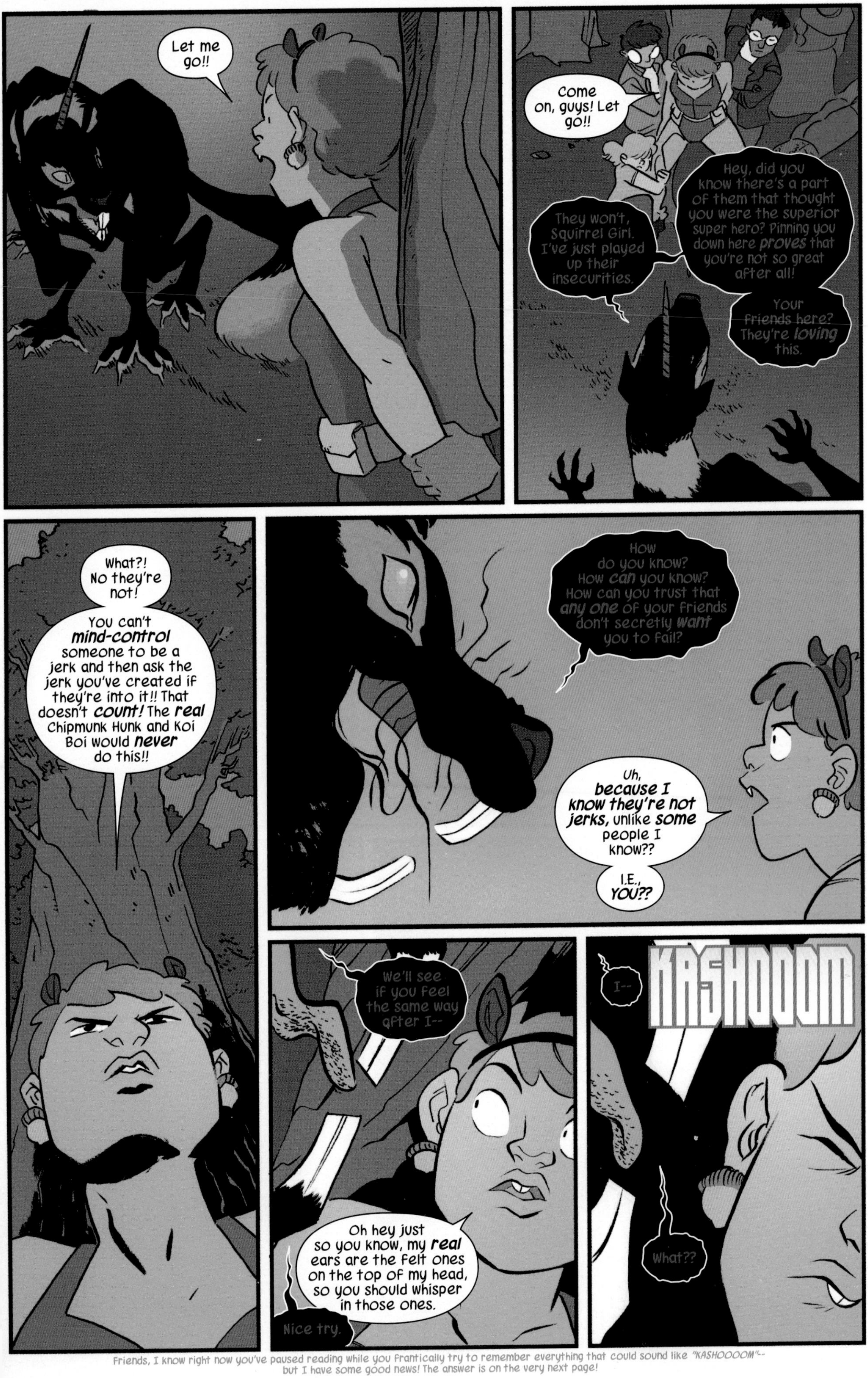
Let me go!!
Come on, guys! Let go!!
They won't, Squirrel Girl. I've just played up their insecurities.
Hey, did you know there's a part of them that thought you were the superior super hero? Pinning you down here proves that you're not so great after all!
Your friends here? They're loving this.
What?! No they're not!
You can't mind-control someone to be a jerk and then ask the jerk you've created if they're into it!! That doesn't count! The real Chipmunk Hunk and Koi Boi would never do this!!
How do you know? How can you know? How can you trust that any one of your friends don't secretly want you to fail?
Uh, because I know they're not jerks, unlike some people I know??
I.E., YOU??
We'll see if you feel the same way after I--
Oh hey just so you know, my real ears are the felt ones on the top of my head, so you should whisper in those ones.
Nice try.
I--
KASHOOOM
What??
Friends, I know right now you've paused reading while you frantically try to remember everything that could sound like "KASHOOOOM"-- but I have some good news! The answer is on the very next page!

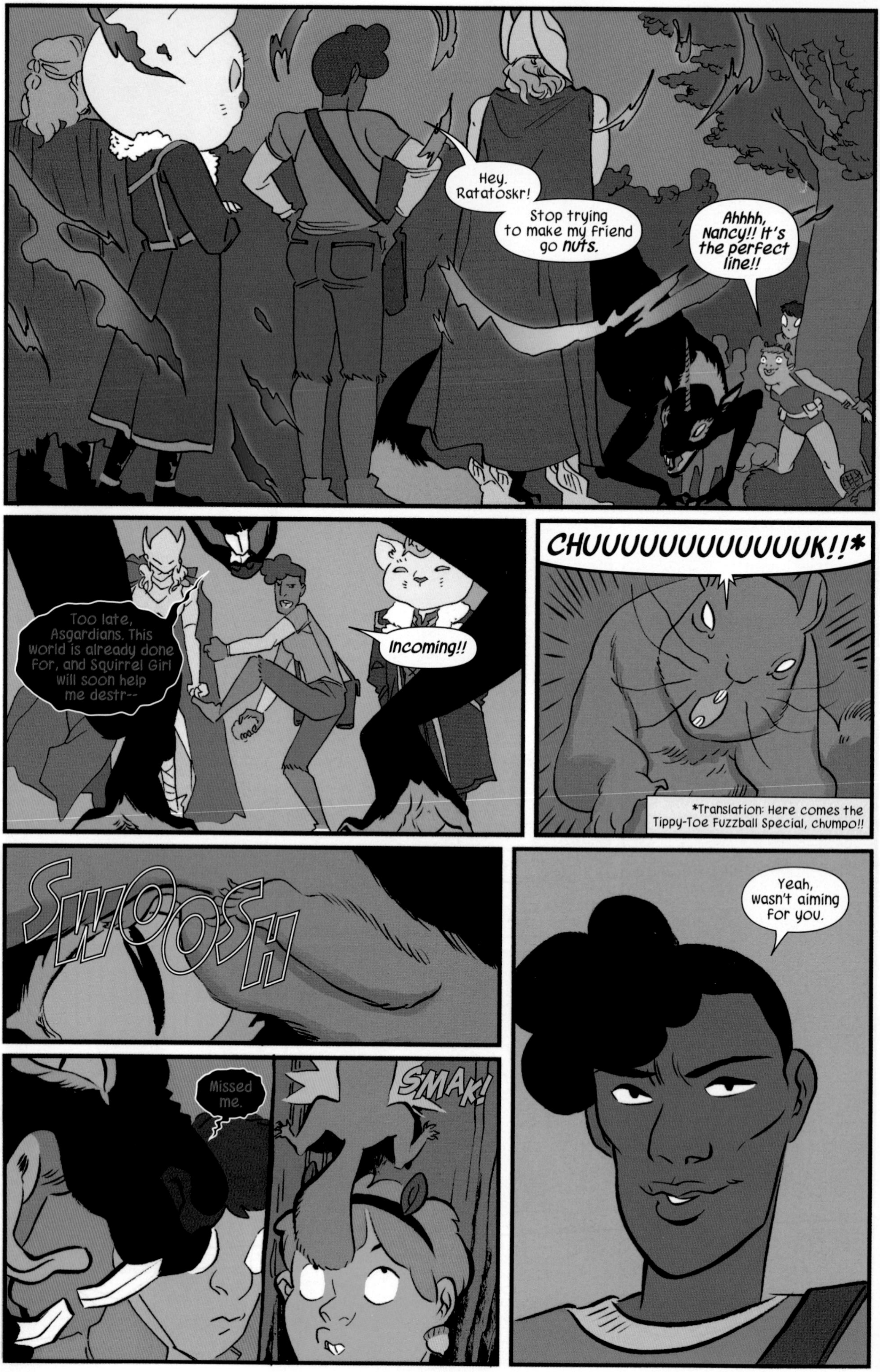
Hey. Ratatoskr!
Stop trying to make my friend go *nuts.*
Ahhhh, Nancy!! It's the perfect line!!
Too late, Asgardians. This world is already done for, and Squirrel Girl will soon help me destr--
Incoming!!
CHUUUUUUUUUUUUK!!*
*Translation: Here comes the Tippy-Toe Fuzzball Special, chumpo!!
SWOOSH
Yeah, wasn't aiming for you.
Missed me.
SMAK!

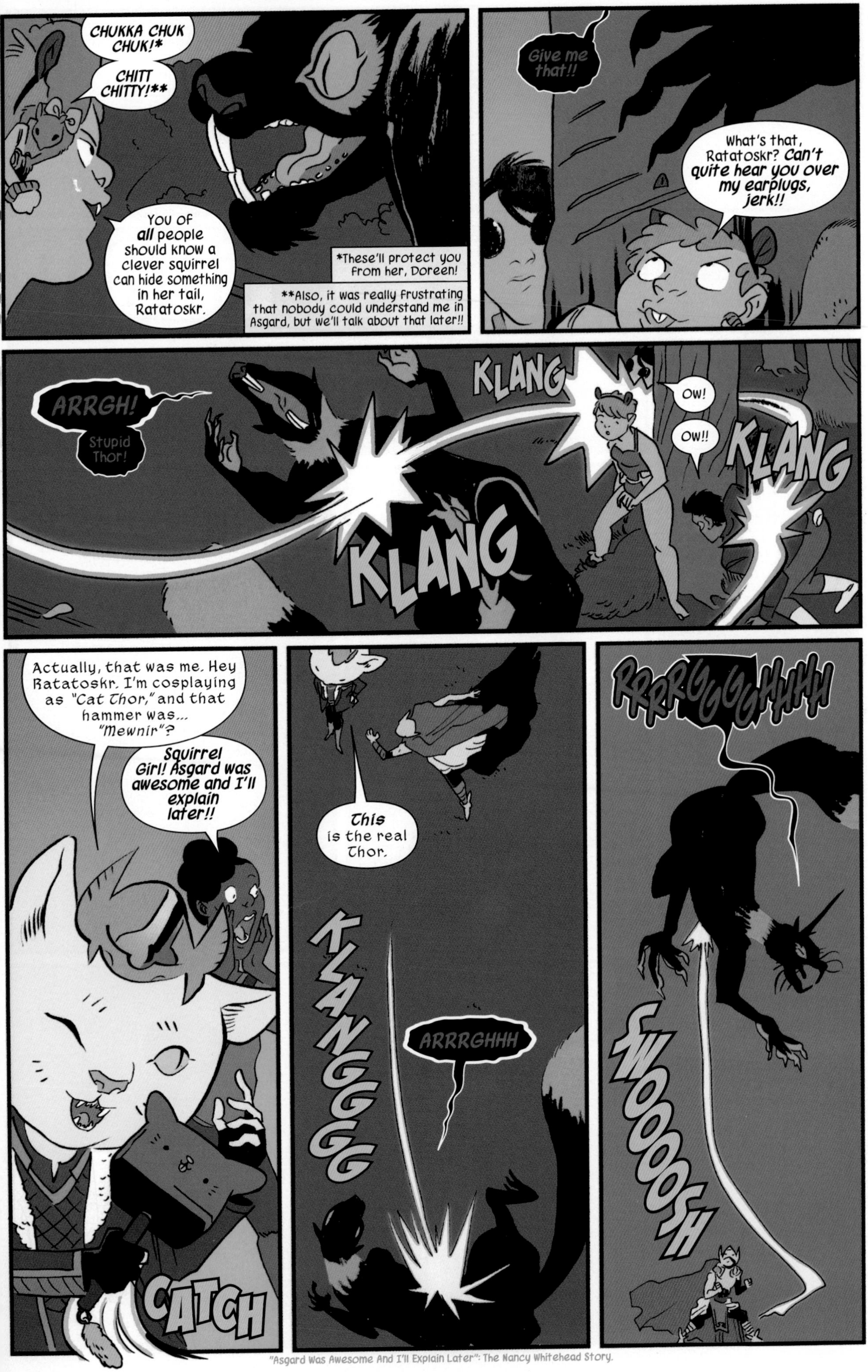
CHUKKA CHUK CHUK!*
CHITT CHITTY!**
You of all people should know a clever squirrel can hide something in her tail, Ratatoskr.
*These'll protect you from her, Doreen!
**Also, it was really frustrating that nobody could understand me in Asgard, but we'll talk about that later!!
Give me that!!
What's that, Ratatoskr? Can't quite hear you over my earplugs, jerk!!
ARRGH!
Stupid Thor!
KLANG
OW!
OW!!
KLANG
KLANG
Actually, that was me. Hey Ratatoskr. I'm cosplaying as "Cat Thor," and that hammer was... "Mewnir"?
Squirrel Girl! Asgard was awesome and I'll explain later!!
CATCH
This is the real Thor.
KLANGGGG
ARRRGHHH
RRRRGGGHHHH
FWOOOOSH

"Asgard Was Awesome And I'll Explain Later": The Nancy Whitehead Story.

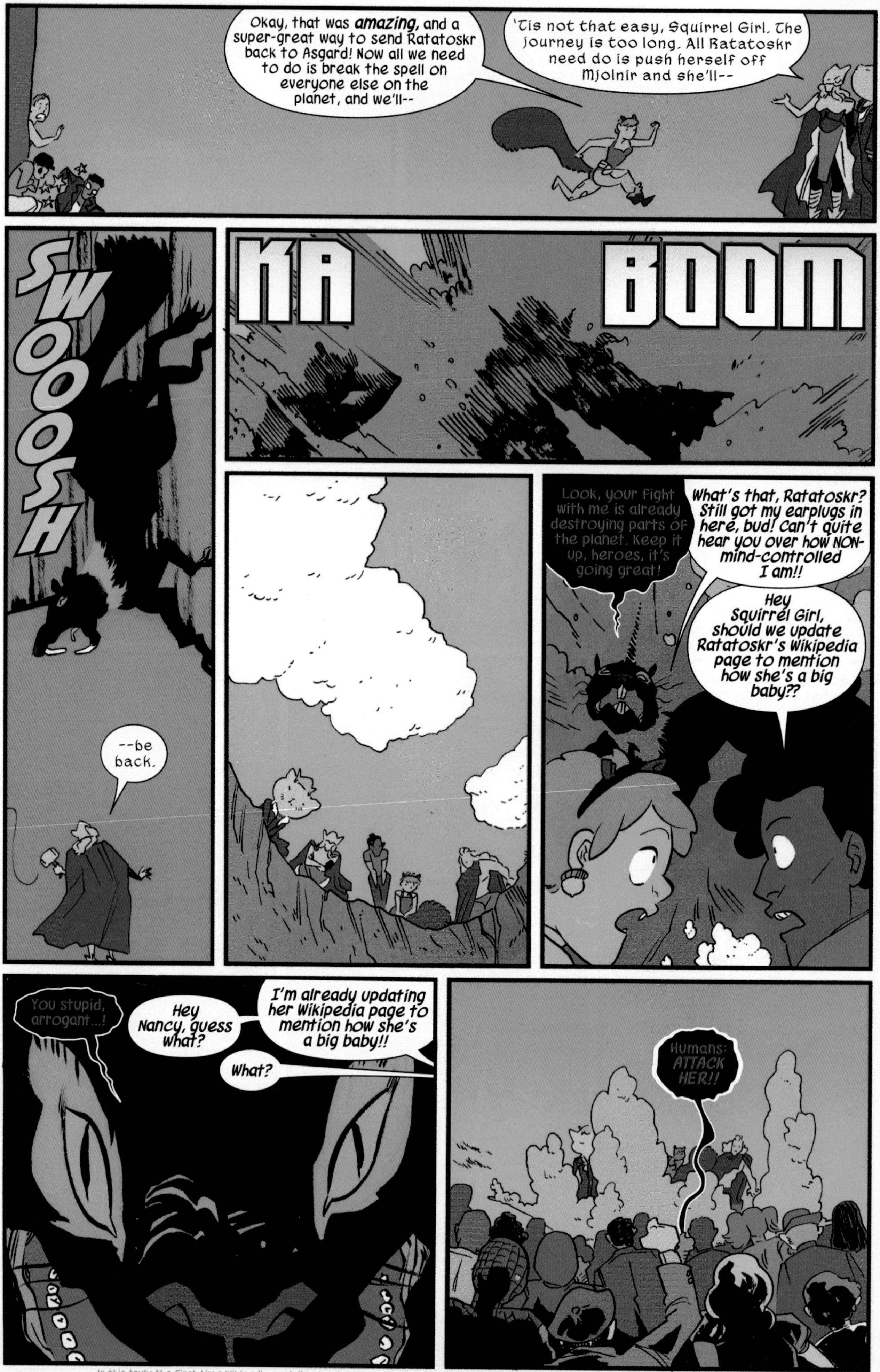

Okay, that was *amazing*, and a super-great way to send Ratatoskr back to Asgard! Now all we need to do is break the spell on everyone else on the planet, and we'll--
'Tis not that easy, Squirrel Girl. The journey is too long. All Ratatoskr need do is push herself off Mjolnir and she'll--
SWOOOSH
KA
BOOM
--be back.
Look, your fight with me is already destroying parts of the planet. Keep it up, heroes, it's going great!
What's that, Ratatoskr? Still got my earplugs in here, bud! Can't quite hear you over how NON-mind-controlled I am!!
Hey Squirrel Girl, should we update Ratatoskr's Wikipedia page to mention how she's a big baby??
You stupid, arrogant...!
Hey Nancy, guess what?
What?
I'm already updating her Wikipedia page to mention how she's a big baby!!
Humans: ATTACK HER!!

Is this truly the first time Wikipedia vandalism has been used in the middle of a super hero fight? Can someone check Wikipedia real quick?

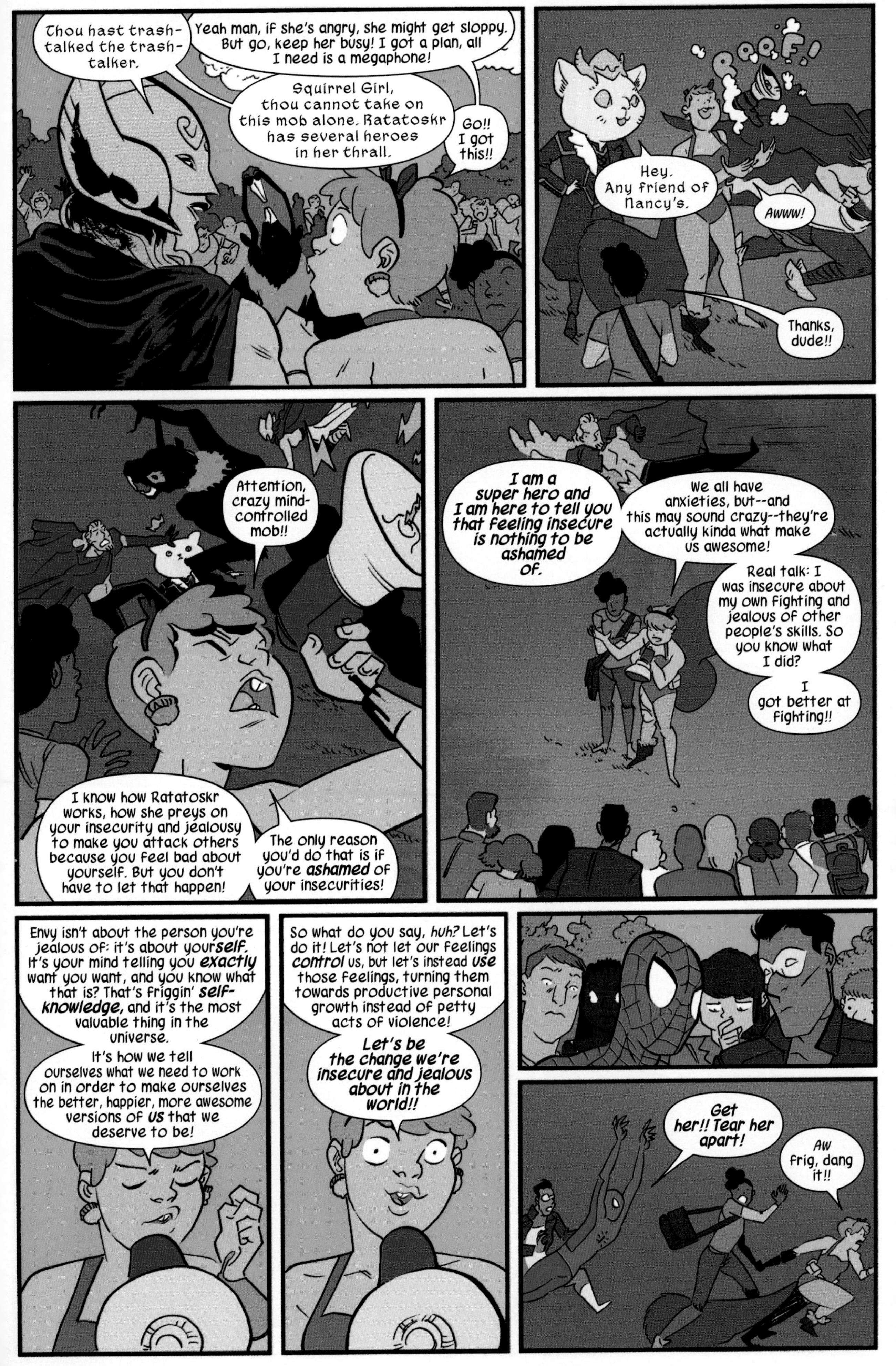

Thou hast trash-talked the trash-talker.
Yeah man, if she's angry, she might get sloppy. But go, keep her busy! I got a plan, all I need is a megaphone!
Squirrel Girl, thou cannot take on this mob alone. Ratatoskr has several heroes in her thrall.
Go!! I got this!!
ROOF!
Hey. Any friend of Nancy's.
AWWW!
Thanks, dude!!
Attention, crazy mind-controlled mob!!
I know how Ratatoskr works, how she preys on your insecurity and jealousy to make you attack others because you feel bad about yourself. But you don't have to let that happen!
The only reason you'd do that is if you're *ashamed* of your insecurities!
I am a super hero and I am here to tell you that feeling insecure is nothing to be ashamed of.
We all have anxieties, but--and this may sound crazy--they're actually kinda what make us awesome!
Real talk: I was insecure about my own fighting and jealous of other people's skills. So you know what I did?
I got better at fighting!!
Envy isn't about the person you're jealous of: it's about your***self.*** It's your mind telling you ***exactly*** want you want, and you know what that is? That's friggin' ***self-knowledge,*** and it's the most valuable thing in the universe.
It's how we tell ourselves what we need to work on in order to make ourselves the better, happier, more awesome versions of ***us*** that we deserve to be!
So what do you say, *huh?* Let's do it! Let's not let our feelings ***control*** us, but let's instead ***use*** those feelings, turning them towards productive personal growth instead of petty acts of violence!
Let's be the change we're insecure and jealous about in the world!!
Get her!! Tear her apart!
Aw Frig, dang it!!

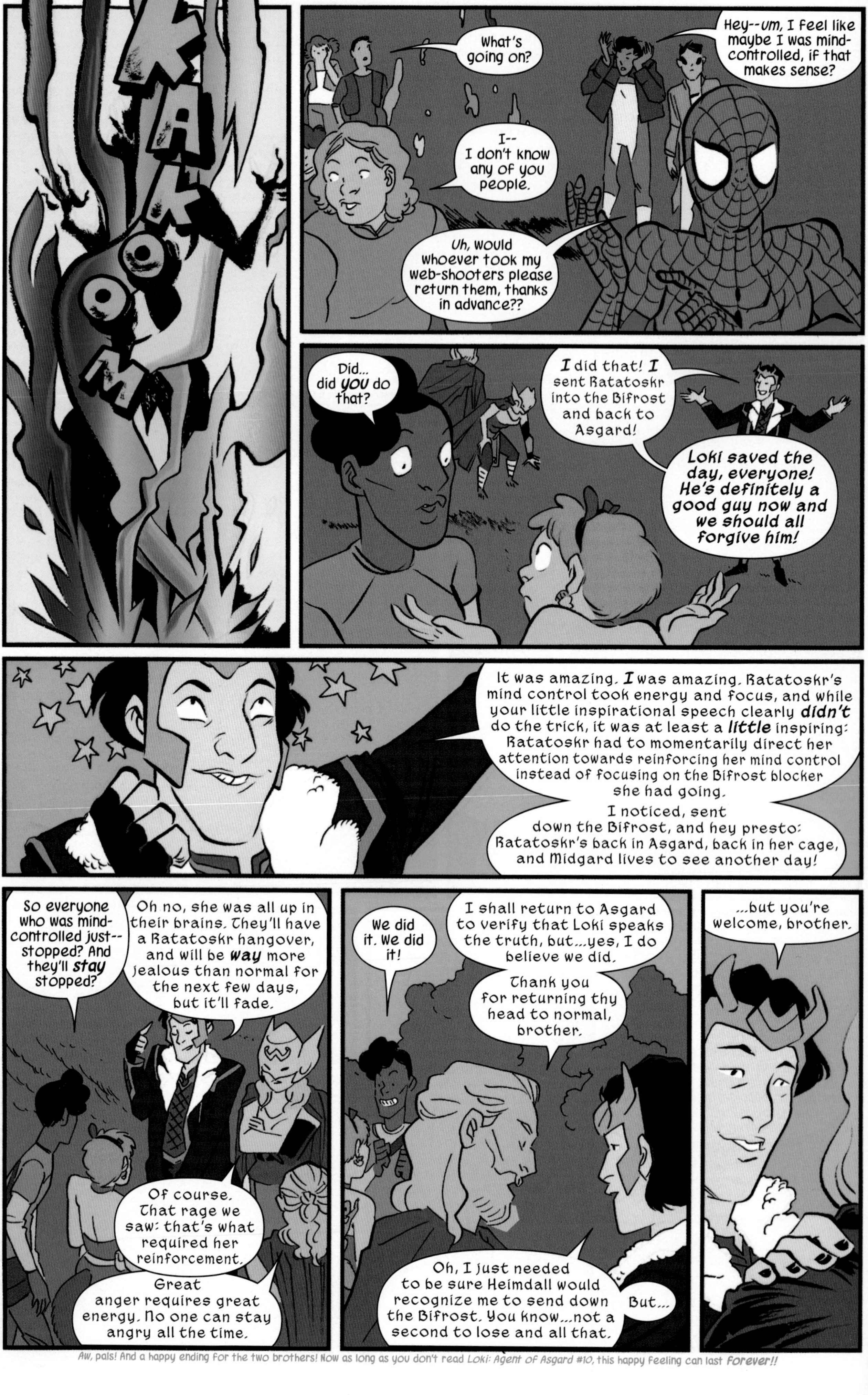
KAPOOM
What's going on?
Hey--um, I feel like maybe I was mind-controlled, if that makes sense?
I-- I don't know any of you people.
Uh, would whoever took my web-shooters please return them, thanks in advance??
Did... did you do that?
I did that! I sent Ratatoskr into the Bifrost and back to Asgard!
Loki saved the day, everyone! He's definitely a good guy now and we should all forgive him!
It was amazing. I was amazing. Ratatoskr's mind control took energy and focus, and while your little inspirational speech clearly didn't do the trick, it was at least a little inspiring: Ratatoskr had to momentarily direct her attention towards reinforcing her mind control instead of focusing on the Bifrost blocker she had going.
I noticed, sent down the Bifrost, and hey presto: Ratatoskr's back in Asgard, back in her cage, and Midgard lives to see another day!
So everyone who was mind-controlled just--stopped? And they'll stay stopped?
Oh no, she was all up in their brains. They'll have a Ratatoskr hangover, and will be way more jealous than normal for the next few days, but it'll fade.
Of course. That rage we saw: that's what required her reinforcement.
Great anger requires great energy. No one can stay angry all the time.
We did it. We did it!
I shall return to Asgard to verify that Loki speaks the truth, but...yes, I do believe we did.
Thank you for returning thy head to normal, brother.
Oh, I just needed to be sure Heimdall would recognize me to send down the Bifrost. You know...not a second to lose and all that.
But...
...but you're welcome, brother.
Aw, pals! And a happy ending for the two brothers! Now as long as you don't read Loki: Agent of Asgard #10, this happy feeling can last forever!!

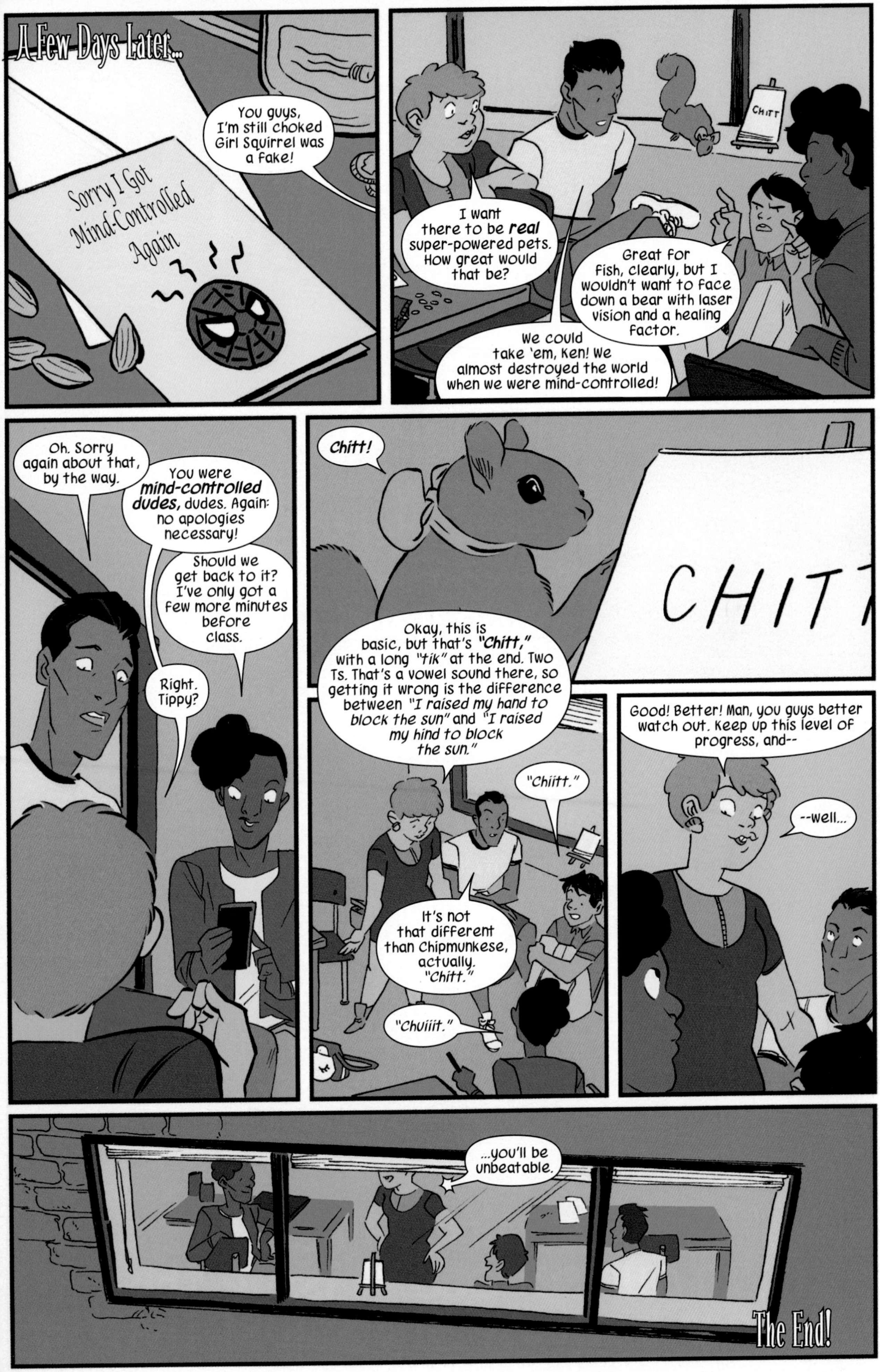
A Few Days Later...
Sorry I Got Mind-Controlled Again
You guys, I'm still choked Girl Squirrel was a fake!
I want there to be *real* super-powered pets. How great would that be?
CHITT
Great for fish, clearly, but I wouldn't want to face down a bear with laser vision and a healing factor.
We could take 'em, Ken! We almost destroyed the world when we were mind-controlled!
Oh. Sorry again about that, by the way.
You were *mind-controlled dudes,* dudes. Again: no apologies necessary!
Should we get back to it? I've only got a few more minutes before class.
Right. Tippy?
Chitt!
CHITT
Okay, this is basic, but that's *"Chitt,"* with a long *"tik"* at the end. Two Ts. That's a vowel sound there, so getting it wrong is the difference between *"I raised my hand to block the sun"* and *"I raised my hind to block the sun."*
"Chiitt."
It's not that different than Chipmunkese, actually. "Chitt."
"Chuiiit."
Good! Better! Man, you guys better watch out. Keep up this level of progress, and--
--well...
...you'll be unbeatable.
The End!

the unbeatable Squirrel Girl #8!

Written by
Ryan North

Art by
Erica Henderson
Color Art by
Rico Renzi

Lettering and Production by
VC's Clayton Cowles

Cover Artist **Erica Henderson**
Assistant Editor **Jon Moisan**
Editor **Wil Moss**
Executive Editor **Tom Brevoort**
Editor in Chief **Axel Alonso**
Chief Creative Officer **Joe Quesada**
Publisher **Dan Buckley**
Executive Producer **Alan Fine**

Squirrel Girl will return... ...in our second #1 issue this year because SHE'S JUST THAT GOOD.

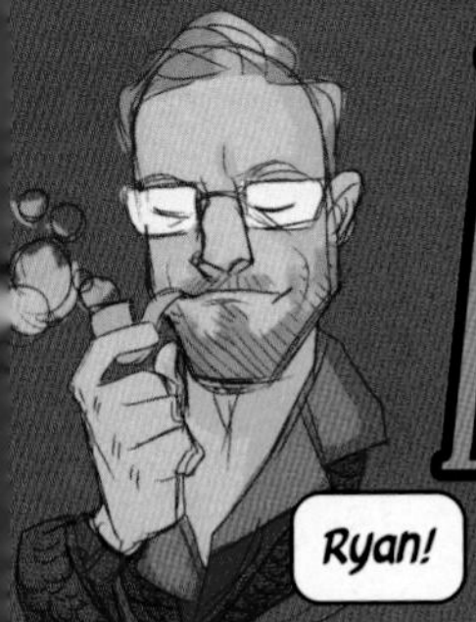

Ryan!

Letters From Nuts

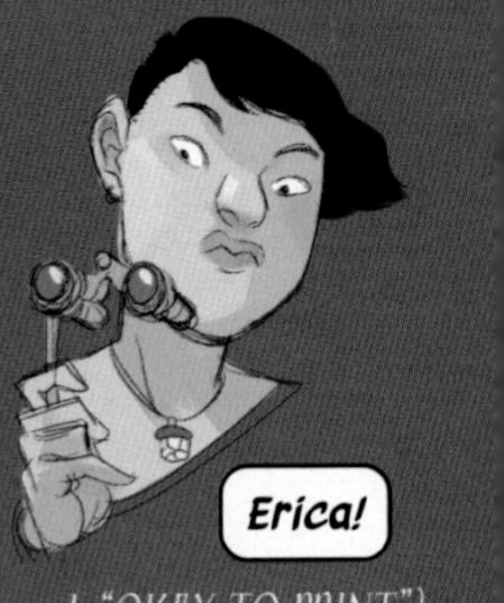

Erica!

Send letters to mheroes@marvel.com or 135 W 50th St, 7th Floor, New York, NY 10020 (Please mark "OKAY TO PRINT")

Dear Ryan and Erica,

I am the paleontologist boyfriend that Amanda the squirrel biologist mentioned when she wrote to you back in issue #5. I study predator-prey arms races in tyrannosaurs and duckbills. Thanks for responding to Amanda's letter. She is now totally obsessed with your comic (which I also think is delightful). Although, I am worried that I should start being a little jealous of that Chipmunk Hunk fellow. I notice that, unlike Doreen, he doesn't have a utility belt. I assume this means that, much like a real chipmunk, he carries all his hero gear in his cheek pouches, which is gross. Yeah, Chipmunk Hunk is gross. Why don't you go ahead and make that canon? Also, is it possible to get any of that sweet "Eat Nuts and Kick Butts" merchandise?

Anyway, I am glad to see you haven't taken Amanda up on her suggestion to introduce a paleontological comic foil who is dreadfully boring in comparison with Squirrel Girl and her other friends. But I do have an alternative suggestion for you. Amanda never told you about her squirrel research. She studies how the personalities of little squirrels relate to their siblings and how their personalities change as the squirrels mature. She does that by catching squirrels (which are complete suckers for peanut butter) and recording their behaviors when placed in a white-walled glass-roofed contraption filled with fake tunnel entrances and mirrors. It's all totally humane, but doesn't that sound like a premise for one of those alien-psychological-observer or hypno/illusionist super villains? Chew it over, and thanks again.

W. Scott Persons, IV

P.S. Erica, thanks for giving your tyrannosaur some protofeathers and for getting your pterosaur's wing membrane attachments right back in issue #5. Yours are much better than in that recently sequeled popular dinosaur movie franchise (the name escapes me, but you know the one I mean).

P.P.S. Attached is a photo of me visiting with one of Amanda's research subjects and also a photo of Amanda and me together, so you'll know that I am who I say I am and not just some nut . . . errr you get the point.

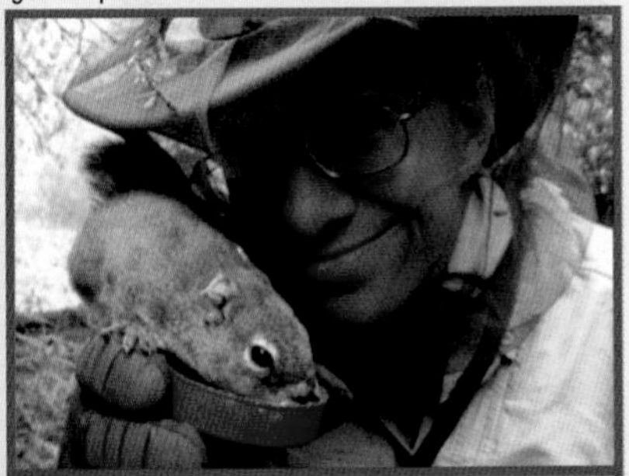

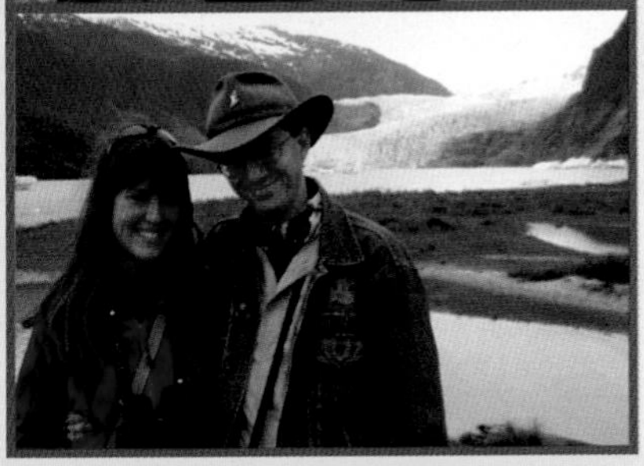

RYAN: Okay this is the best letter ever, and everyone else is now on notice: your letters have to be at LEAST as awesome as this, so please feature a) squirrels b) love and c) interesting squirrel facts in all future letters. I personally just started reading a book about squirrel facts, and did you know there are squirrels on five different continents? They're so widespread that THE SUN NEVER SETS ON SQUIRRELS. There is no way this fact is not making it into a future comic, so uh, when you read it later on try to act surprised.

ERICA: TAKE THAT, HOLLYWOOD. SOME PEOPLE care about being up to date on the latest scientific knowledge on dinosaurs. Listen, we all like Charles Knight, but the golden age of paleontology is over, guys.

P.S. I hope you guys keep writing in.

P.P.S. Now that I know their weakness I'm going to lure in ALL THE SQUIRRELS.

P.P.S. Oh god, are we those people that nobody wants to see movies with because we're going to go on about how Ron Silver being defeated at the end of *Time Cop* makes no scientific sense?

P.P.P.S. Don't watch *Time Cop*.

Dear lovely Erica and Ryan,

Thank you, thank you, thank you for UNBEATABLE SQUIRREL GIRL! With your super-powers combined, you have brought Doreen Green to life in the absolute best way! I love your comic so much, I threw a Marvel themed party for my 30th birthday JUST so I could be Squirrel Girl. And the best part? My best friend Jack surprised me with a squirrel battle against one of Doreen's greatest adversaries...Doctor Doom! Take a look for yourself! #SquirrelSelfie! Thanks Erica and Ryan for doing what you do! Long live Squirrel Girl!

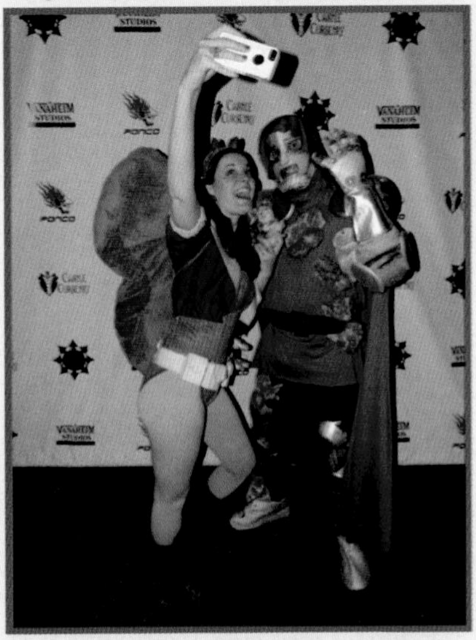

Brittany

R: This is amazing, and I've got to go to way better parties! Great costumes too. I notice Doom's covered in squirrels: confound those wretched rodents!!

E: HM. Next year is my 30th. I may need to steal some ideas from you. PLUS my boyfriend LOVES Doom and does have a couple of teeny scars on his face to make the whole thing even more accurate. HMMMMMMMMMMMMM.

Dear Erica and Ryan,

My dad and I have been reading this awesome comic, and I love it! For this year's Comic-Con in San Diego I tried to get my sister to come dressed as Tippy Toe, but she wouldn't! I have a question though, if Squirrel Girl was in a big crowd of people in her costume, wouldn't her tail keep hitting people in the face? Or would she have to flatten her tail across her back?

Your Inquisitive Fan,
Neva Devine, Age 12

R: I have paid a lot of attention to our cosplaying fans (on account of how they are the best) and most attach the tail via a concealed hook at the back of the vest, which means the tail always stays in place. It shouldn't be hitting people in the face that way, but will still look great! We've reblogged a couple of tutorials, which you can find on the cosplay tag of our unbeatablesquirrelgirl.tumblr.com site!

Anyway, to answer your actual question, yes absolutely Squirrel Girl would hit people in the face with her tail, but only those that deserved it.

E: In a crowd situation I think it would be easier to wrap the tail around herself like in the laser defense system scene in issue #2.

Dear USG team, makers of sheer delight,

I don't have an adorable baby squirrel to send you a photo of, but I do have the second printing of USG #4, which is almost as good, and coincidentally has become my all-time favorite comic issue ever. Of all the times. How will I ever beat that? It's impossible! I really liked how you had Doreen handle Galactus--getting him take-out--Beautiful. I love you crazy nuts for doing this comic. It's uproarious, and I keep getting people to read it. I just finished reading #6, and I can't wait for the next issue. If Squirrel Girl and Magneto form a road-trip duo, I think I'll pop from sheer giggles. Everything about this comic is delightful, and in the midst of the super-serious SECRET WARS and Mister Fantastic's moody melodrama, sheer delight is such a great change of tone. It's immensely needed, and positively needed.

John Polkowske

R: Aw thanks! That's super sweet. I like the idea of Squirrel Girl and Magneto going on a road-trip and the car runs out of gas and Doreen makes Magneto "push" the car with his powers the rest of the way. That's my pitch: a put-upon Magneto and carefree Squirrel Girl discover America, and also...friendship. Marvel, you read your own letters pages, right?? [Ed. note: Only the ones that bag on *Time Cop*.]

E: Hey, he should push the car the whole way. We're not in a place where we should be wasting fuel when we don't have to! Plus, that way, they can tool around in a really sweet vintage ride without worrying about it breaking down all the time.

Hey Squirrel Girl team,

A lot of my friends who are ladies often talk

about their crushes on fictional characters, and it has been something I respected but never really "got." But now that I may or may not have a crush on Squirrel Girl, it's possible that I maaaay see their points. I mean, it is likely that Doreen is super passionate about her interests and would probably have great conversations about squirrels, computer science and squirrel computer science on dates. Plus there is a possibility that she's a super caring, sweet person that would make anyone super happy. It also may be true that she's super cute and strong and awkward in an adorable way? But none of this is, of course, confirmed. Just like my crush on Squirrel Girl. Which is totally up for debate and not confirmed in any way.

(Possibly?) JD Boucher

R: I have a big crush on Commander Data from *Star Trek*, so I understand you. It's more of a friendship crush though. I just want to hang out with robots and the robot-adjacent!

E: I'm pretty sure my first crush ever was on Race Bannon. I totally get it.

Hi Ryan! Hi Erica!
SQUIRREL GIRL is a grand book, yielding laughs and thoughts and an appreciation of pictures. I like it and buy it often.

But I'm afraid there's a bug in your sixth comic. In the front menu, I (naturally) picked Dazzler and Devil Dinosaur as the newest friends of the unbeatable Squirrel Girl, but the "Answer Inside" gave Chipmunk Hunk and Koi Boi. It's 100% reproducible. It even lets me select zero characters but then presents these two.

In case anyone else is facing this issue, I've attached a fix:

Up with squirrels!
Cheston

R: Cheston, I love this. Also: Thank you for the bug report; it has been confirmed on our end and will hopefully be corrected in a future team-up.

E: Marvel IS restarting WHAT IF? Man, I also hope that Marvel reads its own letter columns. [Ed. note: Only the ones with embarrassing *Star Trek* crush revelations.]

Good day, fine folks at Squirrel Girl's headquarters!
This comic brings me more joy than I know what to do with! It's the funniest comic and my absolute favorite. Doreen is my kind of hero--she's so positive, tough, way cool and a total sweetheart. The artwork is endearing, the writing is hilarious, and the animal rhyming names are the best. Thank you so much for this book. You guys are super awesome. My life is better for having read it.

Will you be restarting the series this fall after SECRET WARS ends?? I just looked through the All-New All-Different Marvel Previews and it wasn't in there. I'm worried, to say the least. Are you planning for Superior Squirrel Girl? All-New Squirrel Girl? Old Gal Doreen? Squirrel-Verse event? Squirrel Wars?? I'll take any Doreen Green you wanna serve up.

I've never written in to a comic before, but this

book is so great that getting my picture in an issue of SQUIRREL GIRL is now on my bucket list. Here I am reading my books in a tree, so as to be closer to Tippy Toe and Doreen:

Making Mine Marvel, and wishing you all the nuts,
Molly J. Santa Maria
San Diego, CA

R: This is ALSO amazing. Thank you, Molly! And I have good news: we ARE continuing after SECRET WARS! We're taking a (short!) break, but then we'll be restarting with a new #1 in October. Same characters! Same creative team! Just a new story that builds on everything here. Also, while it's not "Old Man Doreen," you'll be able to get even more Squirrel Girl then, as she'll be in the NEW AVENGERS book too!

E: "Old Man Doreen" is another one for WHAT IF. Also, consider that photo PRINTED.

Erica and Ryan,
Forget all other work commitments, social obligations and personal hobbies, okay? I'm going to need this series to go on FOREVER. Will you accept haikus as a form of reimbursement? Here's a small down payment:
Chik chukka chut chut
Chit chit chukka chitty chut
Chut chitty chukka

Brittany Meredith

R: Ran that by Tippy and she said it was FLATTERING and SAUCY, so thank you!

E: WHAT MAKES YOU THINK WE MIGHT WANT TO STOP?

Erica, Ryan, and Rico,
Hi! I love SQUIRREL GIRL, I've been reading since issue #1, and the story has gotten better and better with each book -- which seems impossible because it's already so amazing. I loved the inclusion of the Avengers in #7. Black Widow and Squirrel Girl in the same panel was like a most wonderful dream... That quickly came to end end because... well...insert spoiler here.I'm really looking forward to the next issue, especially because Ratatoskr is an extremely-scary-looking squirrel with unicorn qualities. An evil unicorn. And I didn't know those types existed.

So yeah, you're all amazing and I love your book and Doreen and Tippy-Toe. Thanks for a great comic book! (:

Brake for squirrels!
Erin

PS: Way back in February when someone at the comic book store told me the person who did the coloring for SQUIRREL GIRL worked at the store, I was blown away and totally geeked out. Thanks Rico!

E: Haha. I liked Black Widow better in #5 because she wasn't mind-controlled into being a jerk. She's so much fun either way though. Ratatoskr is great. I haven't had a chance to draw monsters for a while so it's been a treat!

Friends,
I'm a teacher in North Carolina and picked up the first issues of UNBEATABLE SQUIRREL GIRL for our after school comic club. After reading the

first two comics, SQUIRREL GIRL became a part of my personal pull-list, as well as a title the kids couldn't wait for more of. Thanks for such a fun, positive book!

Additionally, around issue #4 our daughter Penelope was born. I'm pretty sure she's a huge fan because between naps she has been fighting crime under the guise of "Sugar Glider":

Does Squirrel Girl need a sidekick? Keep up the great work.

Joel Richardson,
Washington, NC

R: Can we just turn this letters page into an "adorable pictures of fans" page instead? I am so into this. Welcome to the world, Penelope! I had to wait until I was actually writing a book to be published in a letters page; you've got a huge head start (and awesome costume!).

E: Did you make that or is there a store that sells tiny super hero apparel for babies? Is it in North Carolina? I'm amazed it took this long to break into this untapped market!

Hi Erica and Ryan,
I've been picking up UNBEATABLE SQUIRREL GIRL since the beginning, and it's just terrific (although it takes twice as long to read because of the tiny type at the bottom of the pages). That said, why I'm writing is to thank you on behalf of my five-year-old daughter, Thessaly. She loves comics, and we always read SQUIRREL GIRL together so she can find out what's happening with Tippy-Toe.

A while ago, we played through *Lego Marvel Heroes* together, and after beating the end boss, Galactus, she developed a persistent fear that he was coming to eat her. That same week, SQUIRREL GIRL #4 came out, and as soon as I got home, I handed it to her to read. No more Galactus fears --she even wrote him a note telling him she loved him! Thanks a lot, guys (not only for helping out my girl, but for advancing a plausible theory of just why Galactus can never manage to devour Earth)-- you've earned these two readers.

Bob Britten (and Thessaly)

R: Terrific! And tell Thessaly that when I wrote the story it was after playing that very same game! I took a photo of Galactus and Squirrel Girl together (you can unlock her, she's by the dockyard!) and sent it to my wife with the subject line "story idea."

E: Oh my god, everything about that story is great and I can't even.

New Series. New Avenger (!). Still Eats Nuts and Kicks Butts!

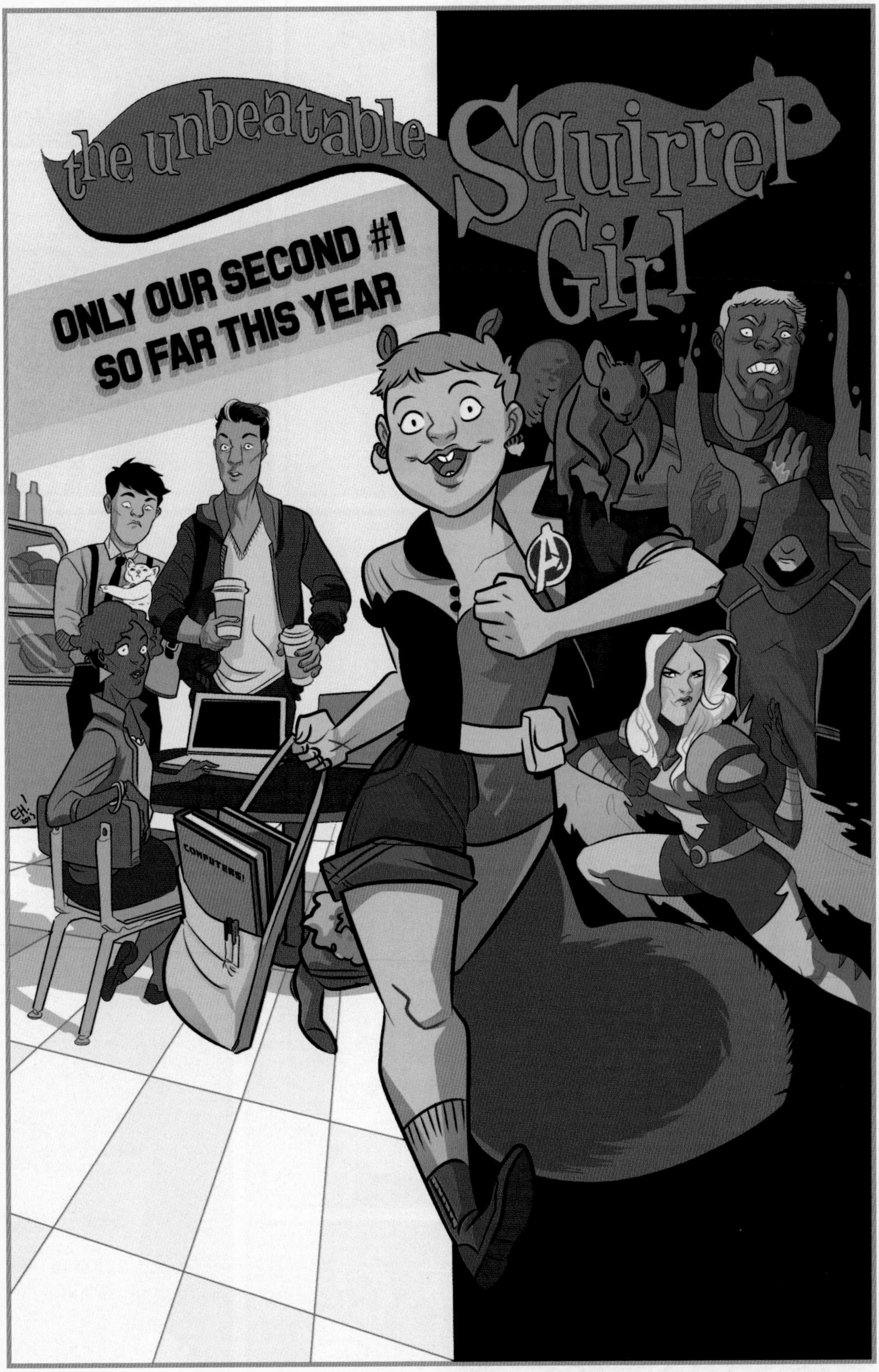

the unbeatable Squirrel Girl
ONLY OUR SECOND #1
SO FAR THIS YEAR
COMPUTERS!

See you in October!
(And keep the letters coming in the meantime!)
- Ryan, Erica, Rico, Clayton, Jon and Wil!

Attention, Squirrel Scouts! Make sure to check out our production blog, **unbeatablesquirrelgirl.tumblr.com**, where we post behind-the-scenes stuff on how the book gets made, along with all sorts of cool things *you* make: fanart, cosplay, whatever!

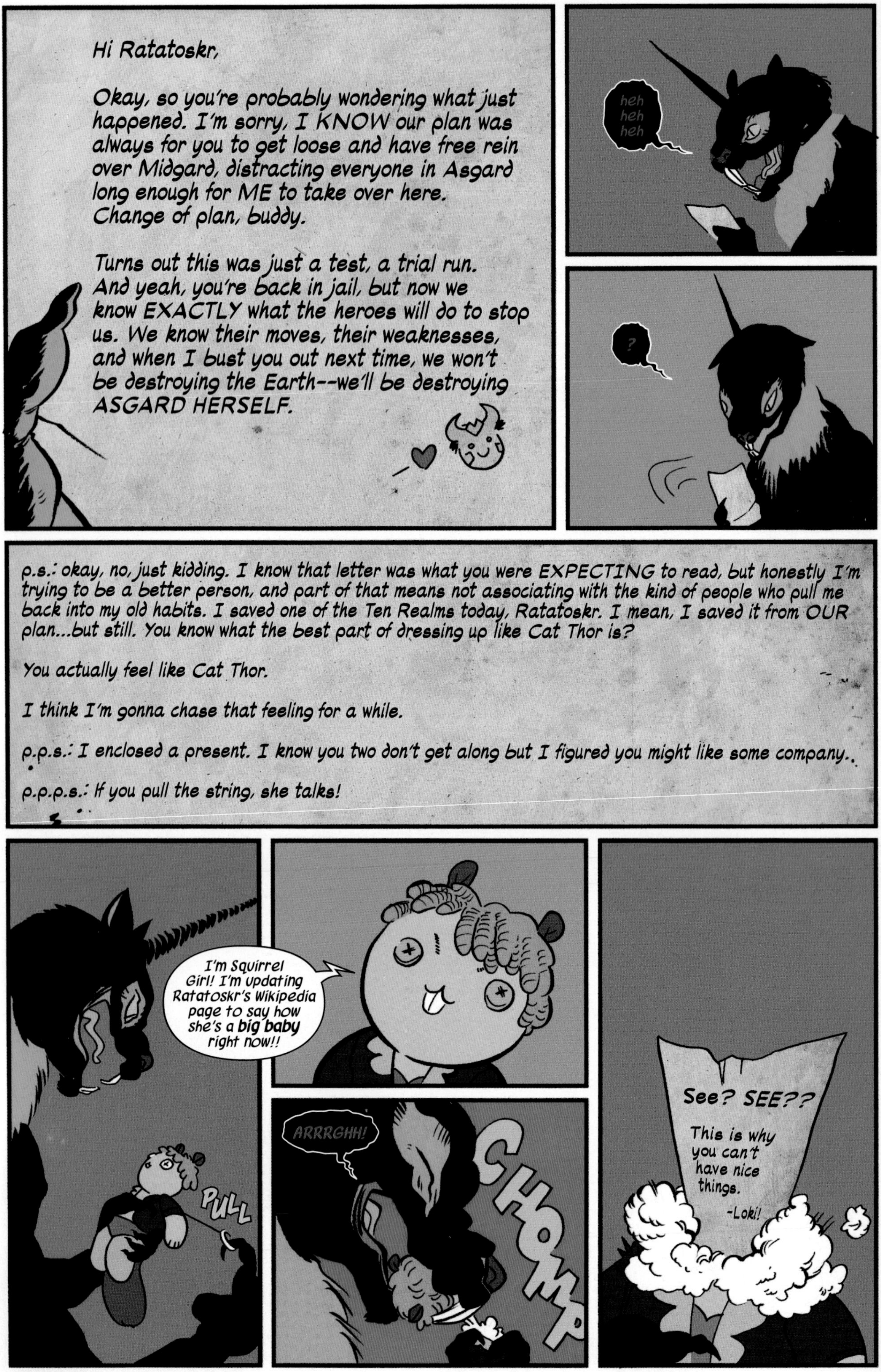
Hi Ratatoskr,
Okay, so you're probably wondering what just happened. I'm sorry, I KNOW our plan was always for you to get loose and have free rein over Midgard, distracting everyone in Asgard long enough for ME to take over here. Change of plan, buddy.
Turns out this was just a test, a trial run. And yeah, you're back in jail, but now we know EXACTLY what the heroes will do to stop us. We know their moves, their weaknesses, and when I bust you out next time, we won't be destroying the Earth--we'll be destroying ASGARD HERSELF.
heh heh heh
?
p.s.: okay, no, just kidding. I know that letter was what you were EXPECTING to read, but honestly I'm trying to be a better person, and part of that means not associating with the kind of people who pull me back into my old habits. I saved one of the Ten Realms today, Ratatoskr. I mean, I saved it from OUR plan...but still. You know what the best part of dressing up like Cat Thor is?
You actually feel like Cat Thor.
I think I'm gonna chase that feeling for a while.
p.p.s.: I enclosed a present. I know you two don't get along but I figured you might like some company.
p.p.p.s.: If you pull the string, she talks!
PULL
I'm Squirrel Girl! I'm updating Ratatoskr's Wikipedia page to say how she's a **big baby** right now!!
ARRRGHH!
CHOMP
See? SEE??
This is why you can't have nice things.
-Loki!

YOU'VE SEEN MY FRIEND DOREEN EAT NUTS AND KICK BUTTS IN THE MARVEL *NOW!*

NOW, REVISIT THE MARVEL *THEN!* FOR SOME EXTRA-SPECIAL BONUS TAILS!

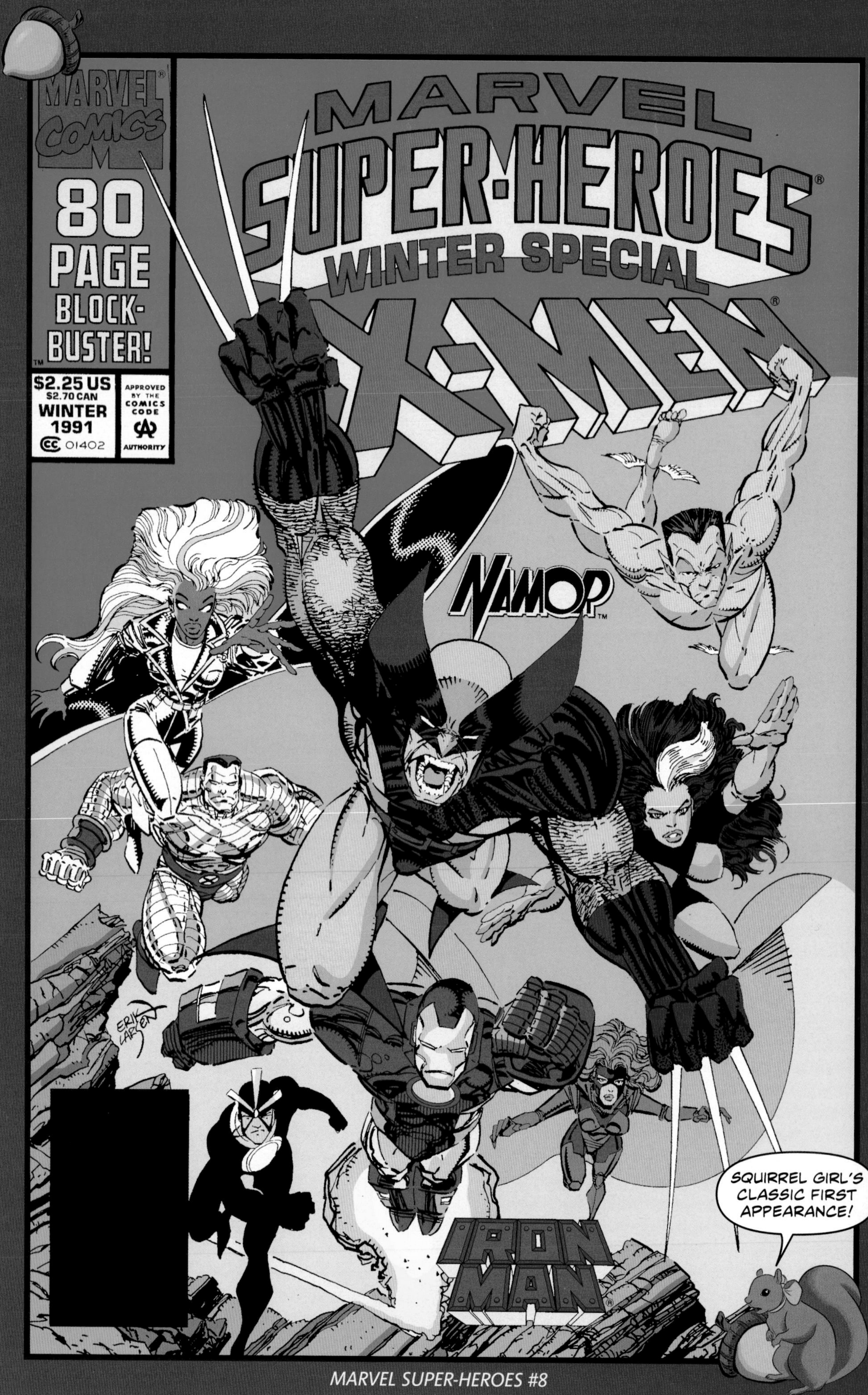
MARVEL COMICS
80 PAGE BLOCK-BUSTER!
$2.25 US
$2.70 CAN
WINTER 1991
APPROVED BY THE COMICS CODE AUTHORITY
MARVEL SUPER-HEROES
WINTER SPECIAL
X-MEN
NAMOR
ERIK LARSEN
IRON MAN
SQUIRREL GIRL'S CLASSIC FIRST APPEARANCE!

MARVEL SUPER-HEROES #8

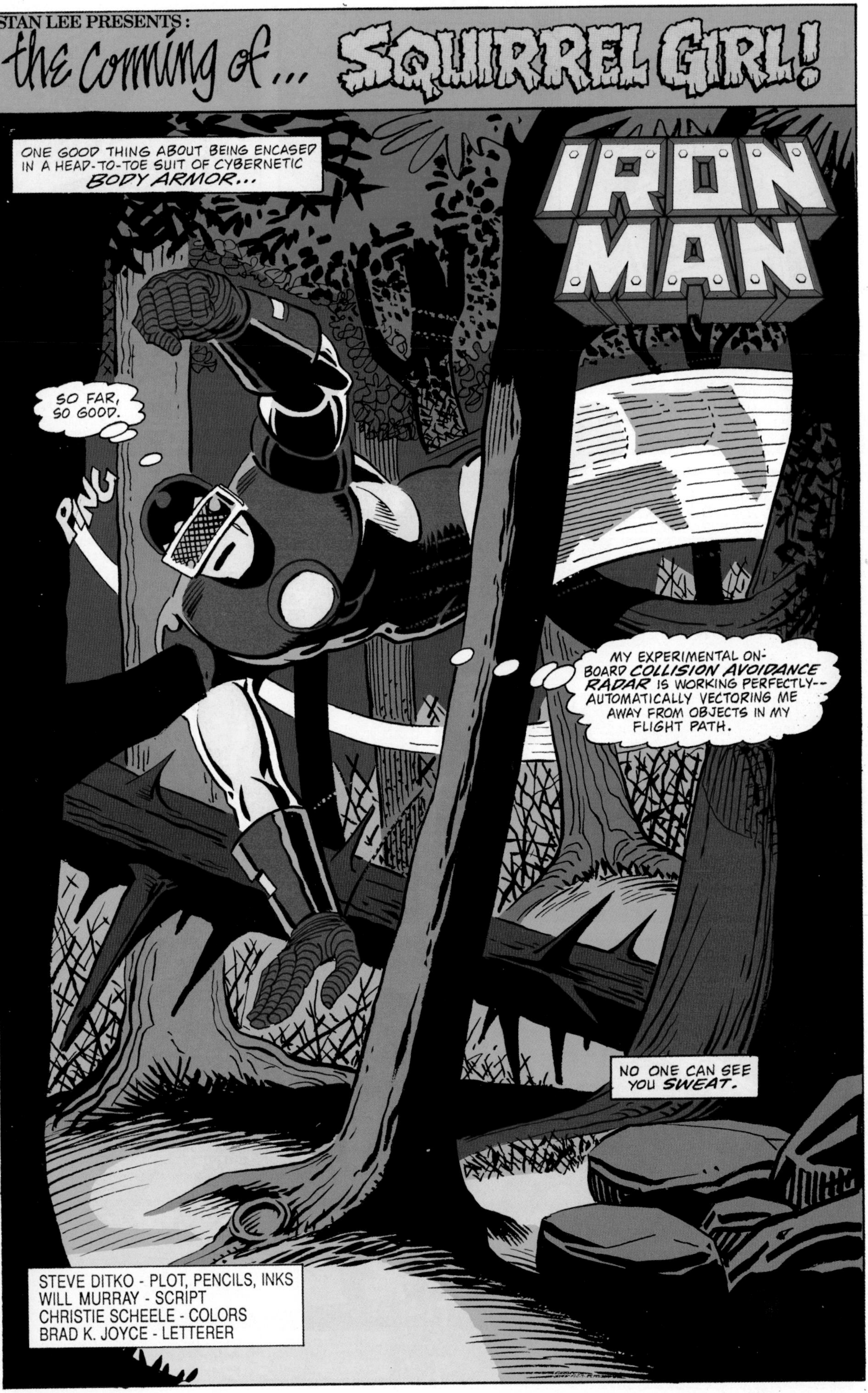

STAN LEE PRESENTS:
the coming of... SQUIRREL GIRL!
IRON MAN
ONE GOOD THING ABOUT BEING ENCASED IN A HEAD-TO-TOE SUIT OF CYBERNETIC BODY ARMOR...
SO FAR, SO GOOD.
PING
MY EXPERIMENTAL ON-BOARD COLLISION AVOIDANCE RADAR IS WORKING PERFECTLY--AUTOMATICALLY VECTORING ME AWAY FROM OBJECTS IN MY FLIGHT PATH.
NO ONE CAN SEE YOU SWEAT.
STEVE DITKO - PLOT, PENCILS, INKS
WILL MURRAY - SCRIPT
CHRISTIE SCHEELE - COLORS
BRAD K. JOYCE - LETTERER

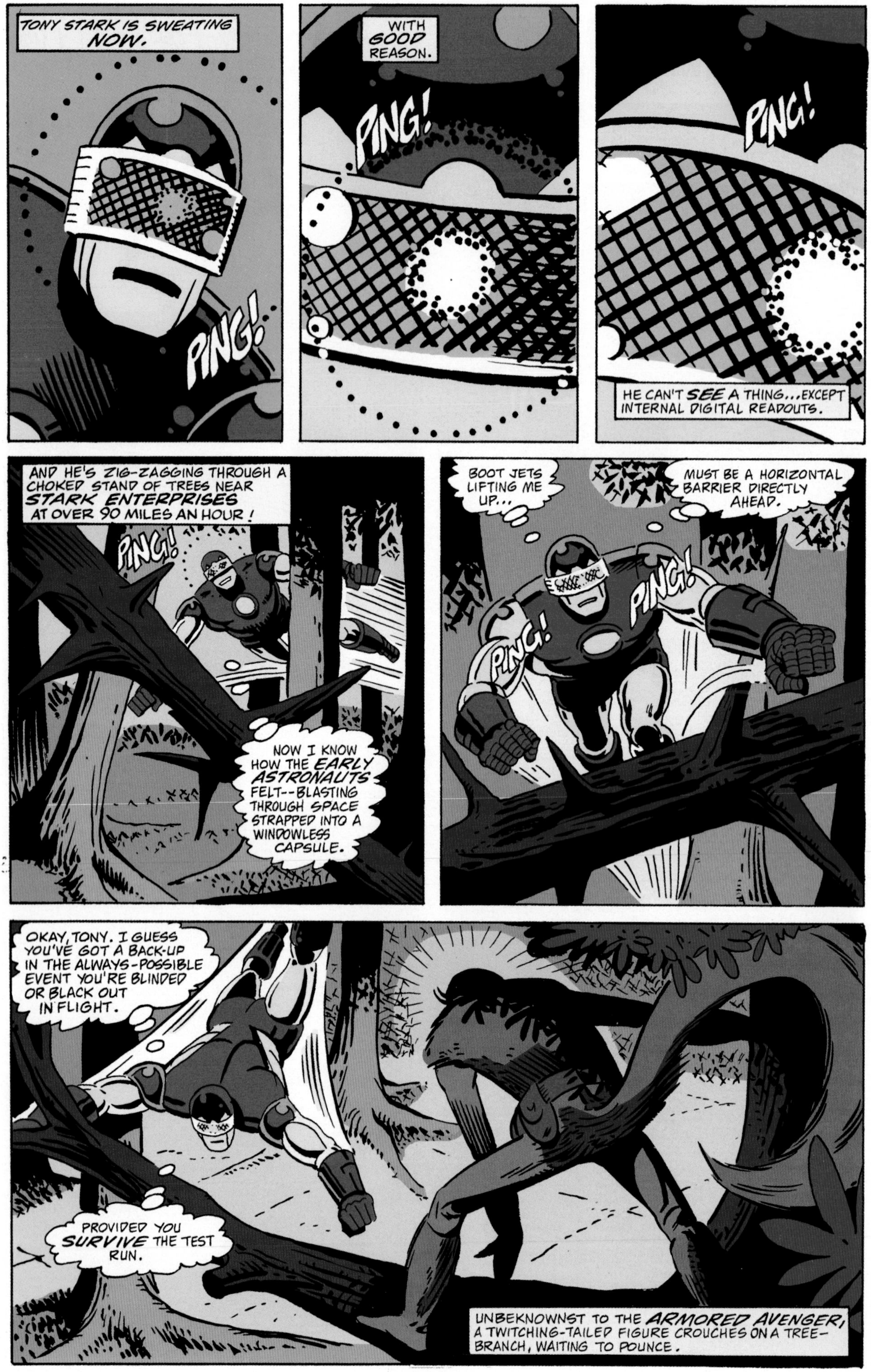

TONY STARK IS SWEATING NOW.
PING!
WITH GOOD REASON.
PING!
PING!
HE CAN'T SEE A THING...EXCEPT INTERNAL DIGITAL READOUTS.
AND HE'S ZIG-ZAGGING THROUGH A CHOKED STAND OF TREES NEAR STARK ENTERPRISES AT OVER 90 MILES AN HOUR!
PING!
NOW I KNOW HOW THE EARLY ASTRONAUTS FELT--BLASTING THROUGH SPACE STRAPPED INTO A WINDOWLESS CAPSULE.
BOOT JETS LIFTING ME UP...
MUST BE A HORIZONTAL BARRIER DIRECTLY AHEAD.
PING!
PING!
OKAY, TONY. I GUESS YOU'VE GOT A BACK-UP IN THE ALWAYS-POSSIBLE EVENT YOU'RE BLINDED OR BLACK OUT IN FLIGHT.
PROVIDED YOU SURVIVE THE TEST RUN.
UNBEKNOWNST TO THE ARMORED AVENGER, A TWITCHING-TAILED FIGURE CROUCHES ON A TREE-BRANCH, WAITING TO POUNCE.

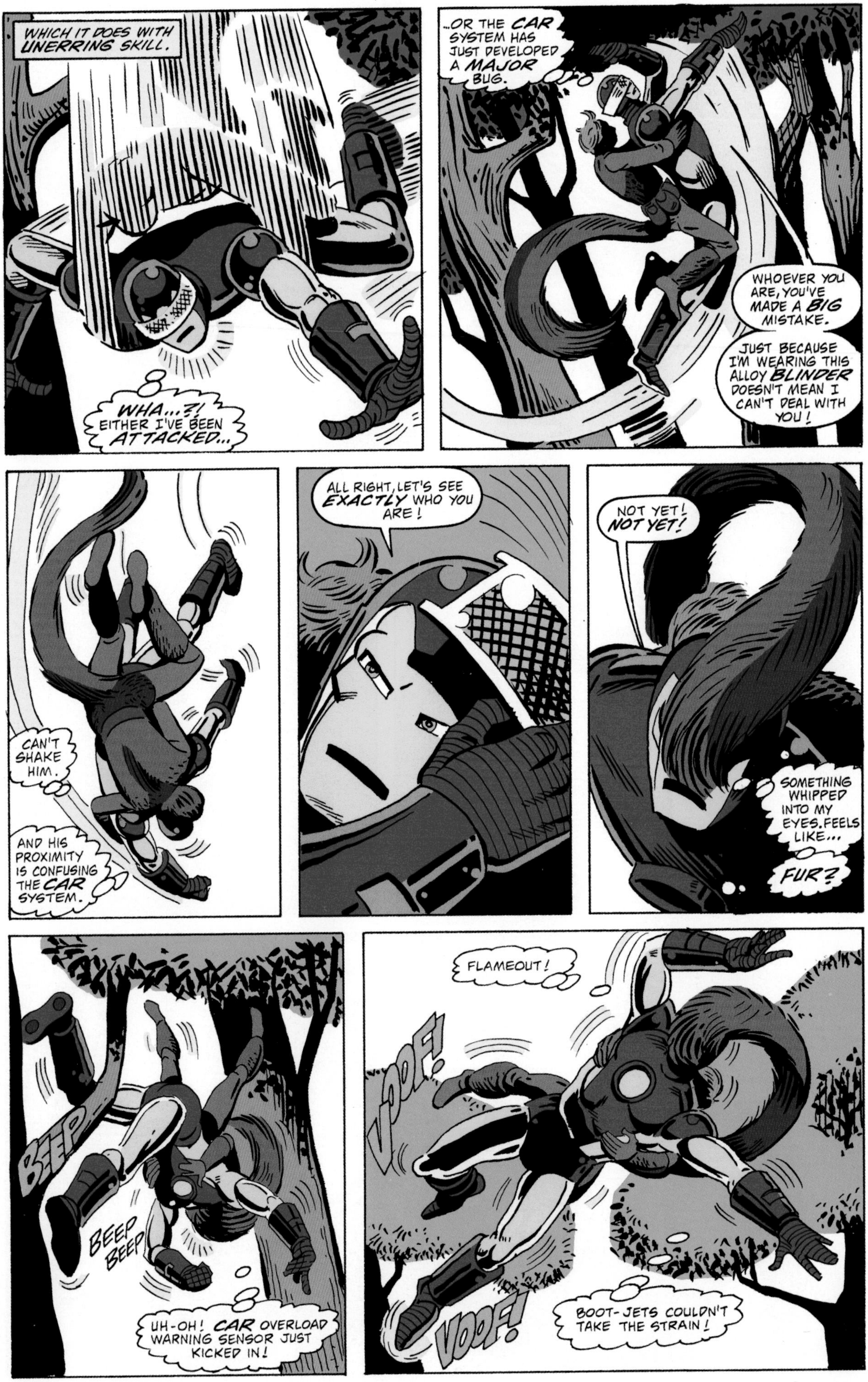

WHICH IT DOES WITH UNERRING SKILL.
WHA...?! EITHER I'VE BEEN ATTACKED...
...OR THE CAR SYSTEM HAS JUST DEVELOPED A MAJOR BUG.
WHOEVER YOU ARE, YOU'VE MADE A BIG MISTAKE.
JUST BECAUSE I'M WEARING THIS ALLOY BLINDER DOESN'T MEAN I CAN'T DEAL WITH YOU!
CAN'T SHAKE HIM.
AND HIS PROXIMITY IS CONFUSING THE CAR SYSTEM.
ALL RIGHT, LET'S SEE EXACTLY WHO YOU ARE!
NOT YET! NOT YET!
SOMETHING WHIPPED INTO MY EYES. FEELS LIKE... FUR?
BEEP
BEEP BEEP
UH-OH! CAR OVERLOAD WARNING SENSOR JUST KICKED IN!
FLAMEOUT!
VOOF!
VOOF!
BOOT-JETS COULDN'T TAKE THE STRAIN!

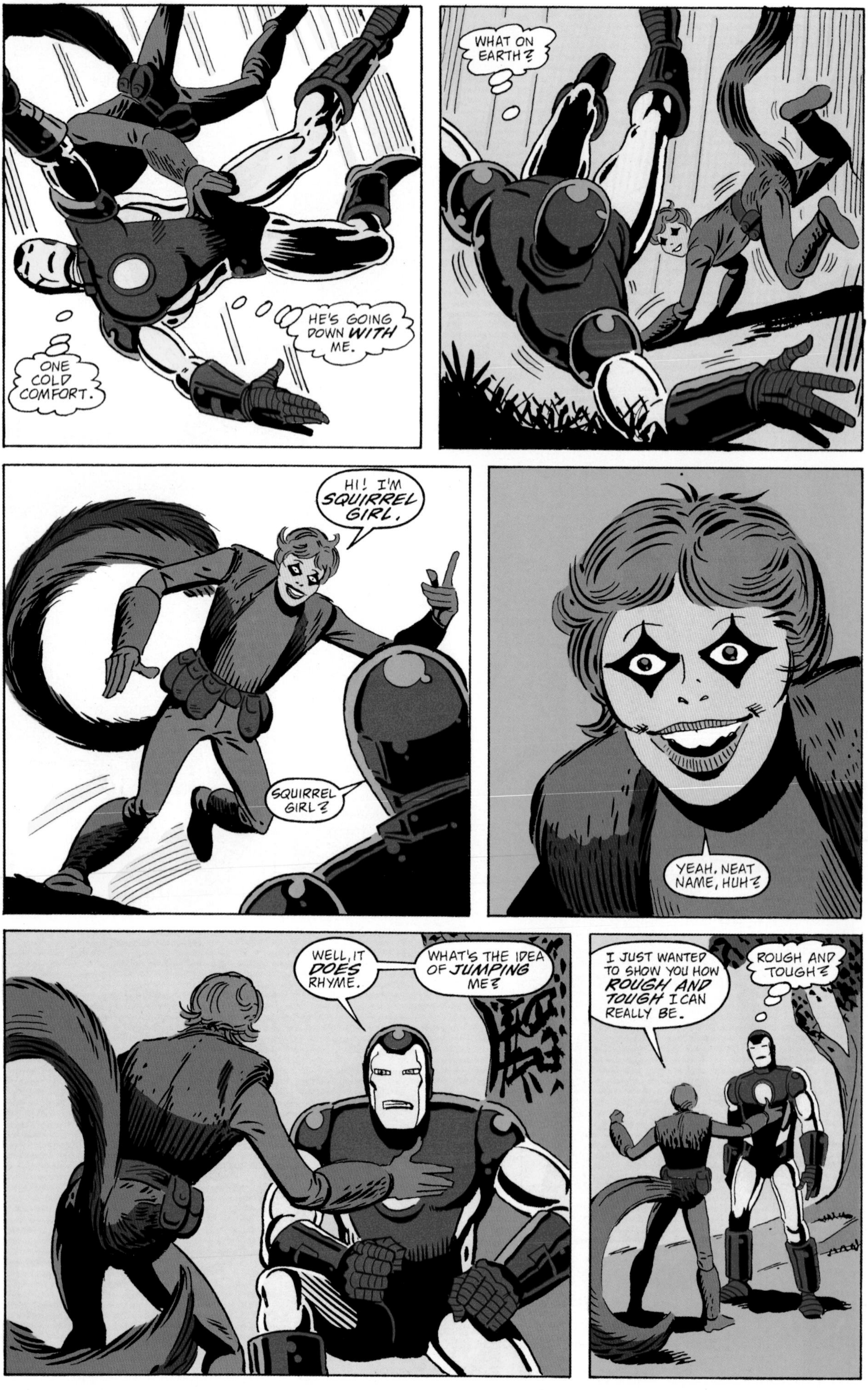
HE'S GOING DOWN WITH ME.
ONE COLD COMFORT.
WHAT ON EARTH?
HI! I'M SQUIRREL GIRL.
SQUIRREL GIRL?
YEAH. NEAT NAME, HUH?
WHAT'S THE IDEA OF JUMPING ME?
WELL, IT DOES RHYME.
I JUST WANTED TO SHOW YOU HOW ROUGH AND TOUGH I CAN REALLY BE.
ROUGH AND TOUGH?

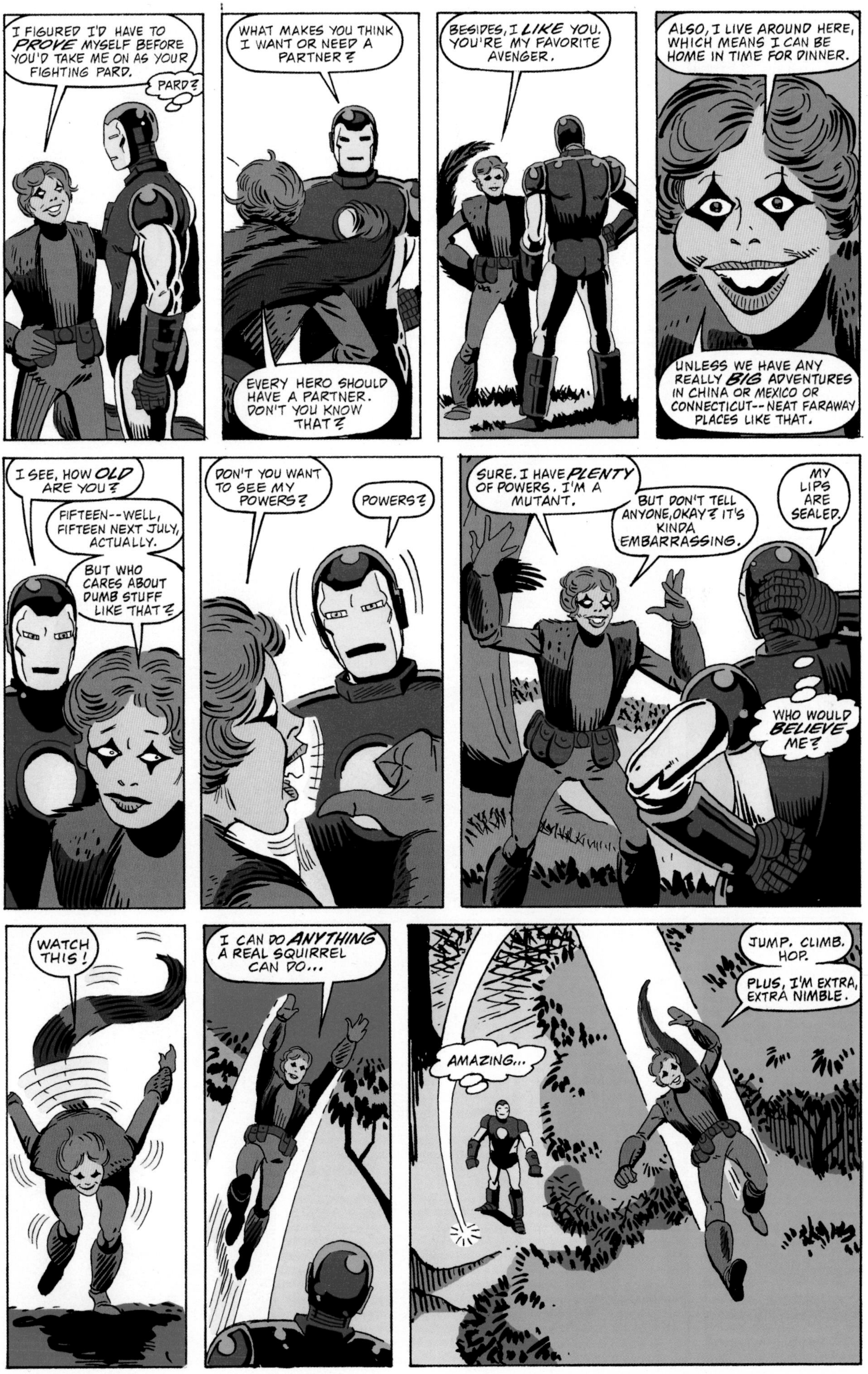
I FIGURED I'D HAVE TO PROVE MYSELF BEFORE YOU'D TAKE ME ON AS YOUR FIGHTING PARD.
PARD?
WHAT MAKES YOU THINK I WANT OR NEED A PARTNER?
EVERY HERO SHOULD HAVE A PARTNER. DON'T YOU KNOW THAT?
BESIDES, I LIKE YOU. YOU'RE MY FAVORITE AVENGER.
ALSO, I LIVE AROUND HERE, WHICH MEANS I CAN BE HOME IN TIME FOR DINNER.
UNLESS WE HAVE ANY REALLY BIG ADVENTURES IN CHINA OR MEXICO OR CONNECTICUT--NEAT FARAWAY PLACES LIKE THAT.
I SEE. HOW OLD ARE YOU?
FIFTEEN--WELL, FIFTEEN NEXT JULY, ACTUALLY.
BUT WHO CARES ABOUT DUMB STUFF LIKE THAT?
DON'T YOU WANT TO SEE MY POWERS?
POWERS?
SURE. I HAVE PLENTY OF POWERS. I'M A MUTANT.
BUT DON'T TELL ANYONE, OKAY? IT'S KINDA EMBARRASSING.
MY LIPS ARE SEALED.
WHO WOULD BELIEVE ME?
WATCH THIS!
I CAN DO ANYTHING A REAL SQUIRREL CAN DO...
JUMP. CLIMB. HOP.
PLUS, I'M EXTRA, EXTRA NIMBLE.
AMAZING...

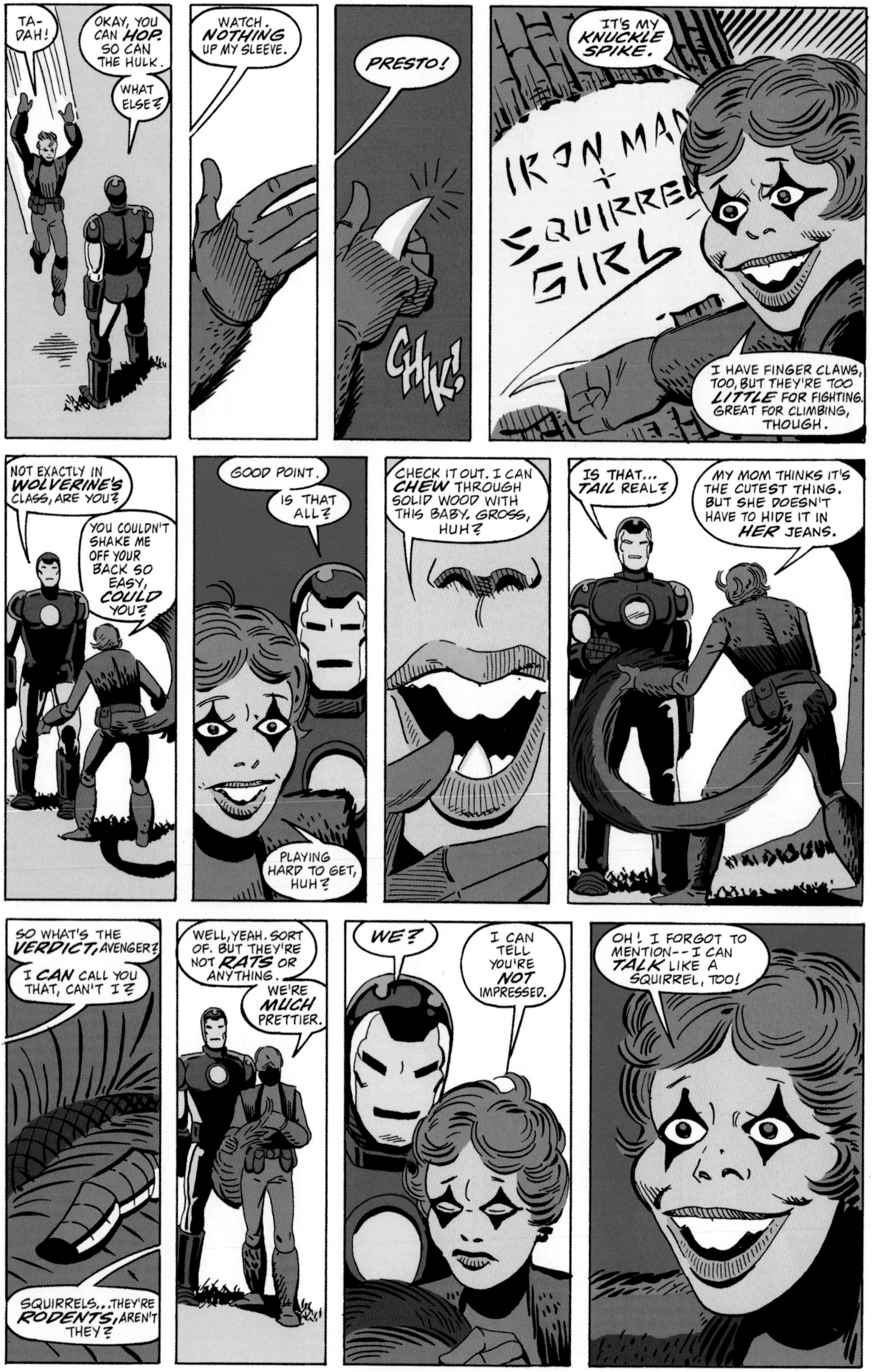
TA-DAH!
OKAY, YOU CAN HOP. SO CAN THE HULK.
WHAT ELSE?
WATCH. NOTHING UP MY SLEEVE.
PRESTO!
CHIK!
IT'S MY KNUCKLE SPIKE.
IRON MAN + SQUIRREL GIRL
I HAVE FINGER CLAWS, TOO, BUT THEY'RE TOO LITTLE FOR FIGHTING. GREAT FOR CLIMBING, THOUGH.
NOT EXACTLY IN WOLVERINE'S CLASS, ARE YOU?
YOU COULDN'T SHAKE ME OFF YOUR BACK SO EASY, COULD YOU?
GOOD POINT.
IS THAT ALL?
PLAYING HARD TO GET, HUH?
CHECK IT OUT. I CAN CHEW THROUGH SOLID WOOD WITH THIS BABY. GROSS, HUH?
IS THAT... TAIL REAL?
MY MOM THINKS IT'S THE CUTEST THING. BUT SHE DOESN'T HAVE TO HIDE IT IN HER JEANS.
SO WHAT'S THE VERDICT, AVENGER?
I CAN CALL YOU THAT, CAN'T I?
SQUIRRELS... THEY'RE RODENTS, AREN'T THEY?
WELL, YEAH. SORT OF. BUT THEY'RE NOT RATS OR ANYTHING.
WE'RE MUCH PRETTIER.
WE?
I CAN TELL YOU'RE NOT IMPRESSED.
OH! I FORGOT TO MENTION--I CAN TALK LIKE A SQUIRREL, TOO!

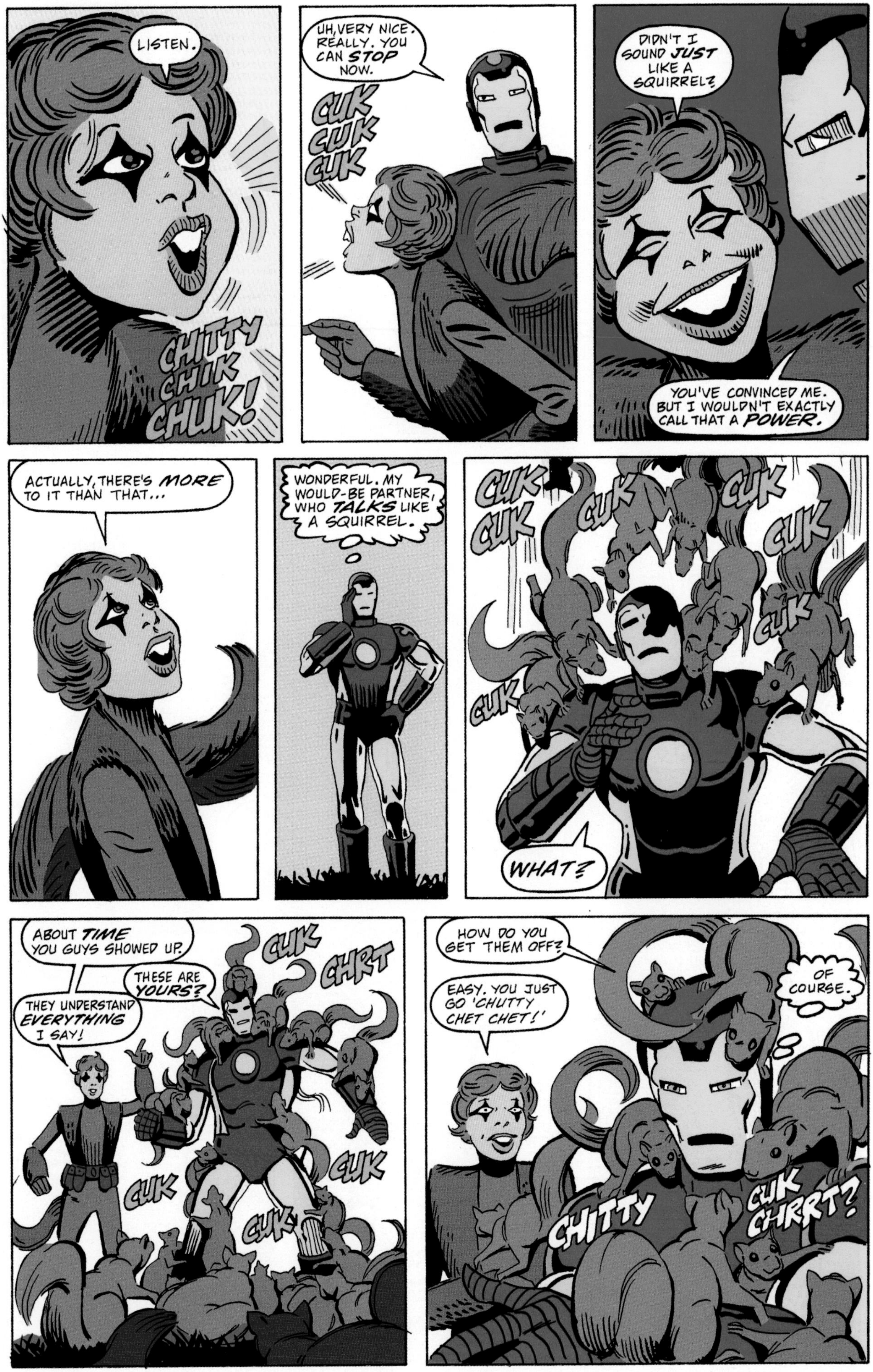

LISTEN.
CHITTY CHIK CHUK!
UH, VERY NICE. REALLY. YOU CAN STOP NOW.
CUK CUK CUK
DIDN'T I SOUND JUST LIKE A SQUIRREL?
YOU'VE CONVINCED ME. BUT I WOULDN'T EXACTLY CALL THAT A POWER.
ACTUALLY, THERE'S MORE TO IT THAN THAT...
WONDERFUL. MY WOULD-BE PARTNER, WHO TALKS LIKE A SQUIRREL.
CUK CUK
CUK
CUK
CUK
CUK
CUK
WHAT?
ABOUT TIME YOU GUYS SHOWED UP.
THEY UNDERSTAND EVERYTHING I SAY!
THESE ARE YOURS?
CUK
CHRT
CUK
CUK
CUK
HOW DO YOU GET THEM OFF?
EASY. YOU JUST GO 'CHUTTY CHET CHET!'
OF COURSE.
CHITTY
CUK CHRRT?

YOU KNOW, I'LL BET THE *X-MEN* WOULD BE VERY, VERY INTERESTED IN TALKING TO YOU.

NO *WAY!*

SPANK

CUK

I DON'T WANT *ANYBODY* TO KNOW I'M A MUTANT.

BESIDES, THEY'RE ALL SO STUCK UP--ESPECIALLY THAT *OBNOXIOUS* KITTY PRIDE.

I KNOW--WHY DON'T I INTRODUCE YOU TO CAPTAIN AMERICA? HE'S USUALLY *OPEN* TO NEW PARTNERS.

CUK CUK

DOWN, MONKEY JOE!

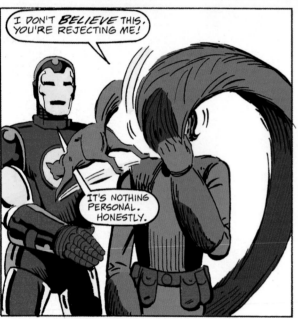

I DON'T *BELIEVE* THIS. YOU'RE REJECTING ME!

IT'S NOTHING PERSONAL. HONESTLY.

I REALLY DON'T *NEED* A PARTNER. IRON MAN IS A SOLO ACT.

BUT...BUT YOU'RE MY PERSONAL HERO! YOU *CAN'T* SAY NO!

AND *YOU'RE* UNDER AGE.

SORRY. I CAN'T BE *RESPONSIBLE* SHOULD SOMETHING HAPPEN TO YOU.

SNIFF!

NOW IF YOU'LL EXCUSE ME, I'M RUNNING LATE.

WAIT! THERE'S ONE OTHER THING.

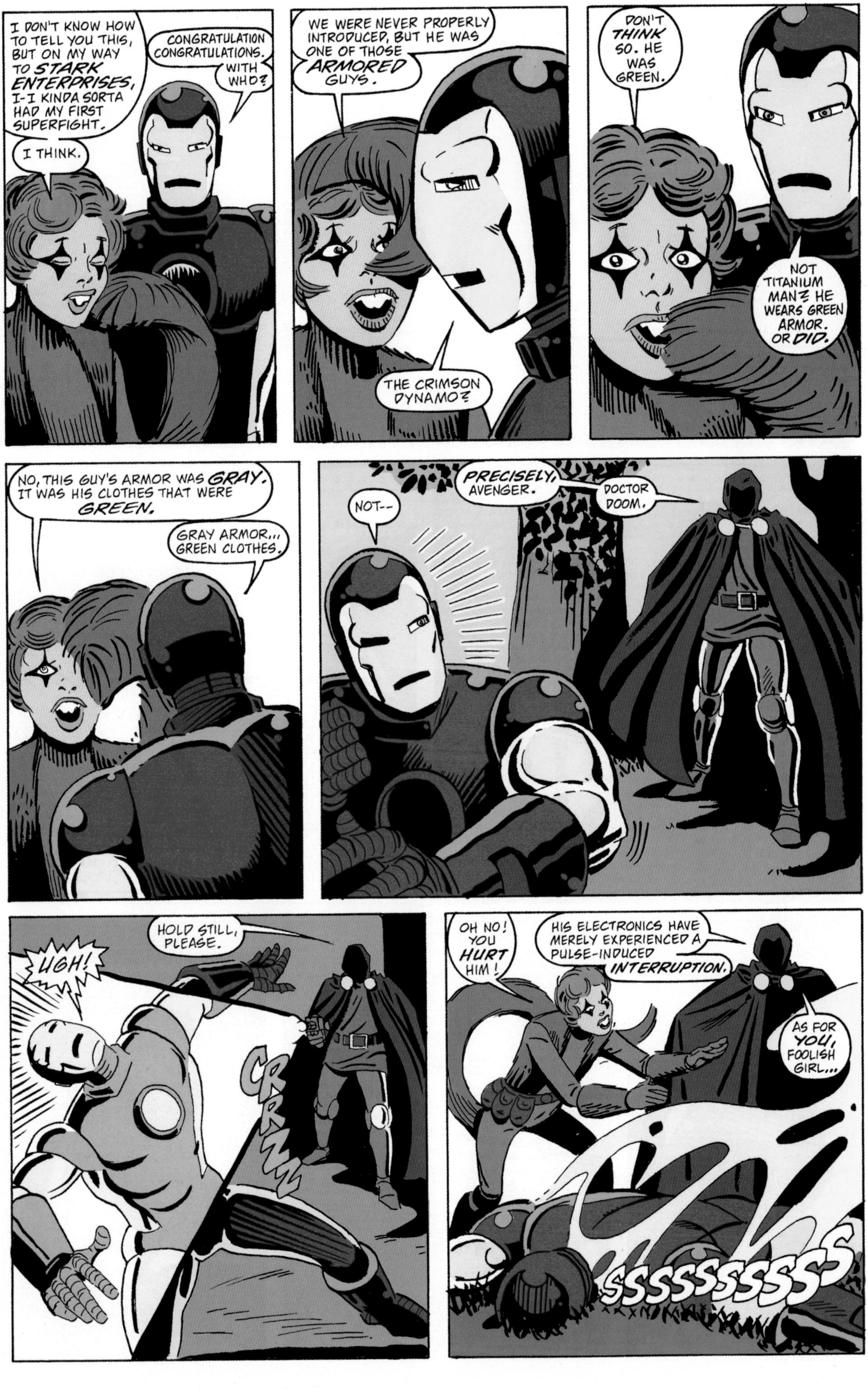
I DON'T KNOW HOW TO TELL YOU THIS, BUT ON MY WAY TO STARK ENTERPRISES, I-I KINDA SORTA HAD MY FIRST SUPERFIGHT.
I THINK.
CONGRATULATION CONGRATULATIONS. WITH WHO?
WE WERE NEVER PROPERLY INTRODUCED, BUT HE WAS ONE OF THOSE ARMORED GUYS.
THE CRIMSON DYNAMO?
DON'T THINK SO. HE WAS GREEN.
NOT TITANIUM MAN? HE WEARS GREEN ARMOR. OR DID.
NO, THIS GUY'S ARMOR WAS GRAY. IT WAS HIS CLOTHES THAT WERE GREEN.
GRAY ARMOR... GREEN CLOTHES.
NOT--
PRECISELY, AVENGER.
DOCTOR DOOM.
HOLD STILL, PLEASE.
UGH!
CRRNNN
OH NO! YOU HURT HIM!
HIS ELECTRONICS HAVE MERELY EXPERIENCED A PULSE-INDUCED INTERRUPTION.
AS FOR YOU, FOOLISH GIRL...
SSSSSSSSSS

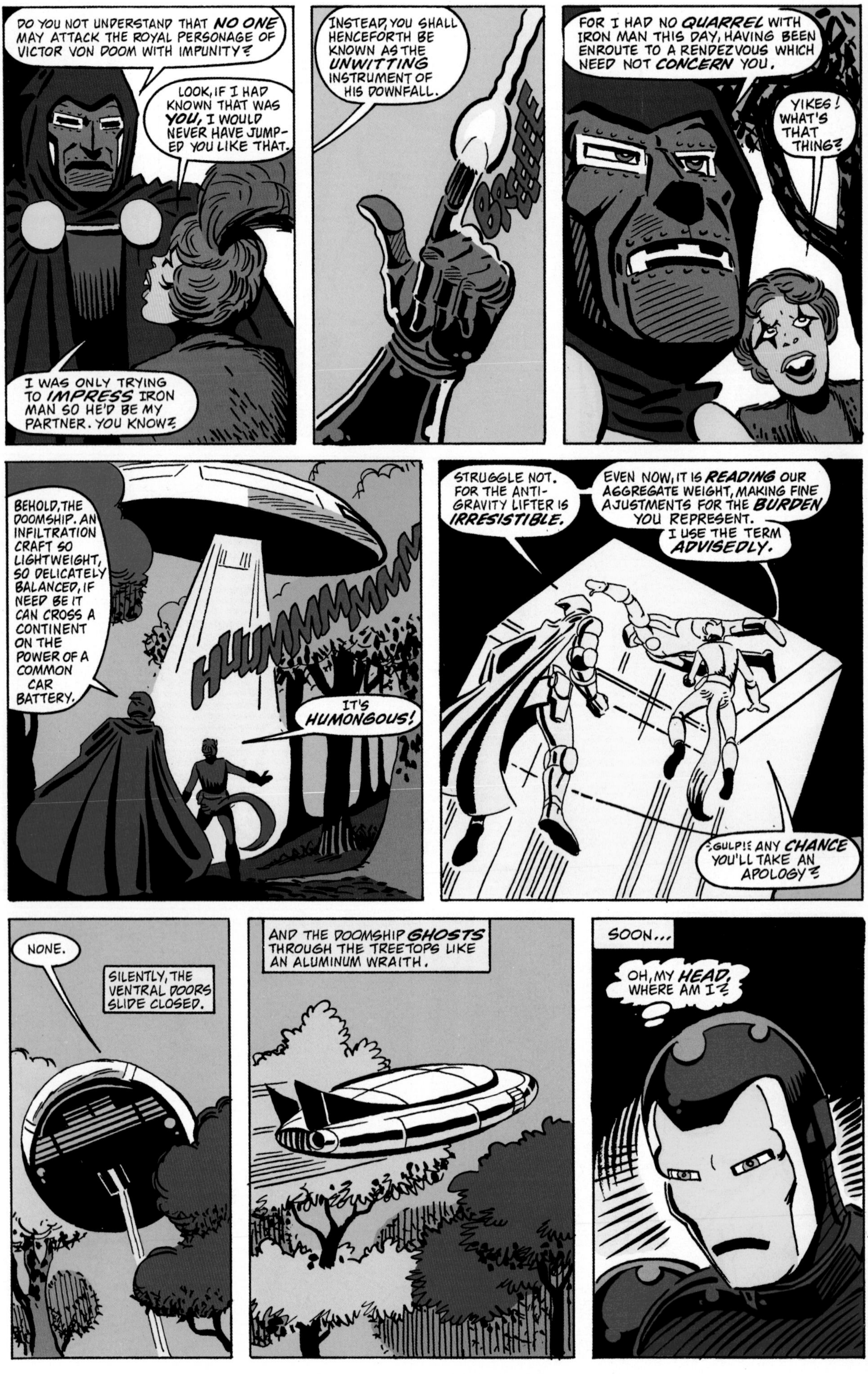
DO YOU NOT UNDERSTAND THAT NO ONE MAY ATTACK THE ROYAL PERSONAGE OF VICTOR VON DOOM WITH IMPUNITY?
LOOK, IF I HAD KNOWN THAT WAS YOU, I WOULD NEVER HAVE JUMPED YOU LIKE THAT.
I WAS ONLY TRYING TO IMPRESS IRON MAN SO HE'D BE MY PARTNER. YOU KNOW?
INSTEAD, YOU SHALL HENCEFORTH BE KNOWN AS THE UNWITTING INSTRUMENT OF HIS DOWNFALL.
BRZZZZ
FOR I HAD NO QUARREL WITH IRON MAN THIS DAY, HAVING BEEN ENROUTE TO A RENDEZVOUS WHICH NEED NOT CONCERN YOU.
YIKES! WHAT'S THAT THING?
BEHOLD, THE DOOMSHIP. AN INFILTRATION CRAFT SO LIGHTWEIGHT, SO DELICATELY BALANCED, IF NEED BE IT CAN CROSS A CONTINENT ON THE POWER OF A COMMON CAR BATTERY.
HUUMMMMMMM
IT'S HUMONGOUS!
STRUGGLE NOT. FOR THE ANTI-GRAVITY LIFTER IS IRRESISTIBLE.
EVEN NOW, IT IS READING OUR AGGREGATE WEIGHT, MAKING FINE AJUSTMENTS FOR THE BURDEN YOU REPRESENT. I USE THE TERM ADVISEDLY.
GULP! ANY CHANCE YOU'LL TAKE AN APOLOGY?
NONE.
SILENTLY, THE VENTRAL DOORS SLIDE CLOSED.
AND THE DOOMSHIP GHOSTS THROUGH THE TREETOPS LIKE AN ALUMINUM WRAITH.
SOON...
OH, MY HEAD. WHERE AM I?

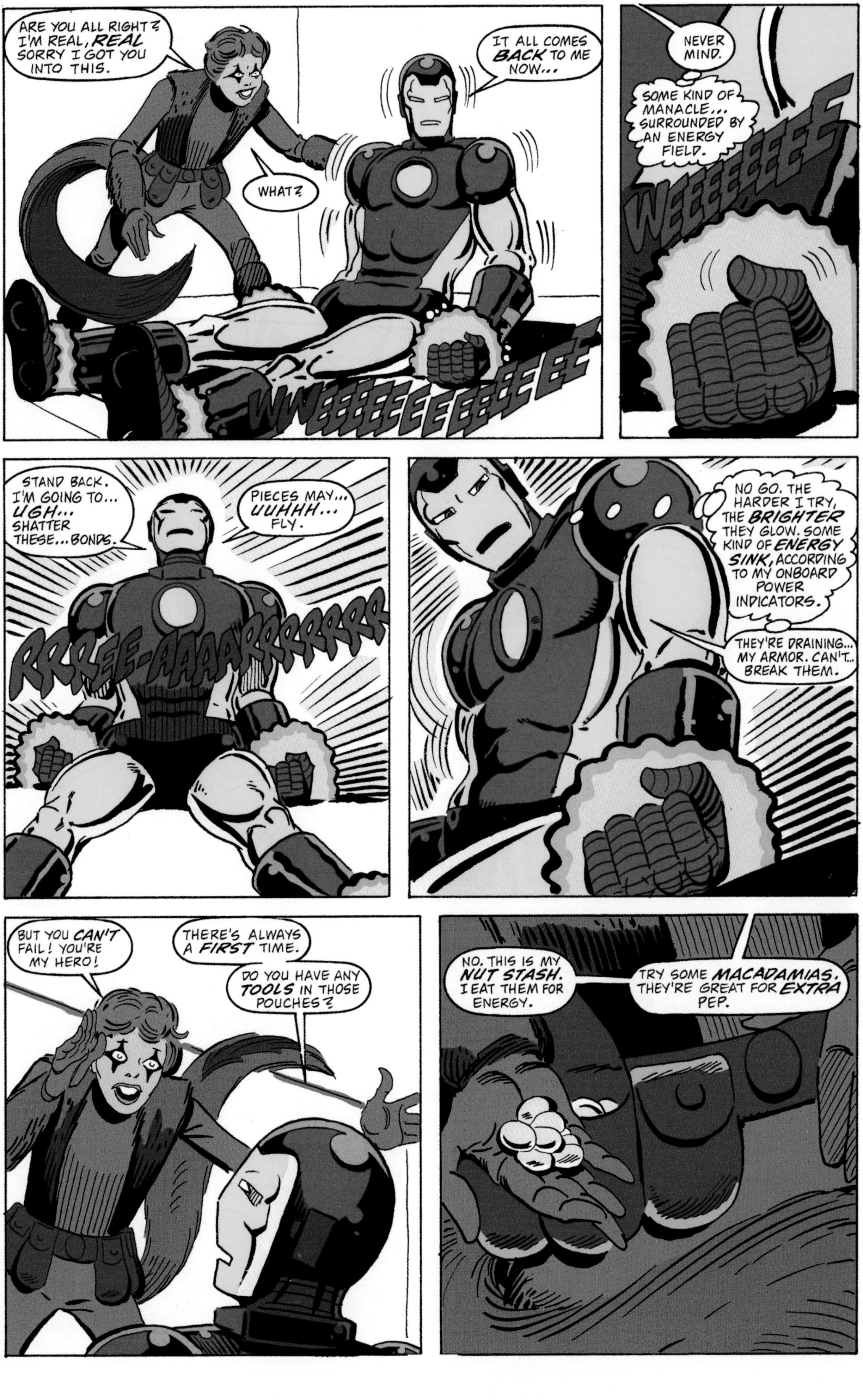
ARE YOU ALL RIGHT? I'M REAL, REAL SORRY I GOT YOU INTO THIS.
IT ALL COMES BACK TO ME NOW...
WHAT?
WWEEEEEEEEEEEEEE
NEVER MIND.
SOME KIND OF MANACLE... SURROUNDED BY AN ENERGY FIELD.
WEEEEEEEEE
STAND BACK. I'M GOING TO... UGH... SHATTER THESE...BONDS.
PIECES MAY... UUHHH... FLY.
RRREE-AAAARRRRRRR
NO GO. THE HARDER I TRY, THE BRIGHTER THEY GLOW. SOME KIND OF ENERGY SINK, ACCORDING TO MY ONBOARD POWER INDICATORS.
THEY'RE DRAINING... MY ARMOR. CAN'T... BREAK THEM.
BUT YOU CAN'T FAIL! YOU'RE MY HERO!
THERE'S ALWAYS A FIRST TIME.
DO YOU HAVE ANY TOOLS IN THOSE POUCHES?
NO. THIS IS MY NUT STASH. I EAT THEM FOR ENERGY.
TRY SOME MACADAMIAS. THEY'RE GREAT FOR EXTRA PEP.

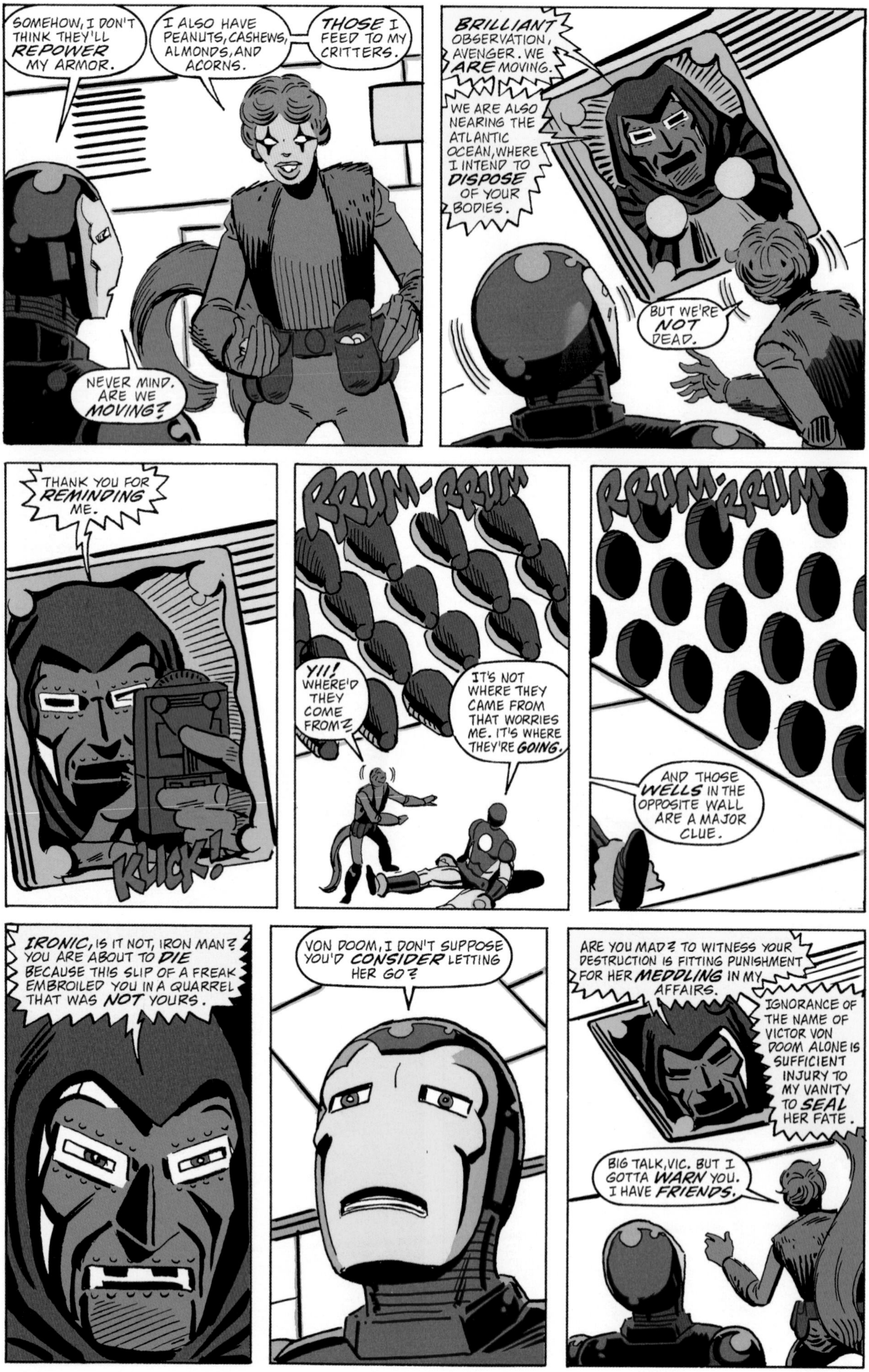

SOMEHOW, I DON'T THINK THEY'LL REPOWER MY ARMOR.
I ALSO HAVE PEANUTS, CASHEWS, ALMONDS, AND ACORNS.
THOSE I FEED TO MY CRITTERS.
NEVER MIND. ARE WE MOVING?
BRILLIANT OBSERVATION, AVENGER. WE ARE MOVING.
WE ARE ALSO NEARING THE ATLANTIC OCEAN, WHERE I INTEND TO DISPOSE OF YOUR BODIES.
BUT WE'RE NOT DEAD.
THANK YOU FOR REMINDING ME.
KLICK!
RRUM-RRUM
YII! WHERE'D THEY COME FROM?
IT'S NOT WHERE THEY CAME FROM THAT WORRIES ME. IT'S WHERE THEY'RE GOING.
RRUM-RRUM
AND THOSE WELLS IN THE OPPOSITE WALL ARE A MAJOR CLUE.
IRONIC, IS IT NOT, IRON MAN? YOU ARE ABOUT TO DIE BECAUSE THIS SLIP OF A FREAK EMBROILED YOU IN A QUARREL THAT WAS NOT YOURS.
VON DOOM, I DON'T SUPPOSE YOU'D CONSIDER LETTING HER GO?
ARE YOU MAD? TO WITNESS YOUR DESTRUCTION IS FITTING PUNISHMENT FOR HER MEDDLING IN MY AFFAIRS.
IGNORANCE OF THE NAME OF VICTOR VON DOOM ALONE IS SUFFICIENT INJURY TO MY VANITY TO SEAL HER FATE.
BIG TALK, VIC. BUT I GOTTA WARN YOU. I HAVE FRIENDS.

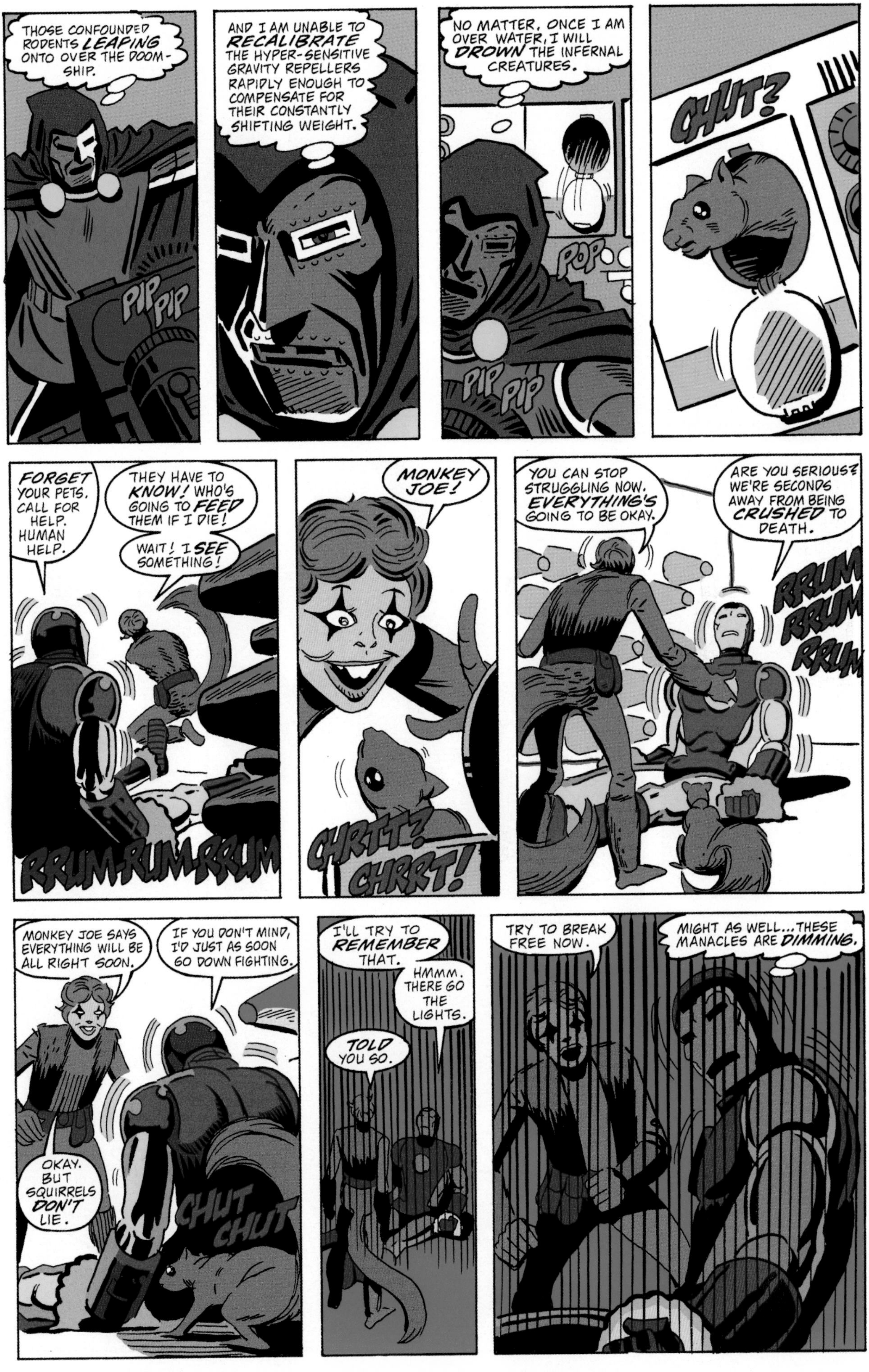
THOSE CONFOUNDED RODENTS LEAPING ONTO OVER THE DOOM-SHIP.
PIP PIP
AND I AM UNABLE TO RECALIBRATE THE HYPER-SENSITIVE GRAVITY REPELLERS RAPIDLY ENOUGH TO COMPENSATE FOR THEIR CONSTANTLY SHIFTING WEIGHT.
NO MATTER. ONCE I AM OVER WATER, I WILL DROWN THE INFERNAL CREATURES.
POP
PIP PIP
CHUT?
FORGET YOUR PETS. CALL FOR HELP. HUMAN HELP.
THEY HAVE TO KNOW! WHO'S GOING TO FEED THEM IF I DIE!
WAIT! I SEE SOMETHING!
RRUM-RUM-RRUM
MONKEY JOE!
CHRTT? CHRRT!
YOU CAN STOP STRUGGLING NOW. EVERYTHING'S GOING TO BE OKAY.
ARE YOU SERIOUS? WE'RE SECONDS AWAY FROM BEING CRUSHED TO DEATH.
RRUM RRUM RRUM
MONKEY JOE SAYS EVERYTHING WILL BE ALL RIGHT SOON.
IF YOU DON'T MIND, I'D JUST AS SOON GO DOWN FIGHTING.
OKAY. BUT SQUIRRELS DON'T LIE.
CHUT CHUT
I'LL TRY TO REMEMBER THAT.
HMMM. THERE GO THE LIGHTS.
TOLD YOU SO.
TRY TO BREAK FREE NOW.
MIGHT AS WELL... THESE MANACLES ARE DIMMING.

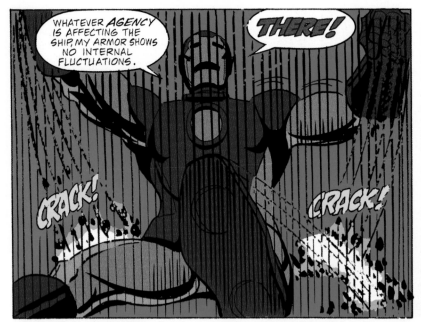

WHATEVER *AGENCY* IS AFFECTING THE SHIP, MY ARMOR SHOWS NO INTERNAL FLUCTUATIONS.

THERE!

CRACK!

CRACK!

IN FACT, I'M BACK TO *FULL* STRENGTH *!*

BRAAACK!

NOW FOR *DOOM!*

CUK

CUK

CUK

CUK

NOT AGAIN!

IT'S OKAY. THEY'RE ON *OUR* SIDE!

CHUT CHIT CHIT CHUT

I JUST TOLD THEM YOU'RE FRIENDLY.

TOO FRIENDLY.

CHRRT

CHRRT

CHRRT

CHRRT

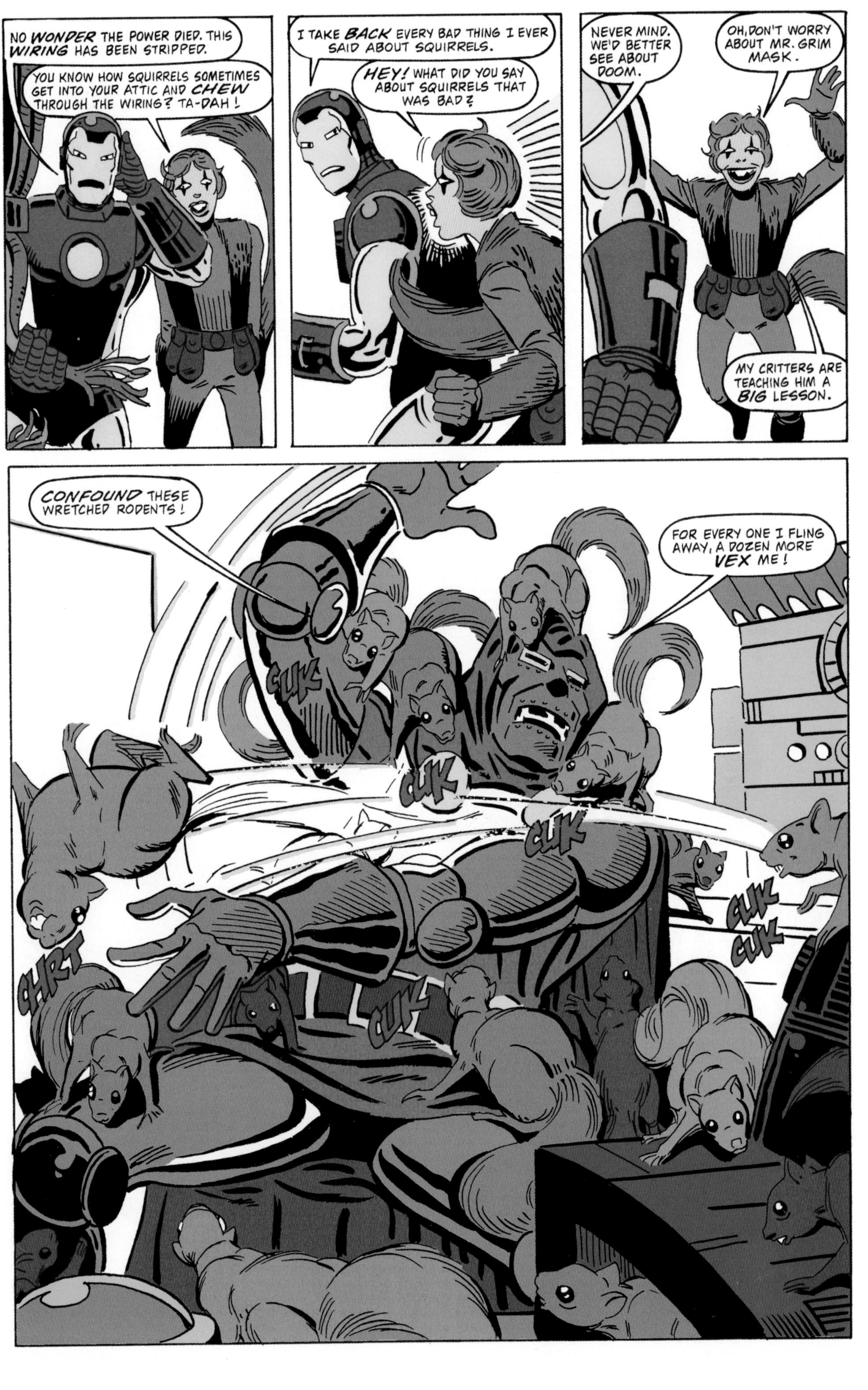
NO WONDER THE POWER DIED. THIS WIRING HAS BEEN STRIPPED.
YOU KNOW HOW SQUIRRELS SOMETIMES GET INTO YOUR ATTIC AND CHEW THROUGH THE WIRING? TA-DAH!
I TAKE BACK EVERY BAD THING I EVER SAID ABOUT SQUIRRELS.
HEY! WHAT DID YOU SAY ABOUT SQUIRRELS THAT WAS BAD?
NEVER MIND. WE'D BETTER SEE ABOUT DOOM.
OH, DON'T WORRY ABOUT MR. GRIM MASK.
MY CRITTERS ARE TEACHING HIM A BIG LESSON.
CONFOUND THESE WRETCHED RODENTS!
FOR EVERY ONE I FLING AWAY, A DOZEN MORE VEX ME!
CUK
CUK
CUK
CUK CUK
CHRT
CUK

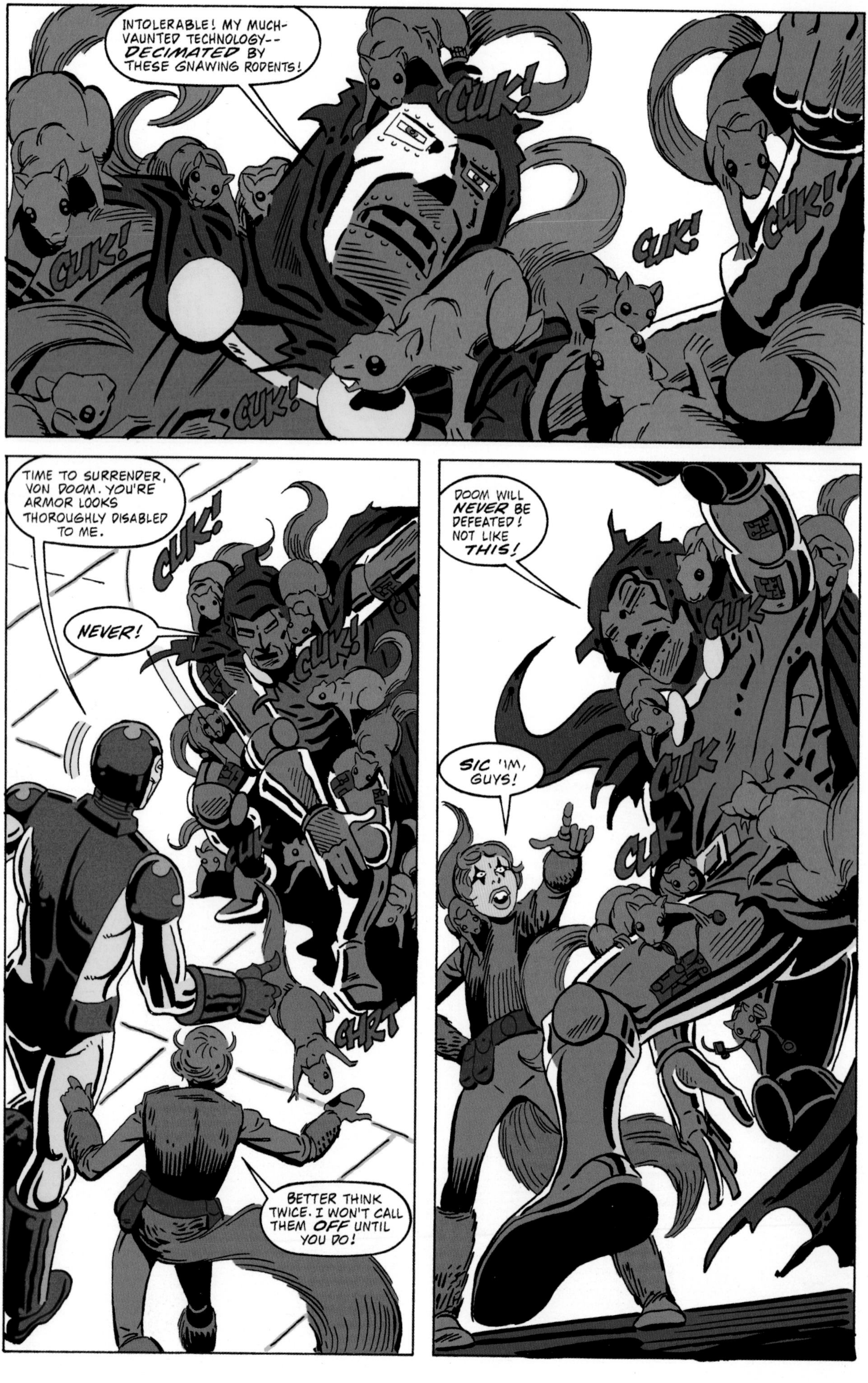

INTOLERABLE! MY MUCH-VAUNTED TECHNOLOGY-- DECIMATED BY THESE GNAWING RODENTS!
CUK!
CUK!
CUK!
CUK!
CUK!
TIME TO SURRENDER, VON DOOM. YOU'RE ARMOR LOOKS THOROUGHLY DISABLED TO ME.
CUK!
NEVER!
CUK!
CUK
CHRT
BETTER THINK TWICE. I WON'T CALL THEM OFF UNTIL YOU DO!
DOOM WILL NEVER BE DEFEATED! NOT LIKE THIS!
CUK
SIC 'IM, GUYS!
CUK
CUK

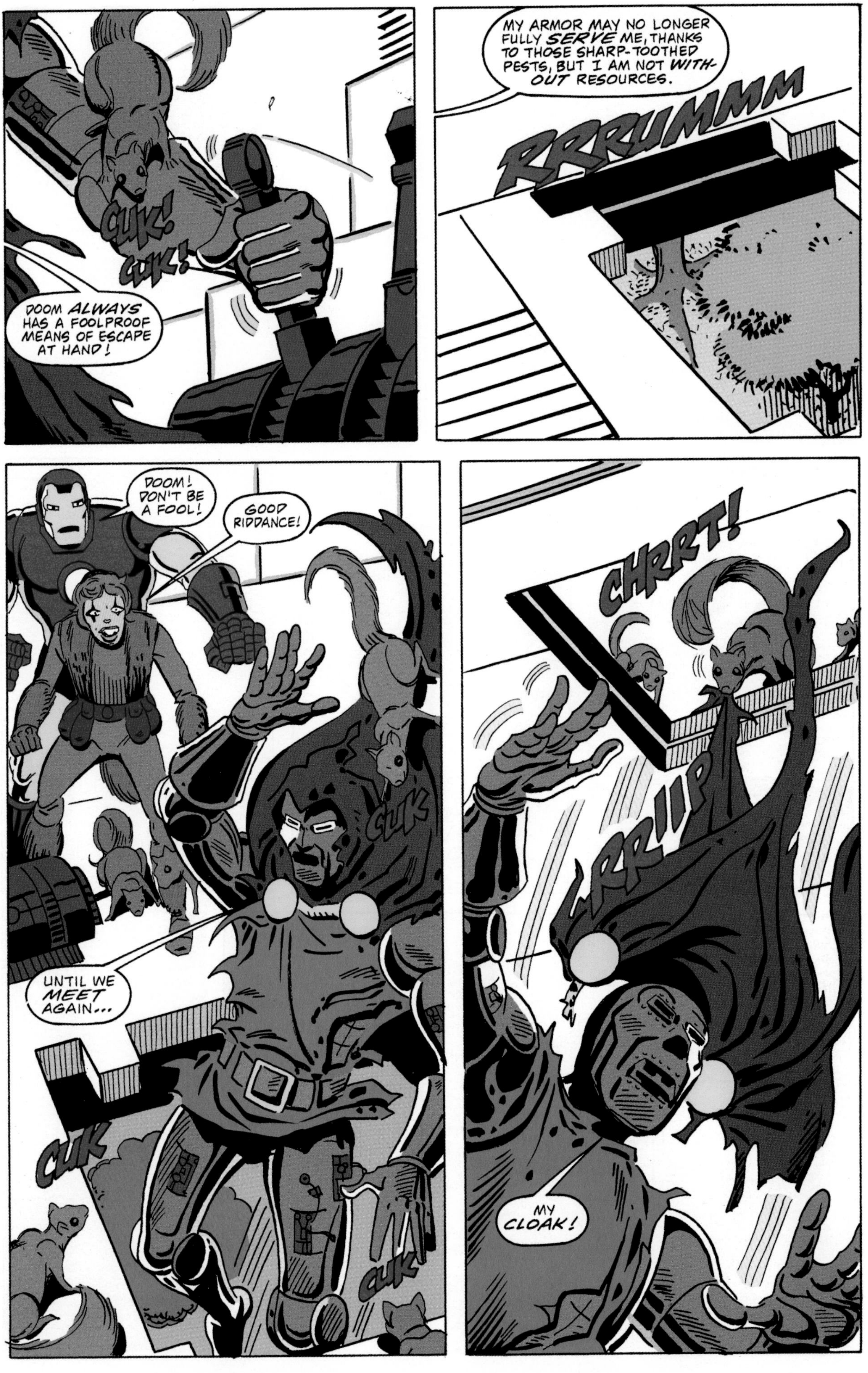
CLIK!
CLIK!
DOOM ALWAYS HAS A FOOLPROOF MEANS OF ESCAPE AT HAND!
MY ARMOR MAY NO LONGER FULLY SERVE ME, THANKS TO THOSE SHARP-TOOTHED PESTS, BUT I AM NOT WITH-OUT RESOURCES.
RRRUMMM
DOOM! DON'T BE A FOOL!
GOOD RIDDANCE!
CLIK
UNTIL WE MEET AGAIN...
CLIK
CLIK
CHRRT!
RRIIP
MY CLOAK!

YOU HAVE NOT HEARD THE *LAST* OF VICTOR VON DOOM! THIS INDIGNITY SHALL BE *AVENGED!*

THE *DOOMSHIP* IS SETTLING. AND THESE WOODS ARE *INFESTED* WITH VICIOUS RODENTS.

I *MUST* ESCAPE!

CUK CUK CUK

WATER AHEAD! MY ONLY CHANCE.

CUK CUK

CUK

VICTOR VON DOOM MUST NOT BE *VANQUISHED* IN THIS IGNOMINIOUS MANNER.

SPLOOSH!!

CHRT!

HE SURE *STIRRED* UP A LOT OF MUD. I DON'T SEE HIM.

HIS BUILT-IN *OXYGEN* SUPPLY IS LIMITED.

ASSUMING IT'S STILL *OPERABLE.*

BLOP!

BLOP!

I DON'T LIKE THE *LOOKS* OF THAT. I'M GOING IN.

STAY PUT.

SPLASH

DON'T *SWEAT* IT. SQUIRRELS ARE GREAT SWIMMERS, BUT I'M *NOT.*

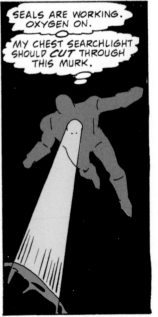

SEALS ARE WORKING. OXYGEN ON.

MY CHEST SEARCHLIGHT SHOULD *CUT* THROUGH THIS MURK.

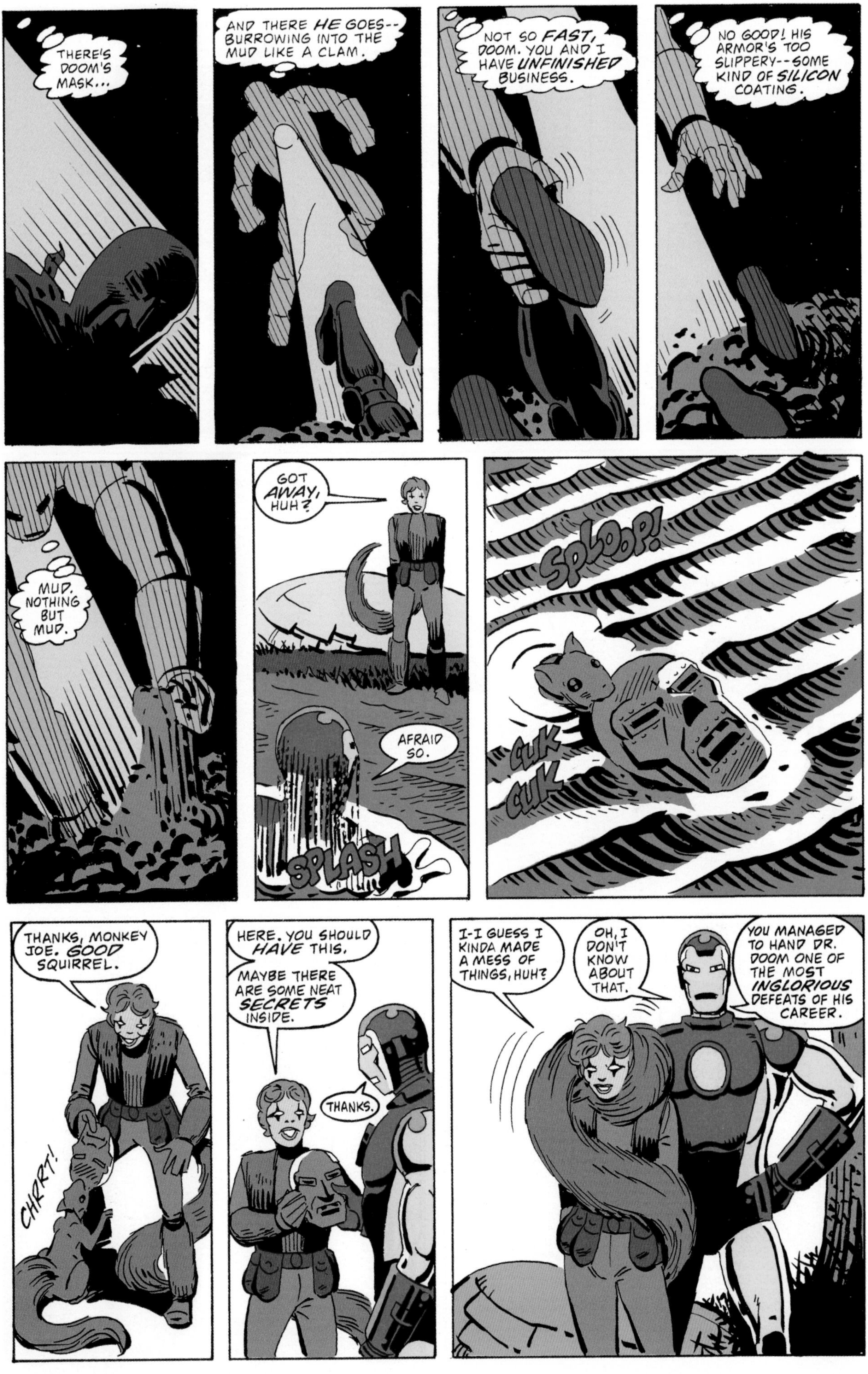
THERE'S DOOM'S MASK...
AND THERE HE GOES-- BURROWING INTO THE MUD LIKE A CLAM.
NOT SO FAST, DOOM. YOU AND I HAVE UNFINISHED BUSINESS.
NO GOOD! HIS ARMOR'S TOO SLIPPERY--SOME KIND OF SILICON COATING.
MUD. NOTHING BUT MUD.
GOT AWAY, HUH?
AFRAID SO.
SPLASH
SPLOOP!
CUK CUK
THANKS, MONKEY JOE. GOOD SQUIRREL.
CHRRT!
HERE. YOU SHOULD HAVE THIS.
MAYBE THERE ARE SOME NEAT SECRETS INSIDE.
THANKS.
I-I GUESS I KINDA MADE A MESS OF THINGS, HUH?
OH, I DON'T KNOW ABOUT THAT.
YOU MANAGED TO HAND DR. DOOM ONE OF THE MOST INGLORIOUS DEFEATS OF HIS CAREER.

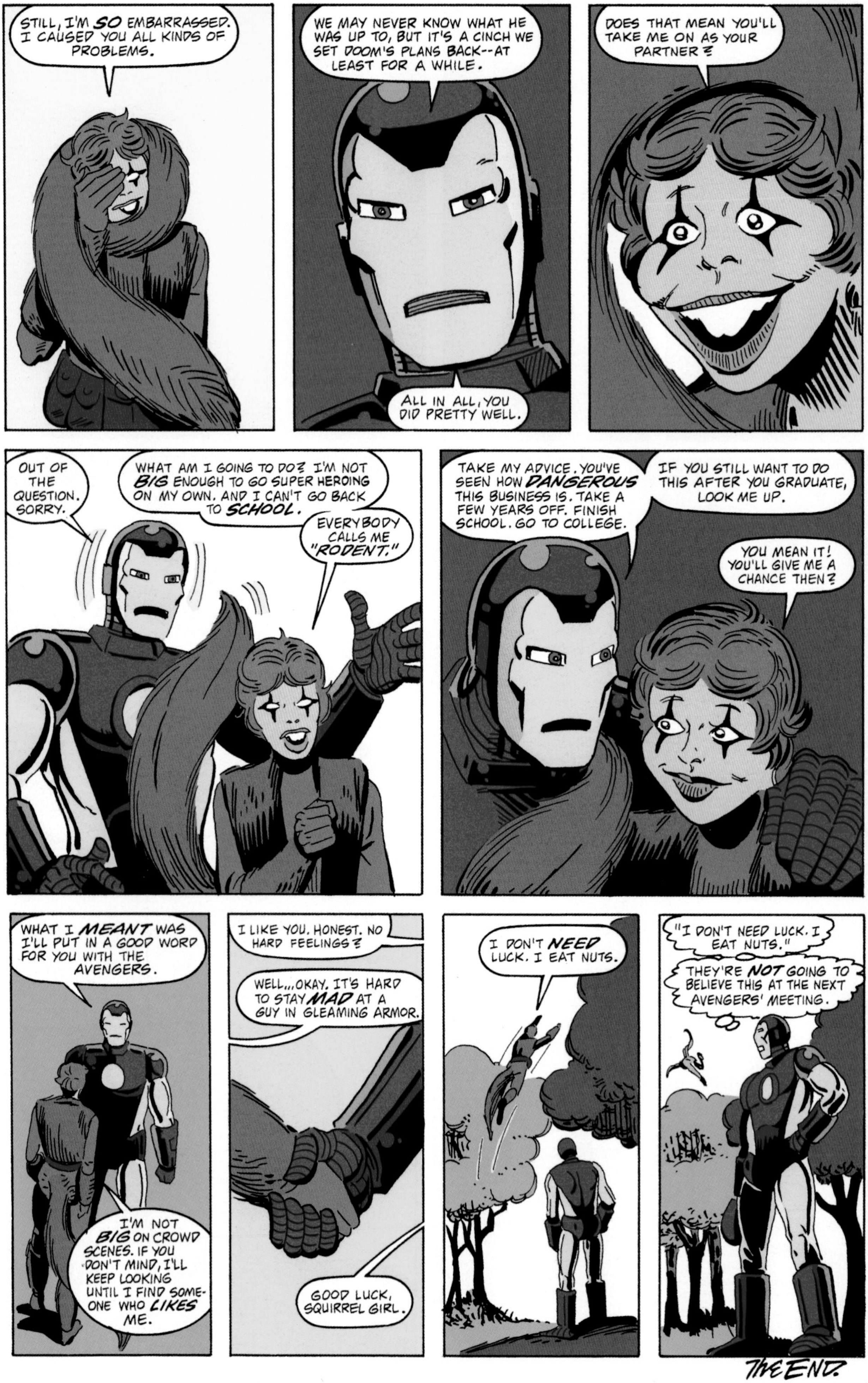
STILL, I'M SO EMBARRASSED. I CAUSED YOU ALL KINDS OF PROBLEMS.
WE MAY NEVER KNOW WHAT HE WAS UP TO, BUT IT'S A CINCH WE SET DOOM'S PLANS BACK--AT LEAST FOR A WHILE.
ALL IN ALL, YOU DID PRETTY WELL.
DOES THAT MEAN YOU'LL TAKE ME ON AS YOUR PARTNER?
OUT OF THE QUESTION. SORRY.
WHAT AM I GOING TO DO? I'M NOT BIG ENOUGH TO GO SUPER HEROING ON MY OWN. AND I CAN'T GO BACK TO SCHOOL.
EVERYBODY CALLS ME "RODENT."
TAKE MY ADVICE. YOU'VE SEEN HOW DANGEROUS THIS BUSINESS IS. TAKE A FEW YEARS OFF. FINISH SCHOOL. GO TO COLLEGE.
IF YOU STILL WANT TO DO THIS AFTER YOU GRADUATE, LOOK ME UP.
YOU MEAN IT! YOU'LL GIVE ME A CHANCE THEN?
WHAT I MEANT WAS I'LL PUT IN A GOOD WORD FOR YOU WITH THE AVENGERS.
I'M NOT BIG ON CROWD SCENES. IF YOU DON'T MIND, I'LL KEEP LOOKING UNTIL I FIND SOMEONE WHO LIKES ME.
I LIKE YOU. HONEST. NO HARD FEELINGS?
WELL... OKAY. IT'S HARD TO STAY MAD AT A GUY IN GLEAMING ARMOR.
GOOD LUCK, SQUIRREL GIRL.
I DON'T NEED LUCK. I EAT NUTS.
"I DON'T NEED LUCK. I EAT NUTS."
THEY'RE NOT GOING TO BELIEVE THIS AT THE NEXT AVENGERS' MEETING.
THE END.

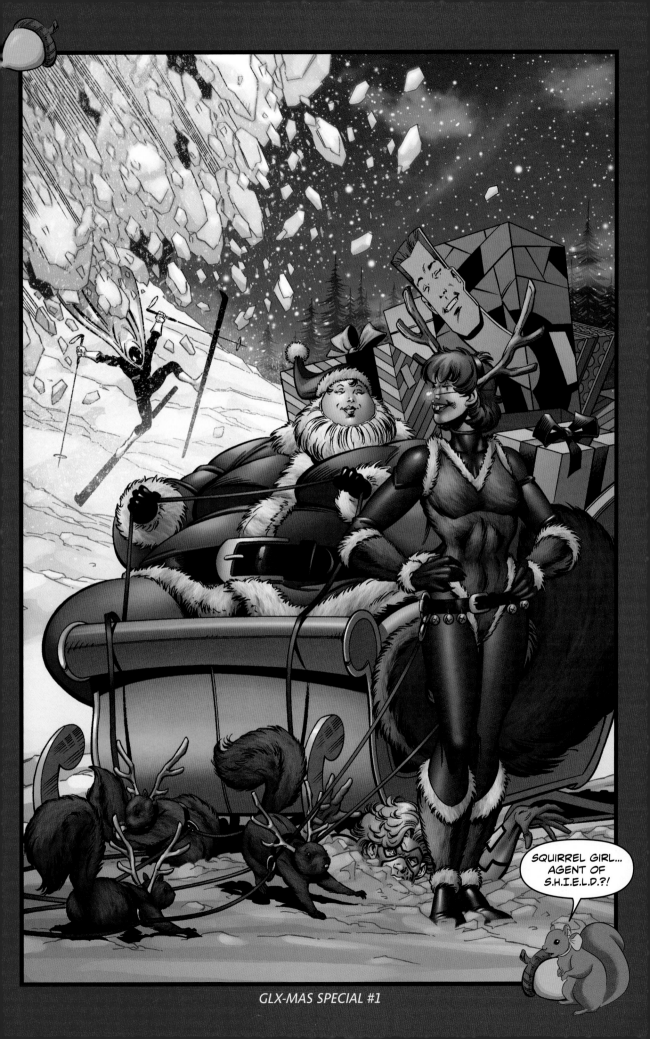

SQUIRREL GIRL... AGENT OF S.H.I.E.L.D.?!

GLX-MAS SPECIAL #1

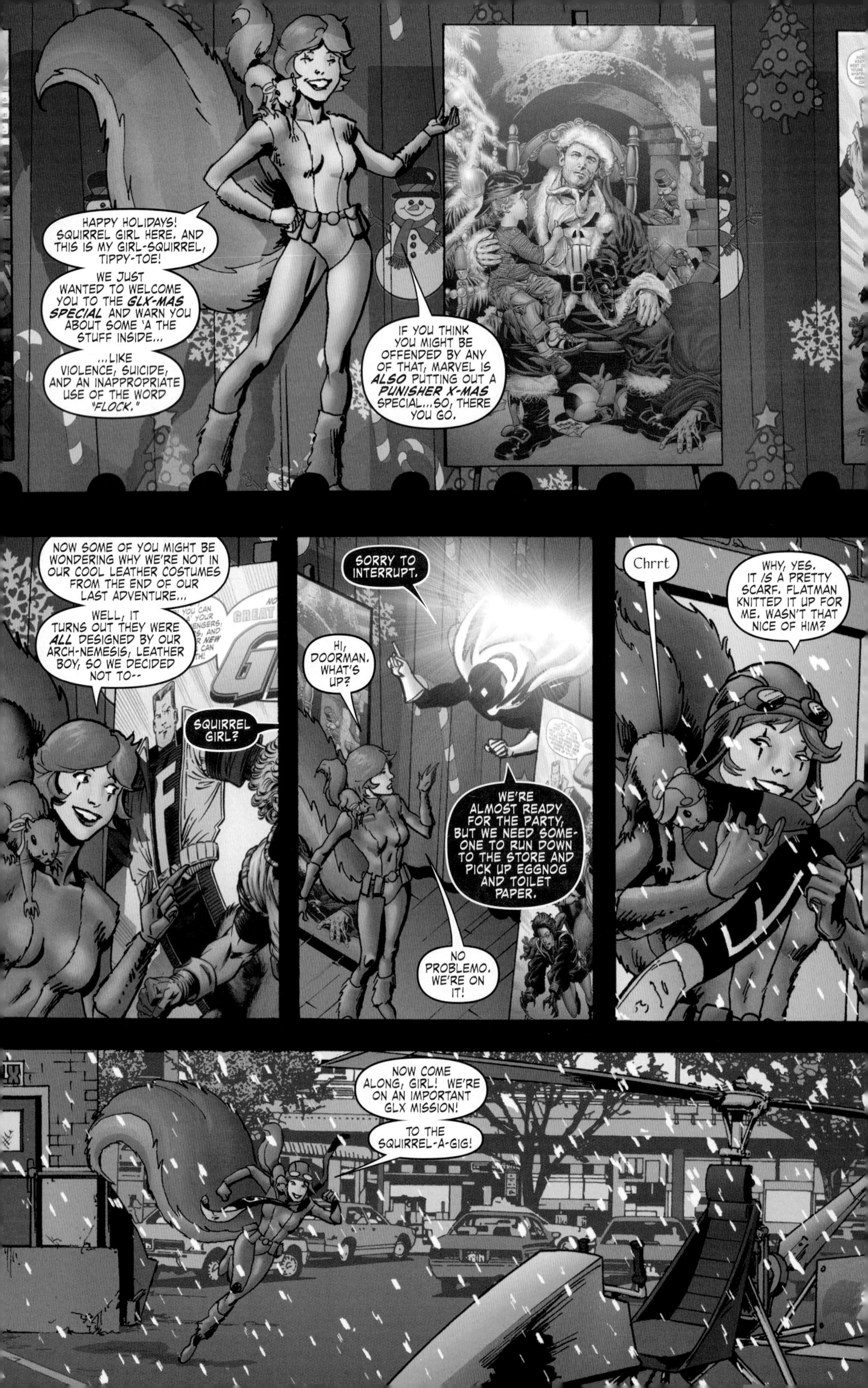
HAPPY HOLIDAYS! SQUIRREL GIRL HERE. AND THIS IS MY GIRL-SQUIRREL, TIPPY-TOE!
WE JUST WANTED TO WELCOME YOU TO THE GLX-MAS SPECIAL AND WARN YOU ABOUT SOME 'A THE STUFF INSIDE...
...LIKE VIOLENCE, SUICIDE, AND AN INAPPROPRIATE USE OF THE WORD "FLOCK."
IF YOU THINK YOU MIGHT BE OFFENDED BY ANY OF THAT, MARVEL IS ALSO PUTTING OUT A PUNISHER X-MAS SPECIAL...SO, THERE YOU GO.
NOW SOME OF YOU MIGHT BE WONDERING WHY WE'RE NOT IN OUR COOL LEATHER COSTUMES FROM THE END OF OUR LAST ADVENTURE...
WELL, IT TURNS OUT THEY WERE ALL DESIGNED BY OUR ARCH-NEMESIS, LEATHER BOY, SO WE DECIDED NOT TO--
SQUIRREL GIRL?
SORRY TO INTERRUPT.
HI, DOORMAN. WHAT'S UP?
WE'RE ALMOST READY FOR THE PARTY, BUT WE NEED SOME-ONE TO RUN DOWN TO THE STORE AND PICK UP EGGNOG AND TOILET PAPER.
NO PROBLEMO. WE'RE ON IT!
Chrrt
WHY, YES. IT IS A PRETTY SCARF. FLATMAN KNITTED IT UP FOR ME. WASN'T THAT NICE OF HIM?
NOW COME ALONG, GIRL! WE'RE ON AN IMPORTANT GLX MISSION!
TO THE SQUIRREL-A-GIG!

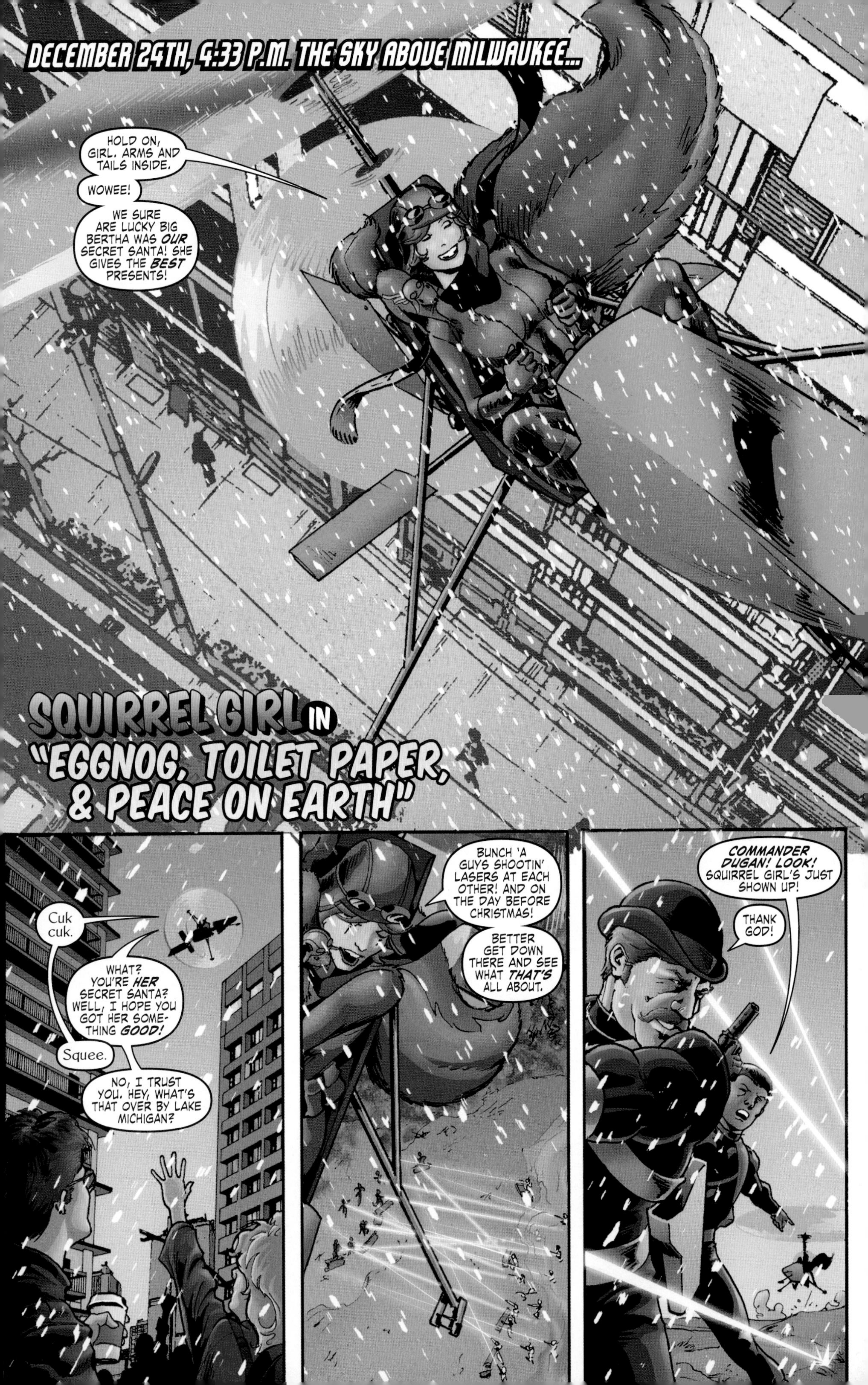
DECEMBER 24TH, 4:33 P.M. THE SKY ABOVE MILWAUKEE...
HOLD ON, GIRL. ARMS AND TAILS INSIDE.
WOWEE!
WE SURE ARE LUCKY BIG BERTHA WAS OUR SECRET SANTA! SHE GIVES THE BEST PRESENTS!
SQUIRREL GIRL IN
"EGGNOG, TOILET PAPER, & PEACE ON EARTH"
Cuk cuk.
WHAT? YOU'RE HER SECRET SANTA? WELL, I HOPE YOU GOT HER SOME-THING GOOD!
Squee.
NO, I TRUST YOU. HEY, WHAT'S THAT OVER BY LAKE MICHIGAN?
BUNCH 'A GUYS SHOOTIN' LASERS AT EACH OTHER! AND ON THE DAY BEFORE CHRISTMAS!
BETTER GET DOWN THERE AND SEE WHAT THAT'S ALL ABOUT.
COMMANDER DUGAN! LOOK! SQUIRREL GIRL'S JUST SHOWN UP!
THANK GOD!

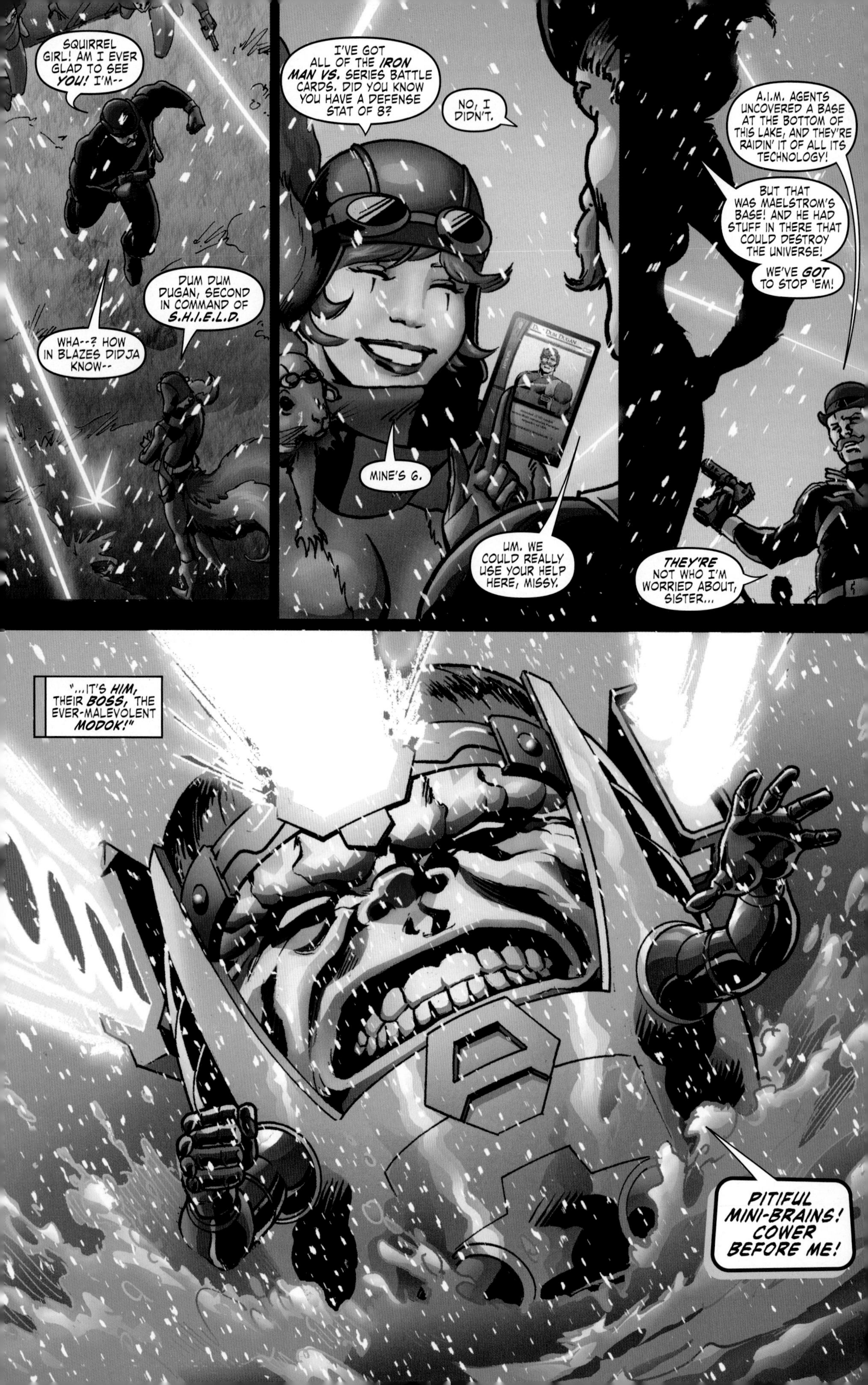
SQUIRREL GIRL! AM I EVER GLAD TO SEE YOU! I'M--
DUM DUM DUGAN, SECOND IN COMMAND OF S.H.I.E.L.D.
WHA--? HOW IN BLAZES DIDJA KNOW--
I'VE GOT ALL OF THE IRON MAN VS. SERIES BATTLE CARDS. DID YOU KNOW YOU HAVE A DEFENSE STAT OF 8?
NO, I DIDN'T.
MINE'S 6.
UM. WE COULD REALLY USE YOUR HELP HERE, MISSY.
A.I.M. AGENTS UNCOVERED A BASE AT THE BOTTOM OF THIS LAKE, AND THEY'RE RAIDIN' IT OF ALL ITS TECHNOLOGY!
BUT THAT WAS MAELSTROM'S BASE! AND HE HAD STUFF IN THERE THAT COULD DESTROY THE UNIVERSE!
WE'VE GOT TO STOP 'EM!
THEY'RE NOT WHO I'M WORRIED ABOUT, SISTER...
"...IT'S HIM, THEIR BOSS, THE EVER-MALEVOLENT MODOK!"
PITIFUL MINI-BRAINS! COWER BEFORE ME!

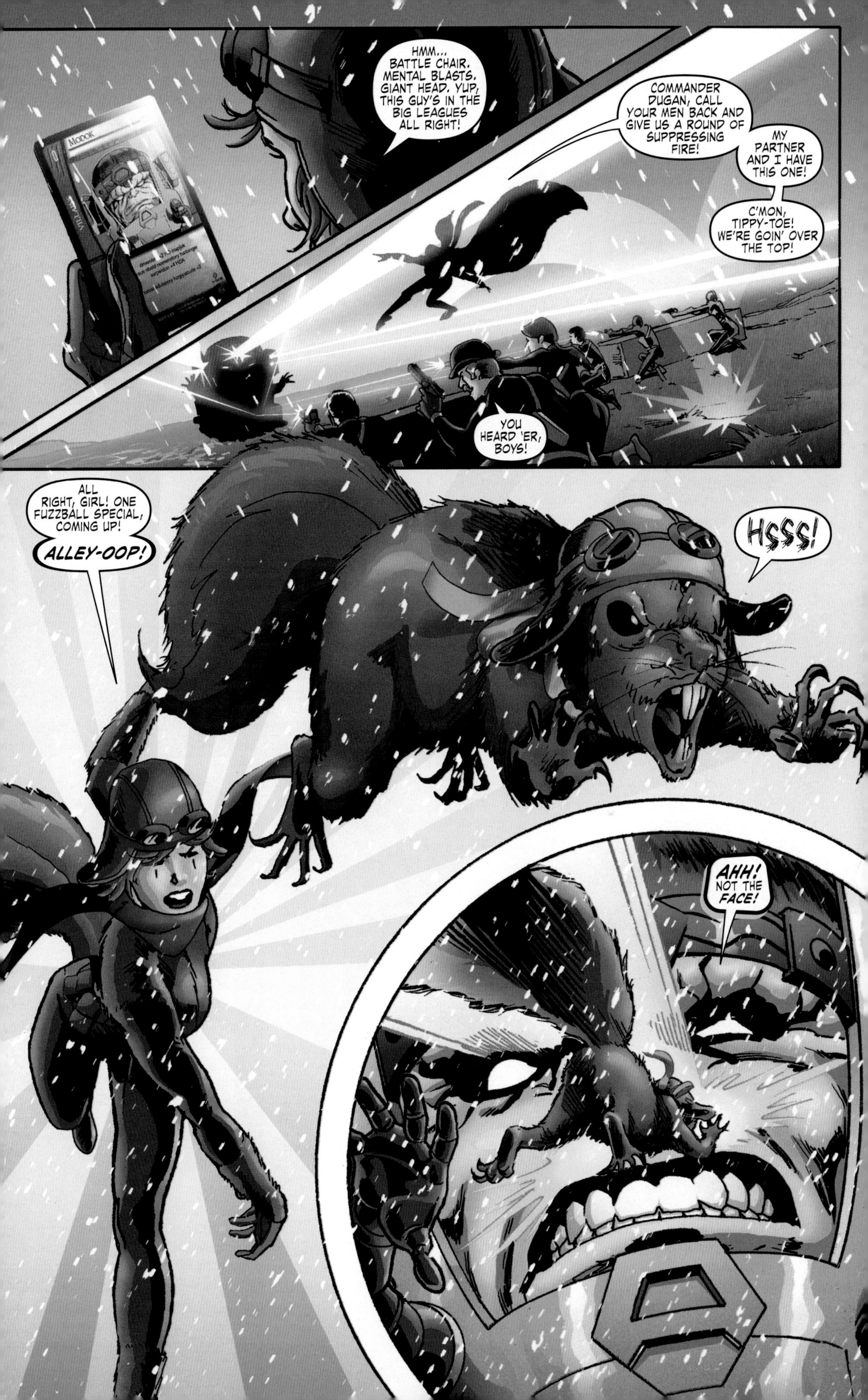
HMM... BATTLE CHAIR. MENTAL BLASTS. GIANT HEAD. YUP, THIS GUY'S IN THE BIG LEAGUES ALL RIGHT!
MODOK
VILLAIN
COMMANDER DUGAN, CALL YOUR MEN BACK AND GIVE US A ROUND OF SUPPRESSING FIRE!
MY PARTNER AND I HAVE THIS ONE!
C'MON, TIPPY-TOE! WE'RE GOIN' OVER THE TOP!
YOU HEARD 'ER, BOYS!
ALL RIGHT, GIRL! ONE FUZZBALL SPECIAL, COMING UP!
ALLEY-OOP!
HSSS!
AHH! NOT THE FACE!

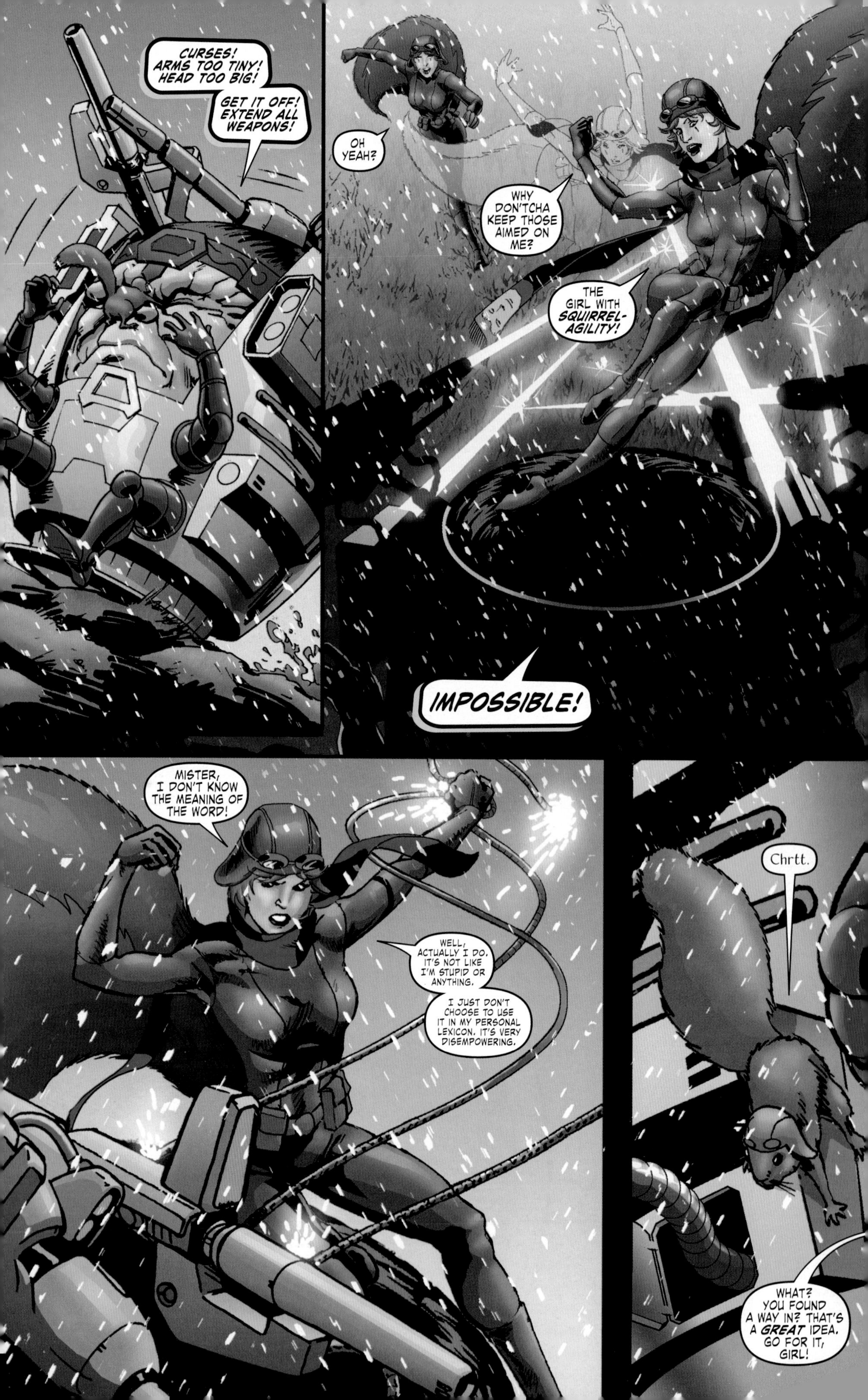
CURSES! ARMS TOO TINY! HEAD TOO BIG!
GET IT OFF! EXTEND ALL WEAPONS!
OH YEAH?
WHY DON'TCHA KEEP THOSE AIMED ON ME?
THE GIRL WITH SQUIRREL-AGILITY!
IMPOSSIBLE!
MISTER, I DON'T KNOW THE MEANING OF THE WORD!
WELL, ACTUALLY I DO. IT'S NOT LIKE I'M STUPID OR ANYTHING.
I JUST DON'T CHOOSE TO USE IT IN MY PERSONAL LEXICON. IT'S VERY DISEMPOWERING.
Chrtt.
WHAT? YOU FOUND A WAY IN? THAT'S A GREAT IDEA. GO FOR IT, GIRL!

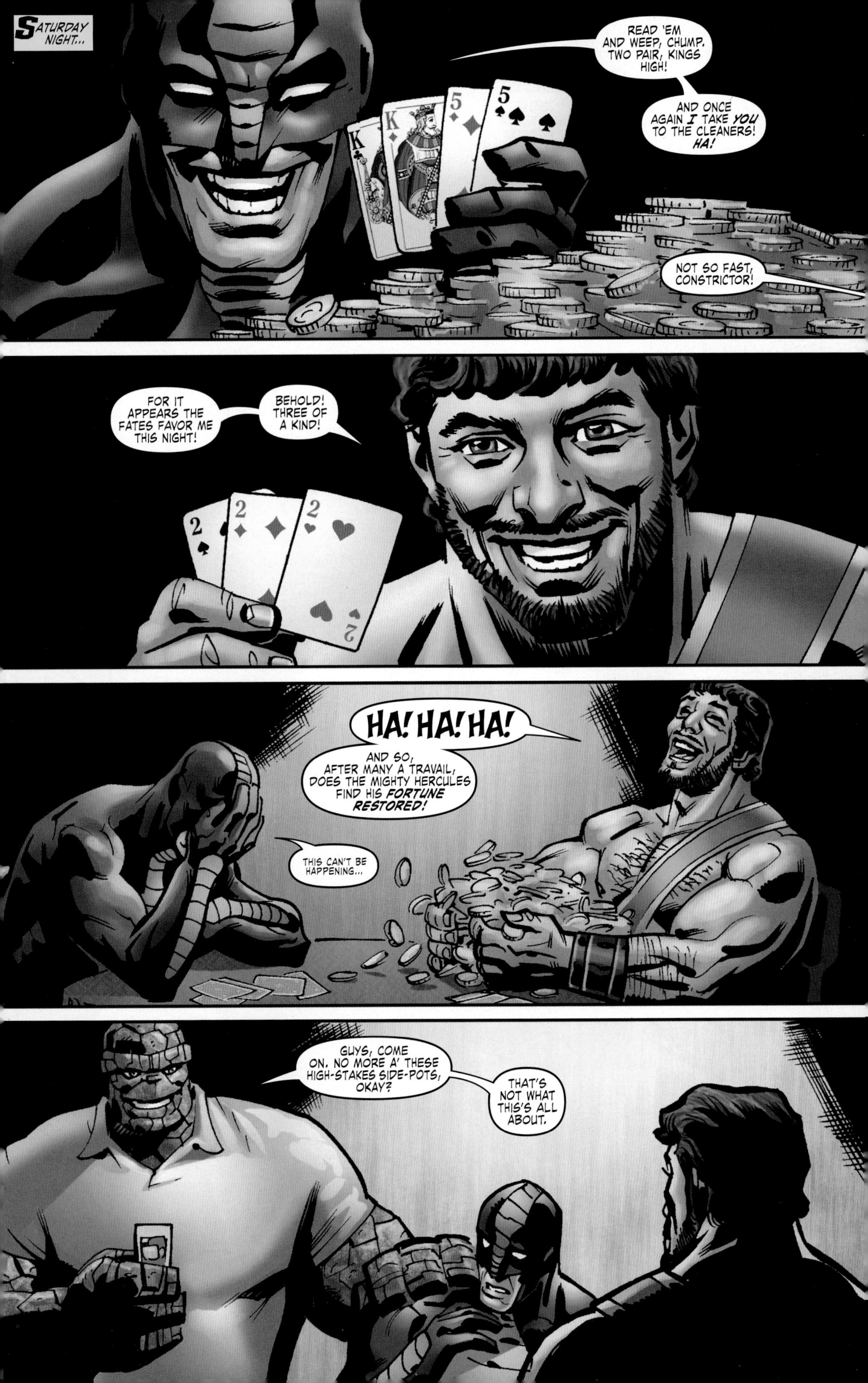
SATURDAY NIGHT...
READ 'EM AND WEEP, CHUMP. TWO PAIR, KINGS HIGH!
AND ONCE AGAIN I TAKE YOU TO THE CLEANERS! HA!
NOT SO FAST, CONSTRICTOR!
BEHOLD! THREE OF A KIND!
FOR IT APPEARS THE FATES FAVOR ME THIS NIGHT!
HA! HA! HA!
AND SO, AFTER MANY A TRAVAIL, DOES THE MIGHTY HERCULES FIND HIS FORTUNE RESTORED!
THIS CAN'T BE HAPPENING...
GUYS, COME ON. NO MORE A' THESE HIGH-STAKES SIDE-POTS, OKAY?
THAT'S NOT WHAT THIS'S ALL ABOUT.

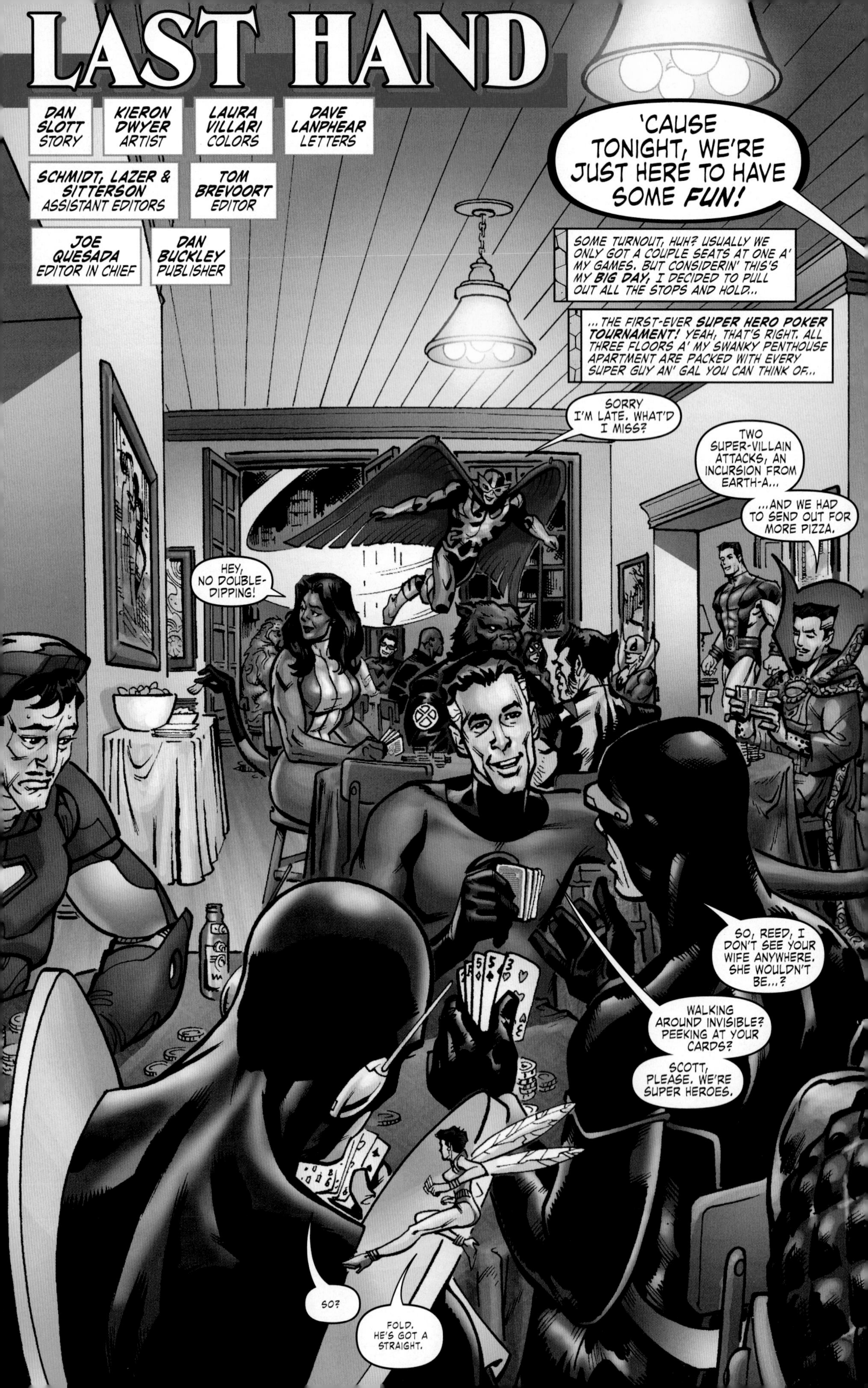
LAST HAND
DAN SLOTT STORY
KIERON DWYER ARTIST
LAURA VILLARI COLORS
DAVE LANPHEAR LETTERS
SCHMIDT, LAZER & SITTERSON ASSISTANT EDITORS
TOM BREVOORT EDITOR
JOE QUESADA EDITOR IN CHIEF
DAN BUCKLEY PUBLISHER
'CAUSE TONIGHT, WE'RE JUST HERE TO HAVE SOME FUN!
SOME TURNOUT, HUH? USUALLY WE ONLY GOT A COUPLE SEATS AT ONE A' MY GAMES. BUT CONSIDERIN' THIS'S MY BIG DAY, I DECIDED TO PULL OUT ALL THE STOPS AND HOLD...
...THE FIRST-EVER SUPER HERO POKER TOURNAMENT! YEAH, THAT'S RIGHT. ALL THREE FLOORS A' MY SWANKY PENTHOUSE APARTMENT ARE PACKED WITH EVERY SUPER GUY AN' GAL YOU CAN THINK OF...
SORRY I'M LATE. WHAT'D I MISS?
TWO SUPER-VILLAIN ATTACKS, AN INCURSION FROM EARTH-A...
...AND WE HAD TO SEND OUT FOR MORE PIZZA.
HEY, NO DOUBLE-DIPPING!
SO, REED, I DON'T SEE YOUR WIFE ANYWHERE. SHE WOULDN'T BE...?
WALKING AROUND INVISIBLE? PEEKING AT YOUR CARDS?
SCOTT, PLEASE. WE'RE SUPER HEROES.
SO?
FOLD. HE'S GOT A STRAIGHT.

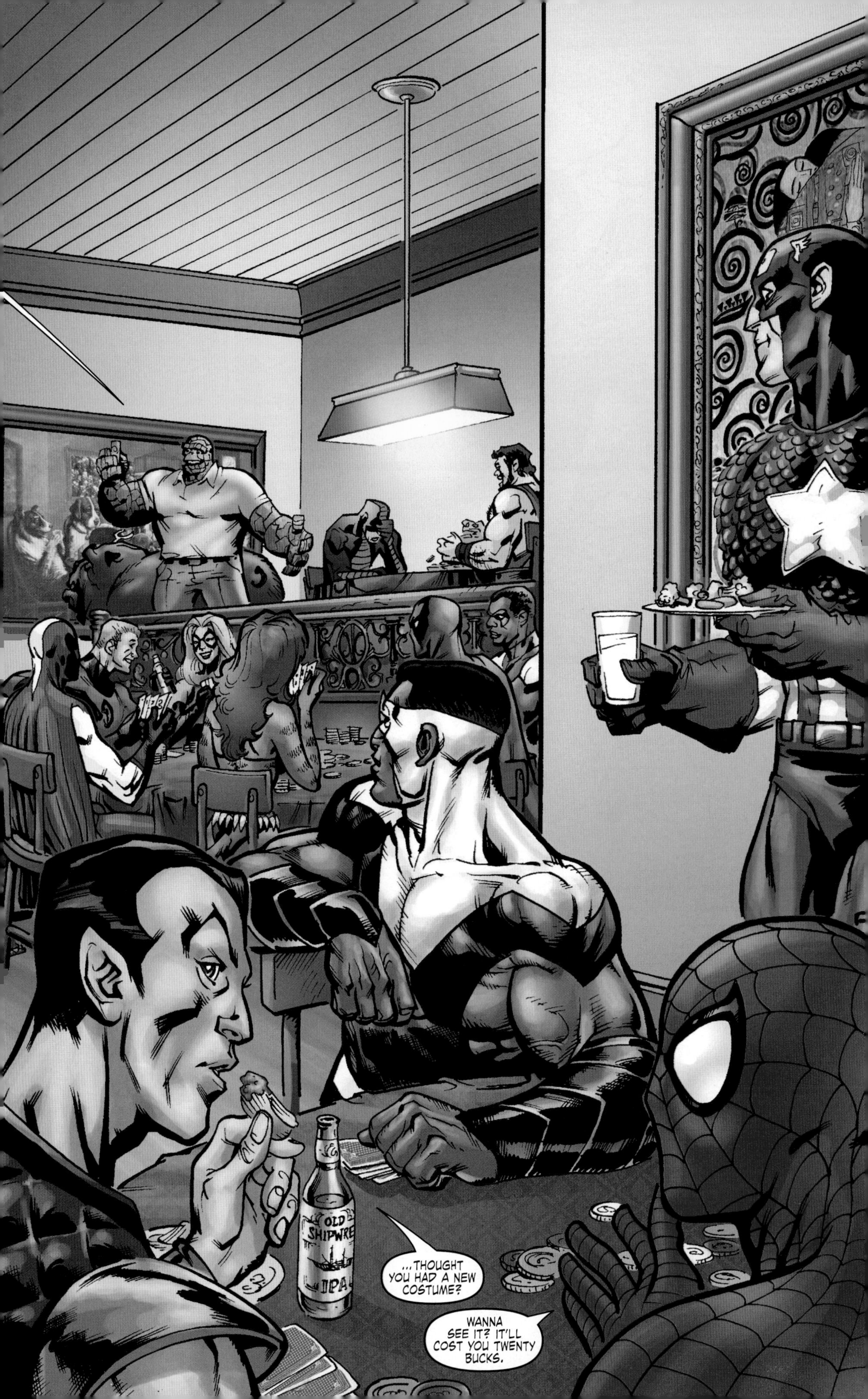
...THOUGHT YOU HAD A NEW COSTUME?
WANNA SEE IT? IT'LL COST YOU TWENTY BUCKS.
OLD SHIPWRE
IPA

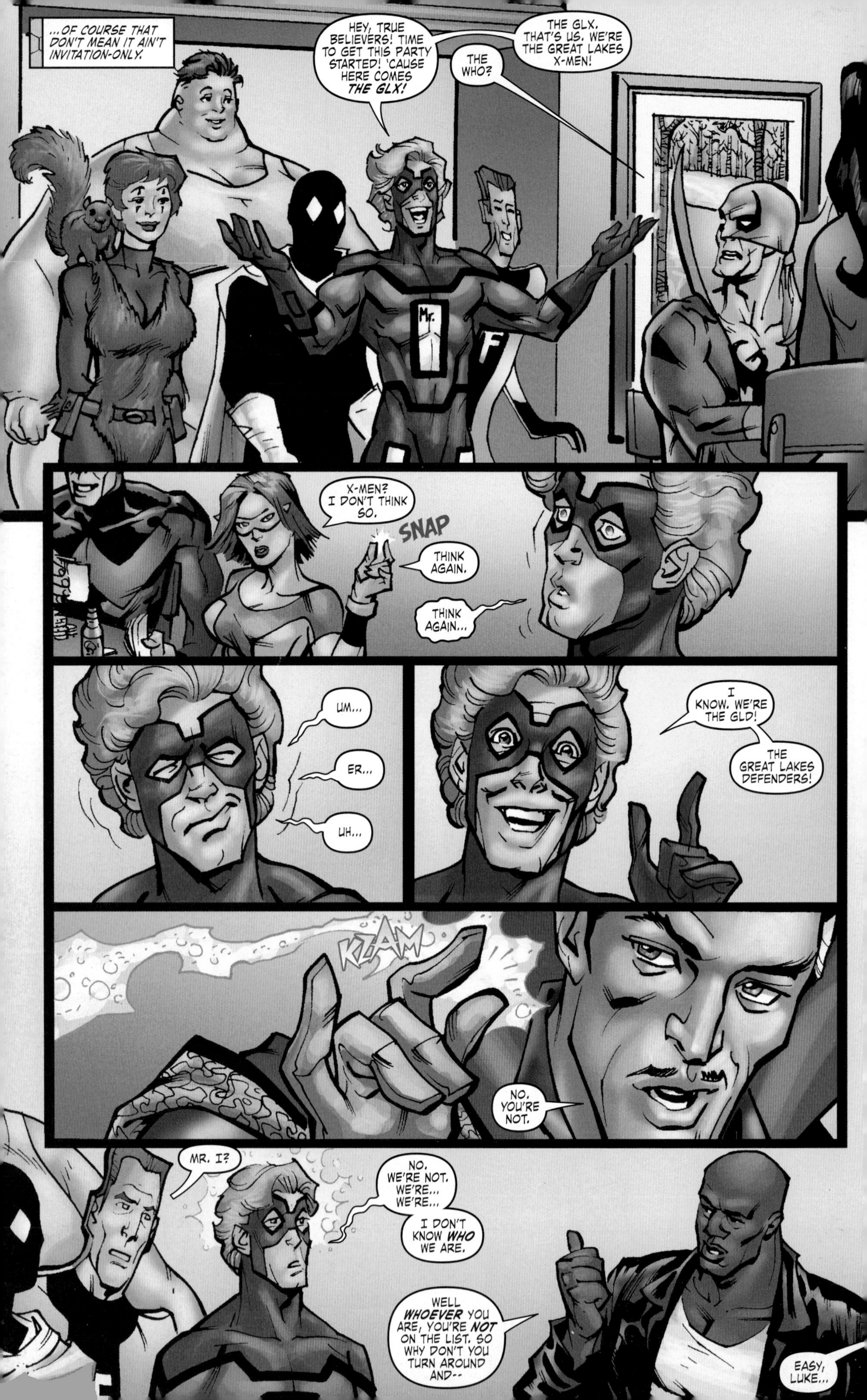
...OF COURSE THAT DON'T MEAN IT AIN'T INVITATION-ONLY.
HEY, TRUE BELIEVERS! TIME TO GET THIS PARTY STARTED! 'CAUSE HERE COMES THE GLX!
THE WHO?
THE GLX. THAT'S US. WE'RE THE GREAT LAKES X-MEN!
X-MEN? I DON'T THINK SO.
SNAP
THINK AGAIN.
THINK AGAIN...
UM...
ER...
UH...
I KNOW. WE'RE THE GLD!
THE GREAT LAKES DEFENDERS!
KLZAM
NO. YOU'RE NOT.
MR. I?
NO. WE'RE NOT. WE'RE... WE'RE...
I DON'T KNOW WHO WE ARE.
WELL WHOEVER YOU ARE, YOU'RE NOT ON THE LIST. SO WHY DON'T YOU TURN AROUND AND--
EASY, LUKE...

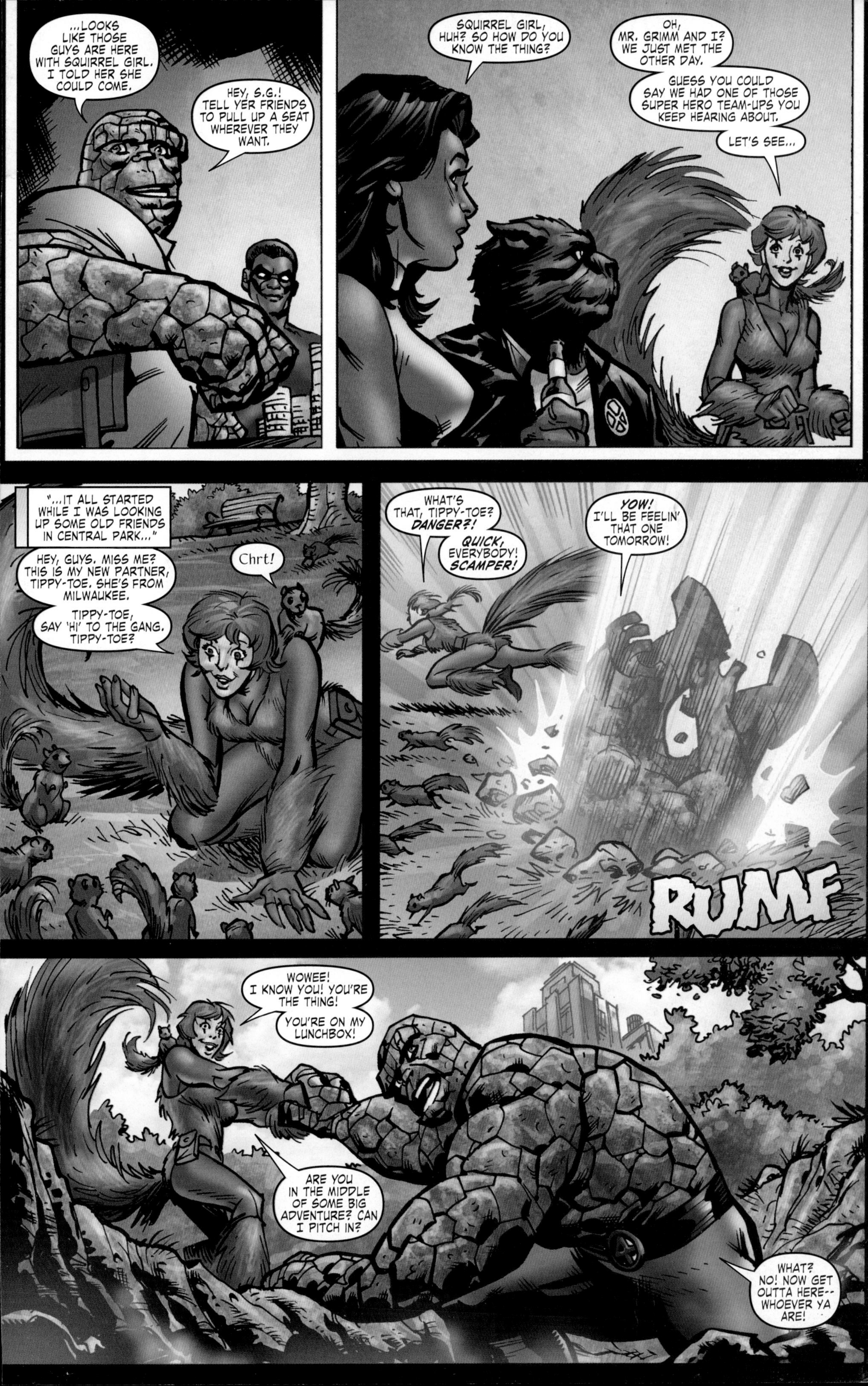
...LOOKS LIKE THOSE GUYS ARE HERE WITH SQUIRREL GIRL. I TOLD HER SHE COULD COME.
HEY, S.G.! TELL YER FRIENDS TO PULL UP A SEAT WHEREVER THEY WANT.
SQUIRREL GIRL, HUH? SO HOW DO YOU KNOW THE THING?
OH, MR. GRIMM AND I? WE JUST MET THE OTHER DAY.
GUESS YOU COULD SAY WE HAD ONE OF THOSE SUPER HERO TEAM-UPS YOU KEEP HEARING ABOUT.
LET'S SEE...
"...IT ALL STARTED WHILE I WAS LOOKING UP SOME OLD FRIENDS IN CENTRAL PARK..."
HEY, GUYS. MISS ME? THIS IS MY NEW PARTNER, TIPPY-TOE. SHE'S FROM MILWAUKEE.
TIPPY-TOE, SAY 'HI' TO THE GANG. TIPPY-TOE?
Chrt!
WHAT'S THAT, TIPPY-TOE? DANGER?!
QUICK, EVERYBODY! SCAMPER!
YOW! I'LL BE FEELIN' THAT ONE TOMORROW!
RUMF
WOWEE! I KNOW YOU! YOU'RE THE THING!
YOU'RE ON MY LUNCHBOX!
ARE YOU IN THE MIDDLE OF SOME BIG ADVENTURE? CAN I PITCH IN?
WHAT? NO! NOW GET OUTTA HERE-- WHOEVER YA ARE!

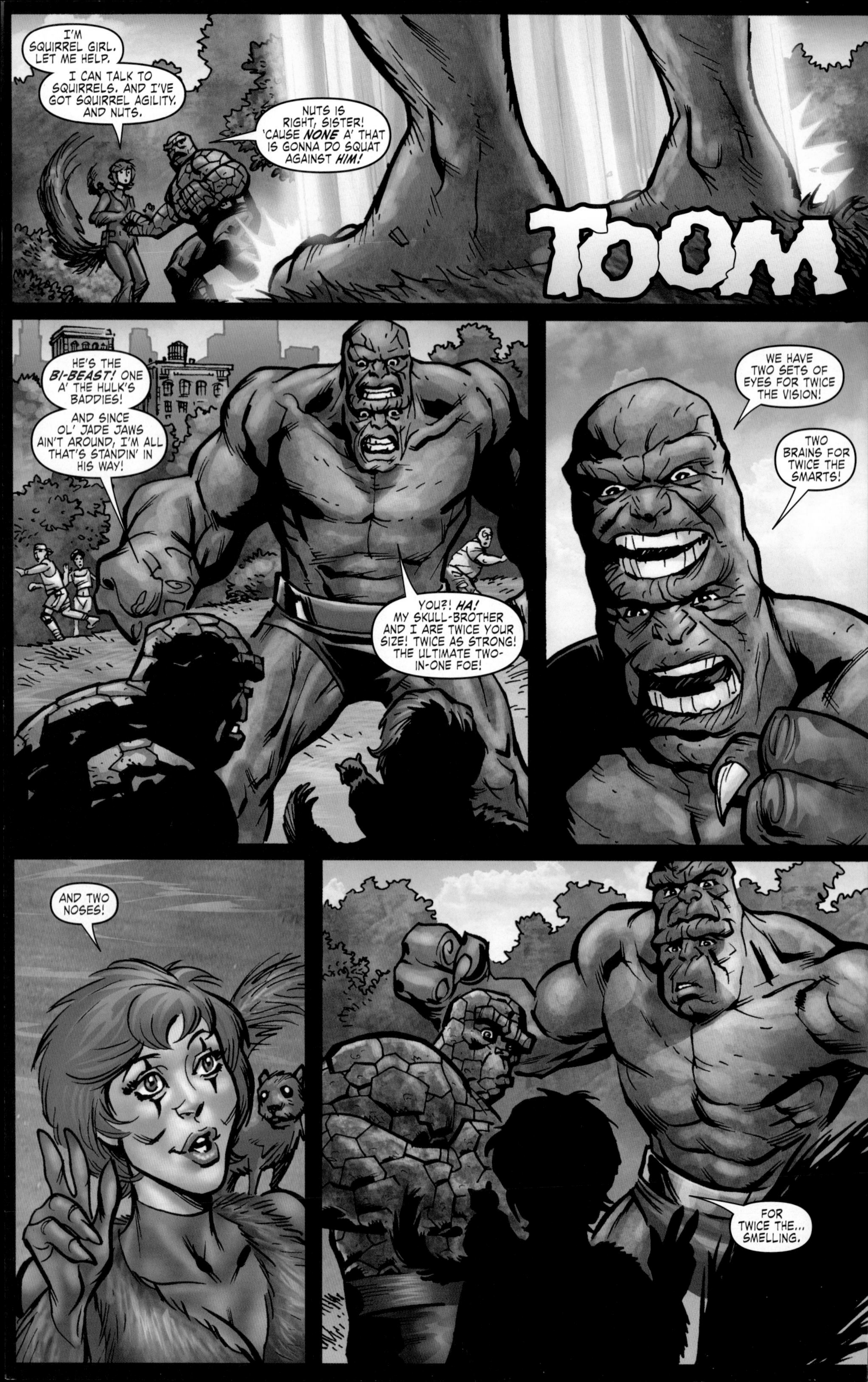
I'M SQUIRREL GIRL. LET ME HELP.
I CAN TALK TO SQUIRRELS. AND I'VE GOT SQUIRREL AGILITY. AND NUTS.
NUTS IS RIGHT, SISTER! 'CAUSE NONE A' THAT IS GONNA DO SQUAT AGAINST HIM!
TOOM
HE'S THE BI-BEAST! ONE A' THE HULK'S BADDIES!
AND SINCE OL' JADE JAWS AIN'T AROUND, I'M ALL THAT'S STANDIN' IN HIS WAY!
YOU?! HA! MY SKULL-BROTHER AND I ARE TWICE YOUR SIZE! TWICE AS STRONG! THE ULTIMATE TWO-IN-ONE FOE!
WE HAVE TWO SETS OF EYES FOR TWICE THE VISION!
TWO BRAINS FOR TWICE THE SMARTS!
AND TWO NOSES!
FOR TWICE THE... SMELLING.

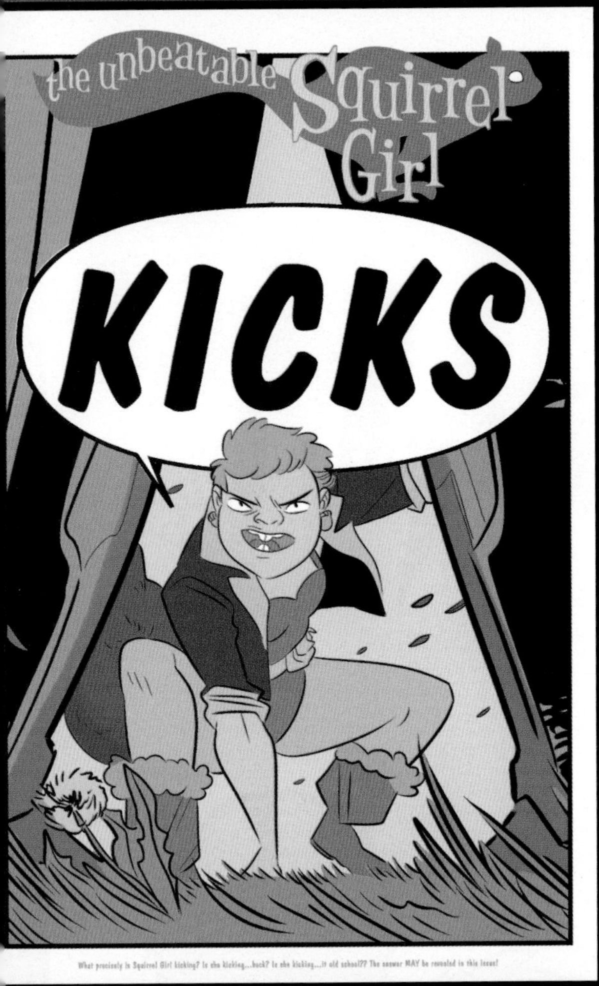
the unbeatable Squirrel Girl
KICKS
What precisely is Squirrel Girl kicking? Is she kicking...back? Is she kicking...it old school?? The answer MAY be revealed in this issue!

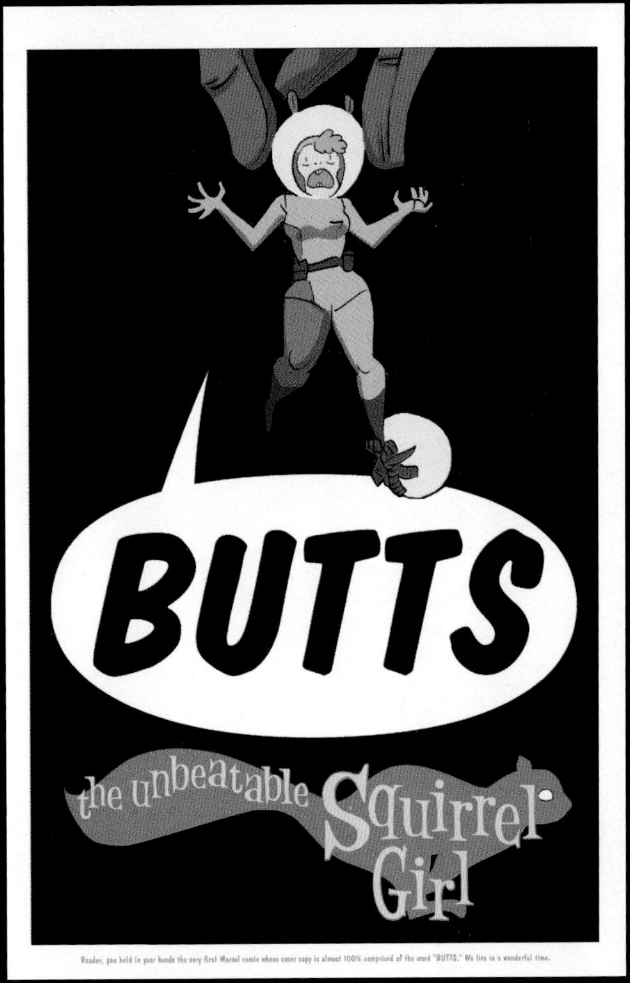
BUTTS
the unbeatable Squirrel Girl
Reader, you hold in your hands the very first Marvel comic whose cover copy is almost 100% comprised of the word "BUTTS." We live in a wonderful time.

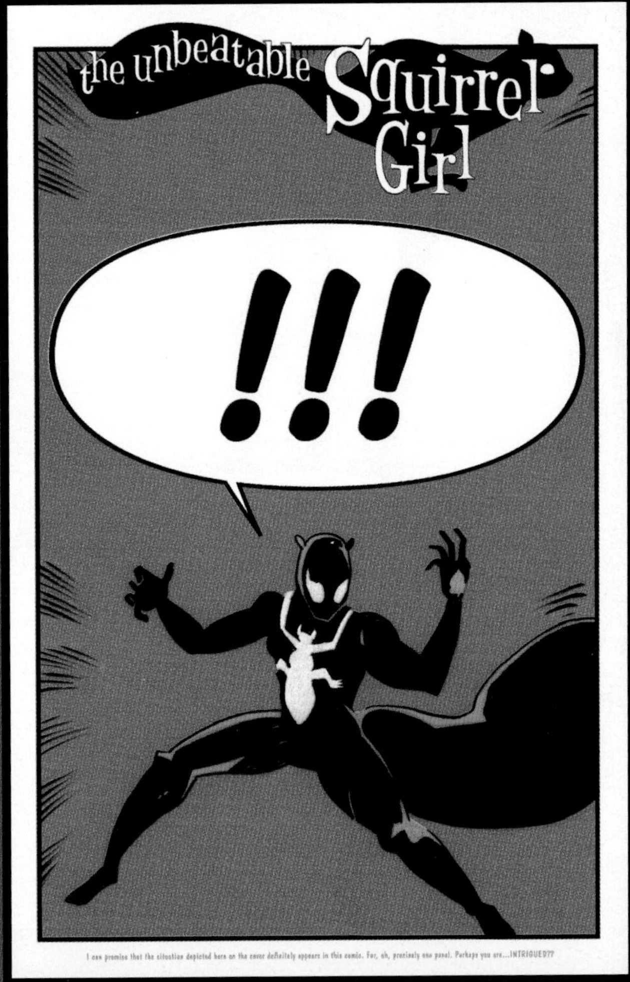
the unbeatable Squirrel Girl
!!!
I can promise that the situation depicted here on the cover definitely appears in this comic. For, uh, precisely one panel. Perhaps you are...INTRIGUED??

TOP ROW, FROM LEFT: ISSUE #1 3RD-PRINTING VARIANT COVER, ISSUE #2 3RD-PRINTING VARIANT COVER, ISSUE #3 2ND-PRINTING VARIANT COVER, ISSUE #4 2ND-PRINTING VARIANT COVER
RIGHT: ISSUE #5 2ND-PRINTING VARIANT COVER

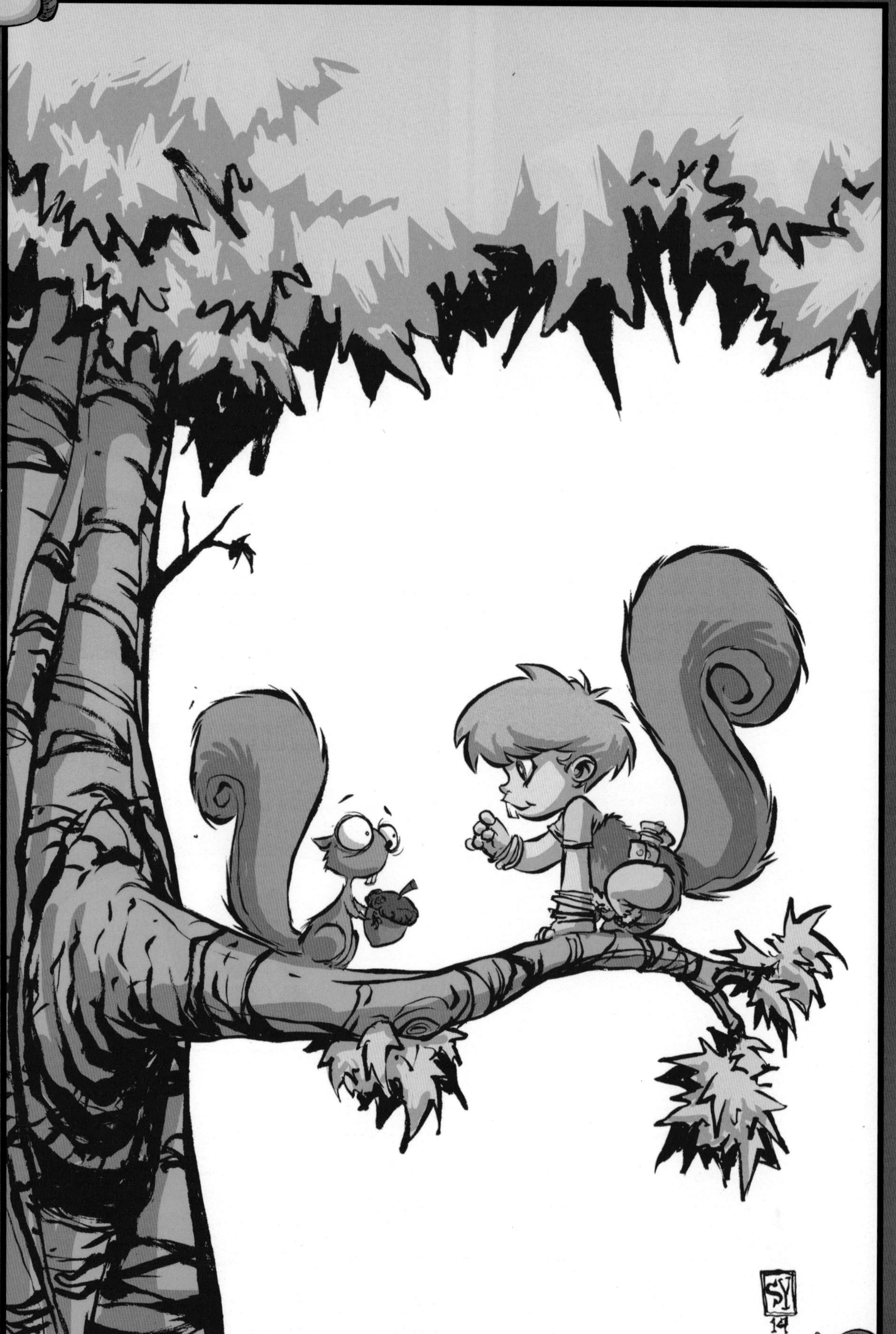

ISSUE #1 VARIANT COVER BY **SKOTTIE YOUNG**

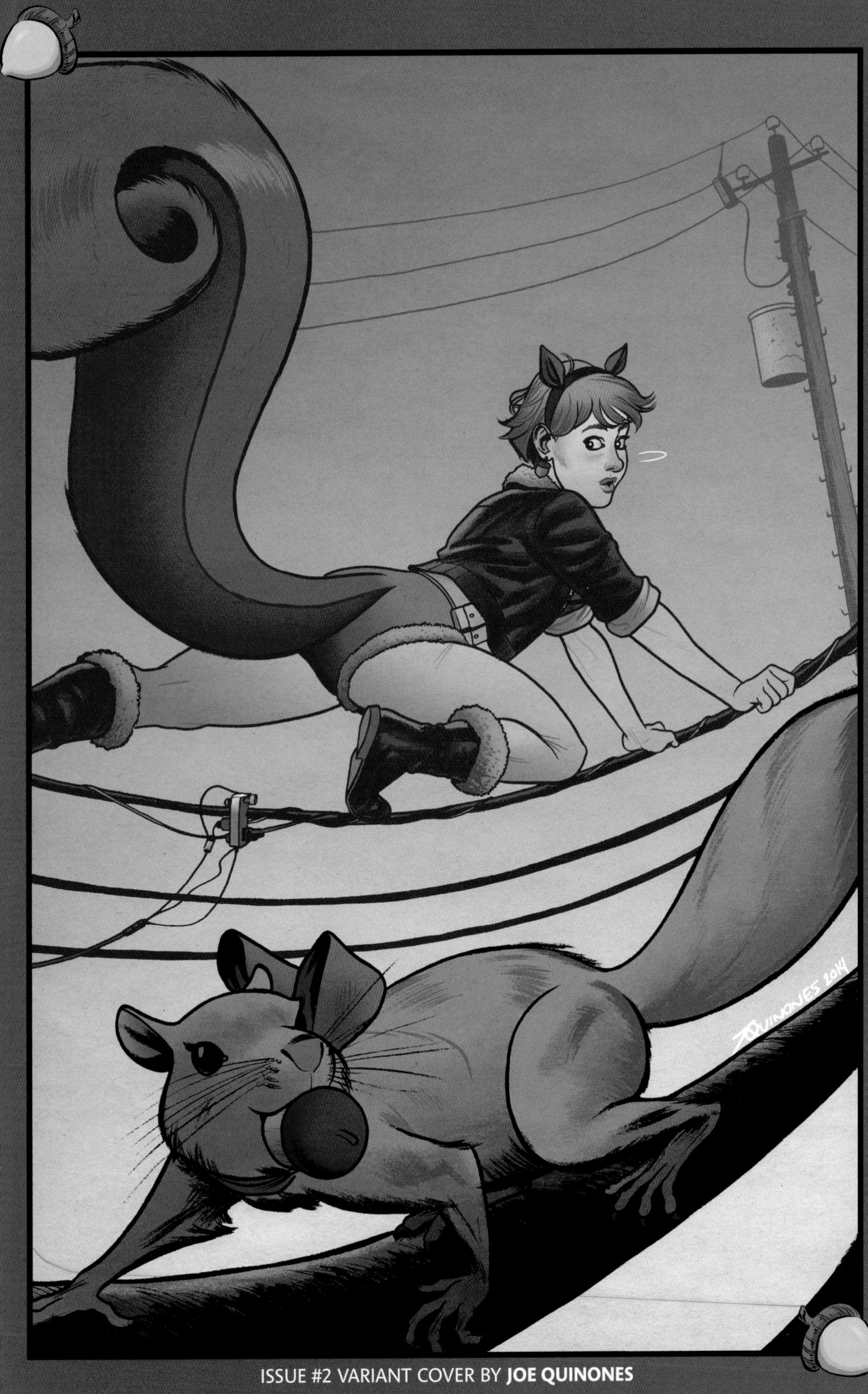

ISSUE #2 VARIANT COVER BY **JOE QUINONES**

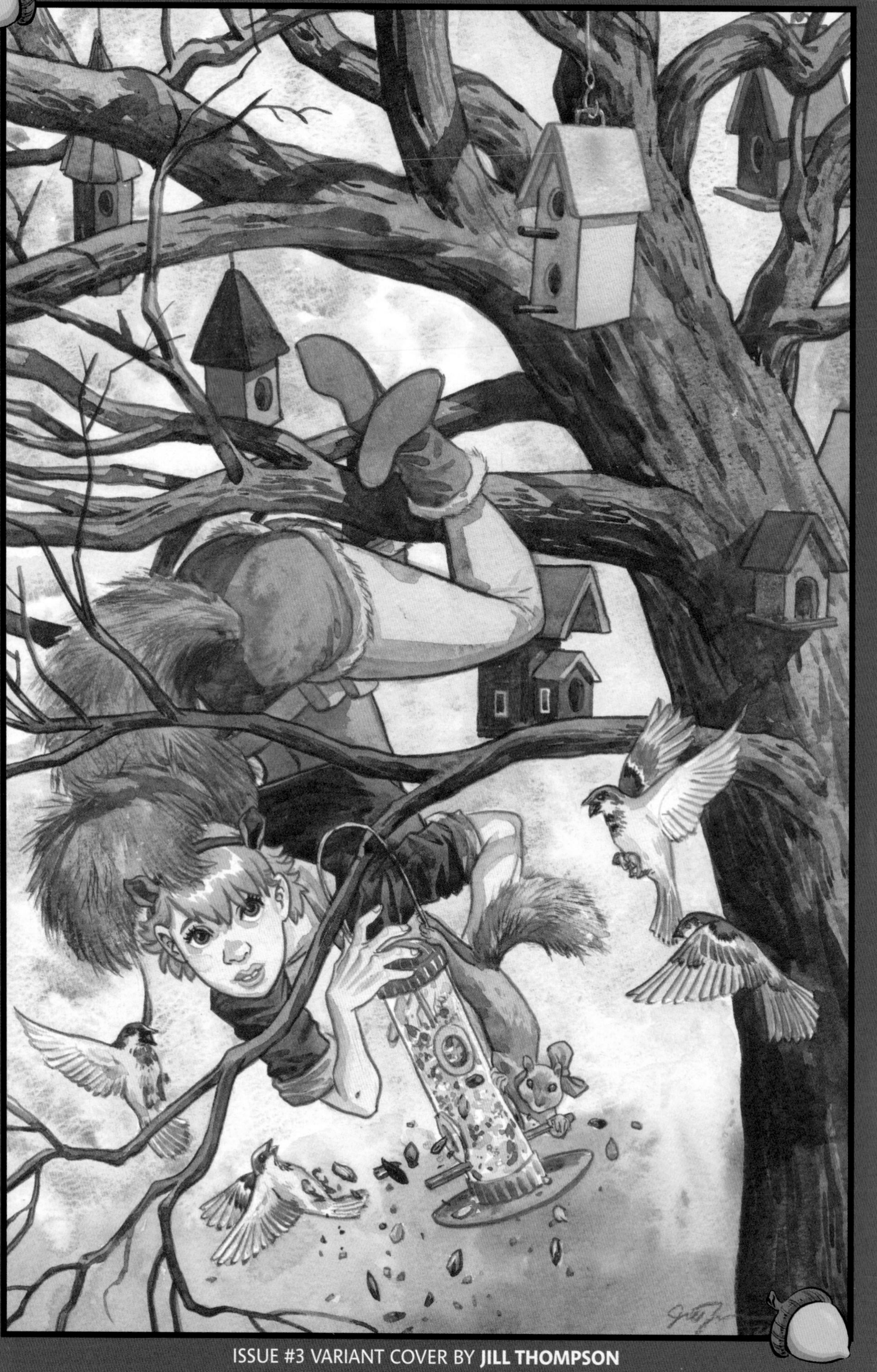

ISSUE #3 VARIANT COVER BY **JILL THOMPSON**

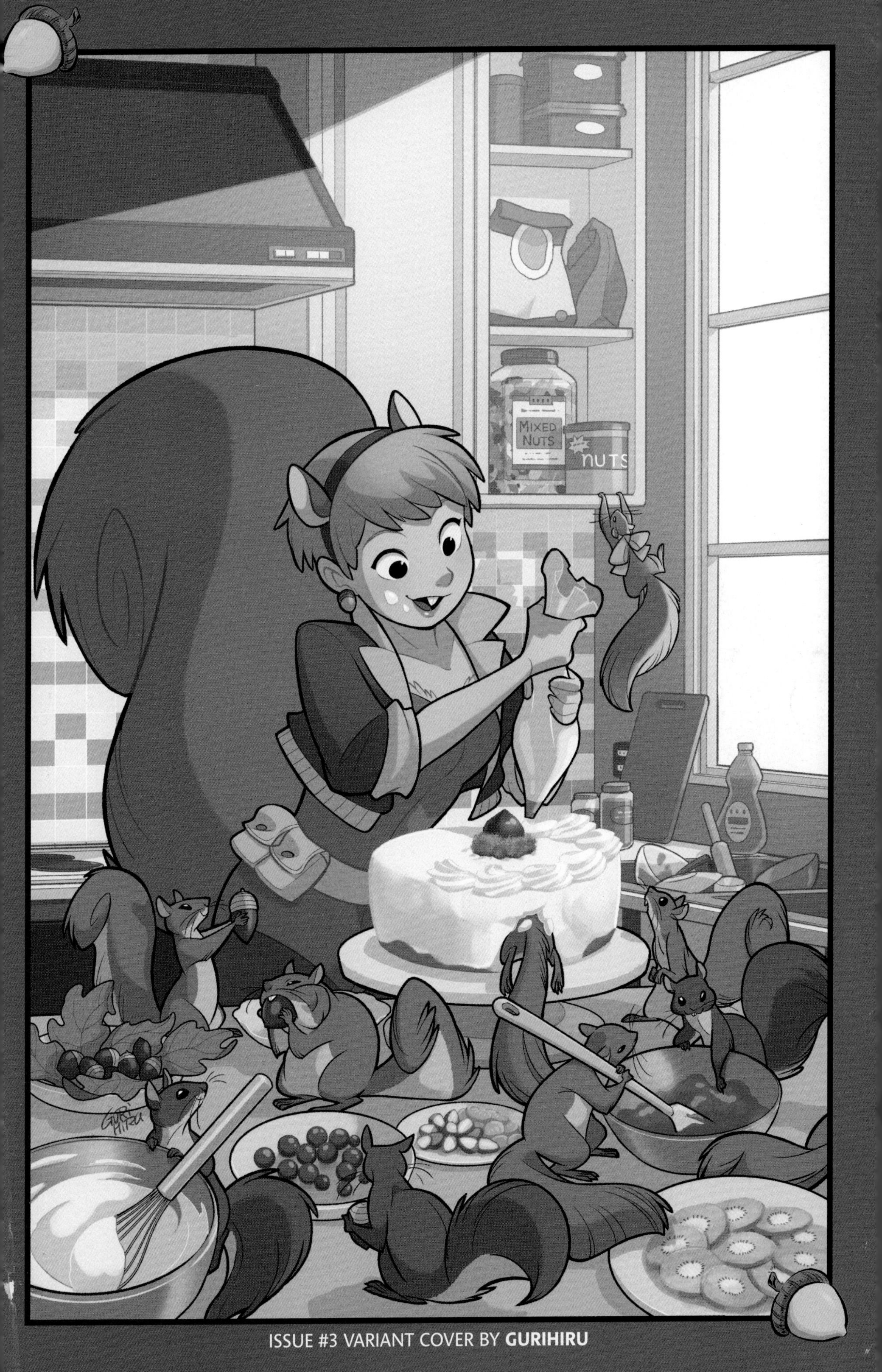
MIXED
NUTS
NUTS
GURI
HIRU
ISSUE #3 VARIANT COVER BY **GURIHIRU**

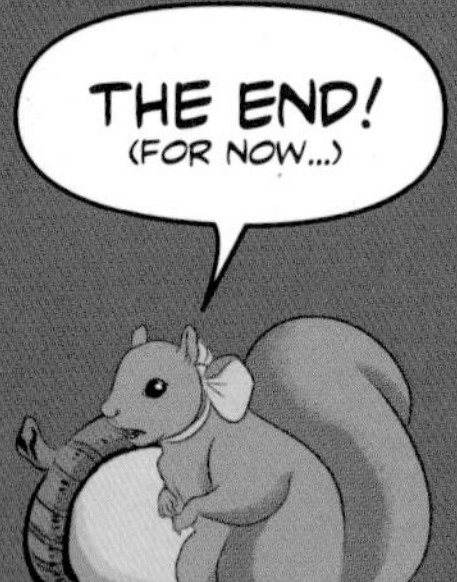
THE END!
(FOR NOW...)